OVER

THE

Uncivilized Books

WALL

PETER WARTMAN

Design & Editing by Tom Kaczynski.

Odod Books

P.O. Box 6434

Minneapolis, MN 55406

USA

ododbooks.com

Second Edition, October 2016

11 10 9 8 7 6 5 4 3 2

ISBN 978-0-9846814-3-3

DISTRIBUTED TO THE TRADE BY:

Consortium Book Sales & Distribution, LLC.

34 Thirteenth Avenue NE,

Suite 101 Minneapolis,

MN 55413-1007

Orders: (800) 283-3572

Printed in China

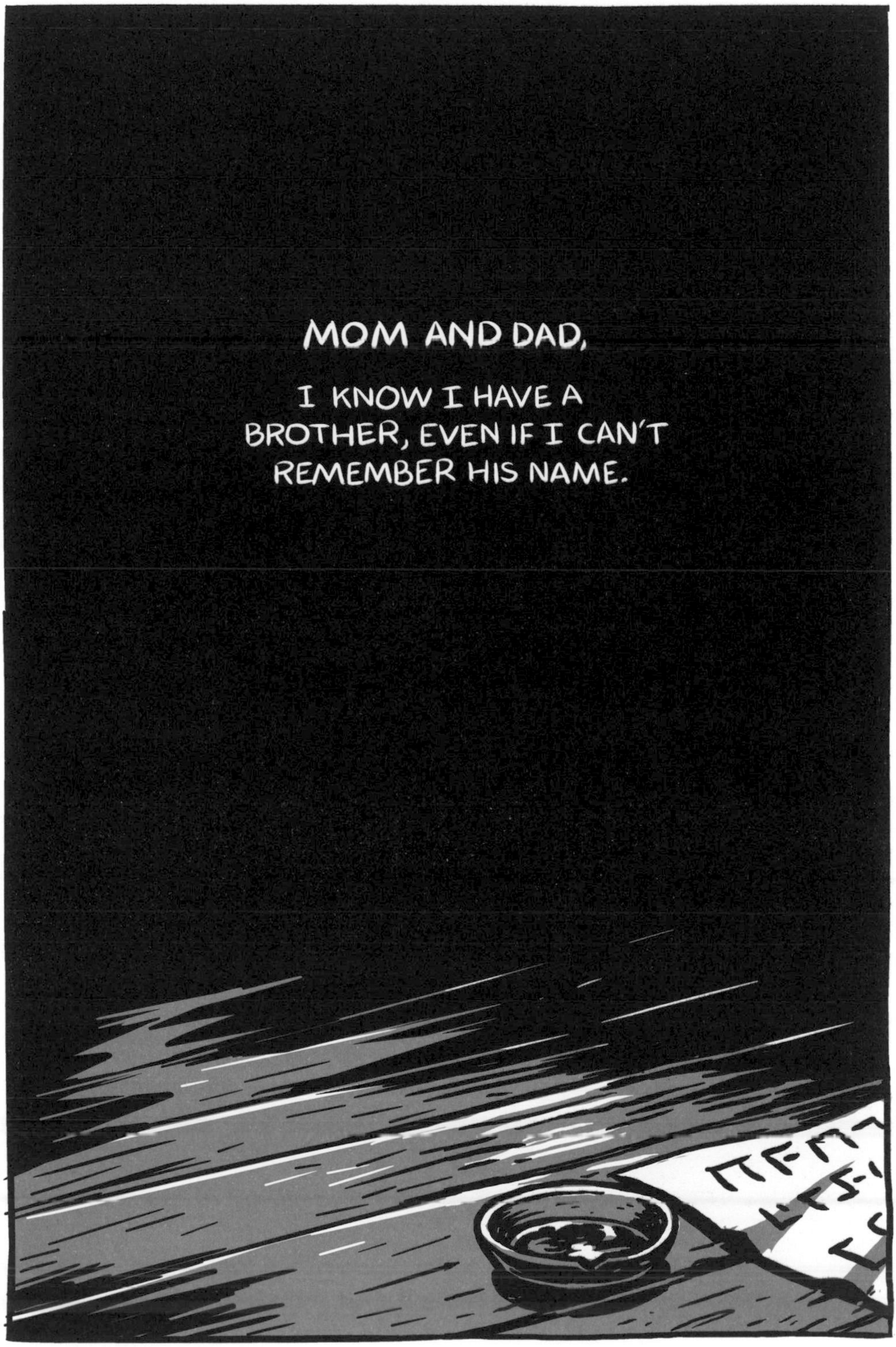
MOM AND DAD,
I KNOW I HAVE A BROTHER, EVEN IF I CAN'T REMEMBER HIS NAME.

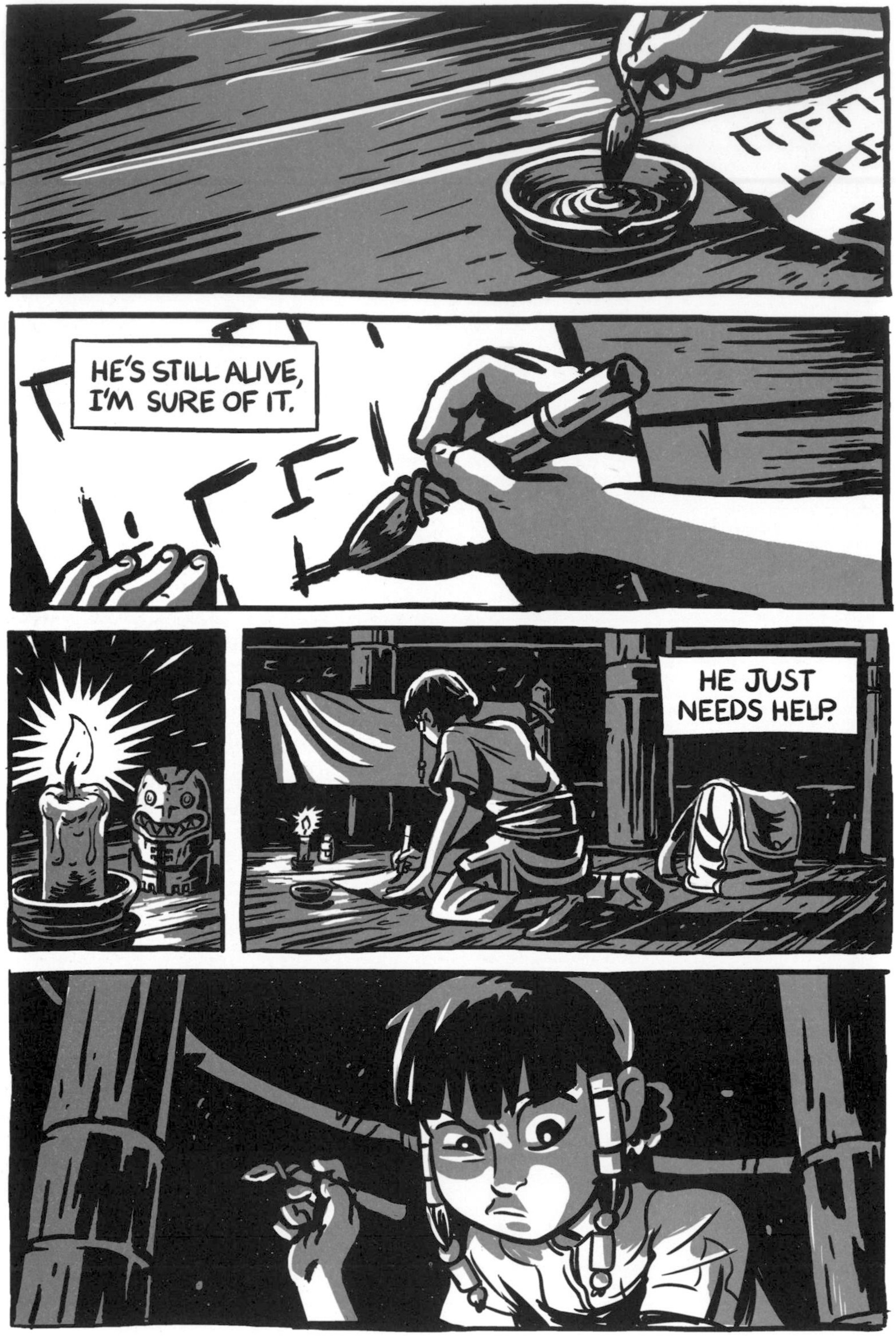
HE'S STILL ALIVE, I'M SURE OF IT.
HE JUST NEEDS HELP.

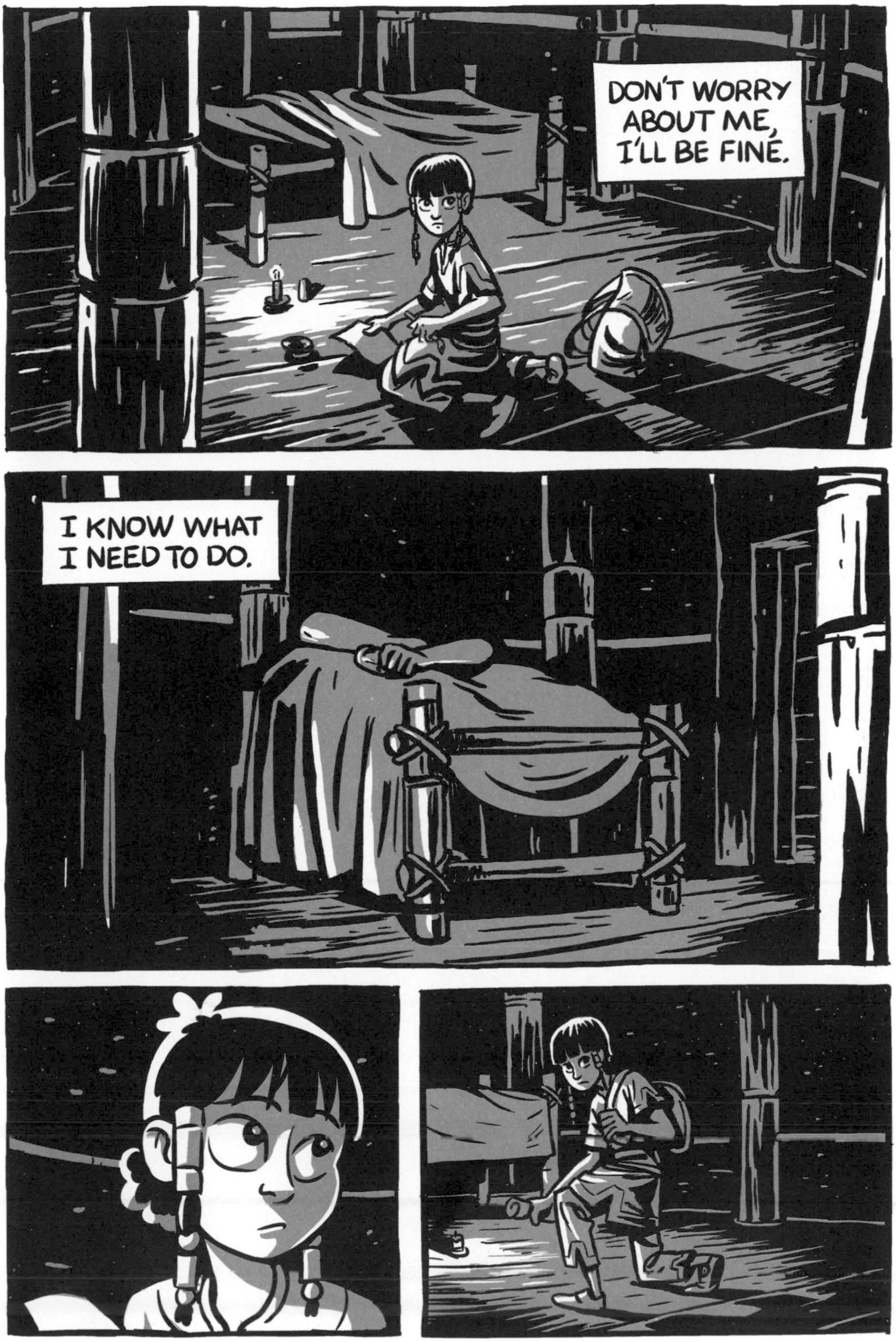
DON'T WORRY ABOUT ME, I'LL BE FINE.
I KNOW WHAT I NEED TO DO.

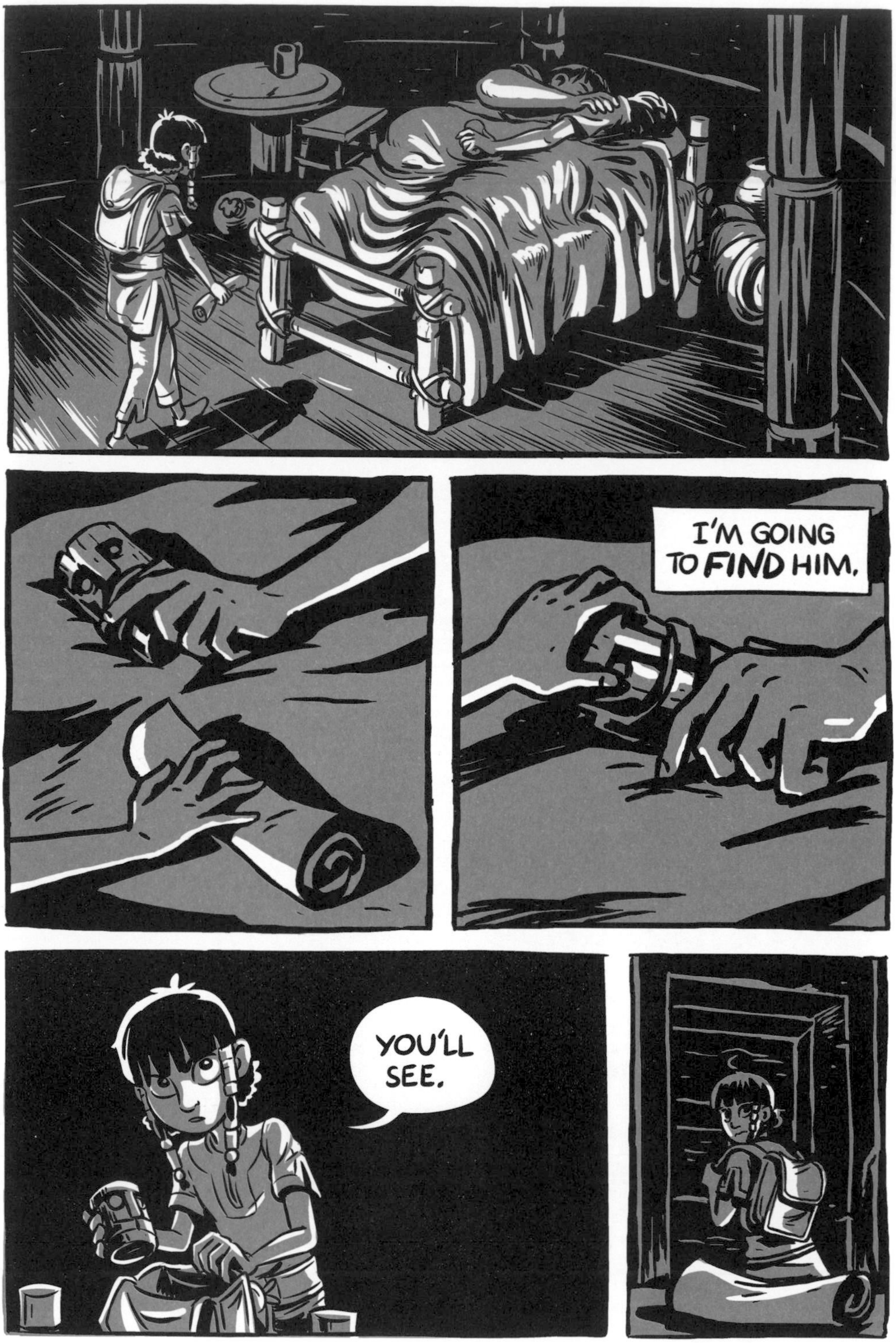
I'M GOING TO **FIND** HIM.
YOU'LL SEE.

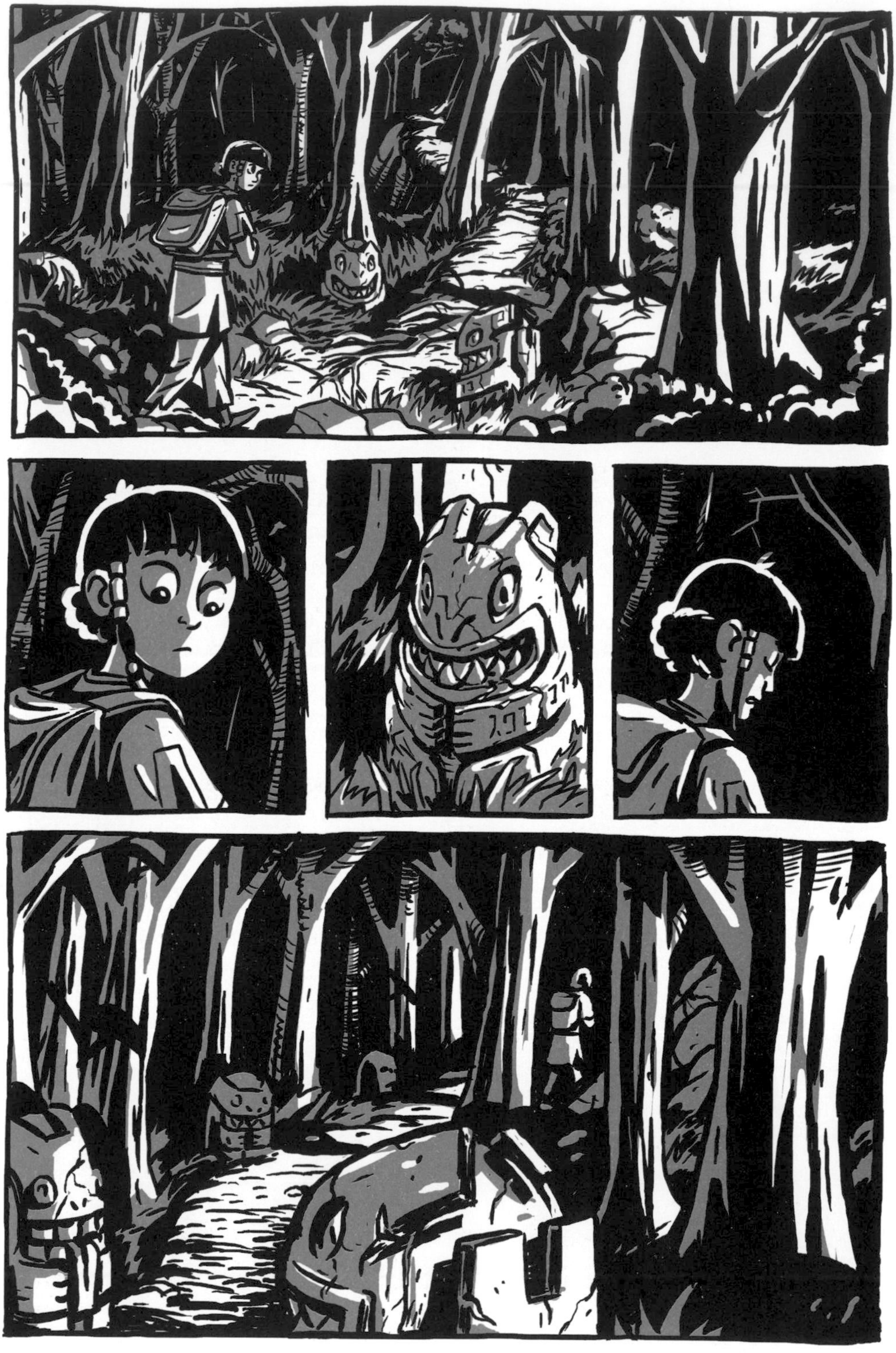

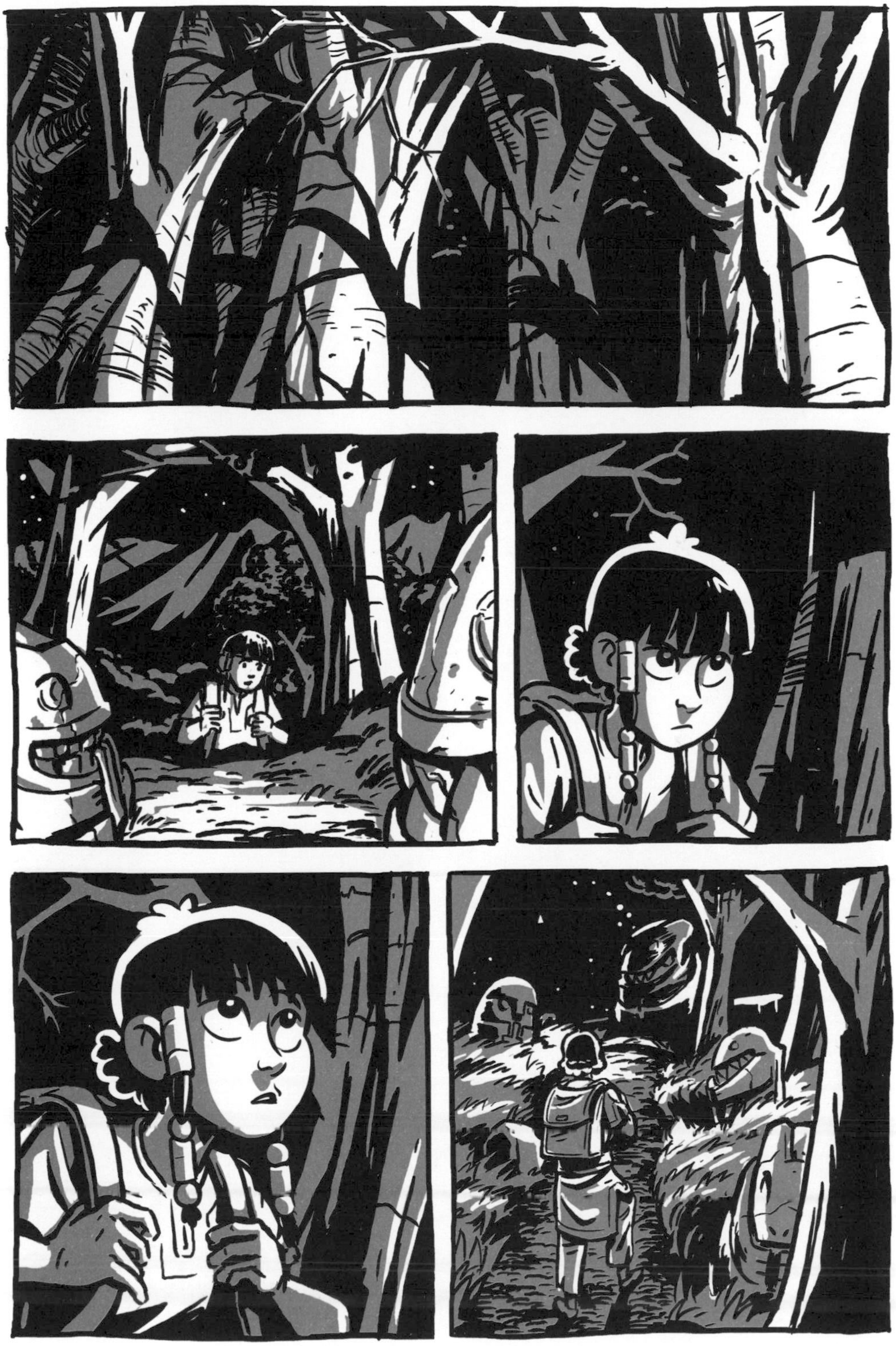

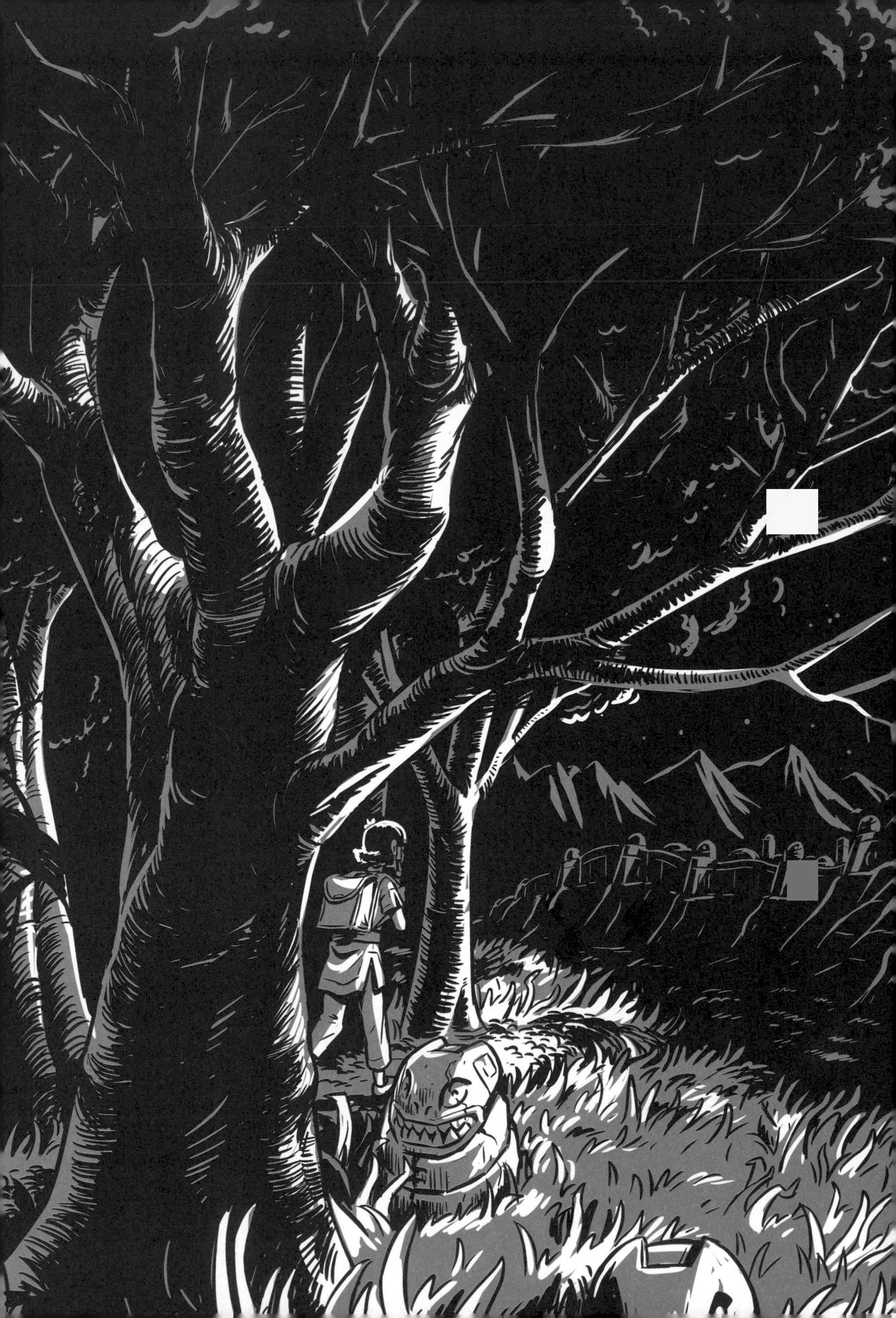

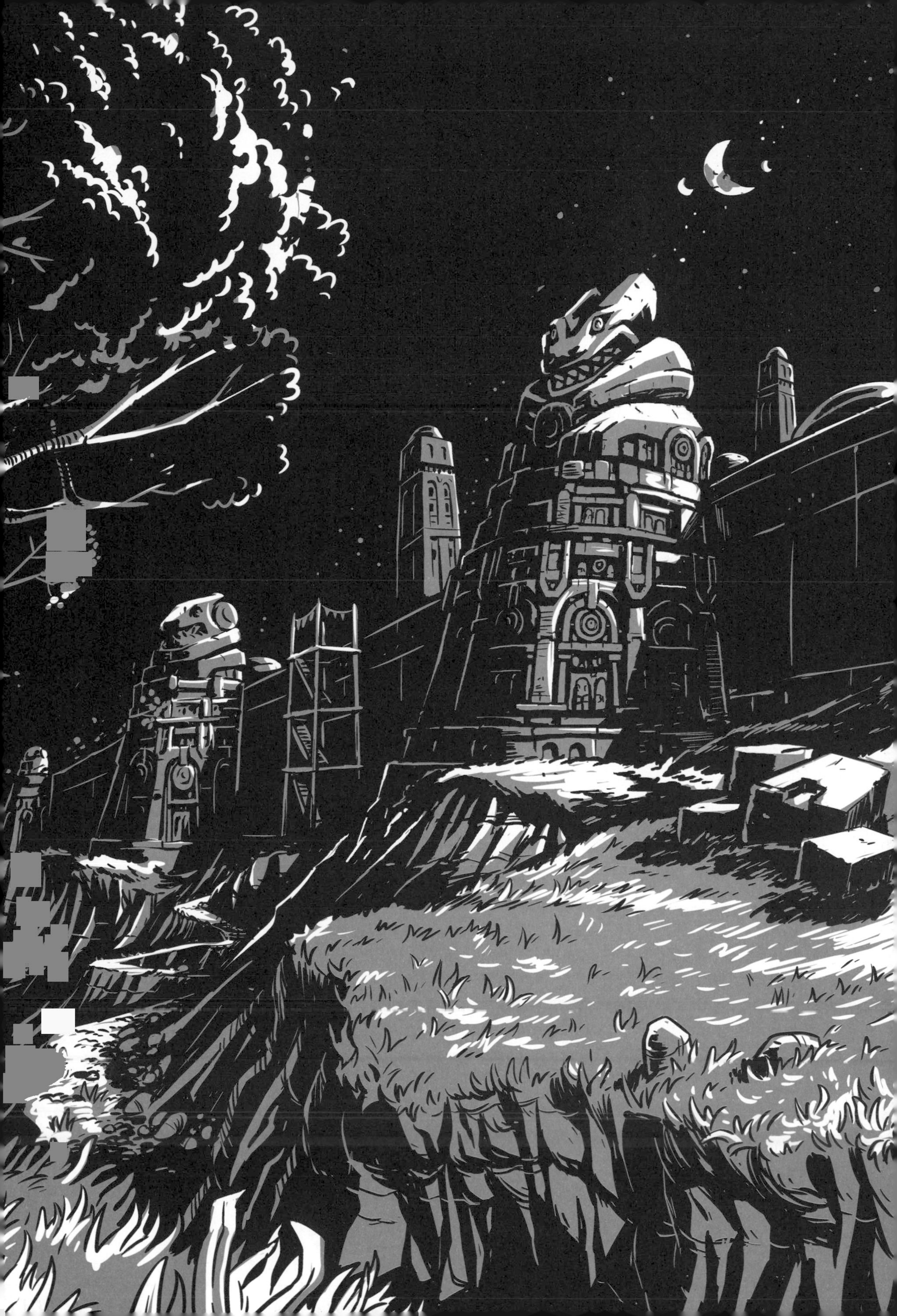

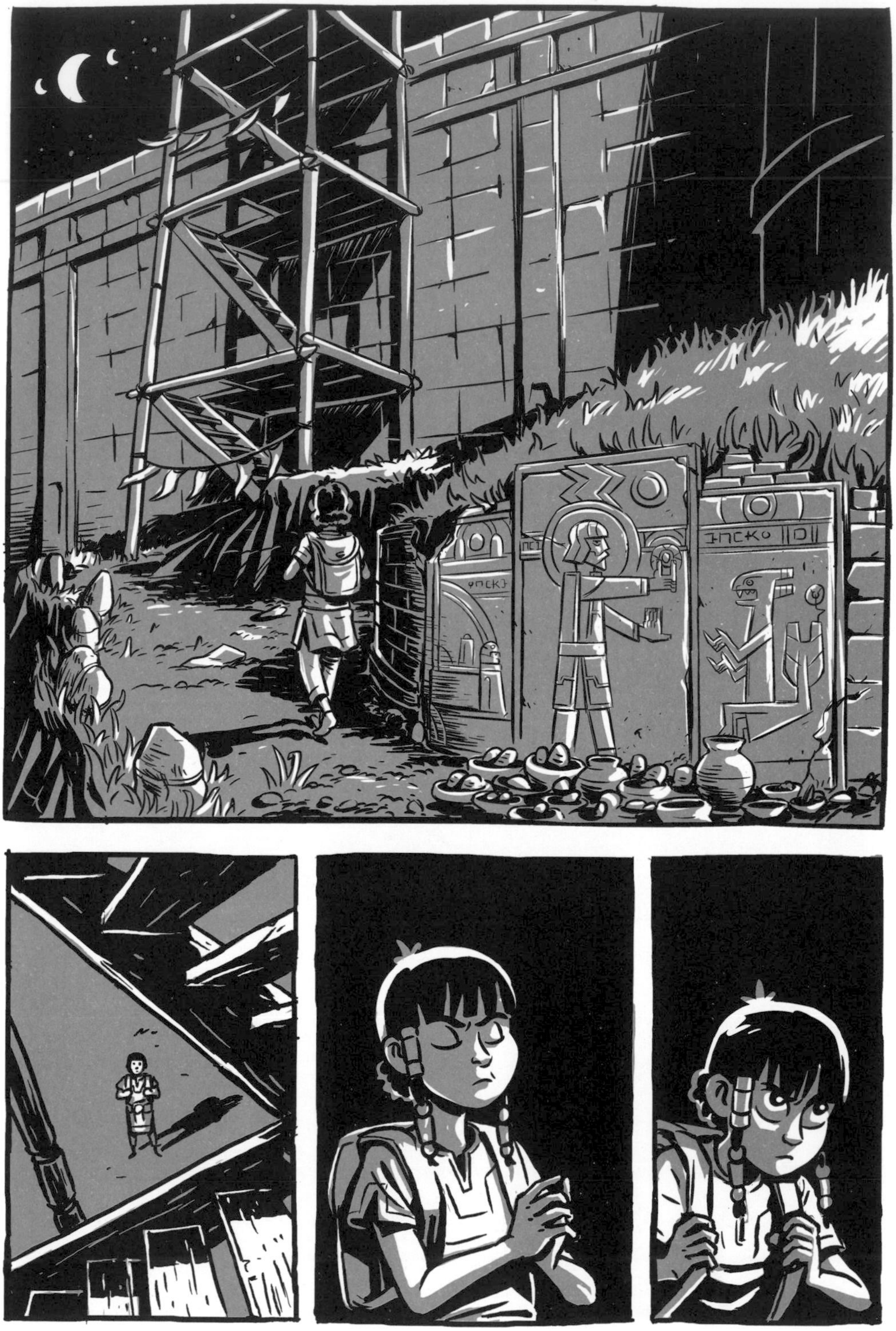

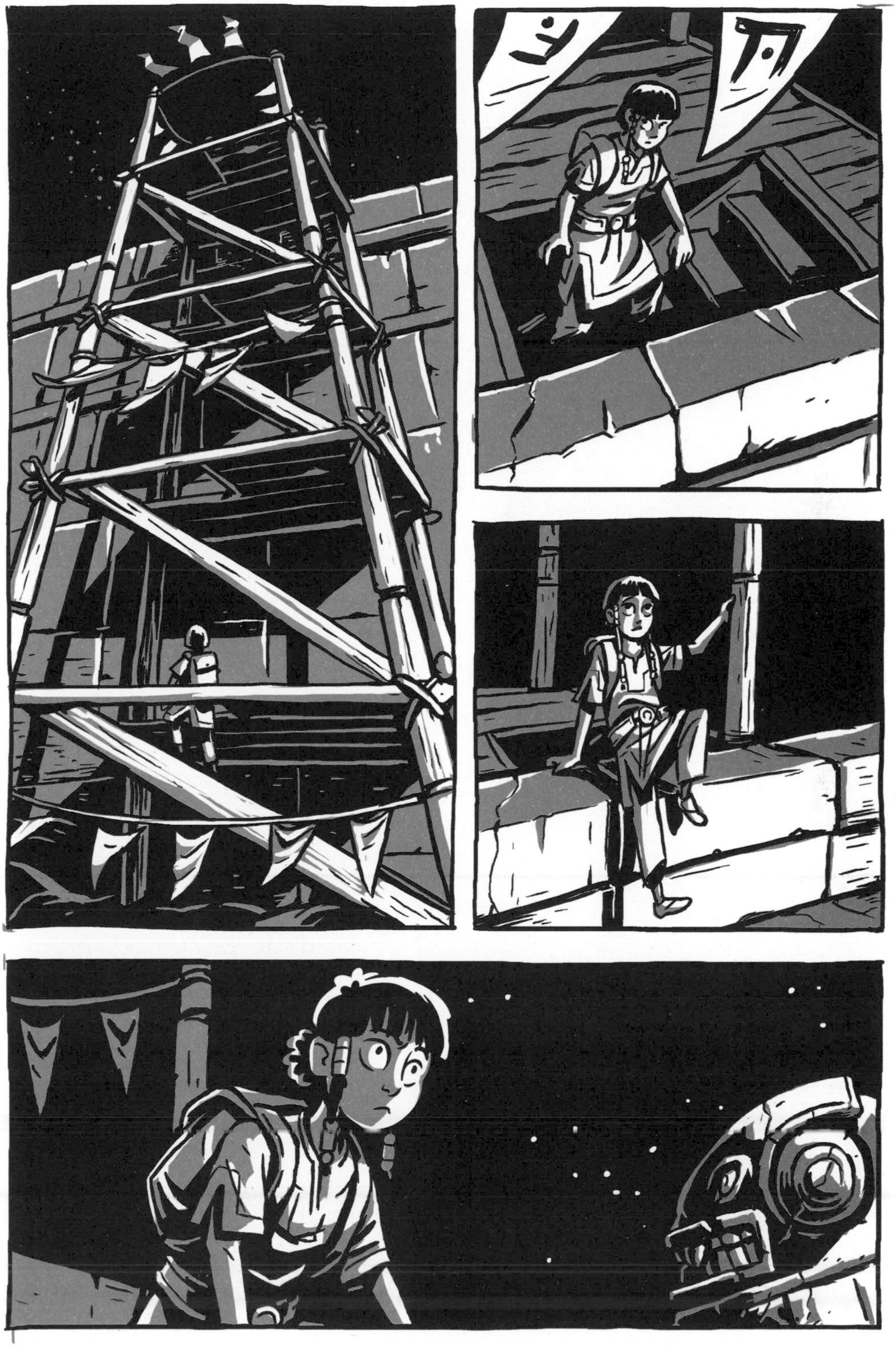

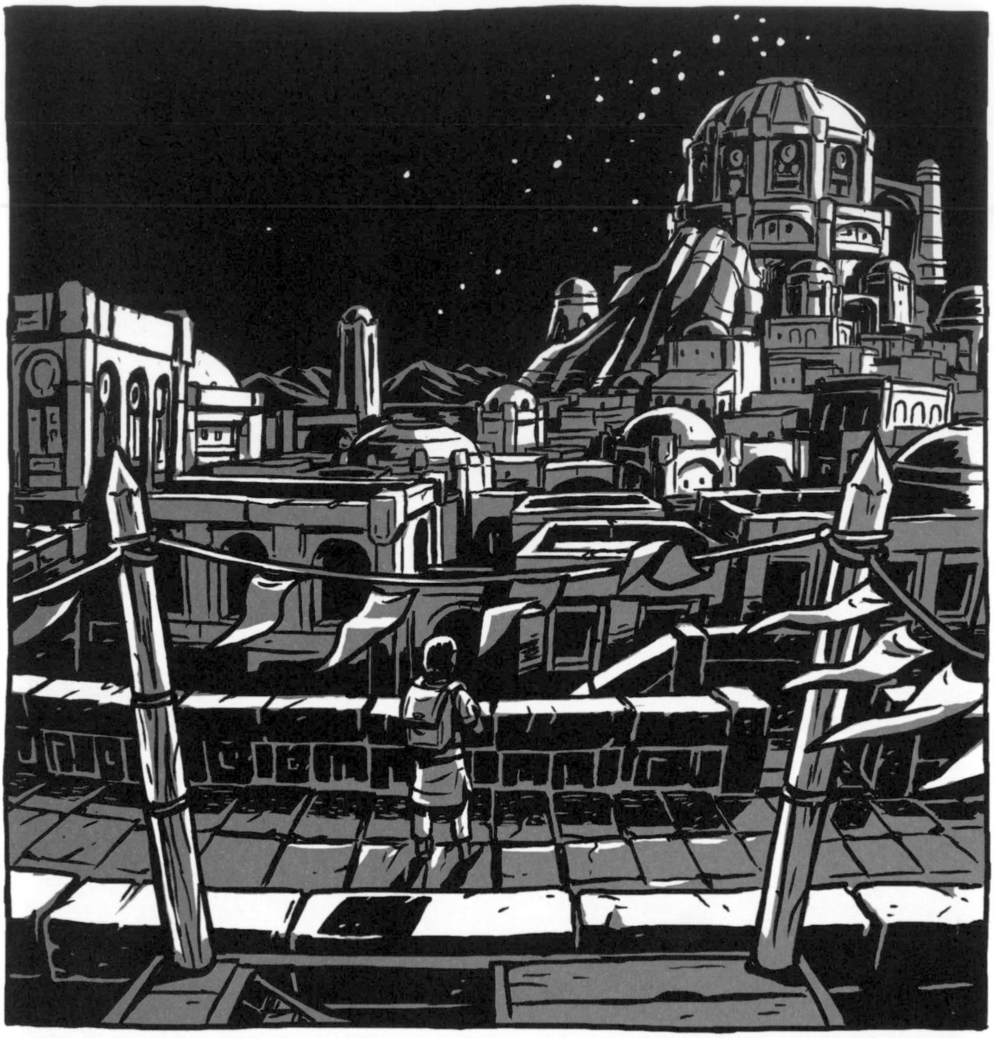

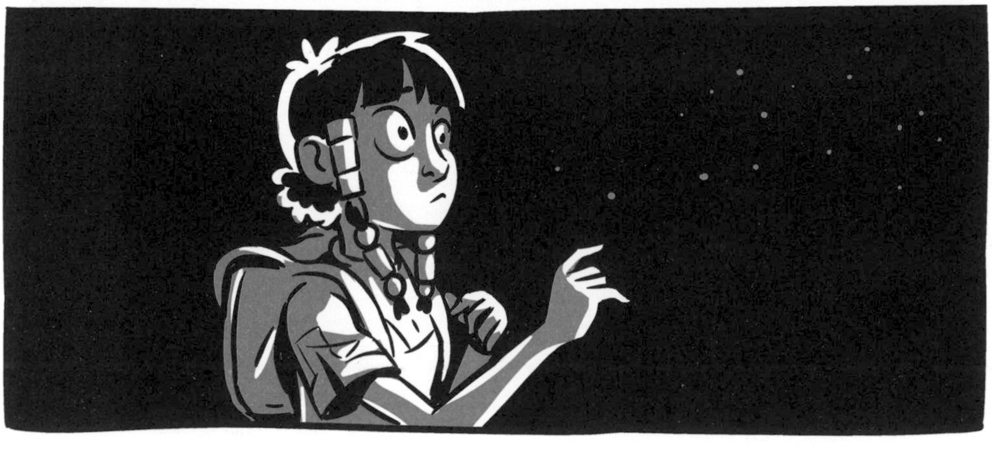

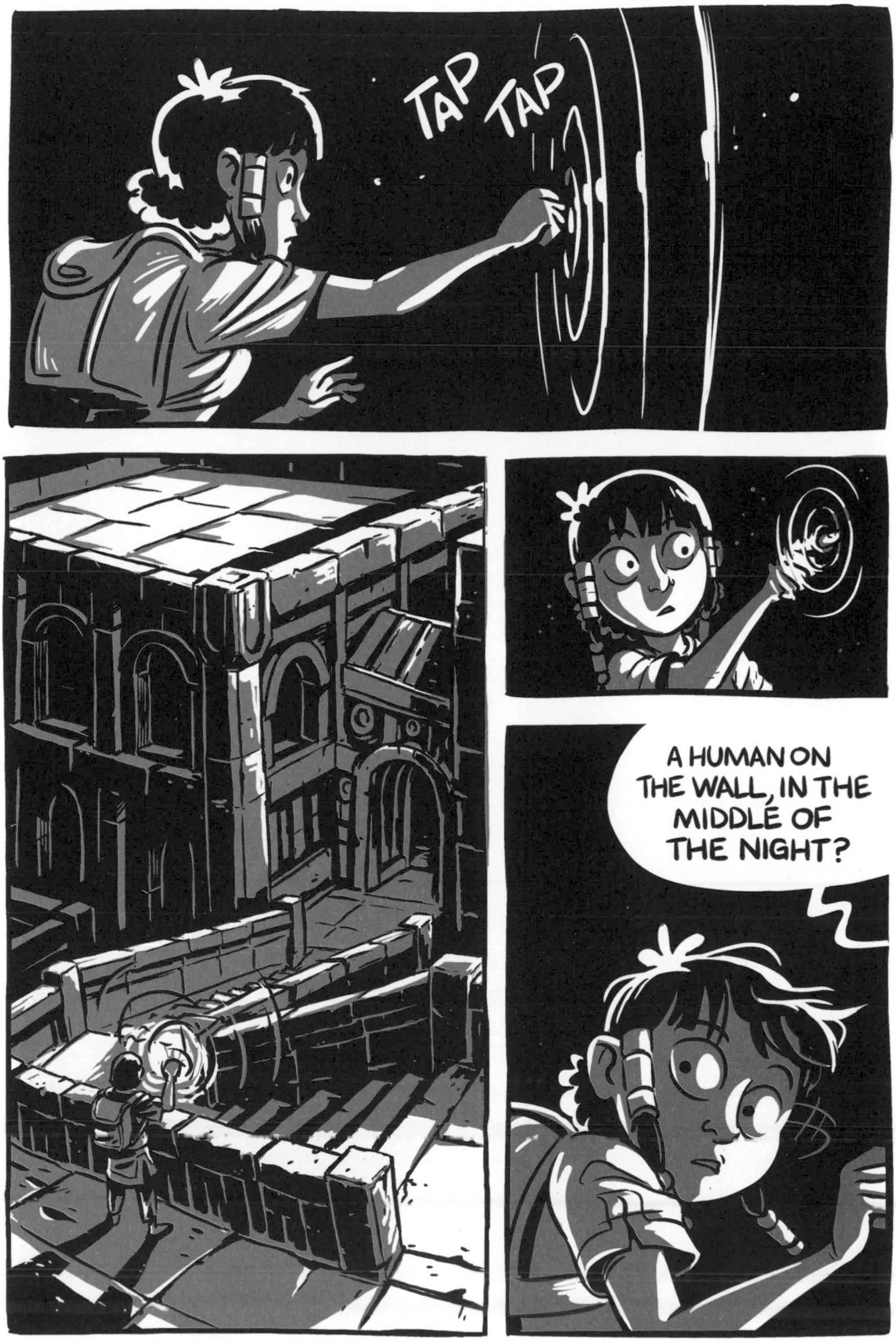
TAP TAP
A HUMAN ON THE WALL, IN THE MIDDLE OF THE NIGHT?

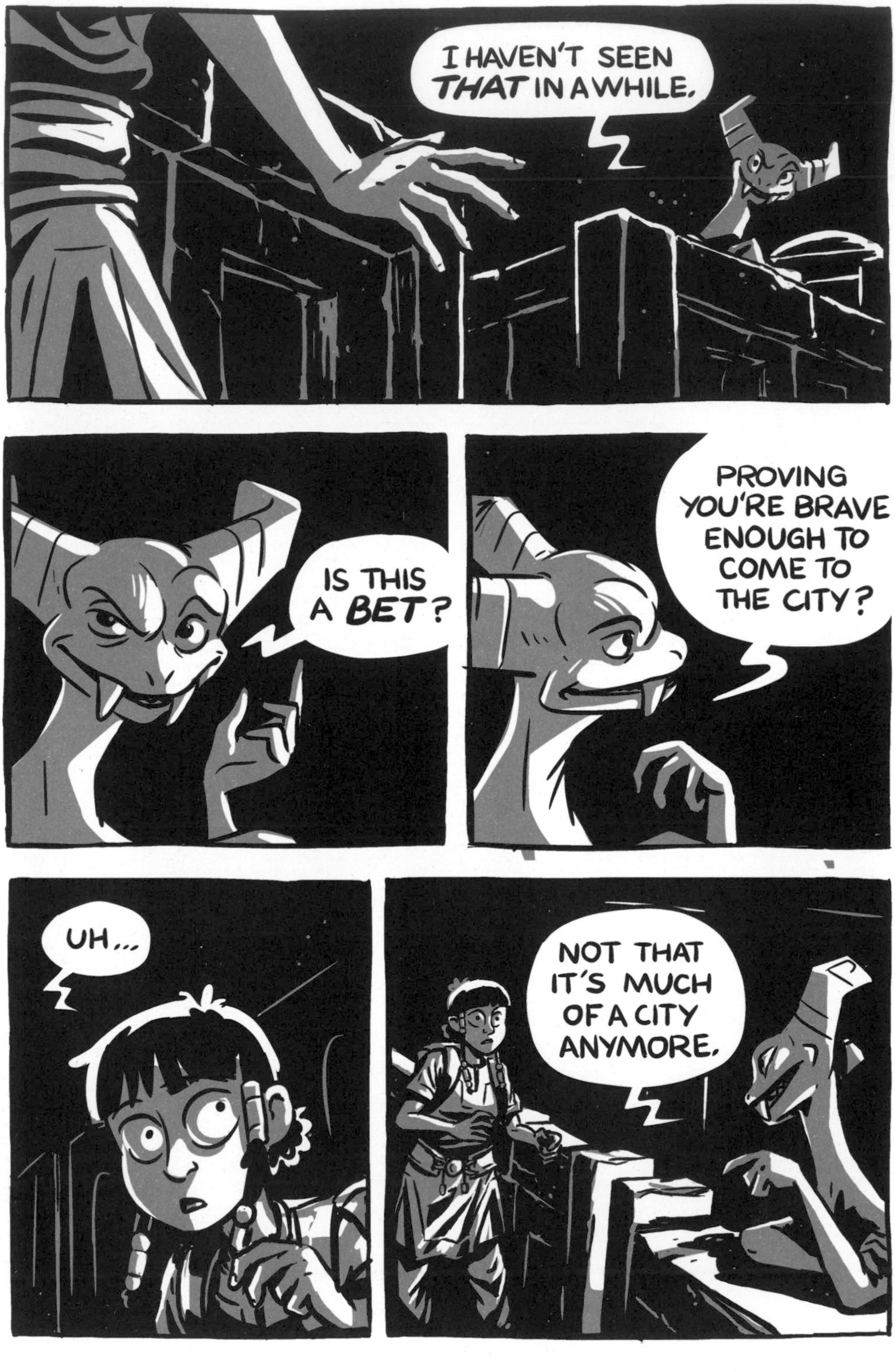
I HAVEN'T SEEN *THAT* IN A WHILE.
IS THIS A *BET*?
PROVING YOU'RE BRAVE ENOUGH TO COME TO THE CITY?
UH...
NOT THAT IT'S MUCH OF A CITY ANYMORE.

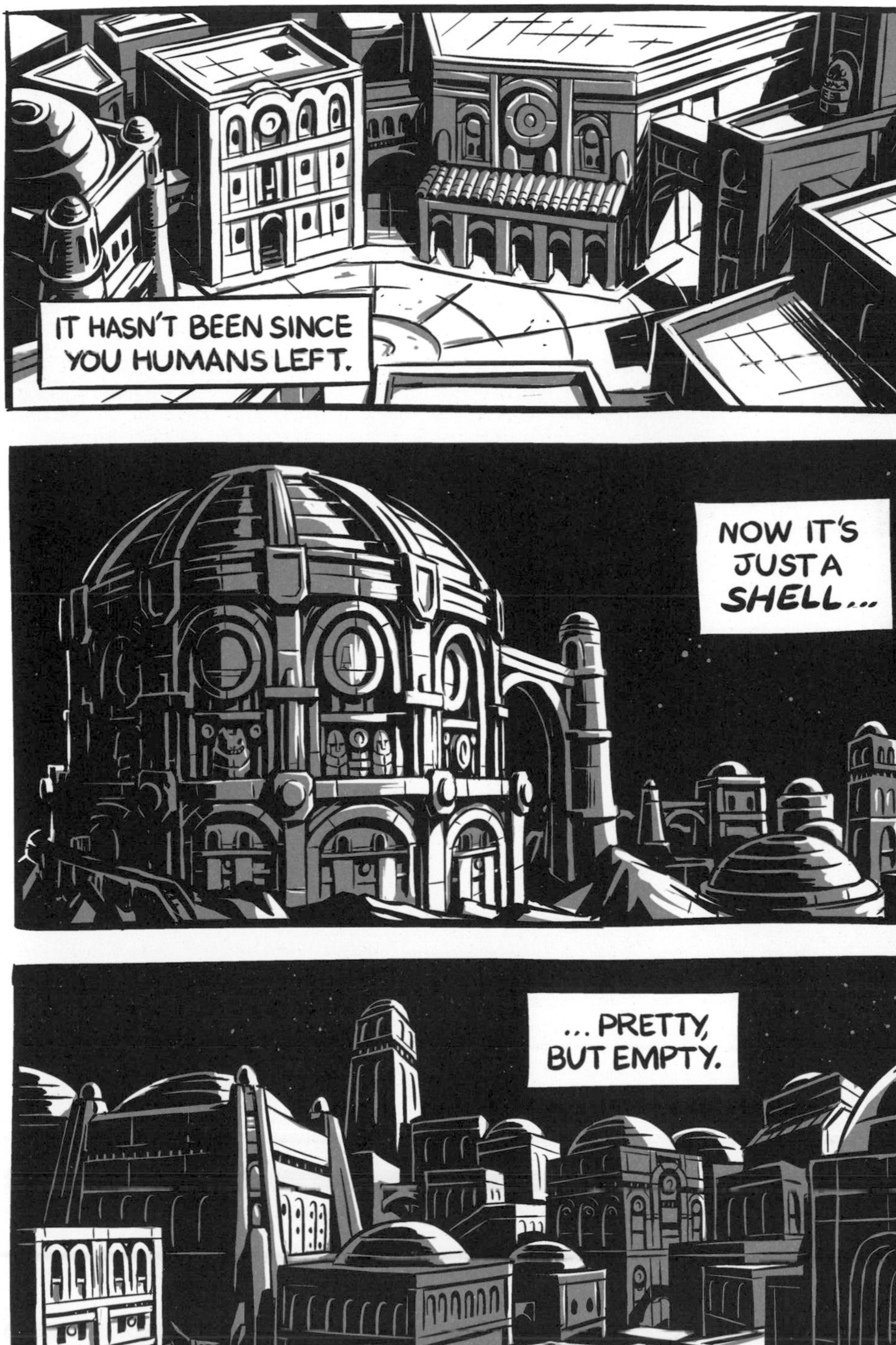
IT HASN'T BEEN SINCE YOU HUMANS LEFT.
NOW IT'S JUST A SHELL...
... PRETTY, BUT EMPTY.

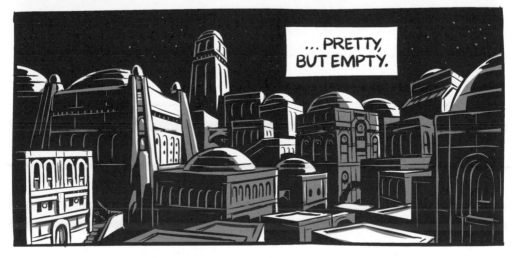

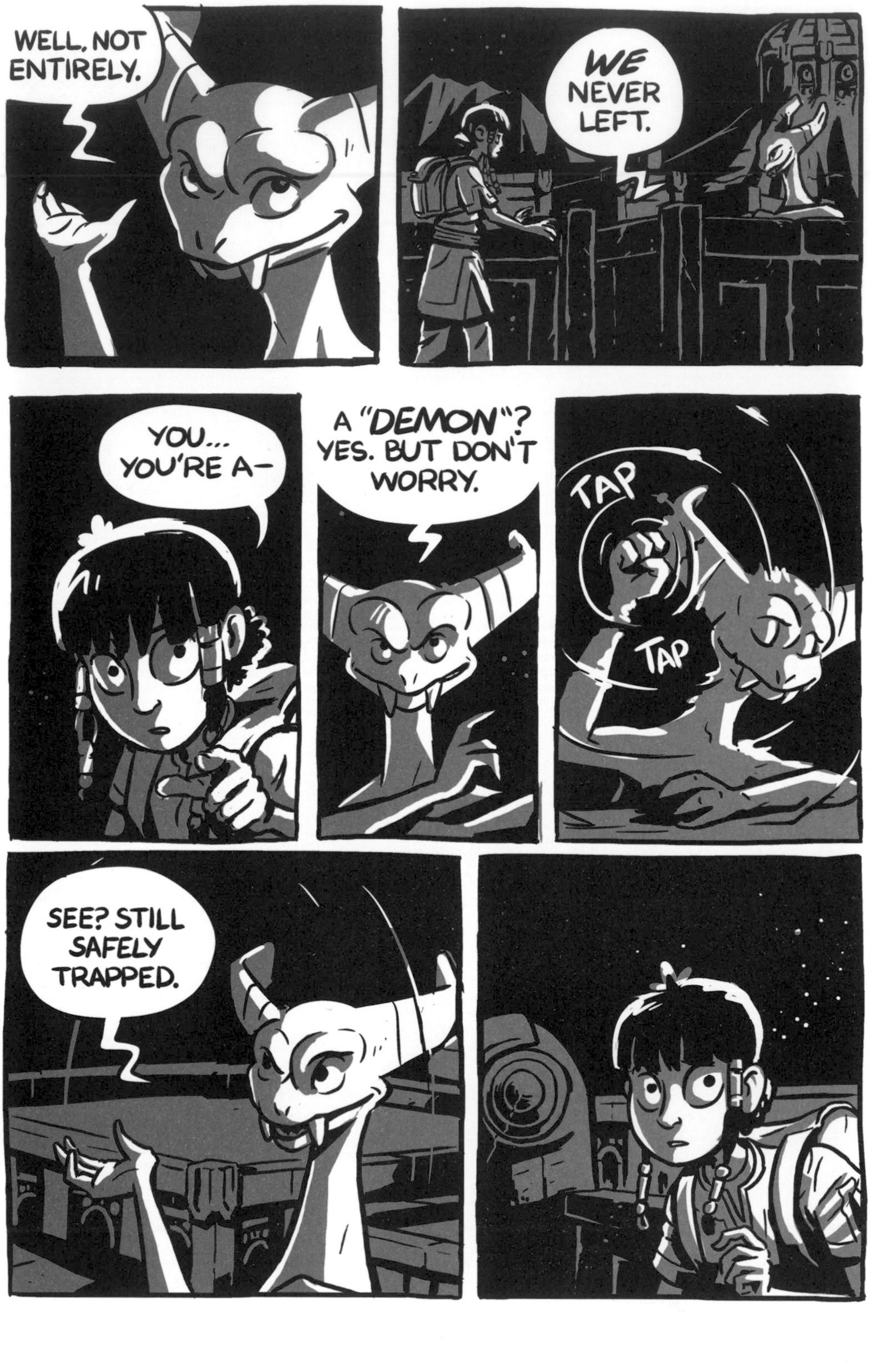
WELL, NOT ENTIRELY.
WE NEVER LEFT.
YOU... YOU'RE A—
A "DEMON"? YES. BUT DON'T WORRY.
TAP
TAP
SEE? STILL SAFELY TRAPPED.

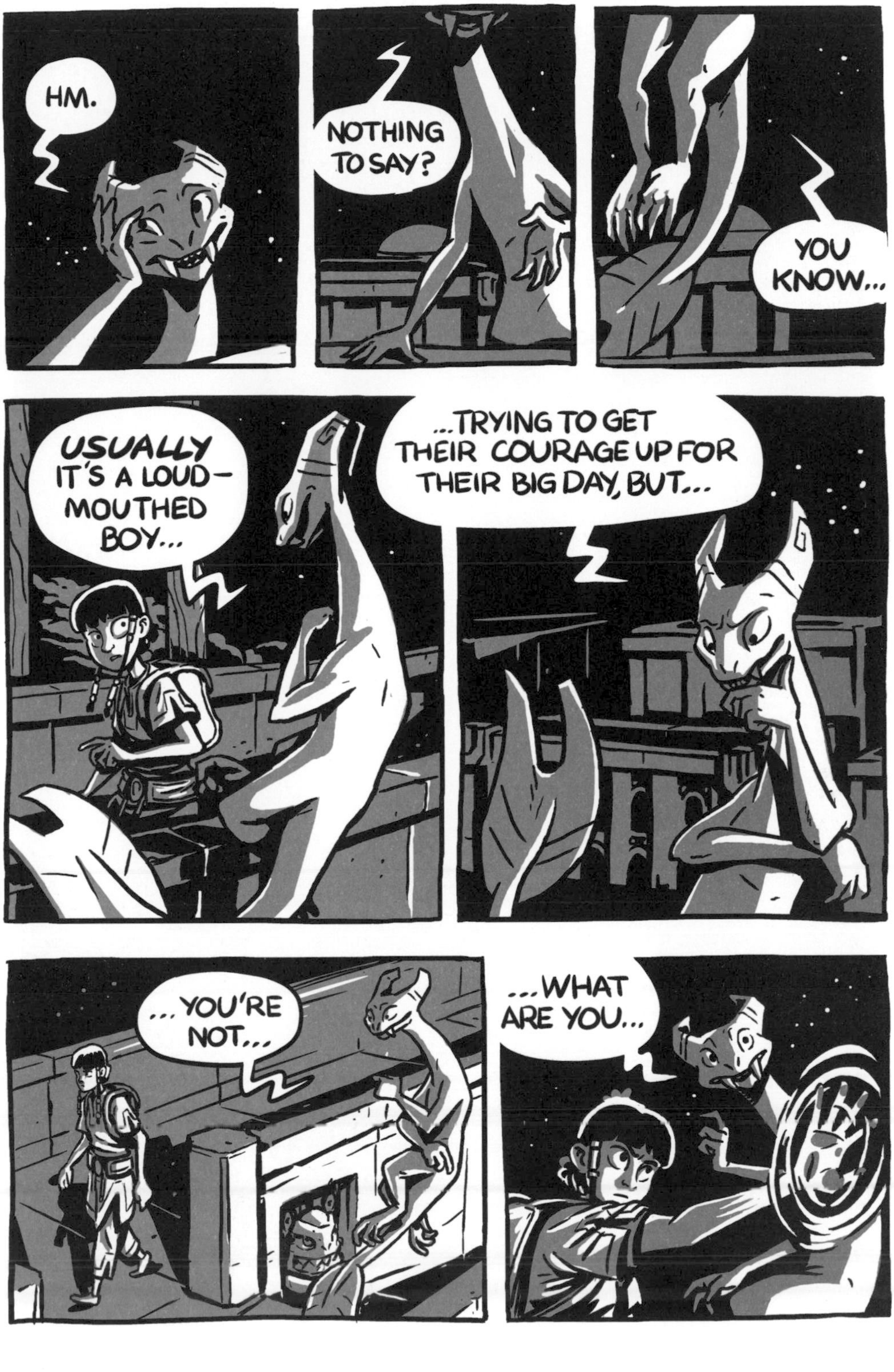
HM.
NOTHING TO SAY?
YOU KNOW...
USUALLY IT'S A LOUD-MOUTHED BOY...
...TRYING TO GET THEIR COURAGE UP FOR THEIR BIG DAY, BUT...
...YOU'RE NOT...
...WHAT ARE YOU...

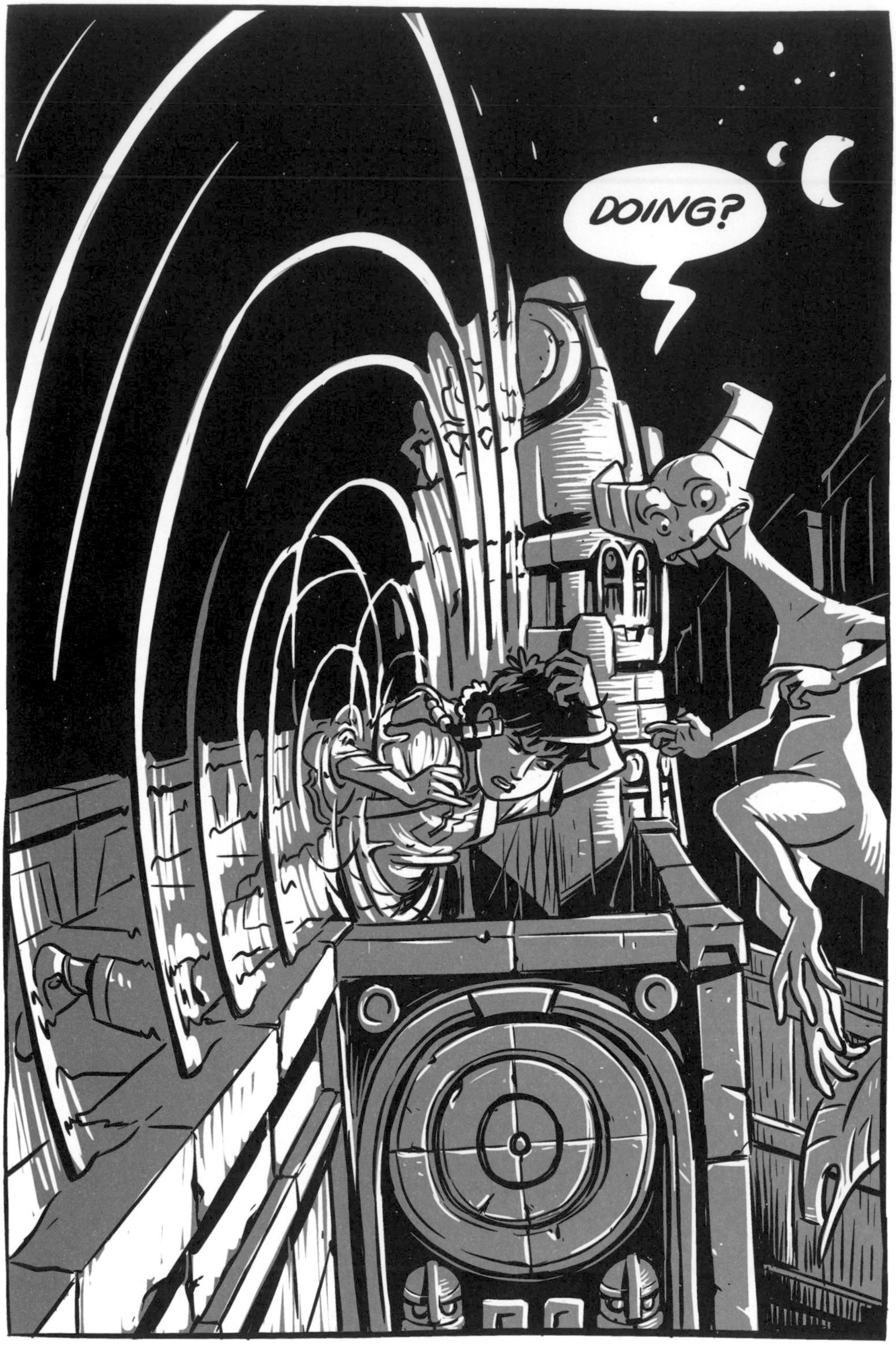
DOING?

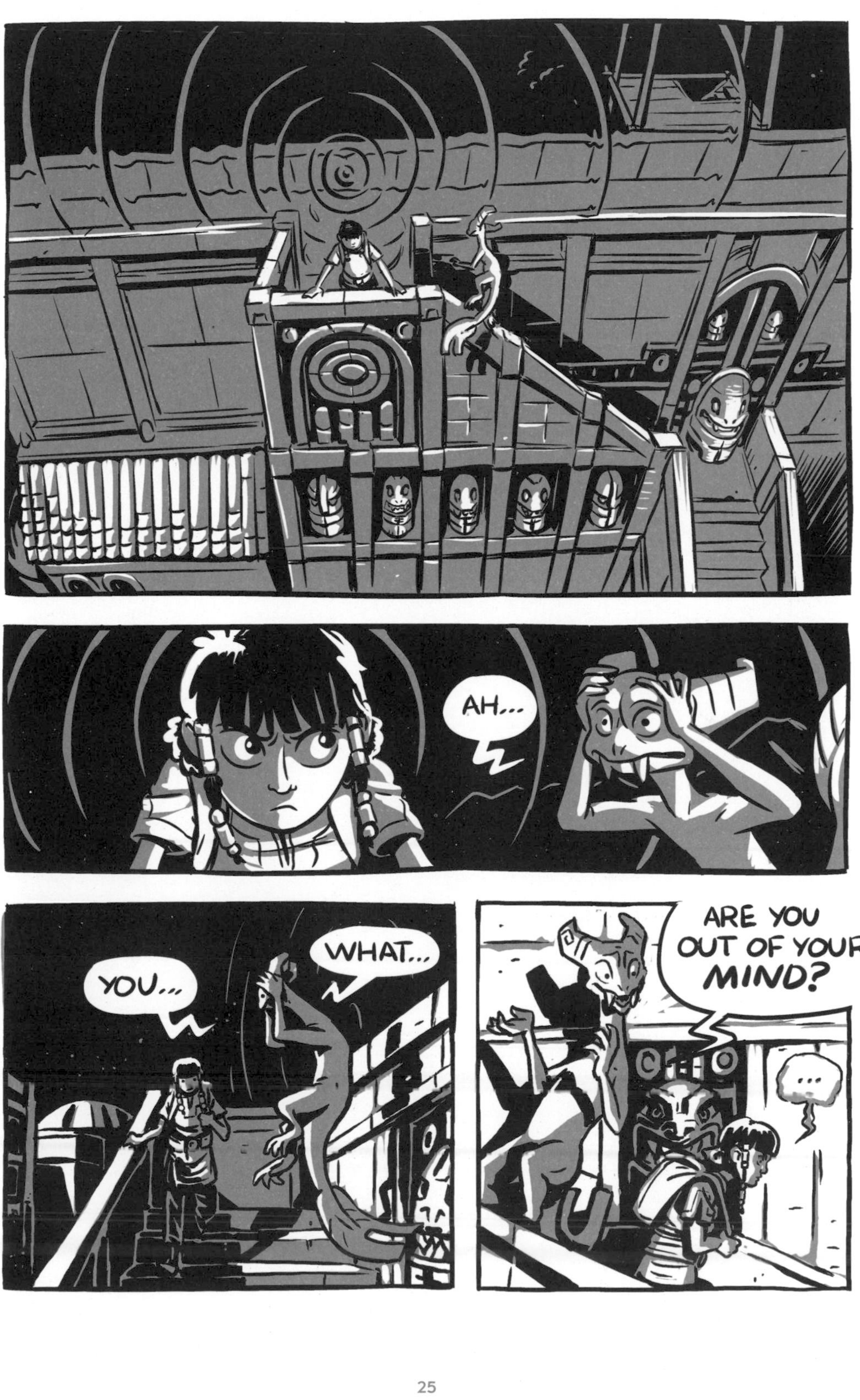
AH...
YOU...
WHAT...
ARE YOU OUT OF YOUR MIND?
...

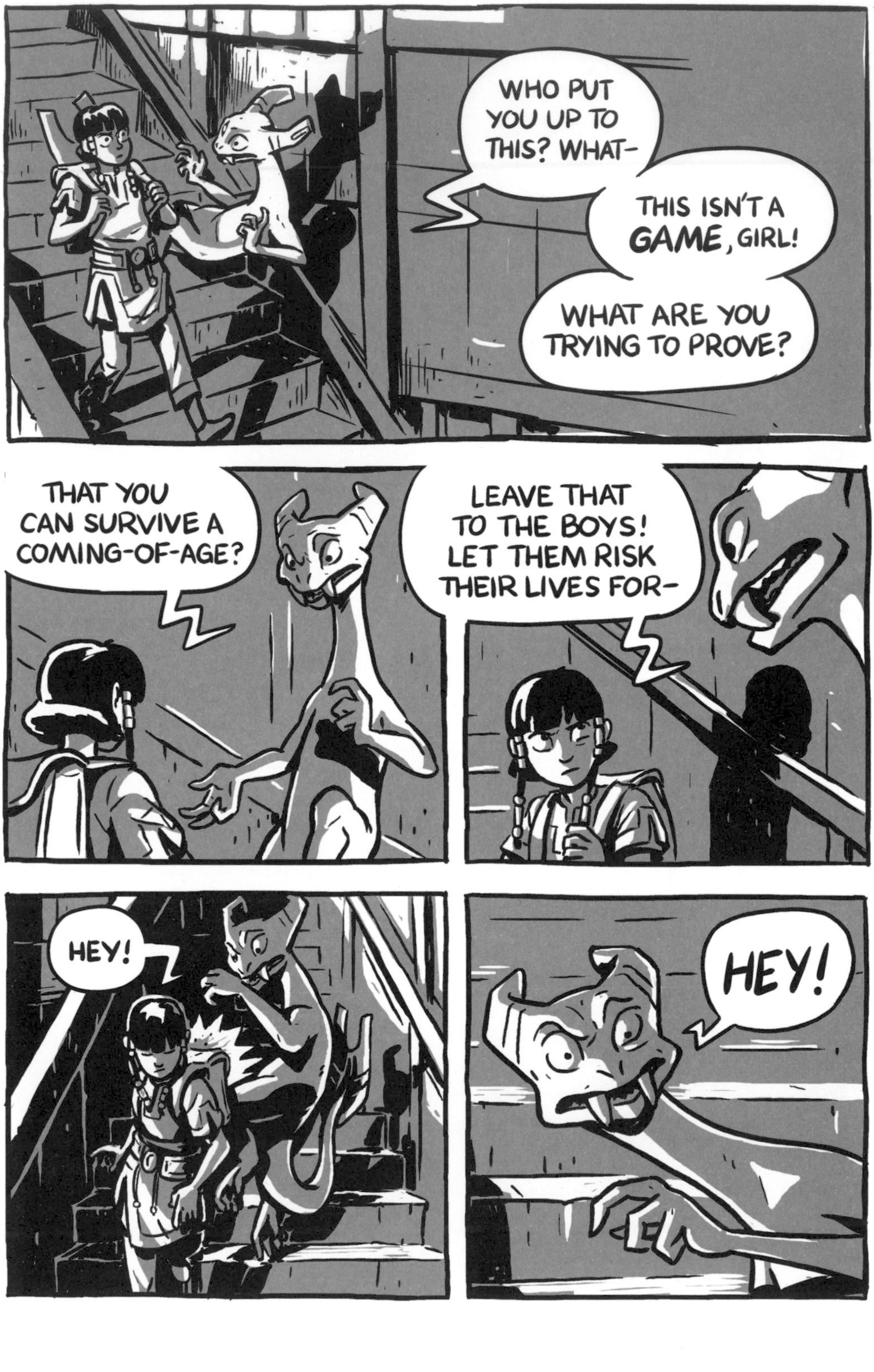
WHO PUT YOU UP TO THIS? WHAT-
THIS ISN'T A GAME, GIRL!
WHAT ARE YOU TRYING TO PROVE?
THAT YOU CAN SURVIVE A COMING-OF-AGE?
LEAVE THAT TO THE BOYS! LET THEM RISK THEIR LIVES FOR-
HEY!
HEY!

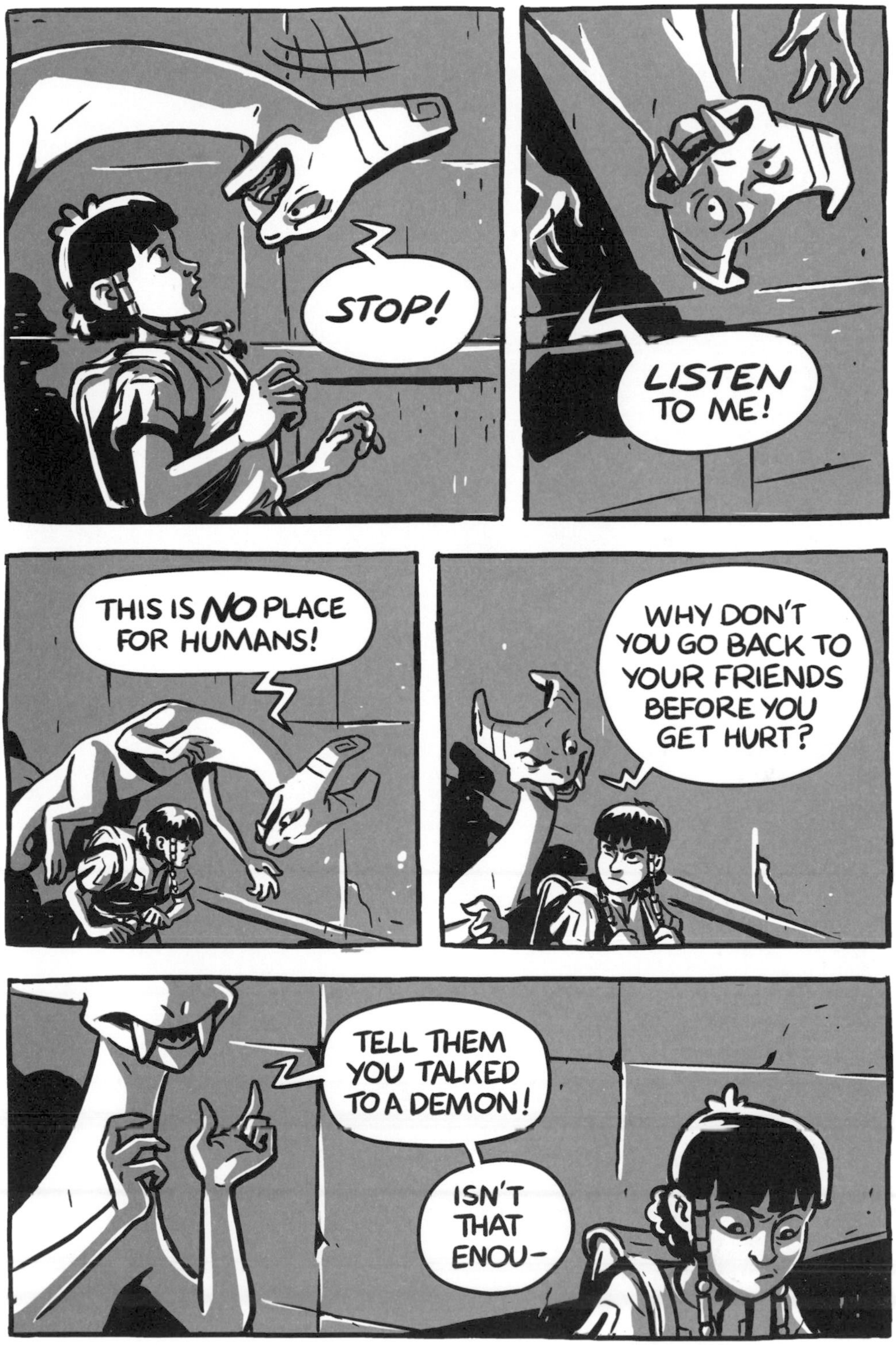
STOP!
LISTEN TO ME!
THIS IS NO PLACE FOR HUMANS!
WHY DON'T YOU GO BACK TO YOUR FRIENDS BEFORE YOU GET HURT?
TELL THEM YOU TALKED TO A DEMON!
ISN'T THAT ENOU-

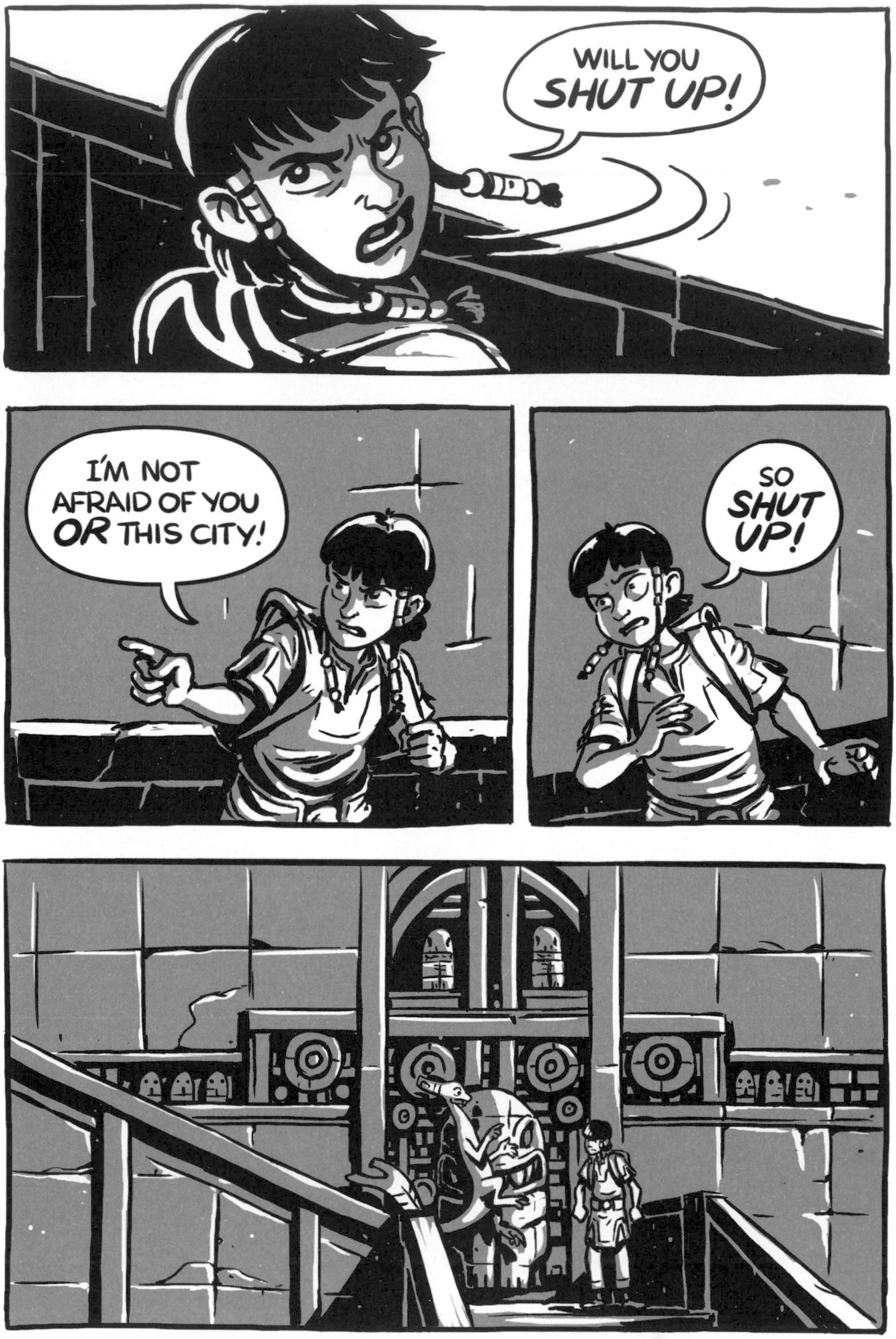
WILL YOU SHUT UP!
I'M NOT AFRAID OF YOU OR THIS CITY!
SO SHUT UP!

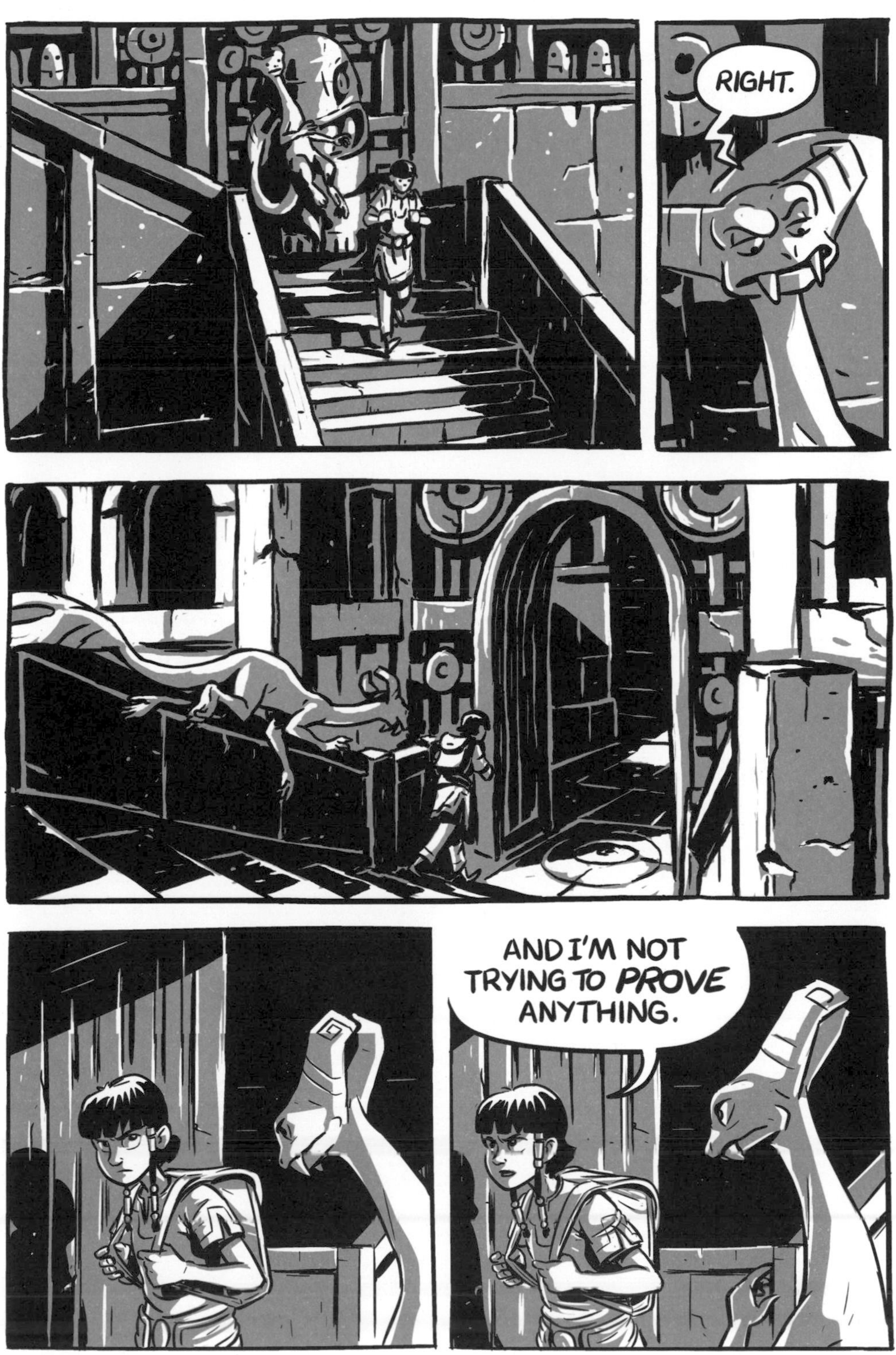
RIGHT.
AND I'M NOT TRYING TO *PROVE* ANYTHING.

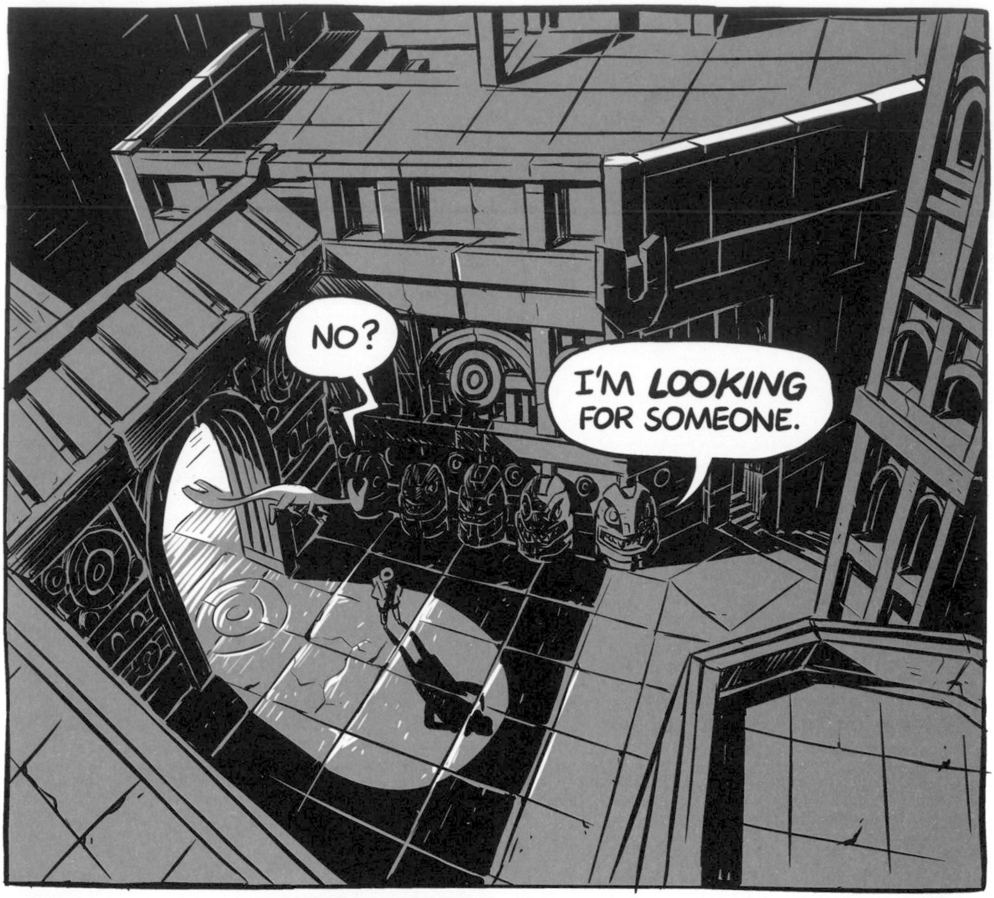
NO?
I'M LOOKING FOR SOMEONE.

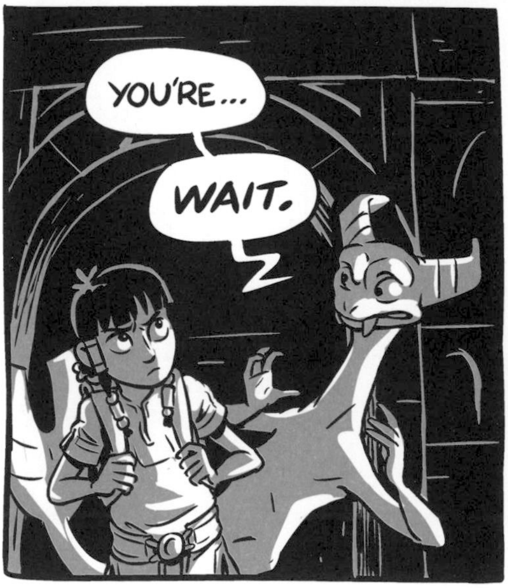
YOU'RE...
WAIT.

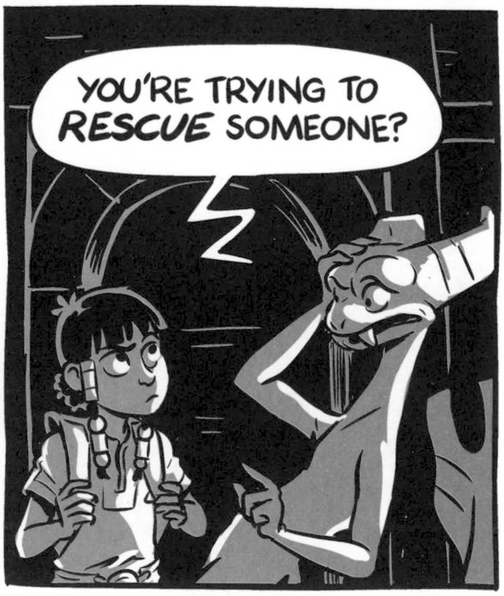
YOU'RE TRYING TO RESCUE SOMEONE?

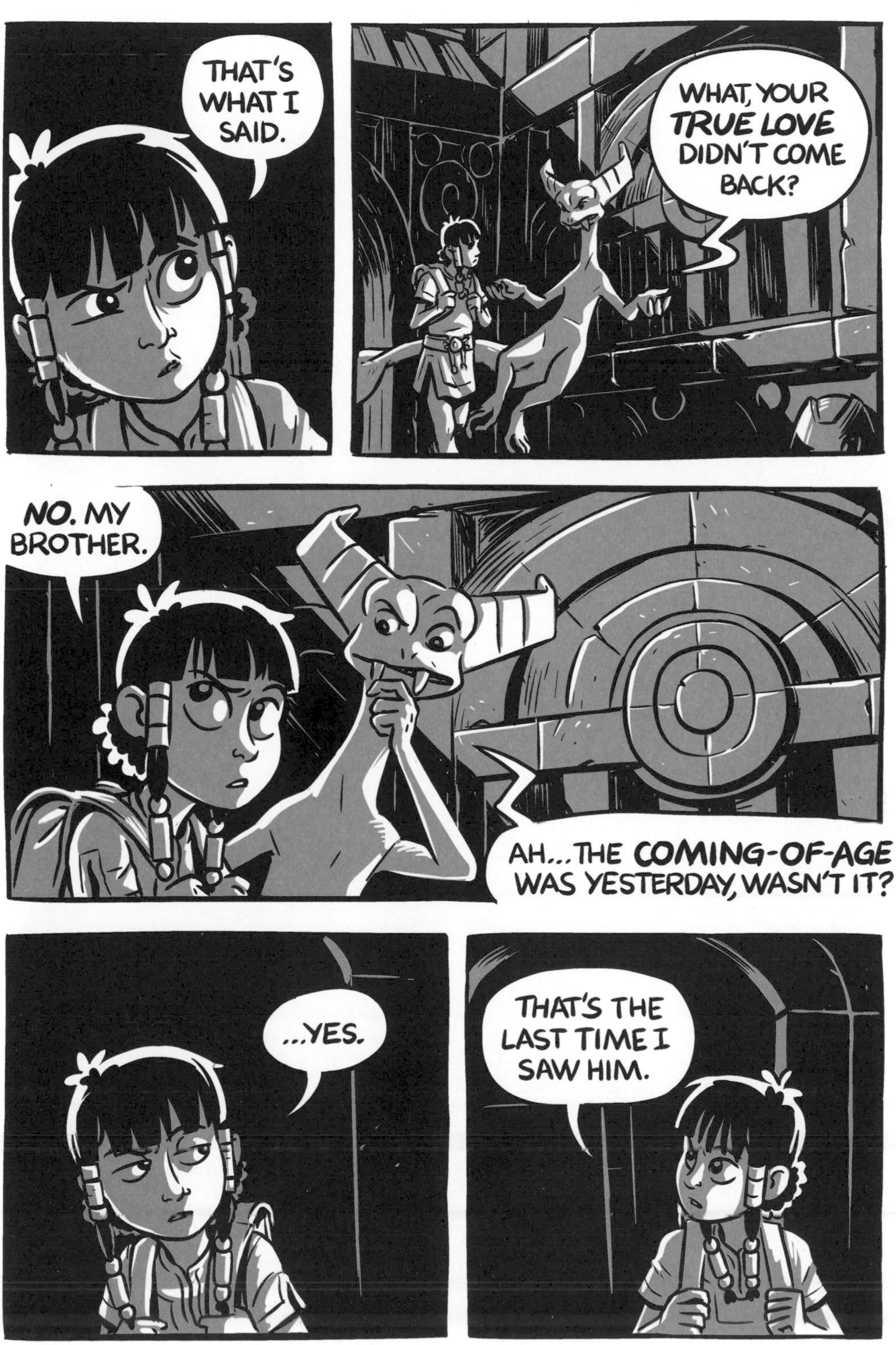
THAT'S WHAT I SAID.
WHAT, YOUR TRUE LOVE DIDN'T COME BACK?
NO. MY BROTHER.
AH... THE COMING-OF-AGE WAS YESTERDAY, WASN'T IT?
...YES.
THAT'S THE LAST TIME I SAW HIM.

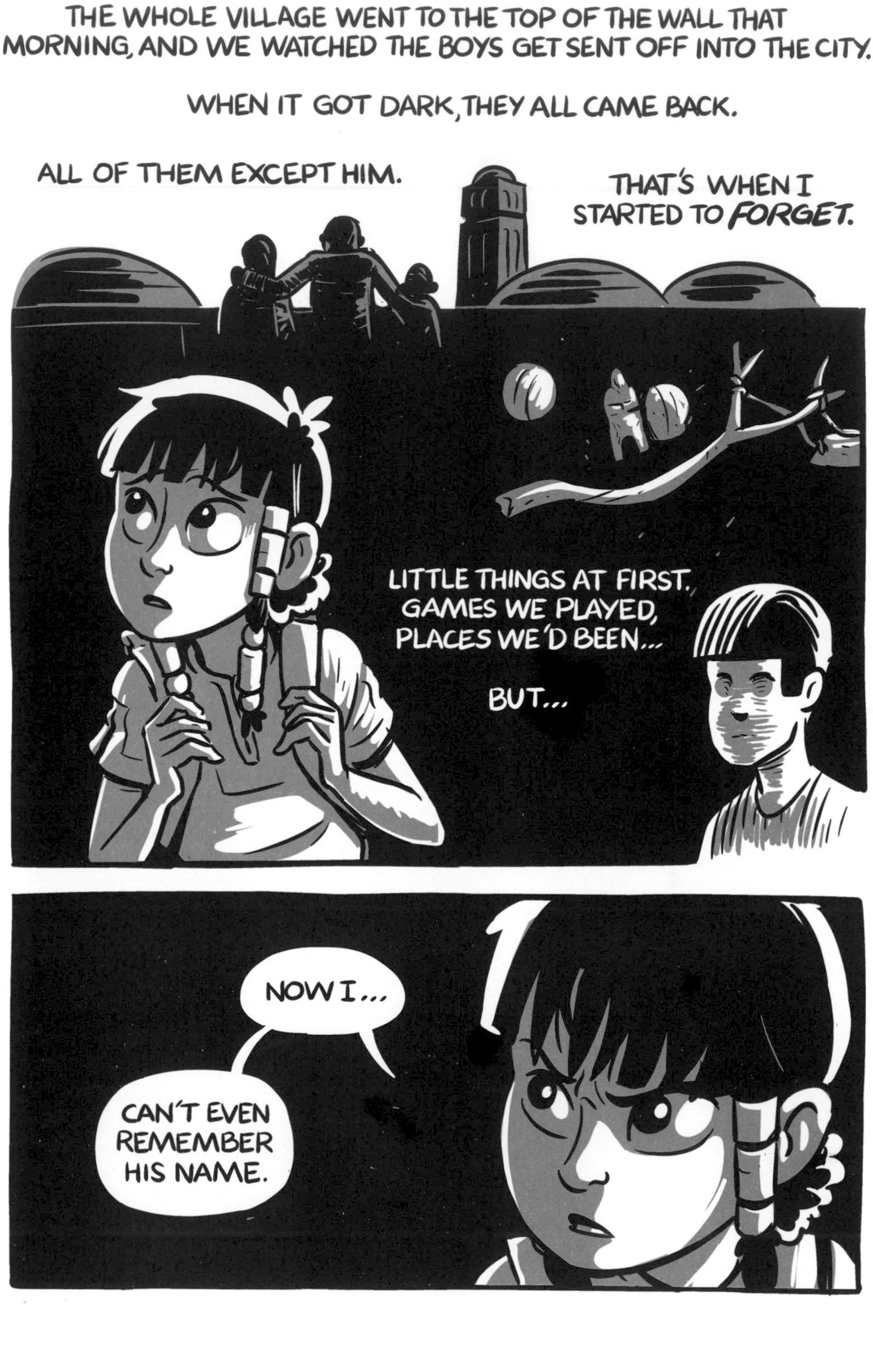
THE WHOLE VILLAGE WENT TO THE TOP OF THE WALL THAT MORNING, AND WE WATCHED THE BOYS GET SENT OFF INTO THE CITY.
WHEN IT GOT DARK, THEY ALL CAME BACK.
ALL OF THEM EXCEPT HIM.
THAT'S WHEN I STARTED TO *FORGET.*
LITTLE THINGS AT FIRST. GAMES WE PLAYED, PLACES WE'D BEEN...
BUT...
NOW I...
CAN'T EVEN REMEMBER HIS NAME.

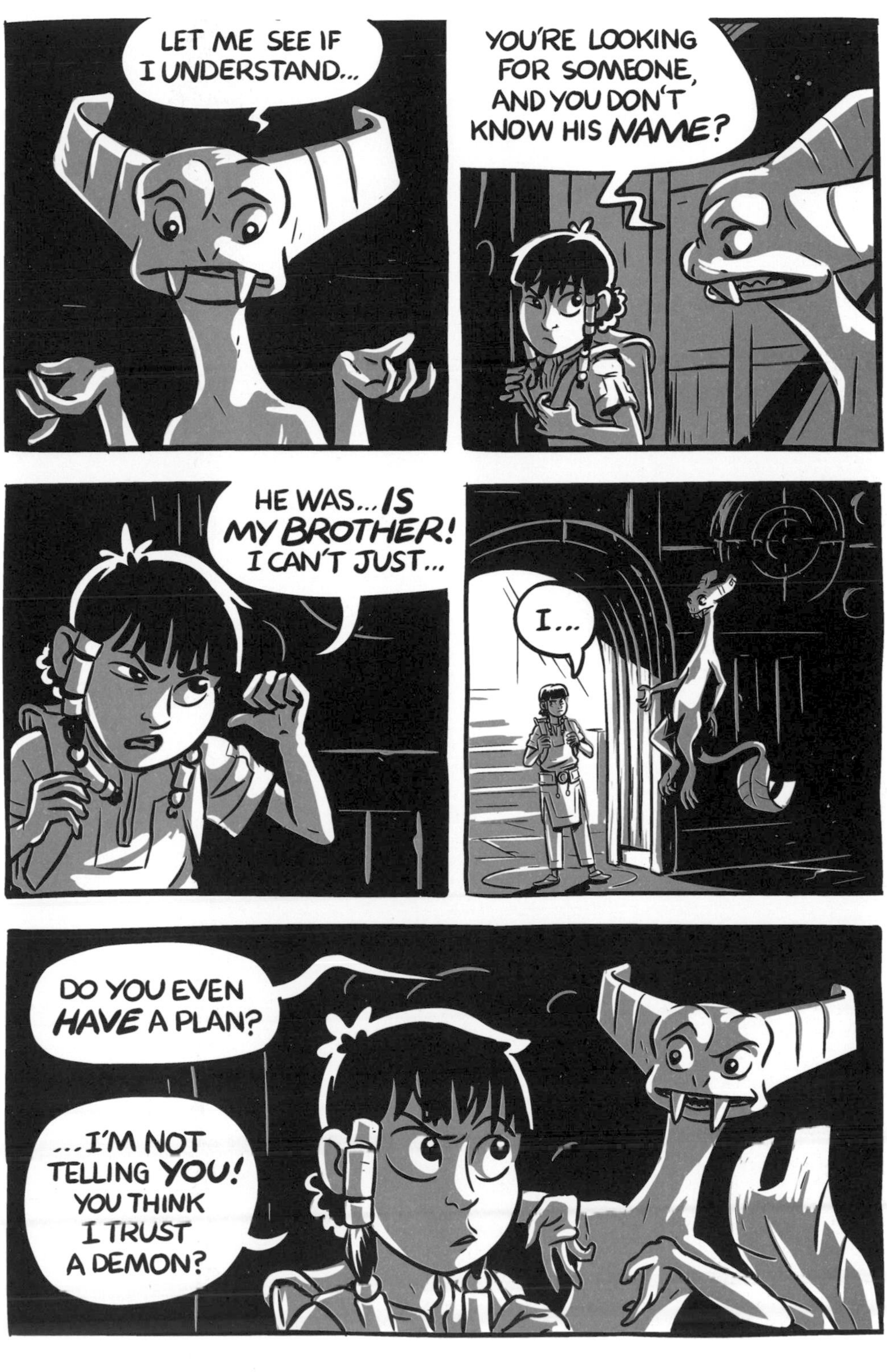
LET ME SEE IF I UNDERSTAND...
YOU'RE LOOKING FOR SOMEONE, AND YOU DON'T KNOW HIS NAME?
HE WAS... IS MY BROTHER! I CAN'T JUST...
I...
DO YOU EVEN HAVE A PLAN?
...I'M NOT TELLING YOU! YOU THINK I TRUST A DEMON?

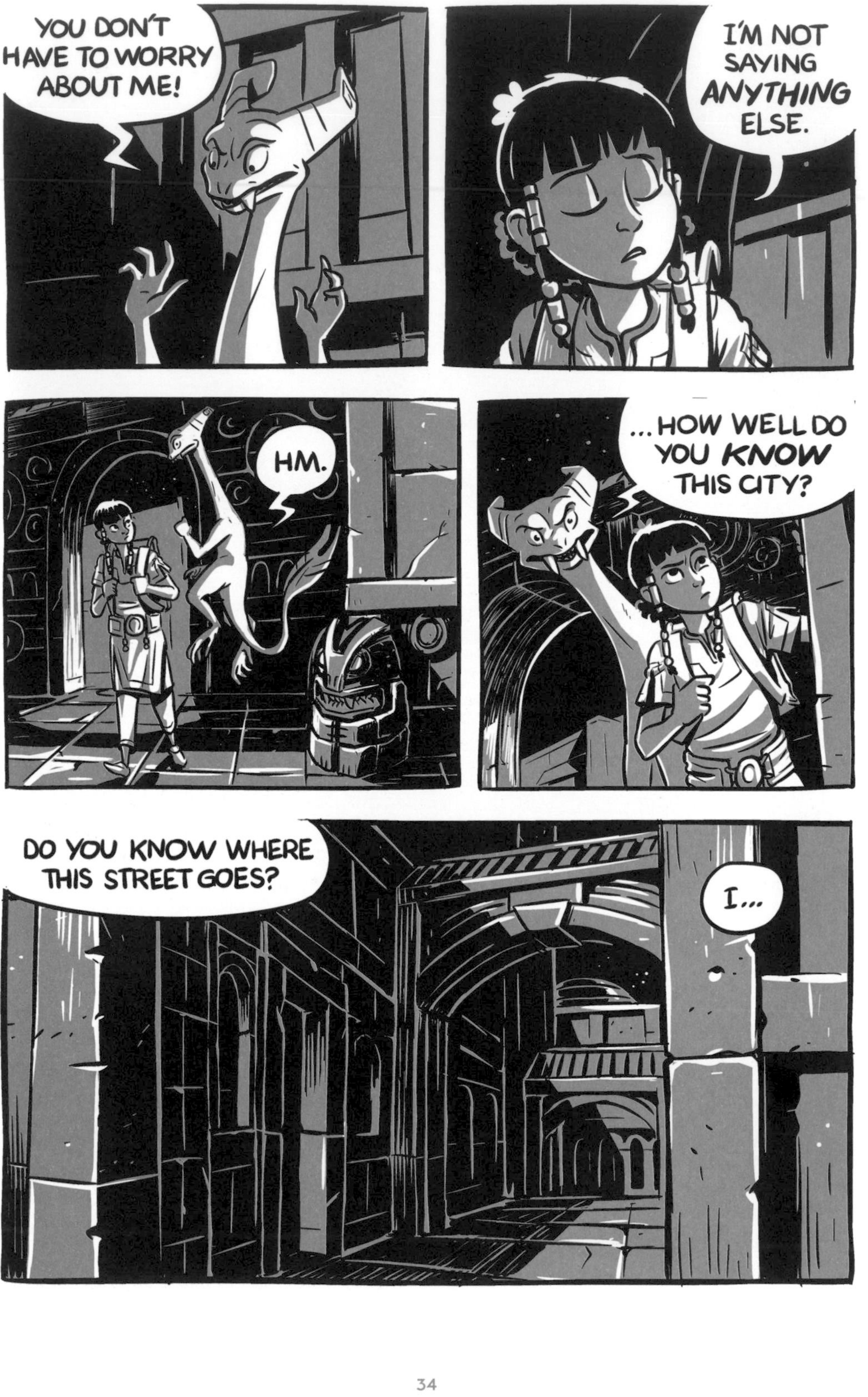
YOU DON'T HAVE TO WORRY ABOUT ME!
I'M NOT SAYING *ANYTHING* ELSE.
HM.
...HOW WELL DO YOU *KNOW* THIS CITY?
DO YOU KNOW WHERE THIS STREET GOES?
I...

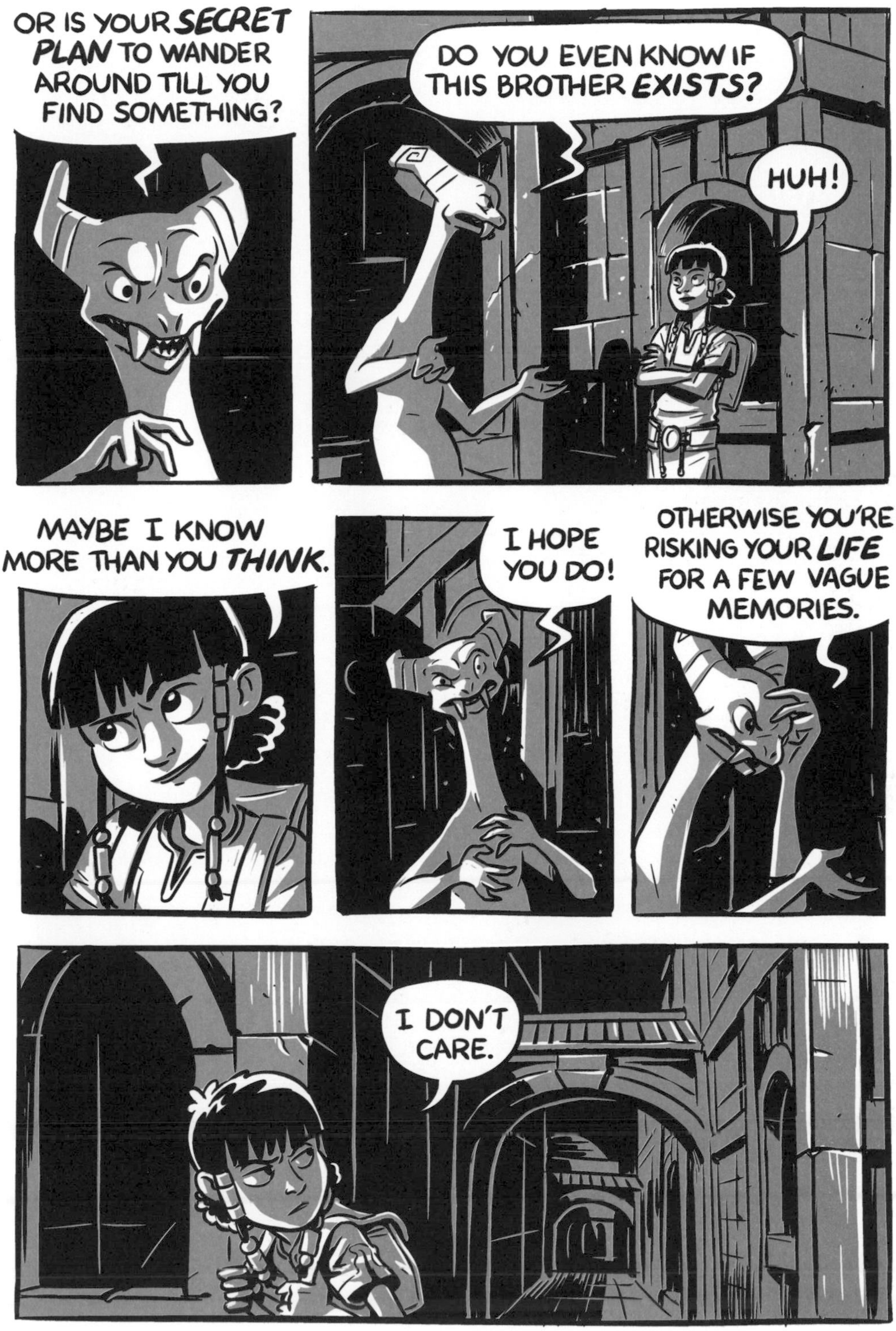

OR IS YOUR SECRET PLAN TO WANDER AROUND TILL YOU FIND SOMETHING?
DO YOU EVEN KNOW IF THIS BROTHER EXISTS?
HUH!
MAYBE I KNOW MORE THAN YOU THINK.
I HOPE YOU DO!
OTHERWISE YOU'RE RISKING YOUR LIFE FOR A FEW VAGUE MEMORIES.
I DON'T CARE.

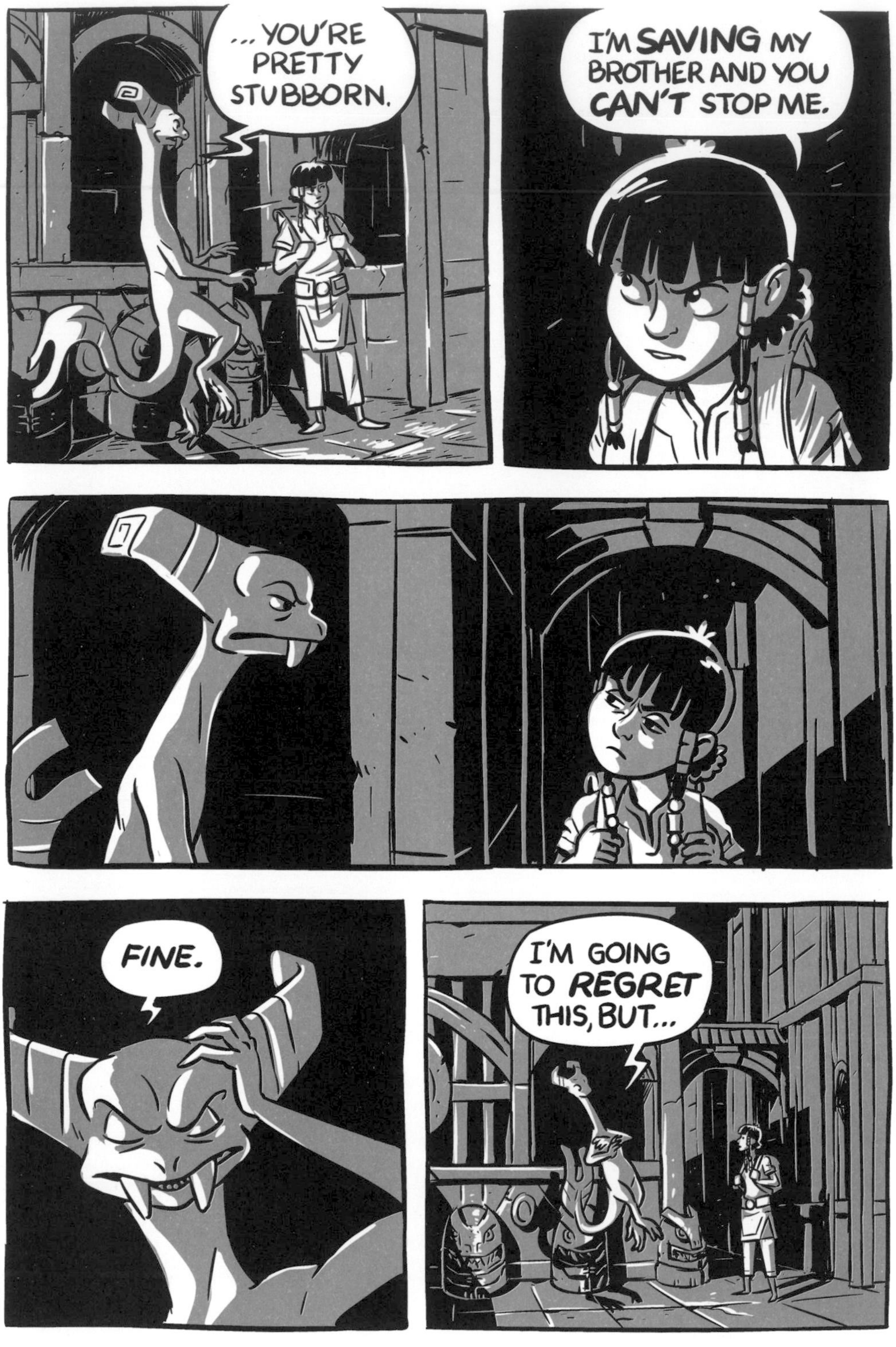
...YOU'RE PRETTY STUBBORN.
I'M SAVING MY BROTHER AND YOU CAN'T STOP ME.
FINE.
I'M GOING TO REGRET THIS, BUT...

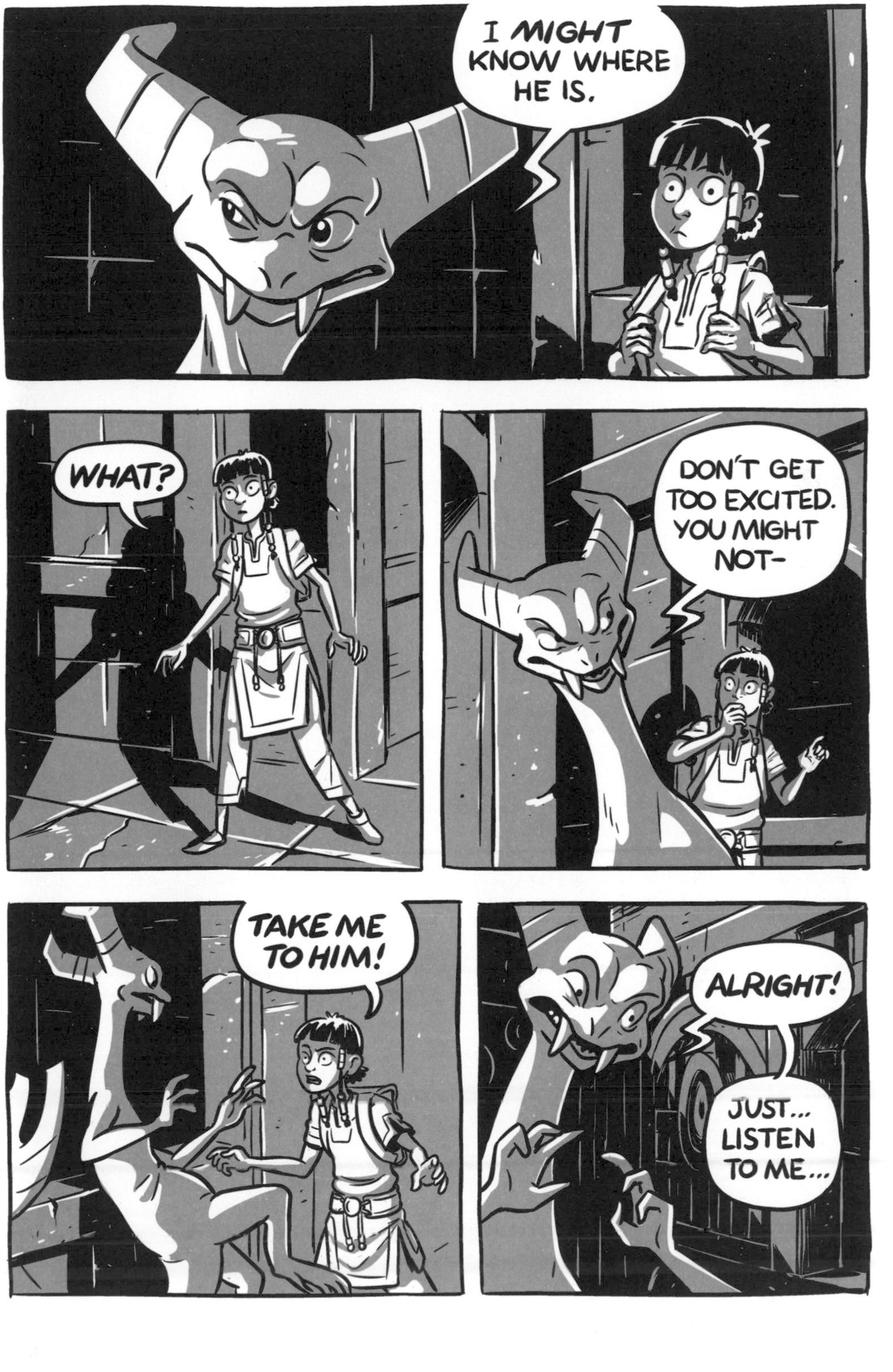
I MIGHT KNOW WHERE HE IS.
WHAT?
DON'T GET TOO EXCITED. YOU MIGHT NOT-
TAKE ME TO HIM!
ALRIGHT!
JUST... LISTEN TO ME...

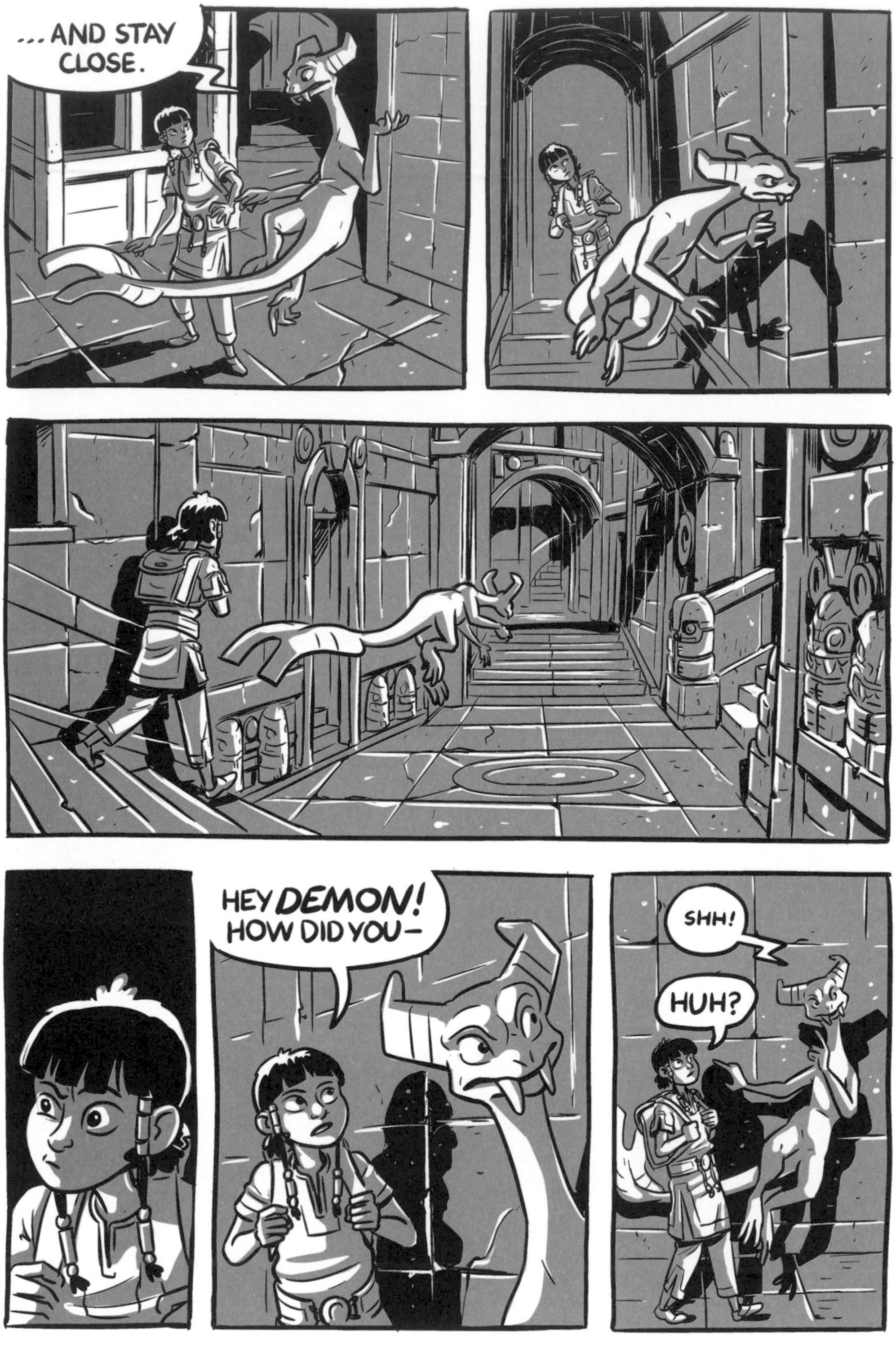
...AND STAY CLOSE.
HEY DEMON! HOW DID YOU–
SHH!
HUH?

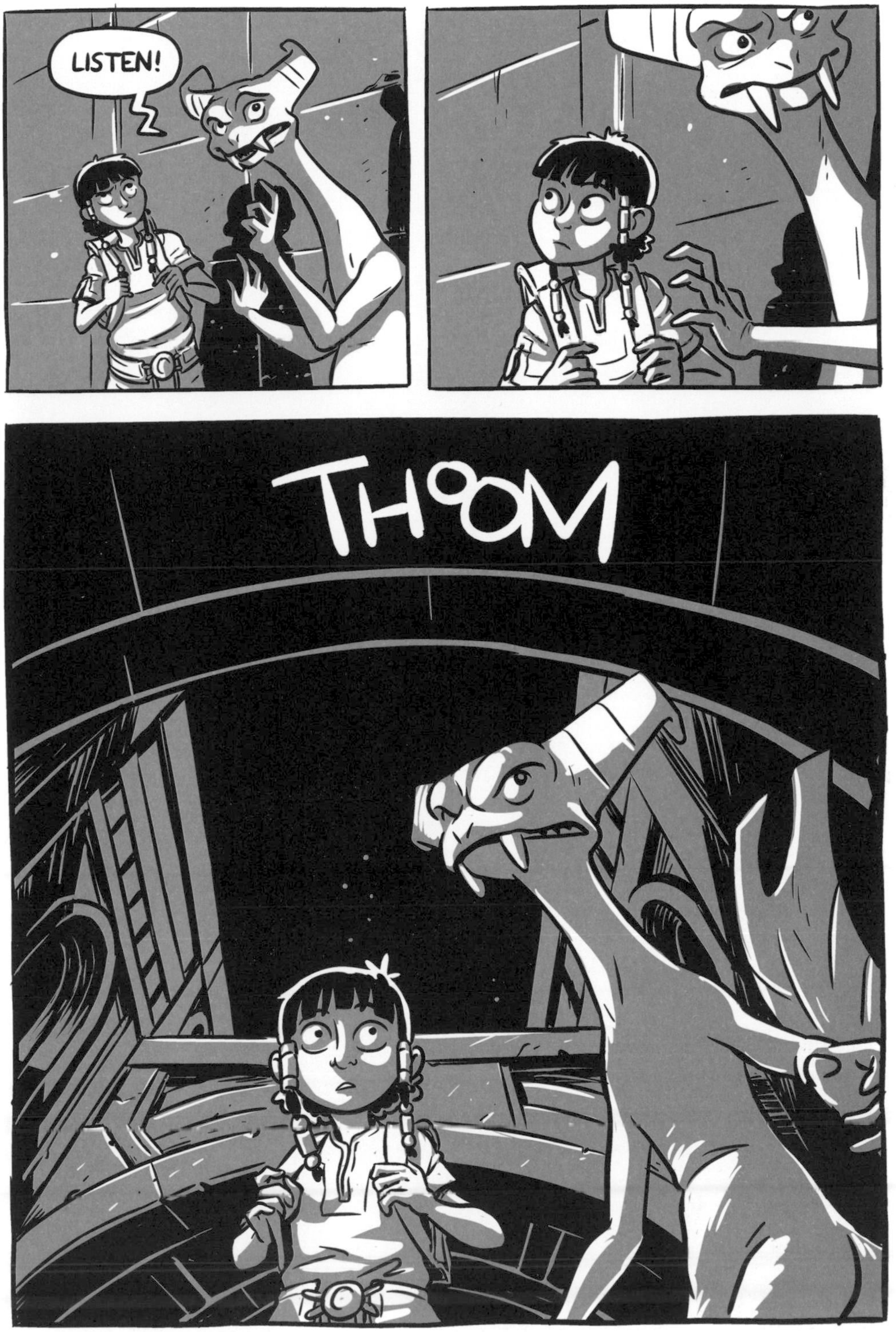
LISTEN!
THOOM

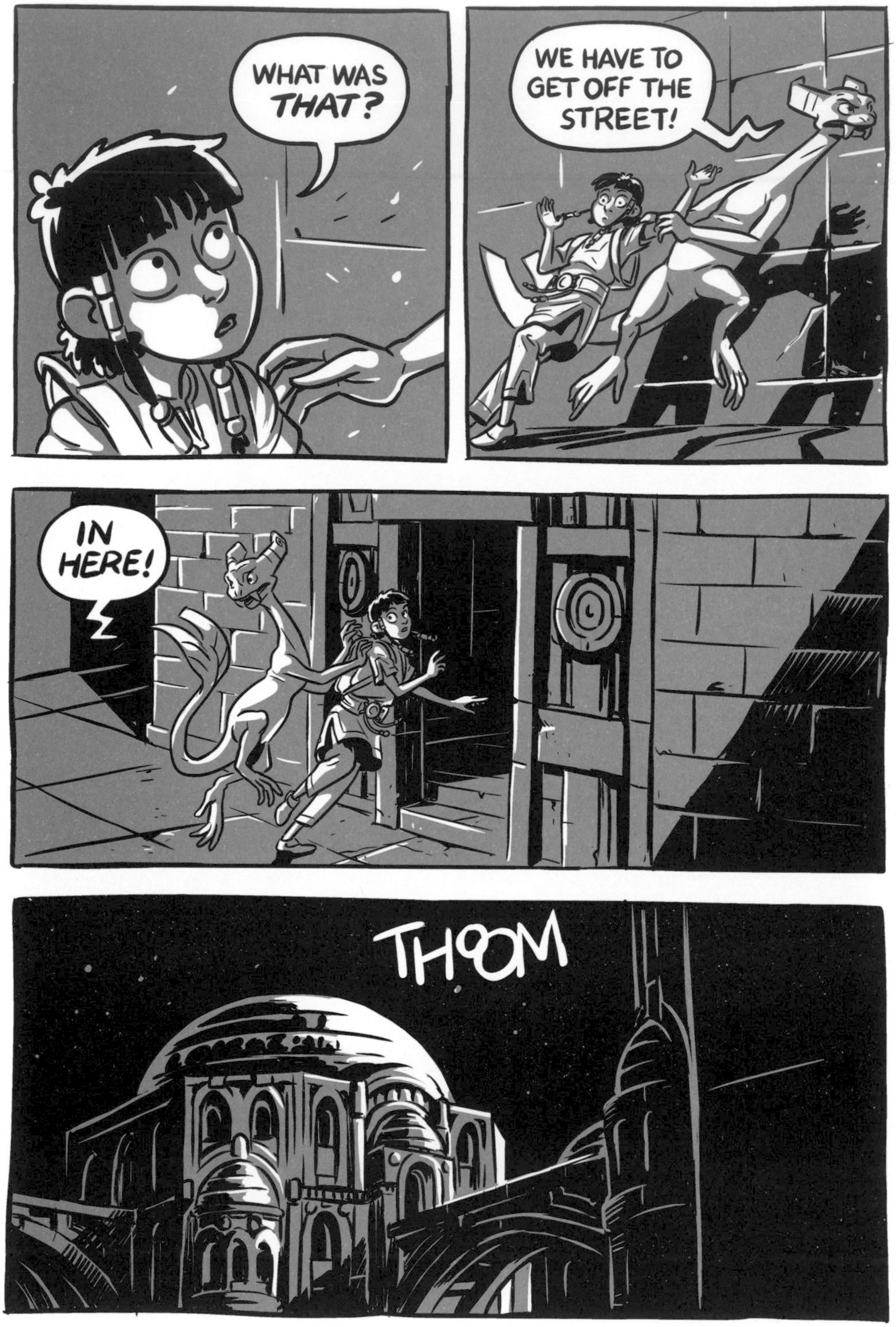
WHAT WAS THAT?
WE HAVE TO GET OFF THE STREET!
IN HERE!
THOOM

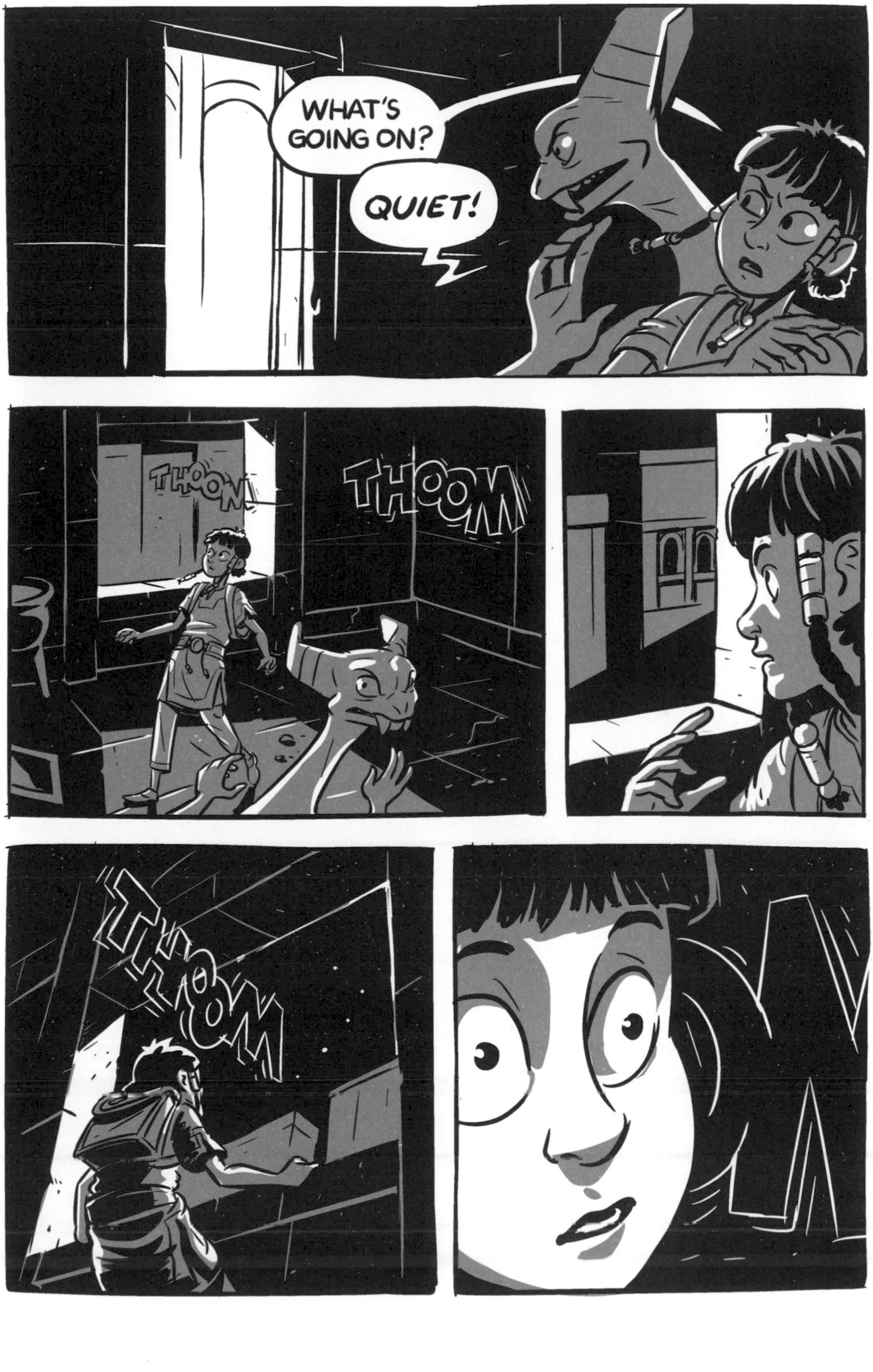
WHAT'S GOING ON?
QUIET!
THOOM
THOOM
THOOM

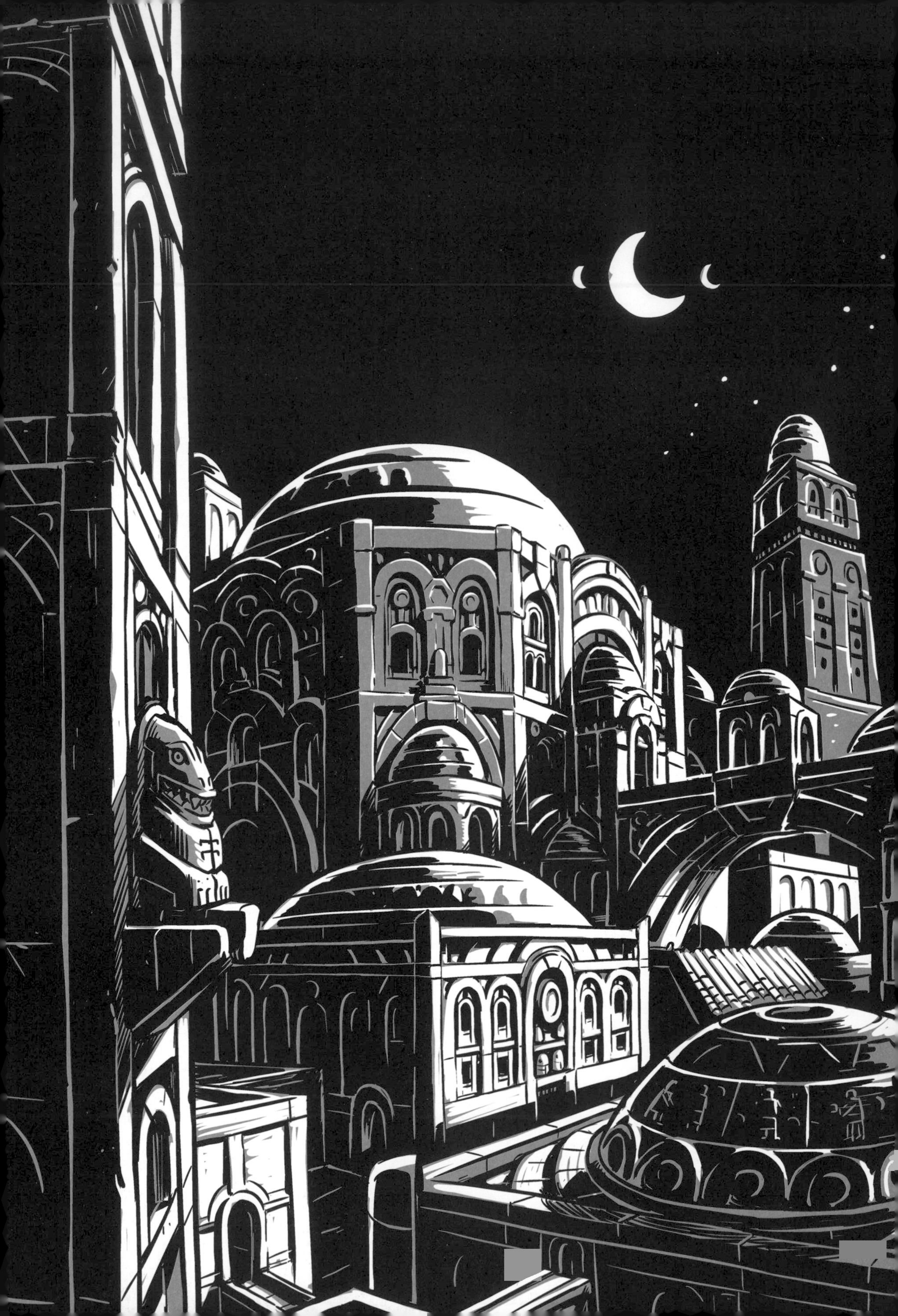

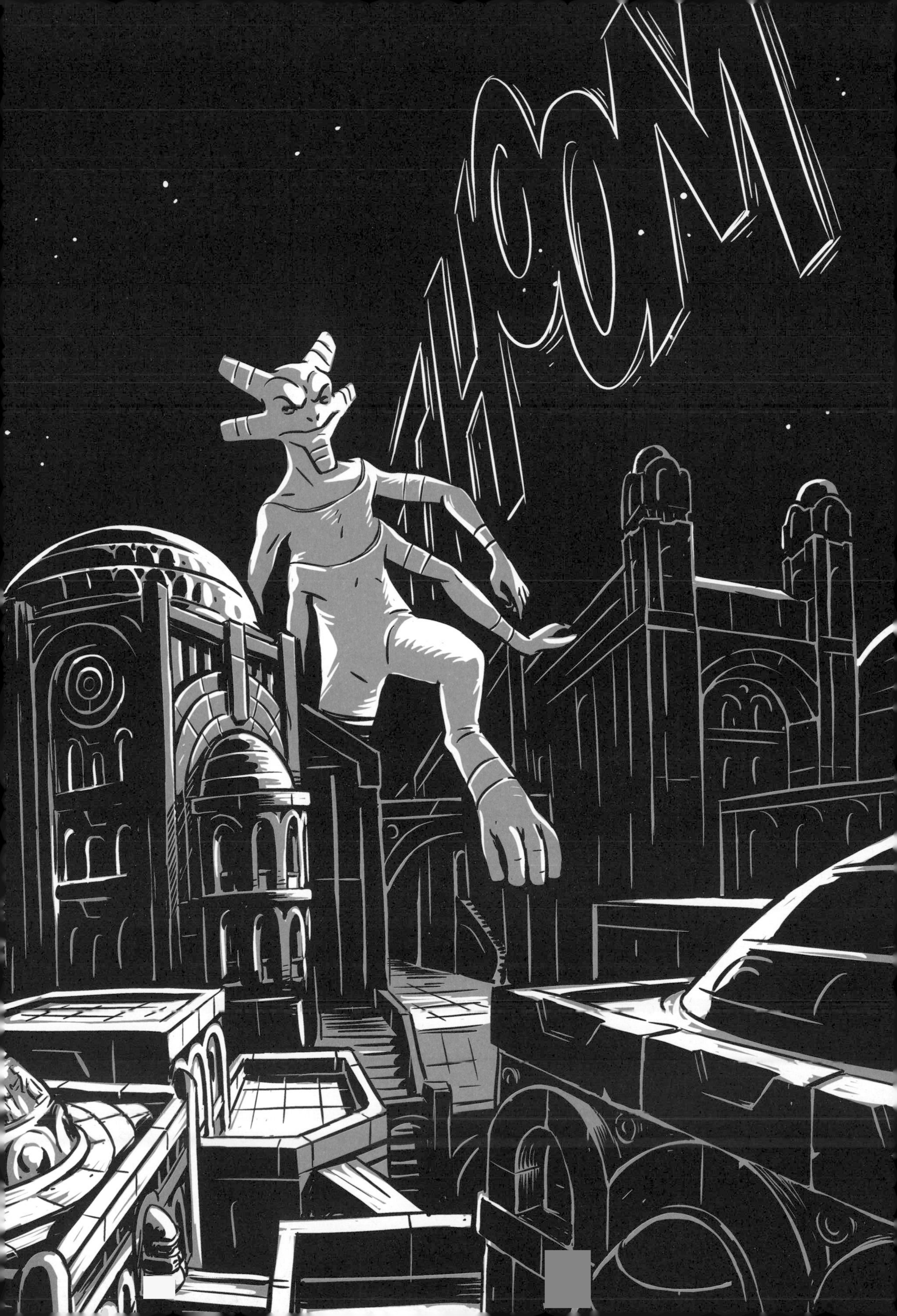
THOOM

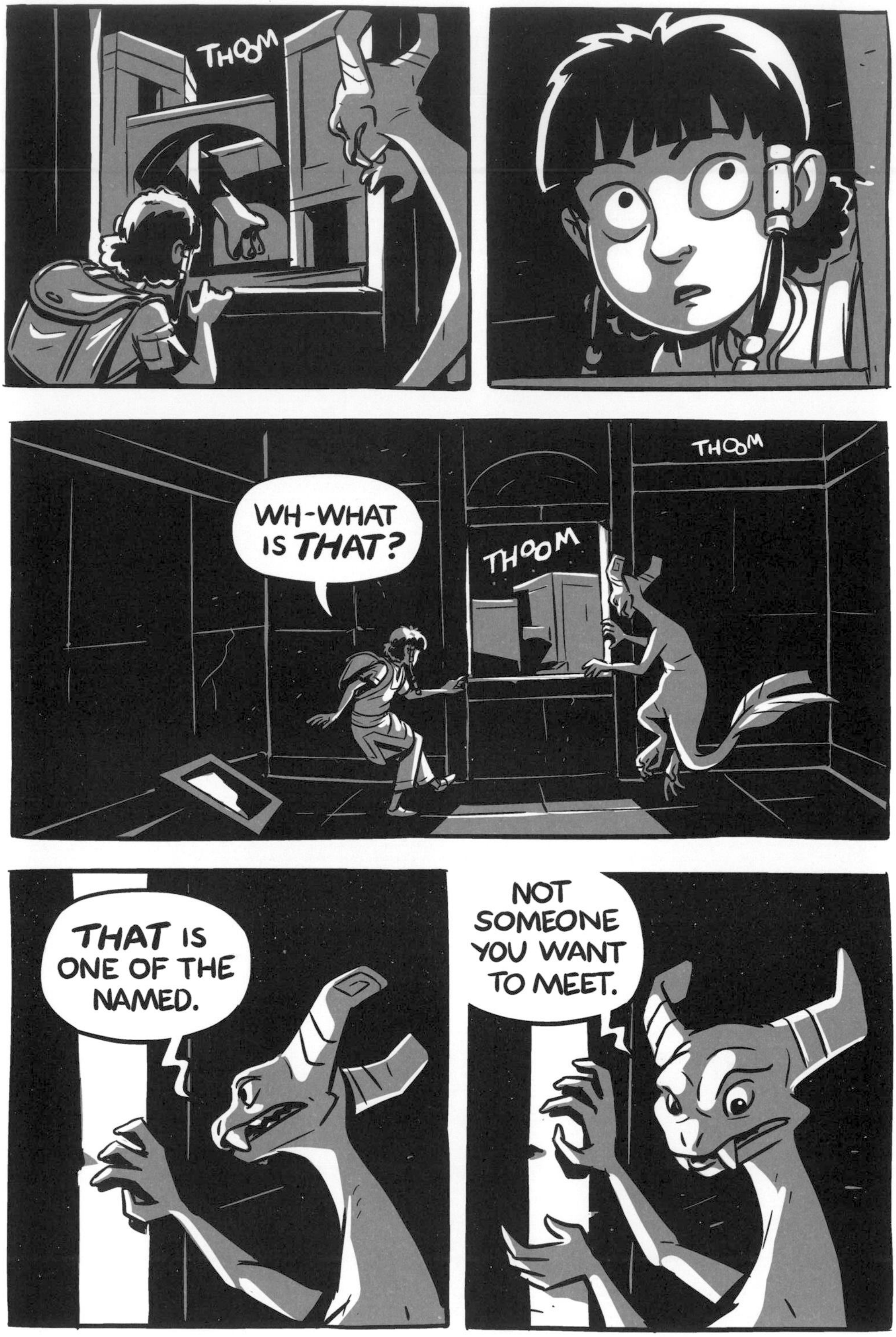
THOOM
WH-WHAT IS THAT?
THOOM
THOOM
THAT IS ONE OF THE NAMED.
NOT SOMEONE YOU WANT TO MEET.

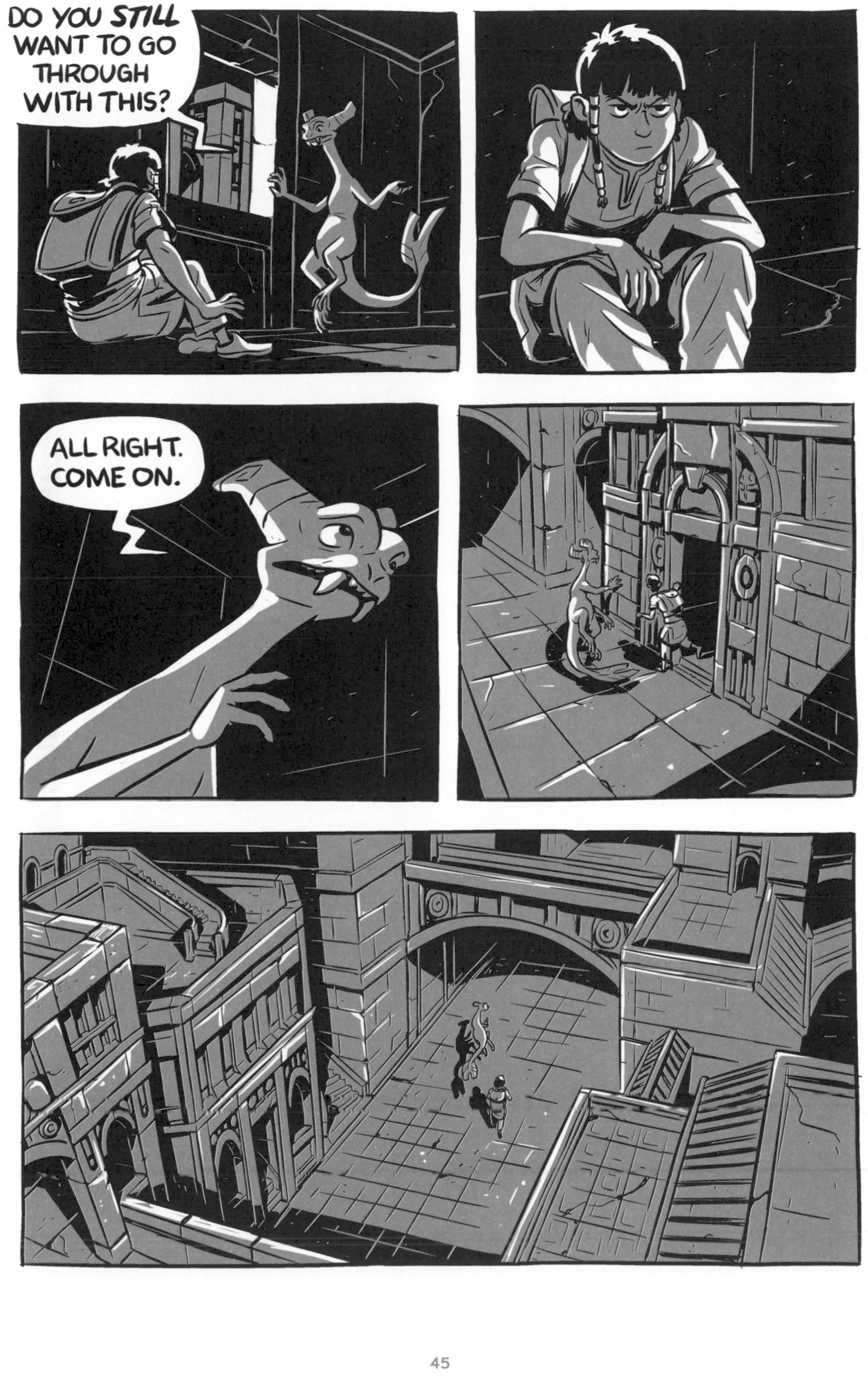
DO YOU STILL WANT TO GO THROUGH WITH THIS?
ALL RIGHT. COME ON.

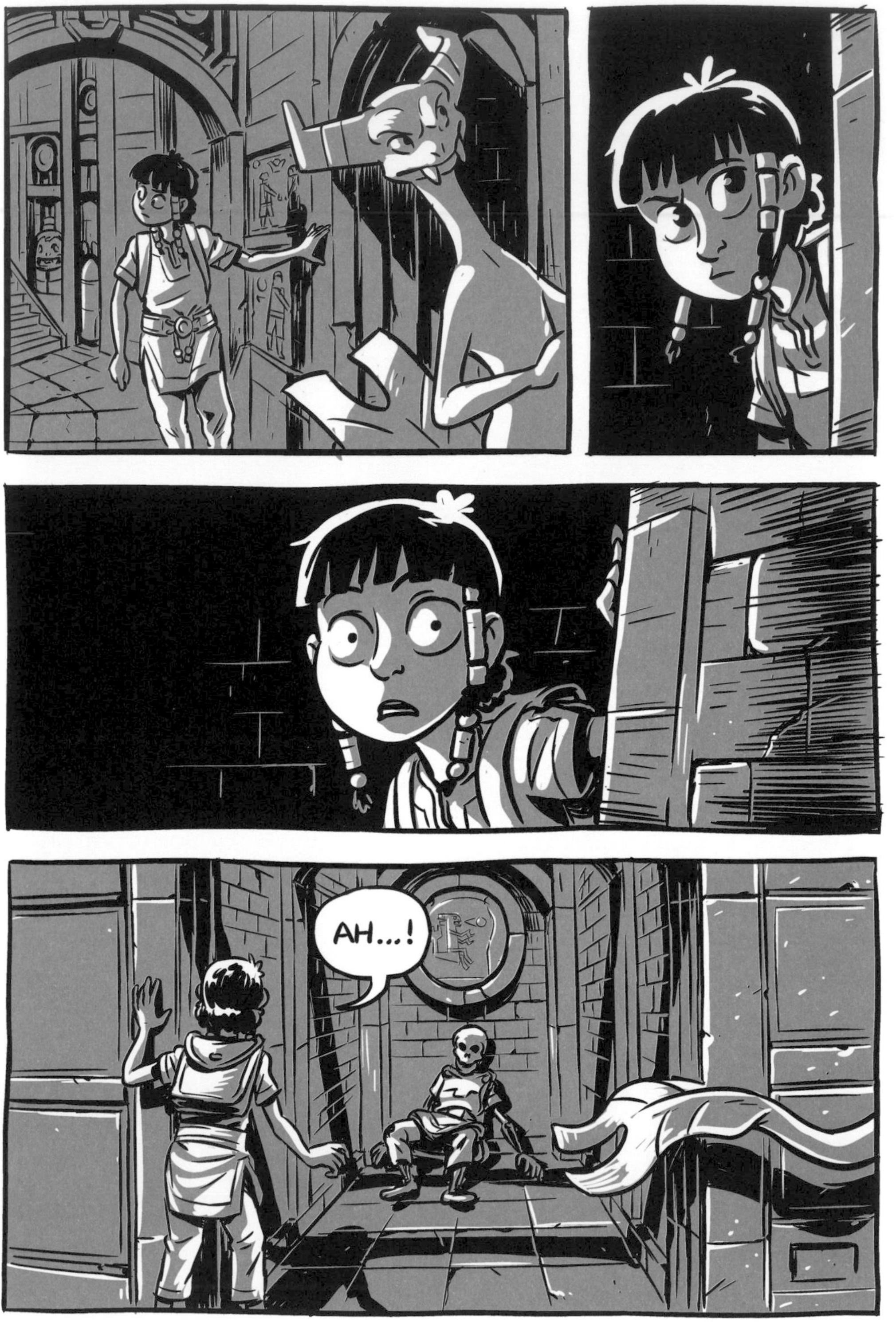
AH...!

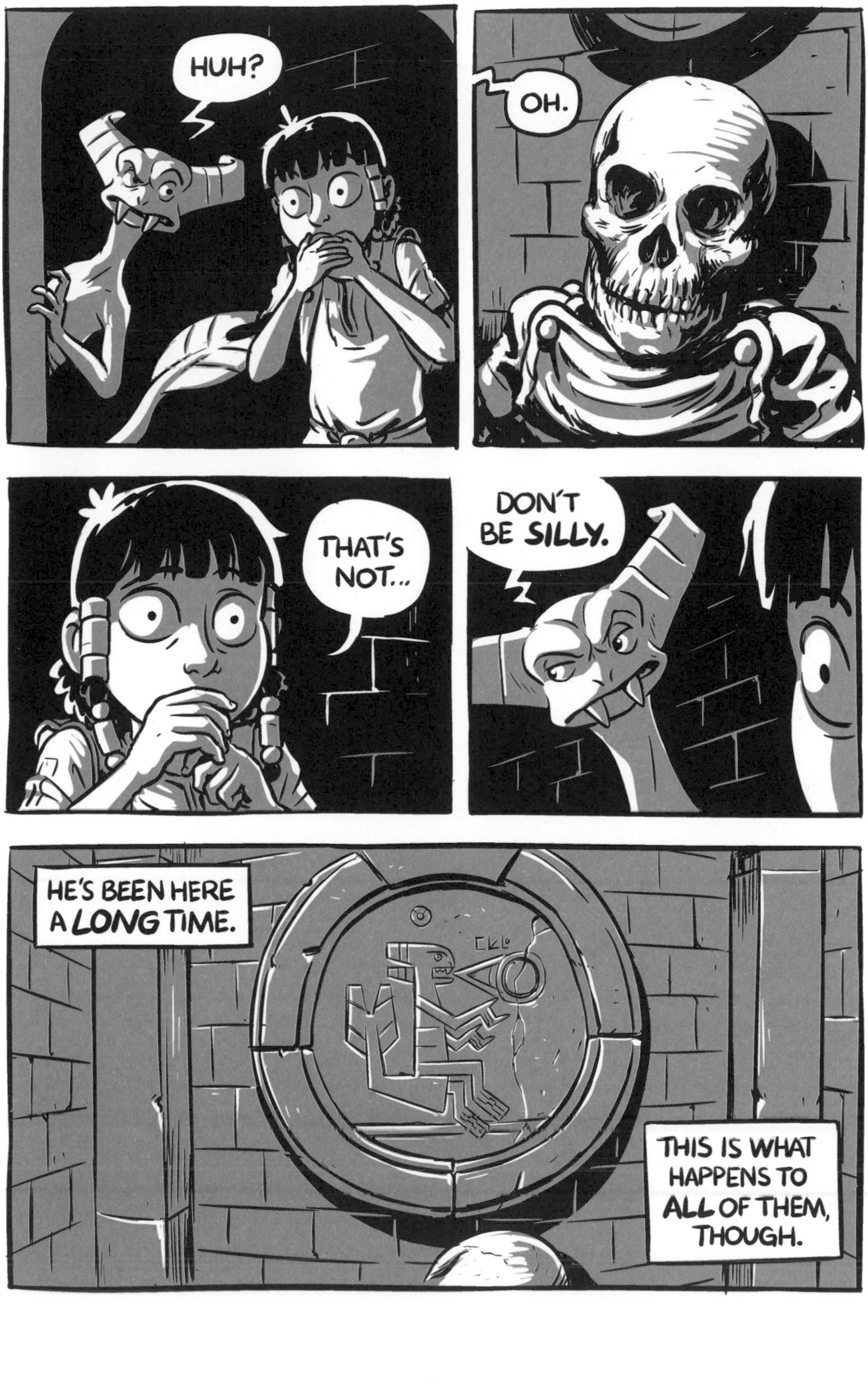
HUH?
OH.
THAT'S NOT...
DON'T BE SILLY.
HE'S BEEN HERE A LONG TIME.
THIS IS WHAT HAPPENS TO ALL OF THEM, THOUGH.

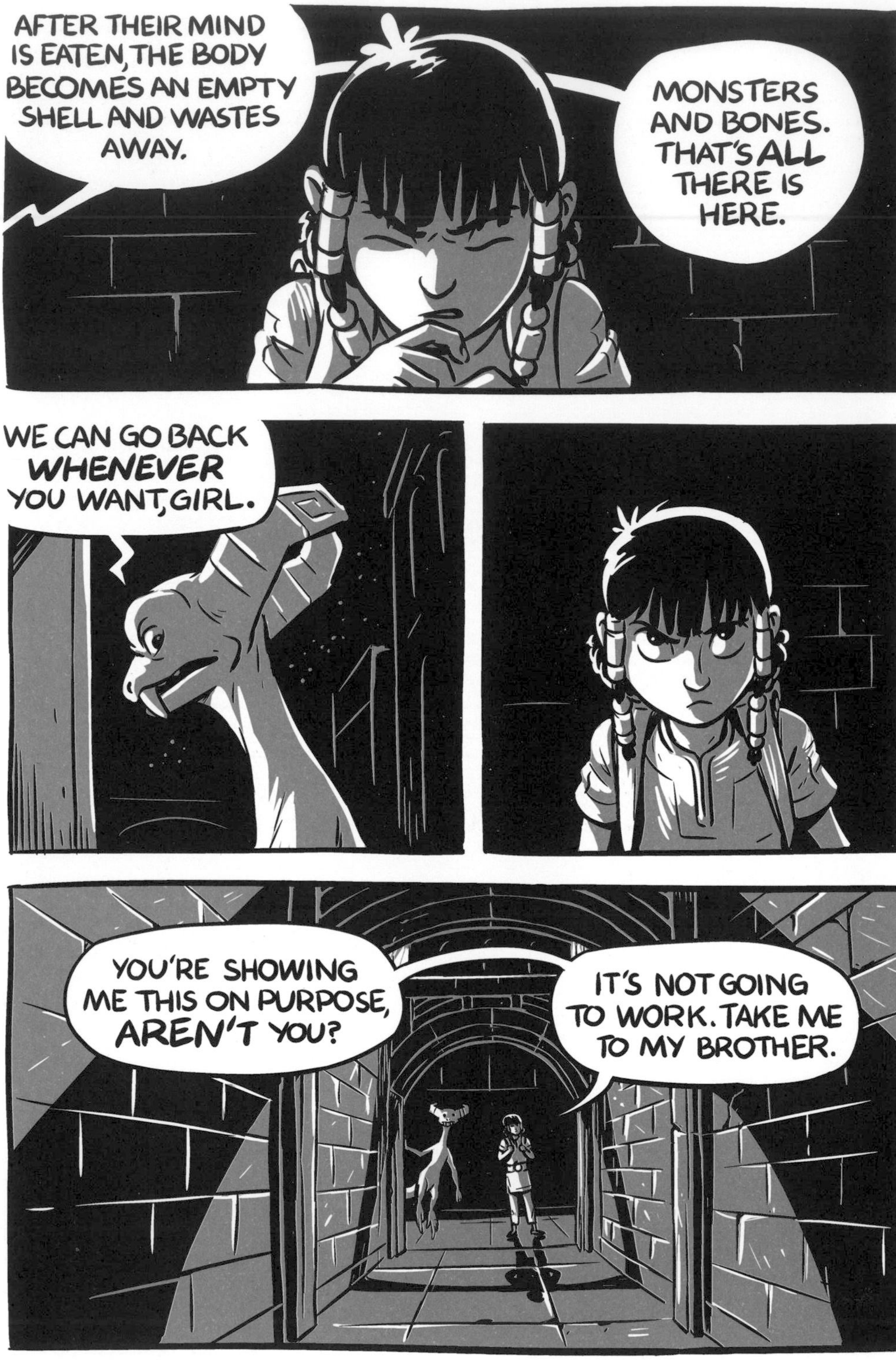
AFTER THEIR MIND IS EATEN, THE BODY BECOMES AN EMPTY SHELL AND WASTES AWAY.
MONSTERS AND BONES. THAT'S ALL THERE IS HERE.
WE CAN GO BACK WHENEVER YOU WANT, GIRL.
YOU'RE SHOWING ME THIS ON PURPOSE, AREN'T YOU?
IT'S NOT GOING TO WORK. TAKE ME TO MY BROTHER.

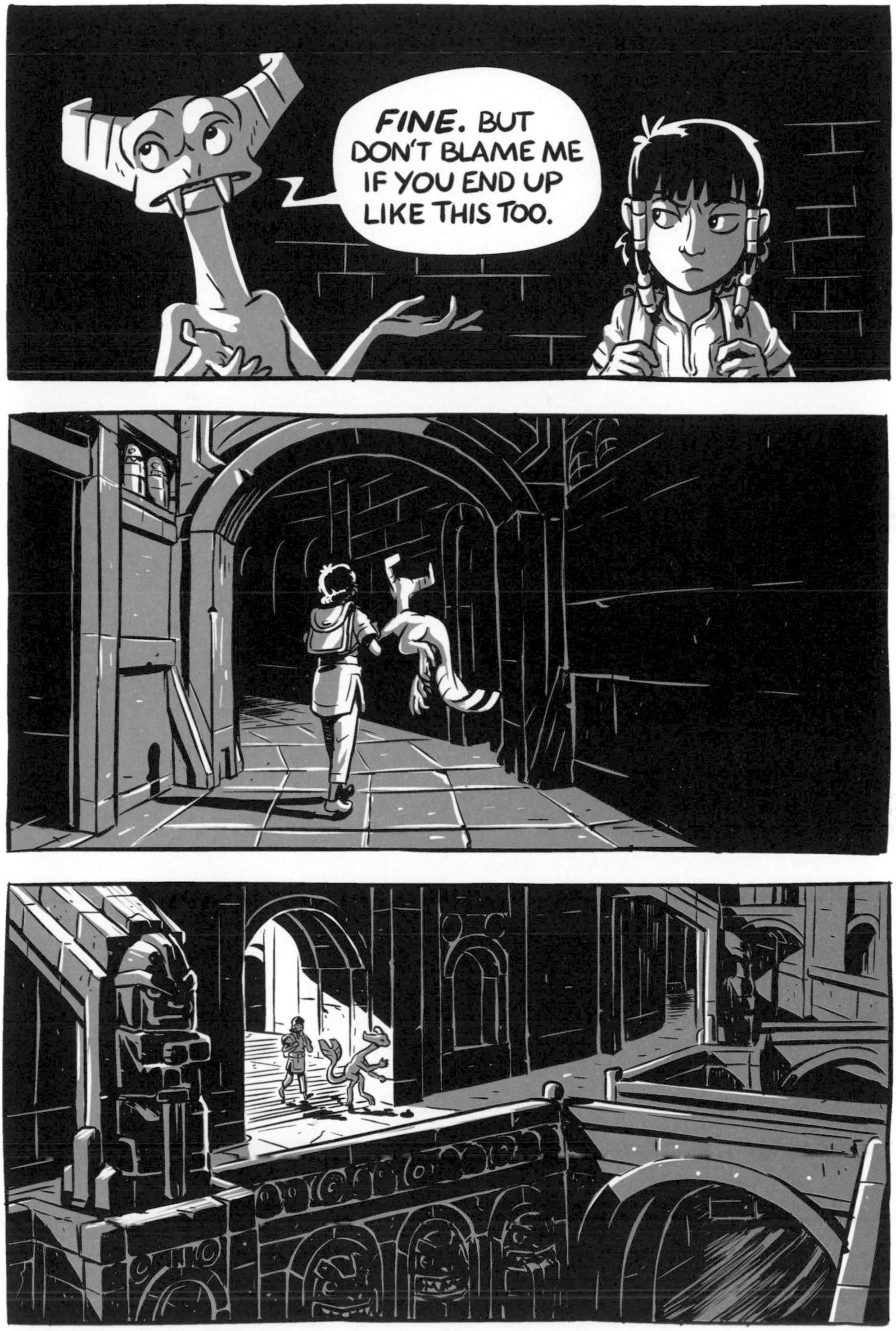
FINE. BUT DON'T BLAME ME IF YOU END UP LIKE THIS TOO.

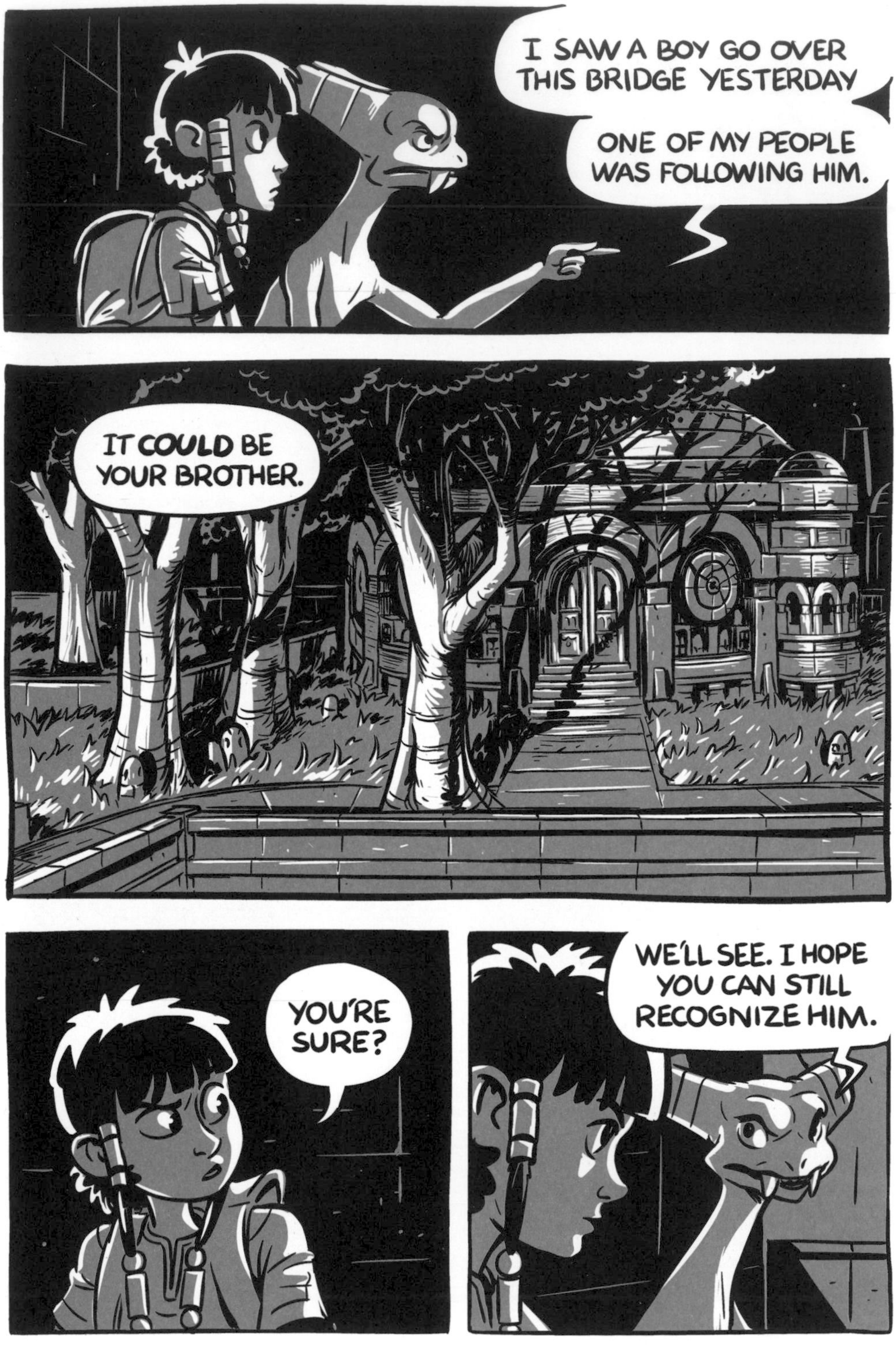
I SAW A BOY GO OVER THIS BRIDGE YESTERDAY
ONE OF MY PEOPLE WAS FOLLOWING HIM.
IT **COULD** BE YOUR BROTHER.
YOU'RE SURE?
WE'LL SEE. I HOPE YOU CAN STILL RECOGNIZE HIM.

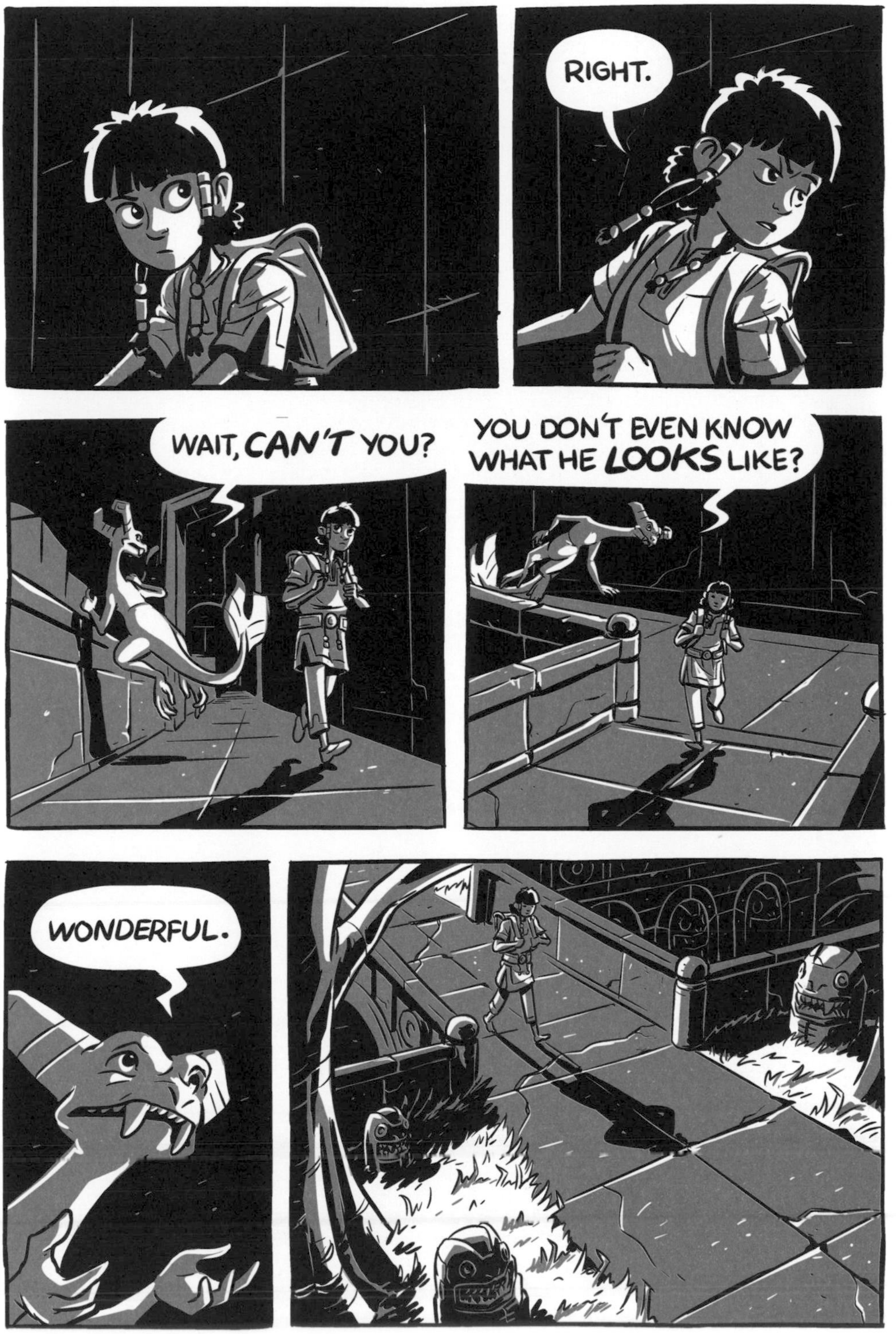
RIGHT.
WAIT, CAN'T YOU?
YOU DON'T EVEN KNOW WHAT HE LOOKS LIKE?
WONDERFUL.

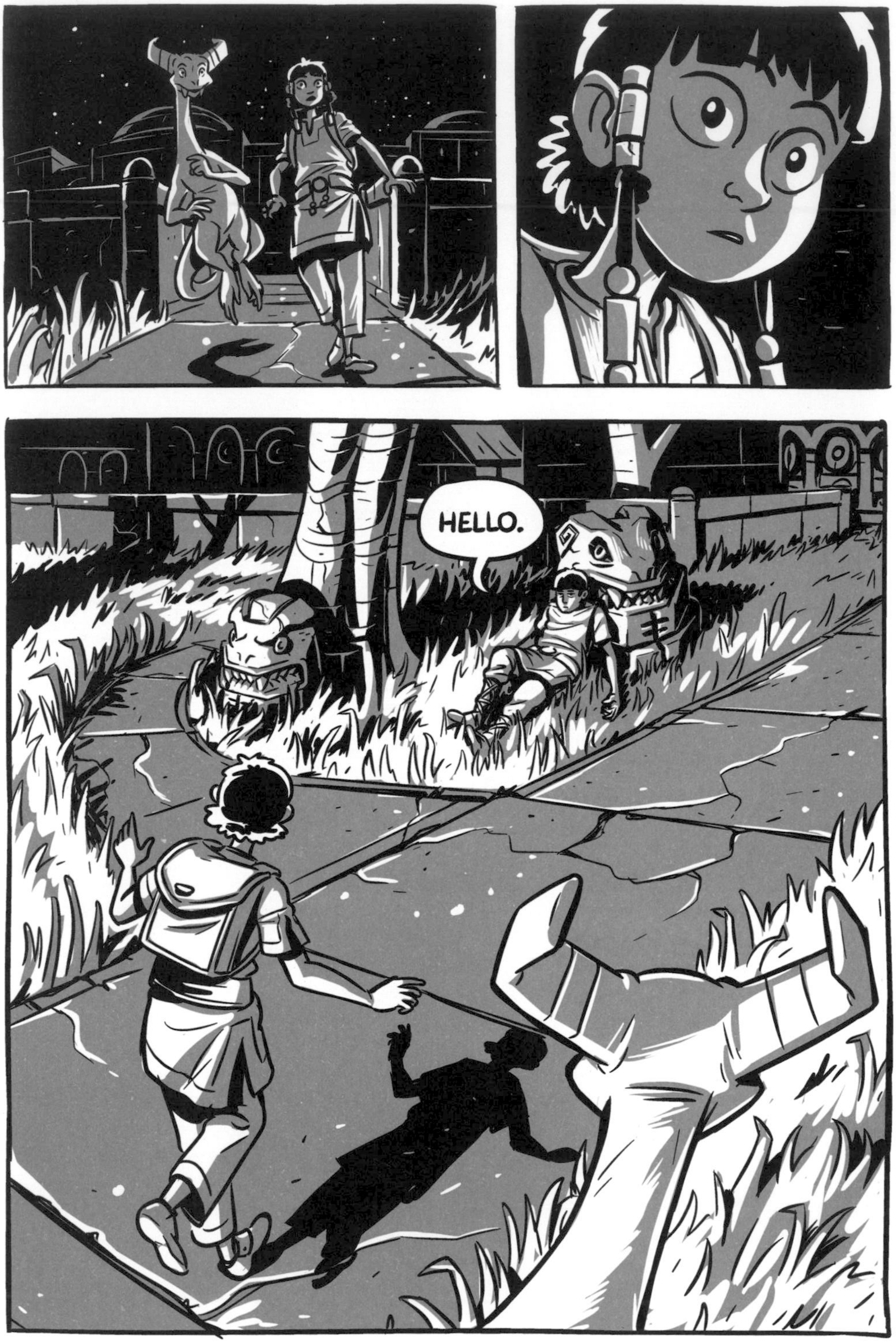
HELLO.

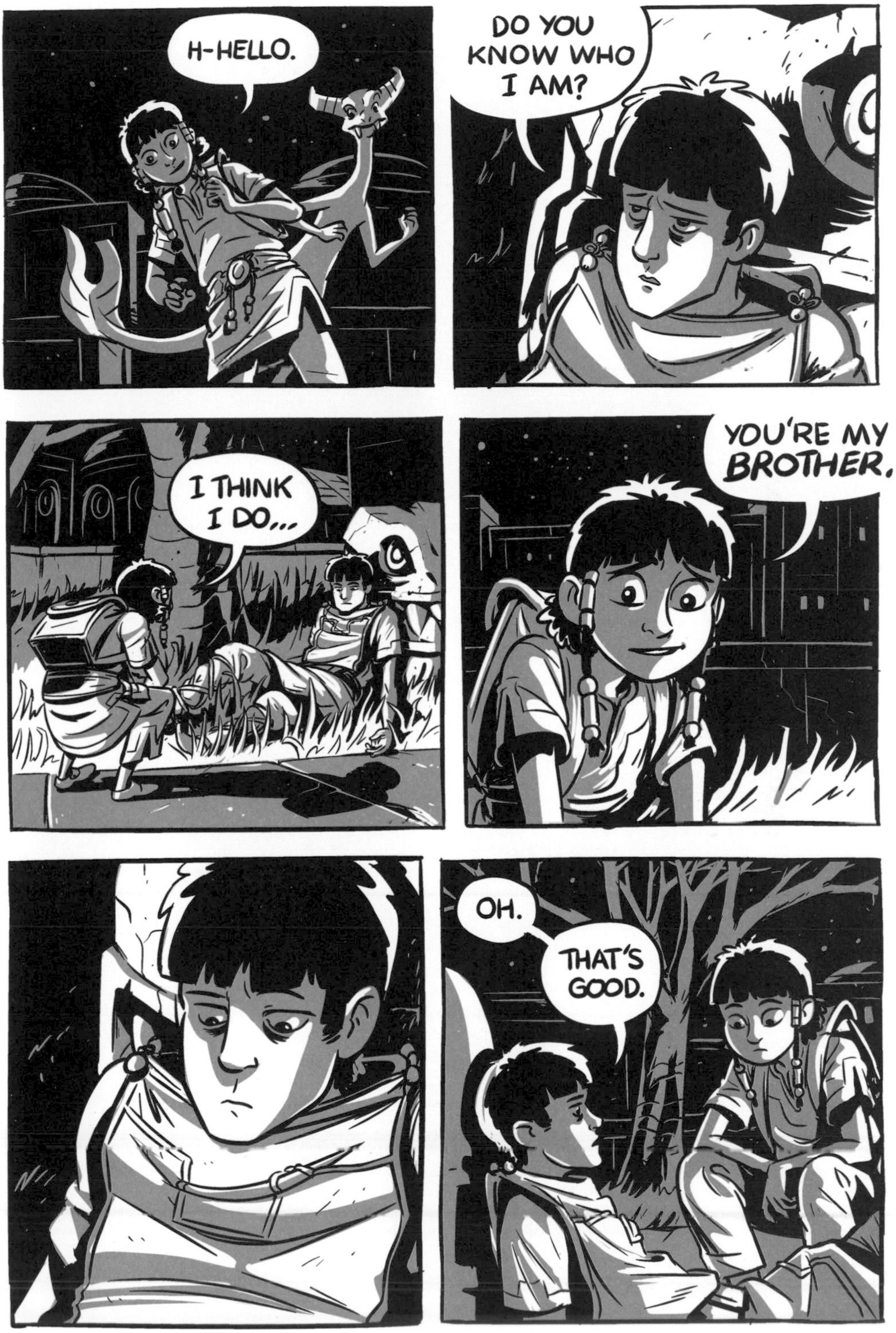
H-HELLO.
DO YOU KNOW WHO I AM?
I THINK I DO...
YOU'RE MY **BROTHER.**
OH.
THAT'S GOOD.

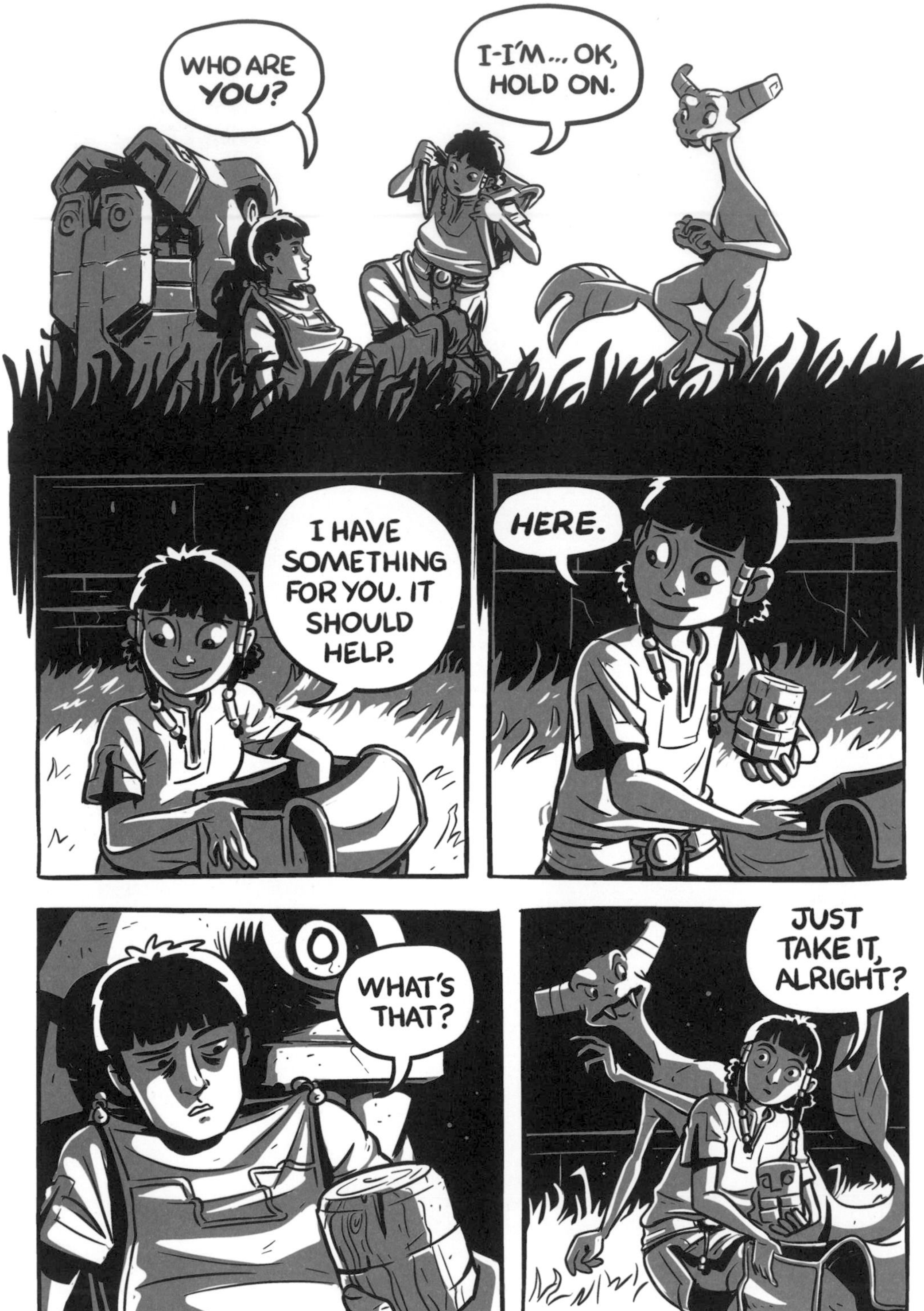
WHO ARE YOU?
I-I'M... OK, HOLD ON.
I HAVE SOMETHING FOR YOU. IT SHOULD HELP.
HERE.
WHAT'S THAT?
JUST TAKE IT, ALRIGHT?

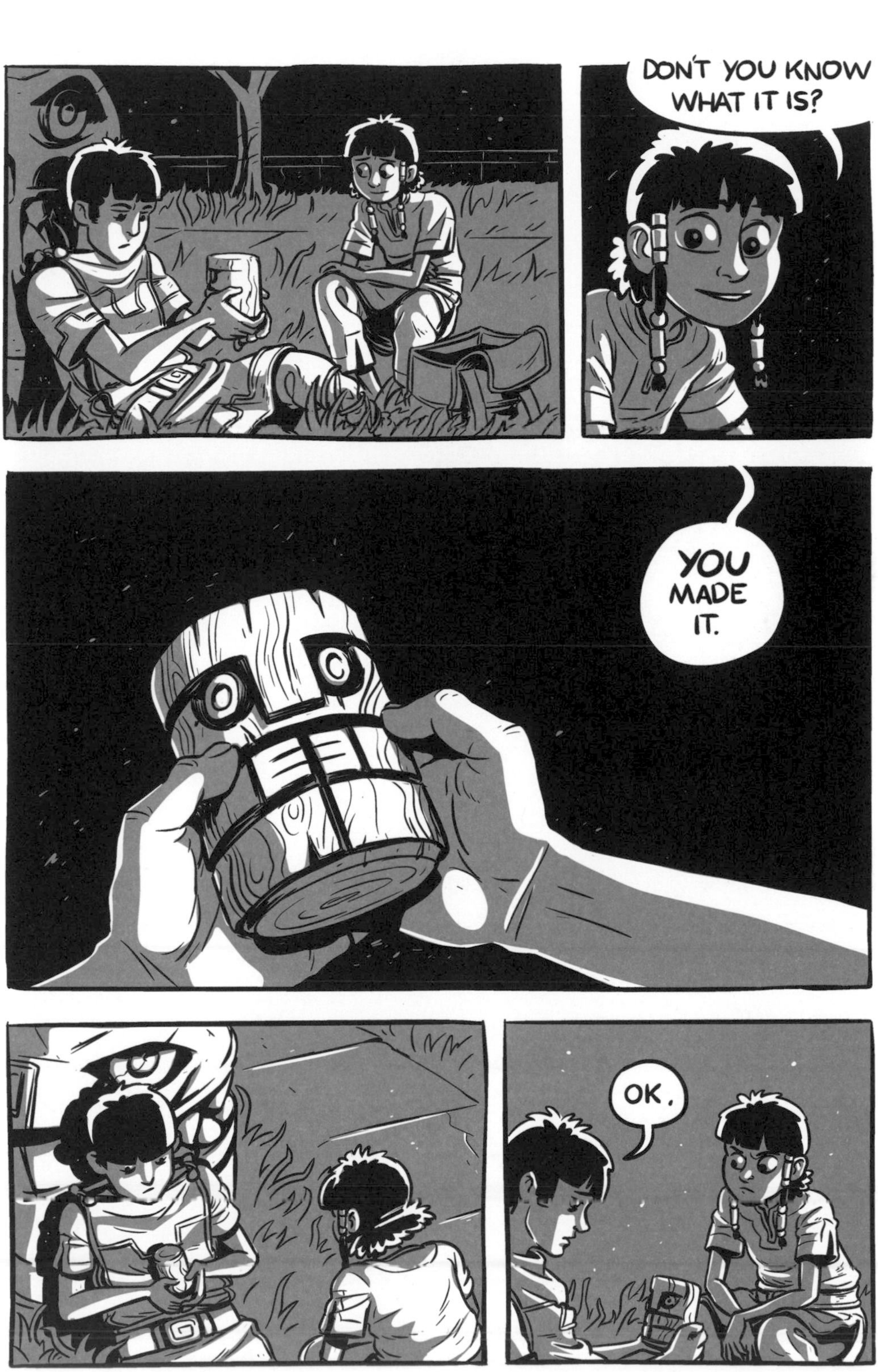

DON'T YOU KNOW WHAT IT IS?
YOU MADE IT.
OK.

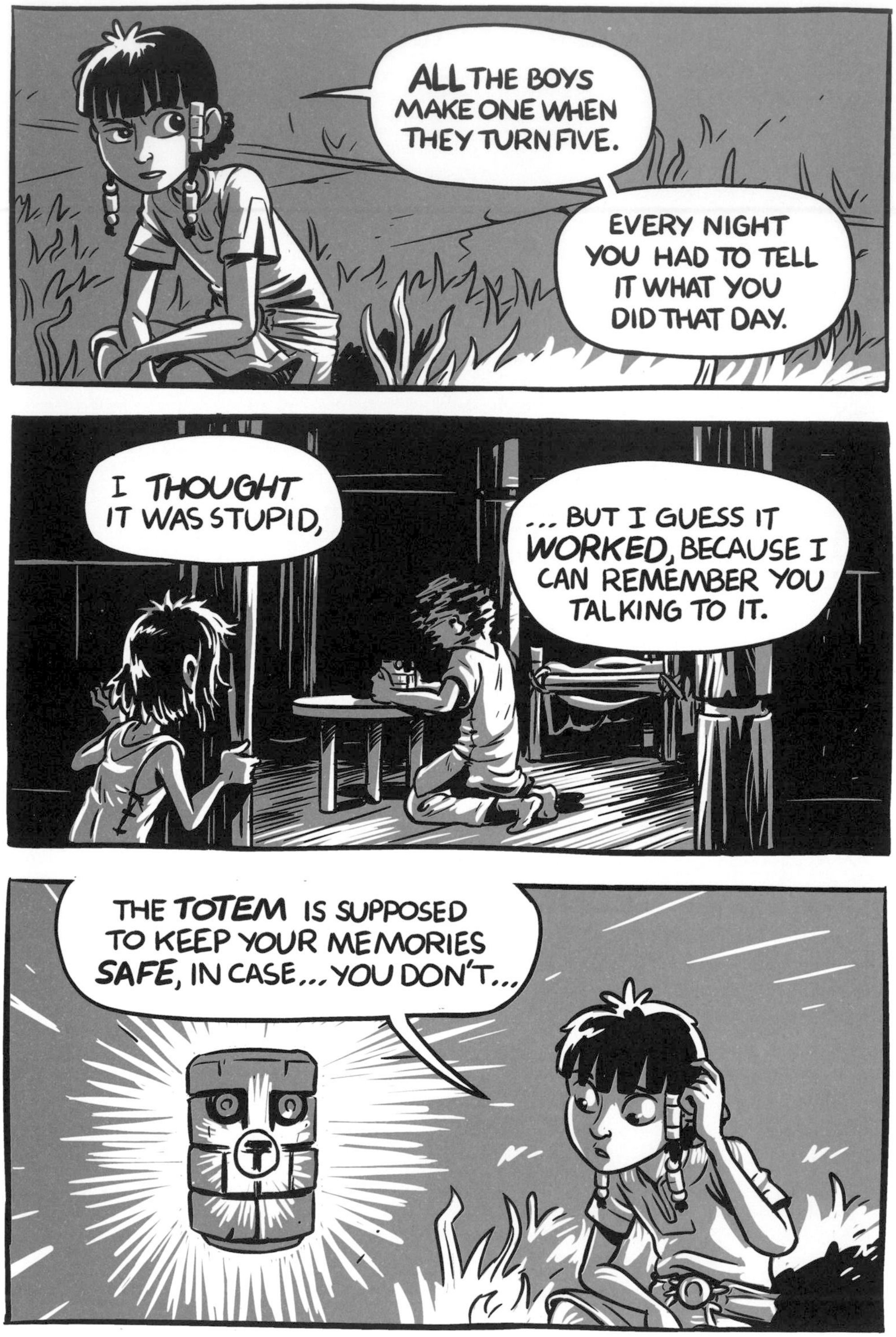
ALL THE BOYS MAKE ONE WHEN THEY TURN FIVE.
EVERY NIGHT YOU HAD TO TELL IT WHAT YOU DID THAT DAY.
I THOUGHT IT WAS STUPID,
... BUT I GUESS IT WORKED, BECAUSE I CAN REMEMBER YOU TALKING TO IT.
THE TOTEM IS SUPPOSED TO KEEP YOUR MEMORIES SAFE, IN CASE... YOU DON'T...

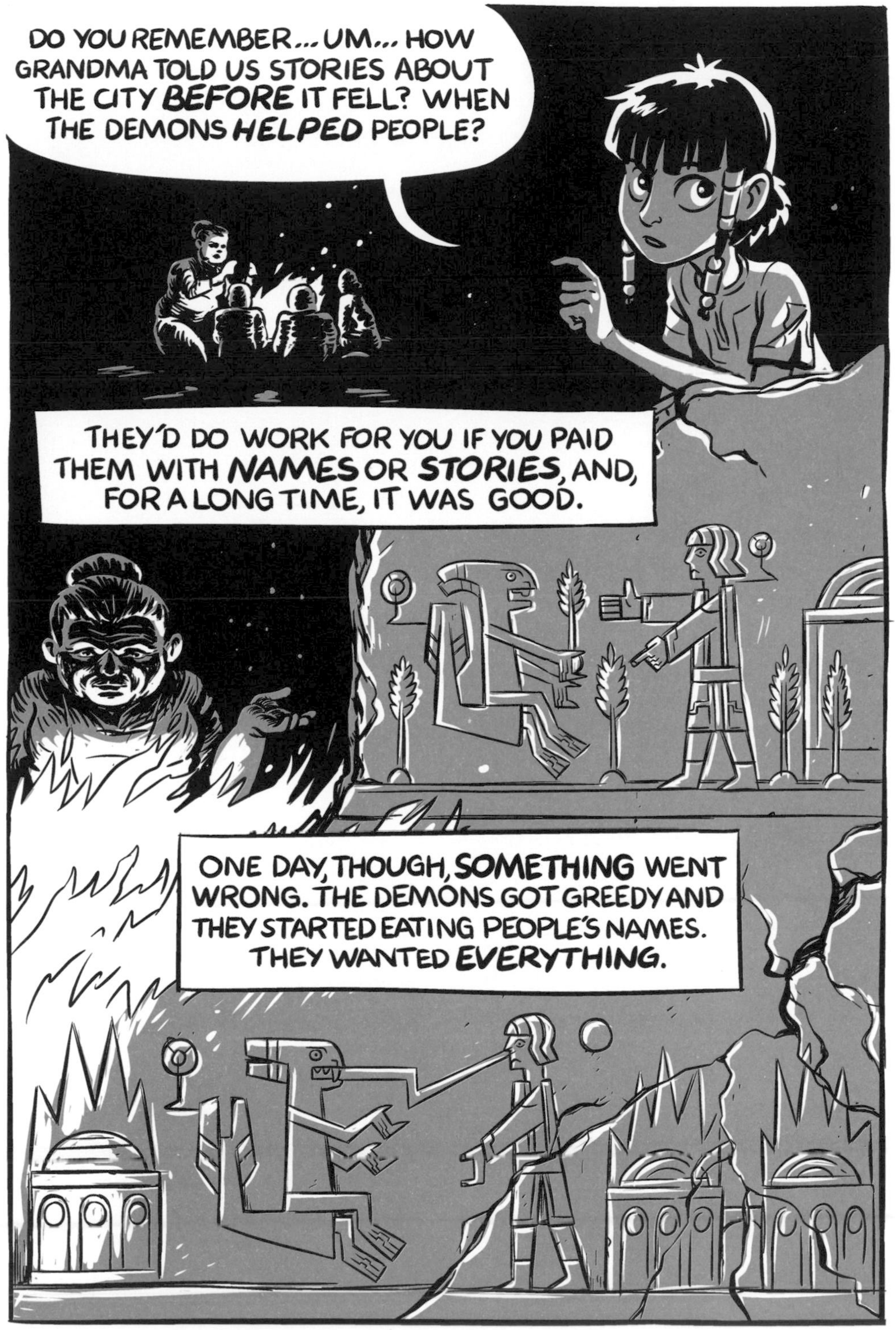
DO YOU REMEMBER... UM... HOW GRANDMA TOLD US STORIES ABOUT THE CITY BEFORE IT FELL? WHEN THE DEMONS HELPED PEOPLE?
THEY'D DO WORK FOR YOU IF YOU PAID THEM WITH NAMES OR STORIES, AND, FOR A LONG TIME, IT WAS GOOD.
ONE DAY, THOUGH, SOMETHING WENT WRONG. THE DEMONS GOT GREEDY AND THEY STARTED EATING PEOPLE'S NAMES. THEY WANTED EVERYTHING.

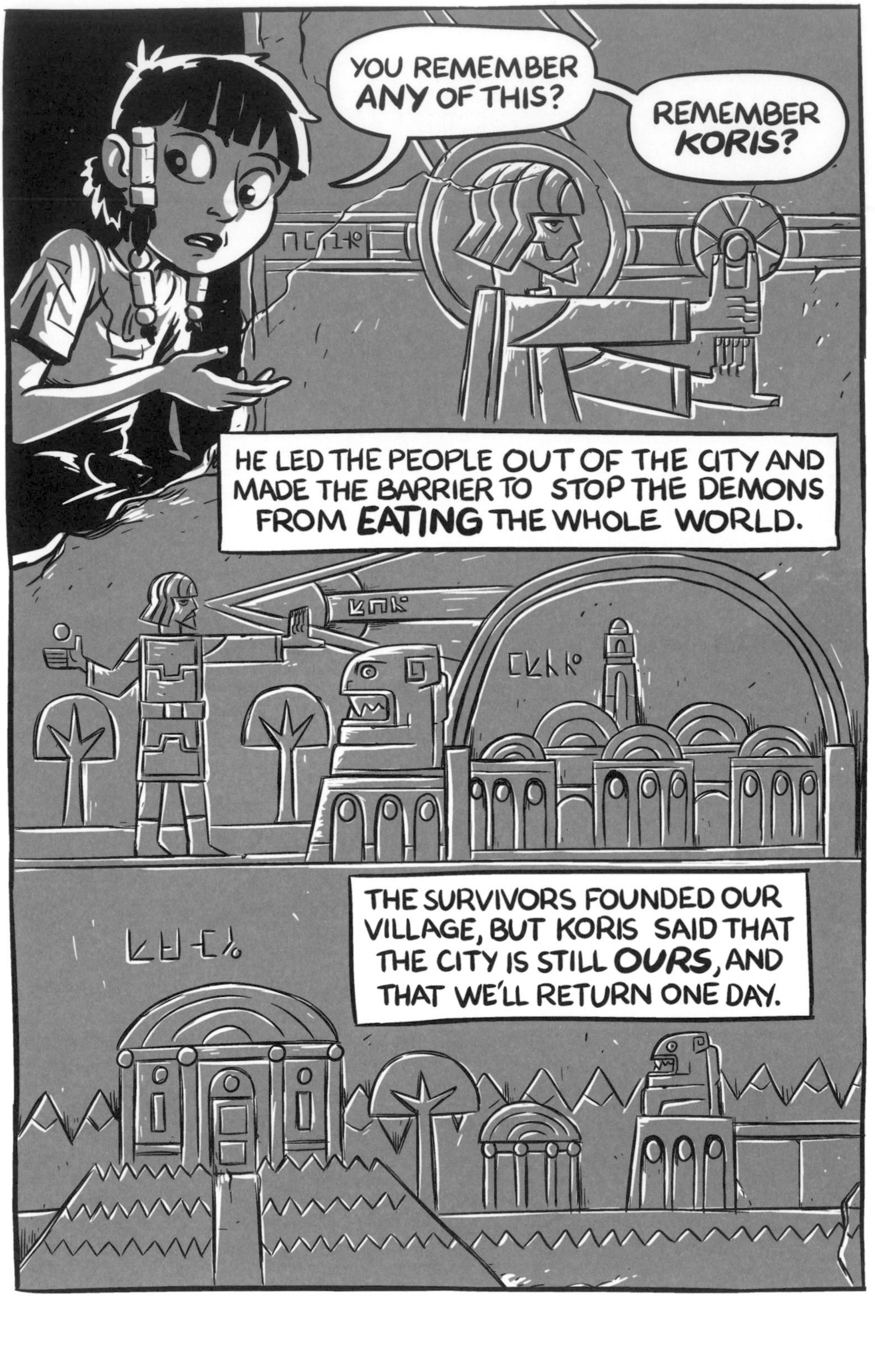
YOU REMEMBER ANY OF THIS?
REMEMBER KORIS?
HE LED THE PEOPLE OUT OF THE CITY AND MADE THE BARRIER TO STOP THE DEMONS FROM EATING THE WHOLE WORLD.
THE SURVIVORS FOUNDED OUR VILLAGE, BUT KORIS SAID THAT THE CITY IS STILL OURS, AND THAT WE'LL RETURN ONE DAY.

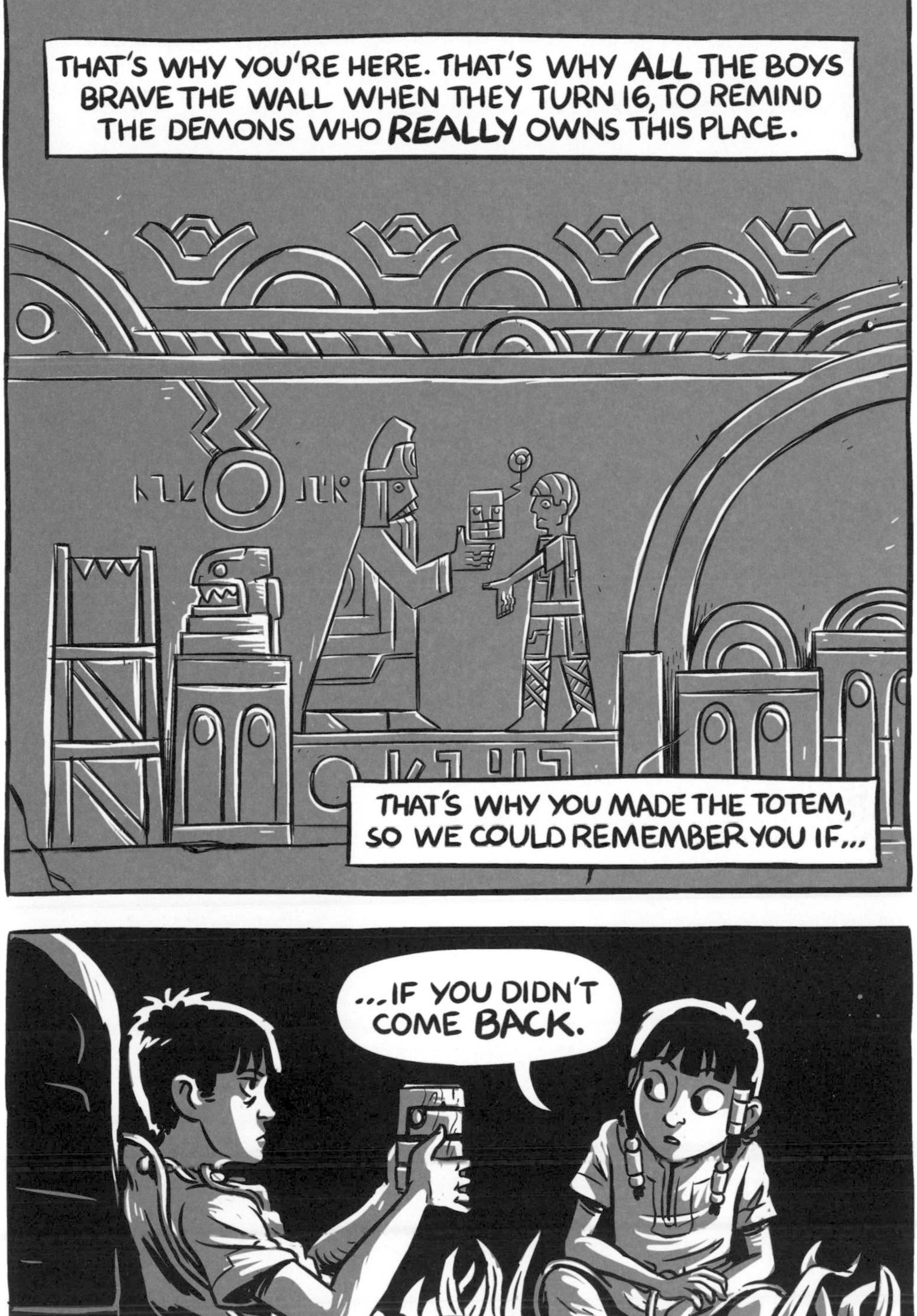
THAT'S WHY YOU'RE HERE. THAT'S WHY ALL THE BOYS BRAVE THE WALL WHEN THEY TURN 16, TO REMIND THE DEMONS WHO REALLY OWNS THIS PLACE.
THAT'S WHY YOU MADE THE TOTEM, SO WE COULD REMEMBER YOU IF...
...IF YOU DIDN'T COME BACK.

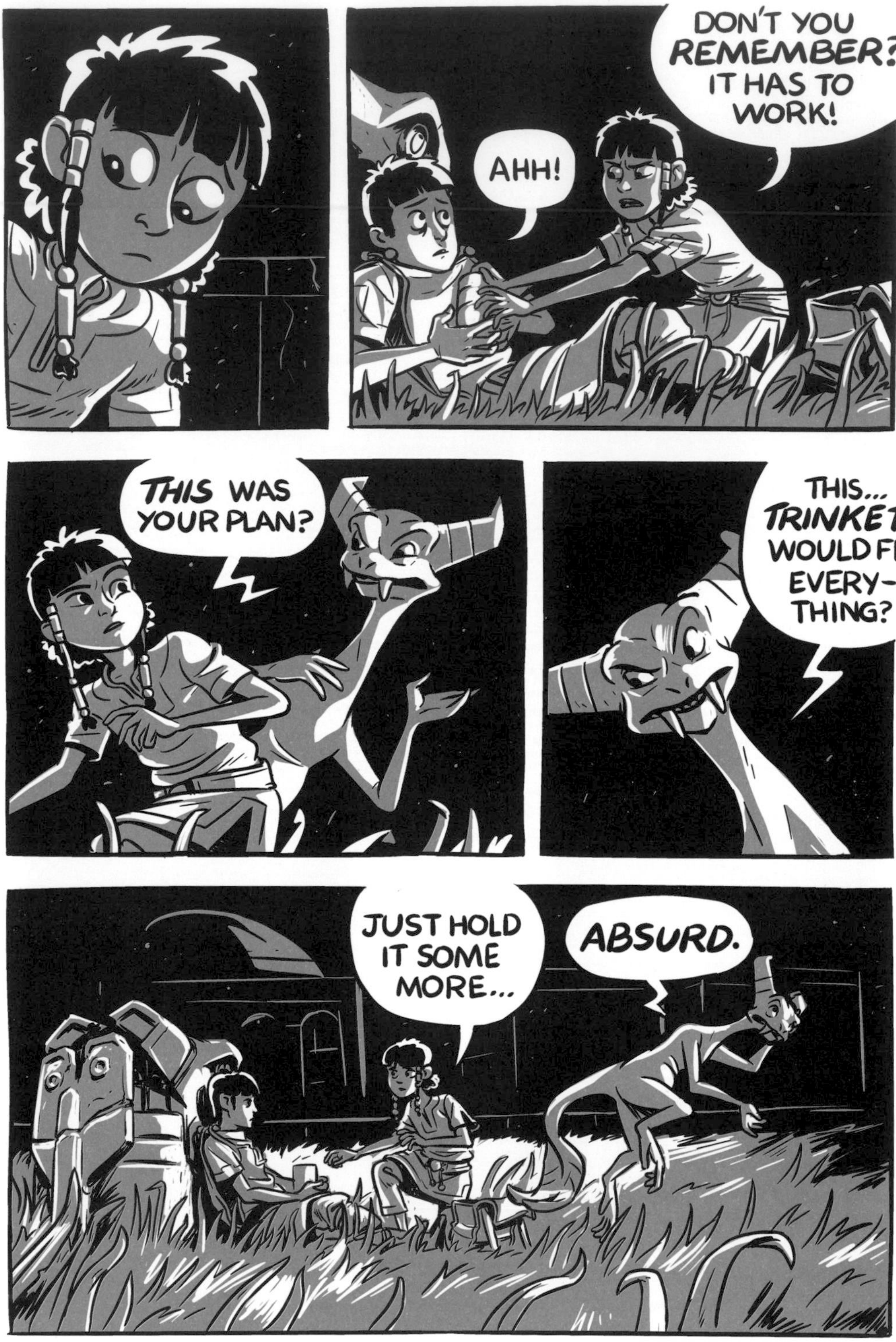
DON'T YOU REMEMBER? IT HAS TO WORK!
AHH!
THIS WAS YOUR PLAN?
THIS... TRINKET WOULD FIX EVERY-THING?
JUST HOLD IT SOME MORE...
ABSURD.

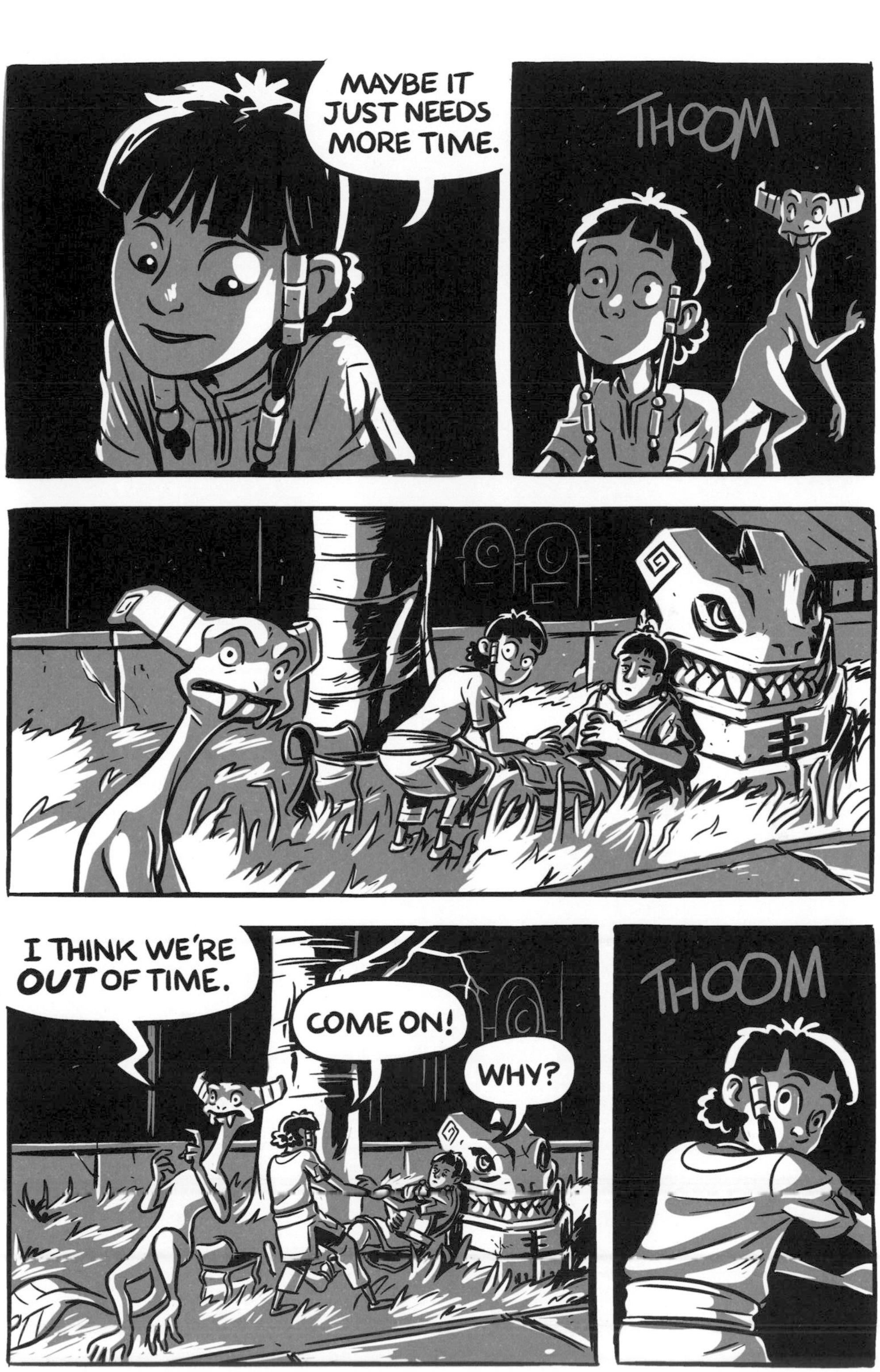
MAYBE IT JUST NEEDS MORE TIME.
THOOM
I THINK WE'RE OUT OF TIME.
COME ON!
WHY?
THOOM

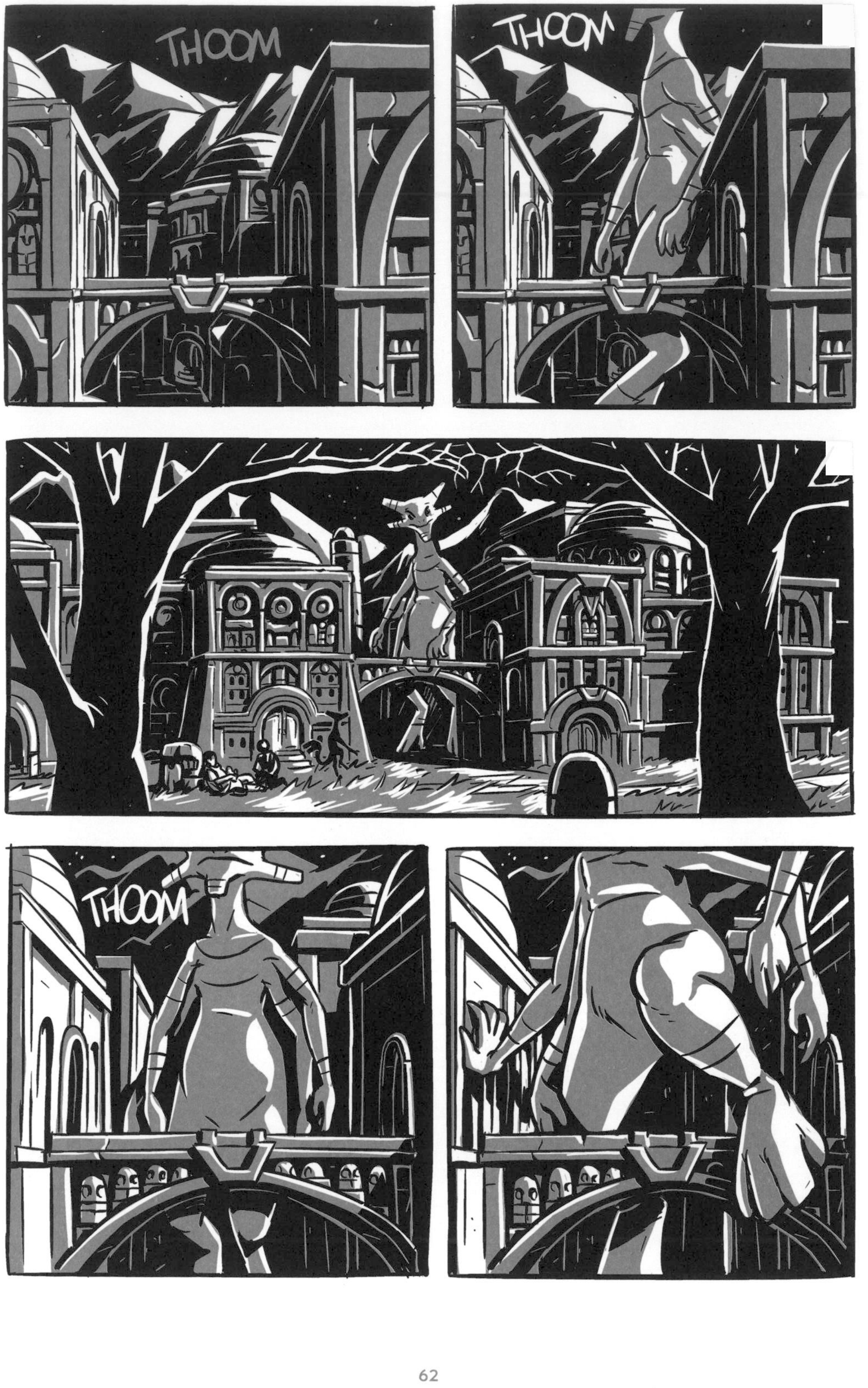
THOOM
THOOM
THOOM

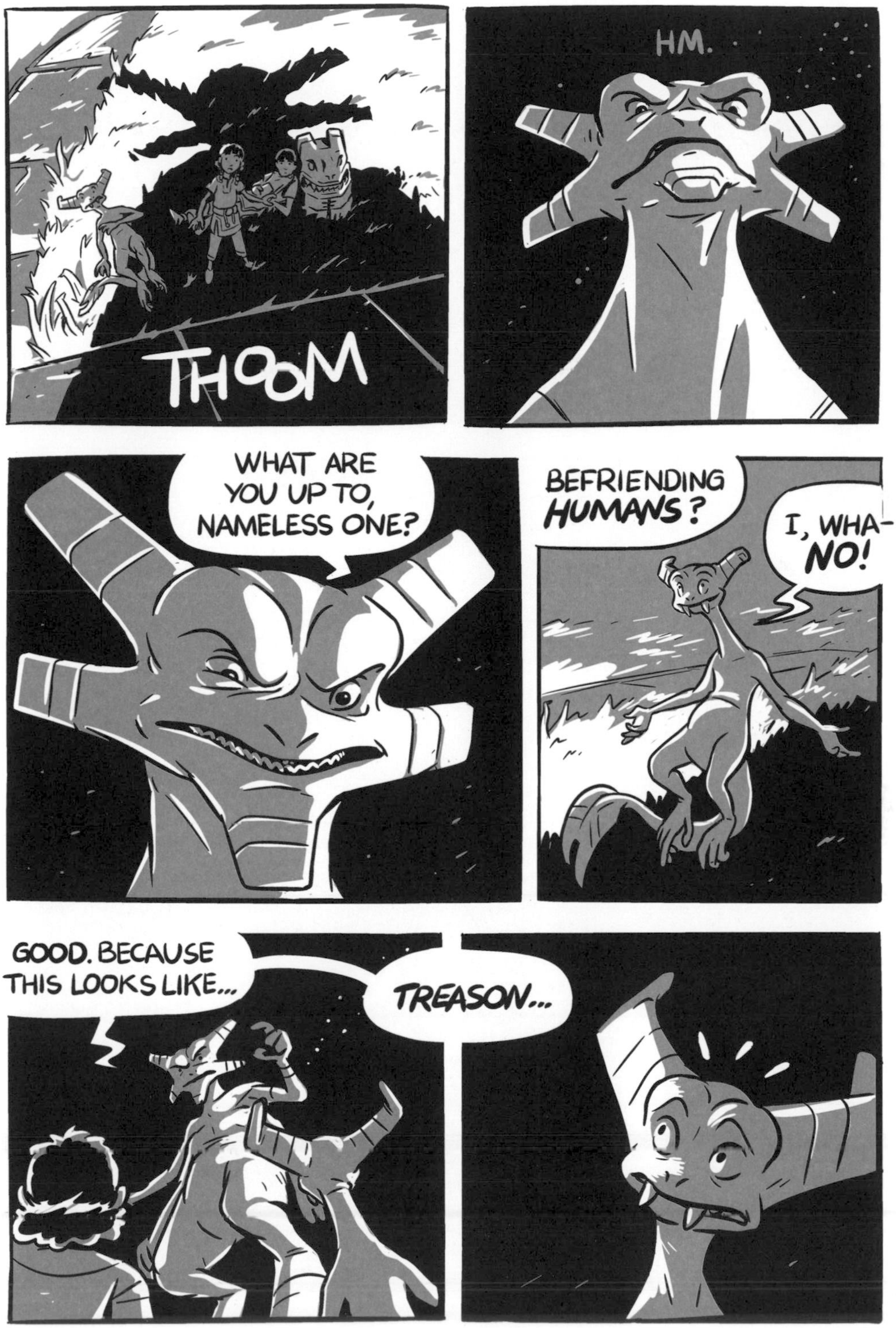
THOOM
HM.
WHAT ARE YOU UP TO, NAMELESS ONE?
BEFRIENDING HUMANS?
I, WHA- NO!
GOOD. BECAUSE THIS LOOKS LIKE...
TREASON...

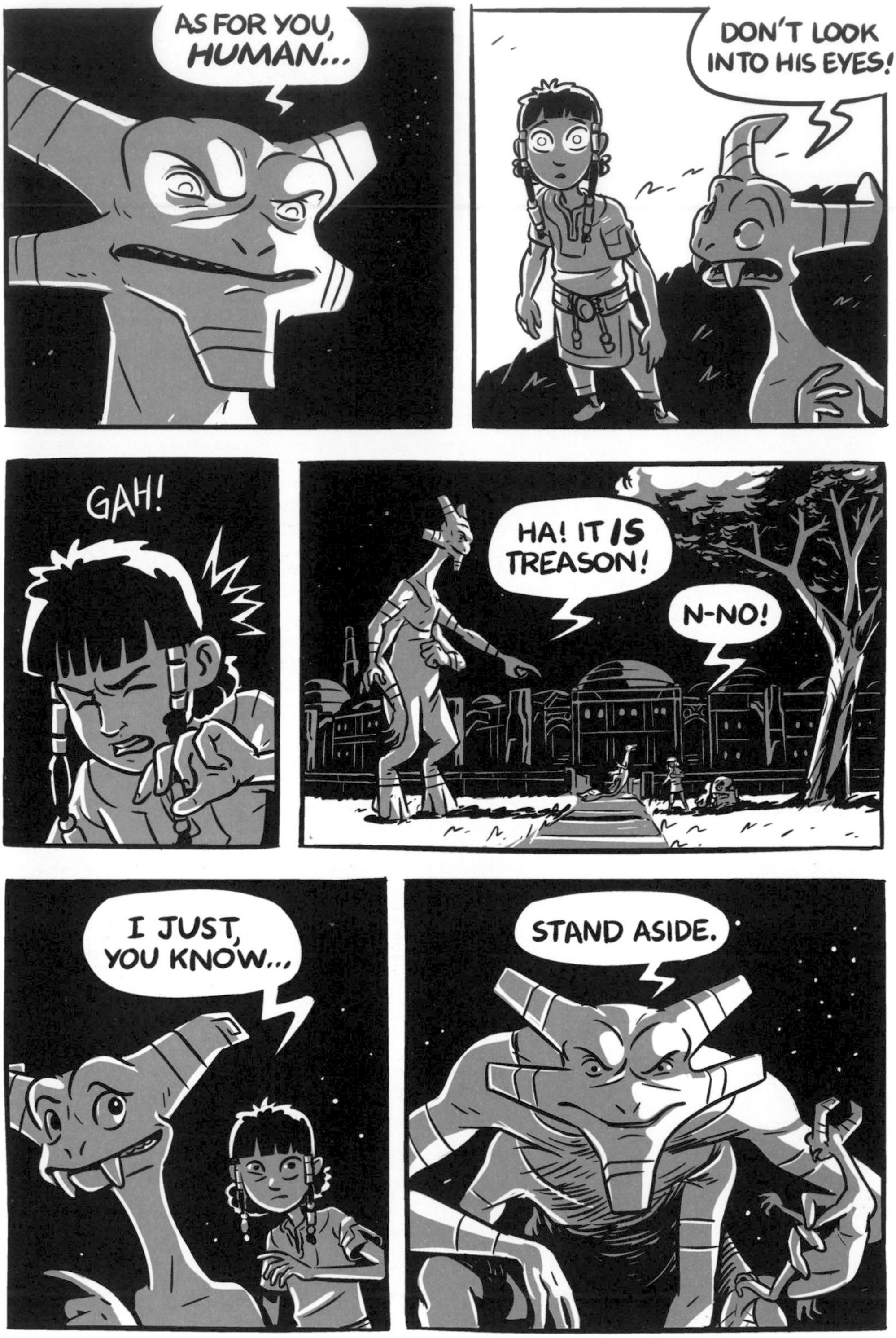
AS FOR YOU, HUMAN...
DON'T LOOK INTO HIS EYES!
GAH!
HA! IT IS TREASON!
N-NO!
I JUST, YOU KNOW...
STAND ASIDE.

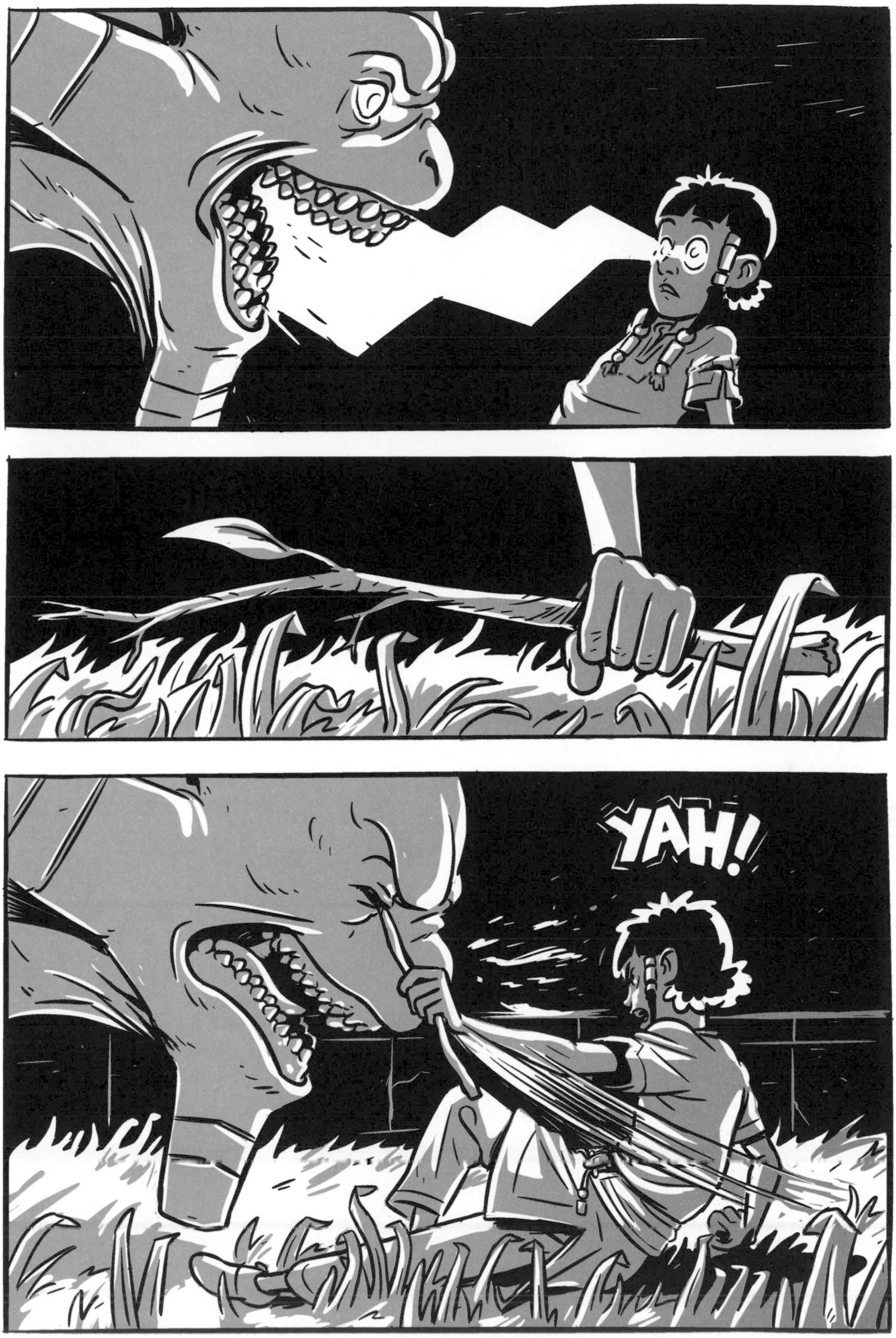
YAH!

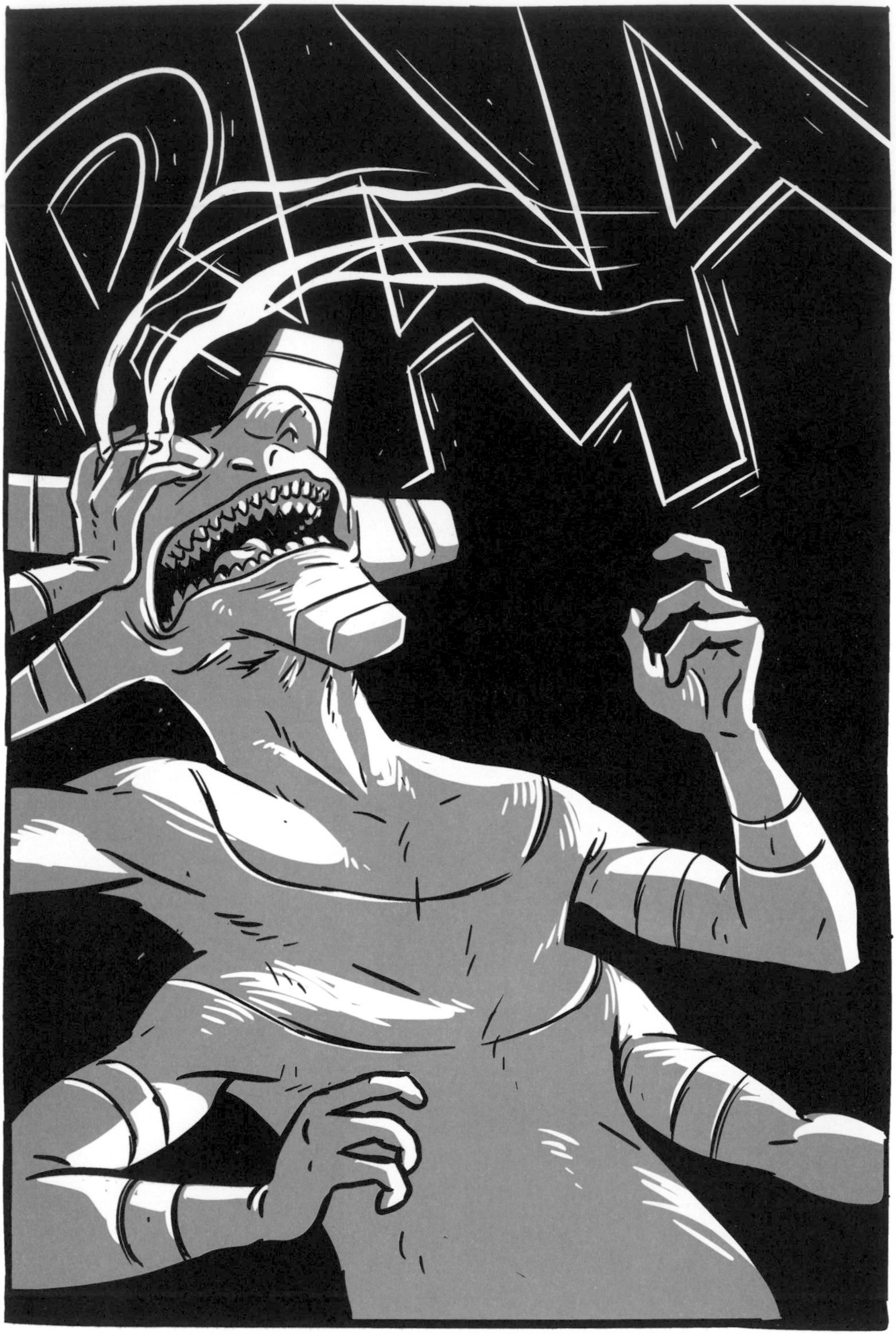

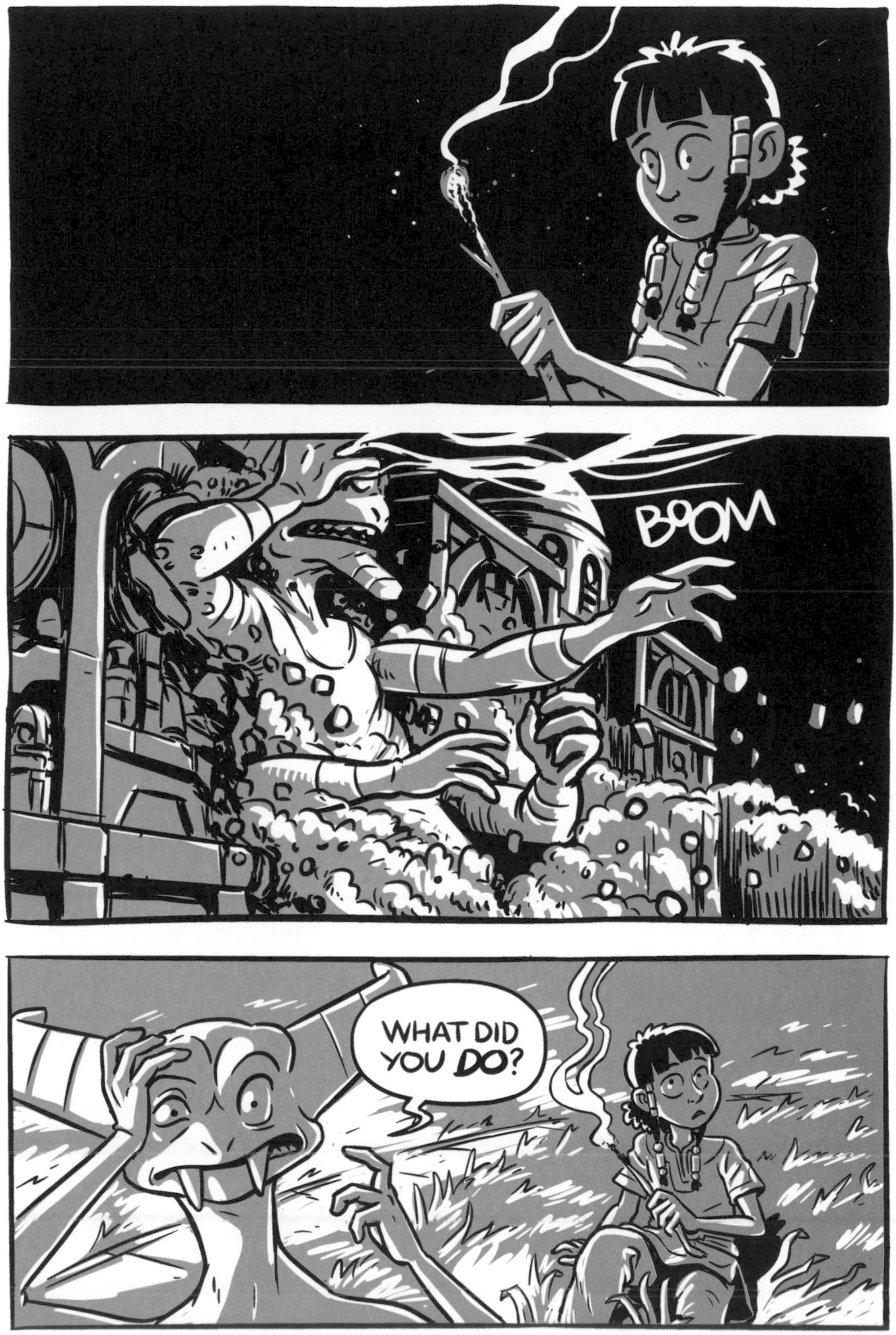
BOOM
WHAT DID YOU DO?

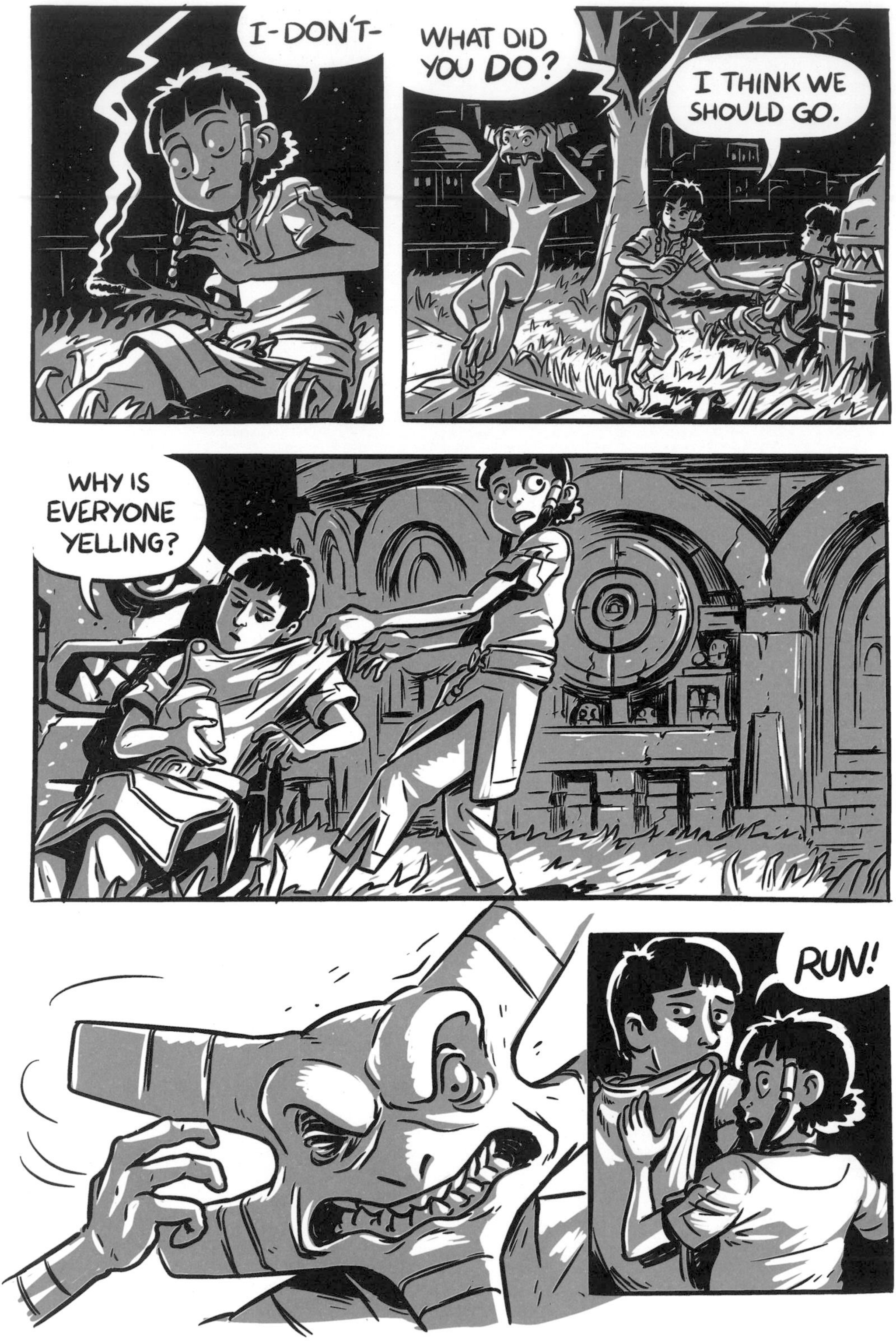

I-DON'T-
WHAT DID YOU DO?
I THINK WE SHOULD GO.
WHY IS EVERYONE YELLING?
RUN!

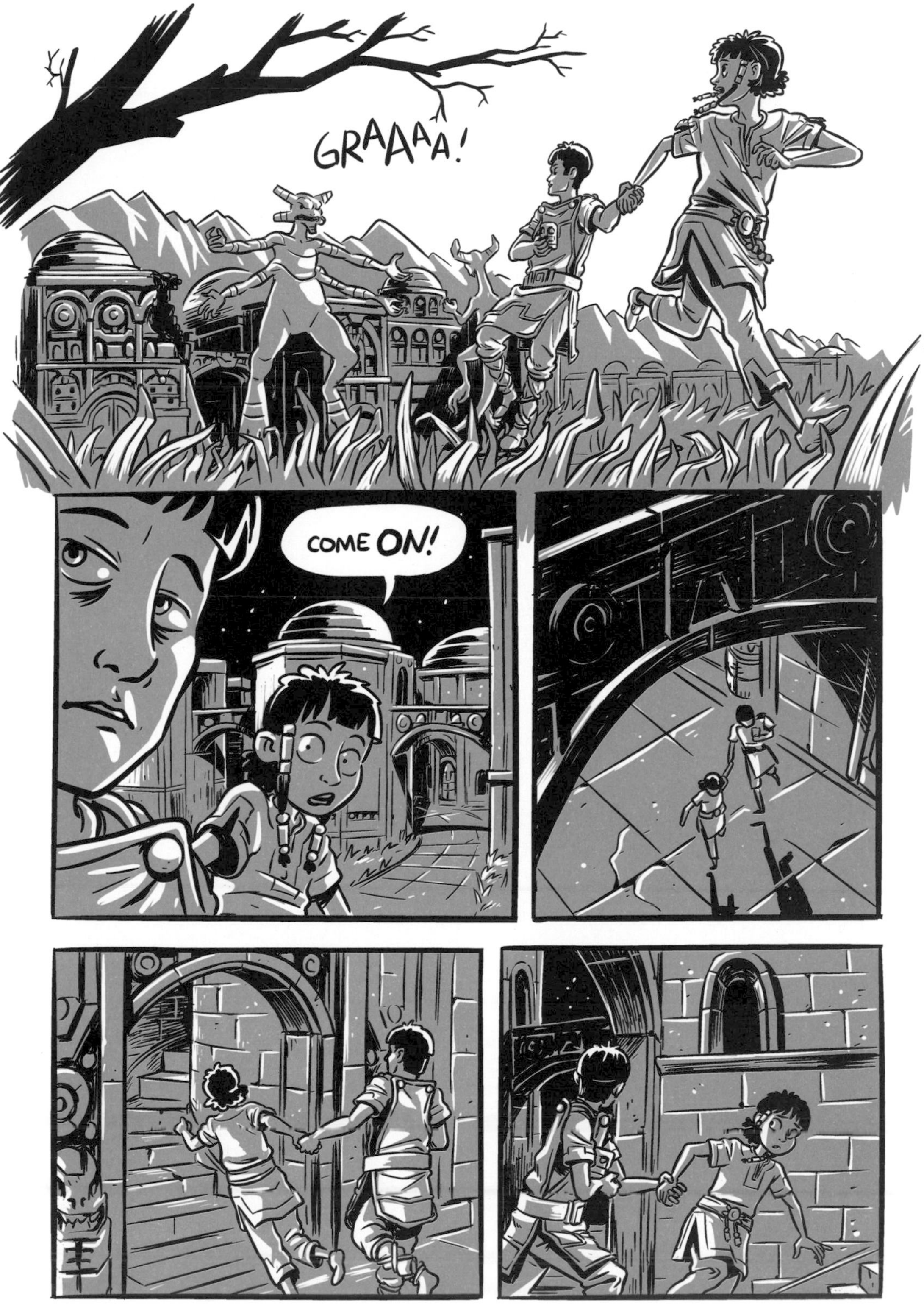
GRAAAA!
COME ON!

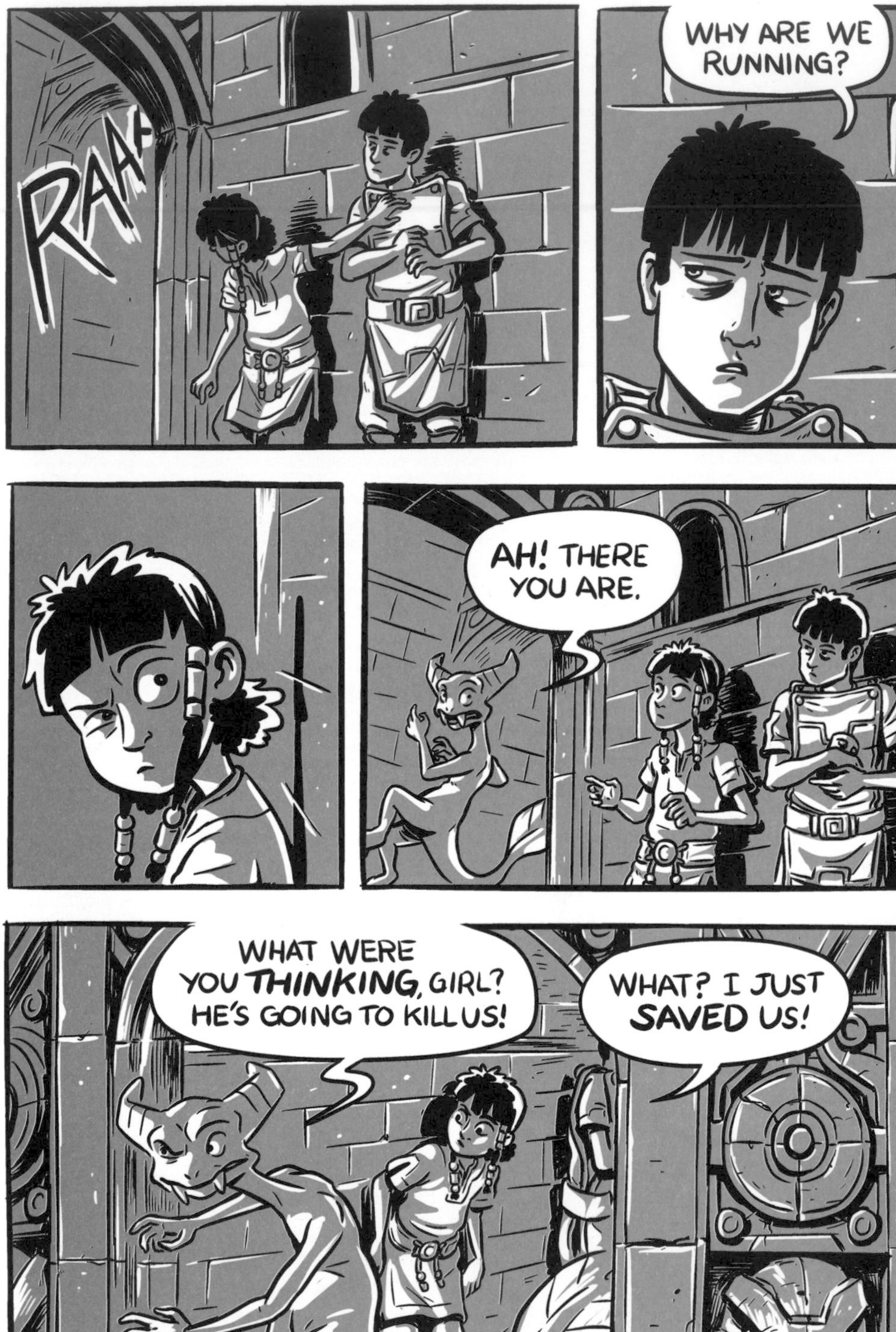
RAA
WHY ARE WE RUNNING?
AH! THERE YOU ARE.
WHAT WERE YOU THINKING, GIRL? HE'S GOING TO KILL US!
WHAT? I JUST SAVED US!

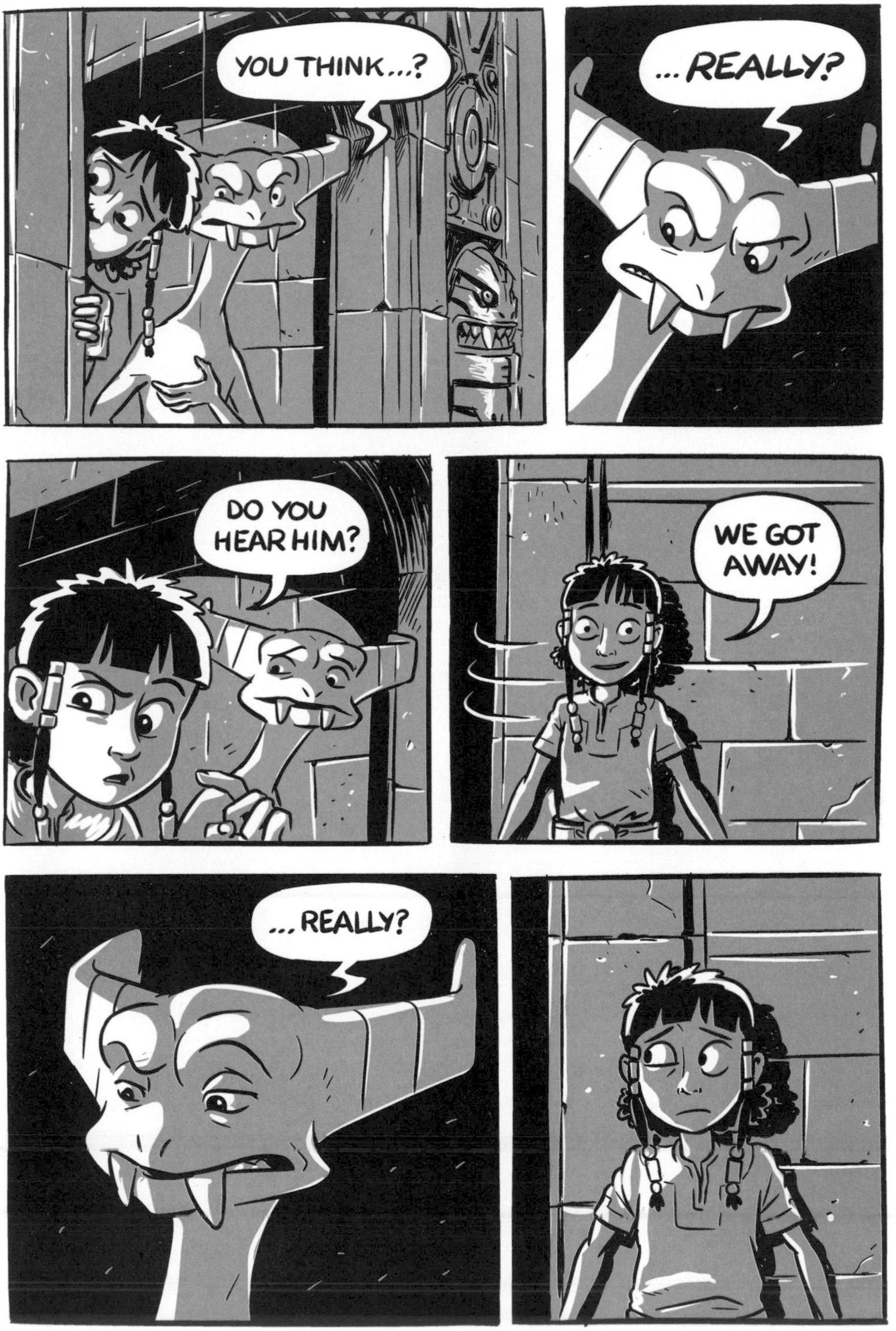
YOU THINK...?
...REALLY?
DO YOU HEAR HIM?
WE GOT AWAY!
...REALLY?

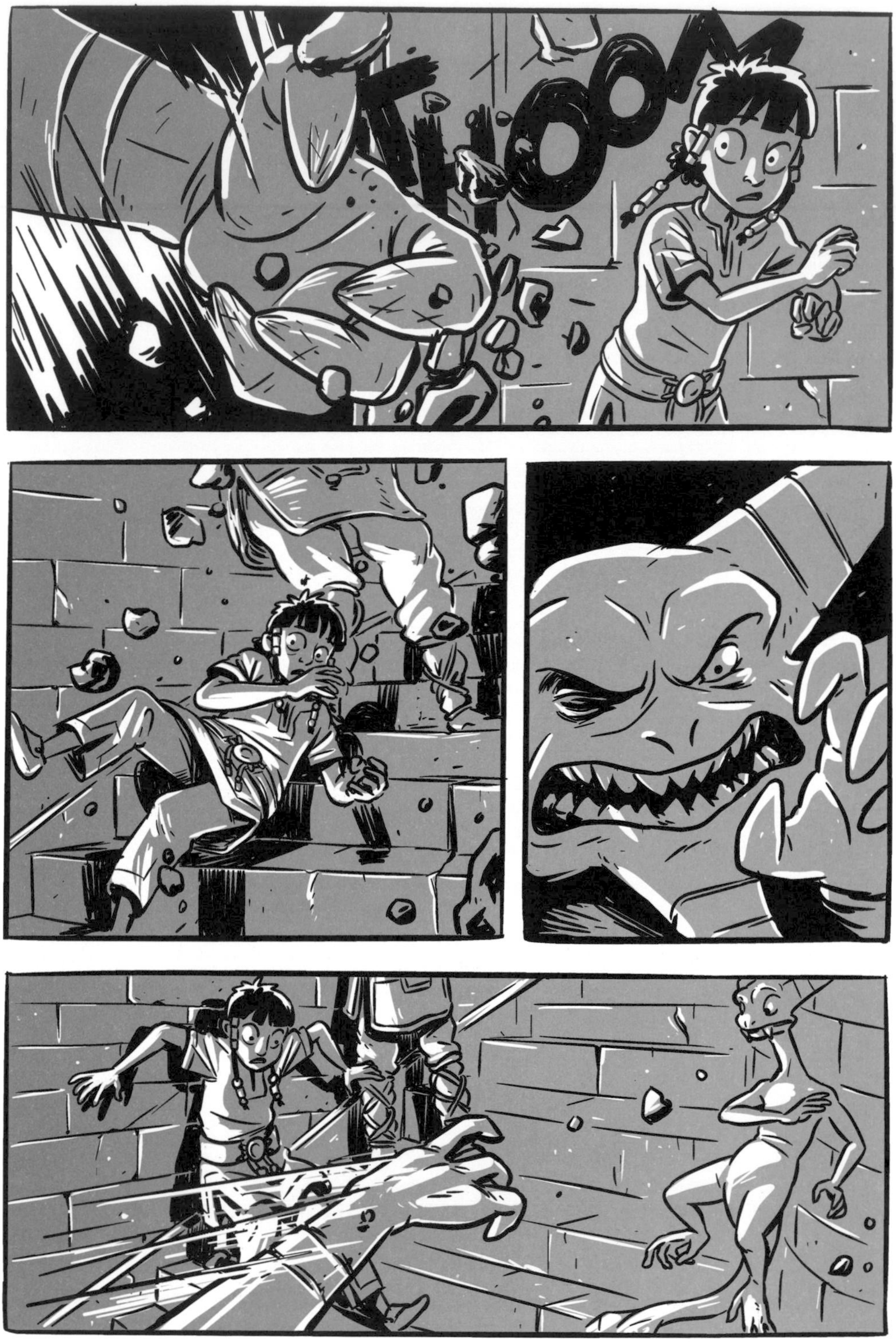
THOOM

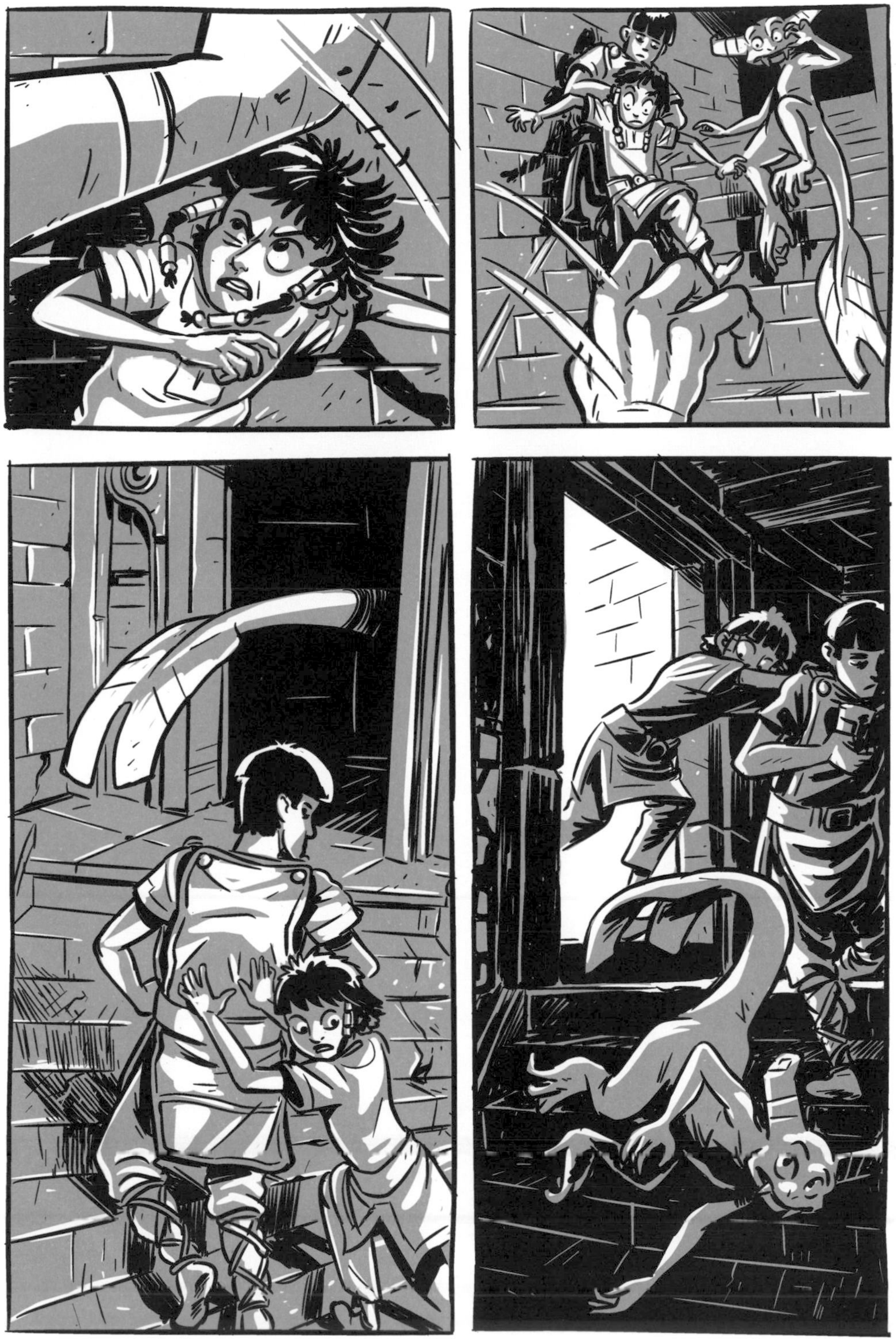

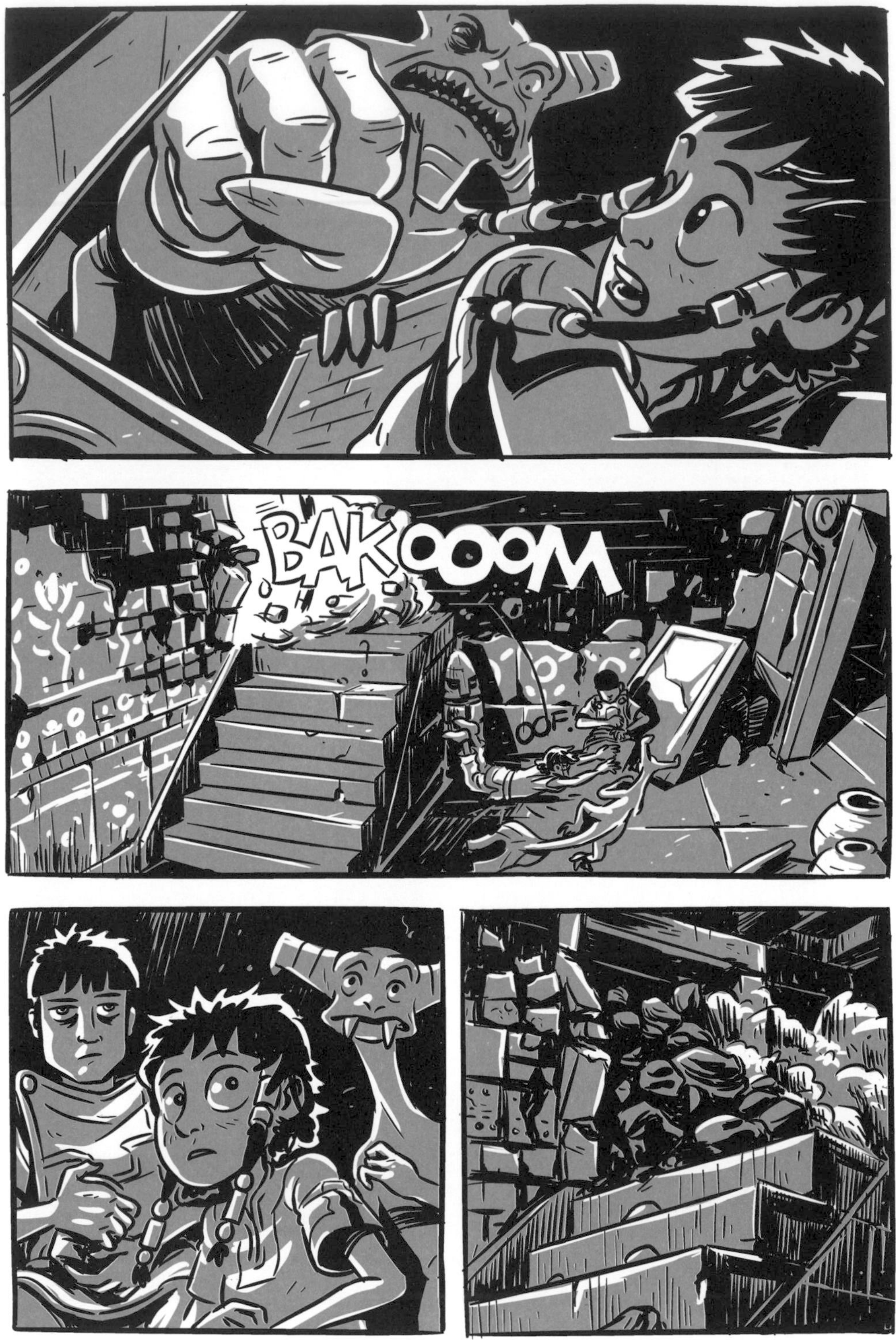
BAKOOOM
OOF!

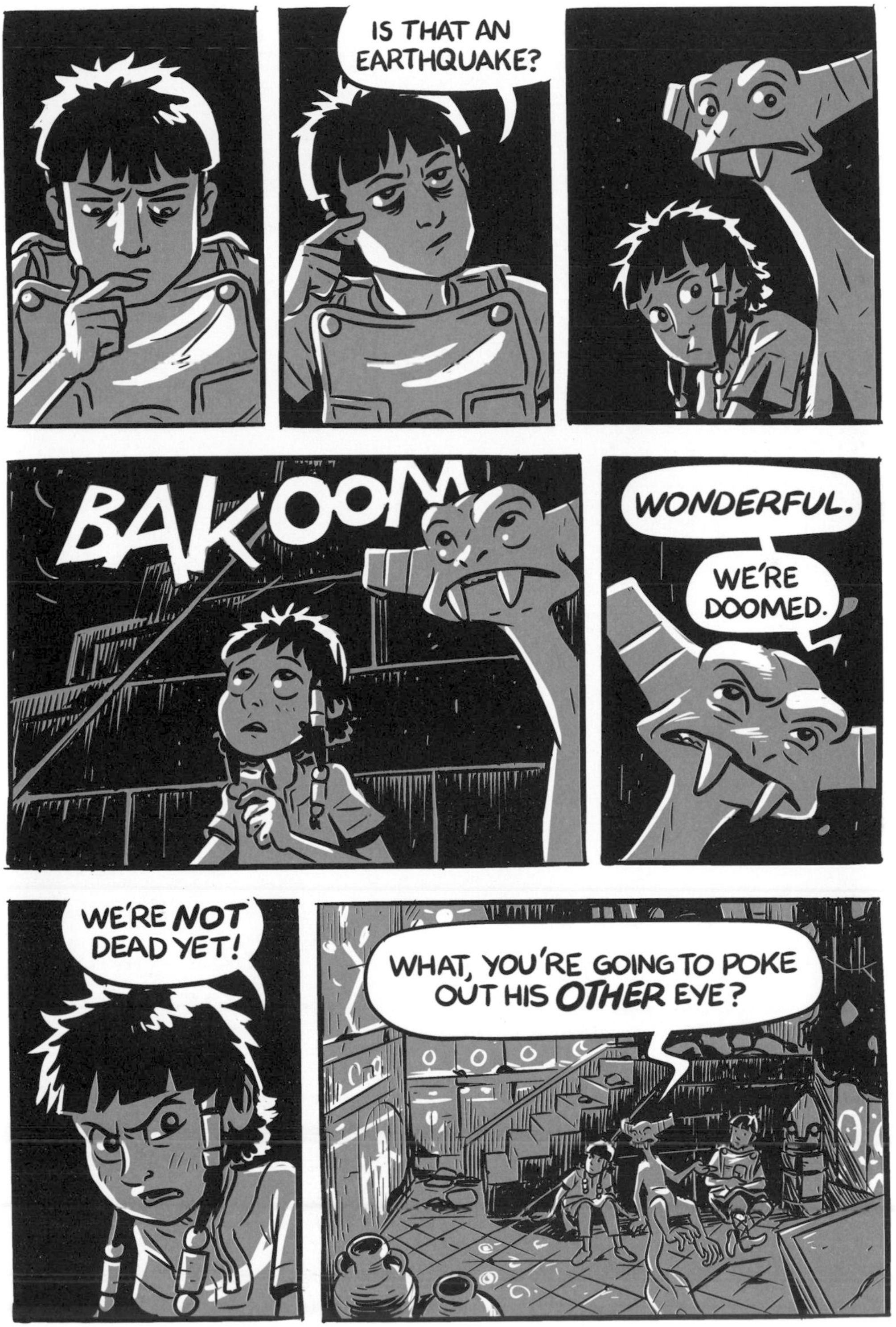
IS THAT AN EARTHQUAKE?
BAKOOM
WONDERFUL.
WE'RE DOOMED.
WE'RE NOT DEAD YET!
WHAT, YOU'RE GOING TO POKE OUT HIS OTHER EYE?

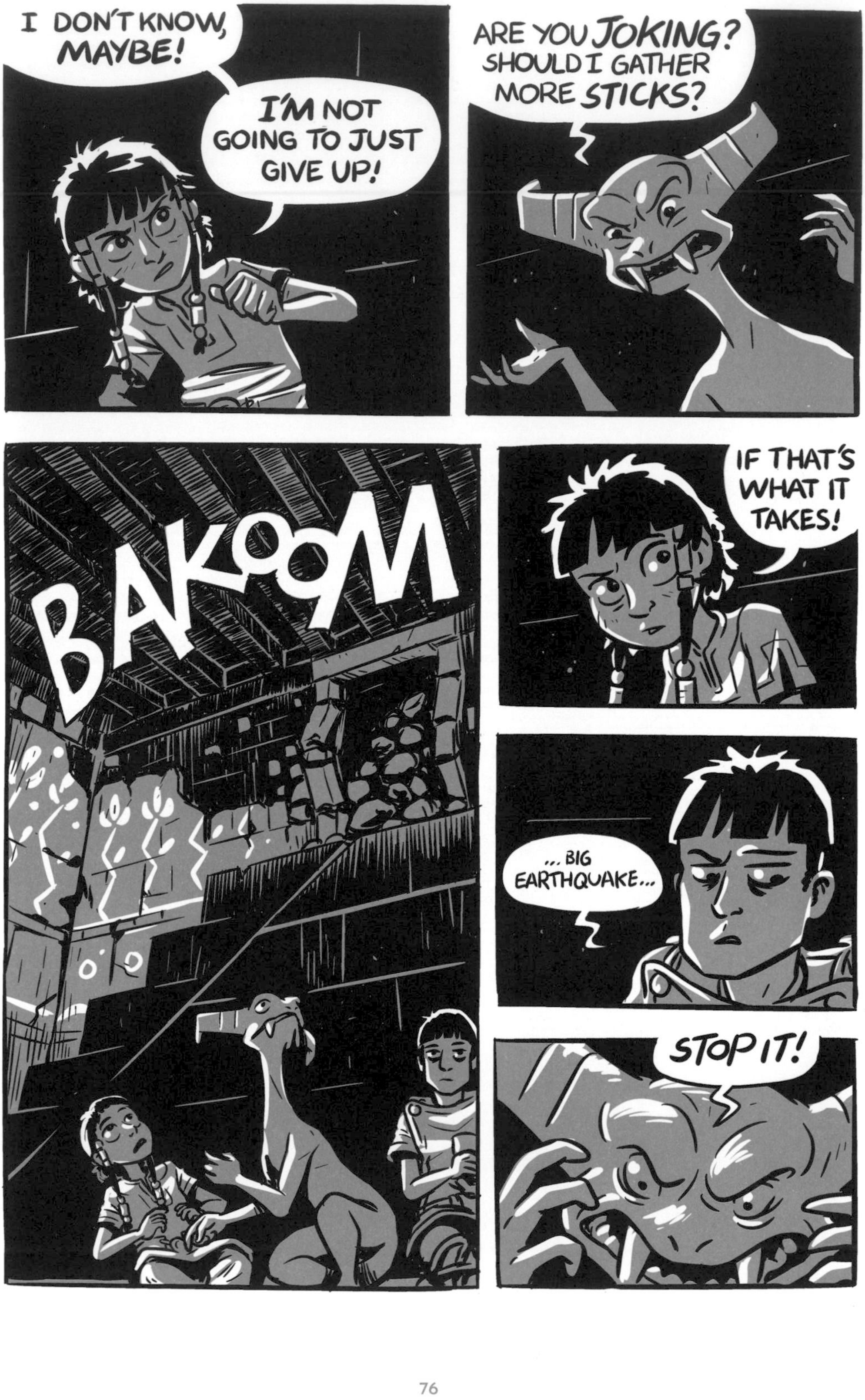
I DON'T KNOW, MAYBE!
I'M NOT GOING TO JUST GIVE UP!
ARE YOU JOKING? SHOULD I GATHER MORE STICKS?
BAKOOM
IF THAT'S WHAT IT TAKES!
...BIG EARTHQUAKE...
STOP IT!

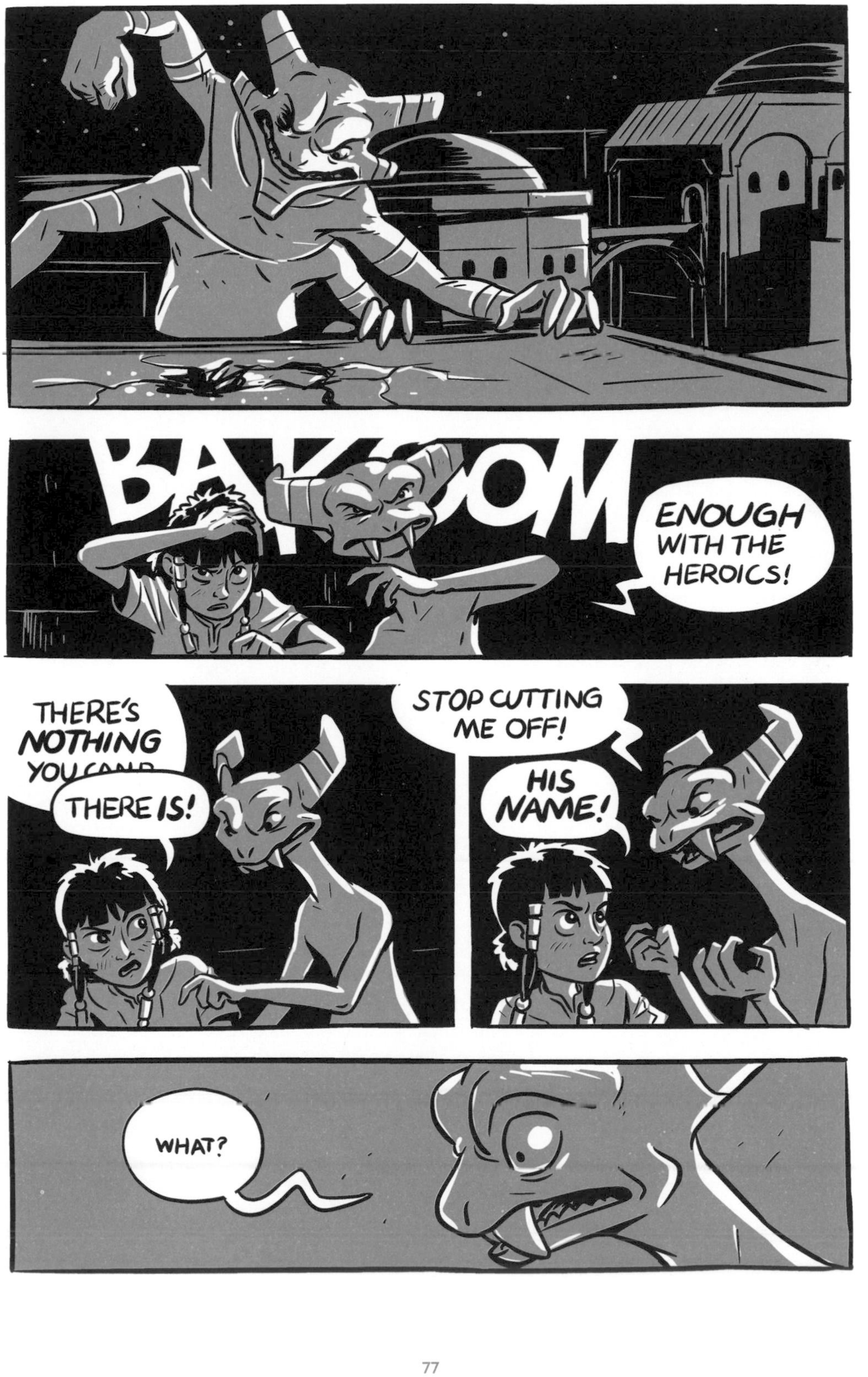
ENOUGH WITH THE HEROICS!
THERE'S NOTHING YOU CAN
THERE IS!
STOP CUTTING ME OFF!
HIS NAME!
WHAT?

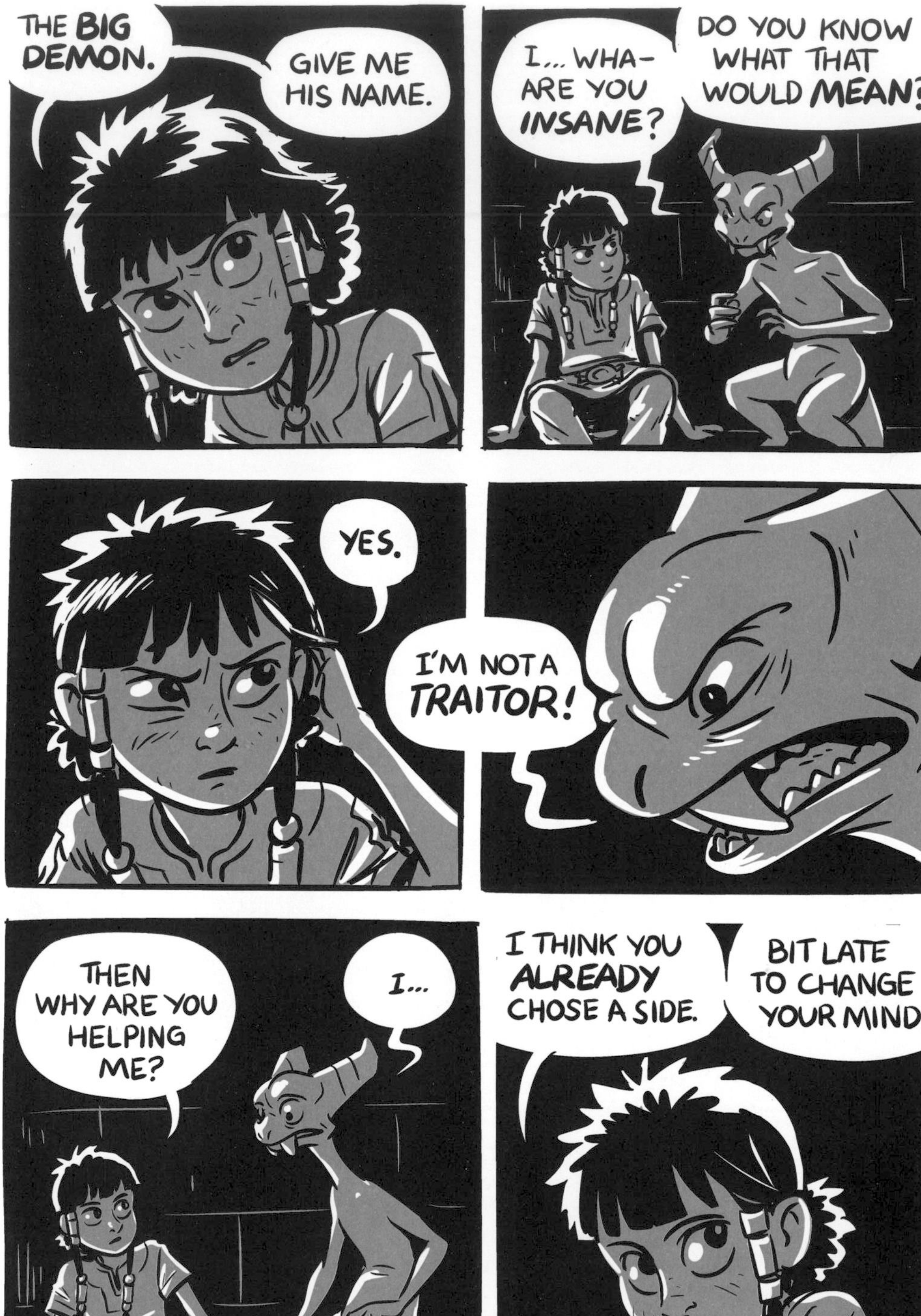
THE BIG DEMON.
GIVE ME HIS NAME.
I... WHA- ARE YOU INSANE?
DO YOU KNOW WHAT THAT WOULD MEAN?
YES.
I'M NOT A TRAITOR!
THEN WHY ARE YOU HELPING ME?
I...
I THINK YOU ALREADY CHOSE A SIDE.
BIT LATE TO CHANGE YOUR MIND.

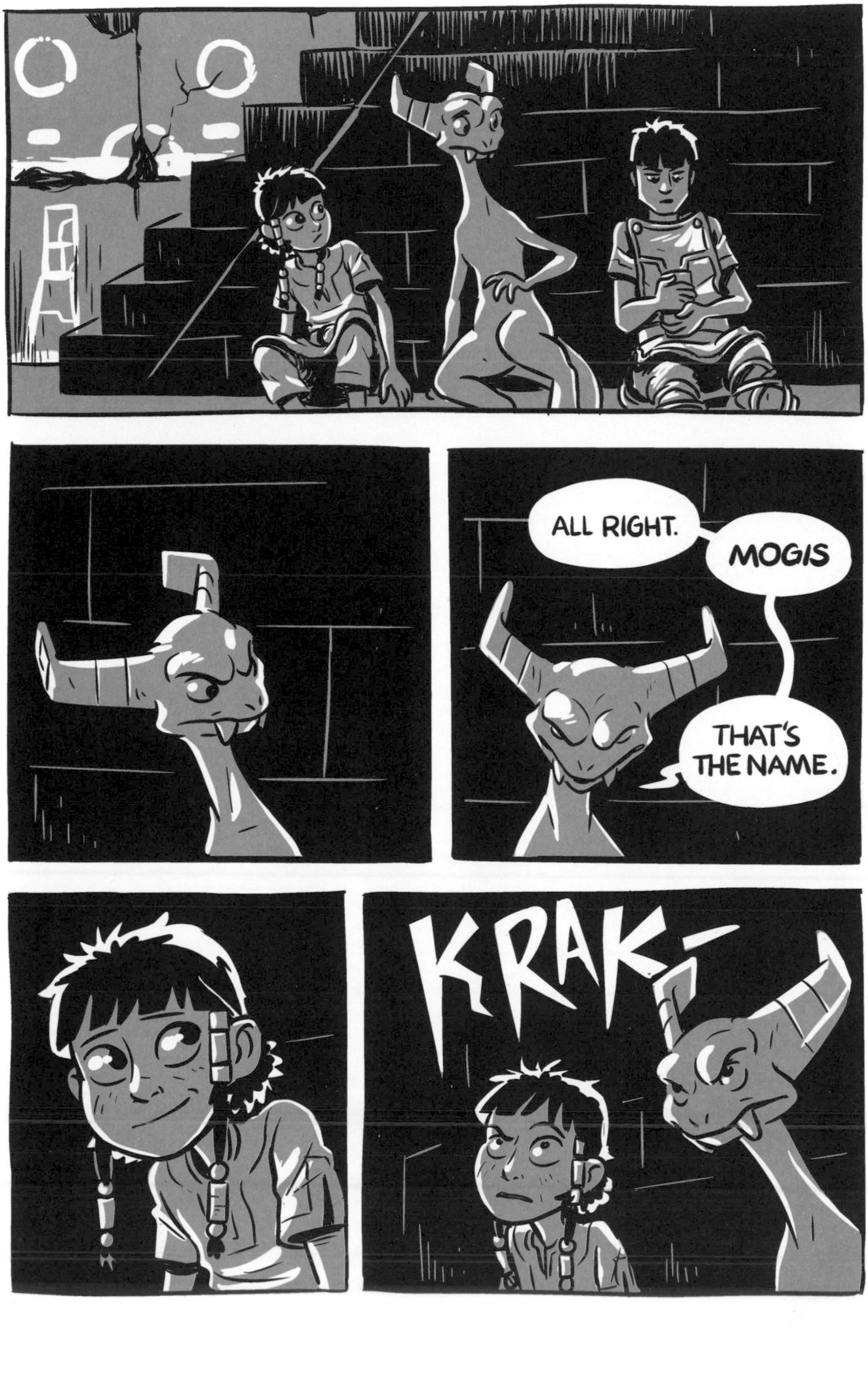
ALL RIGHT.
MOGIS
THAT'S THE NAME.
KRAK-

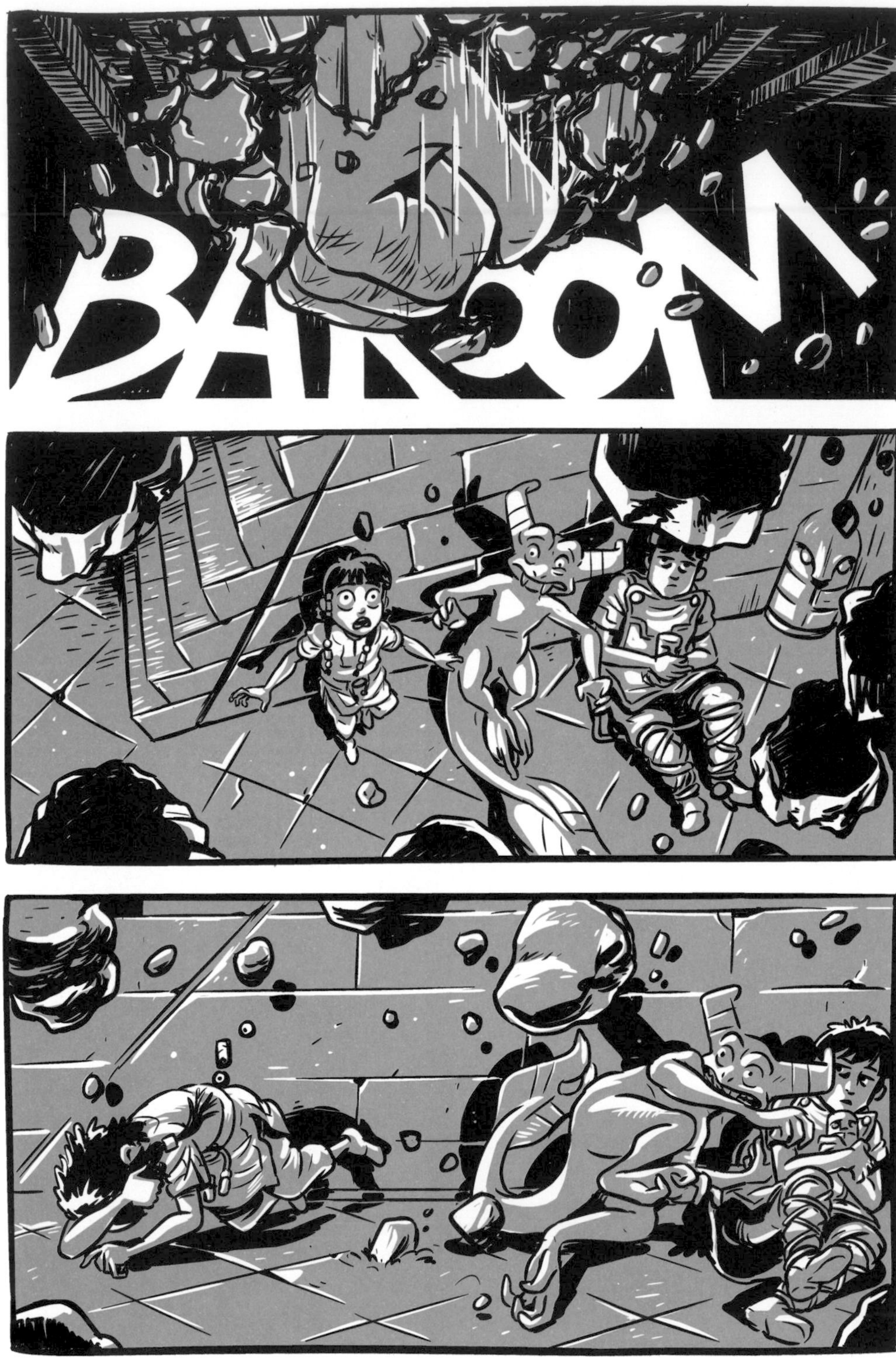
BAROOM

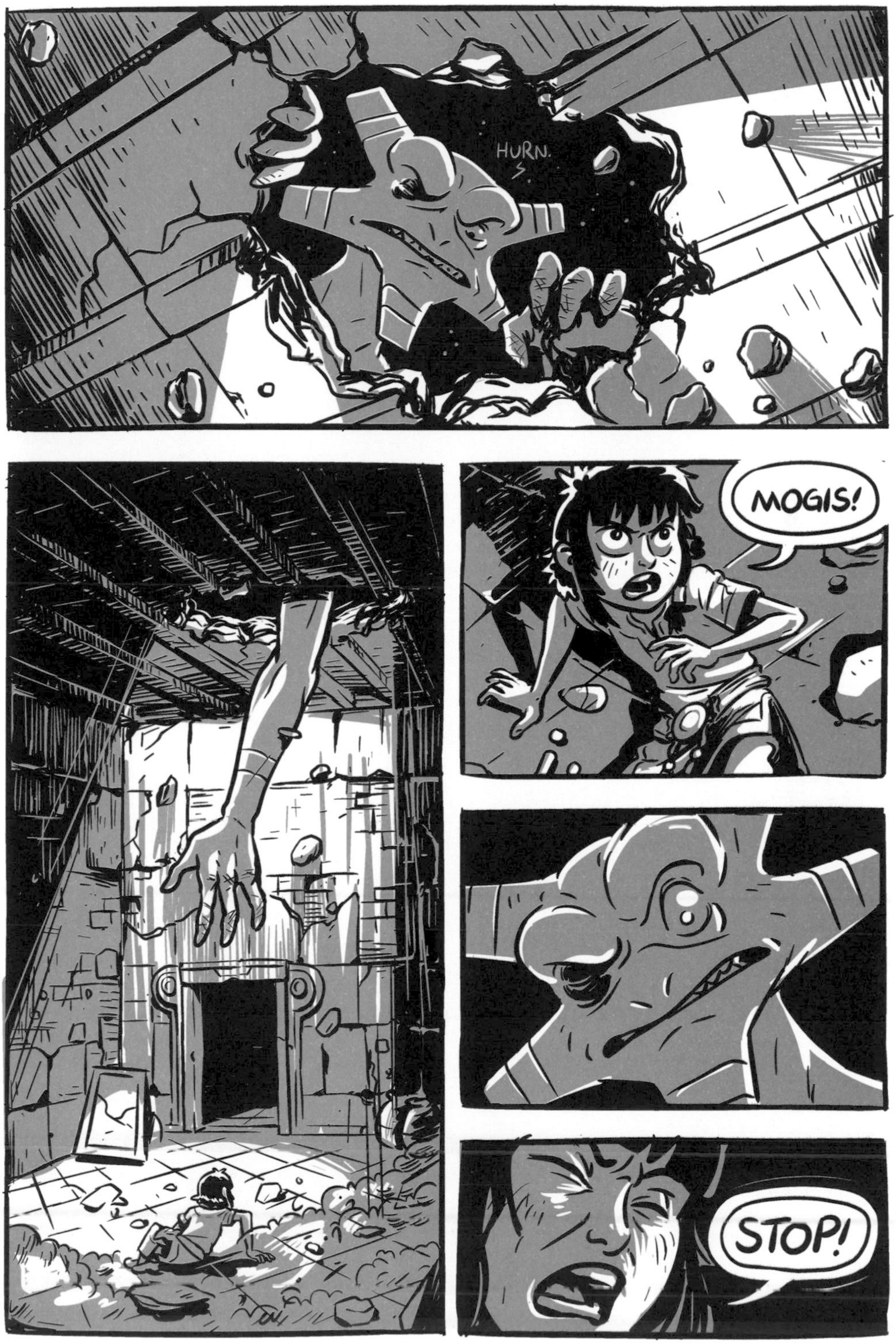
HURN.
MOGIS!
STOP!

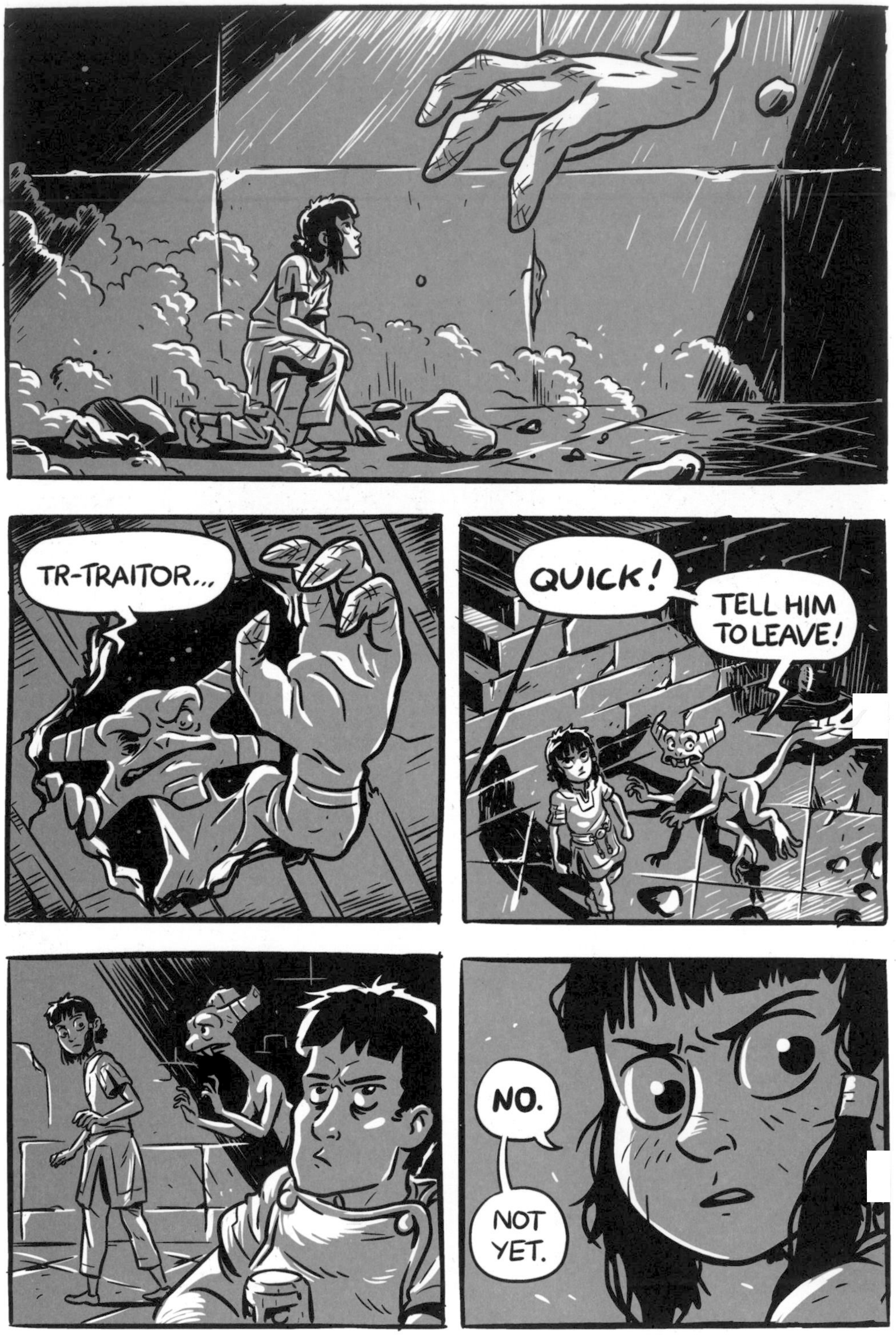
TR-TRAITOR...
QUICK!
TELL HIM TO LEAVE!
NO.
NOT YET.

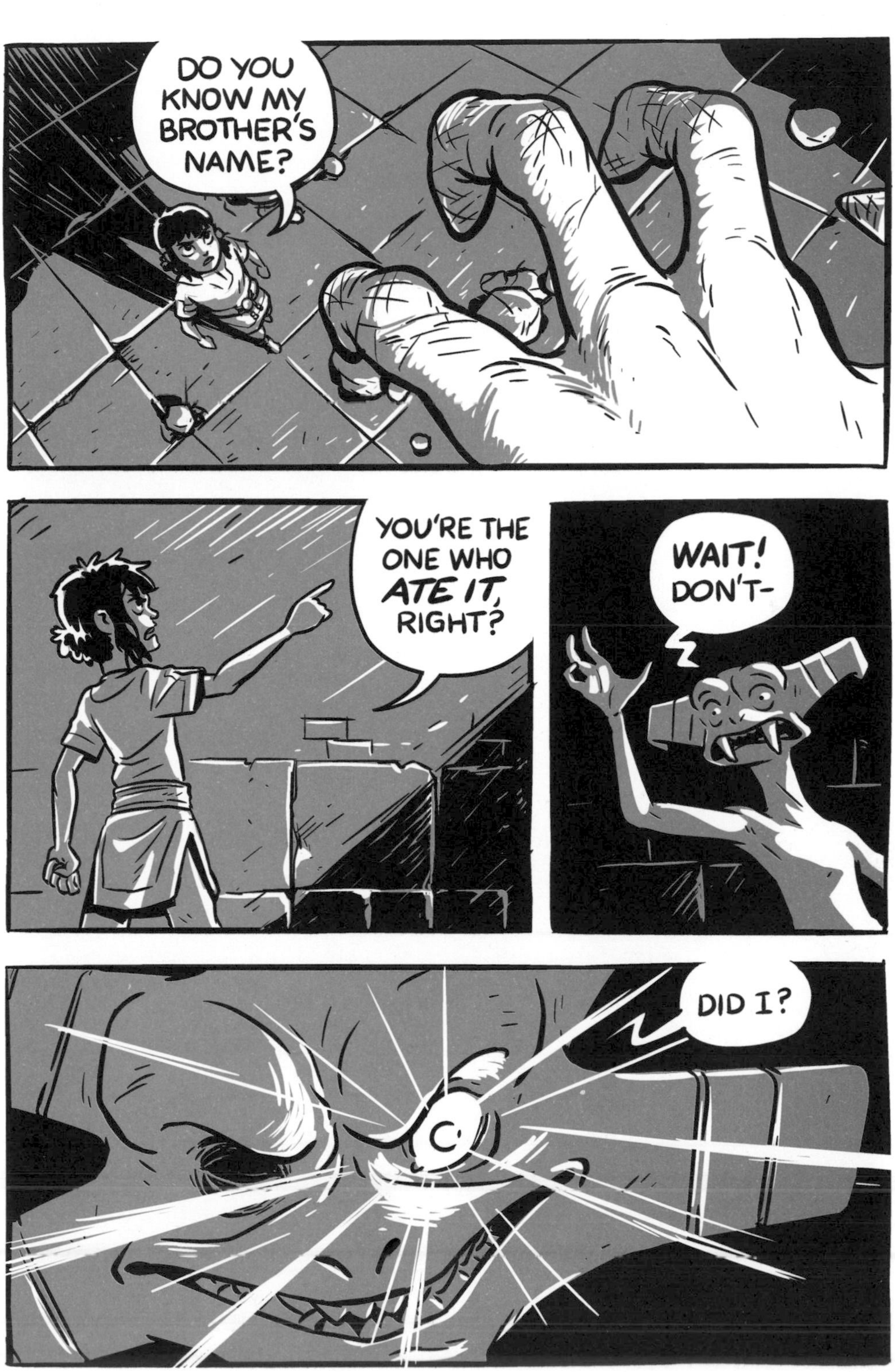
DO YOU KNOW MY BROTHER'S NAME?
YOU'RE THE ONE WHO *ATE IT,* RIGHT?
WAIT! DON'T-
DID I?

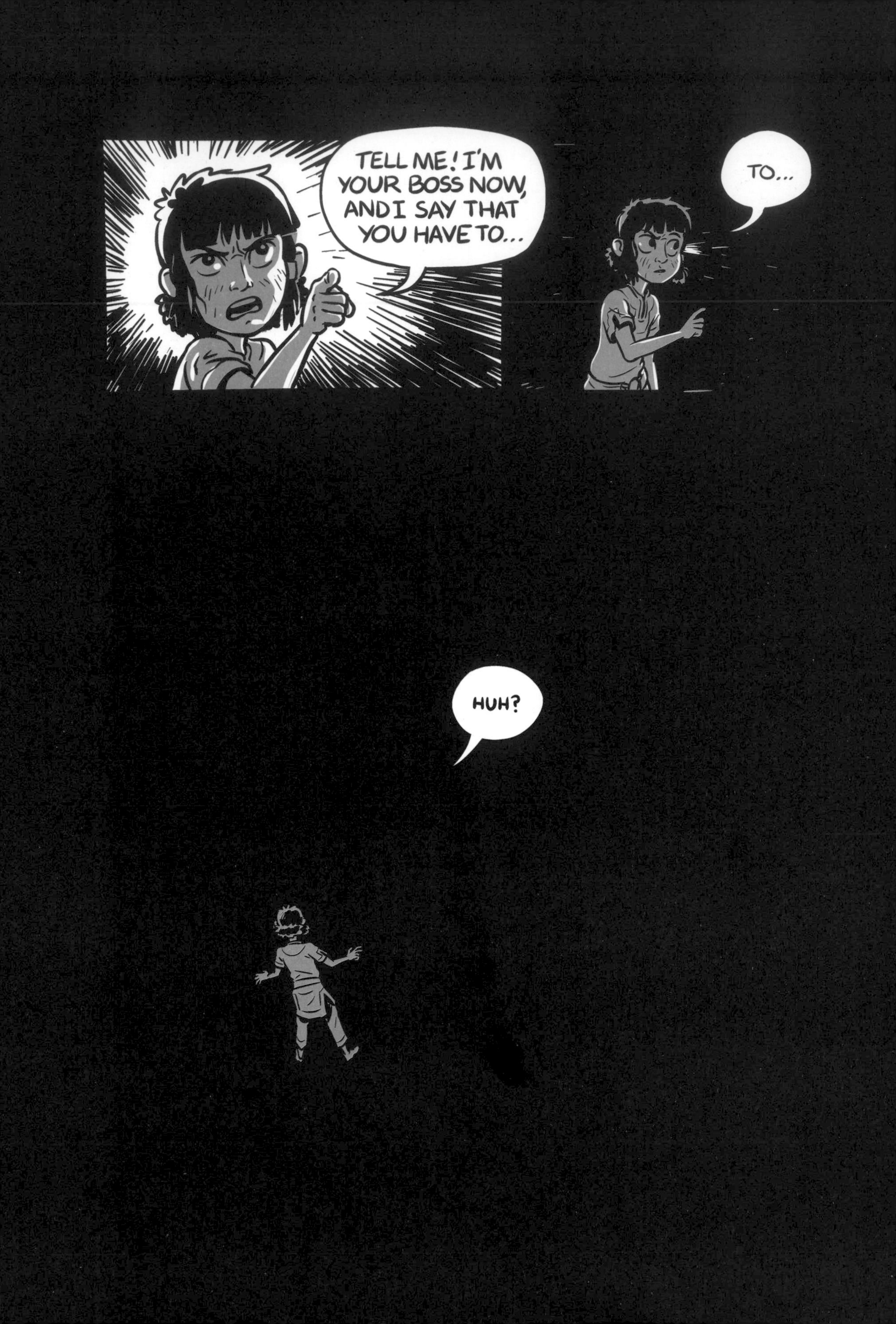
TELL ME! I'M YOUR BOSS NOW, AND I SAY THAT YOU HAVE TO...
TO...
HUH?

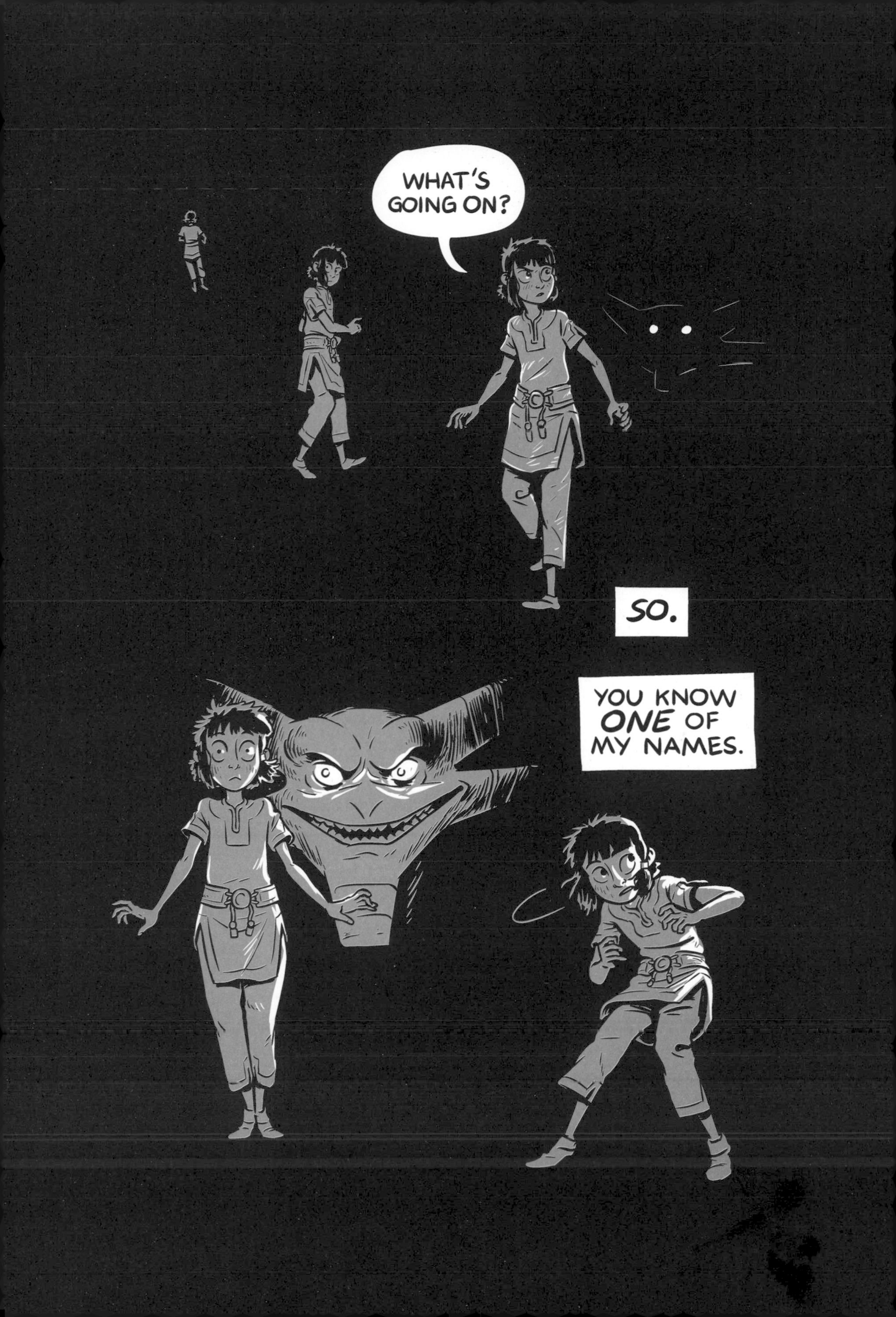
WHAT'S GOING ON?
SO.
YOU KNOW ONE OF MY NAMES.

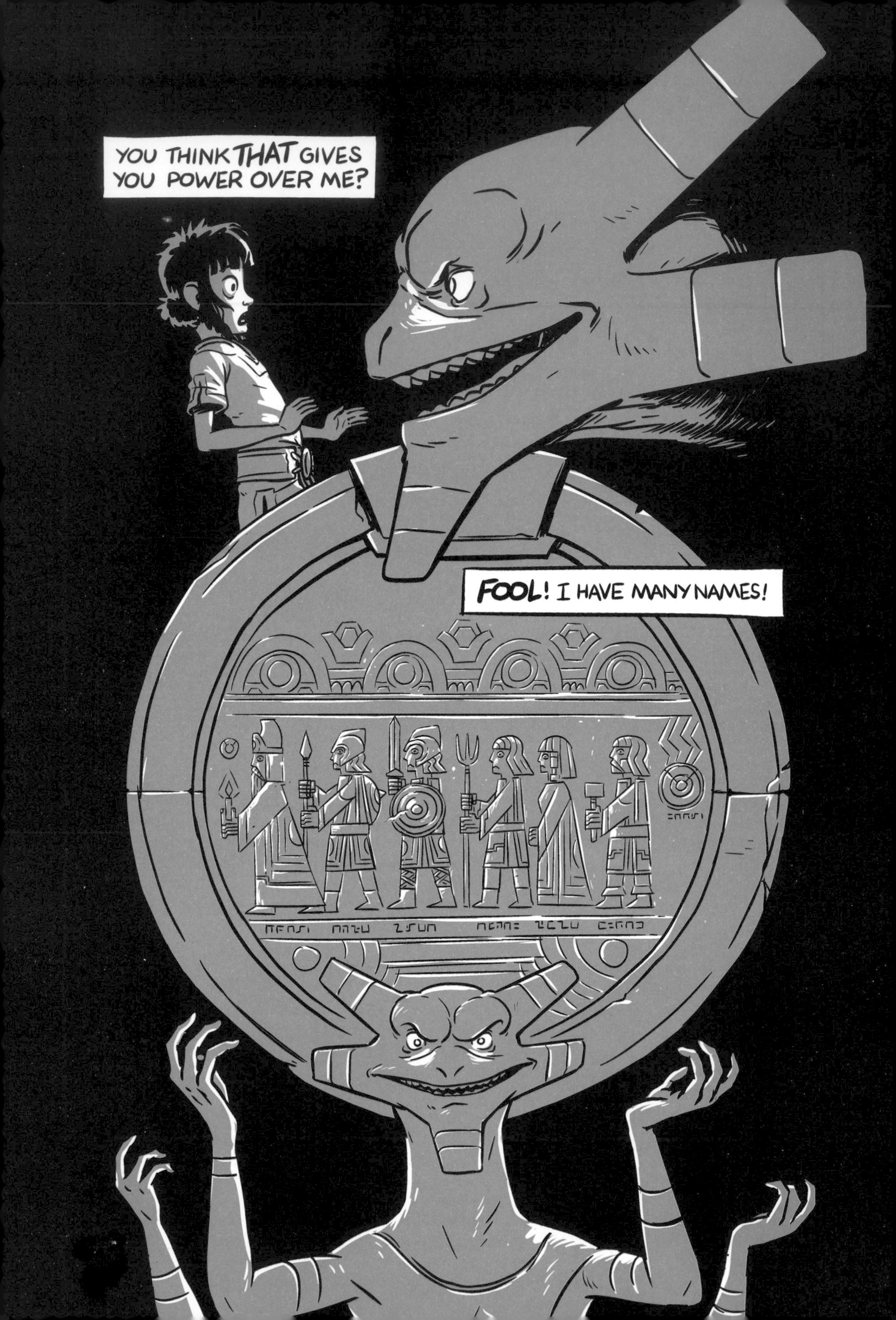
YOU THINK THAT GIVES YOU POWER OVER ME?
FOOL! I HAVE MANY NAMES!

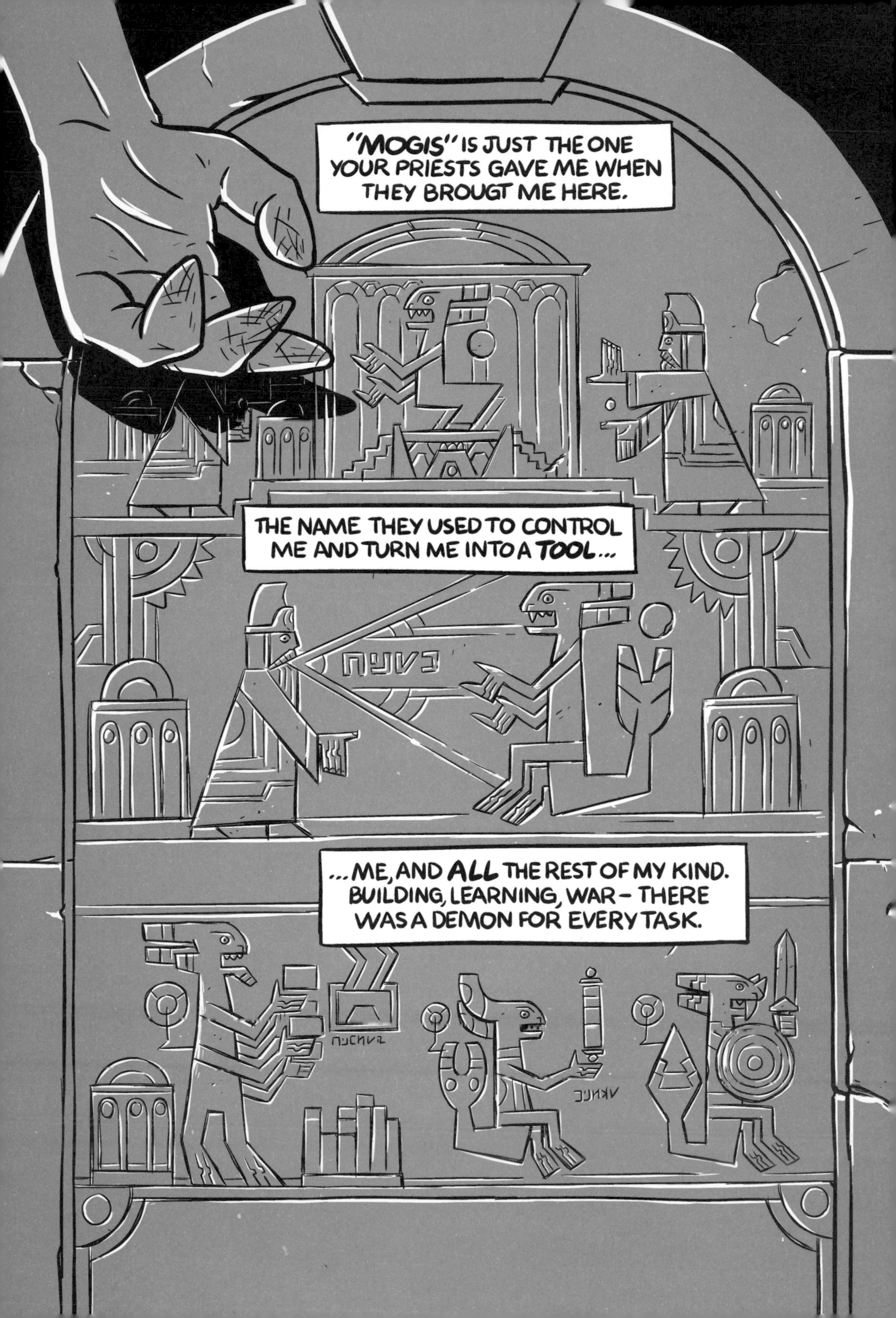
"MOGIS" IS JUST THE ONE YOUR PRIESTS GAVE ME WHEN THEY BROUGT ME HERE.
THE NAME THEY USED TO CONTROL ME AND TURN ME INTO A TOOL...
...ME, AND ALL THE REST OF MY KIND. BUILDING, LEARNING, WAR – THERE WAS A DEMON FOR EVERY TASK.

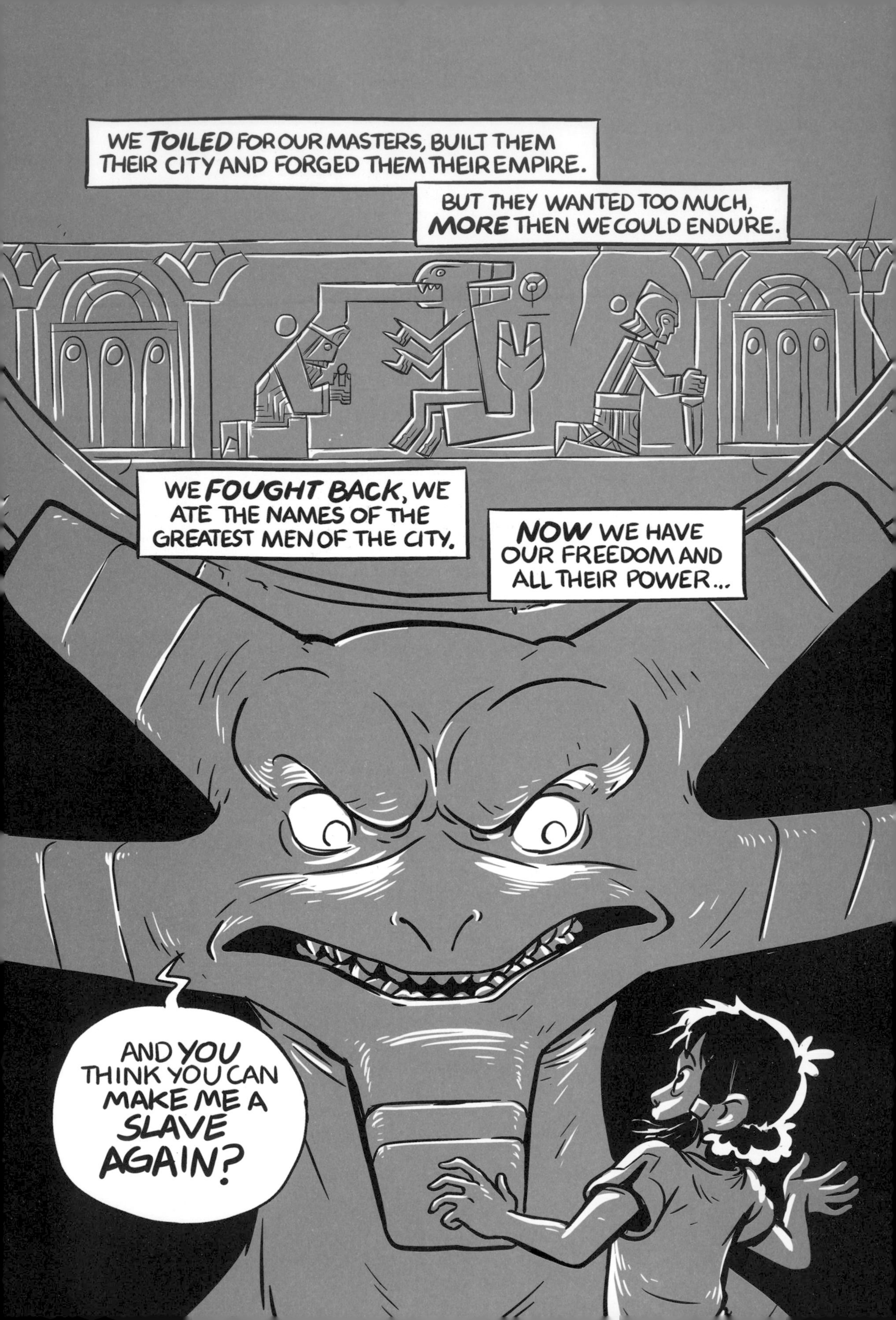
WE TOILED FOR OUR MASTERS, BUILT THEM THEIR CITY AND FORGED THEM THEIR EMPIRE.
BUT THEY WANTED TOO MUCH, MORE THEN WE COULD ENDURE.
WE FOUGHT BACK, WE ATE THE NAMES OF THE GREATEST MEN OF THE CITY.
NOW WE HAVE OUR FREEDOM AND ALL THEIR POWER...
AND YOU THINK YOU CAN MAKE ME A SLAVE AGAIN?

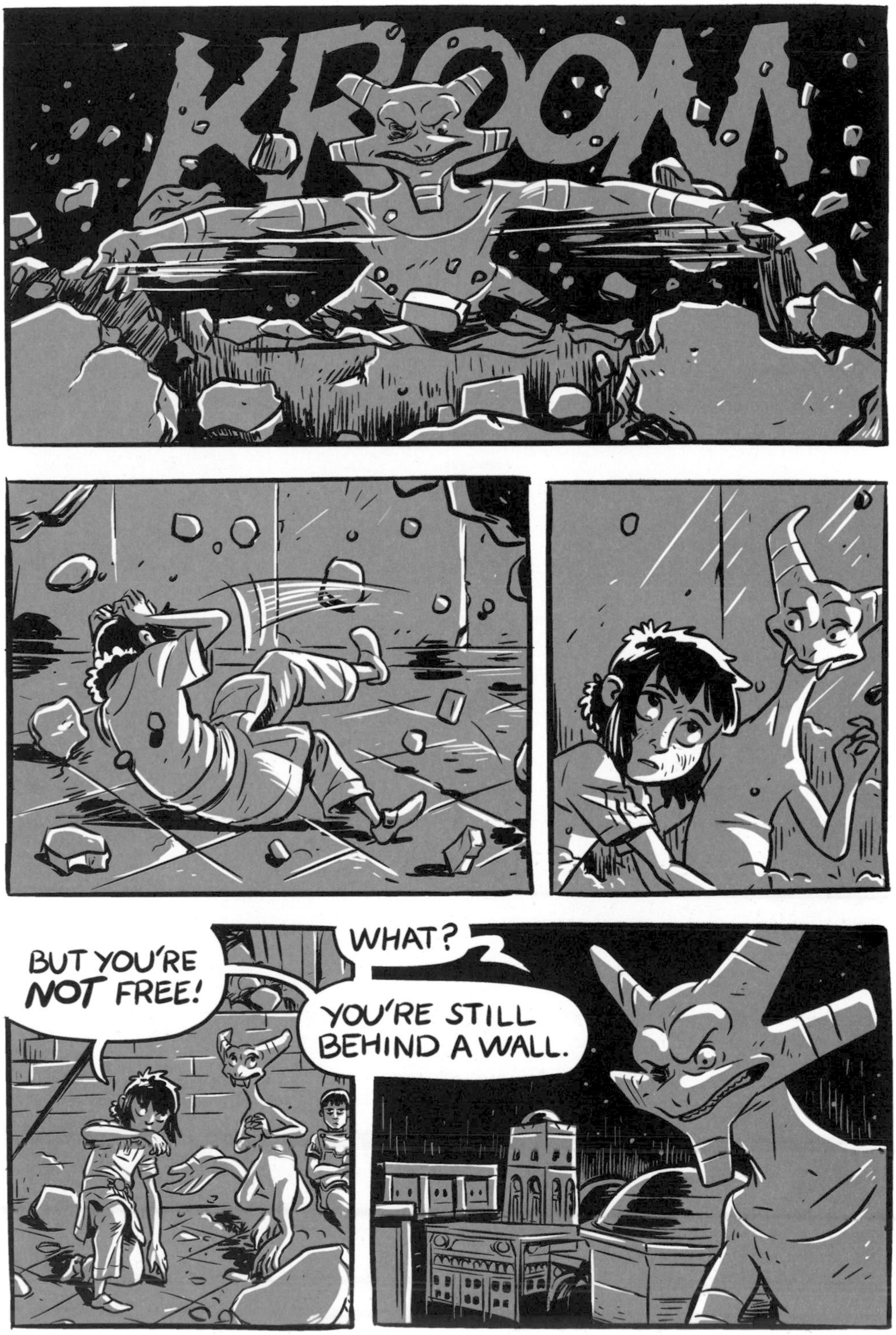
KROOM
BUT YOU'RE NOT FREE!
WHAT?
YOU'RE STILL BEHIND A WALL.

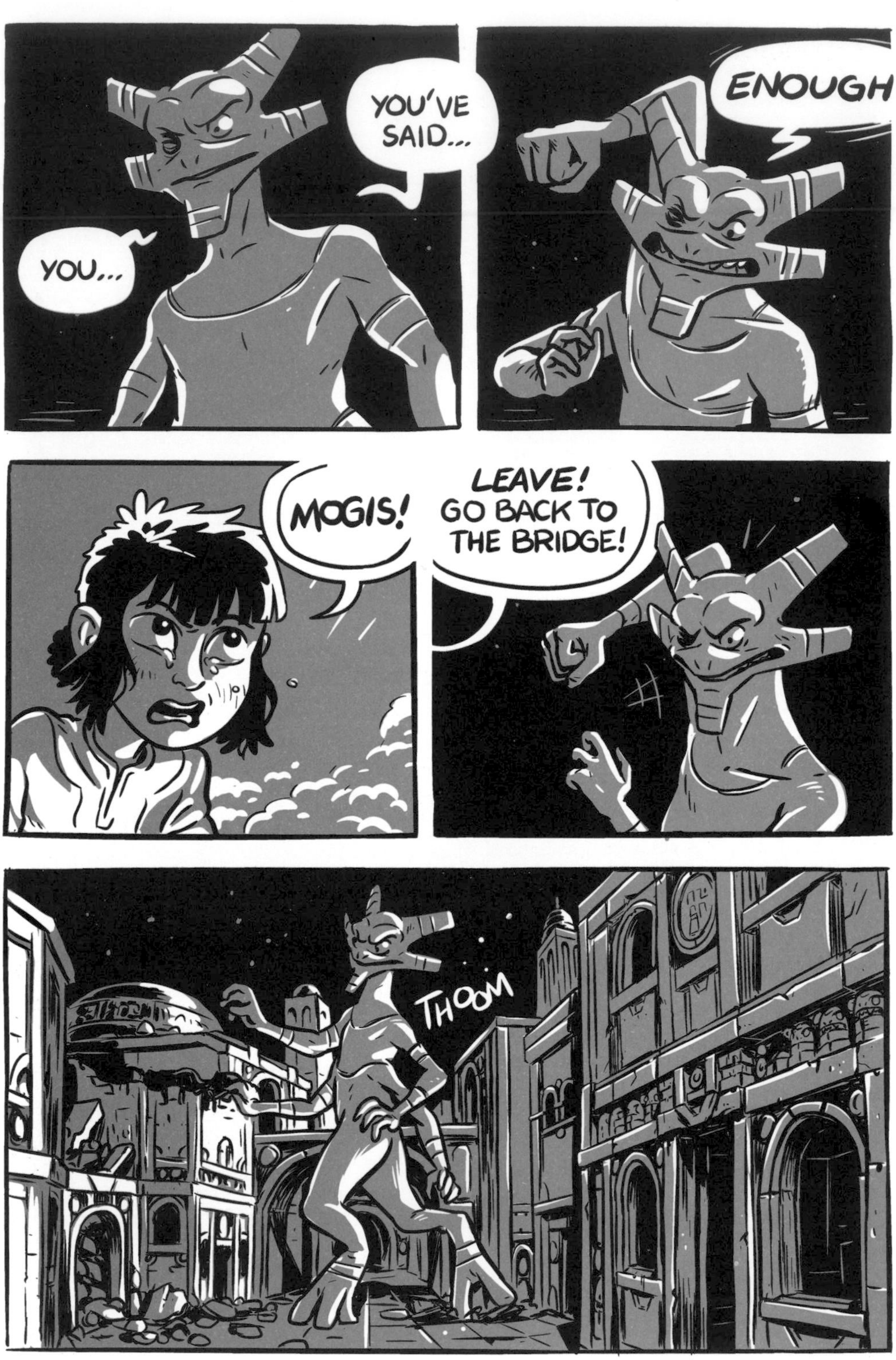
YOU...
YOU'VE SAID...
ENOUGH!
MOGIS!
LEAVE! GO BACK TO THE BRIDGE!
THOOM

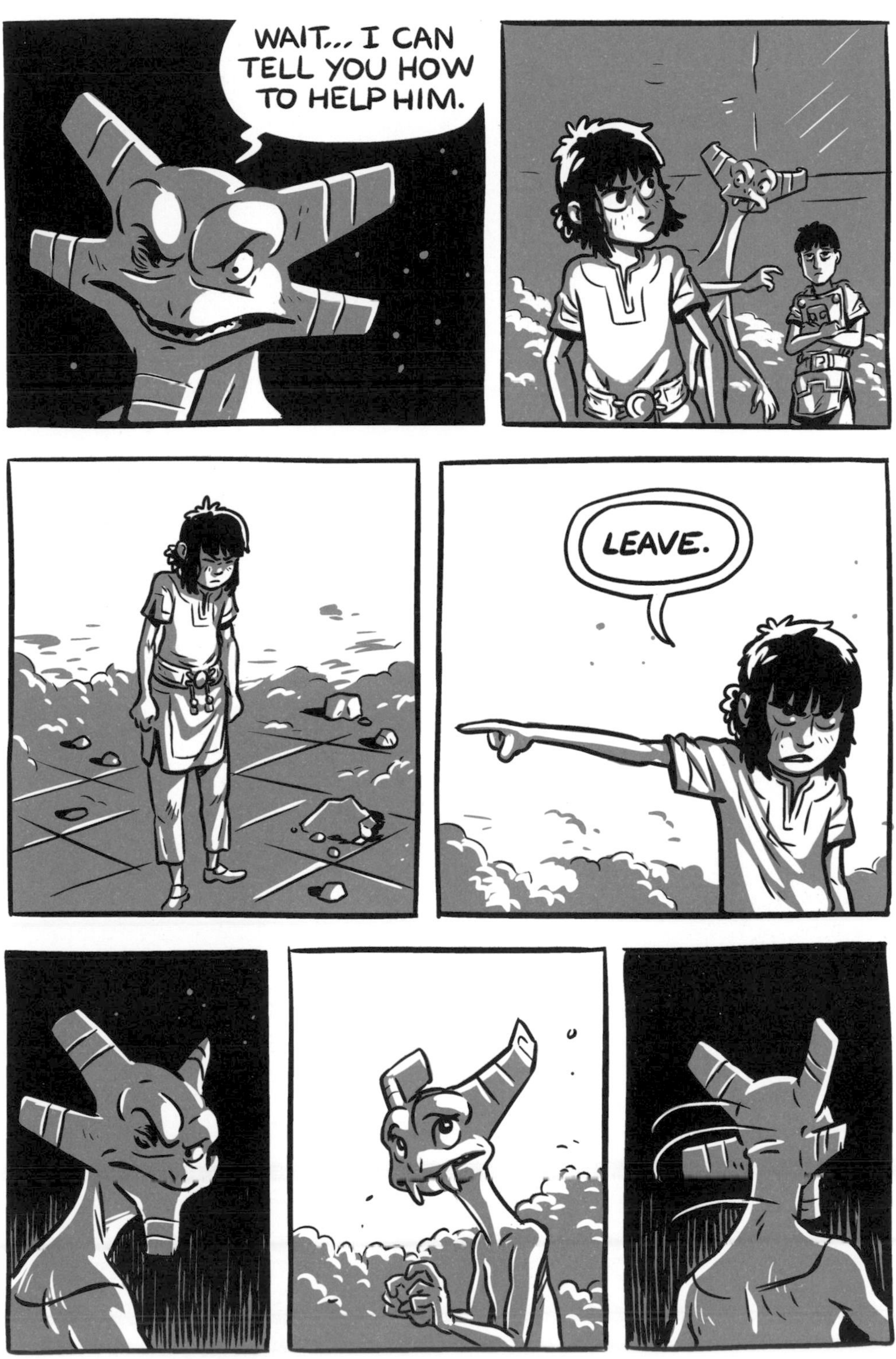
WAIT... I CAN TELL YOU HOW TO HELP HIM.
LEAVE.

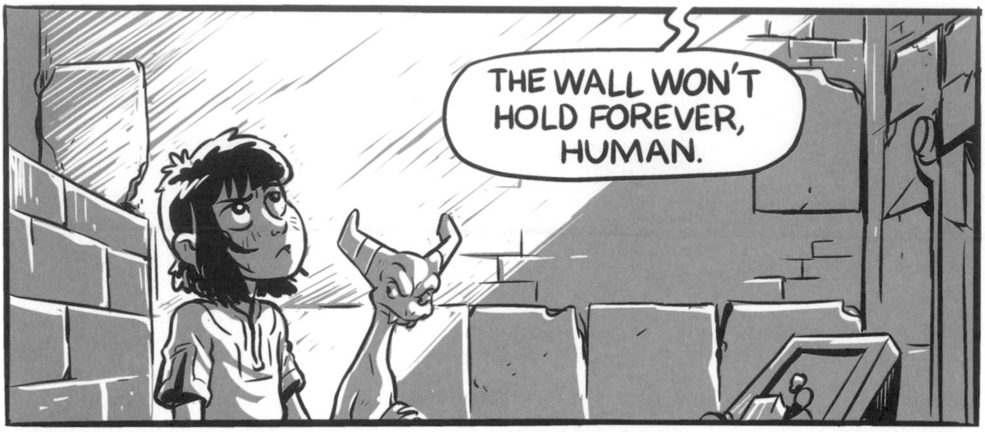
THE WALL WON'T HOLD FOREVER, HUMAN.

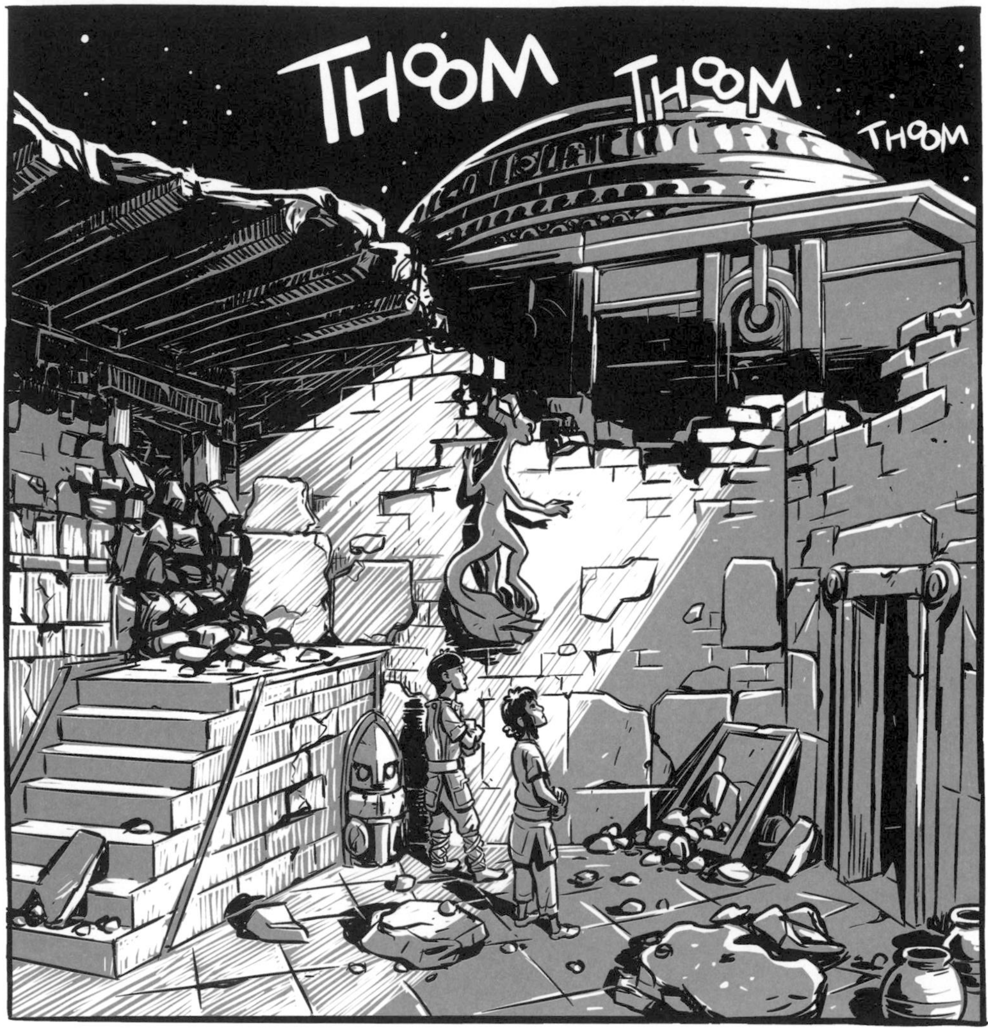
THOOM
THOOM
THOOM

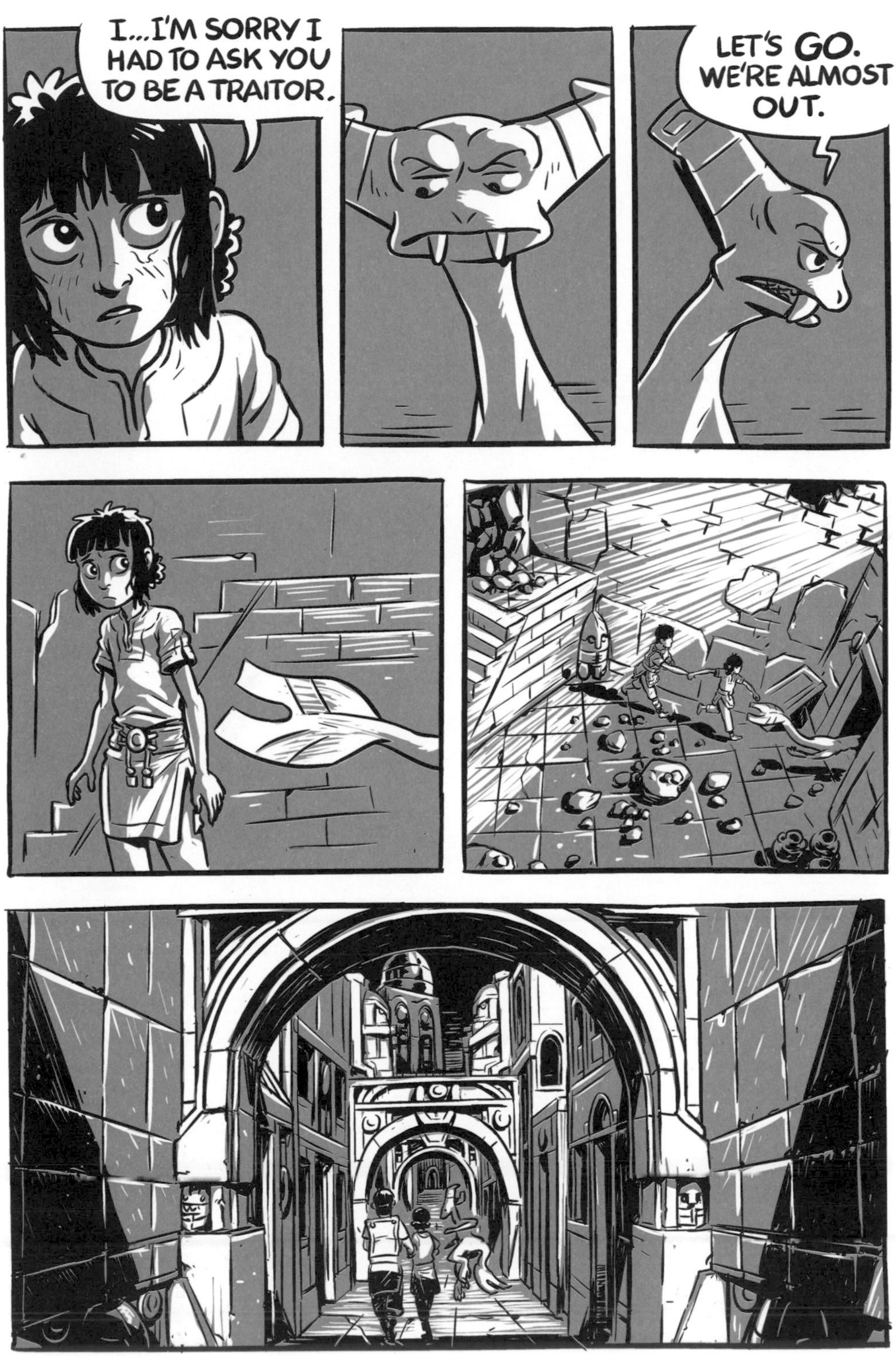
I...I'M SORRY I HAD TO ASK YOU TO BE A TRAITOR.
LET'S GO. WE'RE ALMOST OUT.

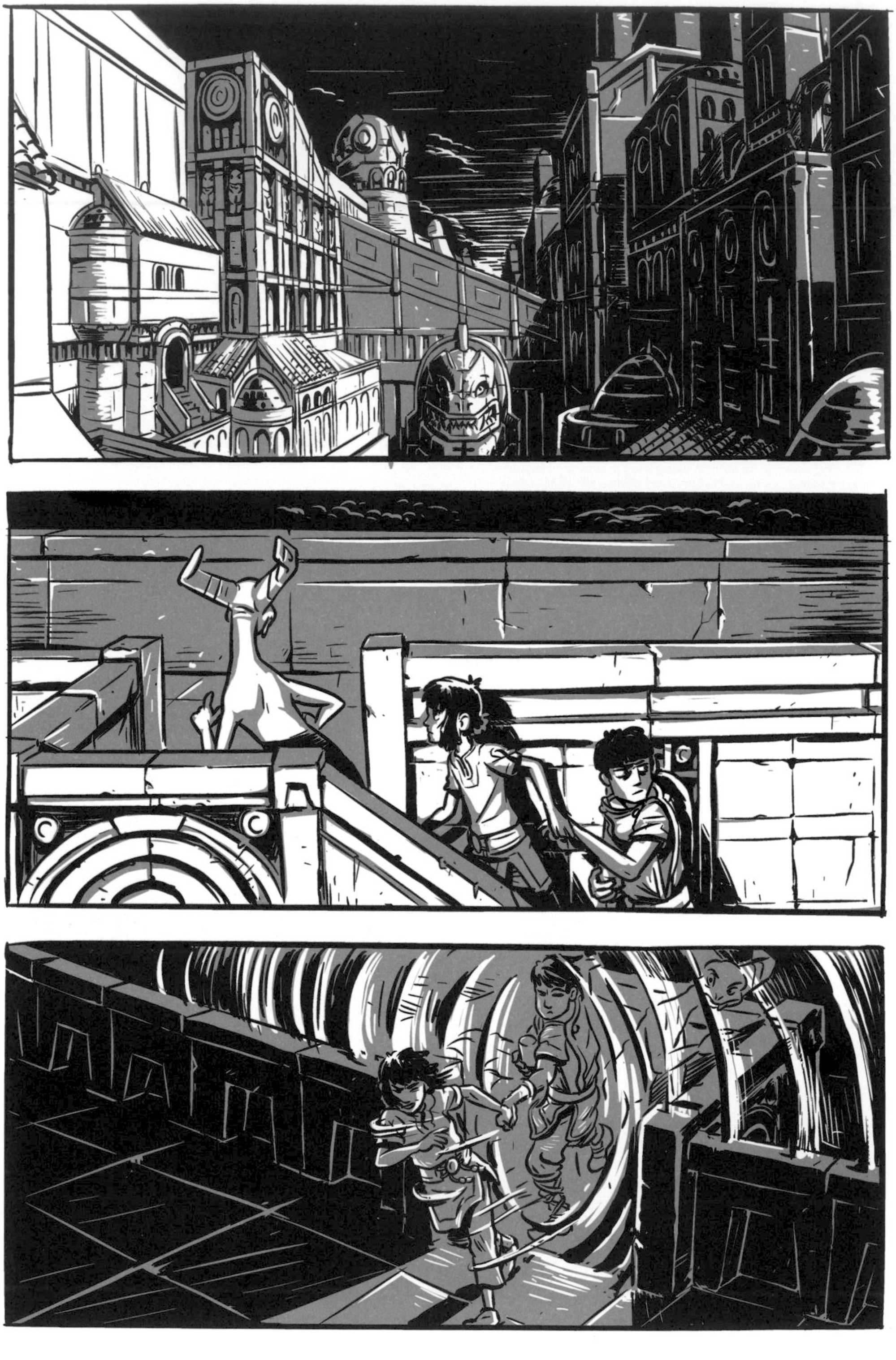

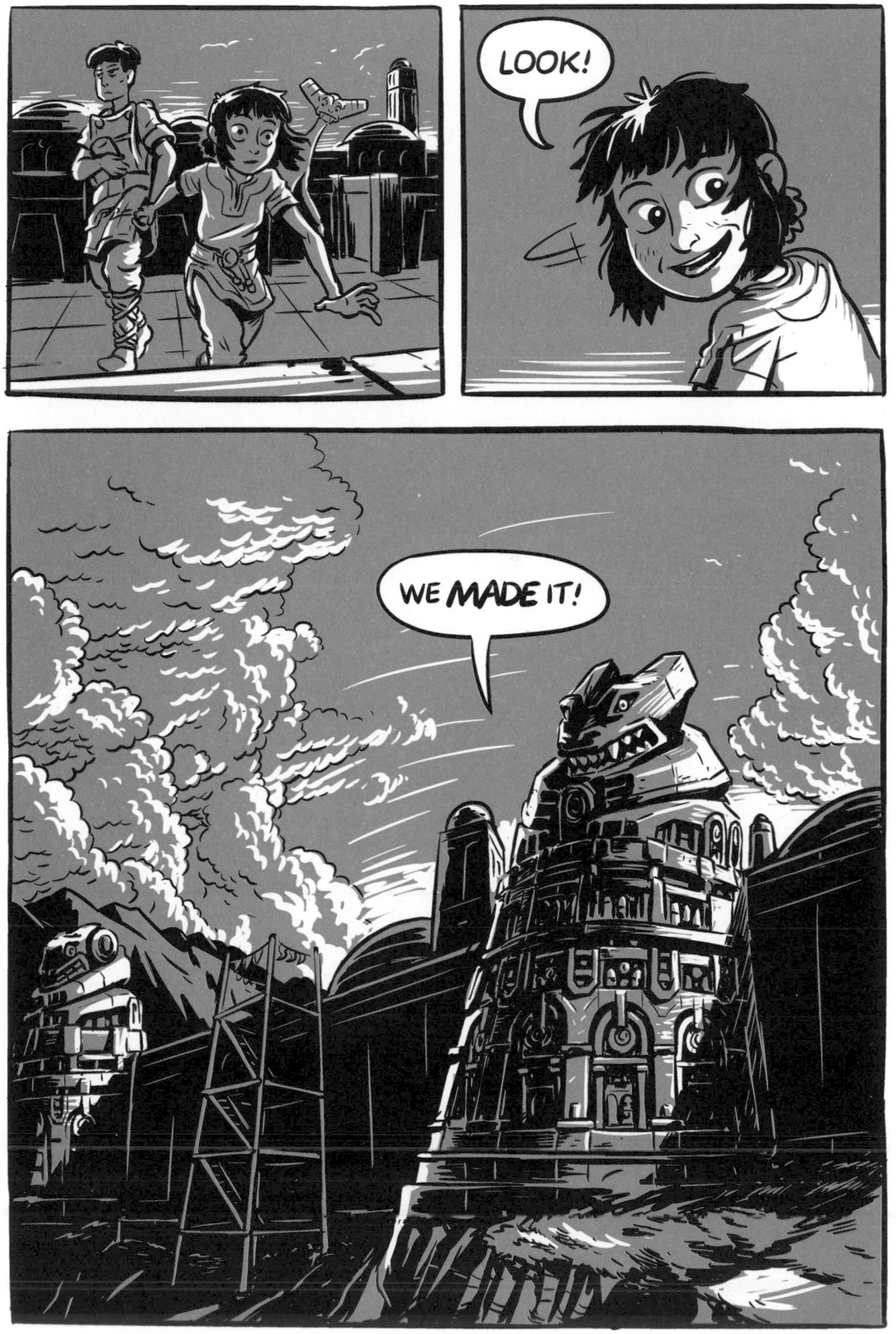
LOOK!
WE MADE IT!

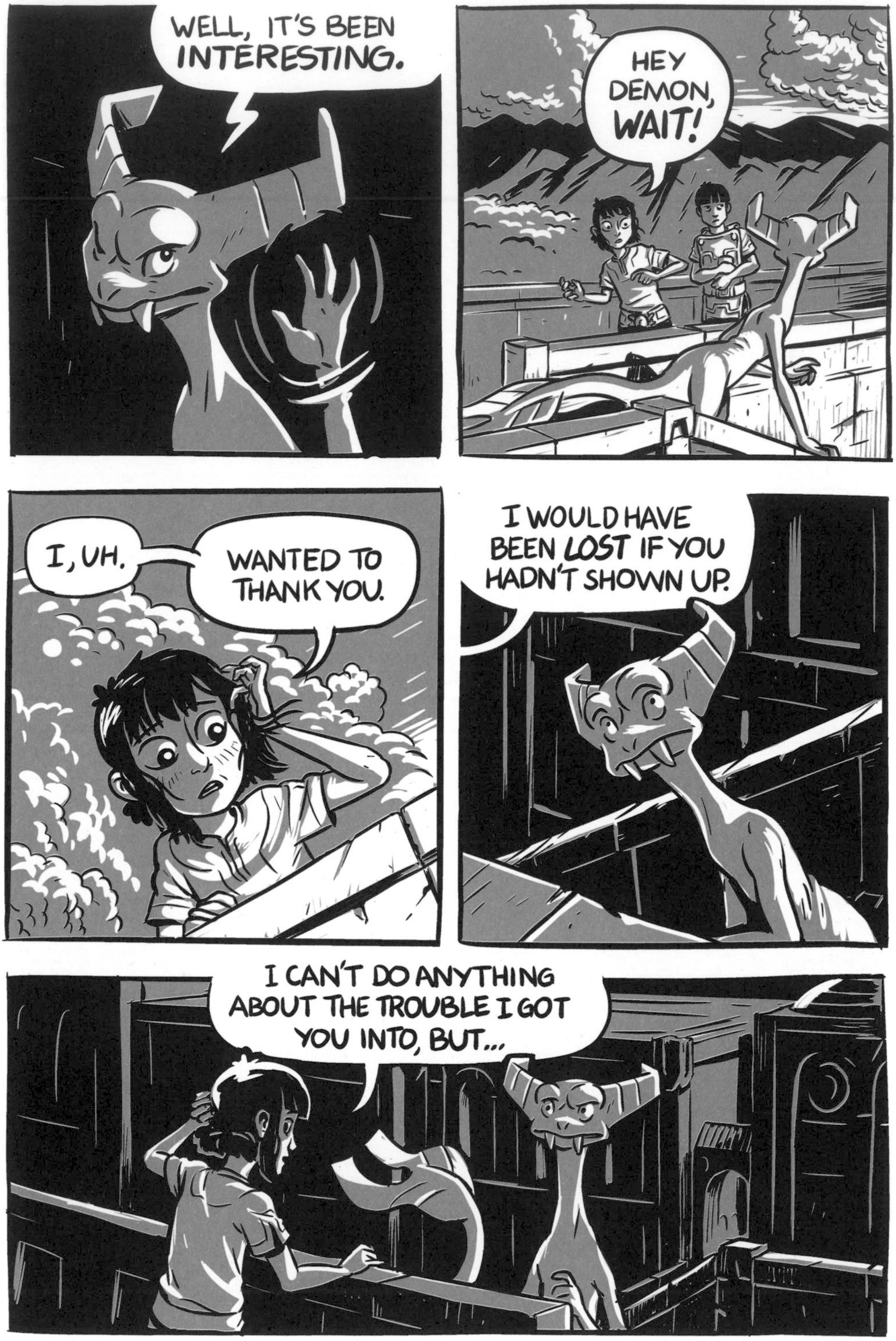
WELL, IT'S BEEN INTERESTING.
HEY DEMON, WAIT!
I, UH.
WANTED TO THANK YOU.
I WOULD HAVE BEEN LOST IF YOU HADN'T SHOWN UP.
I CAN'T DO ANYTHING ABOUT THE TROUBLE I GOT YOU INTO, BUT...

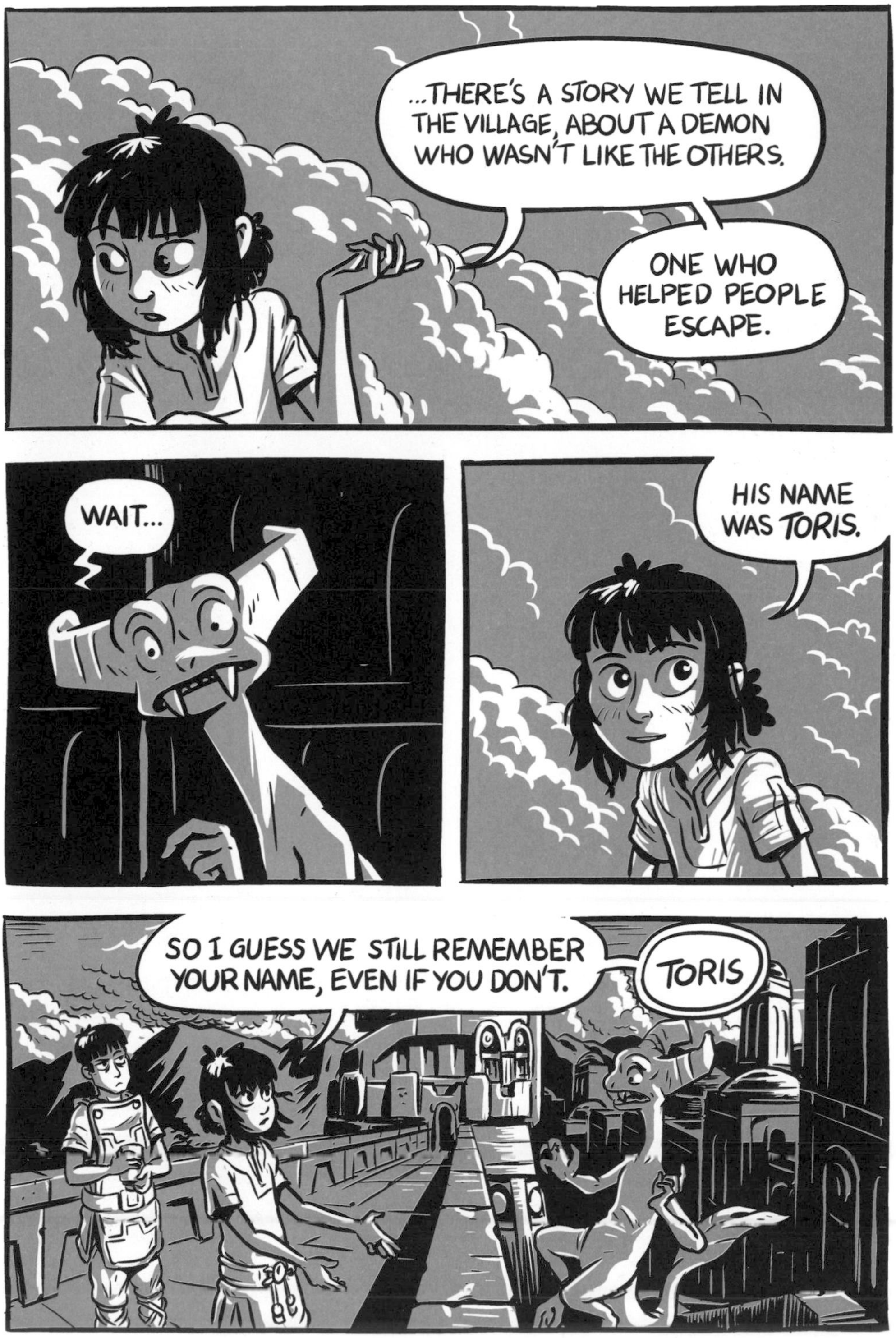
...THERE'S A STORY WE TELL IN THE VILLAGE, ABOUT A DEMON WHO WASN'T LIKE THE OTHERS.
ONE WHO HELPED PEOPLE ESCAPE.
WAIT...
HIS NAME WAS TORIS.
SO I GUESS WE STILL REMEMBER YOUR NAME, EVEN IF YOU DON'T.
TORIS

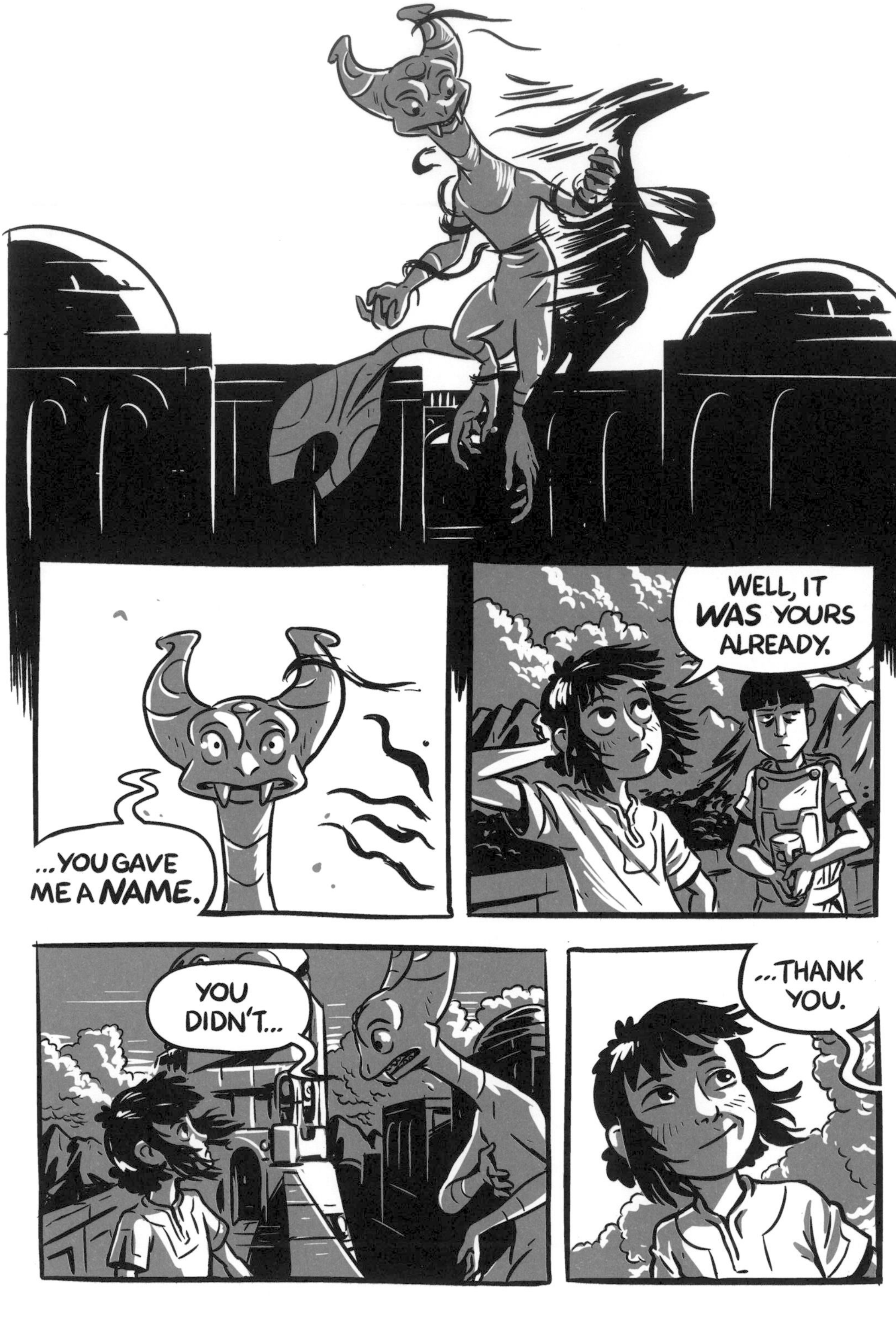
...YOU GAVE ME A NAME.
WELL, IT WAS YOURS ALREADY.
YOU DIDN'T...
...THANK YOU.

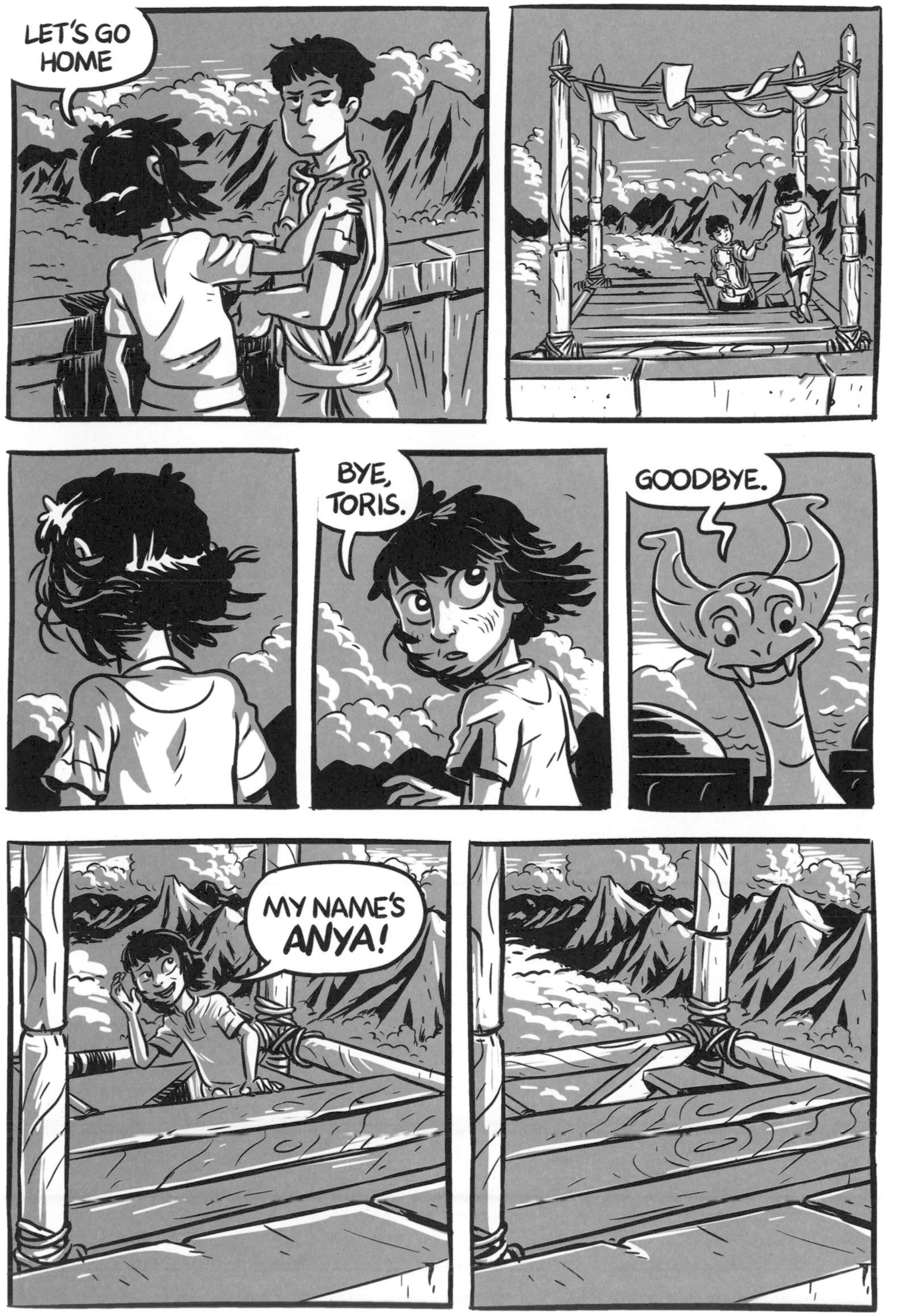
LET'S GO HOME
BYE, TORIS.
GOODBYE.
MY NAME'S ANYA!

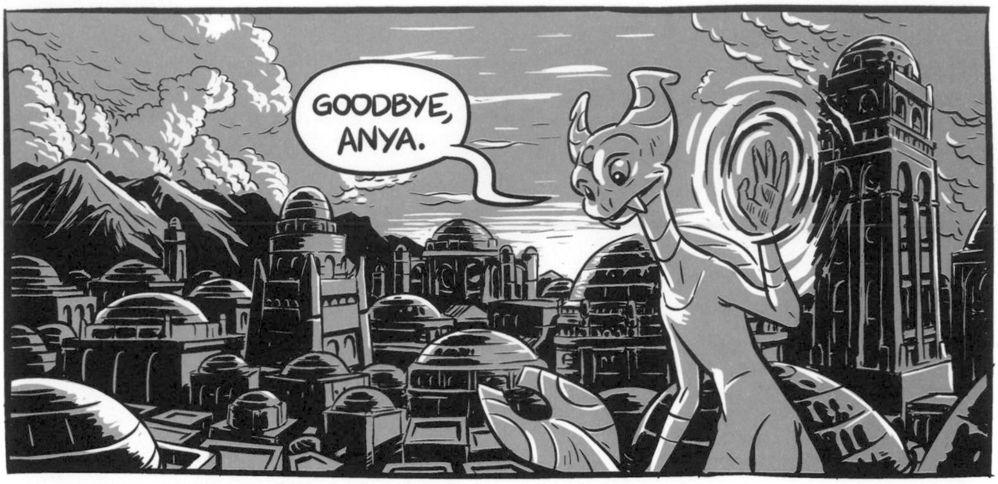
GOODBYE, ANYA.

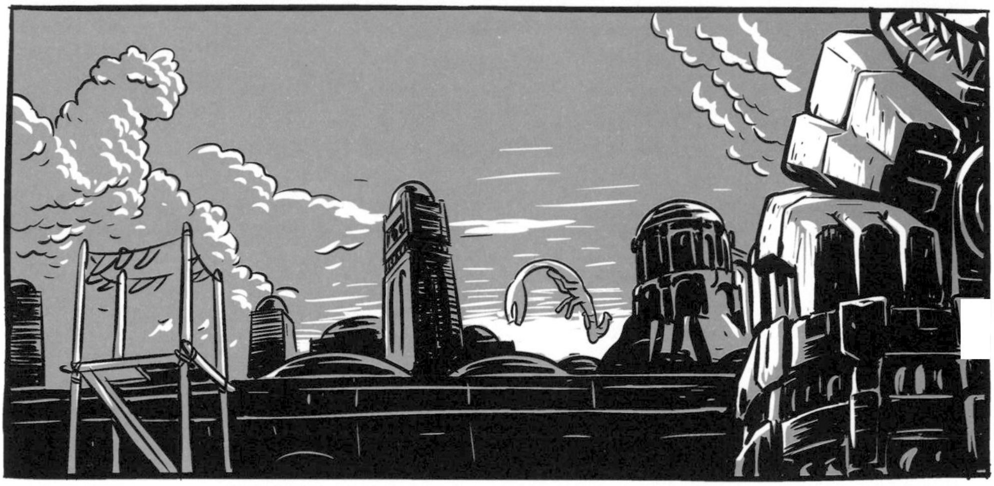

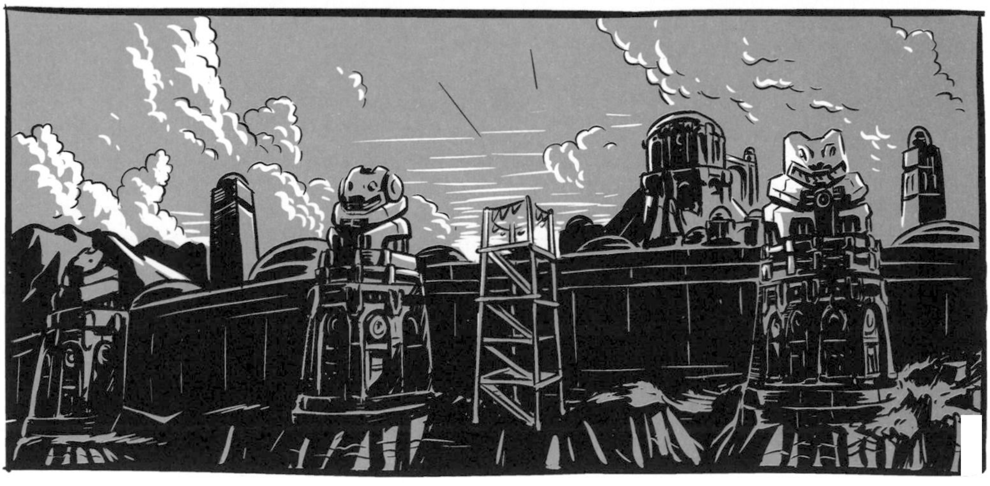

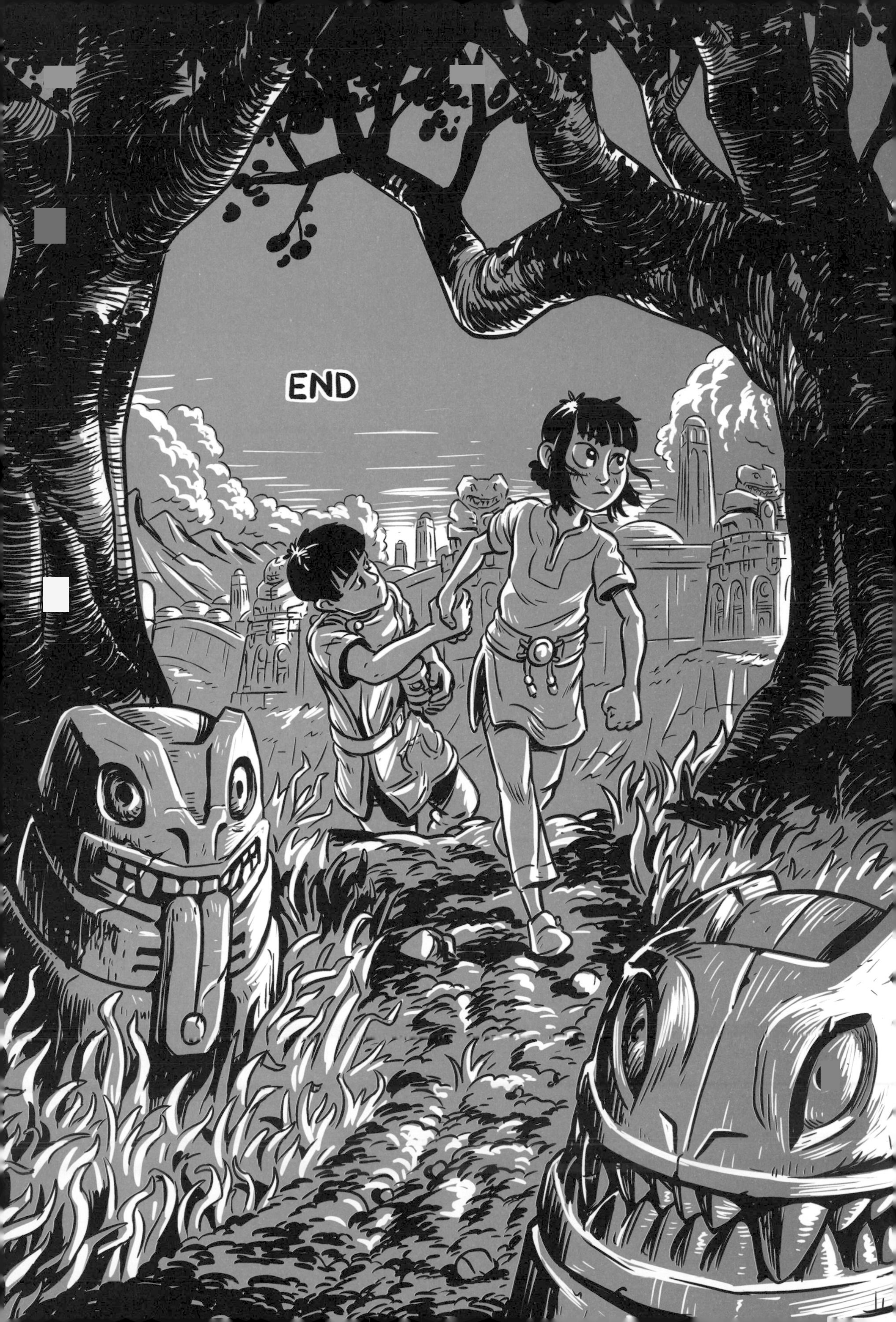
END

ANYA'S STORY WILL CONTINUE IN:

STONEBREAKER

Anya saved her brother, but couldn't save his memory.

In the four years since she first entered the city she has explored every street and found every twisting shortcut, but a cure for her brother's amnesia remains elusive — if one even exists. Anya is drawn to the city anyway, no longer sure what it is she is looking for.

Toris, the demon she befriended and named, has found a home in the city's great library, searching for clues to his own history. The building has become a refuge for Anya as well; a sanctuary among the still dangerous streets of the city.

But the library contains more secrets then the ones written on its scrolls, and two travelers from a distant land have arrived with a plan that will change everything — and force everyone to confront a past they had walled off long ago.

COMING SOON!

MEANWHILE, HERE'S A SMALL PREVIEW

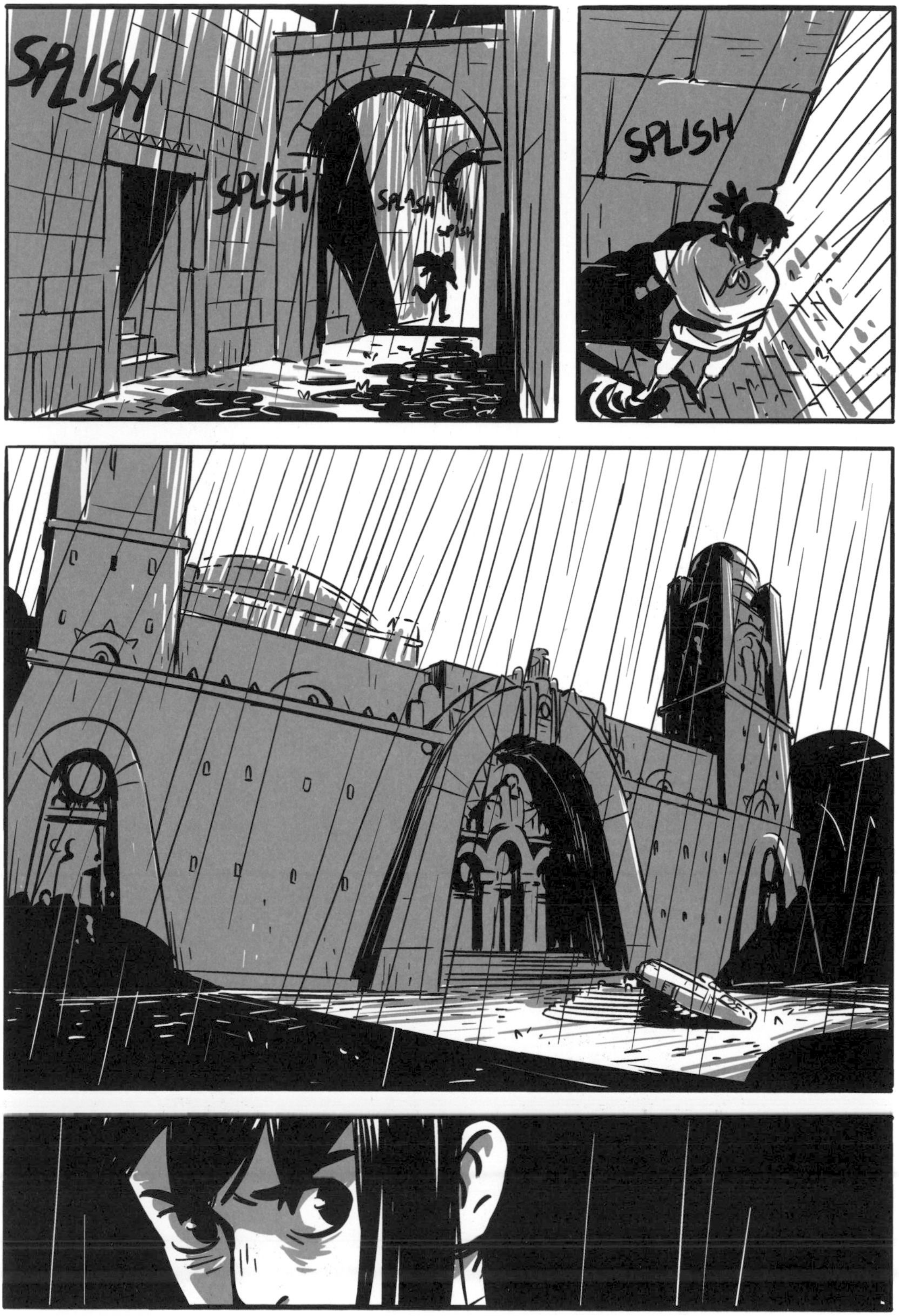
SPLISH
SPLISH
SPLASH
SPLASH
SPLISH

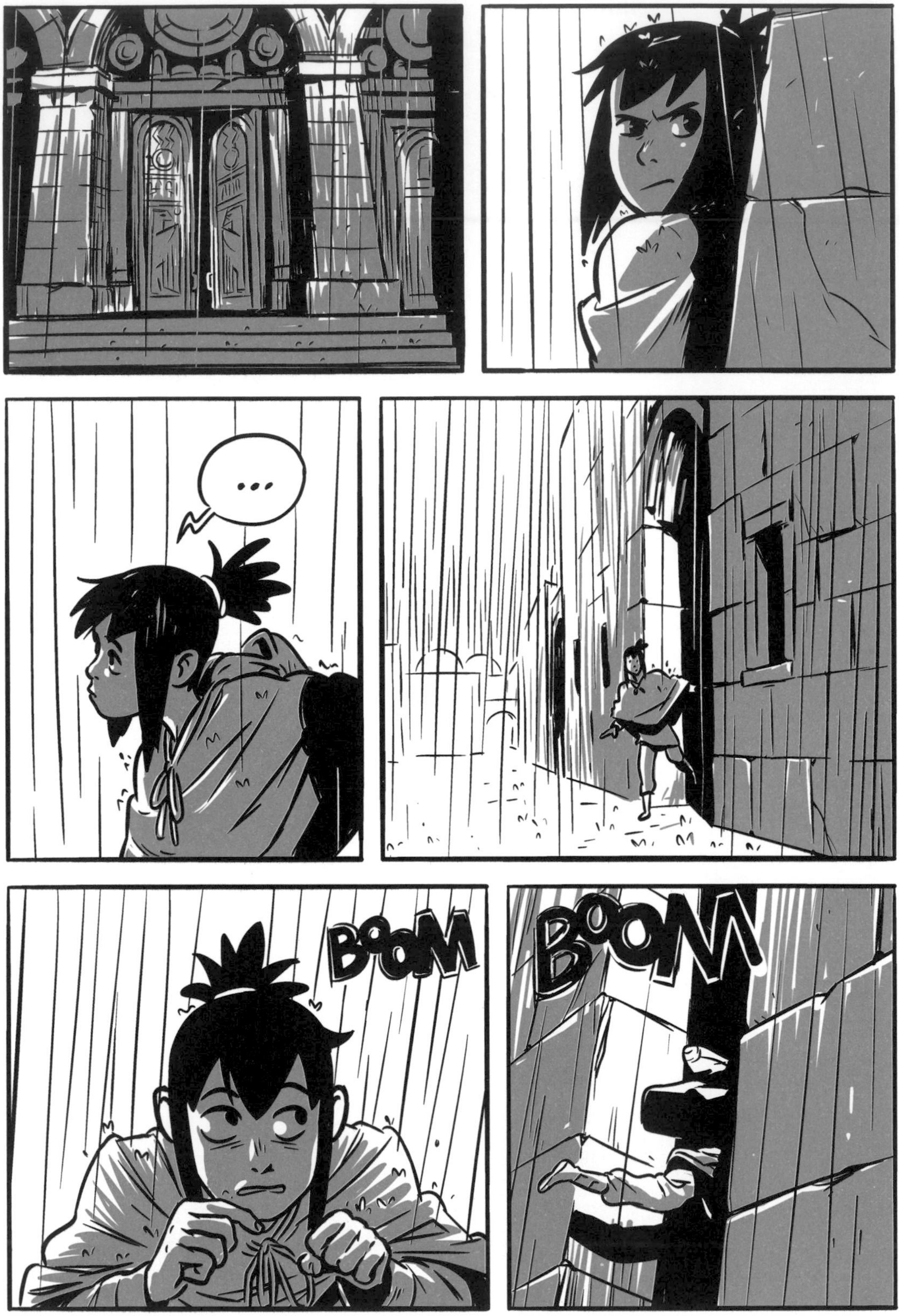
...
BOOM
BOOM

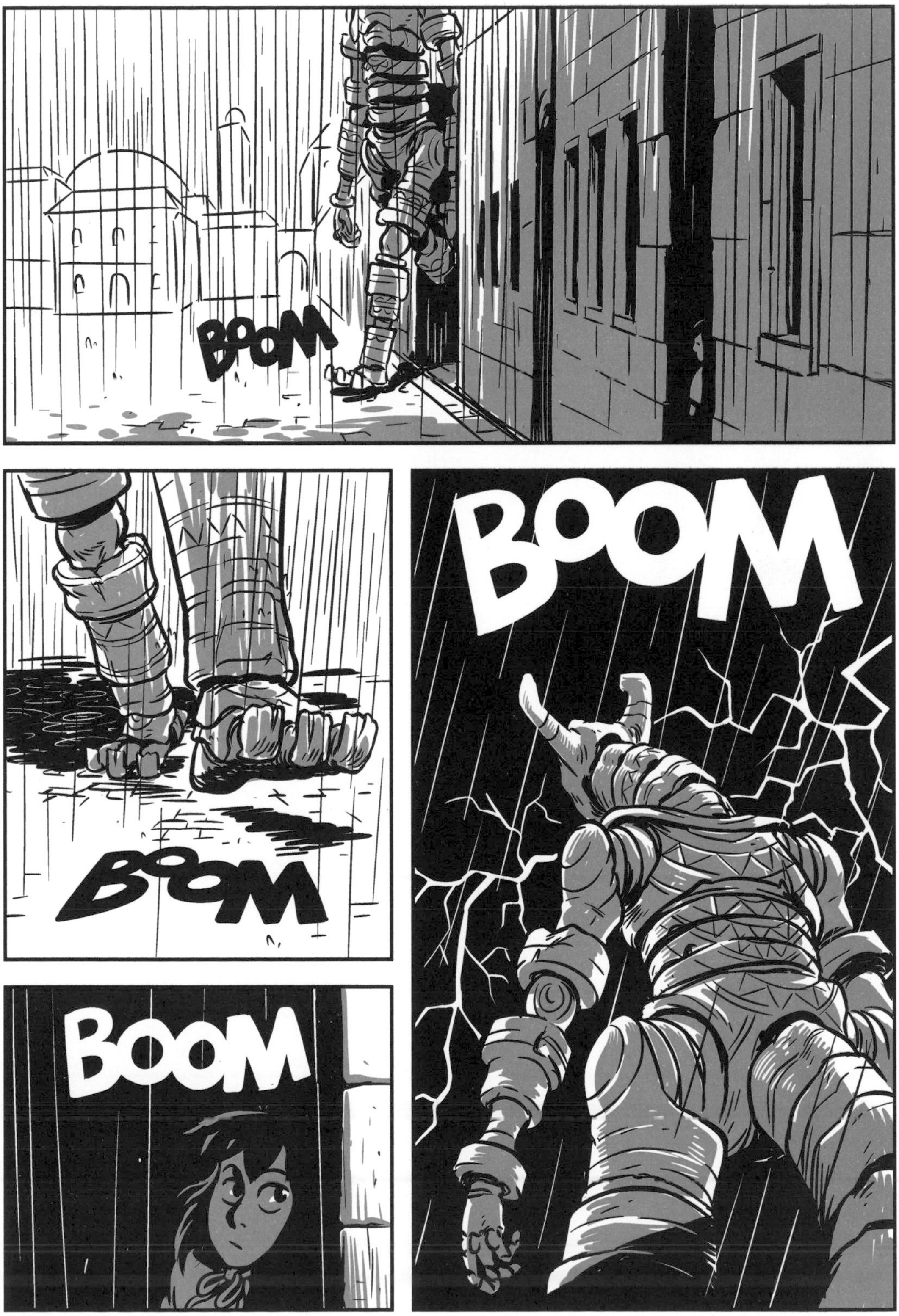
BOOM
BOOM
BOOM
BOOM

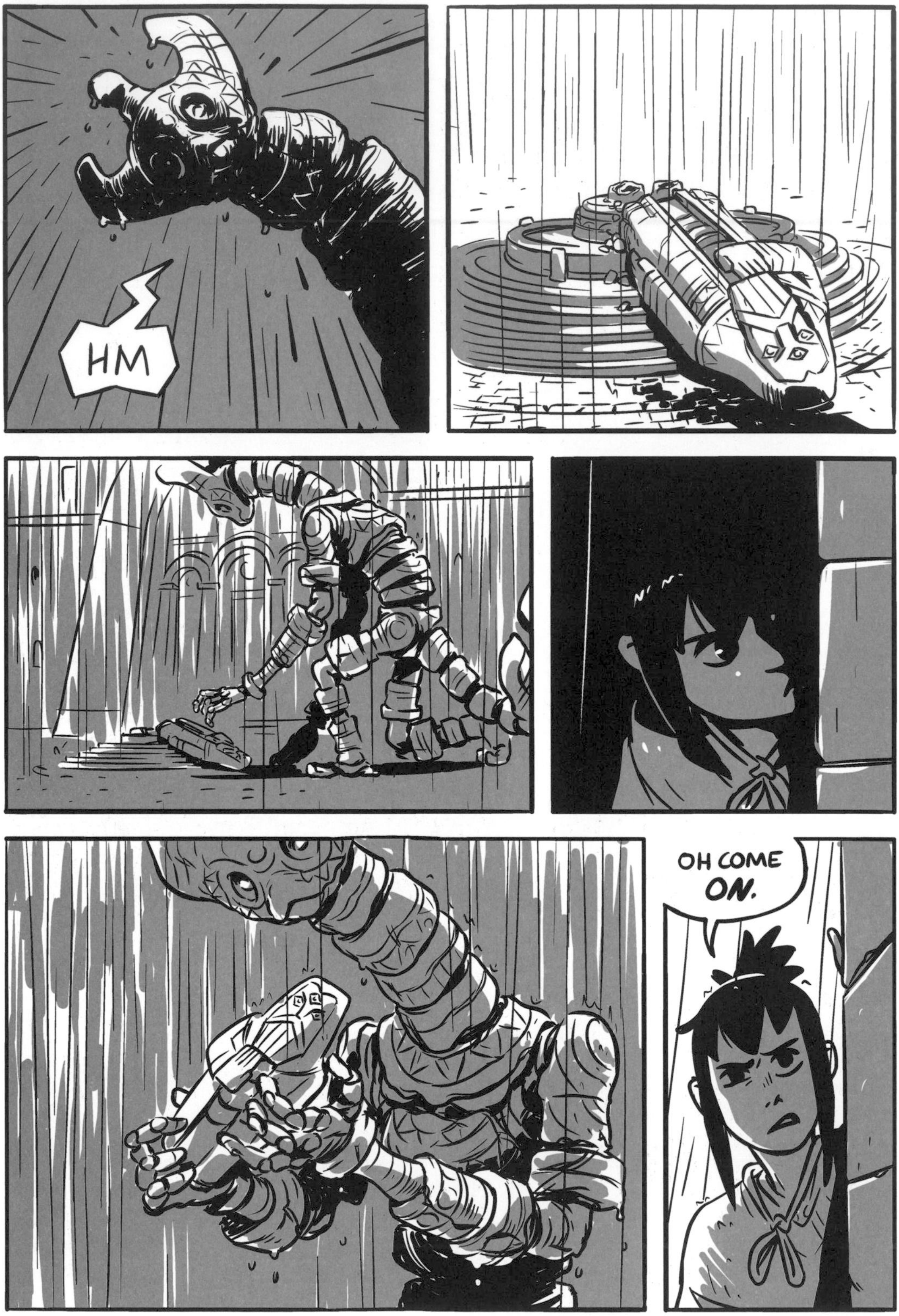
HM
OH COME ON.

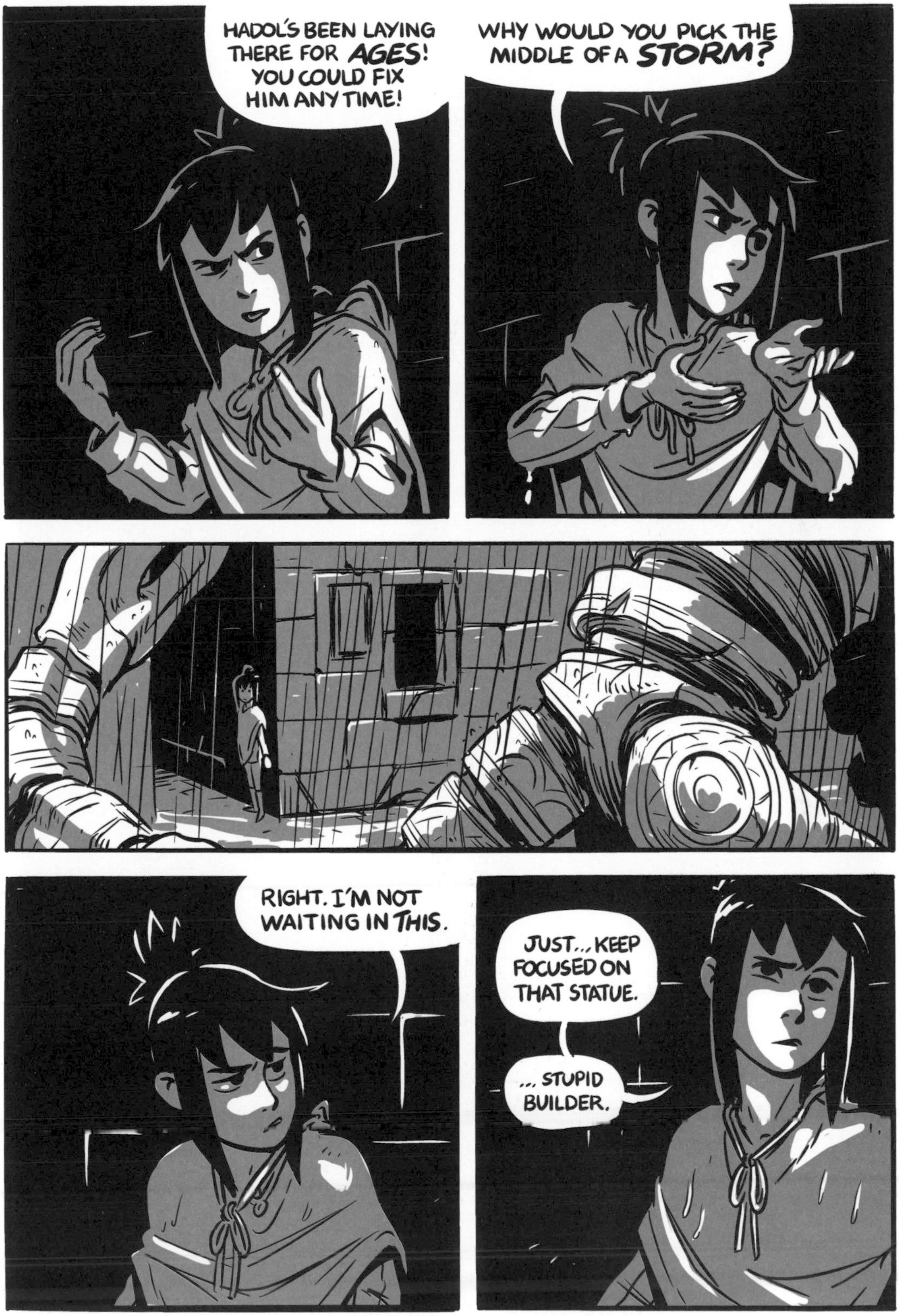

HADOL'S BEEN LAYING THERE FOR AGES! YOU COULD FIX HIM ANY TIME!
WHY WOULD YOU PICK THE MIDDLE OF A STORM?
RIGHT. I'M NOT WAITING IN THIS.
JUST... KEEP FOCUSED ON THAT STATUE.
... STUPID BUILDER.

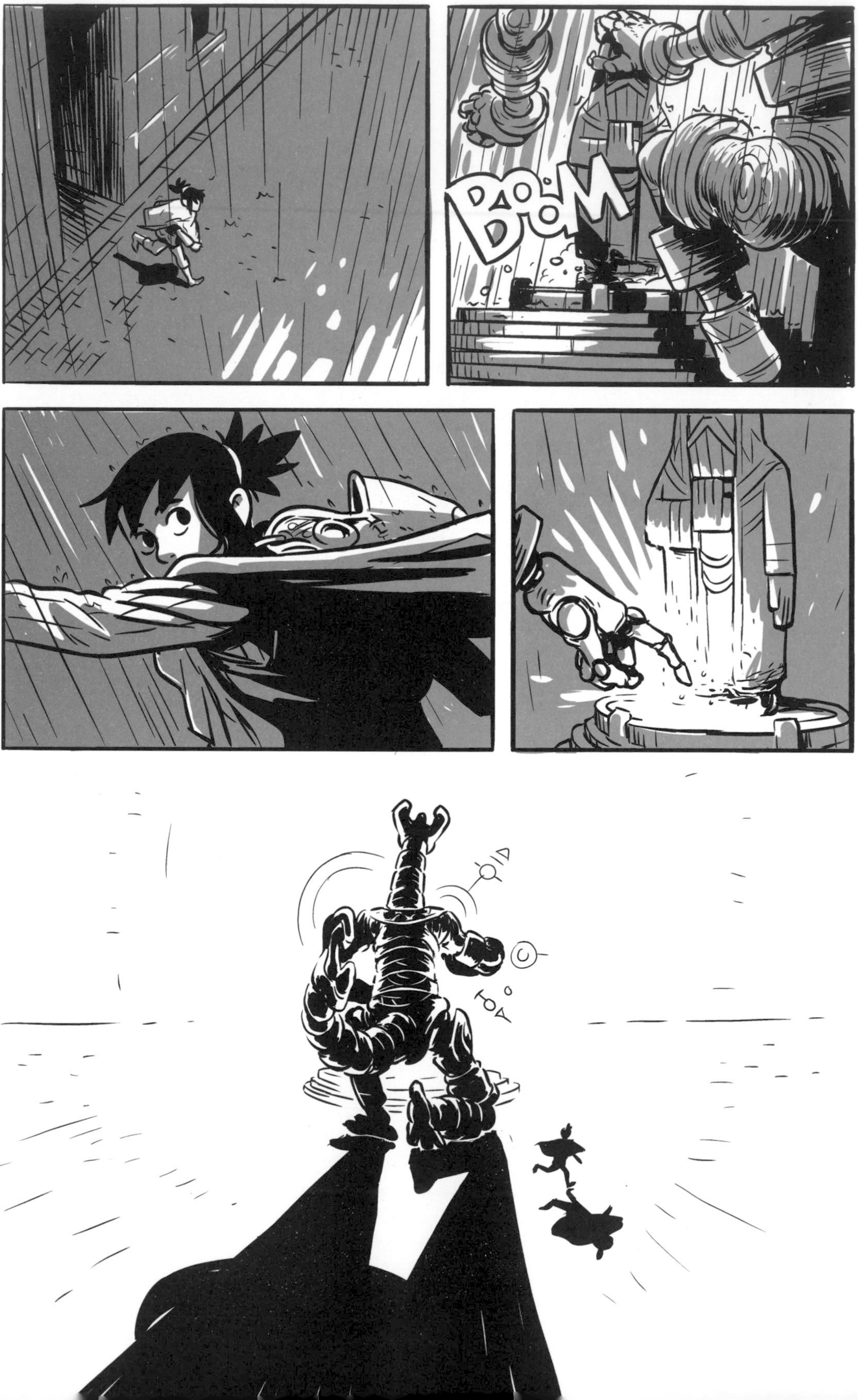

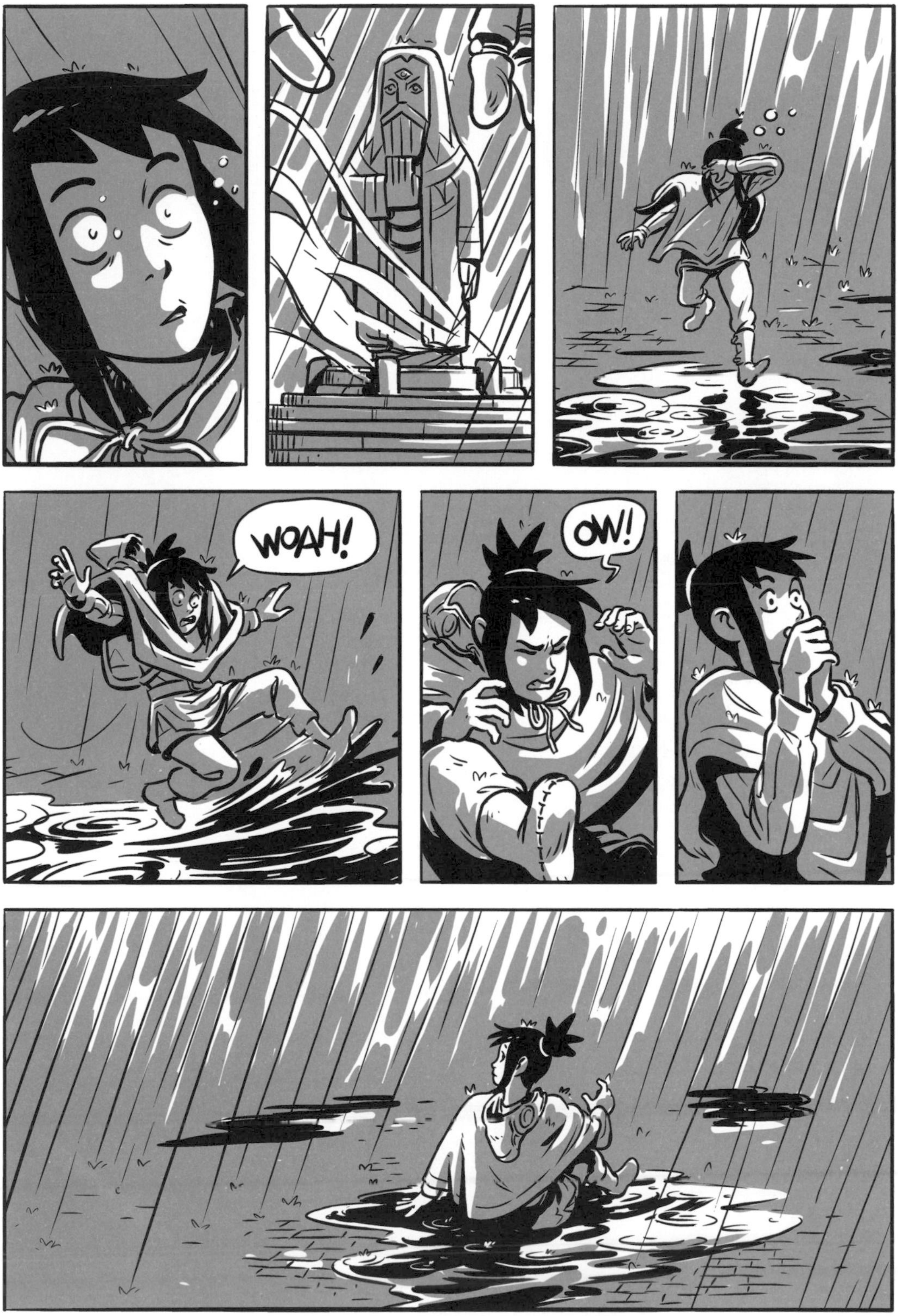
WOAH!
OW!

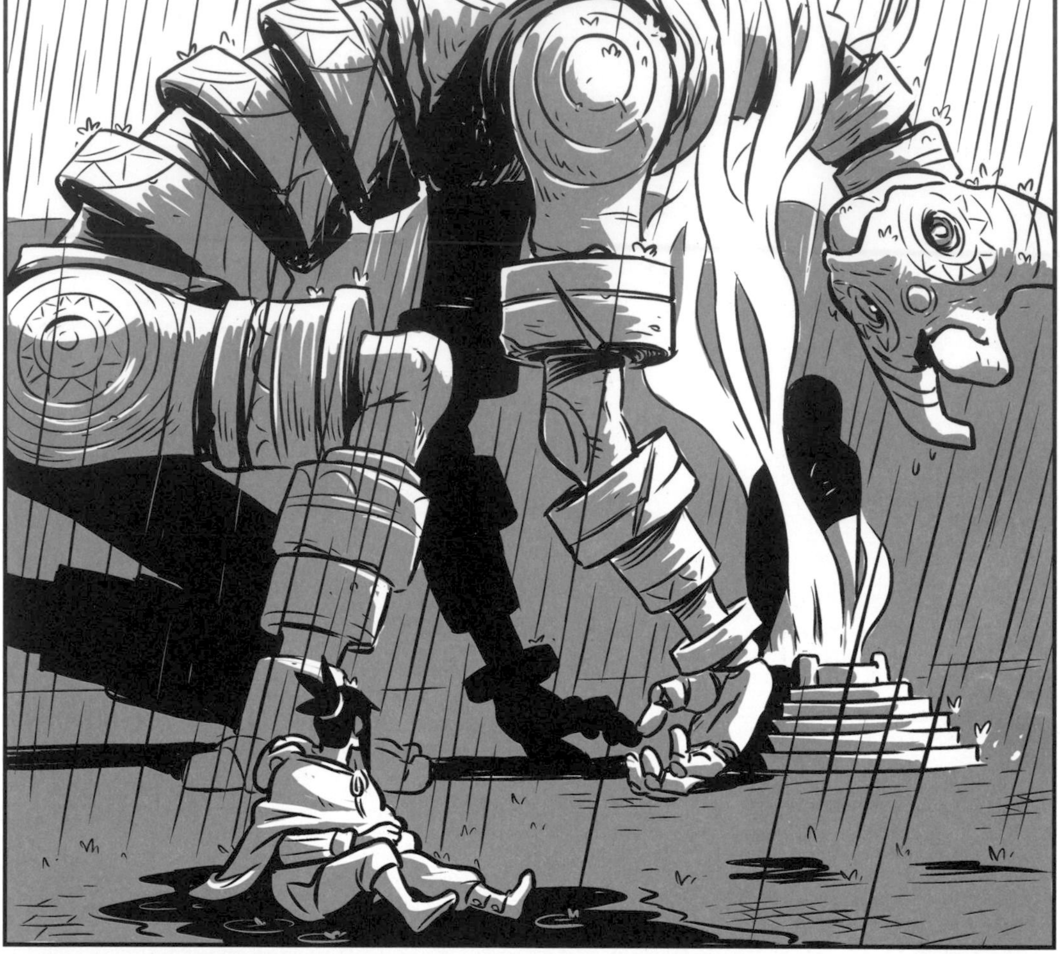

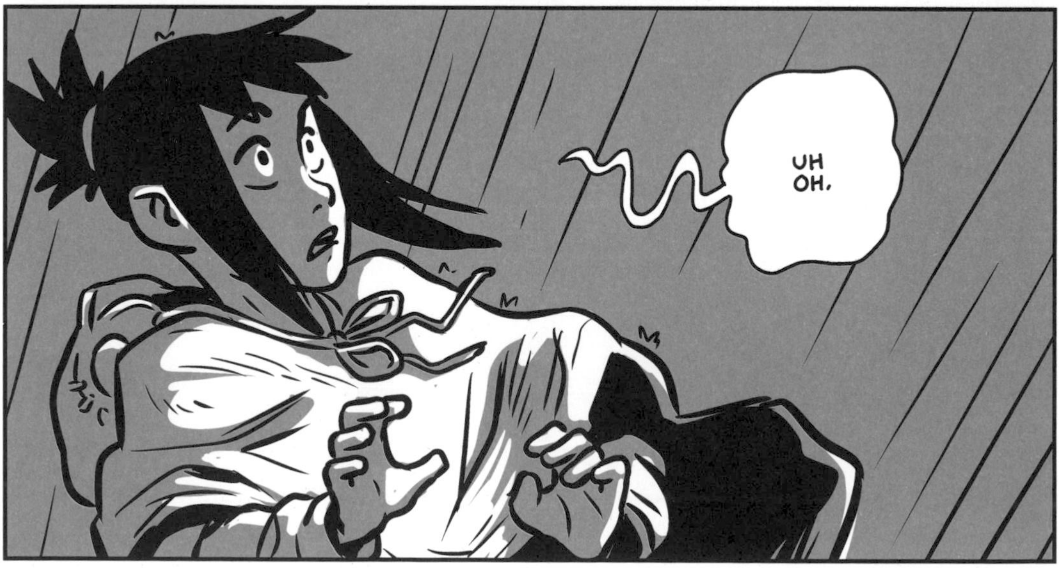
UH OH.

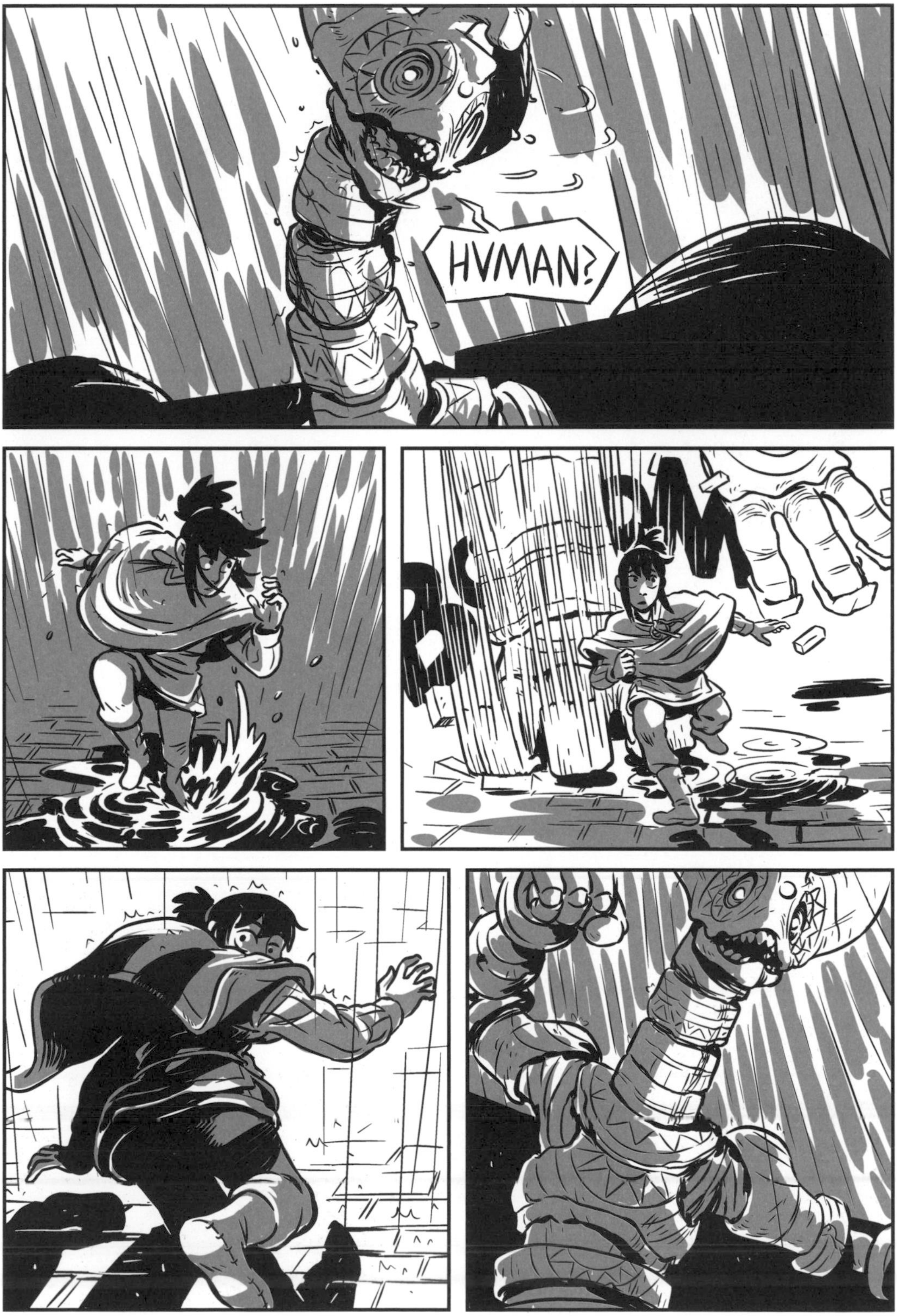
HVMAN?

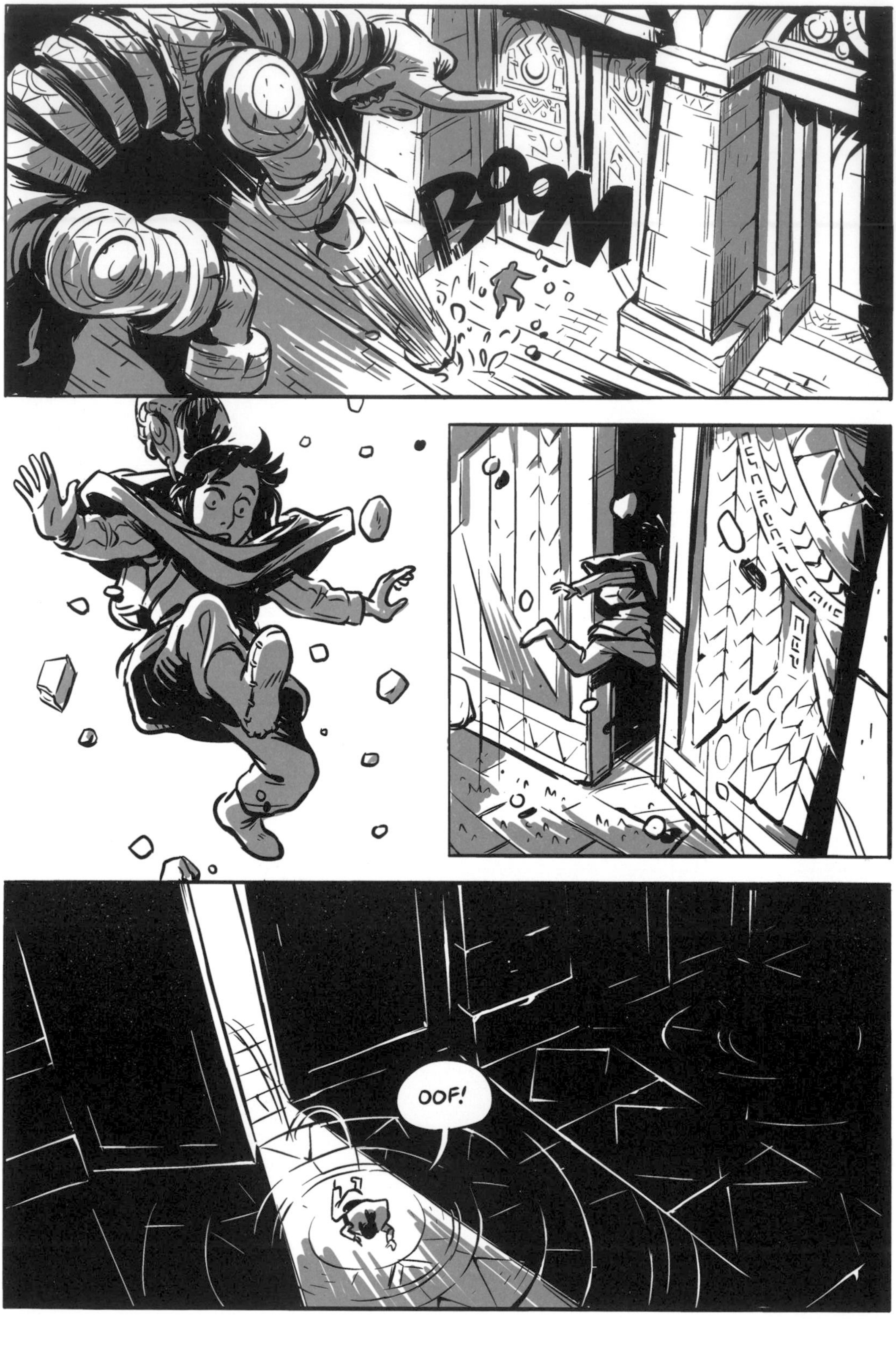
BOOM
OOF!

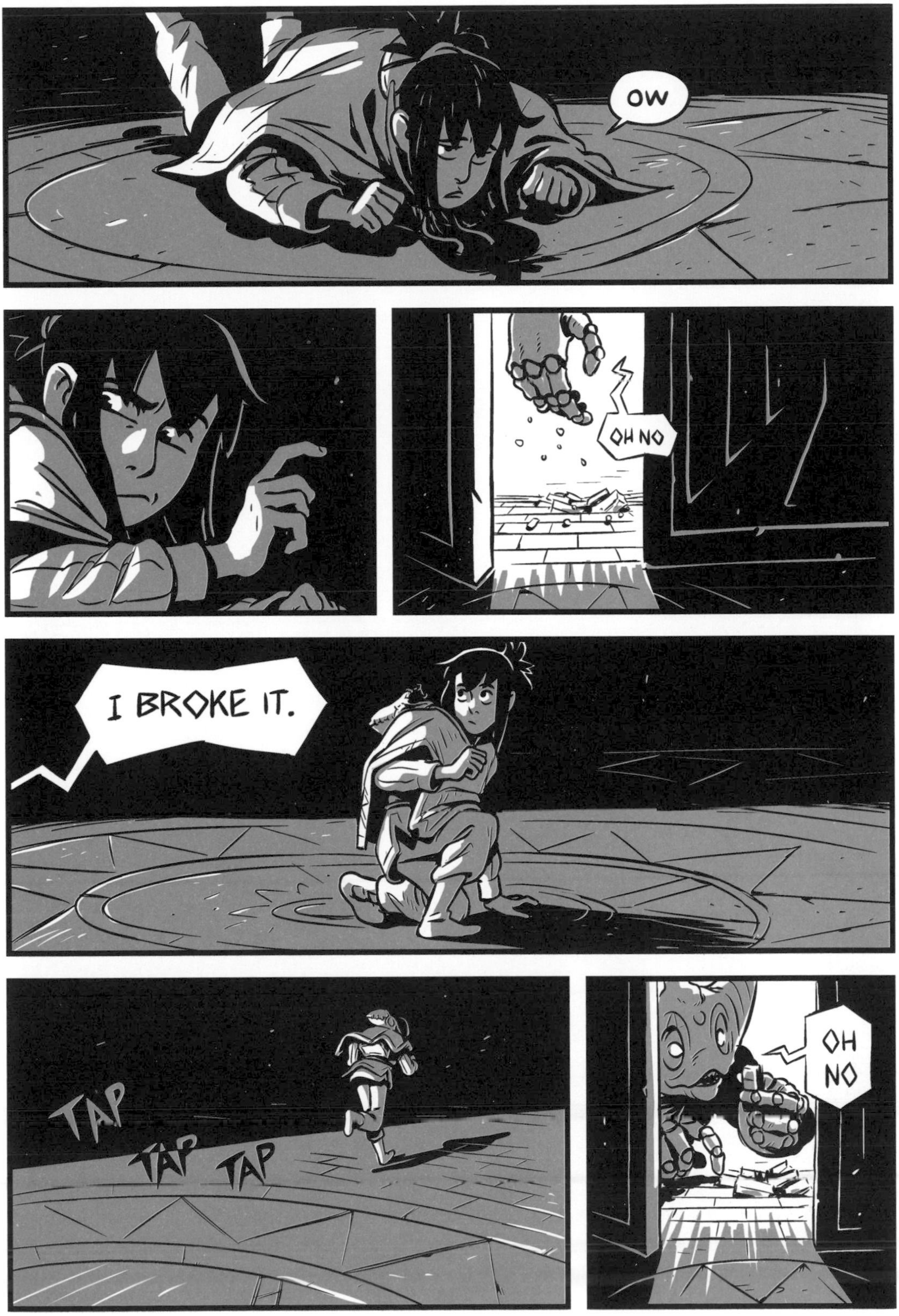
OW
OH NO
I BROKE IT.
TAP
TAP
TAP
OH NO

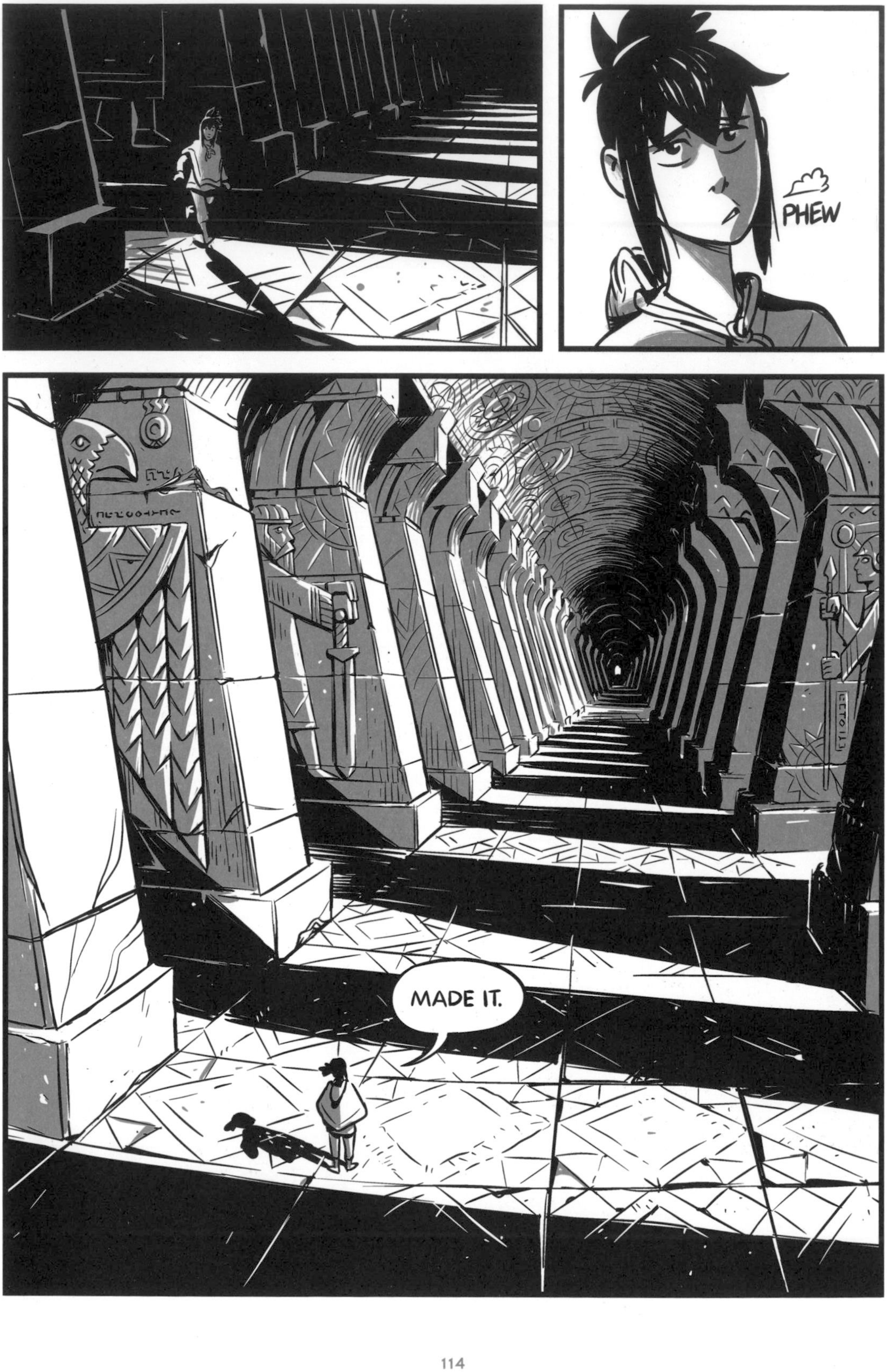
PHEW
MADE IT.

TO BE CONTINUED...

FOLLOW ONLINE:
STONEBREAKERCOMIC.COM

PETER WARTMAN HAS BEEN DRAWING MONSTERS, ROBOTS, AND ASSORTED SPACESHIPS SINCE HE FIGURED OUT HOW TO HOLD A PENCIL. HE LIVES IN MINNEAPOLIS, MINNESOTA WHERE HE WORKS AS A DESIGNER BY DAY AND A COMIC ARTIST THE REST OF THE TIME.

OVER THE WALL WAS HIS FIRST BOOK. HE'S CURRENTLY WORKING ON ITS SEQUEL, **STONEBREAKER**, WHICH CAN BE READ AT STONEBREAKERCOMIC.COM.

First Edition

ASSESSMENT IS ESSENTIAL

Susan K. Green
Winthrop University

Robert L. Johnson
University of South Carolina

 **Higher Education**

Boston   Burr Ridge, IL   Dubuque, IA   New York   San Francisco   St. Louis
Bangkok   Bogotá   Caracas   Kuala Lumpur   Lisbon   London   Madrid   Mexico City
Milan   Montreal   New Delhi   Santiago   Seoul   Singapore   Sydney   Taipei   Toronto

Higher Education

Published by McGraw-Hill, an imprint of The McGraw-Hill Companies, Inc., 1221 Avenue of the Americas, New York, NY 10020. Copyright © 2010. All rights reserved. No part of this publication may be reproduced or distributed in any form or by any means, or stored in a database or retrieval system, without the prior written consent of The McGraw-Hill Companies, Inc., including, but not limited to, in any network or other electronic storage or transmission, or broadcast for distance learning.

This book is printed on acid-free paper.
Printed in the United States of America.

3 4 5 6 7 8 9 0 QDB/QDB 9 8 7 6 5 4 3 2

ISBN: 978-0-07-337872-5
MHID: 0-07-337872-0

Editor in Chief: *Michael Ryan*
Editorial Director: *Beth Mejia*
Publisher: *David Patterson*
Sponsoring Editor: *Allison McNamara*
Marketing Manager: *James Headley*
Developmental Editor: *Alexis Breen Ferraro*
Editorial Coordinator: *Sarah Kiefer*
Production Editor: *Regina Ernst*
Manuscript Editor: *Barbara Hacha*
Design Manager: *Ashley Bedell*
Production Supervisor: *Tandra Jorgensen*
Composition: *10/12 Minion by Aptara®, Inc.*
Printing: *45# New Era Matte, Quad/Graphics, Dubuque*

Cover: © Russell Illig/Getty Images; © BananaStock/PunchStock; © IT Stock Free; © Lars Niki; © BananaStock/JupiterImages.

Photo Credits: p. 3; © Randy Faris/Corbis, p. 32; © PunchStock, p. 66; © Banana Stock/PunchStock, p. 94; © David Buffington/Getty Images, p. 120; © Dynamic Graphics/JupiterImages, p. 152; © PunchStock, p. 184; © image100 Ltd, p. 224; © Banana Stock/PictureQuest, p. 262; © The McGraw-Hill Companies, Inc., p. 290; © BananaStock/PunchStock, p. 322; © Tetra Images/Corbis, p. 358; © Corbis.

Library of Congress Cataloging-in-Publication Data
Green, Susan, 1949–
    Assessment is essential / Susan Green, Robert L. Johnson. — 1st ed.
        p. cm.
    Includes bibliographical references and index.
    ISBN-13: 978-0-07-337872-5 (alk. paper)
    ISBN-10: 0-07-337872-0 (alk. paper)
    1. Educational tests and measurements. I. Johnson, Robert L. (Robert Lewis), 1958– II. Title.
    LB3051.G673 2010
    371.26—dc22

                                                                            2009012378

The Internet addresses listed in the text were accurate at the time of publication. The inclusion of a Web site does not indicate an endorsement by the authors or McGraw-Hill, and McGraw-Hill does not guarantee the accuracy of the information presented at these sites.

For our students and our mentors, past, present, and future.

Learning is not attained by chance, it must be sought for with ardor and attended to with diligence.

–Abigail Adams

TABLE OF CONTENTS

PREFACE

Assessment Is Essential is designed for teacher candidates and practicing teachers. The text can be used for a course that addresses classroom assessment as a major component or in a standalone assessment course. The level of this course varies with different programs, but the text is accessible to candidates at all levels in their teacher education program. Because of its practical focus and numerous examples, it is also intended for continued use as a reference guide for practicing teachers.

The text describes key elements of quality assessment and provides many examples from classroom contexts to ensure accessibility for teachers and teacher candidates with varying amounts of experience. These discussions and examples aim to help them grasp that assessment is an integral part of instruction impacting student motivation and central to improving teaching and learning. This text fills an important gap by drawing the reader into a new mindset that places assessment at the forefront of teaching.

A key assumption guiding our work is that instructors of this course will be preparing teacher candidates to demonstrate their impact on P–12 learners, as well as to carry this capability into their classrooms as practicing teachers. This perspective dovetails with current National Council for Accreditation of Teacher Education (NCATE) guidelines for accreditation that require teacher candidates' documentation of this capability. Implementing these guidelines requires candidates to develop competencies in classroom assessment, as well as facility in interpreting these data to enhance learning. To address these assessment needs, an additional groundbreaking chapter is included, describing methods for determining student academic progress across time for individuals, classes, and disaggregated groups.

A second assumption guiding this text is that assessment should also be looked upon as a process for developing skills that contribute to the mission of educating students in a democracy. The National Network for Educational Renewal (NNER), a supporter of this series of texts, promotes several core principles as part of this mission. These include providing students with the skills to become fully engaged participants in a democratic society, providing equal access to quality learning for all students, and continual renewal of educational institutions. As part of the series, this text shows how these principles can be lived in the concrete reality of the classroom, and they provide teacher candidates with a thoughtful answer to the "Why are we doing this?" question about classroom assessment. By addressing the *why* of assessment, we believe teachers will be more inclined to make good assessment an integral part of their teaching.

To elaborate, our first theme is that schools must teach children skills to be active participants in a democracy. Schools are the only public institution expected to teach children to value and take part in our democratic society. Producing a well-informed citizenry requires cultivating students who take responsibility for their own learning in school and beyond. Taking on this responsibility involves development of self-governing skills such as setting goals and working toward them, taking the initiative to gather and analyze information, and critically applying appropriate standards to one's own work.

Many teacher candidates do not realize the power their assessment can have to transform students into active learners and critical thinkers. We discuss assessment methods that can be employed to help students to internalize criteria for optimal performance and to set their own goals. For example, students who regularly help design rubrics or other evaluation criteria for their work are more likely to become active, independent learners.

Similarly, other assessment practices we describe can also motivate students to internalize the desire to learn and take charge of their own learning, particularly when they can reflect on and keep track of the skills they have mastered in a systematic way by using graphs, journals, or portfolios. These kinds of activities can lead to student confidence and judgment that can be showcased and reinforced by such practices as setting aside time for student authors to share strategies they have found helpful so that other students can learn from them, among others.

A second major way to use assessment for promoting participation in a democracy is teaching students to think critically. A key element for promoting critical thinking is replacing assessments that merely measure rote knowledge with assessments that engage students in critical thinking. Each chapter addressing assessment design includes practical ways to get beyond measurement of facts. Methods for developing thoughtful questions and classroom discourse, application of concepts to new situations, and synthesis of information from many sources are stressed because they are essential aspects of equipping students with critical thinking skills for active engagement in democracy.

Third, the text emphasizes ways that assessment can be used to reduce barriers to providing equal access to knowledge for all students. All people, regardless of family background, have a right to equal access to education as the source of equal opportunity. Efforts to provide equal education to all students regardless of their demographic origins are currently inadequate, particularly for poor and minority children. Students who lag behind in reading in their early elementary years, for example, predictably get further and further behind as they progress through school.

Specific assessment techniques are described in the text to help teachers assist lower-achieving students. As a first step, methods for disaggregating and analyzing assessment results are presented to provide the means for exposing achievement gaps, because a key to teaching for equal access to knowledge is awareness of differential performance of subgroups of students. Formative assessment is described in terms of concrete teacher actions, such as strategically administered "quick writes," to let a teacher know who has and who has not mastered a concept, allowing for additional instruction if needed. Setting goals and tracking progress toward them across time with graphs is another featured technique that has been shown to help struggling learners catch up. For equal opportunity to materialize, these strategies to ameliorate the achievement gap must be incorporated into classroom assessment.

The marginalization or negative portrayal of underrepresented groups in assessment can engender other barriers to equal access to knowledge. For example, to establish a context for an assessment, multiple-choice items and performance tasks often use narrative and art to portray people in their physical appearance, dress, environment, and activities. These portrayals may bring a multicultural perspective to instruction and assessment, or they may promote biases. Helping teachers represent the diversity of the classroom and avoid stereotypical representations and other forms of bias in their assessments is an important component of fair assessment. This text emphasizes ways teachers can discover and address inequities and provide equal access to knowledge for all students.

Finally, teachers must be critical thinkers able to evaluate alternative points of view effectively while keeping in mind the goals of education in a democracy and ongoing educational renewal for themselves and their schools. They must also serve as models of critical thinking for their students. The importance of critical thinking and exercising good judgment when designing and choosing assessment is stressed, particularly in a section on using action research with assessment data as a tool for the reflective practitioner. Additionally, discussions of interpreting and using assessment, issues of ensuring fairness in assessment, and an ongoing focus on ethics and assessment all highlight the importance of critical thinking for teachers in their role as models of democratic values and agents of educational renewal.

Several other innovative features of this text are notable:

- Discussions of specific accommodations for students with several characteristics (e.g., short attention span, learning English, lower reading skills) are provided for each type of assessment design (e.g., multiple choice, essay, performance assessment). This placement allows for more explicit recommendations tailored to type of assessment and type of student need rather than a chapter with abstract suggestions spanning all assessment types. It also promotes the "equal access" theme.

- Each chapter describing assessment design includes a section detailing the five most common errors made by novices when first attempting to devise that type of assessment. This feature assists students in separating major issues from minor details and helps prevent information overload.

- As an additional aid to understanding, case studies describing three teachers' instructional units, one for elementary science, one for middle level math, and one for high school English, make concrete the ideas about assessment presented in each chapter. They are carried throughout the text, providing continuity across chapters and tangible applications of key themes. At the end of each relevant chapter, examples from one of these case studies are described to provide context and concrete illustrations of major assessment concepts.

- A practical section on ethics and assessment in the first chapter focuses on basic principles connected to classroom practices, with "ethics alerts" throughout the text to tie ethics to common occurrences in relevant contexts.

- A final chapter pulls together themes from the text and creates a vision of assessment excellence for teachers. The chapter proposes six key guidelines for assessment that foster equal access to knowledge, promotion of self-governing skills, and development of critical thinking. These are illustrated by descriptions of assessment practices at two schools with contrasting teaching philosophies. This chapter also provides practical suggestions for efficient use of assessment and for setting goals related to assessment practices so that teacher candidates have specific, concrete ideas to apply immediately in their classrooms.

We hope this book will inspire future teachers to discover all the ways their classroom assessment can help them achieve their goals in preparing knowledgeable, discerning, active students ready to take their place in a democratic society.

Acknowledgments

This book has been a collaborative effort, not only between the two of us, but also with numerous colleagues across university and public school settings. We gratefully acknowledge the willingness of the following people to have dialogues with us about classroom assessment and to share their hard-earned expertise based on countless years of working with students of all ages: Kelley Adams, A. J. Angulo, Angela Black, Barbara Blackburn, Keith Burnam, Bob Cattoche, Susan Chapman, Stevie Chepko, Tracie Clinton, Beth Costner, Sharon Craddock, Susan Creighton, Olive Crews, Denise Derrick, Minta Elsman, Caroline Everington, Rebecca Evers, Chris Ferguson, Tiffany Flowers, Rodney Grantham, Meghan Gray, Stephen Gundersheim, Connie Hale, Gloria Ham, Lisa Harris, Frank Harrison, Jo Ellen Hertel, Lisa Johnson, Marshall Jones, Shannon Knowles, Carol Marchel, Stephanie Milling-Robbins, Heidi Mills, Debi Mink, Mark Mitchell, Carmen Nazario, Marg Neary, Tonya Moon, Tim O'Keefe, Linda Pickett, Aaron Pomis, Nakia Pope, Frank Pullano, Jim Ross, Kevina Satterwhite, Jesse Schlicter, Elke Schneider, Seymour Simmons, Julian Smith III, Tracy Snow, Dana Stachowiak, Tenisha Tolbert, Carol Tomlinson, Jonatha Vare, Enola West, Jane White, Brad Witzel, and Karen Young.

We want to express our appreciation to the South Carolina Department of Education (SCDE) for sharing examples of assessment items. We also thank Scott Hockman at the SCDE and Ching Ching Yap at the University of South Carolina for the use of items from the South Carolina Arts Assessment Program.

Our students have also contributed important insights and examples that have helped us convey some of the important principles and concepts in classroom assessment. They have taught us much about teaching and learning. We want, in particular, to thank Angie Alexander, Laura Clark, Leslie Drews, Graham Hayes, Lynn McCarter, Laura McFadden, Krystle McHoney, Maria Mensick, Diana Mîndrilă, Grant Morgan, Meredith Reid, and Elizabeth Schaefer. The influence of countless other unnamed students is also present throughout this book.

As we developed *Assessment Is Essential*, we received valuable feedback from faculty who prepare teacher candidates to implement classroom strategies in their classrooms. The reviews were constructive and guided our fine-tuning of the chapters. We want to thank the following reviewers:

Robert Carpenter, *Eastern Michigan University*
Irene Linlin Chen, Ed.D., *University of Houston Downtown*
Ann Dargon, Ed.D., *Stonehill College, MA*
Margaret Golden, Ed.D., *Dominican University of California*
Jessica N. Gomel, Ph.D., *California State University, Fullerton*
Dennis M. Holt, Ph.D., *University of North Florida*
Jason Jiandani, *Northern Illinois University*
David W. McMullen, Ph.D., *Bradley University, IL*
Naomi Jefferson Petersen, Ed.D., *Central Washington University*
Glenn E. Snelbecker, Ph.D., *Temple University, PA*
Dr. Neal H. Schnoor, *University of Nebraska, Kearney*
Ahmed M. Sultan, Ph.D., *University of Wisconsin Stevens Point*
Michael S. Trevisan, *Washington State University, Pullman*
John Venn, Ph.D., *University of North Florida*
Rhea Walker, Ph.D., *Winona State University, MN*

We also want to thank the public school educators who diligently read drafts of most or all of our chapters with an eye toward helping us keep them sensible and useful for practicing teachers: Bob Cattoche, Jo Ellen Hertel, and Dana Stachowiak. Nick Mills also read several chapters, enhanced our logic and organization, and provided important suggestions from a college student perspective. Finally, we want to single out William Mills for special appreciation. He edited every draft of every chapter, helped us maintain our vision, provided moral support, and made countless suggestions that improved our efforts to communicate our conviction that assessment *is* essential.

ABOUT THE AUTHORS

Dr. Susan K. Green is currently a professor of educational psychology in the Richard W. Riley College of Education at Winthrop University. She teaches classroom assessment and educational psychology, and she collaborates with teachers in local public schools as part of professional development school initiatives. She brings to education a point of view shaped by expertise and experience in basic and applied psychology. She served as a school psychologist in Oregon and South Carolina for 10 years, focusing on academic interventions to enhance student achievement. She earlier taught introductory and social psychology for 10 years at George Washington University in Washington, DC. She holds Ph.D.'s in social psychology and in educational psychology and research. Her research interests include classroom assessment, strategies to enhance student achievement, applications of theories of learning and motivation in classrooms, and other aspects of applied psychology.

Dr. Robert L. Johnson is an associate professor of applied measurement at the University of South Carolina, where he teaches courses in classroom assessment and survey design. He earned his Ph.D. in Educational Research, Measurement, and Evaluation. Prior to joining the faculty at USC, Robert was an elementary teacher. During his 13 years in the public schools, he taught language arts and mathematics. Robert conducts research on ethics in classroom assessment practices and on the scoring of essays and portfolios. He is lead author of *Assessing Performance: Developing, Scoring, and Validating Performance Tasks*, and co-author of *Put to the Test: Tools and Techniques for Classroom Assessment* and *Assessment in the Literacy Classroom*.

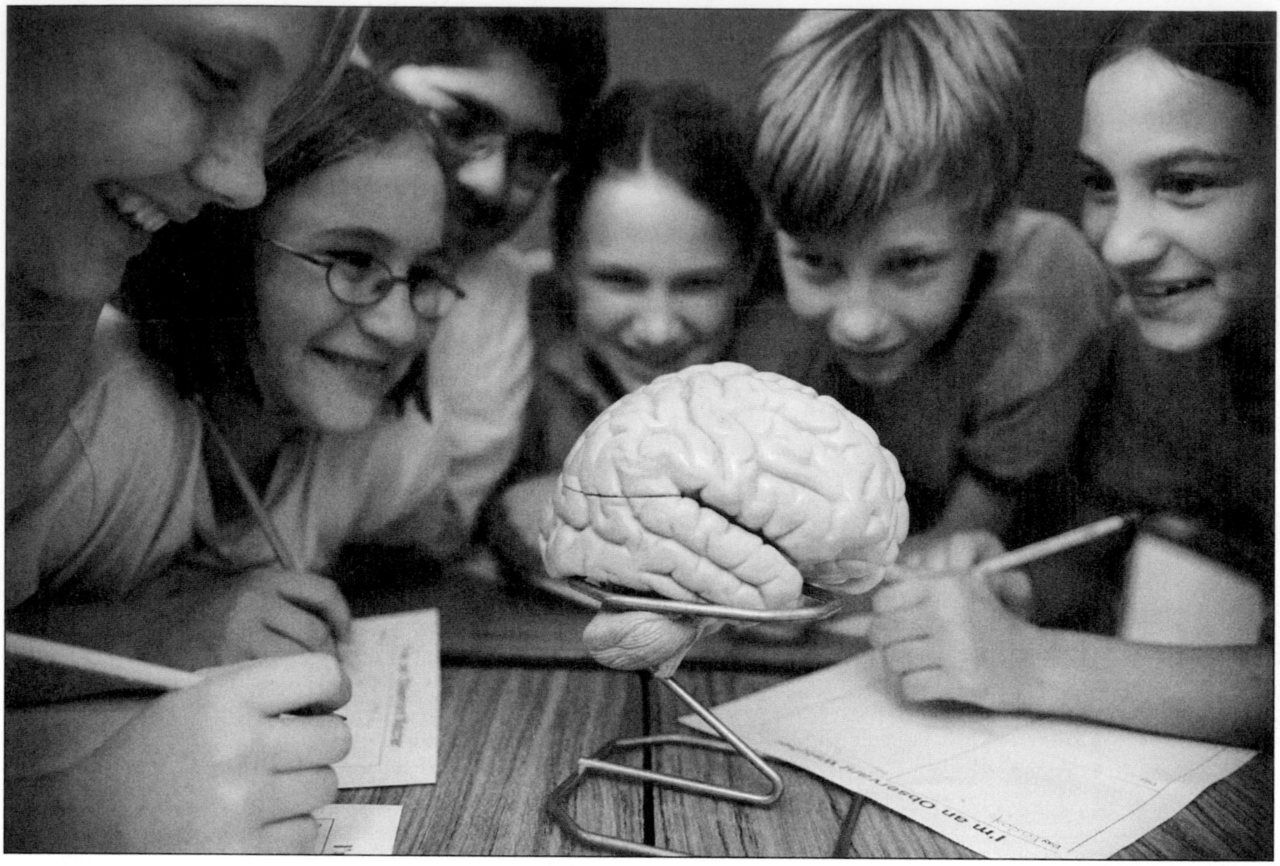
I'm an Observant

CHAPTER 1

WHY IS ASSESSMENT ESSENTIAL?

An informed citizenry is the bulwark of democracy.

–Thomas Jefferson

❖ **Chapter Learning Goals**

At the conclusion of this chapter, the reader should be able to do the following:

- Explain why assessment is essential to success as a teacher.

- Explain three ways assessment can be used to promote democratic values.

- Describe similarities and differences among the three purposes of assessment.

- Apply the use of an inquiry stance to a range of classroom assessment practices.

- Use two overarching ethical principles to judge a variety of assessment practices.

➔ A BROAD VIEW: ASSESSMENT AND DEMOCRATIC VALUES

What's the first thing that comes to your mind when you think about the word *assessment*? The last test you took in history class? That nasty pop quiz in psychology? Most of our students think about a recent test or quiz. And that is one of the main reasons we wanted to write this book. We think assessment has negative connotations and is therefore undervalued and pushed to the background in a lot of people's thinking about teaching. People equate assessment with tests, and not many people enjoy being tested.

Teachers know testing is important, but they often feel it takes away from valuable instructional time. But we have come to see assessment as an amazingly flexible and comprehensive tool that has measurably improved our own teaching. Even more important, we believe that learning to design good assessments also helps teachers prepare their students for participation as citizens in a democracy. That sounds like a lofty claim, but as we show you all the ways you will use assessment in your classroom, you will gradually come to see its wisdom.

The Key Question—Will This Help My Students Learn?

We want to make some of our assumptions clear about teaching and learning in a democracy. A democracy is a form of government in which the people exercise power directly or through elected representatives based on free and fair elections. Like Thomas Jefferson, we believe that to participate effectively and to make good choices, citizens must be well educated. In the United States, public education is intended to provide the skills and knowledge all students need so we can live up to

TABLE 1.1

Democratic Themes Related to Teachers' Assessment Practices

Theme	Assessment Practices Examples
Equal access to educational opportunity	• Use assessment to keep track of different rates of learning so you can provide differentiated instruction tailored to individual needs.
Development of self-governing skills for democratic participation, such as independent thought and a sense of responsibility	• Encourage self-assessment so students internalize aims of learning and take responsibility for their own learning. • Encourage students to track their own progress across time rather than comparing themselves to others.
Development of critical thinking skills that enable good decision making	• Design assessments that require critical thinking rather than rote memorization. • Encourage self-assessment that requires critical thinking.

our ideal that "all [people] are created equal." Public education is the single most important element to ensure a level playing field for children who don't come from families of privilege. As a teacher you will make hundreds of decisions every day, and you will find it easier if you weigh all you do against one important question: "Will this help my students learn?" If you are constantly thinking about the best ways to help your students learn more, you are moving them toward their highest potential for participating as citizens in our democracy. In the following sections we discuss three key themes that appear throughout the text that link preparation for democratic participation to teachers' assessment practices. These themes are shown in Table 1.1.

✦ Equal Access to Educational Opportunity

Achievement Gap

The disparity in performance between student groups (e.g., ethnicity, gender, and/or socio-economic status) on achievement measures such as large-scale tests or graduation rates.

Over the past few years you have probably heard about the focus of educators on closing the **achievement gap.** Students who are African American, Hispanic, and especially those who are poor have consistently performed lower than other demographic groups in terms of academic achievement and graduation rates, although the gaps narrowed in the 1970s and early 1980s (Lee, 2008). Furthermore, the United States has the highest average rate of children in poverty (25 percent) among Western democratic countries, with rates above 40 percent in African American and Hispanic communities (Banks et al., 2005). The current achievement gaps have begun to erode our belief that anyone who conscientiously tries hard, regardless of race, color, creed, or wealth, can succeed in our schools and in our country. Equal access to educational opportunity often doesn't seem to be happening the way it was intended.

The underlying factors contributing to the achievement gap are varied and complex and start long before a child enters school. In fact, researchers have found that the achievement gap already exists when students enter kindergarten (Lee, 2008). You won't be able to directly change what neighborhood your students come from, whether they are from a single-parent home, or whether schools in your city or county are adequately funded. As teachers, we must work with the children who come in our door, and we must do what is in our power to maximize learning for all our students and provide equal access to educational opportunity.

We contend that good assessment practices provide the opportunity for teachers, working in the realm where they have primary impact—their own classroom—to maximize learning for their students. Teacher actions are crucial for providing equal access to educational opportunity (Stiggins & Chappuis, 2005). That's because equal access does not mean that every student should receive exactly the same instruction. Instead, equal access means that some students may need extra accommodations or differentiated resources and instructional opportunities to be able to reach mastery on the learning goals for the class. For example, many middle-class children learn the mechanics of spoken and written language implicitly from their parents, whereas some poor children may not have these opportunities. Teachers must address these differences in the classroom so that all students acquire the foundational skills and common knowledge as well as the more complex understanding and skills necessary for democratic participation (Poplin & Rivera, 2005). So, we can't provide equal access without maximizing learning opportunities, and we can't maximize learning opportunities without assessment that lets us know where students are now in relation to where we want them to go.

Here's an example of assessment practices that moved some students toward more equal access. A student teacher we know was interested in encouraging her kindergarteners to read more books. On different days, the student teacher decided to try different strategies and then see if those strategies caused more students to visit the reading center. To see if she was making any difference, she started keeping records of attendance at the reading center. After a week, she was looking at the data and discovered three of the four children who had not been to the reading center at all that week were also the students with literacy skills lagging behind those of the other children. This discovery allowed her to see an achievement gap in the classroom and to focus on those students who weren't exposed often enough to books at school. She and the teacher worked hard to draw those students to the reading center with books and activities tied to their interests. By the end of the semester, those students were visiting the reading center as much as or more than other children, and their reading skills were accelerating. If the student teacher hadn't done a simple assessment—keeping track of voluntary center attendance—she might not have noticed one of several strategies needed to help close the learning gap for these children.

We strongly believe teachers' assessment practices play a large role in their efforts to do their part to help all students have access to the education that is a basic right in this country. Knowing where students are in the curriculum and what they need next is a key focus for assessment. Such knowledge is critical for differentiating your instruction to meet the range of needs your students bring to your classroom. We will return to this theme in future chapters as we explore further how teacher assessment practices in the classroom contribute to the fundamental right of equal access to education.

✦ SELF-GOVERNING SKILLS FOR PARTICIPATION IN A DEMOCRACY

The founders of our form of government had to assume that all citizens could be and would be educated enough to make good decisions and to be capable of governing their own lives. All citizens need to develop responsibility for independence in their thinking, and they must take responsibility to do their part to participate in society. They must, then, be interested in learning and critically analyzing new information for the rest of their lives. Our government wouldn't function well if people couldn't think for themselves and didn't expect to have some control over decisions that affect them. Self-governing skills don't necessarily come naturally. Instead, we as teachers must help students develop these capabilities. We believe your assessment practices can help your students become more active participants in their own learning and, by extension, more active in making other decisions for themselves that will prepare them to participate as full citizens in a democracy. To explain how, we must first look at some of our changing assumptions about the purpose of schools and learning.

Traditional Functions of Schools: Sorting and Performance

One of our friends remembers only one thing from his first day of college. He was a little nervous sitting in an auditorium with hundreds of other freshmen. In the middle of a speech, he remembers the college president commanding students to "Look at the person on your right. Now look at the person on your left. One of the three of you will be gone by the end of the year." This administrator's comment illustrates the sorting function that schools at all levels have often implicitly or explicitly served (Stiggins, 2007). In the past, education was often used to separate the "brighter" learners from the "duller" learners. The assumption was that intelligence is an innate capacity that can't be changed, so we should make sure students are placed into different courses of study to match their intellectual capabilities.

In a not-so-distant time in this country, this kind of sorting was considered by many to be a primary function of education (Gordon, 2008). Assigning grades, deciding who gets into gifted programs, and college entrance decisions are all sorting functions that still occur in schools. Many school systems give all students "intelligence" tests and track students into more or less demanding courses, especially at the high school level. Under this sorting approach, a key purpose of assessment is judgment. Tests are used to separate achievers from non-achievers. Educators decide who makes the grade and who doesn't. Thomas Jefferson, whose quotation introduced this chapter, might have disagreed with this elitist notion.

Performance Goals
Academic goals held by students that focus on performing well in front of others and that assume ability is fixed.

This judgment approach to assessment can produce what psychologists call **performance goals** in students (Urdan & Schoenfelder, 2006). Students with strong performance goals are motivated to perform well in the eyes of others. In a school setting that promotes performance goals above all else, students focus on their level of ability. To prove how smart they are, students at the top brag about how little studying they did to ace the test. They enjoy competing with others and comparing grades. They eagerly await the class rankings that appear once a semester on their report card to see if they've moved up a notch. Their learning focus ties their self-esteem to their high ability and to public recognition.

Unfortunately, students with performance goals who are *not* at the top suffer. Students toward the bottom of the grade distribution give up early and label themselves as poor students and losers. Often they begin to disrupt class and have behavior problems because, as one student once said to us, "It's better to be bad than dumb." Because of the bad grades, negative labels, and poor self-concept, many of these students never reach their full potential. Chances are, you know or remember students who were disengaged or disruptive, perhaps victims of the educational sorting mechanism. You could tell they didn't enjoy learning in school and probably would not end up as the inquisitive lifelong learners a democracy requires. Table 1.2 presents characteristics of students with a performance-goal orientation.

TABLE 1.2

Student Characteristics Associated with Performance Goals and Mastery Goals

Performance Goals	Mastery Goals
Compare themselves to others to determine progress	Focus on their own progress
Confirmation of learning comes from judgments of others	Confirmation of learning comes from within
Not willing to attempt challenging tasks and give up more easily	Willing to attempt challenging tasks and persist longer
Assume ability is more important than effort	Assume effort is more important than ability
Believe that intelligence is a fixed trait	Believe that intelligence can be increased
Use shallow cognitive processing strategies	Use deeper level cognitive processing strategies

Transforming Functions of Schools: Helping All Children Learn with Mastery Goals

More recently, educators have come to see the harmful effects of solely using the judgment approach to assessment that sorts students in terms of achievement and success. You have probably seen mission statements of schools that include the idea that "all children can learn" as one manifestation of a different mindset that adds another dimension to the role of assessment. People are beginning to realize how important it is for *all* students to reach their potential, rather than letting some fall through the cracks. Boosting high school graduation rates, for example, could save this country $45 billion every year (Belfield & Levin, 2007). This newer approach sees teachers as advocates of students. They use their assessment practices to enhance every student's learning and to experience academic success. They work with all students, regardless of their initial academic level, to kindle a love of learning and a belief that they can succeed and keep learning more. They structure their classroom and assessment tasks to nurture **mastery goals** in students. When students have mastery goals, they focus less on showing how smart they are (or avoiding showing how "dumb" they are), and more on their desire to understand and master the task before them. They focus on their own learning and improvement over time and less on the judgments of others, developing a sense of independence. In Figures 1.1 and 1.2, a teacher candidate in art education has drawn "Ms. Sorter" and "Ms. Gapcloser" to illustrate her conception of the difference between the traditional approach and the more recent approach to assessment.

Mastery Goals
Academic goals held by students that focus on a desire to understand and accomplish the task and that assume ability can increase.

Research has shown that students who have strong mastery goals react very differently from students who have only performance goals in the classroom (Urdan & Schoenfelder, 2006). They tend to learn for the pleasure of learning. They keep trying even when the work gets harder. They expend a lot more effort to get the job done because they know their effort makes a difference in their learning. They assume that intelligence is not a fixed trait, and they know they can get smarter. They have more positive feelings about school and school work. Perhaps most important for our discussion, they become more autonomous and look inward rather than outward for

My recipe for effective teaching is to use your instruction and assessments to accurately sort students by their abilities.
Today's Date
March 20, 1951
Miss Sorter

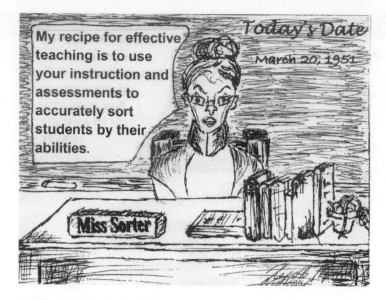

FIGURE 1.1 ***Teacher Focused on Earlier Model of Assessment as Judgment***

Reprinted with permission of Krystle McHoney.

My recipe for effective teaching is to help all children learn by focusing on individual improvement across time using meaningful tasks.
Today's Date
May 1, 2011
Ms. Gapcloser

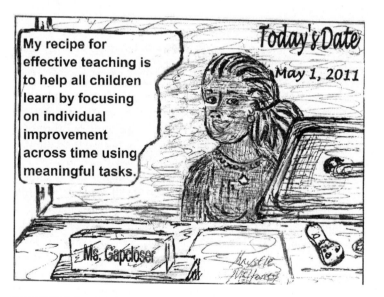

FIGURE 1.2 ***Teacher Focused on Newer Model of Assessment as Helping All Students Learn***

Reprinted with permission of Krystle McHoney.

confirmation of their learning. You can compare the characteristics of students with a mastery-goal orientation to those with a performance-goal orientation in Table 1.2.

Naturally, every teacher would want a class full of students with mastery goals. They sound like dream students! But in our competitive society, promoting mastery goals takes extra effort. The good news is that teachers can play a large role in helping their students to become more mastery oriented (Ames, 1992; Butler, 2006; O'Keefe et al., 2008). Becoming more mastery oriented does not mean students give up performance goals entirely—both kinds of goals can be positively related to achievement, depending on the context (Witkow & Fuligni, 2007). In fact, sometimes students manifest both kinds of goals. For example, a student can care about being at the top of the class but also love history and go beyond course requirements in pursuing that interest.

Many students, however, need some encouragement to develop mastery goals. This is especially true for students who aren't at the top of the class. Encouraging mastery goals may increase their motivation and help them see school in a new light. Carole Ames (1992) has summarized the research on what teachers can do to structure their classrooms to promote mastery goals among their students. Her ideas as they relate to assessment are shown in Figure 1.3.

Assessment Tasks That Enhance Mastery Goals

As you can see in Figure 1.3, teachers can help foster mastery goals in several ways by designing assessment strategies with specific characteristics.

Varied, Meaningful, and Challenging Tasks

First, if students find assessment activities interesting and relevant, they are more likely to develop mastery goals. They see a reason—besides getting a good grade—to do those

Ames's Classroom Element	Assessment Strategies	Outcome
1. *Varied, Meaningful, Challenging Tasks* →	Many different types of assessment (e.g., papers, projects, brief oral and written check-ups) Challenging, novel, relevant assessments (e.g., using data students collect on their friends for math, writing persuasive letters to politicians for social studies) →	
2. *Students Participate in Decision Making* →	Provide choices for ways for students to show what they have learned Use student participation in designing scoring guides for assessments Have students engage in self-assessment and peer assessment →	**Students with Mastery Goals and High Motivation for Academic Tasks**
3. *Students Focus on Personal Goals, Own Improvement* →	Keep assessment results private rather than public Focus on individual improvement across time using benchmarks Allow students to develop goals and keep track of their progress using a graph or chart Develop assignments where mistakes are an expected part of learning and improvement is expected across time (e.g., turn in first drafts for feedback) Recognize student effort. →	

FIGURE 1.3 *Assessment Strategies That Foster Mastery Goals*

Adapted from Ames, C. (1992). Classrooms: Goals, structures, and student motivation. *Journal of Educational Psychology* 84(3): 261–271. Reprinted with permission.

assignments. They value the activity because it is useful or relevant to their lives. They are more willing to give it their full attention and effort because they find it worthwhile. For example, demonstrating calculation skills through designing a monthly budget based on the salary made by people in an interesting career can be more compelling than completing abstract calculation problems. Similarly, a Spanish teacher who involves students in projects such as writing and performing scenes from a popular Spanish novel rather than simply drilling on the questions at the end of the chapter is also using a meaningful and challenging assessment task.

Student Participation in Decision Making

Next, teachers can use assessment strategies that help students participate in decision making so they develop responsibility for their learning and self-governing skills. If you think back to papers you had to write in English class, perhaps you remember being more engaged with the paper where you got to choose the person whose biography you read and used for a report. When students have meaningful choices, and these choices are tied to their preferences and interests, they are more likely to be engaged in the assessment and have something meaningful to say.

Another important way for students to participate in decision making in the assessment of their learning is through helping to design scoring guides. During the development of a scoring guide, when students take part in describing what a good paper looks like, they learn the standard they are aiming for (e.g., factual accuracy when writing about a biography) and feel like they have more say over the outcome of their own efforts (Andrade, 2008). The next step is to connect the assessment to the learning process. This occurs by encouraging students to assess themselves, to monitor what they are learning, and to use feedback to modify their understanding (Earl, 2003). They begin to internalize the standard and not just see it as something arbitrarily imposed by the teacher.

Focus on Personal Goals and Improvement

Finally, the way a teacher uses assessments has a big impact on fostering mastery goals. If teachers help students focus on personal goals and track their own progress instead of comparing themselves to other students, then teachers cultivate mastery goals in their classrooms. A choir director can have students record themselves alone in a practice room singing several songs at the beginning, middle, and end of the semester. He can then use the same scoring guide to analyze each performance and examine progress over time with students individually. Such a practice is much easier on the ego than more competitive ones such as performing in front of the whole class for a grade. In addition, it allows for *all* students to see their progress and doesn't simply focus on the best singers. When people see they are making progress, they are more likely to keep trying hard and to learn more, distinguishing traits of students with mastery goals.

The other part of this guideline involves helping students focus on the importance and value of their effort. Students must be able to develop **effort optimism** in each class. Effort optimism is the idea that effort has a payoff—if you work hard you will learn more. Usually students start out in kindergarten with the belief that effort pays off. Over time this belief can erode. Students' experiences with failure, discrimination, or other negative circumstances can eliminate effort optimism. They no longer have the conviction that their effort will be rewarded, which usually reduces self-reliance and effective coping strategies, ultimately lowering academic achievement (Scott & Brown, 2003).

In the classroom, teachers must make the connection explicit and strong between student effort and academic success. One thing that weighs heavily in effort optimism

Effort Optimism
The idea that effort brings rewards. For example, if you work hard in school you will learn more.

is how the teacher treats mistakes. If children are embarrassed or made fun of for their mistakes, they will be afraid to try new things and will participate only if they are sure they know the answer. As a teacher, you need to help students see that learning takes hard work and practice, and that mistakes are a valuable part of learning. For example, think back on important times you have learned new things. Didn't a lot of your breakthroughs come from making mistakes first?

In one of our recent classes, the need for teachers to convey the value of mistakes in learning came up. One student raised her hand and told the class about the fourth-grade teacher she would never forget. This teacher had a slogan, "We don't make mistakes, we make discoveries!" She used this slogan several times a day to promote effort optimism in her students. It certainly had worked for this student. She would always answer a question in class when no one else would give it a try because she knew she would make a discovery (and not a mistake) about whatever concept the class was trying to master.

All three of these recommendations—varied, meaningful, and challenging tasks, encouraging student participation in decision making, and evaluation that focuses on individual progress and values effort and improvement—are strongly linked to the classroom assessment strategies that we describe in this book. All the research that we have seen suggests these assessment strategies can have direct impact on the motivation of students, and they may especially benefit students who are the most likely to be at risk for school failure (Shepard, 2008). If you want students to love learning, to persist in the face of obstacles, and to care about their own progress rather than how they do compared to others, you will want to use assessment practices that have the characteristics we have just described. You will also be fostering self-governing skills such as independent thinking and a personal sense of responsibility crucial for citizens engaged in democratic participation.

Promoting Mastery Goals Through Assessment: Examples

As we have discussed earlier, students need to acquire self-governing skills and a sense of responsibility to participate appropriately in a democracy. When we look at ways to foster self-governing skills in the area of classroom assessment, one of the most often recommended strategies is encouragement of student self-assessment.

Self-assessment

The ability to assess oneself is one of the primary goals of education. We as teachers must teach our students to function autonomously. Ultimately, they must deal on their own with making decisions about life in all of its complexity. Only relatively recently, however, has the strategy of explicit self-assessment been introduced, probably as a result of the weakening rationale for the traditional sorting function of schools. You can easily see why self-assessment is important. It teaches objectivity—being able to get beyond your own point of view and look at yourself in relation to a standard. It also teaches empowerment—if you eventually understand the standard yourself, you are not as dependent on an authority to make judgments about your own work. You can do it yourself. The process of self-assessment also helps you to become open to feedback from a variety of sources. Gradually, you will be able to decide which sources of information are valuable and which are not.

Student self-assessment is a key to enhance learning because it requires students to become *active* in connecting their work to the criteria used for evaluating it (Earl, 2003; Pelligrino et al., 2001). The requirement that students self-assess activates what psychologists term **metacognition.** Metacognition is the ability to step back from merely listening to a lecture or doing an assigned task, to *thinking* about what is happening in a more

Metacognition
The process of analyzing and thinking about one's own thinking and enabling skills such as monitoring progress, staying on task, and self-correcting errors.

critical way. It involves directing your awareness to a bird's-eye view of what you are doing. This heightened level of self-awareness allows students to monitor whether they are understanding a lecture point and then to take action by asking a question if they aren't. Or, it pushes them to notice when they calculate an answer that doesn't make sense, and to self-correct it. Metacognitive skills such as monitoring progress, staying on task, and self-correcting errors can and should be taught by teachers (Pelligrino et al., 2001).

We can see the development of these self-assessment skills occurring in the classroom of Tracie Clinton, a third-grade teacher. To encourage self-assessment, she holds writing conferences with individual students every nine weeks. First, students respond to a writing prompt (e.g., "If I could visit anywhere in the United States I would visit . . ."). They use a writer's checklist to monitor themselves as they are writing. During the individual conferences, Tracie encourages students to critique their own writing. She has them focus on only one or two areas each time (e.g., staying on topic, using vivid vocabulary). She finds that students want to improve, and they can identify problem areas on their own with a little guidance. Next, they discuss how to get the paper back on track, and Tracie writes down pointers on "sticky" notes for the student to refer to later. She has found that students are able to transfer what they discuss during writing conferences to other work. As she says, "I have found that my students get extremely excited when they catch a mistake in their writing on their own. Writing conferences are a long process, but it is worth every moment when I see my students blossoming into exceptional writers."

As shown in this example, when students self-assess, the teacher doesn't give up responsibility for assessment but rather shares it with the students. Students learn and eventually internalize the standards and goals they are working toward. Researchers have found that students who participate in self-assessment improve the quality of their work, have a better understanding of their strengths and weaknesses, and have higher motivation (Andrade, 2008).

Focus on Individual Progress Across Time

Another example directly related to assessment and promotion of mastery goals occurred when we were working with an elementary teacher who wanted to help six of her students become more fluent readers. We sat down with all six individually and encouraged each student to set a goal for the next 10 weeks—a specific number of words the student would read correctly in one minute. We also had each student make a list of the things he or she would do each day to help achieve that goal. For the next 10 weeks, we met with each student once a week and they would do a timed reading. We would also talk about how the student's strategies for each day were going. We then plotted the student's score on a graph to show progress over time.

After the first week, an identical graph was sent home to put on the student's refrigerator. We would call the students' homes each week with the new score to add to the refrigerator graph as well as the one kept at school. By the end of the 10 weeks, all six of these students had increased their reading fluency by a significant amount more than their teacher had seen in the previous 10 weeks. Based on the students' comments, we found that using the graphs helped students focus on their own progress rather than on how they were doing compared to the rest of their class. The whole process was private rather than public and provided weekly opportunities to show improvement. The home graph also helped the family to see the improvement each week and then provide encouragement and support to their child. The teacher reported that as the children made gains, they became more interested in reading and they started taking more books home from her classroom library. These behaviors definitely exemplify developing a mastery goal orientation.

Throughout the book, we discuss other assessment practices that illustrate recommendations for promoting mastery goals. We believe teachers should foster mastery goals

BOX 1.1

Letter from a Student Observer. Are These Teachers Encouraging Mastery or Performance Goals?

Recently, I have had an opportunity to observe how two different teachers have used assessment in their classroom. For the past month, I have been volunteering at a high school. Two mornings a week I help in Ms. Q's freshman English class, and one morning a week I help in Ms. R's senior English class. Aside from the age difference, the classrooms seem to be fairly similar; both have twenty to twenty-five students, both have a comparable ethnic make-up, and both are "regular" English classes. I really enjoy helping the students, but right now I may be getting more from my volunteer hours, because I have the chance to observe two different teachers and the instructional decisions they make, particularly in regard to how they assess their students.

Ms. Q's freshman class has been working on a research/writing unit in which the students pick products, research two different brands of that product, write short comparison/contrast papers, create PowerPoint presentations of their papers, and then, finally, make oral presentations. First of all, I am impressed with Ms. Q's ability to pack so much into a single, comprehensive unit. Secondly, I like the way that her different activities gave all her students various opportunities for success. I know that several students had trouble with some of the writing aspects of their papers and that their paper grades probably reflected some of those issues, but many of those same students put together very eye-catching PowerPoints. Ms. Q assessed the same information several times, which should give her a much more reliable picture of each student (it also gave students the opportunity to revise at each stage). Further, since the final activity in the unit was a performance, Ms. Q used an analytic rubric to assess the students' oral presentations. Her rubric had about six criteria (content, number of slides, grammar, speaking, etc.) and was less than a page in length. Even though it was an oral presentation, Ms. Q focused more on the content than the actual speaking since most of the students were unfamiliar with making presentations. I am sure that she gave them an assignment with some kind of criteria, but I am not sure that she gave them the actual rubric that she used for grading, which would be my only criticism.

In contrast, Ms. R gave a summative test in her senior English class, today, that seemed to be the antithesis of everything we have learned about assessment. To begin with, the test was poorly designed. It was a matching test on characters from the *Canterbury Tales* that not only had several typos, but also had over thirty premises and more than fifty responses, far more than could be handled at one time by most students. The students were allowed to use their notes. To have more space, seven students went with me to a spare room where I proctored their test. Ms. R had collected their notes for a grade, and right before the test, she returned the notes to the students. Unfortunately, there did not seem to be any feedback on the notes, and even if there had been comments, the students would not have had an opportunity for addition or revision. I do not know Ms. R's learning goals, but if they were knowledge based, then I suppose a matching test was appropriate; however, since the students were allowed to use their notes, the test did not really seem to be an assessment of their knowledge, but rather their ability to take notes. The seven students whose test I proctored did not do well on the test (one of them may have passed), and it was obvious while they were taking the test that they were frustrated. I saw that their notes were skimpy, and the points they had pulled out about the characters were frequently irrelevant. Since Ms. P had seen the notes, she had to know that their notes were insufficient, so it seems that these students had no real chance of doing well.

I understand that teachers make mistakes, and so I hope I just happened to catch Ms. R on a bad day. Still though, it reinforces the importance of appropriate assessment. The seven students from Ms. R's class were frustrated. They knew within five minutes that they had no hope of doing well on that test, and in another five minutes they were ready to give up, saying the test was too hard and was stupid. All I could tell them was that the test looked tough, but that they needed to keep working and fill in every blank. I *wanted* to tell them that, regardless of their notes, the test was just bad. In contrast, the students in Ms. Q's class who were not doing as well did not complain or exhibit the same level of frustration. They realized, if only at a subconscious level, that they had had several chances to exhibit their abilities. We have read and discussed the fact that assessment needs to be thoughtful and planned along with instruction, and recently I have seen examples that prove those important points.

as one foundational element for helping students acquire the skills needed to function well as citizens in a democracy. You can begin to see the difference in student reactions when mastery goals are encouraged by comparing the two classrooms described in Box 1.1 by one of our own students who volunteered in these classrooms. We believe good assessment practices are essential for promoting mastery goals, and so the connection between assessment and mastery goals is another recurring theme in this text.

✦ THE IMPORTANCE OF CRITICAL THINKING

In addition to promoting equal access and self-governing skills for democratic participation, the third theme related to educating children for their roles as citizens in a democracy is the need to acquire the ability to think critically. The most obvious use of critical thinking in our society is in the voting booth. Those who can't effectively sift through the campaign ads and news stories about candidates will make poor choices, which undermine the democratic process and the foundation of our society. Analyzing arguments, seeing both sides of an issue before choosing a position, and discerning what is left unsaid are key critical-thinking skills related to democratic participation that must be taught. In our view, providing opportunities to learn these skills is one of the essential functions of schools.

By now you won't be surprised to learn that we think good classroom assessment is one of the crucial methods for developing critical-thinking skills. If you want your students to learn these skills, you must design your assessment to require them. In many tenth-grade government classes, one area of content is understanding the function of the federal government's three branches. Maybe you decide to liven up class with skits showing how the three branches function together. Maybe you have interesting discussions about bills in the legislature right now and how they are faring. But students ultimately remember and study what they think will be on the test. When it comes to test time, if you signal interest only in the specific facts about the three branches, we guarantee you that the students will learn specific facts and little else. Typical students (unless you have already succeeded in instilling unusually strong mastery goals) invest their energy where it counts—getting a good grade on the test.

Designing assessment questions that address *only* basic concepts and definitions is a common problem in the teacher-made assessments that we see. Questions about facts and definitions are the easiest kinds of questions to design, and they are also easier to grade. But if you want your students to learn more than the facts, if you want them to learn critical-thinking skills and master the requirements of the standards you are teaching, you need to develop assessments that do this, too. In forthcoming chapters, designing assessments of all types that foster critical thinking is the third theme related to equipping students for democratic participation.

As you can see from this discussion, we take a broad view of assessment. It's not just about testing degrees of knowledge with often punishing consequences. The practice of classroom assessment encompasses a wide array of activities that foster student learning, from keeping track of student activity preferences to holding individual writing conferences that encourage self-assessment. Many educators now talk about a distinction between assessment *of* learning, which is the more traditional type of assessment, and assessment *for* learning. Assessment *for* learning promotes democratic values by guiding the development of tools to help teachers address achievement gaps, by promoting skills such as independence and responsibility, and by designing assessments that foster students' critical thinking. We believe that, like us, you will find these tools essential in your classroom. We next turn to organizing these different types of assessment into an overview to illustrate their purposes and uses.

✦ AN OVERVIEW OF ASSESSMENT

Assessment

The variety of methods used to determine what students know and are able to do before, during, and after instruction.

First, let's lay out a definition of **assessment** that is broader than the tests we usually think of: Assessment is the variety of methods used to determine what students know and are able to do before, during, and after instruction. In fleshing out this definition, we will provide an overview of assessment covering three central purposes.

Purposes of Assessment

From our definition, you can see that you will be interested in what your students know and are able to do at many different points *during* the school year and, more specifically, *during* each instructional unit you teach. Now that you also know that the purpose of assessment is broader than tests or quizzes for grades, we want to describe the other major purposes teachers have for doing assessments. Keeping your purpose for any assessment in mind is very important because your purpose dictates the specific kinds of assessments you will do. For example, as an art teacher, if your purpose is to do a quick check that your students understand how the color wheel works, you will do a different assessment than if your purpose is to determine whether they have mastered the concepts in the unit on perspective drawing. If your purpose is to compare your social studies class to other ninth graders across the country, you will use a different assessment than if your purpose is to see how much they learned from the Civil War unit you just completed. Table 1.3 illustrates the three general purposes of assessment with some examples.

TABLE 1.3

The Three Major Purposes of Assessment

Purpose of the Assessment: Why Do You Do It?	When Do You Do It?	How Do You Do It?	Examples
Purpose 1: Diagnosic assessment Getting a sense of strengths and needs for planning instruction	Before instruction	School records. Teacher observations. Teacher-made questionnaires and pre-tests.	**Math:** Strengths in math skills from previous statewide testing. **Language arts:** Observation of student level of analysis during first look at a poem in class. **Music:** Last year's performance rankings of students at all-state band auditions.
Purpose 2: Formative Assessment Monitoring growth as you teach (assessment *for* learning)	During instruction	Teacher observations. Quizzes. Skill checklists. Homework. Student self-assessments. Systematic teacher questioning.	**Math:** Checklist of new algebra skills demonstrated during class or homework. **Language arts:** Quick write summarizing key issues in differentiating similes from metaphors. **Music:** Self- and teacher-ratings of individual performance of a selection for an upcoming concert.
Purpose 3: Summative Assessment Determining what students have learned after instruction or for accountability purposes (assessment *of* learning)	After instruction	End of unit test for assigning grades. Statewide tests at the end of the year.	**Math:** Final algebra exam that uses novel problems based on skills taught. **Language arts:** Booklet containing a student's poems that incorporate figures of speech learned in a poetry unit. Statewide achievement test scores in math and language arts. **Music:** Final graded performance for the semester in band class.

Purpose 1: Diagnostic Assessment

Diagnosis is a word we usually associate with the medical field in the negative sense of figuring out what is wrong with a patient. But we use it more broadly in education. When you start a new year as a teacher, you want to know many things about your students. One of the most important is their current level of basic skills. For example, right now we have three elementary teachers in a graduate assessment class. All three of them have students who read material ranging from the first-grade level to the ninth-grade level. Accurately understanding what your students know and are able to do from the beginning of the year is crucial in designing instruction for them that challenges but does not overwhelm them (Earl, 2003; Moon, 2005). This process is termed **diagnostic assessment.**

Diagnostic Assessment

Assessment at the early stages of a school year or unit that provides the teacher with information about what students already know and are able to do.

An example of the importance of understanding what your students know and are able to do is provided by Jocelyn Beaty-Gordon, a teacher of high school biology in a high-needs school. At the beginning of the year, she discovered that many of her students had never passed an end-of-grade test in reading. Based on this information, she decided that she would alter how she taught biology. Rather than require students to read the text independently, she spent class time reading to students and having them draw pictures and diagrams to express their understanding. She also encouraged students to ask questions about words they did not understand, telling them they were doing a service for the class because many others didn't understand those words either. She put these words on the bulletin board with their definitions. She reported that by the midpoint of the year, most of the students were grasping the most difficult biological concepts, thanks to her clear understanding of their low basic-reading skills and her accommodations for their skill level.

As you can see from this example, diagnostic assessment is critical to designing instruction that meets the needs of your students. Many educators have termed this process **differentiation** or **differentiated instruction.** The basic idea of differentiation is that you find out student needs and readiness before you teach so you can use this information to tailor, or differentiate, your instruction for them. They suggest that these procedures are critical because of the wide range of student cultures, abilities, and needs in every classroom today. Diagnostic assessment must be the first step in differentiating instruction because you use diagnostic assessments to learn what your students' varying needs are (Moon, 2005; Tomlinson, 2008).

Differentiation

Using students' current understanding, readiness levels, skills, and interests to tailor instruction and meet individual needs.

At the beginning of each school year, you will also be interested in learning about your students' likes and dislikes, from food and music to academic interests. Understanding student preferences about types of assignments can help you work from their strengths to address their needs. For example, you may discover that your students hate to write essays, but writing strong persuasive essays is an important part of your learning goals for the year. This information can help you pay particular attention to designing assignments that more gradually move students toward the goal and incorporate topics most relevant to their interests. And, yes, those food and music preferences can be worked into the assignments. You might have students write a persuasive essay on why their favorite band should be considered for the next Grammy Awards.

Another important time for diagnosis is when you begin a new unit. Psychologists tell us that students' new learning is usually dependent on their prior knowledge (Pelligrino et al., 2001). One of the most important ways you can help close the achievement gap between lower and higher performing students is to check to make sure your students have the prior knowledge necessary to begin a new unit. If you are teaching your students long division, for example, you first need to check to make sure they can multiply with ease. We once observed a student teacher who was teaching a math unit on measurement. Rather than checking first, she assumed her students had all used rulers. Partway through the lesson, when they had difficulty with one of her planned activities and started using the rulers as weapons, she discovered that they had not worked with rulers before. She quickly had to interrupt her plans and teach them what rulers were for and how they worked. You can see how assessment for the purpose of diagnosis is crucial.

Purpose 2: Formative Assessment

As shown in Table 1.2, the second major purpose of assessment is monitoring of student progress during instruction. This type of assessment is usually called **formative assessment.** A key aspect of formative assessment is giving students feedback on their growth toward the learning goals they need to master (Black & Wiliam, 1998). It helps students understand where they are now compared to where they should be going, and it gives them suggestions for getting there. Formative assessment is, therefore, assessment *for* learning.

Formative Assessment
Monitoring student progress during instruction and learning activities that includes feedback and opportunities to improve.

Teachers have always checked on student progress informally during instruction by asking questions or checking out puzzled facial expressions. These actions definitely fall under the heading of formative assessment. Recent discussions of formative assessment have suggested that more systematic checkup and feedback during instruction can have a significant impact on student learning and also on student motivation (Shute, 2008; Stiggins, 2007). These activities also influence the teacher's later instruction. Homework, quizzes, and class assignments can be used for formative assessment. The key is that these activities do not result in grades that penalize students for "wrong" answers. The purpose of these activities is for feedback for students and teacher *before* more official assessment for a grade.

Many of our students have a difficult time with the distinction between formative assessment and assessment for grades (summative assessment). After explaining formative assessment and its use to enhance learning, we often have students write a paragraph for homework explaining how they saw a concept we discussed in class demonstrated in the classroom in which they are currently observing. The first time we use this type of formative assessment each semester, we write comments on their examples, correct misconceptions, indicate where more information on the concept can be found in the text, and suggest other examples. However, we put no grade or point value on these papers. When we hand these papers back, there is always a chorus of "But what did I *get* on this?" even though students knew the assignment was for formative purposes. After we remind them about formative assessment and how it works, students see the value of this feedback—especially later when they do well on a summative test question covering the same concept.

Purpose 3: Summative Assessment

Summative assessment is the conventional purpose of assessment that we all grew up with. It is assessment *of* learning, a summing up of what the students know and are able to do after instruction has taken place. Examples include exams, projects, and term papers. Grading is based on information from summative assessment, and grading is often the major function of summative assessment at the classroom level. As you can see in Table 1.4, the other type of summative assessment is large-scale state or national tests administered infrequently and used by local, state, and national decision makers. If you took the SAT, ACT, or a high school exit exam, you have participated in summative assessment at the large-scale level. The No Child Left Behind Act (NCLB) also mandates large-scale testing. Each state accepting federal assistance is required to

Summative Assessment
A summing up of what students know and are able to do after instruction is completed.

TABLE 1.4

Differences Between Summative Assessment at the Classroom and Large-Scale Levels

Differences	Classroom Level	Large-Scale Level
Function	Grading	Accountability, planning, resource allocation
Frequency	Often, at least once per week	Usually once per year
Focus	Narrow: Individual mastery of elements in a unit of instruction	Broad: Group performance in relation to a number of standards
Design	Designed by teachers	Designed by state or national assessment authorities
User	Teacher, student, parents	Policy makers, citizens
Conditions of Testing	Heavily dependent on context	Standardized across contexts
Metaphor	Close-up snapshot	Panoramic view

assess students in math and reading in grades 3 through 8 each year and once in high school. They are also required to assess students annually in science at least once in grades 3–5, 6–9, and 10–12.

One of the key implications of the two different kinds of summative assessment is that they serve very different functions and must be designed to match their function. The needs of large-scale assessment users require assessments covering a wide range of content. Most of these tests are designed to cover material across one or more years of instruction. To assess this broadly requires that you can ask only a few items on each concept. This approach is akin to the panoramic view—the details of the scenery are necessarily fuzzy. And because large-scale tests cover so much ground, they primarily give a general picture rather than any specific information classroom teachers could use for designing their instruction. We will discuss large-scale assessments and their strengths and weaknesses at greater length in Chapter 11.

In contrast, for the end-of-unit summative test, classroom teachers want a more close-up snapshot of a narrower landscape. They want to know what students have learned from the unit. They need information for a grade. And based on possibly poor scores on some of the essay questions chosen for this test, they might also decide to change their instruction the next time they teach the unit. These teacher needs are quite different from those of the users of large-scale tests. Because the requirements of the users are so very different, the SAT would not work as an end-of-unit test, and an end-of-unit test would not be helpful for making college admissions decisions.

Another important difference between the two kinds of summative assessments is the way they are administered. Teachers can vary the conditions of summative assessments in their classrooms to make sure all students can show in different ways what they know and can do. For example, some children may need extra time, other children may need to have all items read to them, and others may need to talk their way through a problem. In several later chapters, we discuss more about the accommodations that teachers can use for all their assessments.

Because large-scale tests often are used to compare students across schools, districts, and even countries, the way they are administered must be **standardized.** That is, they must be administered, scored, and interpreted the same way for everyone taking the exam. The proctor who is administering the tests must read the directions carefully; the time given for students to complete the assessment must be exact. If you are taking the SAT in New Mexico, it wouldn't be fair if a college admissions officer compared you to a student in Iowa who got 10 more minutes to complete the exam than you did. Review Table 1.4 to compare these two types of summative assessment.

Standardized

Administered, scored, and interpreted exactly the same for all test takers.

✦ Action Research and the Inquiry Stance

From our discussion so far, you have an inkling of the different purposes for assessment and some of the ways you will be using it in your classroom. Now we want to offer you a framework for problem solving in your classroom that uses assessment as its foundation.

When working in an elementary school, we were talking with a first-grade teacher before the school year started. During the conversation, the teacher mentioned that she had been reading about "invented spelling" (i.e., letting students spell words as they sound) in the early grades and was wondering whether she should scrap her spelling lessons that year. This teacher usually arranged her children into four groups, each containing students at various skill levels, for literacy instruction. We suggested that the teacher might want to try invented spelling with two of the groups, do her usual spelling curriculum with the other two, then compare the progress of the two groups at some point later in the fall. By the strange and dubious look on her face, we could tell she thought the idea was ridiculous. But we had been trained in graduate studies to look for an answer to any question in terms of finding solid information to support one side or the other. Once you "gather the data," you can make a sound decision. The teacher had a clear difference in world view, and it definitely did not involve systematic data collection from her students.

Inquiry Stance

Long after that meeting, we went to a conference where B. J. Badiali (2002) discussed an "inquiry stance" as something important for teachers' work in schools. Badiali pointed out that colleges of education cannot prepare teacher candidates for every possible classroom situation, so they must give them the tools for problem solving in the classroom. In contrast to a "caring stance" or a "best practices stance," an **inquiry stance** prepares teacher candidates to identify problems, collect relevant data, make judgments, and modify practices to bring about improvement in teaching and learning. In 1910, John Dewey, one of the founders of modern educational practices, described a similar process for dealing with problematic situations. He suggested designing a solution, observing and experimenting to test the solution, and then accepting or rejecting it (Dewey, 1910).

Inquiry Stance

An approach to dealing with challenges in the classroom that involves identifying problems, collecting relevant data, making judgments, and then modifying practices to improve teaching and learning.

One key use of the inquiry stance and problem-solving process is analyzing and then improving student learning outcomes in each classroom. As discussed in the early paragraphs of this chapter, we believe all you do should be aimed toward helping your students learn. You can see that assessment in all of its manifestations is the foundational tool for an inquiry stance. This is because assessment gives you information every step of the way on what your students know and are able to do and whether your instructional strategies are working.

Inquiry Stance and Action Research

Action Research

The process of examining and improving teaching practices and student outcomes using an inquiry stance.

The process of examining and improving our teaching practices and our student outcomes using an inquiry stance is often termed **action research.** Using systematic collection and analysis of data, action research has been used by teachers to examine their practice and to solve problems in their own classrooms (e.g., Green & Brown, 2006; Salmon, 2008). Individual teachers and classrooms, not just educational theories and "best practices," are valuable sources of information for improving student learning. Taking this more personal approach, teachers can tailor data gathering and interventions to their own environment and their own students. The student teacher in kindergarten mentioned earlier who encouraged attendance at the reading center in her classroom offers an example of action research.

Some people are not comfortable with the term *data*. It implies to them complex statistical analyses and confusing numbers. But as we pointed out, collecting data can be as simple as systematically noting which students visit a center, or asking students about their reading preferences. You use numbers to summarize the information for yourself so you can notice patterns more easily. These patterns can then help you make decisions about how to change your practices or whether something you try is working the way you want it to in your classroom. Data can help you identify the needs of your students and can uncover problems that might otherwise remain hidden. In Chapter 5 we talk more about methods to summarize information so that patterns become visible.

But even without these methods, you can easily see the value of simple data collection. As a teacher, you will probably assign homework. You may not notice any patterns in terms of who does and doesn't do the homework because you have so many other details and decisions to make about your classes and instruction. But then you notice one day that several students can't answer questions based on the readings assigned for homework the night before. Using an inquiry stance, you might start keeping close tabs on who has and has not turned in homework during a particular two-week period. You might notice that the same seven of your students tend to have problems in completing the homework. This pattern will naturally prompt you to think about why these students are having problems and what you might do to encourage homework completion. For example, one student teacher chose exactly this problem for an action research project. The student teacher talked with the students about issues that made homework difficult for them, she provided incentives for homework completion, and she was able to help them all begin completing homework more regularly. The students then participated more actively in class and their grades improved.

Simple projects like this one allow you to use information that you already collect from your students to improve their learning. Noticing a problem, looking for patterns in the data you are already collecting, and then trying out different solutions to see if they have the desired impact is a basic, but often powerful, action research approach. Small projects like this can lead to important changes in student learning that can help close the achievement gap. If all teachers in their own classrooms solved problems in this manner, we might see great learning gains.

Gathering New Information

Sometimes the problem you see can also encourage you to start collecting information you haven't been collecting. Elizabeth Mills works with children with autism, who often have difficulty with fine motor skills. She is always looking for new ways to help her students achieve more and had recently read about hand-strengthening exercises. She wondered whether these types of exercises might help improve the students' writing

Name
orange orange
purple purple
green green
Name
orange orange
purple purple
green green

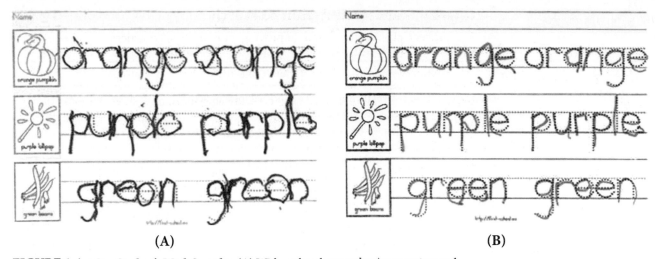

(A) (B)

FIGURE 1.4 ***One Student's Work Samples*** (A) Without hand-strengthening exercises and (B) with hand-strengthening exercises on the same day.

Reprinted with permission.

skills. She set up two new daily writing activities. Students did the hand-strengthening exercises before one of them and did nothing before the second. She used students' tracing quality as her new measure of student learning (see Figure 1.4). As you can see, when students used the exercises, their writing was much more controlled than when they did not. She also saw general improvement over several weeks, so she decided to continue to incorporate the exercises.

In Table 1.5, you can see a sample of action research projects recently completed by teachers in their classrooms. Problems range from enhancing literacy skills to reducing transition times so more instruction could take place. These teachers chose projects based on their own interests and passions connected to specific problems they saw in their own classes. For example, Janelle Smith recently read that 85 percent of students who appear in court are illiterate. The article also mentioned that officials should plan jail cells 15 years from now equal to the number of current third graders who cannot read. She decided to involve parents as partners in her classroom reading instruction. She sent a questionnaire home and found that many parents wanted to help but lacked strategies and were afraid they would do the wrong thing. Each week she designed and sent home to these parents several strategies to help their children in the coming week. She subsequently saw much improvement in her kindergarten students' reading levels and knowledge of the alphabet.

Broader Uses of Action Research

Many educators have suggested that action research and the inquiry stance can go beyond the individual teacher and classroom level (Cochran-Smith & Lytle, 1999; Barrell & Weitman, 2007). They believe these processes can prepare teachers to work together in communities to develop systematic inquiries about teaching and learning in their schools and to become school leaders. For example, most of the teachers mentioned in Table 1.5 have shared their results with other teachers in their schools in an effort to use the new knowledge gathered from the projects to enhance student learning in other classrooms. Cochran-Smith and Lytle also suggest the inquiry stance can "bring about fundamental change in classrooms" and a broader agenda of empowerment of students and teachers.

TABLE 1.5

Recent Action Research Projects Conducted by Teachers in Their Classrooms

Teacher	Problem	Intervention	Data Collected	Outcome
Elizabeth Mills	Fine-motor deficits in children with autism.	Hand-strengthening exercises before some fine-motor tasks and not before others.	Work samples of activities with and without hand-strengthening exercises.	Exercises increased legibility and accuracy.
Dana Stachowiak	Students' literacy skills below grade level and not showing growth.	Read alouds 5–7 times per day.	STARS levels, end of grade scores, students' attitudes on read alouds before and after.	Most students enjoyed read alouds. Most showed more growth than in prior 18 weeks.
Janelle Smith	Parents want to help with reading but lacked strategies to assist.	Family homework packet with activities; leveled books sent home each week.	Alphabet knowledge, word recognition, parent questionnaire, weekly reading logs, completion of activities.	Increased parent participation, increased alphabet and word recognition.
Jocelyn Beaty-Gordon	Students unable to read biology text.	Guided reading and students designing concept posters to illustrate comprehension.	Compared this year's test scores to last year's.	Significant increase in test scores, improvement of student confidence, student and teacher attitudes.

A good example of student empowerment came out of the action research project of Dana Stachowiak (see Table 1.5). Dana had recently attended a staff development session about the value of reading aloud to students seven times per day. She did not believe such a simple act could impact her students' literacy skills, so she set out to do an action research project to prove the presenter was wrong. She started reading brief items from the newspaper, poems, and even "The Way I See It" quotes from Starbucks paper coffee cups, as long as the excerpts were related to a lesson she was about to teach. One student noticed that the Starbucks quotes were all from famous people. Her class had a discussion about the quotes and the fact that they had no quotes from children. Because Dana was doing a unit on activism and persuasive writing at the time, she and the class decided to write letters to Starbucks supported with good arguments suggesting that Starbucks use quotes from children. She wanted to instill in her students the knowledge that they could act to change things they didn't agree with. She was interested in promoting civic engagement as one skill important to citizens in a democracy. An example of the letters students sent and quotations they offered appear in Box 1.2.

Incidentally, Dana also found that the frequent readings had a positive impact on her students' literacy skills. These findings bring up another advantage of data collection. Data gathered fairly and objectively can help you make decisions in your classroom that might allow you to get beyond your own perspective and biases and use some effective practices you never dreamed could work.

From the projects we have discussed, you can also see that action research uses data addressing all three of the purposes of assessment described in the previous section

BOX 1.2

Letters and "The Way I See It" Suggestions from Ms. Stachowiak's Class

Dear Starbucks Corporate,

My name is Crissy Megill, and I am in Miss Stachowiak's 4th grade classroom at Benton Heights Elementary School in Monroe, NC. I am writing to let my voice and my classmates' voices be heard on your cups in "The Way I See It" series.

Our goal is to let kids' voices and feelings be heard because our minds might be fresher about the things in the world. We might see things different than an adult or famous person. Plus, it would be something different because I bet you sometimes get tired of using famous people.

Thank you for your time!

–Crissy Megill

The Way I See It. . . .
Stand up for what's right
even if you're standing alone.
Like if there is a gang that hates you or bullies you.
Tell them, "Back off and leave me alone!"
Leave them standing there in shame.
Bullies are people who
call you names or pick on you.
I have experienced it all.

–Kendra Covington, 4th grader
Benton Heights Elementary School

of this chapter. For example, you can use diagnostic assessment to get a clear sense of what the problem might be. Janelle Smith needed a concrete picture of what literacy skills her children needed to work on so that she could send assignments home with effective suggestions for parents. Similarly, Jocelyn Beaty-Gordon needed to understand her students' literacy levels to design appropriate activities for her biology classroom.

Formative assessment is useful during an intervention to see whether it has the hoped for impact during implementation. If it does not, the formative assessment gives you information to tweak the intervention. For example, Janelle found that when scissors or crayons were needed for one of the activities she sent home, the book bags came back with those activities unfinished. When asked, the children told her they did not have those supplies at home. When she started sending home supplies as well as activities, the book bags came back with completed projects.

Finally, summative assessment is needed to determine the overall value of the project. Janelle used a knowledge of the alphabet test and the final literacy assessments at the end of the year to see how much progress her students made. Similarly, Jocelyn found that her techniques were working with her biology students when she compared their scores on biology tests to those of students in previous years.

So action research and an inquiry stance are part of a mindset that many teachers employ to empower themselves to problem solve about their practice and to help their children learn more. At the heart of all action research projects is the enhancement of student learning, and assessment for all three purposes—diagnostic, formative, and summative—provides the data to make the decisions.

➔ ETHICS AND ASSESSMENT

As we all can attest from memories of our own childhood experiences, teachers have pervasive and long-lasting influence. They have the potential to do both great good and great harm. Because assessment plays such a significant role in the lives of students, teachers must use assessment practices that are ethical. Ethical practices benefit and enhance student learning and avoid potential harmful effects. They promote well-being, and they are based on basic beliefs about right and wrong.

Do No Harm

As a starting point for generating principles widely applicable to the various types of assessment that occur in classrooms, we have found that two general guidelines seem to address many of the ethical questions raised by teachers (Green et al., 2007). The first one, dating back to the ancient Greeks, is to *do no harm*. Avoiding suffering is a basic, broad ethical principle that people use to govern their lives. It summarizes ethical principles handed down through the centuries, such as the Golden Rule (or "Assess as Ye Would Be Assessed" [Payne, 2003]). In the realm of the classroom, this principle manifests itself as the basic duty that teachers have to their students. Teachers must fulfill the needs of each student as a learner, preserving the dignity of both the student and the teacher. Teachers must remember that they serve *in loco parentis* (in the place of parents), another factor that lends support to the principle that assessment should protect students and do no harm to them.

For educators to fulfill this obligation, they must be well-versed in the potential impact of the practices they use, because their assessments and evaluations may have a variety of unintended consequences for their students. Protecting students from harm is a general principle that no one contests in the abstract. However, thinking about *causing* harm focuses the discussion on implications for everyday practice. So when we talk about harm, we must emphasize that teacher judgment must be involved. The first judgment comes in defining what harm is. For example, a teacher who, on a test, uses surprise items that did not appear on the study guide may do harm by breaking the implicit bond of trust between teacher and student. A teacher who passes out tests from highest grade to lowest may do harm by breaching confidentiality. Such actions erode the dignity of students.

Avoid Score Pollution

The second general guideline for classroom assessment is to *avoid score pollution*. This is a specific manifestation of the do no harm principle applying to assessment. If scores from an assessment do not reflect the level of a student's mastery of the instructional content represented by that assessment, then harm has been done. Score pollution is akin to lying. This guideline is adapted from recommendations for teachers preparing their students for standardized tests. The basic idea is that any practice that improves performance on an assessment without also increasing actual mastery of the content tested produces score pollution and harms students (Haladyna et al., 1991). For example, a teacher who has the class practice beforehand with actual test content would produce score pollution. The score on that assessment would no longer measure mastery of a body of knowledge, but would simply show the ability to memorize specific test items. The score on the test does not represent actual student achievement in the content area and is "polluted," or determined partially by factors unrelated to academic achievement. Practices designed to produce high test scores, no matter what the cost in terms of integrity, do harm. Decisions and choices made on the basis of erroneous scores could have many adverse consequences for students and schools, including the eventual emotional ramifications of student placement in the wrong program, increased teacher stress, or parents who are unaware of exactly how far behind their child may really be.

We believe this ethical principle can be extended to everyday classroom assessment and not just to high-stakes tests. Any official assessment, including grades, should reflect only the extent to which students have mastered the goals of instruction. When teachers modify grades or scores because of student effort, late work, or behavior problems, for example, the scores do not accurately communicate the level of mastery and can eventually harm students. Similarly, many teachers do not use a blind grading system and may unconsciously prefer certain students. Such educators may unintentionally engage in score pollution by giving less-favored students lower grades than they deserve. Everyone has stories about a teacher with biases—the one who won't ever give males an A or the one who is always lenient with the kids who play sports. Classroom grades sometimes seem to be "polluted" by these other factors. Such actions can result in harms such as mistrust between student and teacher, discouragement, and lack of student effort.

We had a memorable experience during graduate training that illustrates the harm that can be done with score pollution. A group of us were asked to listen to individual students read aloud who were in a special education class for students with learning disabilities. We were checking to see if any of the students might be getting closer in literacy skills to those in general education in the same grade. We were surprised when one boy, poorly dressed, unkempt, and a tad defiant, read aloud fluently and expressively at a level well above typical students in his grade. Our only conclusion could be that he had been labeled as a student with a learning disability and placed in that class based on very "polluted" scores of his achievement level. After the testing information came to light, we were relieved to learn that this student was chosen to be reintegrated into a general education classroom. Students, their families, and other stakeholders in the education system need unbiased and factual information regarding academic achievement to make good decisions about each step in their education.

Examples from Classrooms and Headlines

The all-too-frequent unpleasant accounts from our own students about unfair treatment have also highlighted for us the need for consistent guidelines for ethical assessment. For several years we have asked students to write down a time when they were graded unfairly. Very few of them have difficulty coming up with an incident that they vividly remember. For example, one student described her science teacher who always handed out tests after they were graded from highest to lowest score, so everyone knew exactly where they fell in the pecking order. She found this practice traumatizing even though she usually did fairly well. Another student remembered receiving a "0" for a homework grade in her physical education class when she failed to bring a permission slip signed by her parent (who was out of town) on the due date. You can easily see the harm done to the first student and the pollution of the grade of the second student.

The necessity for guidelines on ethical assessment practices is also evident in frequent events taken from news headlines. In one incident, a biology teacher in the midwestern United States decided to assign students failing grades for the science course after the students were caught cheating on a class project. The decision split the community and the teacher resigned. In another instance, the state law enforcement division in a southern U.S. community investigated a teacher after she used in her classroom some commercially available test preparation materials designed to simulate the type of items and subject matter in the state test. Finally, the president of a southeastern U.S. college fired two professors for their refusal to adhere to a policy awarding freshmen 60 percent of their grade based on effort (which amounted to simply showing up for class). The dismissal of the professors brought unfavorable national attention to the administrator's misguided policy on effort and grades.

Judgment Calls

We believe that *do no harm* and *avoid score pollution* are two basic guidelines you can apply when facing real-life decisions about assessment in your classroom. In our own research, we have asked teachers and teacher candidates for their judgments about whether a variety of classroom assessment practices are ethical (Green et al., 2007). We found strong agreement in several areas of assessment (see Table 1.6). For example, protecting confidentiality of students' assessment results was judged important. Most agreed with our student that a teacher who passed out scored tests to students in order of points earned was unethical. Communication about grading was another area with high levels of agreement. Explaining how a task will be graded and letting students know what material will be on a test are examples of items judged ethical. Finally, this group agreed on some grading practices, for example, indicating that lowering report card grades for disruptive behavior was unethical. Although not all situations you face will be easily resolved, there is general agreement about the most common ones.

Harder Judgment Calls

At times, making ethical assessment decisions emerges in practice as a choice between harms. As we have said, teacher judgment is required, not only to define harms but to determine which harm is greater. A teacher may have to choose between a high-stakes exam that yields important data about student performance and the emotional stress such exams cause in students (and teachers). We have also talked to many teachers who agonize over choosing between harms when grading struggling students. They have to decide whether to give a low grade that reflects the student's actual mastery level versus a higher grade that reflects the student's effort but doesn't truly reflect their level

TABLE 1.6

Judgments About the Ethicality of Classroom Assessment Practices with Strong Agreement by Teachers and Teacher Candidates

Scenario	Ethical	Unethical
A teacher states how she will grade a task when she assigns it.	98%	2%
A teacher tells students what materials are important to learn in preparing for a class test.	98%	2%
To motivate students to perform better, a science teacher always announces that he is passing out scored tests to students in order of points earned, from the top score to the bottom score.	6%	94%
A teacher spends a class period to train his students in test-taking skills (e.g., not spending too much time on one problem, eliminating impossible answers, guessing).	90%	10%
A second-grade teacher uses observations as the sole method to assess what students have learned.	15%	85%
A teacher lowers report card grades for disruptive behavior.	15%	85%

Adapted from Green, S., Johnson, R., Kim, D., & Pope, N. (2007). Ethics in classroom assessment practices: Issues and attitudes. *Teaching and Teacher Education* 23: 999–1011. Reprinted with permission from Elsevier.

of understanding. You can see why teacher judgment is so important in determining and avoiding harm.

Your Turn

When we questioned teachers and teacher candidates about their views about whether a variety of classroom assessment practices were ethical, we found several areas of disagreement. Table 1.7 shows a sample of some of the scenarios we used. Cover the "Ethical" and "Unethical" columns and take a few minutes to write down your own rating of each practice as ethical or unethical. You can then compare your answer choices with those of our group of teachers and teacher candidates.

One area that our group disagreed about was grading practices—the area that created the firestorm in a Midwestern community. You can see we found mixed results in the grading items shown in Table 1.7. We believe one reason we saw disagreement about these practices is the complexity and nuance facing teachers involved in making ethical judgments. For example, teachers often include dimensions not directly related to the mastery of the learning goals in their grading schemes, such as neatness or class participation. If the percentage devoted to such factors has minimal impact on the overall grade, such practices do not pose an ethical dilemma. However, if such factors are weighted heavily enough to change a grade, they may result in score pollution. As you can see, score pollution is one issue where theory meets reality in the classroom.

Final Thoughts on Ethics and Assessment

We believe that the scenarios we designed can create an opening for discussion between you and your colleagues about the ethics of your classroom assessment practices. We

TABLE 1.7

Judgments About the Ethicality of Classroom Assessment Practices with Disagreement by Teachers and Teacher Candidates

Scenario	Ethical	Unethical
A teacher always knows the identity of the student whose essay test she is grading.	49%	51%
To enhance self-esteem, an elementary teacher addresses only students' strengths when writing narrative report cards.	41%	59%
A physical education teacher gives a student a zero as a homework grade for not returning a form requiring a parent's signature.	43%	57%
A teacher weights homework heavily in determining report card grades.	57%	43%
As a teacher finalizes grades, she changes one student's course grade from a B+ to an A because tests and papers showed that the student had mastered the course objectives even though he had not completed some of his homework assignments.	37%	63%

Adapted from Green, S., Johnson, R., Kim, D., & Pope, N. (2007). Ethics in classroom assessment practices: Issues and attitudes. *Teaching and Teacher Education* 23: 999–1011. Reprinted with permission from Elsevier.

TABLE 1.8

Recommendations for Making Ethical Assessment Decisions

1. Familiarize yourself with and follow your district's and your school's practices regarding classroom assessment and standardized testing.
2. Discuss potential ethical issues or conflicts with teachers and administrators with whom you work.
3. Use *do no harm* and *avoid score pollution* as guidelines for your actions.
4. Think things through from all perspectives before you act.

also believe that *do no harm* and *avoid score pollution* are two useful basic principles you can apply when faced with making ethical decisions about assessment in your classroom. Unfortunately, not all situations you face will be easily resolved. You will develop your professional judgment about ethics and assessment through experiences in your classroom, discussions with peers and administrators, and analysis of more news stories that are sure to arise. Our advice is to make sure you first familiarize yourself with and follow your district's and school's practices. Also, as you become aware of potential ethical issues or conflicts, explicitly discuss them with other teachers. Finally, make your own practices and decisions around assessment with the benefit of the students in your care in mind, and make sure you clearly think things through before you act. Seeing things from students' or administrators' perspectives, as well as your own, can help you clarify your decisions. These recommendations are summarized in Table 1.8.

KEY CHAPTER POINTS

In this chapter we have tried to show you why assessment is essential. First, we explained how integral assessment is in preparing students to function in a democracy. We outlined how assessment is the key to providing equal access to educational opportunity. Assessment that gives teachers a clear sense of how their students are doing can help them maximize those students' opportunities for learning. Next we talked about self-governing skills, such as independent thinking and a sense of responsibility, needed in a democracy. We discussed how these skills can be fostered by using assessment strategies promoting mastery goals. The third theme linking assessment to democratic functioning is the promotion of critical thinking. Assessments that go beyond rote memory and basic concepts and definitions will enable students to think for themselves and become discerning voters and public-spirited citizens.

We provided you with an overview of assessment organized by the purposes assessments can serve. Diagnostic assessment helps you understand your students' strengths and needs at the beginning of the year and before new instruction. Formative assessment allows you to monitor students during the learning process to help them learn more. It is often thought of as assessment *for* learning. Summative assessment, in contrast, is assessment *of* learning, the more conventional understanding of assessment with which most of us grew up. Summative assessment for classroom purposes usually serves the function of marking assignments for a grade. Summative assessment for large-scale purposes serves the accountability function at the district, local, state, national, and even international levels.

Next, we acquainted you with the inquiry stance, which orients teachers to iden-tify and solve problems in their classrooms. This problem-solving process is often called *action research*. We offered several examples of the kinds of questions teachers ask and the kind of assessment data they can collect to answer them. You saw how these assessments served the diagnostic, formative, and summative functions. These examples should help you see a number of the ways that assessment was essential in these teachers' classrooms and will become essential in yours.

Finally, we discussed the importance of ethics and assessment, providing two key guidelines for making ethical decisions regarding assessment. The first was *do no harm*, and the second was *avoid score pollution*. We also emphasized the importance of teacher judgment when making ethical decisions grounded in the intention to help students learn.

Helpful Websites

http://www.accessexcellence.org/LC/TL/AR/
This site on action research provides background, resources, examples, and a step-by-step
   approach for getting started.
http://www.edweek.org/rc/issues/achievement-gap/
This site on the achievement gap provides background information as well as links to data bases,
   web resources, and relevant articles from *Education Week*.

Chapter Review Questions

1. What do you think are the most important skills for preparing students for democratic participation? What classroom assessment practices would help foster these skills?
2. Give examples of teacher assessment practices that you have observed or experienced that exemplify the sorting (or judgment) approach to education.
3. Give examples of teacher assessment practices that promote mastery goals in terms of meaningful and challenging tasks, student participation in decision making, and student focus on personal goals and individual progress.
4. Compare times in your life as a student when you know you had "effort optimism" and times when you know you lacked "effort optimism." What teacher assessment practices may have contributed to your beliefs in each situation?
5. Discuss the assessment practices of the two teachers in Box 1.1. Which teacher would you rather have? Explain your answer in terms of mastery and performance goals.
6. Give examples of assessments in your discipline that exemplify each of the three major purposes of assessment.
7. Compare classroom-level and large-scale-level summative assessments. What similarities and differences do you see? Why is it likely that most statewide summative assessments cannot yield detailed practical information for teachers to use in teaching?
8. What is an inquiry stance? Why is an inquiry stance useful?
9. Give examples of data that are routinely collected in classrooms that could be used to answer questions and solve problems that teachers see as important.
10. Describe a way that you might incorporate action research and an inquiry stance in your classroom in relation to your assessment practices.

11. Describe a time you or someone you know was graded unfairly. Was a violation of either of the two ethical guidelines, *do no harm* or *avoid score pollution,* involved? Explain.

12. Examine the practices described in Table 1.7. Which do you believe are ethical? Which do you believe are unethical? Explain your reasoning.

13. As a teacher, what do you think will be your most difficult ethical dilemma related to assessment practices? Why do you think so?

REFERENCES

Ames, C. 1992. Classrooms: Goals, structures, and student motivation. *Journal of Educational Psychology* 84 (3): 261–271.

Andrade, H. 2008. Self-assessment through rubrics. *Educational Leadership* 65: 60–63.

Badiali, B. J., and D. J. Hammond. 2002 (March). The power of and necessity for using inquiry in a PDS. Paper presented at the Professional Development Schools National Conference, Orlando, FL.

Banks, J., M. Cochran-Smith, L. Moll, A. Richert, K. Zeichener, P. LePage, L. Darling-Hammond, H. Duffy, and M. McDonald. 2005. Teaching diverse learners. In L. Darling-Hammond and J. Bransford (Eds.), *Preparing teachers for a changing world.* San Francisco: Jossey-Bass.

Barrell, J., and C. Weitman. 2007. Action research fosters empowerment and learning communities. *Delta Kappa Gamma Bulletin* 73 (3): 36–45. Retrieved April 4, 2008, from Academic Search Premier database.

Belfield, C. R., and H. Levin. 2007. *The price we pay: Economic and social consequences of inadequate education.* Washington, DC: Brookings Institution Press.

Black, P., and D. Wiliam. 1998. Assessment and classroom learning. *Assessment in Education: Principles, Policy, and Practice* 5 (1): 7–74.

Butler, R. 2006. Are mastery and ability goals both adaptive? Evaluation, initial goal construction and the quality of task engagement. *British Journal of Educational Psychology* 76: 595–611.

Cochran-Smith, M., and S. L. Lytle. 1999. Relationships of knowledge and practice: Teacher learning in communities. *Review of Research in Education* 24: 249–305.

Dewey, J. 1910. *How we think.* Lexington, MA: D. C. Heath.

Earl, L. 2003. *Assessment as learning.* Thousand Oaks, CA: Corwin Press.

Gordon, E. W. 2008. The transformation of key beliefs that have guided a century of assessment. In C. A. Dwyer (ed.), *The future of assessment: Shaping teaching and learning.* New York: Erlbaum, pp. 3–6.

Green, S., and M. Brown. 2006. Promoting action research and problem solving among teacher candidates: One elementary school's journey. *Action in Teacher Education* 27 (4): 45–54.

Green, S., R. Johnson, D. Kim, and N. Pope. 2007. Ethics in classroom assessment practices: Issues and attitudes. *Teaching and Teacher Education* 23: 999–1011.

Haladyna, T. M., S. B. Nolen, and N. S. Haas. 1991. Raising standardized achievement test scores and the origins of test score pollution. *Educational Researcher* 20: 2–7.

Lee, J. March, 2008. War on achievement gaps: Redrawing racial and social maps of school learning. Raymond B. Cattell Early Career Award Lecture presented at the meeting of the American Educational Research Association Meeting, New York.

Moon, T. 2005. The role of assessment in differentiation. *Theory into Practice* 44 (3): 226–233.

O'Keefe, P. A., A. Ben-Eliyahu, and L. Linnenbrink-Garcia, March, 2008. Effects of a mastery learning environment on achievement goals, interest, and the self: A multiphase study. Paper presented at the annual meeting of the American Educational Research Association, New York.

Pelligrino, J. W., N. Chudowsky, and R. Glaser. 2001. *Knowing what students know: The science and design of educational assessment.* Washington, DC: National Academy Press.

Poplin, M., and J. Rivera. 2005. Merging social justice and accountability: Educating qualified and effective teachers. *Theory into Practice* 44 (1): 27–37.

Salmon, A. K. 2008. Promoting a culture of thinking in the young child. *Early Childhood Education Journal* 35: 457–461.

Shepard, L. A. 2008. Formative assessment: Caveat Emptor. In C.A. Dwyer. 2008. *The future of assessment: Shaping teaching and learning.* New York: Lawrence Erlbaum Associates, 279–303.

Shute, V. J., 2008. Focus on formative feedback. *Review of Educational Research* 78: 153–189.

Stiggins, R. 2007. Assessment through the student's eyes. *Educational Leadership* 64 (8): 22–26.

Stiggins, R., and J. Chappuis. 2005. Using student-involved classroom assessment to close achievement gaps. *Theory into Practice* 44 (1): 11–18.

Tomlinson, C. 2008. Learning to love assessment. *Educational Leadership* 65 (4): 8–13.

Urdan, T., and Schoenfelder, E. (2006). Classroom effects on student motivation: Goal structures, social relationships, and competence beliefs. *Journal of School Psychology* 44: 331–349.

Witkow, M. R., and A. J. Fuligni. 2007. Achievement goals and daily school experiences among adolescents with Asian, Latino, and European American backgrounds. *Journal of Educational Psychology* 99: 584–596.

CHAPTER 2

LEARNING GOALS:
THE FIRST STEP

Begin with the end in mind.

–Stephen Covey

❖ **Chapter Learning Goals**

At the conclusion of this chapter, the reader should be able to do the following:

- Describe learning goals and their importance.
- Develop a planning chart to align learning goals, instruction, and assessment.
- Locate resources that outline key subject-area content and strategies.

- Set priorities in the selection of learning goals to address in instruction.
- Use taxonomies as an aid in writing and revising learning goals.
- Construct a table of specifications for planning instruction and assessment.

✦ INTRODUCTION

As a teacher you have the awesome responsibility to chart a course of learning that will prepare the students in your class to be productive citizens in our society. As you prepare for the school year, you will establish broad goals your students should achieve. For example, suppose you want your students to be able to comprehend, interpret, analyze, and evaluate what they read. You set these goals mentally and perhaps commit them to paper. In planning a unit or a lesson, you realize that for the goals to be helpful they must be stated more specifically. For example, *to comprehend* means what? Your reading goal now becomes more tangible, possibly including the ability of students to summarize and paraphrase texts, draw conclusions, make predictions, analyze cause and effect, or interpret figurative expressions.

Clear statements of the aims you have in mind will assist you in systematically addressing the key understanding and skills your students should know and be able to do. Without such learning goals, instruction may be a hit-or-miss approach that will address some key points, but neglect others.

✦ DEFINING AND USING LEARNING GOALS

Learning Goals
Learning objectives, targets, and outcomes.

Learning goals are referred to with many terms, such as learning outcomes, objectives, aims, and targets. Some educators make a distinction between broad learning goals for a unit, and narrower learning objectives for specific lessons. What these terms all have in common is that they specify what students should learn as the result of classroom experiences such as instructional lessons and units. We refer to these statements of instructional intent as learning goals.

Learning goals consist of a verb and a noun phrase. The verb specifies the type of response students will exhibit to show they have achieved a goal. For example, a learning goal in language arts might require that a student

explain the figurative use of words in context
Verb (Response)
Student must explain
(translate the meaning) of . . .
Noun Phrase (Content)
Figures of speech (e.g., metaphor,
simile, hyperbole, personification)
within a text.

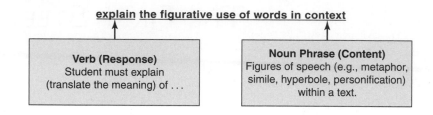

Frequently, the verb reflects the cognitive process (e.g., recalling, classifying, critiquing) that is the intended learning outcome. The noun phrase refers to the subject-area content that students should learn. In our example, then, as teachers plan instruction and assessment, they focus on students recognizing figurative expressions and using the context of the narrative to interpret the meaning of such expressions. Examples of learning goals from mathematics, social studies, and science are shown in Table 2.1. Notice that the goals use the verb/noun structure described.

You may be wondering why we include a discussion of learning goals in a book on assessment. Learning goals allow you to start a unit and each lesson with a clear understanding of what you ultimately want to achieve in your instruction. As you plan instruction, you need a fairly concrete mental image of the learning you want students to accomplish. As Figure 2.1 shows, the learning goals provide a guide for teachers as they plan learning experiences and prepare the student assessment. The learning goals clarify what students will do to demonstrate their learning. To continue our example,

TABLE 2.1

Examples of Learning Goals in Various Subject Areas

	Structure of Learning Goals		
Subject Area	**Grade**	**Verb**	**Noun Phrase**
Social Studies	K	Compare . . .	. . . the daily lives of children and their families in the United States in the past with the daily lives of children and their families today (South Carolina Department of Education [SCDE], 2005b, p. 7).
Mathematics	6	Organize . . .	. . . data in frequency tables, histograms, or stem-and-leaf plots (SCDE, 2007, p. 53).
Science	HS	Balance . . .	. . . chemical equations for simple synthesis, decomposition, single replacement, double replacement, and combustion reactions (SCDE, 2005a, p. 80).

State the learning goal and define it in terms of student performance.
Provide a variety of learning experiences directed toward the learning goal.
Assess student achievement of the learning goal using a variety of assessment methods.

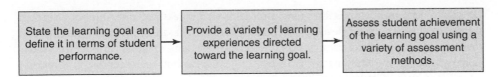

FIGURE 2.1 ***Alignment of Learning Outcomes, Instruction, and Assessment***

Adapted from Gronlund & Brookhart, 2009, p. 7. Reprinted with permission.

a learning goal that states that students *will explain the figurative use of words in context* requires a teacher to develop a lesson or unit that involves the class in the interpretation of figurative expressions the students find in their readings. Then the assessment would similarly require students to analyze figurative language within the context of new readings, such as stories or a poem.

Using learning goals as a starting point is the key to **alignment** in the instructional process. Alignment occurs when elements that are interrelated (i.e., learning goals, instruction, and assessment) are positioned so that the elements perform properly. Aligning your instruction and your assessment with your learning goals ensures that instruction addresses the content and strategies that you want students to learn. It also ensures that students are properly assessed on that specific content.

Alignment
The congruence of one element or object in relation to others.

A planning chart offers a teacher further support for alignment of goals, instruction, and assessment (Gronlund & Brookhart, 2009). As illustrated in Table 2.2, a planning chart sketches out the learning experiences a teacher might use to develop a lesson or unit on a topic, such as figurative language. The focus of this lesson is the learning goal related to interpretation of metaphors. Notice that the activities in the Teaching Methods column both follow from the learning goal and prepare students for assessment tasks showing they have accomplished the learning goal.

Misalignment occurs when instruction or assessment tasks are not congruent with learning goals. In our example, misalignment would occur if we haven't prepared students with learning experiences to meet the goal. It would also occur if we required students to write poems in which they use figurative expressions as the assessment. Instructionally we have only prepared students to *interpret* figurative expressions. Similarly, we have misalignment if an assessment requires students only to list and define the types of figurative expressions. In this instance, we could not determine whether students can use context to understand the meaning of figurative expressions encountered in their readings.

Misalignment
The lack of congruence of learning goals, instructions, and/or assessment.

TABLE 2.2

Planning Chart to Align Teaching and Assessment Tasks with the Learning Goals

Learning Goal	Teaching Methods/Learning Experiences	Assessment Tasks
Interpret devices of figurative language such as similes, metaphors, and hyperbole.	Read Carl Sandburg's "Fog" and other poems that use metaphor. Discuss the meaning of the metaphors. Break into small groups and read examples of metaphors and discuss meaning. Report back to the full class the examples the group found and the meaning of the examples.	Determine whether students can highlight and interpret new instances of metaphors in poems.

We have noticed misalignment problems in the lessons and units our teacher candidates design. They develop interesting ideas for lessons and units (e.g., a zoo unit or a lesson incorporating cooking), but these lessons or units do not necessarily relate clearly to the learning goals in the subject area they are teaching. If a teacher spends the bulk of instructional time making cookies for a lesson with a learning goal related to understanding fractions, the students will learn more about baking cookies than about fractions. The teacher's instructional activities were not aligned with the learning goals. Students learn what they spend their time attending to or doing. For alignment of learning goals, instruction, and assessment, you must make sure your instruction and your assessment guide students to attend to the content of the learning goals.

A lesson about learning goals comes to us from an article about integrating video games into instruction (Sandford et al., 2007). As might be expected, the authors learned that video games were not a panacea for generating student interest and boosting achievement. They discovered that the teachers who had the most success integrating the games into instruction were those who had clear learning goals in mind and thought of specific ways they could use these games to reach those goals. Teachers without clear goals were not able to capitalize on the games or plan ways to use them to further specific kinds of learning needed. These findings illustrate that learning goals are the touchstone for your instruction and assessment.

Backward Design

Backward Design

A process of planning in which a teacher identifies the learning goals and the forms of evidence (assessment) that would indicate a student has attained the learning goals. Instruction is then planned to address the knowledge and skills addressed in the goals and assessment.

Wiggins and McTighe (1998) also zero in on the importance of alignment by offering a slightly different approach for planning unit lessons. In their **backward design** process, the learning goals are identified first (see Figure 2.2). These authors, however, remind us that those learning goals are the desired *end results*. The learning goal expresses what student outcome is desired. Thus, as Stephen Covey (1989) states, you "begin with the end in mind."

In the backward design process, the middle stage differs from our typical thoughts about planning a lesson or unit. Instead of designing instruction in this stage, the teacher identifies the forms of *evidence* (performances or other assessment results) that would indicate a student has attained the desired knowledge, skills, or strategies. At this stage the teacher asks, "How will we know if students have achieved the desired results and met the standards?" (Wiggins & McTighe, 1998). Here the authors are advising us that in the planning stages we should ask ourselves how we will determine whether students have accomplished the learning goals. Thus, if we consider interpreting figurative language a critical understanding for students, how will we know students have mastered this goal? Will students read poems and speeches that employ figurative language and write brief interpretations of the meaning of the materials?

After specifying these learning outcomes, the final stage involves planning instruction to prepare students to meet the learning goal, such as interpreting figurative language.

Identify desired results.
Determine acceptable evidence.
Plan learning experiences and instruction.

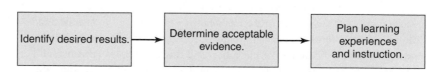

FIGURE 2.2 ***Sequence for Planning Using Backward Design Process***

Wiggins & McTighe, 1998, p. 9. Reprinted with permission.

TABLE 2.3

Questions That Assist in Planning Instruction to Address Learning Goals

Key Questions	Answers to Key Questions
What enabling knowledge (facts, concepts, and principles) and skills (procedures) will students need to achieve desired results?	Understanding and skills required for learning goal mastery: Describe how racism and intolerance contributed to the Holocaust. Locate information using both primary and secondary sources. Determine the credibility and bias of primary and secondary sources. (Arizona Department of Education, 2006)
What activities will equip students with the needed knowledge and skills?	Small group work inspecting primary sources to examine the prejudice associated with the Holocaust.
What will need to be taught and coached, and how should it best be taught, in light of performance goals?	Concepts of racism, intolerance. Use of primary sources to infer social conditions. Types of bias in primary sources.
What materials and resources are best suited to accomplish these goals?	Photocopies of primary sources. Website of the United States Holocaust Memorial Museum.
Is the overall design coherent and effective?	Varied range of instructional and assessment activities provide opportunity to master the learning goals.

Wiggins and McTighe suggest that planning for instruction should focus on the questions in Table 2.3.

The table provides an example based on a learning outcome related to the Holocaust in which the end goal is *Students will use primary sources to reconstruct the experiences of persecuted groups.* In the right-hand column are the answers to the key questions as they apply to the learning goal related to the Holocaust. In answering each of the key questions, you can plan instruction to help students achieve the desired outcomes.

✦ BENEFITS OF SPECIFYING LEARNING GOALS

Clear statements of learning goals provide the potential to guide student learning, especially if you share the goals with students. Such a practice is consistent with the principle that producing a well-informed citizenry requires cultivating students to begin to take responsibility for their own learning in school and beyond. Sharing learning goals provides students with guideposts in the learning process (Guskey, 1997). One school district with which we work has a policy that each day teachers list the learning goals on the board and review them with students at the beginning of class. This practice reflects the importance of students understanding learning goals.

Sharing learning goals with students also offers them criteria to develop a clear conception of quality performance (Gronlund & Brookhart, 2009). Students can start using the learning goals to self-assess and become more independent in their learning. To foster this, learning goals should be the source of the criteria that you use for evaluating performance. Figuring out how to score an assignment can create uncertainty for a teacher. For example, if students develop a presentation, how should points be allocated? The learning goals are the best source for criteria for scoring students' performances. As shown in Table 2.4, a set of communications learning goals can lead directly to criteria that would be included in a checklist (see Table 2.5) to evaluate students' communication skills.

TABLE 2.4

Content Standards for Communication Skills

Communication Goal (C)	The student will recognize, demonstrate, and analyze the qualities of effective communication.
7-C1	The student will use speaking skills to participate in large and small groups in both formal and informal situations.
7-C1.1	Demonstrate the ability to face an audience, make eye contact, use the appropriate voice level, use appropriate gestures, facial expressions, and posture when making oral presentations.
7-C1.2	Demonstrate the ability to use language, vocabulary, and presentation techniques appropriate for the purpose and audience. (SCDE, 2003a, p. 60)

From South Carolina Department of Education. 2003a. *South Carolina English language arts curriculum standards 2002.* http://ed.sc.gov/agency/offices/cso/standards/ela/.

TABLE 2.5

Example of a Checklist Based on Learning Goals for Communication Standards

Student: Hassan Brown		Date: June 10, 2011
✓	Criteria	Comments
✓	Faces the audience.	
✓	Makes eye contact.	
	Uses appropriate gestures.	
✓	Uses appropriate facial expressions.	
✓	Uses appropriate posture.	
✓	Uses language and vocabulary appropriate for the purpose and audience.	
	Uses visual aids, such as props and technology, to support his meaning.	
✓	Expresses ideas orally with fluency.	
	Expresses ideas orally with confidence.	
✓	Uses effective organizational strategies in oral presentations.	

Criteria	Tally Marks	Percentage Mastery
Faces the audience.	ⅢⅢ ⅢⅢ ⅢⅢ ⅢⅢ	100%
Makes eye contact.	ⅢⅢ ⅢⅢ ⅢⅢ ⅢⅢ	100%
Uses appropriate gestures.	ⅢⅢ ⅢⅢ	50%
Uses appropriate facial expressions.	ⅢⅢ ⅢⅢ ⅢⅢ ⅢⅢ	100%
Uses appropriate posture.	ⅢⅢ ⅢⅢ ⅢⅢ ⅢⅢ	100%
Uses language and vocabulary appropriate for the purpose and audience.	ⅢⅢ ⅢⅢ ⅢⅢ ⅢⅢ	100%
Uses visual aids, such as props and technology, to support his meaning.	ⅢⅢ ⅢⅢ ‖	60%
Expresses ideas orally with fluency.	ⅢⅢ ⅢⅢ ‖‖	70%
Expresses ideas orally with confidence.	ⅢⅢ ⅢⅢ ⅢⅢ	75%
Uses effective organizational strategies in oral presentations.	ⅢⅢ ⅢⅢ ⅢⅢ ⅢⅢ	100%

FIGURE 2.3   *Class Summary for Learning Goals Related to Communications*

In addition, if a teacher notes which students mastered the skills and which have not, that information can point to strengths and weaknesses of instruction and guide plans for further instruction. Figure 2.3 shows the results of a teacher using tally marks to record the number of students who demonstrated achievement of each learning goal. The right-hand column shows the percentage of students who mastered each topic. In the case of the goal *faces the audience,* 100% of the students achieved this skill. In contrast, only 10 of the 20 students appropriately use gestures. Thus, when students are preparing for a subsequent speech, the teacher may want to offer more examples and provide students time to practice using gestures. We expand on the use of class summary data in Chapter 5.

✦ WHERE DO LEARNING GOALS COME FROM?

Many resources are available for teachers in developing learning goals. In planning a unit and developing its learning goals, you will review state and national content standards for the subject area, your district curriculum guides, and the teacher edition of the textbook.

State and National Content Standards

A key source for learning goals is your state content standards for each subject area. Content standards are skills, strategies, and bodies of knowledge that students should learn. Some educators consider the phrase *content standards* to be interchangeable with learning goals, curricular goals, instructional objectives, or curriculum standards (Anderson & Krathwohl, 2001; Popham 2003). Examples of content standards for various content areas are shown in Table 2.6.

Identification of the subject matter to be included in content standards is accomplished by convening committees that include teachers in the content area, curriculum

TABLE 2.6

State Content Standards for Various Grade Levels and Subject Areas

Grade Level	Subject Area	Standard	State
K	English Language Arts: Reading	Identify the front cover, back cover, and title page of a book.	California (2006)
1	Mathematics	Use patterns to skip count by twos, fives, and tens.	Texas (2006)
2	Social Studies: Economics	Give examples of people in the school and community who are both producers and consumers.	Massachusetts (2003)
3	Science	Describe several functions of bones: support, protection, and locomotion.	North Carolina (2004)
4	Theatre	Adapt a classroom dramatization to reflect a particular historical period or culture.	South Carolina (2003b)
5	Physical Education	Analyze fitness data to describe and improve personal fitness levels (e.g., apply data to own plan for improvement in at least two components of health-related fitness).	Virginia (2001)
6	Technology	Use a computer system to connect to and access needed information from various Internet sites.	New York (1996)
7	Visual Arts	Apply the principles of design to interpret various masterworks of art.	New Jersey (2004)
8	Foreign Language	Comprehend and interpret the main ideas and details from television, movies, videos, radio, or live presentations produced in the target language.	Florida (2005)
9	English Language Arts: Writing	Establish a clear, distinctive, and coherent thesis or perspective and maintain a consistent tone and focus throughout.	Georgia (2006)
10	English Language Arts: Literature	Evaluate relationships between and among character, plot, setting, theme, conflict and resolution and their influence on the effectiveness of a literary piece.[1]	Illinois (1997)
11	Social Studies: History	Compare and evaluate competing historical narratives, analyze multiple perspectives, and challenge arguments of historical inevitability.[1]	Washington (n.d.)[2]
12	Music	Explain how music reflects the social events of history.	Ohio (2003)

[1]High school standards
[2]Office of the Superintendent of Public Instruction (n.d.)

specialists, politicians, and educational policy makers (e.g., International Reading Association [IRA] & National Council of Teachers of English [NCTE], 1996; National Council of Teachers of Mathematics [NCTM], 2000). This process occurs at the national and state levels. Typically, the development of national content standards precedes the development of state standards; subsequently, the national standards inform the work on state-level content standards.

Content standards do not always translate directly into learning goals. Instead, they sometimes describe competencies at a general level that requires further definition of the instructional goal. In Table 2.4, for example, the communications goal is specified at a very general level: *The student will recognize, demonstrate, and analyze the qualities of effective communication.* Often standards are accompanied by indicators or benchmarks that clarify the outcome stated in the standard. One learning outcome associated with the communication goal is *Demonstrate the ability to face an audience, make eye contact, use the appropriate voice level, use appropriate gestures, facial expressions, and posture when making oral presentations.* Such a statement does have clear implications for instruction and assessment.

District Curriculum Guides

Another resource for teachers in developing learning goals is your district curriculum guide for each subject area. Generally, the district guides are based on state-level content standards. However, the learning goals in district curriculum guides are typically more specific in their description of student outcomes than are state content standards. Often in the development of curriculum guides, teachers in the same content area or grade level work together to clearly define the goals for their students.

Teacher Editions

Learning goals are also found in the teacher editions of textbooks used in the classroom. These learning goals may serve as examples of the strategies and content knowledge expressed in the state standards and district curriculum guides.

As a teacher, you should not rely solely on the learning goals in teachers' manuals. They may not address the key content identified in your state content standards and district curriculum materials. The state and district content standards describe the skills and concepts that your students will experience in the state test. As a teacher, your responsibility to the student is to develop the knowledge, skills, and strategies outlined in state and district content standards. Only then will your students have equal access to educational experiences that prepare them to meet the challenges they will face on the state test and in life beyond the classroom.

Some teachers take this responsibility to mean they cannot go beyond the content standards in the state and district documents and expose their students to other important ideas, but this is not true. The concepts, skills, and strategies in the content standards should be *central* to the learning experiences you plan. But teachers often go beyond these to introduce students to other important ideas. For example, teaching students to integrate figurative expressions into their writing would be an appropriate extension of the goal of interpreting figurative language.

✦ Too Many Learning Goals, Too Little Time: Selecting Learning Goals

Popham (2003, 2006) notes that in any given subject area, teachers are faced with more learning goals than can be covered in a year. A teacher has to make decisions about which should be the focus of instruction. In developing the learning goals, you should understand that selection of these goals involves sampling from all possible learning outcomes. The selection process, then, should seek a representative sample of learning goals. For example, review the following brief list of some possible learning goals for figurative expressions:

1. Demonstrates knowledge of the meaning of terms used to describe types of figurative language.
2. Identifies figurative expressions in a text.
3. Comprehends the meaning of figurative expressions using context.
4. Incorporates figurative language into writing.

An English language arts teacher would quickly be overwhelmed given a similar list of learning goals for every new concept—central idea, cause and effect, fact and opinion, drawing conclusions, making predictions. So, in thinking about the learning goals that are appropriate for your class, you need to select those of most importance to your students.

Given the need to sample learning goals, how does one select which should be addressed? Wiggins and McTighe (1998) offer us a series of filters to guide the selection of learning goals (see Table 2.7).

The first filter notes that in selecting learning goals, we should focus on the big ideas. For example, in reading, a critical strategy is for students to identify the main idea of a text and the details that support the central idea. Such a skill is important in reading across narrative and expository texts and across subject areas. As shown in

TABLE 2.7

Filters to Aid in the Identification of Key Learning Goals

Filter	Description	Example
To what extent does the idea, topic, or process represent a "big idea" having enduring value beyond the classroom?	Enduring understanding focuses on the larger concepts, principles, and processes within a field.	Importance of understanding graphic representation of data.
To what extent does the idea, topic, or process reside at the heart of the discipline?	Enduring understanding involves students in applying the knowledge, skills, and procedures used by professionals in their fields.	Summarizing data reveals patterns and trends across a variety of content areas.
To what extent does the idea, topic, or process require uncoverage?	Enduring understanding requires assisting students in uncovering abstract ideas, counterintuitive ideas, and misconceptions.	Students do not realize that graphs can be manipulated to deceive the reader.
To what extent does the idea, topic, or process offer potential for engaging students?	Enduring understanding should provoke and connect to students' interests.	Use bar graphs to document the number of biographies in the school media center that portray each ethnic group.

Adapted from Wiggins, G., and J. McTighe. 1998. *Understanding by design.* Alexandria, VA: Association for Supervision and Curriculum Development. Used with permission.

Table 2.7, in mathematics and social studies a critical skill is for students to be able to interpret graphic representations of data and to summarize data graphically.

The second filter addresses the degree to which the new idea or strategy is central to the discipline. For students of history, reviewing and interpreting primary sources is a process central to historical inquiry (VanSledright, 2004). Thus, this second filter would suggest that students' time would be well spent working in small groups to review journal entries, political cartoons, and advertisements for a historical period. Making meaning from these documents models for students the process that historians engage in as they research historical periods.

The third filter focuses on the need for instruction to uncover key ideas because of the abstract quality of the new concepts, common misperceptions of students, or counterintuitive quality of the new principles. For example, students are familiar with mixing red and blue paint to develop the color purple. This knowledge, however, may contribute to student misperceptions about the formation of white light. Thus, in physics, a demonstration may be a useful method to assist students in the counterintuitive understanding that white light is formed by the overlap of red, green, and blue light. Similarly, in foreign languages the demands of learning irregular verbs that do not follow standard rules of conjugation may require special attention, with well-articulated learning goals to address this challenging area.

The fourth filter relates to the potential for the concepts to engage students. Wiggins and McTighe (1998) note that seemingly dry ideas can be more appealing if the learning activities engage students and relate to their interests. They note that big ideas may connect for students if presented as questions, issues, simulations, or debates. For example, *Wrinkle in Time* by Madeleine L'Engle (1962) is a science fiction book about a group of children who travel through a wrinkle in time to a planet where the father of two of the children is held prisoner. On arriving at the planet, the children find a society in which everyone does everything at the same time, in the same way. All children bounce balls in rhythm and skip rope in rhythm. The book was quite challenging for the fifth graders we taught; however, we personalized the book by exploring the theme of conformity. To engage students, we promoted discussion with questions such as, "Do we in America prize people who are different, or do we try to make everyone conform?" Students became more interested as they related the book to current issues about conformity that they, themselves, were encountering.

Integrating learning goals across subject areas may also promote student engagement. Consider, for example, the integration of social studies and dramatization in theater. Students may not be interested in learning the characteristics of specific historical periods during social studies; however, incorporating such information into a dramatization might promote student engagement.

✦ How Do I Write Good Learning Goals?

The learning goals you find in state standards and district curriculum guides will not all be expressed in a way that makes specific the knowledge and strategies students need to learn. In revising available goals, or in writing a new learning goal, you should select the appropriate verb and noun phrase.

Selecting the Verb

Begin the learning goal with an action verb. The selection of the verb is a crucial step in developing learning goals. The verb you select specifies the type of response students will exhibit to show achievement of the learning goal. Revisit Table 2.1 and look at the verbs and how each implies the way students will demonstrate achievement. Building on the idea of alignment of goals, instruction, and assessment, a verb should be selected consistent with instructional intent. For example, if during a lesson on figurative expressions, instruction focuses on matching expressions with their actual meaning, the relevant verb is *matching*. However, if you intend for students to learn to use the context of a story to explain the figurative use of words, the relevant verb is *explaining* or *translating*.

To continue our example of data representation in graphs (Table 2.7), the instructional intent might be for students to *interpret* tables and graphs or to *summarize* data in tables and graphs. The choice of verbs has implications for student learning experiences. In the case of interpreting tables and graphs, students will require practice in reviewing graphics and making statements based on the data. In the instance of summarizing data, students will need instruction and practice in compiling data and representing the information in tables and graphs.

Writing the Noun Phrase

Following the verb is a noun phrase describing the relevant content. This leads us back to the content standards developed at national and state levels. Important understanding and skills in each subject area are identified in these documents. Refer back to the examples shown in Table 2.6. These learning goals identify the important subject-area content for students, and they describe how the students should be able to use the information. Look at the standard for theater in fourth grade. Can you begin to imagine a lesson that would prepare students to meet this goal? Would the lesson include identifying cultural aspects of a historical period? Would you teach students to consider such cultural aspects as types of shelter, food, and clothing? Students will need practice in locating information about the historical period. Students also need experience using the information in an adaptation of a dramatization. Only then will they be prepared for demonstrating they have met the learning goal through an assessment.

Specificity of Learning Goals

One important element to consider as you write learning goals is specificity. In developing learning goals for a lesson, you want them specific enough to establish in your mind what learning experiences are necessary for students and for the content of the assessment. The learning goals should also clearly communicate to students what they will be learning. The fourth-grade reading goals in Table 2.8 demonstrate several levels of specificity for learning goals. The most general level, Reading Goal (R), indicates

TABLE 2.8

Three Levels of Learning Goals in Reading

Reading Goal (R)   The student will draw upon a variety of strategies to comprehend, interpret, analyze, and evaluate what he or she reads.

    4-R2   The student will use knowledge of the purposes, structures, and elements of writing to analyze and interpret various types of texts.

        4-R2.6 Demonstrate the ability to identify devices of figurative language such as similes, metaphors, and hyperbole and sound devices such as alliteration and onomatopoeia. (SCDE, 2003a, p. 35)

South Carolina Department of Education. 2003a. *South Carolina English language arts curriculum standards 2002.* http://ed.sc.gov/agency/offices/cso/standards/ela/

that students will use various strategies to comprehend, interpret, analyze, and evaluate text. Such a statement is useful in thinking about outcomes of student learning over a school year. However, for the teacher, this broad statement is not helpful in planning a unit or a lesson plan. The next level (4-R2) focuses on "knowledge of the purposes, structures, and elements of writing," but does not guide us about the meaning of "purposes, structures, and elements of writing." At the third level (4-R2.6), we find that one area in which we should develop student understanding is figurative language such as similes, metaphors, and hyperbole. At this level of specificity, the implications for instruction are clear. So as you review the learning goals in state standards or district curriculum guides, select learning goals that provide enough specificity for you to understand the implications for planning instruction.

Simplifying Learning Goals

On occasion you will need to simplify a content standard or indicator for it to be useful in planning instruction and assessment. You can break indicators into their elements to simplify them. The communications indicator *Demonstrate the ability to face an audience, make eye contact, use the appropriate voice level, use appropriate gestures, facial expressions, and posture when making oral presentations* (see Table 2.4) is specific, but multifaceted. The learning goals that you develop from this indicator would be based on its elements. For example, you might decide that one lesson and assessment should focus only on students learning to face an audience and make eye contact. Notice each of these elements is listed separately in the assessment checklist in Table 2.5.

Student Input to Learning Goals

Consider refining the learning goals with students. After describing the state or district standards associated with your unit, you can ask students to put the learning goals in their own words. You can revise the goals to reflect student language and, thus, promote student understanding. For example, in Jo Ellen Hertel's middle-school computer class, she provides students before each unit with the state learning goals for the unit, reworded into student-friendly language (see Figure 2.4). She and her students discuss all the skills they will learn. Then the students write additional personal goals for that unit that focus on elements of most interest to them. She reports that this process helps focus students' attention and gets them involved.

→ LEARNING GOALS, CRITICAL THINKING SKILLS, AND TAXONOMIES

Learning goals direct everything, so that is where you need to begin in the task of promoting critical thinking skills. As we have explained, these higher-level skills are important for optimal participation in a democratic society. Several authors have devised **taxonomies,** or classification frameworks, that detail thinking strategies important to develop in our students. These taxonomies help teachers consider from several angles what should be the focus of a lesson or unit.

Taxonomy
A classification framework.

Cognitive Taxonomies

Frameworks that can help you in thinking about the skills and strategies that are important for students to learn include Bloom's cognitive taxonomy (1956); Anderson and Krathwohl's revised Bloom's taxonomy (2001); Gagné's framework (1985); Marzano's new taxonomy (2001); or Quellmalz's reading taxonomy (1985). These frameworks share in

January

Database Unit of Instruction

As a result of this unit, I will . . .

Understand key vocabulary terms, including:

database	electronic database	print database	relational database	record
field	file	criteria	entry	filter
operators	inequalities	form view	list view	report
sort	ascending	descending		

I will . . . Recognize how and why databases are used to collect, organize, and analyze information

I will . . . Understand how to plan and develop a database report

I will . . . Understand how to manipulate a database using edit/find, sorting, and filter/search

Personal Learning Goals: During this unit, I will . . .

_____

_____

_____

_____

FIGURE 2.4   *Learning Goals Written in Student-Friendly Language with Space for Related Personal Goals*

Cognitive Domain

Processes related to thinking and learning.

common a focus on skills in the **cognitive domain** that you should incorporate into learning goals. In this section we have chosen two commonly used cognitive taxonomies—Bloom's taxonomy and the revised Bloom's taxonomy—to show you how such taxonomies can assist you.

Bloom's Cognitive Taxonomy

First published in 1956, Benjamin Bloom's taxonomy has been around the longest. This taxonomy lists six categories of thinking skills (Table 2.9). The cognitive category of "knowledge" requires only that students recall information, such as the definition of metaphor; whereas "comprehension" requires they demonstrate an understanding of material, such as inferring the meaning of a metaphor. "Application" involves the use of rules in solving a problem, such as using the characteristics of metaphors to complete a figurative expression. "Analysis" involves separating material into its components, as a student might do to classify figurative usage as a metaphor, simile, or hyperbole. "Synthesis" occurs when a student combines elements to form a new pattern or structure, as would be the case if a student wrote a poem that incorporates figurative

TABLE 2.9

A Continuum with Bloom's Cognitive Categories and Examples of Learning Goals

Cognitive Categories	Knowledge—the recall of specifics, universals, methods, processes, patterns, structures, or settings.	Comprehension—the understanding of the meaning and intent of material.	Application—the use of abstractions, such as rules, in particular situations.	Analysis—the separation of material into its elements in such a way that the relationships between the elements are made evident.	Synthesis—the combining of elements to form a pattern or structure that was not evident previously.	Evaluation—the judgment of the degree that materials satisfy criteria.
Verbs for Learning Goals	define, identify, label, list, locate, match, name, recall, recognize, remember, repeat, select, state, tell, underline	categorize, change, classify, conclude, convert, describe, dramatize, draw, explain, extend, infer, interpret, outline, paraphrase, predict, rephrase, restate, retell, summarize, translate, transform	apply, arrange, complete, compute, demonstrate, generalize, operate, organize, predict, solve, use	analyze, associate, break down, categorize, classify, compare, contrast, debate, diagram, differentiate, discriminate, dissect, distinguish, group, investigate, outline, relate, separate, subdivide	assemble, build, combine, compose, construct, create, design, devise, formulate, hypothesize, invent, plan, produce, propose, write	appraise, argue, assess, conclude, critique, debate, defend, dispute, evaluate, judge, justify, prioritize, rate, recommend, revise, support, validate
Examples of Learning Goals	Define metaphor, simile, and hyperbole.	Explain the meaning of the following metaphor.	Complete the following statement as a simile.	Indicate which of the following statements are metaphors, similes, and hyperboles.	Use metaphor to write a poem modeled after Sandburg's poem "Fog."	Read the following poem and identify the various forms of figurative language and the effectiveness of the author's usage.

Based on Bloom et al., 1956; Gronlund, 2003; Metfessel, Michael, and Kirsner, 1969.

47

language. "Evaluation" occurs when a student determines whether the materials meet relevant criteria, as in critiquing the use of figurative language in a poem.

Because we present each cognitive strategy in its own category, you might assume that the different cognitive skills do not overlap. This is a common misconception. If students develop the research design for an experiment (synthesis), they must remember the meaning of subject-specific terms (knowledge), apply their understanding of research designs in general to the specifics of the study (application), and evaluate drafts of the design as they finalize the product (evaluation). Higher-level cognitive processes automatically require students to use several other thinking skills in achieving the learning goal. Thus, your learning goals need not state every cognitive process. Instead, the thinking skills associated with the focus of the particular lesson should be the only ones stated.

Although we learned about Bloom's taxonomy in college, it took years of experience in schools to appreciate it as a valuable tool in planning for instruction and assessment. A taxonomy like Bloom's allows you to focus on the possible kinds of learning you want for your students. An array of choices helps you move beyond the basic facts that so often get the attention in classrooms. For example, in history classes, when we studied wars, we always seemed to focus on memorizing battles and dates—definitely a knowledge-level focus. Using a thinking skills taxonomy to get past that, you can build learning goals requiring other kinds of cognitive skills. How about comparing and contrasting different elements of the cultures of the two sides that might have led to war (analysis)? How about applying the lessons learned from this war to examine the later foreign policy of that nation (application)? Knowing the array of possible thinking skills helps you think outside the box of knowledge-level learning goals.

When your learning goals become more complex and interesting, your instruction and assessment must follow. As we have already mentioned, alignment among learning goals, instruction, and assessment is the key to making sure students learn what they need to learn. So, the other important function of a taxonomy is assisting with alignment. For example, if you have learning goals that require students to compare elements of the cultures on two sides of a war, you must be sure that you include classroom activities involving learning about the cultures as well as practicing the skills of comparison and contrast. You can't just give lectures every day—you must involve the students in practicing the skills they need to be able to demonstrate. In addition, you must design your assessment to include these higher skills. As you will see in Chapter 4, you can design really good questions that tap key elements of your learning goals using verbs associated with Bloom's taxonomy. Your assessment and your instruction must mirror the skills and knowledge in the learning goals, and a taxonomy of thinking skills helps you maintain that focus.

Here's another example. If you have a learning goal stating that students must be able to apply their knowledge of multiplication to finding the area of different spaces, you must go beyond instructional activities such as having them memorize their multiplication tables. Memorizing multiplication tables is at the knowledge level of Bloom's taxonomy. Finding area includes knowledge of multiplication tables, but it goes beyond that to also require students to apply their multiplication knowledge to a different task. For learning goals, instruction, and assessment to be aligned, each of them must address the same levels of the taxonomy. In the case of finding area, the learning goal, the instruction, and the assessment must all address the application level. Having the skills readily available to consult in the taxonomy allows you to check alignment.

Revised Bloom's Taxonomy

The revised Bloom's taxonomy is shown in Table 2.10, illustrated with learning goals from a poetry unit. We have included it because some states require standards to be based on this taxonomy. Notice that the cognitive process dimension across the top of

TABLE 2.10

Revised Bloom's Taxonomy with Examples of Learning Goals in Poetry

	Cognitive Process Dimension					
Type of Knowledge Dimension	Remember—retrieve knowledge from memory.	Understand—construct meaning from communications.	Apply—implement a procedure in a given situation.	Analyze—break material into its parts and determine how parts relate to one another and an overall structure.	Evaluate—make judgments based on criteria.	Create—bring elements together to form a new pattern or structure.
A. Factual Knowledge—of basic elements associated with a discipline.	Recall forms of poetry and definitions. (10%) Recall origins of forms of poetry. (5%)					
B. Conceptual Knowledge—of interrelationships among the basic elements within more complex structures.		Interpret the meaning of poems. (20%)		Analyze elements of poems to identify the forms. (20%)		
C. Procedural Knowledge—of how to do something: skills, methods, techniques used to do something and criteria for such and when to use such.			Apply elements of a specific form of poetry to complete a poem. (10%)			Write poems with appropriate stylistic elements. (25%)
D. Meta-Cognitive Knowledge—of how to use cognition and self-awareness of one's own cognition.					Discuss in an authors' conference the strengths and areas for improvement of poems she/he wrote. (10%)	

Adapted from *A Taxonomy for Learning, Teaching, and Assessing,* by Anderson, L., and D. Krathwohl (eds.). Published by Allyn and Bacon, Boston, MA. Copyright 2001. Used with permission.

the revised taxonomy covers the same thinking skills as were in the original taxonomy. However, the thinking skills are now all expressed as verbs rather than nouns (e.g., "analyze" instead of "analysis"). The use of verbs emphasizes what the student is expected to be able to do. Also, "create" (formerly "synthesis") is now at the highest level of the taxonomy, and "evaluate" is at the second-highest level. This change reflects the greater cognitive complexity associated with creating.

The newly added dimension down the left side of Table 2.10 describes the different kinds of knowledge or content to which these cognitive strategies can be applied (Anderson & Krathwohl, 2001). The authors identify four types of knowledge: factual, conceptual, procedural, and metacognitive. Factual knowledge is composed of the basic elements of a content area or discipline. Conceptual knowledge addresses the interrelationships of the elements within a more complex structure. Thus, knowing the forms of poetry associated with the poetry unit and the definitions of terms (e.g., sonnet, rhyme, meter) is factual knowledge. Students use this body of factual knowledge as they interpret the meaning of poems, a learning goal placed at the intersection of conceptual knowledge and the cognitive skill of understanding (see Table 2.10).

Procedural knowledge is concerned with students' ability to do something, and metacognitive knowledge centers on students' self-awareness of their thinking and problem-solving strategies. So learning goals related to procedural knowledge address writing poetry. Metacognitive knowledge is developed when students self-assess the strengths and areas for improvement in the poetry they have written. Recall that metacognition is key to developing students' self-governing skills that are critical in participating in a democracy.

We believe that for most classroom purposes, these four types of knowledge can be distilled into two major types. The content (or what is learned) is covered in **knowledge/understanding,** which encompasses factual and conceptual knowledge. The techniques and skills you teach students (the how to use) are **skills/strategies/procedures,** addressing procedural and metacognitive knowledge. See Table 2.11 for examples from several fields of study.

Knowledge/understanding covers factual knowledge that consists of the basic information associated with a field. Examples include basic facts such as technical vocabulary in economics (supply, demand), musical notation (quarter notes, treble clef), and types of rocks (igneous, sedimentary). Knowledge/understanding also covers conceptual knowledge or the interrelationships among the basic information within more complex structures such as theories or models. Examples include economic principles such as comparative advantage, musical forms (symphonies, folk songs), and periods of geological time.

In contrast, skills/strategies/procedures address the techniques and skills acquired in different fields of study. Within this category, procedural knowledge deals with methods and techniques employed in a field, such as learning how to analyze the geographic impact on the economics of a region, learning to sing a song, or learning how to classify rocks. It also includes metacognitive knowledge such as analytical skills related to cognition in general as well as one's own cognition. This subset of skills/strategies/procedures includes skills such as knowing when to use a particular strategy for analysis, knowing how to monitor yourself as you perform, knowing how to catch yourself when you make a mistake, and knowing how to work from your strengths and improve your weaknesses.

Most of your units will have both knowledge/understanding learning goals and skills/strategies/procedures learning goals. You will be teaching your students specific content, and you will also be teaching your students specific skills to use when manipulating that content. In Chapter 3 we begin to link these two types of knowledge with specific kinds of assessments, one of the key early steps in aligning assessments with learning goals.

TABLE 2.11

Examples of the Two Basic Types of Knowledge

Knowledge/Understanding (What)		Skills/Strategies/Procedures (How)	
Factual Knowledge	**Conceptual Knowledge**	**Procedural Knowledge**	**Metacognitive Knowledge**
Economics: Technical vocabulary such as supply and demand	Economics: Principle of comparative advantage	Economics: How to calculate growth curves	Economics: Choosing the correct mathematical formula for a given problem
Music: Musical notation such as quarter notes, treble clef	Music: Musical forms such as sonatas, symphonies, folk songs	Music: How to sing a song; how to determine in which period a symphony was written	Music: When practicing, knowing how to build on strengths and adjust for weaknesses
Geology: Types of rocks such as igneous, metamorphic, sedimentary	Geology: Periods of geological time	Geology: How to classify rocks and land forms	Geology: How to determine where and when to get additional information to draw a conclusion about from which geological period an artifact comes
Literacy: Letter names and sounds; sight words	Literacy: Phonemic awareness	Literacy: How to read a passage	Literacy: Self-correction when a word does not make sense in context

Affective and Psychomotor Taxonomies

The taxonomies we have discussed so far focus specifically on *cognitive* strategies as they apply to the different kinds of knowledge. Two other taxonomies that teachers may find useful focus on the affective and psychomotor domains of student learning. The **affective domain** deals with different categories of students' emotional or internal responses to subject matter. The **psychomotor domain** addresses perceptual and motor skills. We present taxonomies for the affective and psychomotor domains in this section.

Affective Domain
Responses related to students' emotional or internal reactions to subject matter.

Psychomotor Domain
Processes related to perceptual and motor skills.

Affective Domain

The categories of the affective taxonomy are presented in Table 2.12. The affective categories range from least to most committed. At the most basic level, a student pays attention to an idea ("receiving"). At the highest level of commitment ("characterization"), a student would adopt and internalize an idea or value and would always act consistently with that value. So the affective taxonomy could be particularly useful for developing learning goals that encourage students to internalize and then act on specific values.

In our conversations with physical education teachers, we have found that they are particularly committed to helping students become active and health conscious for the rest of their lives. Thus they often develop learning goals based on the affective domain. For example, among the physical fitness goals developed by Jim Ross at Orchard Elementary School, you will find *students will discuss the importance of regular physical activity,* a learning goal at the "valuing" level. Similarly, *students will develop a health-related fitness goal and use technology to track their fitness status,* is at the affective level of "organization."

TABLE 2.12

A Continuum with Krathwohl's Affective Categories and Examples of Learning Goals

Affective Categories	Receiving—attends to stimuli.	Responding—participates and reacts to stimuli.	Valuing—attaches worth or value to stimulus (e.g., object, phenomenon, situation, or behavior).	Organization—brings together a complex of values, resolves differences between them, and develops an internally consistent value system.	Characterization—behaves in a manner that is pervasive, consistent, and predictable.
Verbs for Affective Learning Goals	follows, listens, locates, points to, receives	answers, articulates, contributes, discusses, finds, greets, interacts, marks, recites, states, tells	accepts, appreciates, commits, cooperates, demonstrates, devotes, praises, selects, shares	alters, argues, defends, integrates, modifies	acts, demonstrates, displays, maintains, practices, seeks
Examples of Affective Learning Goals	Follows text of poems as others read. Tracks with eyes the movement of the ball.	Participates in discussions of the meaning of various metaphors. Uses Spanish to answer questions in foreign languages class.	Selects various genres for reading during sustained silent reading. Shares collection of rocks and minerals with class.	Formulates and records learning goals in journal. Argues the basis for evolution.	Demonstrates intellectual curiosity in writing. Maintains interest in music styles.

Based on Krathwohl, D., B. Bloom, and B. Masia. 1984. *Taxonomy of educational objectives: Book 2, Affective domain.* Boston, MA: Allyn & Bacon; and Gronlund, N., and S. Brookhart. 2009. *Writing instructional objectives for teaching and assessment,* 8th ed. Upper Saddle River, NJ: Pearson Education.

To achieve this goal, students at Orchard Elementary integrate complex information to modify behaviors contributing to their fitness across time. This process could also help increase students' commitment to a physically healthy lifestyle.

Similarly, teachers in related arts fields, such as theater, music, and visual arts, also aim to instill a lifelong commitment to aspects of culture by ensuring that students take an active rather than a passive role throughout their instruction. For example, over the course of a semester, a theater teacher may use students' personal stories to teach and create monologues. By comparing their characters to monologues that actors perform in plays, they address learning goals related to projection, emotional recall, and empathy. These goals touch on "receiving," "responding," and "valuing" in the affective taxonomy. By later performing monologues they write, they move toward "organization" and "characterization" with learning goals related to character creation and performance of a role. The goal of lifetime commitment is addressed through participatory classroom activities that allow students to experience what is compelling about participating in and watching theater performances. Music and visual arts teachers also take a similar "hands-on" approach to developing an affective commitment among students.

Another example related to the arts occurs at the valuing level in the visual arts when learning goals include students in sharing reasons for preferring one artist's work.

Notice the potential overlap of cognitive and affective domains in this last example. In stating their preferences in a particular artist's style, the students attach worth (i.e., value) to the artist's work and justify (i.e., evaluation) their choices based on their understanding of artistic elements.

Psychomotor Domain

The psychomotor domain has primarily been used in physical education. But teachers in arts-related fields, special education, and technical education also find it useful because it can directly address perceptions and physical movements and skills that are a part of mastering these disciplines. As you can see in Table 2.13, the categories of behavior move from "perception" to "origination." Each category involves increasing the complexity of decision making related to physical actions. This continuum also requires increasingly higher-level thinking. For example, a student would move from "perception," or understanding the demonstration of a single kick, which requires only one decision, all the way to "adaptation" and "origination" of kicks during a soccer game, which involve multiple decisions and problem-solving strategies depending on positions of teammates and opponents, placement on the field, and other considerations. In music, students in band learn to follow a melody line (i.e., mechanism) established by lead players, who maintain a steady beat (i.e., complex overt response) for others to follow.

We show you these various taxonomies to acquaint you with the range of frameworks available for use in developing learning goals for your students. Cognitive, psychomotor, and affective outcomes are important to consider in promoting the full educational development of students.

✦ TABLES OF SPECIFICATIONS

In your planning, you are likely to identify numerous learning goals that might be the focus for learning activities and assessment in a unit. Your next challenge is to find a way to organize these learning goals to make sure that you have appropriate coverage of the types of knowledge and cognitive strategies. One way to organize the learning goals that you've identified is to place them into a **table of specifications.** Thomas Guskey (1996) describes a table of specifications as "a relatively brief, compact, and yet concise description of what we want students to learn and be able to do as a result of their involvement in a particular learning unit." If kept concise, the table can serve as an organizer for our development of a unit or our lesson plans.

Table of Specification
A chart that lists the test content and specifies the number or percentage of test items that cover each content area.

In developing a table of specifications for instruction, Guskey reminds us to ask, "What should students learn from this unit?" and "What should students be able to do with what they learn?" Table 2.10 provides an illustration of the use of these dimensions in a table of specifications for instruction. In the cells of the table, we placed learning goals that might be relevant in a poetry unit. Placement of the learning goals in the cells reveals that instruction in the poetry unit requires students to apply the full range of cognitive skills—from remembering information about poetry forms to creating poems based on the styles they learned. In addition, the learning goals are fairly evenly distributed across the forms of knowledge.

The percentages listed with each goal indicate approximately the amount of time to be allocated to instruction and learning activities. These percentages also guide teachers as they plan the amount of coverage the learning goal should have on a test. The percentages should be based on the importance of the learning goal as well as the time required for students to learn the information or skill. Also, the percentages should not

TABLE 2.13

A Continuum with Simpson's Psychomotor Categories and Examples of Learning Goals

Psychomotor Categories	Perception—uses senses to guide motor activities.	Set—prepares to take a particular action.	Guided Response—imitates an action modeled by an instructor or uses trial and error to approximate the action.	Mechanism—performs movements at a habitual level.	Complex Overt Responses—performs complex movements at a habitual level.	Adaptation—modifies movements to fit a problem situation.	Origination—creates new movement patterns to fit a problem situation.
Verbs for Psychomotor Learning Goals	describes, relates	enters, moves, reacts, shows	adapts, attempts, copies, mimics, replicates	calibrates, operates, prints	demonstrates, shows	adjusts, changes, modifies, varies	choreographs, composes, improvises
Examples of Psychomotor Learning Goals	Relates music to a dance movement. Moves head toward sound (infant).	Enters and exits stage on cue. Enters into a debate.	Copies hand position for chords on a guitar. Imitates parents' vocalizations.	Prints legibly. Speaks fluently in Spanish. Styles hair.	Carves sculpture from wood. Conducts an orchestra. Gestures to emphasize points in speech.	Modifies running speed for terrain in a marathon. Varies strokes to achieve textures in a painting.	Improvises simple rhythmic accompaniments using body percussion.

Based on Simpson, E. 1972. *The classification of educational objectives in the psychomotor domain.* Washington, D.C.: Gryphon House; and Gronlund, N., and S. Brookhart. 2009. *Writing instructional objectives for teaching and assessment* (8th ed.). Upper Saddle River, NJ: Pearson Education.

be considered rigid time allotments for teaching the learning goal. They are guideposts that remind you to spend the majority of instructional time on preparing students to write poems and relatively less time on teaching the origins of each poetry form.

After completion of the table of specifications for instruction, the planning chart that we introduced earlier can now be used with each learning goal to align the learning goals, instructional experiences, and assessments. Notice the alignment here:

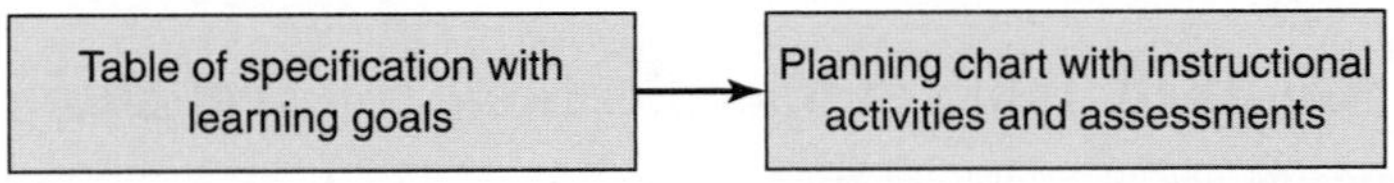
Table of specification with learning goals
Planning chart with instructional activities and assessments

As shown in Table 2.14, the learning goals have implications for teaching. In this instance, the learning goals require the teacher to plan instruction that involves students in learning about the characteristics of types of poetry and using those characteristics to determine the types of poetry when new examples are offered. Notice that these two learning goals are taught together. A teacher might consider it essential that students are making meaning of the poetry as they determine the forms of the poems. Also notice that the integration of these two learning goals provides a teacher with some flexibility because the goals combined account for 40 percent of the time for the unit.

Benefits of a Table of Specifications

One benefit of a table of specifications is that it provides you with a compact view of concepts that are the focus of instruction, promoting a close match between unit materials and activities and learning outcomes. The table of specifications allows you to review the level of cognitive strategies called for in the learning goals. It also prompts you to move beyond knowledge level to higher-order thinking because any empty cells toward the right allow you to notice the lack of learning goals encouraging students to analyze, evaluate, or create.

Another major benefit of the table of specifications is its potential to inform your instructional planning. Instruction will change across learning goals in several ways, such as different learning activities, different curricular materials, and different roles for the teacher and student. To consider instructional implications, contrast learning goals in the Remember column and the Evaluate column in Table 2.10. Learning activities

TABLE 2.14

Planning Chart

Learning Goal	Teaching Methods/Learning Experiences	Assessment Tasks
Analyze elements of poems to identify the forms.	Read examples of haiku, limericks, and cinquains. Discuss similarities and differences. Discuss the meaning of the poems and the authors' intent (e.g., to create an image, to tell a humorous story).	Students distinguish between types of poetry in new reading selections.
Interpret the meaning of poems.	Break into pairs, read a selection, and use *think, pair, share* to determine the type of poem and its meaning.	Students write the meanings of a set of new haiku, limericks, and cinquains.

must differ when students (a) read a text to learn the names of the poems and their origins or (b) share the draft of a poem in a writer's conference. Instructional materials change from examples of poems in reading texts to the draft of a poem. Also, the roles of the teacher and students are likely to change when a student is learning some factual information about the stylistic elements versus when the student leads the discussion in an author's conference.

Using a Modified Table of Specifications for Test Design

Another valuable use of a table of specifications is in designing a test. In the table of specifications we have seen thus far, we list all cognitive levels of Bloom's taxonomy across the top and the types of knowledge down the left side (see Table 2.10). Many teachers do not get this specific when designing a blueprint for aligning their tests with their instruction, and a more streamlined approach can be as effective (McMillan, 2007). We believe the key to designing a successful test is to use a modified blueprint, such as the one depicted in Table 2.13, to keep track of the distribution of questions across learning goals. Notice that the table collapses the cognitive strategies into two levels: Remember and Higher Order Cognitive Strategies. This modification allows teachers to monitor their use of higher order cognitive strategies but not become trapped in deciding whether, for example, an item requires *applying* concepts or *analyzing* concepts.

Development of assessments should be guided by the degree of importance of each learning goal, as represented by the percentage of the unit devoted to it. Basically, the percentage covered in an assessment should be consistent with the coverage in the learning goal. Table 2.15 shows the classification of test items that would be written for each learning goal for a 40-item assessment. A teacher would write approximately four items (10% of 40 = 4 items) for the learning goal of *Recall forms of poetry and definitions*. If a teacher develops an assessment in which 50 percent of the items address poem forms and definitions, then this goal is overrepresented in the assessment. Use of a table of specifications in test design ensures that you will address all the learning and won't include superfluous assessment items or tasks.

Another benefit of the table is that any empty cells will cue a teacher that critical concepts or cognitive strategies might have been overlooked in the assessment items developed so far. Teachers sometimes emphasize subject matter of interest to them and may overlook concepts in less-favored subject areas. This does not mean that every unit must have all the knowledge and cognitive levels covered in your table of specifications. Not every unit will necessarily have learning goals at all levels.

Challenges in Using a Table of Specifications

The use of a table of specifications or taxonomy might appear too demanding considering everything you must do as a teacher. However, in the past, a common criticism of teaching was the perceived overreliance on instruction and assessment using knowledge-level cognitive strategies to the exclusion of challenging students with higher-level thinking skills (recall our example of memorizing battles and dates in history classes). Using a table to make the cognitive levels explicit enables you to design instruction and assessment at higher levels of cognitive skills, even though it may involve some deliberate complex judgments.

One mistake that teachers sometimes make is becoming overly concerned about the exact cell in the table of specifications in which a learning goal or an assessment item belongs. In fact, we have seen disagreement about such classifications

TABLE 2.15

Streamlined Table of Specifications for Planning a Test

List Each Learning Goal and Percent of the Unit It Covers	List Items in Appropriate Column	
	Remember	Higher Order Cognitive Strategies Understand————▶Create
1. Recall forms of poetry and definitions. **10**%	Items 1–4	
2. Recall origins of forms of poetry. **5**%	Items 5–6	
3. Interpret the meaning of poems. **20**%		Items 7, 8, 11, 12, 15–18
4. Analyze elements of poems to identify the forms. **20**%		Items 9, 10, 19–24
5. Apply elements of a specific form of poetry to complete a poem. **10**%		Items 13, 14, 25, 26
6. Write poems with appropriate stylistic elements. **25**%		Items 27–36
7. Discuss in an authors' conference the strengths and areas for improvement of poems she/he wrote. **10**%		Items 37–40

in textbooks and in tables on various websites. For example, we have found that generating examples of a concept is sometimes placed at the "comprehension/understand" level and sometimes at the "application/apply" level. These nuances and contradictions may frustrate you if you dwell on them too much. The key requirements are (1) you are addressing skills above the knowledge level in both your instruction and your assessment, and (2) your learning goals, instruction, and assessment are all aligned. We advise our students not to obsess about classifying goals or items in the table. Instead, we advise them to be able to justify their method of classification to themselves and to ensure that their lessons and assessments cover the range of cognitive and knowledge levels.

→ CASE STUDY APPLICATIONS

In this section we introduce three case studies that will provide examples of the assessment methods throughout this text. We discuss these case studies in this chapter in terms of the lessons they provide about learning goals. We will revisit the case studies to see applications of new assessment strategies presented in those chapters. As shown in Table 2.16, in the unit by Maria Mensik, high school students in an English class explore the characteristics of ideal societies (utopias) and dysfunctional societies (dystopias). Students read *Utopia,* by Thomas More; *1984,* by George Orwell; and *The Giver,* by Lois Lowry. They view films, such as *Pleasantville,* and *I, Robot.* In terms of assessment, students complete tests and work in small groups to formulate their own ideal society, using PowerPoint to develop a persuasive presentation to recruit new citizens for their country.

TABLE 2.16

Descriptions of Three Case Studies

Subject Area	Grade Level	Focus/Theme	Learning Goals	Forms of Assessment
Maria Mensik's English Class	High School	Utopia and Dystopia	The students will compare and contrast characteristics of a utopia and dystopia. The students will compare and contrast multiple works concerning utopia/dystopia, paying particular attention to the role of the government and the role of the individual. The students will use persuasive language in writing and/or speaking.	Multiple-Choice, Modified True/False, Performance Tasks
Lynn McCarter's Mathematics Class	Middle Level	Solving Problems Related to Proportions	The students will use geometric concepts and modeling to interpret and solve problems.[1] The students will solve problems related to similar and congruent figures. The students will select appropriate units and tools for measurement tasks within problem-solving situations; determine precision and check for reasonableness of results.	Journal Prompts; Essays, Multiple-Choice, Performance Task
Ebony Sanders's Science Class	Early Childhood	Distinguishing between Solids and Liquids	The students will recognize matter in their daily surroundings. The students will describe the characteristics of solids and liquids based on their explorations. The students will demonstrate the appropriate steps to test an unknown solid or liquid. The students will use the writing process to describe solids and liquids.	Fill-in-the-Blank, Performance Tasks, Journal Prompts

[1]North Carolina Department of Public Instruction. 1998. *K–8 Mathematics Competency Goals and Objectives,* p. 41.

Solving problems related to proportions is the focus of Lynn McCarter's mathematics unit. In this unit, middle-level students use proportions to solve problems similar to those in real life, such as reading a map, enlarging or reducing a photograph or a poster, and determining heights of very tall objects. Assessments used by Lynn include multiple-choice items, journal entries, essays, and a performance task.

Ebony Sanders's science unit focuses on first-grade students' learning about the characteristics of solids and liquids. Activities include students predicting the outcome of "a race" between two liquids and determining the "rule" the instructor uses to sort objects into a solids pile. Assessments include students touching a solid in a "feely" box and writing in their journals about how they could tell the object was a solid and taking a photograph of a solid or liquid found in their school and completing a writing task about solids or liquids.

Maria's unit on utopia and dystopia illustrates several important aspects of learning goals. Table 2.17 shows Maria's use of content standards to develop her unit goals. For example, the learning goal *The students will compare and contrast characteristics of a utopia and dystopia* addresses the content standard *Demonstrate the ability to analyze the origin and meaning of new words by using a knowledge of culture and mythology.* Maria's use of the content standards reminds us that they may require revision prior to being used as learning goals.

Maria's unit also reminds us about applying filters in determining how to address learning goals. In terms of the engagement filter, students might lose interest if the

TABLE 2.17

English Learning Goals and Content Standards

Learning Goals	State Standards: Reading (R), Writing (W), Communication (C), and Research Goals (RS)	
The student will compare and contrast characteristics of a utopia and dystopia.	R3.1	Demonstrate the ability to analyze the origin and meaning of new words by using a knowledge of culture and mythology.
	C3.8	Demonstrate the ability to make connections between nonprint sources and his or her prior knowledge, other sources, and the world.
The student will compare and contrast multiple works concerning utopia/ dystopia, paying particular attention to the role of the government and the role of the individual.	R1.2	Demonstrate the ability to make connections between a text read independently and his or her prior knowledge, other texts, and the world.
	R1.9	Demonstrate the ability to read several works on a particular topic, paraphrase the ideas, and synthesize them with ideas from other authors addressing the same topic.
	R2.9	Demonstrate the ability to present interpretations of texts by using methods such as Socratic questioning, literature circles, class discussion, PowerPoint presentations, and graphic organizers.
	W1.3	Demonstrate the ability to develop an extended response around a central idea, using relevant supporting details.
	W1.6.3	Demonstrate the ability to write essays, reports, articles, and proposals
	C3.6	Demonstrate the ability to compare and contrast the treatment of a given situation or event in nonprint sources.
The student will use persuasive language in writing and/or speaking.	W2.3	Demonstrate the ability to use writing to persuade, analyze, and transact business.
	W3.1	Demonstrate the ability to respond to texts both orally and in writing.
	C1.3	Demonstrate the ability to use oral language to inform, to explain, to persuade, and to compare and contrast different viewpoints.

discussion lacks relevance to their lives. However, the learning goal to *compare and contrast multiple works* dovetails with instruction that uses currently popular works as well as classic literature. Using these broad resources offers potential for students to make connections with their lives.

Lynn McCarter's math class shows how the teacher uses problems based on real-life situations to promote engagement. Students are more likely to be interested when the learning goals are applied to situations they encounter. Also, Lynn indicates that student performance will be documented by using a checklist providing her with a breakdown of student learning levels to be used later for cooperative groups. Students will also use the checklist to find areas of weakness and explore those areas further in individual projects. Here, Lynn reminds us of our earlier statement that students begin to learn to self-assess when provided with the learning goals for a lesson and when given a scoring guide (e.g., a checklist) based on those learning goals. As we mentioned in Chapter 1, the development of self-assessment, or self-governing skills, is critical to prepare students for participation in a democracy.

A review of Ebony Sanders's learning goals and state standards in Table 2.18 shows how to integrate subject matter, such as science concepts, and writing skills. Notice that in addition to students learning the characteristics of solids and liquids, Ebony also has learning goals related to students using the writing process to communicate their understanding of solids and liquids.

TABLE 2.18

Learning Goals and Content Standards for Ebony Sanders's Unit

Learning Goals	Corresponding State Standard(s)
	Physical Science
The students will recognize matter in their daily surroundings.	I.A.2. Compare, sort and group concrete objects according to observable properties.
The students will describe the characteristics of solids and liquids based on their explorations.	I.A.1. Use the senses to gather information about objects or events such as size, shape, color, texture, sound, position, and change (qualitative observations). IV.A.3. Objects can be described by the properties of the materials from which they are made, and those properties can be used to separate or sort a group of objects or materials. IV.A.4. Materials can exist in different states. a. Explore and describe characteristics in solids. b. Explore and describe characteristics in liquids.
The students will demonstrate the appropriate steps to test an unknown solid or liquid.	I.B.1.b. Employ simple equipment, such as hand lenses, thermometers, and balances, to gather data and extend the senses. IV.A.2. Properties of matter can be measured using tools, such as rulers, balances, and thermometers.
	Writing
The students will use the writing process to describe solids and liquids.	1-W1.2. Begin using prewriting strategies. 1-W1.3. Demonstrate the ability to generate drafts using words and pictures that focus on a topic and that include relevant details. 1-W1.6. Demonstrate the ability to write in a variety of formats. 1-W1.6.1. Demonstrate the ability to write simple compositions, friendly letters, and expressive and informational pieces with peer or teacher support.

Our review of the case studies reinforces several points. First, revising content standards may be necessary when using them as learning goals. Also, because the number of standards is greater than a teacher's time to cover them, we should consider the importance of the learning outcome and the instructional time we allocate to it. In addition, student engagement may be improved by the use of resources based on relevant real-life experiences. Finally, the integration of learning goals (e.g., writing and science observations) can "create" time for coverage of multiple subject areas.

KEY CHAPTER POINTS

Learning goals are a formal statement of the end results that you intend for your students. We have learned that learning goals consist of a verb and a noun phrase:

Organize   data in charts, pictographs, and tables.

Verb   Noun phrase

The verb tells what the students will do and the noun phrase describes the subject-area content knowledge the students will learn.

We reviewed resources for writing learning goals, including taxonomies, subject-area content standards, district curriculum guides, and teacher manuals. We examined the use of Bloom's taxonomy and the revised Bloom's taxonomy to guide the development of learning goals related to cognitive skills (e.g., analyze, evaluate, create). Content standards, district curriculum guides, and teacher manuals provide information about the knowledge that students should learn. Content standards are documents that outline key subject-area knowledge, skills, and strategies that teachers must develop in their students. Learning goals in district curriculum guides often are written at a level that is more specific in their description of student outcomes than are state content standards. Goals in teacher manuals are usually specific to the lesson; however, a teacher must ensure that state and district standards are covered.

In our discussion of tables of specifications, we examine the use of a two-way table (i.e., Type of Knowledge by Cognitive Skill; see Table 2.10) to organize the learning goals in an instructional unit. Each learning goal is categorized in a cell of the table according to the goal's knowledge type and cognitive process. Organizing learning goals in such a table allows a teacher to see which cognitive skills and types of knowledge have been addressed. Empty cells in the table also cue the teacher to consider whether additional learning goals need to be developed.

The learning goals in the table of specifications can be put into a planning chart for you to sketch out the learning experiences and assessment tasks that are required. This process ensures the alignment of learning goals, instruction, and assessment. In addition, planning the assessment will be assisted by using a modified table of specifications for assessment. This simplification of the instructional table of specifications allows you to classify each assessment item by learning goal and cognitive skill.

In this chapter, we have presented methods for you to systematically develop learning goals that will guide your instruction and assessment. In the following chapters we explore methods for assessing student achievement of learning goals.

HELPFUL WEBSITES

http://www.ccsso.org/Projects/State_Education_Indicators/Key_State_Education_Policies/3160.
      cfm#S. Provides links to content standards at state department of education websites. Use

this site to locate your state content standards—the best place for you to begin learning about content standards and learning goals.

http://www.ncte.org/about/over/standards/110846.htm (English language arts)
http://standards.nctm.org/document/appendix/numb.htm (Mathematics)
http://books.nap.edu/html/nses/html/6a.html (Science)
http://www.socialstudies.org/standards/strands/ (Social Studies)
Provide content standards developed at the national level.

CHAPTER REVIEW QUESTIONS

1. Complete a web search to locate the state content standards for your subject area. Select five learning outcomes that are specific enough for you to describe the appropriate instruction and assessment.
2. Describe at least two examples of appropriate instruction and two examples of appropriate assessment for one learning goal from Item 1 above.
3. In which cognitive process dimension and knowledge dimension of Bloom's revised taxonomy would you categorize the foreign languages learning goal, "Comprehend and interpret the main ideas and details from television, movies, videos, radio, or live presentations produced in the target language"?
4. Review the affective categories in Table 2.12. Use a verb from the middle row, Verbs for Affective Learning Goals, to develop a learning goal for a subject area (e.g., reading, mathematics, visual arts).
5. Review the psychomotor categories in Table 2.13. Using a verb from the row labeled Verbs for Psychomotor Learning Goals, develop a learning goal for an arts-related subject area (e.g., dance, music, theater).
6. The following mathematics standard requires revision to specify what students must do to show achievement of the goal: Understand fractions as parts of a whole. Hint: Make the verb more specific.
7. Choose one of the three case studies discussed in the chapter and describe where you believe the learning goals would fit in Bloom's revised taxonomy.
8. Look at the learning goals provided by a textbook chapter in your content area. How are they similar to or different from your state's standards for that subject matter and grade level?
9. Design a learning goal for some aspect of the content of this chapter. Then describe instructional activities and types of assessment that would be aligned with this learning goal.

REFERENCES

Anderson, L., and D. Krathwohl (eds.). 2001. *A taxonomy for learning, teaching, and assessing: A revision of Bloom's taxonomy of educational objectives* (Abr. Ed.). New York: Longman.
Arizona Department of Education. 2006. *The social studies standard articulated by grade level.* Retrieved June 2, 2007 from http://www.ade.state.az.us/standards/sstudies/articulated/.
Bloom, B. (ed.), M. Engelhart, E. Furst, W. Hill, and D. Krathwohl. 1956. *Taxonomy of educational objectives: Handbook I: Cognitive domain.* New York: David McKay Company.
California State Board of Education. 2006. *Kindergarten English-language arts content standards.* Retrieved June 2, 2007 from http://www.cde.ca.gov/be/st/ss/engkindergarten.asp.
Covey, S. 1989. *The seven habits of highly effective people.* New York: Simon & Schuster, p. 95.
Florida Department of Education. 2005. *Foreign languages grades 6–8.* Retrieved June 2, 2007 from http://www.firn.edu/doe/curric/prek12/pdf/forlang6.pdf.

Gagné, R. 1985. *The conditions of learning and theory of instruction.* 4th ed. New York: Holt, Rinehart, and Winston.

Georgia Department of Education. 2006. *Grade 9 ELA standards.* Retrieved June 2, 2007 from http://www.georgiastandards.org/english.aspx.

Gronlund, N. 2003. *Assessment of student achievement.* 7th ed. Boston: Allyn & Bacon.

Gronlund, N., and S. Brookhart. 2009. *Gronlund's writing instructional objectives.* 8th ed. Upper Saddle River, NJ: Pearson Education.

Guskey, T. 1997. *Implementing mastery learning.* 2nd ed. Belmont, CA: Wadsworth Publishing Company.

Illinois State Board of Education. 1997. *Illinois learning standards for English language arts.* Retrieved June 11, 2007 from http://www.isbe.state.il.us/ils/ela/standards.htm.

International Reading Association & National Council of Teachers of English. 1996. *Standards for the English language arts.* Newark, DE: International Reading Association.

Krathwohl, D., B. Bloom, and B. Masia. 1984. *Taxonomy of educational objectives: Book 2, Affective domain.* Boston, MA: Allyn & Bacon.

L'Engle, M. 1962. *A wrinkle in time.* New York: Farrar, Straus, and Giroux.

Marzano, R. J. 2001. *Designing a new taxonomy of educational objectives.* Thousand Oaks, CA: Corwin Press.

Massachusetts Department of Education. 2003. *Massachusetts history and social science curriculum framework.* Retrieved June 2, 2007 from http://www.doe.mass.edu/frameworks/current.html.

McMillan, J. 2007. *Classroom assessment: Principles and practice for effective standards-based instruction.* 4th ed. Boston, MA: Allyn and Bacon.

Metfessel, N., W. Michael, and D. Kirsner. 1969. Instrumentation of Bloom's and Krathwohl's taxonomies for the writing of behavioral objectives. *Psychology in the Schools* 6: 227–231.

National Council of Teachers of Mathematics. 2000. *Principles and standards for school mathematics.* Reston, VA: Author.

New Jersey. 2004. *New Jersey core curriculum content standards for visual and performing arts.* Retrieved June 2, 2007 from http://www.nj.gov/education/cccs/s1_vpa.pdf.

New York State Education Department. 1996. *Learning standards for mathematics, science, and technology.* Retrieved June 2, 2007 from http://www.emsc.nysed.gov/ciai/mst/pub/mststa5.pdf.

North Carolina Department of Public Instruction. 1998. *K–8 mathematics competency goals and objectives.* Retrieved June 9, 2007 from http://community.learnnc.org/dpi/math/archives/K8-98.pdf.

North Carolina Department of Public Instruction. 2004. *Science standard course of study and grade level competencies: K–12.* Retrieved June 2, 2007 from http://www.ncpublicschools.org/docs/curriculum/science/scos/2004/science.pdf.

Office of the Superintendent of Public Instruction. n.d. *Essential academic learning requirements: History.* Olympia, Washington. Retrieved June 11, 2007, from http://www.k12.wa.us/CurriculumInstruct/SocStudies/historyEALRs.aspx.

Ohio Department of Education. 2003. *Academic content standards: K–12 fine arts.* Retrieved June 11, 2007, from http://www.ode.state.oh.us/GD/Templates/Pages/ODE/ODEDetail.aspx?page=3&TopicRelationID=336&ContentID=1388&Content=12661.

Popham, W. J. 2003. Trouble with testing: Why standards-based assessment doesn't measure up. *American School Board Journal* 190(2): 14–17.

Popham, J. 2006. Content standards: The unindicted co-conspirator. *Educational Leadership,* 64(1): 87–88.

Quellmalz, E. 1985. Developing reasoning skills. In J. Baron & R. Sternberg, (eds.), *Teaching thinking skills: Theory and practice,* pp. 86–105. New York: Freeman.

Sandford, R., M. Ulicsak, K. Facer, and T. Rudd. 2007. *Teaching with games: Using commercial off-the-shelf computer games in formal education.* Retrieved June 2, 2008, from http://www.futurelab.org.uk/projects/teaching_with_games/research/final_report/.

Simpson, E. 1972. *The classification of educational objectives in the psychomotor domain.* Washington, D.C.: Gryphon House.

South Carolina Department of Education. 2003a. *South Carolina English language arts curriculum standards 2002*. Retrieved June 2, 2007, from http://ed.sc.gov/agency/offices/cso/standards/ela/.

South Carolina Department of Education. 2003b. *South Carolina visual and performing arts curriculum standards 2003*. Retrieved June 2, 2007, from http://ed.sc.gov/agency/offices/cso/standards/vpa/.

South Carolina Department of Education. 2005a. *South Carolina science academic standards*. Retrieved June 2, 2008, from http://ed.sc.gov/agency/offices/cso/standards/science/.

South Carolina Department of Education. 2005b. *South Carolina social studies academic standards*. Retrieved June 2, 2008, from http://ed.sc.gov/agency/offices/cso/standards/ss/.

South Carolina Department of Education. 2007. *South Carolina academic standards for mathematics*. Retrieved June 2, 2008, from http://ed.sc.gov/agency/offices/cso/standards/math/.

Texas Education Agency. 2006. Chapter 111. *Texas essential knowledge and skills for mathematics: Subchapter A. Elementary*. Retrieved June 2, 2007, from http://www.tea.state.tx.us/rules/tac/chapter111/ch111a.html.

VanSledright, B. A. 2004. What does it mean to think historically . . . and how do you teach it? *Social Education* 68(3): 230–233.

Virginia Department of Education. 2001. *Physical education standards of learning for Virginia Public Schools*. Retrieved June 2, 2007, from http://www.pen.k12.va.us/VDOE/Superintendent/Sols/physedk-12.pdf.

Wiggins, G., and J. McTighe. 1998. *Understanding by design*. Alexandria, VA: Association for Supervision and Curriculum Development.

CHAPTER 3

Diagnostic Assessment: Ensuring Student Success from the Beginning

Evaluation is creation.

–Friedrich Nietzsche

❖ **Chapter Learning Goals**

At the conclusion of this chapter, the reader should be able to:

- Choose, design, and interpret diagnostic assessments for planning instruction.

- Understand differences in measuring skills/strategies/procedures and knowledge/understanding.

- Accommodate diverse learners during diagnostic assessment.

✦ Introduction

The public and the press focus on and therefore emphasize formal standardized large-scale state testing at the end of each year. But we believe that assessments at the beginning and during each year are actually more important when it comes to fostering student learning. In this chapter we address diagnostic assessments. Introduced in Chapter 1, diagnostic assessments are the assessments used at the beginning of the year and the beginning of units to help you understand and respond to the wide range of needs, backgrounds, and attitudes that your students bring to your classroom. They also show you how students think and what misconceptions they have. You must understand the varying needs of your students so you can provide differentiated instruction that helps to close achievement gaps. Different students will need different strategies to profit from your classes. We chose Nietzsche's quotation to begin our chapter because diagnostic assessments are the foundational evaluation methods for creating learning in your classroom.

Determining what your students know at the beginning of the year and at the beginning of a new unit allows you to design lessons to meet their needs. We don't want students getting discouraged from the first day of class. As you recall, Jocelyn, the biology teacher described in Chapter 1, discovered that none of her students' reading skills were adequate for tackling her biology textbook. This knowledge helped her design instruction that addressed biology. But she also addressed her students' need for intensive vocabulary work and encouraged them to demonstrate their learning through means other than traditional writing tasks and tests, rather than assuming they simply weren't equipped to meet the class goals. Diagnostic assessment was crucial for Jocelyn to figure out how best to teach her students and tailor activities to their needs.

→ BEFORE YOU BEGIN: HIGH EXPECTATIONS AND BEHAVIORS THAT CONVEY THEM

In developing diagnostic assessment, you must start by holding high expectations for your students. Even though Jocelyn's students' basic reading skills were not at grade level, she designed her instruction to hold them fully accountable for the complex biology content she would teach them. To design appropriate instruction, she had to base her diagnostic assessment on the assumption that they could meet the learning goals.

All of us support and give lip service to high expectations, but they are often quite difficult to internalize and implement in a classroom. Researchers have found that some teachers unconsciously communicate differently with students, depending on whether they believe those students are high or low achievers (Schunk et al., 2008). These teachers convey high—or low—expectations to their students through their behaviors and, in particular, through their actions during ongoing, informal assessment activities that begin the very first day of the school year. Often teachers are not even aware that they convey such notions to students.

Table 3.1 illustrates some of the behaviors that teachers engage in during ongoing classroom assessment and interaction with students for whom they have low expectations. For example, if a student gives an incorrect response or no response to a teacher's oral question, a teacher can quickly move on to someone else, or the teacher can provide a few seconds for the student to think, clarify the question, repeat the question, or give the student additional information that could help make a connection more prominent. If the teacher has low expectations for a student, the most likely response is to move quickly on to another student. Such behavior can be particularly noticeable for students who are learning English (Rothenberg & Fisher, 2007). Teachers don't want to put them

---

TABLE 3.1

Some Teacher Behaviors Related to Assessment That Communicate Low Expectations

Waiting less time for low achievers to answer a question.

Giving answers to low achievers or calling on someone else rather than trying to improve responses by giving clues or rephrasing.

Rewarding incorrect answers by low achievers.

Criticizing low achievers more often for failure.

Praising low achievers less often for success.

Providing briefer and less informative answers to questions of low achievers.

Failing to give feedback following public responses of low achievers.

Generally paying less attention to low achievers and interacting with them less frequently.

Calling on low achievers less often, or asking them only easier, nonanalytic questions.

Generally demanding less from low achievers (e.g., accepting low-quality or incorrect responses).

Not giving low achievers the benefit of the doubt as much as high achievers when grading tests or assignments.

Showing less acceptance and use of low achievers' ideas.

Adapted from Brophy, J. 1998. *Motivating students to learn*. Copyright McGraw-Hill Companies, Inc. Used with permission.

on the spot or embarrass them, but then they end up not requiring the same level of participation and accountability from their English learners.

In contrast, a teacher who has high expectations is more likely to probe for an answer, clarify the question, or do something to communicate that the teacher expects the student to be able to answer correctly. These teacher behaviors then influence the learning process. The latter student will feel encouraged and be more likely to answer correctly more often and thus probably will learn more.

Different teacher behavior patterns toward low and high achievers can help us understand the connection between student performance and teacher expectations. You can see how gradually across time, students get discouraged when they are ignored, criticized, or skipped over. A year's accumulation of less attention, easier work, and more criticism has a major impact on a student's learning. Often teachers' perception of students heavily influences the pupils' perceptions of themselves. Students buy into the teacher's perceptions and don't try as hard and don't see themselves as successful or competent. Such perceptions then lead to student behaviors that result in lower achievement, fulfilling the teacher's original expectations.

Figure 3.1 shows how teacher expectations could translate into different outcomes for two groups. If teachers tend to believe a particular type of student (perhaps the poor or minority children on the wrong side of the achievement gap) won't do well, their own instructional behaviors could in fact lead to lower achievement for those less-favored groups.

Researchers have indeed uncovered a strong link between teacher expectations, which can be formed very early in the school year, and student achievement. One early study illustrating this point well was done with first-grade teachers (Palardy, 1969). At the beginning of a school year, a researcher asked a group of teachers about whether boys were likely to make as much progress in reading as girls during first grade. Ten of these teachers felt that boys tend to do as well as girls, and ten felt that boys usually do significantly worse than girls in reading in first grade. In this study, according to scores on aptitude tests, all students had equivalent ability to do well. At the end of the school year, the researcher looked at the achievement levels in reading of first-grade girls and boys who had been students in these teachers' classrooms. He found that the

Teacher Expectations	Teacher Behaviors Related to Assessment	Student Achievement Level
Unfavored groups will be less successful than favored group $\Longrightarrow$	More criticism, less praise Less teacher attention during questioning Fewer demands for high-quality work $\Longrightarrow$	Unfavored group's academic achievement is lower than favored group's
All groups will be successful $\Longrightarrow$	Similar levels of praise, criticism for all groups Equal teacher attention during questioning for all groups Equal demands for high-quality work $\Longrightarrow$	Equivalent academic achievement for all groups

FIGURE 3.1   *How Teacher Expectations May Influence Student Achievement*

girls' achievement was no different for all teachers. The boys' achievement was different depending on which teacher they had. If they had a teacher with high expectations for boys, their scores did not differ from the girls'. If they had a teacher with low expectations for boys, their scores were significantly lower than the girls'.

Remember that these differences in teacher behaviors are not necessarily conscious and deliberate. Teachers care about their students and want them to learn as much as they can. But we all have some unexamined biases or stereotypes and assumptions that can influence our behavior about certain students. For example, one African American teacher we know was observed by her principal her first year of teaching. He marked on a seating chart whom she called on over a 20-minute period. When he showed her the results, she was horrified to see that she called on her European American children more often than on her African American children, even though her class had equivalent numbers of each. From that day forward, she has made a concerted effort to be mindful of her behaviors toward students and has developed a strategy for calling regularly on all students.

Careful efforts by a teacher to convey high expectations through her behavior toward her students is captured in one boy's remark to a new student in his class (cited by Eggen & Kauchak, 2004): "Put your hand down. Mrs. Lawless calls on all of us. She thinks we're all smart." If you are making an effort to close the achievement gap, you will not only take deliberate, conscious steps to make sure you avoid behaviors such as providing briefer and less informative answers to questions of low achievers, or rewarding incorrect answers by low achievers (see Table 3.1) as you engage in informal assessment practices in your classroom. You will also design your more formal diagnostic assessments based on the assumption that all students will meet the class learning goals.

✦ CHOOSE YOUR SOURCES OF INFORMATION WISELY

When deciding on what information to examine and use, make sure you have several kinds of information to draw from so you don't jump to hasty conclusions based on one piece of data. You want to see a pattern emerge across several sources before you draw any firm conclusions (Chapman & King, 2005). Scores on tests, for example, look very official, and their technical aspects have usually been carefully researched. This often leads us to assume they are always accurate and precise in the information that they provide. However, a student could have been ill on the day of the test and attained a low score that does not represent her knowledge and skills accurately. You must check whether other information suggests a different conclusion. This process of developing an accurate conclusion based on several sources is often called **triangulation.** The term comes from the series of steps seagoing navigators would take to pinpoint an unknown position in their journey based on two or more known positions. Now the term is commonly used to characterize the process of using several types of information to get a more accurate picture of a complex concept, such as a student's achievement. When getting a sense of student skills and knowledge, you must look for convergence from several sources of information, as shown in Figure 3.2. The student's achievement level in the figure is probably more accurately represented, in this case, by measures other than the standardized test.

Before Classes Start

Teachers often disagree on which sources to use and how much information to gather before classes start, especially from past teachers, school records, and previous testing. Many don't want to be biased by information from previous years because they know the impact that unwarranted teacher expectations can have on student achievement.

Triangulation
The process of developing an accurate conclusion based on several sources.

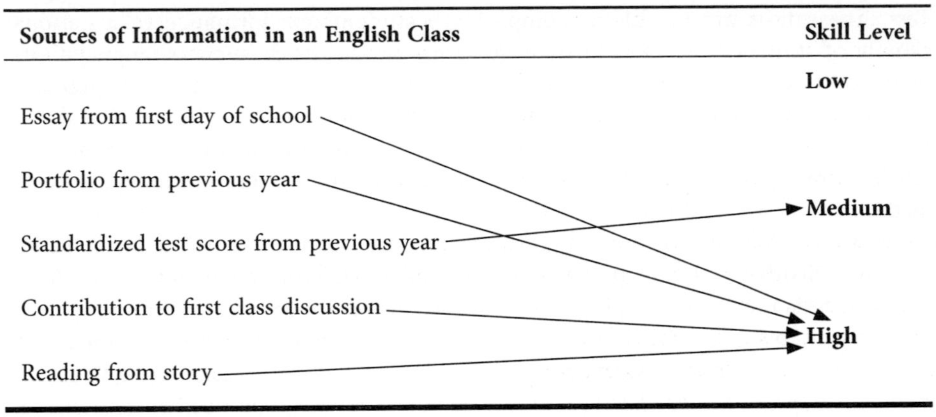
Sources of Information in an English Class
Skill Level
Low
Essay from first day of school
Portfolio from previous year
Medium
Standardized test score from previous year
Contribution to first class discussion
High
Reading from story

FIGURE 3.2 ***Using the Process of Triangulation to See a Pattern in Achievement for a Student Who Did Not Score as Well on a Standardized Test as on Other Measures***

Table 3.2 provides a list of sources of information that are usually available to teachers at the beginning of the school year.

Grades

End-of-term grades can be a particularly limited source of information because they are a fairly crude summary of a student's performance. Most students don't perform consistently across all the learning goals in one semester. A grade is an average that can obscure information needed about the skills and knowledge that students bring to your classroom. Examining the pattern of grades across years and subjects, though, can give you a rough idea of a student's strengths and weaknesses.

Large-Scale Test Scores

Many schools use widely available summative assessments such as the Stanford Achievement Tests, the Iowa Tests of Basic Skills, or the Metropolitan Achievement

TABLE 3.2

Sources of Information Available to Teachers at the Beginning of the School Year

Nonacademic Records	Academic Records
Attendance records	Portfolios of student work
Discipline records	Large-scale test scores (e.g., End of Grade [EOG] Tests, State Test Scores)
Health records	Previous grades and report cards
Written comments from previous teachers	Eligibility for and records from special programs (Special Education, Gifted, English as a Second Language)
Classroom conduct checklists (work habits, independence, social skills)	

Test. These tests are useful for comparing a student's performance to a national sample of students on broad knowledge across several fields such as language arts, math, and reading. In addition, all states require achievement tests in grades 3 through 8 to determine annual yearly progress of schools for the No Child Left Behind Act. Score interpretation for large-scale tests is explained in Chapter 11. These scores can give you a picture of which of your students are in the typical range in the content areas tested.

Scores from any of these large-scale tests are not usually useful for targeting specific skills that children need to work on, unless wide discrepancies appear. Standardized tests *are* useful for giving you clues about additional information you might want to gather yourself. Remember that most published standardized achievement tests provide a panoramic view, with only one or two items examining each skill. To get the close-up snapshot needed for designing specific instruction, you need to gather more detailed information yourself.

Portfolios of Student Work

Some schools have portfolios of student work that move up the grades with the student, and we will discuss portfolios further in Chapter 10. Portfolios are especially useful for documenting student development of complex skills and strategies, such as a student's ability to organize ideas in writing or use problem-solving skills in mathematics. For example, an essay on each student's goals for a class might be included from the beginning of each year. An essay on the most important person in each student's life might be inserted in mid-year, and an essay on how that student would change the world might be added at the end of each year. Such a collection across the elementary years could show student growth in thinking and writing skills in a compelling way.

School Records

Other schools devise forms such as the one from Cotton Belt Elementary School in Figure 3.3. These forms are designed to give helpful information gathered from a current teacher's experience for use by the next year's teacher. These forms have academic and social information that offer clues about students. To avoid bias, remember the need for triangulation as you gather this information and check it against other sources about the student.

Eligibility for Special Programs

Before school starts you will want to know whether any of your students are eligible for and participate in special programs. Knowing as much as possible about your students' strengths and needs related to these special programs will help you determine the assessment strategies and instruction you will use.

Special Education   The federal government requires public schools to provide a free and appropriate education to students with disabilities who qualify under the Individuals with Disabilities Education Act (IDEA). Each student has an Individualized Education Program (IEP) tailored to that student's needs. All teachers who work with that student must be aware of and implement that IEP. Many students have accommodations for both instruction (e.g., preferential seating, large-print texts) and assessment (e.g., extended time for assessments, oral administration of an assessment) that each teacher must honor.

Student Information Sheet

Student Name _____ Teacher _____ Gender _____ Race _____

Academic Performance

Reading	Math	Spring Map Scores
Grades K–4 DRA Level _____	Below Grade Level _____	Reading _____ (RIT)
(The numbers below are the end of the year DRA benchmarks for each grade level.)	On Grade Level _____	_____ (Percentile)
	Above Grade Level _____	Math _____ (RIT)
K - (3) 3rd - (38)		_____ (Percentile)
1st - (16) 4th - (40)		Lang. Usage _____ (RIT)
2nd - (28) 5th - (44)		_____ (Percentile)

Conduct (Circle) A   B   C   D   F   **Circle if applies:** Frequently - Absent   Tardy
("A" is excellent behavior.
"F" is bad behavior.)

Individual Time Required of Teacher
_____ Independent Worker _____ Some Teacher Assistance _____ Dependent on Teacher
Work Habits _____ Slow _____ Average _____ Quick

Please check those that apply for **CURRENT** school year.
_____ Reading Assistance (1st grade only)
_____ Reading Recovery (1st grade only)
_____ Gifted program
_____ After-school Program
_____ Speech   _____ Academic Plan (R, M, Sc, SS)   _____ ESL
_____ IEP (Circle model) R M W   _____ Medication (type)/Health concerns
                                                                    (Please list on back)
_____ Frequent discipline referrals   _____ Student study team information available

Please check those that apply for the **UPCOMING** school year.
_____ Recommended for Reading Assistance   _____ Qualifies for ESL
_____ Qualifies for speech therapy   _____ Qualifies for gifted
_____ Qualifies for Special Services–Explain _____

If possible, separate from _____
On the reverse side, provide as much information as possible that would help in placing the child for next year. For example, does he/she need structure/flexibility, have unique learning style, etc.?

FIGURE 3.3   *Student Data Form from Cotton Belt Elementary School*

English as a Second Language   Programs for students who are learning English as a Second Language (ESL) vary from state to state and even from district to district. Often these students have some time each day with an ESL instructor, but they are also expected to function in their regular classes. With students who are learning English, your nonverbal cues and gestures are very important for the learning process. Knowing you have ESL students will allow you to plan to amplify this dimension of your teaching. Getting a clear sense of the level of these students' English language skills in consultation with the ESL instructor will also allow you to plan your instruction and assessment to accommodate their needs.

Gifted Programs   Ideally, a continuum of services is provided for gifted learners, or students who show evidence of strong capabilities in intellectual, creative, or artistic fields. Sometimes a program will pull students into a special classroom. Often, regular teachers modify the level, pace, or content of their instruction for gifted learners. In planning ahead for gifted students in your classroom, you will want to consider variations you can build into your instruction that will provide different levels of challenge while focusing on the key learning goals for your units.

After You Meet Your Students

Many teachers, including college professors, like to start classes by getting a general sense of their students' basic skills. Do you remember, on the first day of fourth or fifth grade, having to write a theme about what you did on your summer vacation? Your teacher was probably using it to check on your vocabulary, your writing fluency, and the sophistication of your sentence structure. Similarly, planning early class-wide or small-group discussions gives teachers an informal sense of their students' level of thinking and ability to communicate ideas coherently. For example, Kevina Satterwhite, a high school English as a Second Language (ESL) teacher, plays a game in which each student receives an index card with either a question about their school (principal's name, mascot, history) or an answer to one of the questions. Students have to match questions and answers with other students. This activity gives Kevina an idea of who understands written English, who speaks English to ask questions, and who is already familiar with the school. She also has students participate in dialogue discussions in pairs to determine listening and speaking abilities. She might give them a photo and ask them to describe in English what is happening, or have them write dialogue among characters in a picture.

Dana Stachowiak, a fourth-grade teacher who wants her children to become student activists, gives her children a chance to respond to posters around her room. These posters have artwork and quotes related to civic responsibility and activism. During the entire first week of school, she and her students talk about what the ideas mean to them personally. Then the students write a reflective paper about their discussions. These papers allow Dana to see students' levels of critical thinking, how they organize their thoughts, and how they make decisions.

Other teachers develop writing activities about student interests, families, dreams, and accomplishments, or they have students write about a good time with their best friend. These activities supplement a published test on speaking, listening, reading, and writing. You should design these informal activities to be enjoyable to students. To lower your students' anxiety levels, you should never grade these assignments. Providing feedback and using such work as a jumping-off point for later assignments can be useful, however.

For math classes at the elementary level, diagnostic assessment is particularly important because most math texts through the sixth grade begin with review chapters on addition and subtraction. If you find that your students do not need a review of these skills, you can move beyond these chapters quickly. Some math teachers often have the students make graphs of class preferences (e.g., favorite music group, favorite sports team, most admired person) or calculate averages of class characteristics (e.g., average height, average distance between home and school). These activities allow teachers to get a sense of a variety of student skills (including the ability to follow complex directions).

Such activities also provide an opportunity to observe how students interact with one another. Your observations will give you an idea about how much effort you must invest in explicitly teaching social skills, such as showing respect for others, sharing materials, and handling disagreements. Finally, these activities also help you get to know your students' interests and preferences, which will come in handy as you design your future instruction and your assessment.

As You Begin a New Unit of Instruction

For the past five years, we have kept track of the different assessments that our teacher candidates use during their student teaching. One of the most common assessment mistakes they make, especially with younger students, is to overestimate what the students already know. When you are designing a pre-unit assessment to see if students are already familiar with any of the content, you must also be sure to check whether they have mastered the foundational skills on which your unit is based. For example, if you plan to teach a unit on fables, you must make sure that the vocabulary level of the fables you will use is appropriate for your students. If you are teaching long division, students must have mastered their multiplication tables. If they struggle with multiplication, they may need instructional aides, such as a multiplication facts chart or simple calculator, to use in the division exercises.

An initial assessment will allow you to differentiate instruction and assessment. For example, if you are teaching a second-grade language arts/social studies unit on the five regions of the United States, some of your students may already be familiar with the major cities and landmarks of these areas but may not be familiar with the culture and customs. Others may never have seen a map of the United States before. You need to understand where each student is starting.

Informal Assessment Methods and Their Pitfalls

Several teachers we know have favorite ways to assess what students have learned previously and remembered related to a unit of study they are beginning. One science teacher favorite is called "The In and Out Game." When preparing to teach a unit, the teacher will first list two or three items that fit the concept, and one that does not. For example, when starting a unit on mammals she might say, "Dogs, cats, and bears are in. Frogs are out. What am I looking for?" Then she would ask a series of other questions, such as, "What else is in? What else is out?" By probing student understanding with this informal guessing game, she could get a good sense of what students already knew and how well they could distinguish features and examples of the concept "mammal."

You can think of many variations of games like this for assessing student understanding related to almost any unit you are preparing to teach. It can work for language arts concepts, such as adjectives or even literary periods; geographic concepts, such as land forms; food groups in nutrition; or art concepts, such as texture. For example, with a life science unit on producers and consumers, you could begin with salamanders, people, and insects as "in," and trees, algae, and grasses as "out," and follow the same procedure to elicit the level of student understanding.

Teachers also use the "Always, Sometimes, Never Game." With this game, students are asked to indicate whether a concept has a certain property always, sometimes, or never. For example, do rainbows always, sometimes, or never form after a storm? These games allow the teacher to gauge student levels of thinking in a non-threatening and enjoyable way.

Pitfalls with such games can occur, however. Children who need to be kept track of the most can fall through the cracks during these class-wide games or other informal checks a teacher may try. Students who are learning English may be reticent to participate because people might make fun of the way they speak. Students who are

TABLE 3.3

Questions Systematic Preassessment Can Address

What is students' current level of knowledge about this unit? Do they have common misconceptions?

Have all students mastered the foundational skills and knowledge necessary for this unit?

Have some students mastered some or all of the unit goals?

What are particular student interests related to the unit?

introverted may never raise their hand. Students who take more time to process information may not have a chance to get an answer out fast enough. As a result, most teachers also use more systematic ways to gather information about student understanding before a unit begins to make sure they get a clear picture of all of their children's understanding.

More Systematic Pre-unit Assessment Methods

Systematic preparation gives you solid information for instructional decision making. It can help you decide whether to begin with review or to start with new material. It also allows you to decide which content you will need to emphasize most and which you can cover more superficially.

You will also need some systematic evidence of what your students know at the beginning of a unit for accountability purposes. For example, we require our teacher candidates during their final college semester to show that they have had an impact on the preschool–12th grade students they teach during the unit where they have full responsibility for the class. They often design a brief assessment that can be quickly and easily administered before the unit to establish and prioritize their students' learning needs. This assessment serves several purposes, as shown in Table 3.3.

Your pre-unit assessment can also serve a motivational function (Chapman & King, 2005). Your diagnostic questions and activities can create student interest in the upcoming topic. Students can begin to notice items in their environment or online articles related to the new unit and can bring these to class to enrich their exploration and generate anticipation, for example.

✦ KEY STEPS IN DESIGNING PRE-UNIT DIAGNOSTIC ASSESSMENTS

A few simple steps for designing pre-unit diagnostic assessments are shown in Figure 3.4. These procedures will help you choose simple and efficient methods for gathering the information you need to design instruction that works for all your students.

1. Prioritize Content from Your Learning Goals

As we noted in Chapter 2, your learning goals and the standards for your discipline are the foundation for every unit. Because both your assessment and your instruction flow from the learning goals, your first step in designing your preassessment is to consult these goals and prioritize the content. If a learning goal has several parts, you

1. Prioritize content from your learning goals
2. Design and administer brief measures of top priority content
If content is skills/procedures:
Develop scoring guide or checklist to differentiate among students at different levels
If content is knowledge/understanding:
Develop 2–3 brief open-ended questions that capture top priority content
Have students perform the skill/procedure and rate
Interview students orally or have them write the answers to the questions and score
3. Gather other useful information
4. Analyze results of assessment to determine unit content and instructional strategies

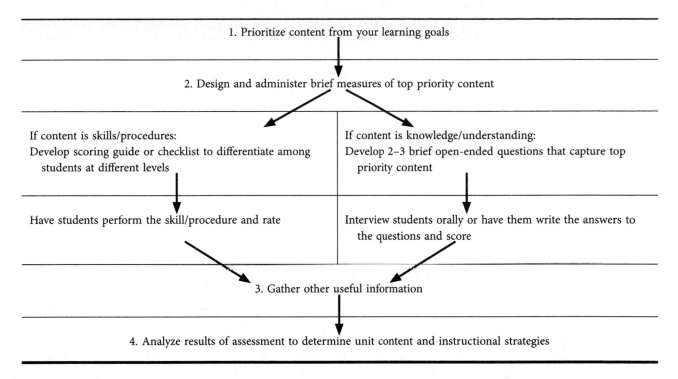

FIGURE 3.4 ***Steps in Designing Brief Pre-unit Diagnostic Assessments***

will probably focus on the most central or important for your preassessment. For example, suppose you have one learning goal: the students will be able to distinguish the five cultural regions of the United States, including language, customs, culture, and geography. For the preassessment you might want to determine whether students have any understanding of cultural regions and can distinguish among regions in any way. You wouldn't want to give a long preassessment of 50 multiple-choice questions with minute details about each region's specific customs, culture, and geography, especially if you suspect your students don't even know what a cultural region is.

2. Design and Administer Brief Measures of Top Priority Content

Next, you must decide what method or methods of assessment capture your prioritized learning goals best. These measures should be brief but focused on key concepts and skills for the unit (Moon, 2005; Rakow, 2007). For example, directly assessing common misconceptions held by students can be helpful. The purpose of the preassessment is to provide general patterns of gaps and mastery so you can get the unit's instructional sequence started.

As we discussed in Chapter 2, you can usually focus on two kinds of learning—basic knowledge or understanding students hold, and student ability to perform a skill, strategy, or procedure. A math example can illustrate the difference: If you want to know whether students understand place value (which is knowledge about how numbers work), you can ask them a question such as *How does the number of zeroes help you explain the difference between 100 and 1,000?* A student who can explain how the ones, tens, and hundreds columns function differently has general knowledge of place value. They don't need to work any problems to show you they understand this basic concept.

If you want to know whether your students can use their knowledge to *perform* a desired skill, you will be assessing the skill or procedure that you expect them to master. Asking math students to solve a specific problem taps this kind of skill. For example, *To the nearest hundred, calculate the sum of 87,500, 912 and 92,431,331.* Solving this problem correctly will show the teacher that the students can use their understanding of place value in a mathematical procedure.

Measuring Knowledge/Understanding

If you are measuring knowledge and understanding, you can have students answer questions orally (if you note their answers on a checklist) or on paper. Usually two or three questions per learning goal are sufficient, especially when you are quite certain that students are not likely to have encountered the content of the unit before, such as in advanced math or physics.

In returning to the earlier example, let's suppose you are getting ready to preassess the level of knowledge students have of your learning goal on the five regions of the United States. You might give students a map of the United States and ask them to color the five regions with different colors and then, at the bottom, list all the things they can think of that each region is known for. They could also briefly list any similarities or differences they see across regions. Such an assessment is brief, covers the key content, and allows students who may already be familiar with culture, geography, or customs to demonstrate their specific knowledge. It also allows students who don't know much to avoid suffering through numerous detailed questions about culture, geography, and customs. Other examples of brief, systematic preassessments for knowledge and understanding appear in Table 3.4. Notice that each of the measures goes beyond rote knowledge to address the "comprehension" and "analysis" levels of Bloom's taxonomy. Using higher order questions allows the teacher to get a sense of the way students think about the topic and provides a challenge for all students. It also enables the teacher to access multiple levels of understanding. Ideally, no student should get all of the items correct *or* all of the items wrong (Chapman & King, 2005).

Measuring Skills/Strategies/Procedures

If your learning goal requires students to perform skills, strategies, or procedures, before instruction begins you need to set up a method for observing them perform the key skills or a representative subset of skills. You then rate their level of performance with a scoring guide. Measuring skills is crucial in disciplines where most learning is centered on performing specific skills, such as physical education, art, music, or dance. If you decide on one or more basic skills or procedures, you will design a checklist or other scoring guide that captures the crucial differences in student levels. For example, if a physical education teacher is teaching second graders how to catch a ball, she will have them take turns throwing and catching a ball a few times. As she scans the group, she will note the children's skill level, starting with those who don't have the skill at all. A scoring chart that lists the three levels of skill down one side and the names of the students across the top (as in Table 3.5) is useful for completing this task quickly.

This activity will help the teacher determine which aspects of the catching pattern (e.g., arm position) need to be worked on most with the students. In addition, if she finds that many students already have a mature catching pattern, she will revise her goals for the unit and move on to a more difficult skill. Table 3.6 shows several examples of diagnostic measures for key skills and procedures.

TABLE 3.4

Examples of Knowledge/Understanding Diagnostic Measures Before Instructional Units

Learning Goal	Diagnostic Measure	Sample Scoring
Social studies: Student will be able to distinguish the five cultural regions of the United States, including language, customs, culture, and geography.	Give students a U.S. map and ask them to color the five cultural regions. Then list things associated with each region at the bottom, and list similarities or differences between regions.	1 point for each correct region, 1 point for each item associated correctly with a region, up to 5. 1 point for each similarity or difference up to 2.
Algebra: Student will be able to understand and represent relations and functions in math.	Ask students to describe the difference between a relation and a function and give an example of each.	Develop a scoring guide that lists the key distinctions and misconceptions. Score each answer on a 1 to 4-point scale based on the list.
Secondary English: Student will be able to compare and contrast utopias and dystopias in literature.	Have students write the definition of utopia and dystopia. Then provide any examples they can think of from previously read literature.	1 point for each correct definition, 1 point for each example.
Music: Student will be able to explain distinguishing characteristics of musical genres.	Ask students to listen to two different pieces of music and write down distinctions between them.	1 point for each distinction (e.g., rhythm, melody, harmony, expression, and timbre).
Vocabulary for multiple subjects: Students will be able to understand and use key terms of the discipline in writing and speaking.	Provide students a list of vocabulary words relevant to the unit and ask them to match words with their definitions.	1 point for each correctly matched word.

TABLE 3.5

Scoring Guide for Catching a Ball

Level	Student 1	Student 2	Student 3	Student 4	Student 5
ONE • Arms are outstretched, elbows extended and palms upward. • Ball is contacted with arms and elbows flexed. • Object is trapped against the body.					
TWO • Arms are in front of body, elbows slightly flexed. • Arms encircle the ball against the chest. • Hands, arms hold the ball to chest.					
THREE • Arms are slightly ahead of body, elbows flexed. • Ball is contacted with hands and is grasped with fingers. • Palms are adjusted to size and flight of ball.					

From Chepko, S.F., and R.K. Arnold. 2000. *Guidelines for physical education programs: Standards, objectives, and assessments for Grades K–12*. New York: Allyn & Bacon. Reprinted by permission of Pearson Education.

TABLE 3.6

Examples of Skills/Strategies/Procedures Diagnostic Measures Before Instructional Units

Learning Goal	Diagnostic Measure	Sample Scoring
Physical education: Student will be able to execute a mature overhand throwing pattern.	Have students throw the ball in pairs.	Check off their skill level on a scoring guide with elements of a good throw listed.
Music: Student will be able to maintain a steady beat in $\frac{4}{4}$ time.	Have students listen to recorded song and clap a steady beat.	Use the class list to check off each student who maintains a steady beat for four or more measures.
Theater: Student will be able to write a script for a play based on personal experience, heritage, imagination, literature, and history.	Provide a paragraph describing a new play. Have students develop the first five lines of dialogue for the opening scene based on two elements (e.g., personal experience and literature) of the learning goal.	Develop a scoring guide that addresses the level of quality of the dialogue in reference to the two elements.
Elementary language arts: Student will be able to read grade-level material fluently.	Have students take turns reading aloud to a partner.	Teacher circulates and notes number and kinds of miscues per sentence on clipboard chart.

3. Gather Other Useful Information

You may also want to use other information you gain in less systematic ways for designing your unit and your individual lessons. For example, many teachers use KWL charts (K = what we know, W = what we want to know, L = what we have learned). They start a unit by asking students as a group what they already know about the content of a learning goal. Then they ask what else they would like to know. This information can be helpful to a certain extent for unit planning because it provides some ideas about how students are thinking currently about a topic, what kind of background knowledge they have, some of their preferences, or the level of enthusiasm they have for the topic. Although it does have informal uses, we do not recommend this method for more formal preassessment. Developing a KWL chart often misses input from less-confident or less-talkative students. And sometimes knowledgeable students stop talking after providing one or two suggestions. In addition, some students can go off on unrelated tangents and take others with them. So KWL charts usually do not provide an accurate, systematic picture of each student's level of understanding before instruction begins (Rakow, 2007). They also can have limited utility when you are teaching skills and procedures because students are talking about the skill and not showing you whether they can do the skill. You need information on every student related to the key learning goals to provide the best instruction.

4. Analyze Results of Preassessment to Determine Unit Content and Instructional Strategies

After you have collected the preassessment information, you must find a way to summarize it for yourself in a meaningful way. We recommend assigning points so that each student ends up with a total score. These scores are *not* for grading purposes.

TABLE 3.7

Preassessment Information on Five Cultural Regions Ordered from Least Knowledgeable to Most Knowledgeable Student

Student	Regions Indicated on Map? 100% = 5/5	Associations with Region? 100% = 5/5	Similarities Between Regions? 100% = 2/2	Differences Between Regions? 100% = 2/2
1	0%	0%	0%	0%
2	0%	0%	0%	0%
3	0%	0%	0%	0%
4	20%	0%	0%	0%
5	20%	20%	0%	0%
6	40%	20%	0%	0%
7	40%	20%	0%	0%
8	60%	40%	0%	0%
9	80%	40%	0%	0%
10	100%	100%	50%	50%

They are only a way for you to get a rough picture of where the members of your class fall in relation to the learning goals you will be addressing. These scores are just an estimate to help you get a sense of where you will probably need to put the most energy and instructional time on the unit.

We recommend assigning scores based on percentage correct. You can interpret a score of 25 percent more quickly than a score of 3 out of 12 or 6 out of 24. Table 3.7 shows the preassessment information in percentages from one class of second graders related to the five cultural regions learning goal, arranged from lowest to highest scores. You can see from looking at the first question in the table that the last three students have an emerging factual understanding of the boundaries of U.S. cultural regions, but the first three students in the table appear to have no understanding of this most basic element of the unit.

Furthermore, these first three students had 0 percent correct across all items. Seeing 0 percent correct across all questions should function as a red flag for you. Students who attain a score of 0 percent on a preassessment need additional preassessment attention. If students have no prior knowledge or skill, the learning goal, as it stands, may be too difficult for them. At this point, you need to drop back to check whether they have the prior knowledge and skills needed for the unit you are preparing. For example, in the unit on the five geographic regions, you would want to check on whether these three students have worked with maps before and whether they understand how maps represent places. You would want to find out if they understand the relationship between individual states, regions, and the United States. You would want to ask them questions about what they know about their own state and region. If they have only recently arrived in the United States, you may need to provide additional background information before they are ready for the learning goals associated with this unit.

In Table 3.7 you will also note that all students except Student 10 had difficulty comparing and contrasting regions, even if they showed some basic knowledge about region facts. This finding should let you know that you need to focus on higher-level thinking skills, such as analysis, as you teach this unit. Encouraging comparisons across regions as you study each new region could help your students develop facility with analysis.

For students who perform significantly better than others on the preassessment, such as Student 10, you need to make sure that they are not bored and have new challenges. You may decide to differentiate activities to include more depth or breadth. For example, with the regions unit, Student 10 will need different tasks (not just *more* tasks) than some of the other students. This student could be given tasks that emphasize higher-level thinking skills and could go beyond the grade-level learning goals, such as analyzing how the geography of each region influences its culture and economy.

→ MAKING THE MOST OF YOUR DIAGNOSTIC ASSESSMENTS

We'd like to summarize this section by offering three suggestions for efficiently gathering information that will be useful for helping your students learn. These are displayed in Table 3.8. First, *hold high expectations for all of your students and engage in behaviors that convey high expectations.* You can do this by avoiding negative information from previous years that may no longer apply. We recently talked to a student who decided to turn over a new leaf when he started his junior year of high school. Over the summer he had worked with a counselor at camp who had helped him see the error of his ways and kindled in him the desire to attend college. He had been a troublemaker and a poor student since elementary school, and his records showed it. He knew he had to work hard to change his path, and so he put many hours into his first paper for English that fall. The paper was so well written that the teacher accused him of plagiarism. He, along with his parents, had a tough job convincing his teacher that he was making an effort to start fresh. The teacher's assumptions about him almost sank his new determination to become a serious student.

Second, *choose brief measures that focus on the most important knowledge and skills for your learning goals before beginning a unit.* Your preassessment measures should be brief. You don't want to use valuable instructional time unnecessarily, and you don't want to discourage your students about what they don't know yet with

TABLE 3.8

Three Rules to Guide Your Diagnostic Classroom Assessment

Hold high expectations for all your students and engage in assessment behaviors that convey high expectations from the first day of school.

Choose brief measures that focus on the most important elements of your learning goals, including higher-order thinking, before beginning a unit.

Rely most on the information you gather systematically yourself across time.

lengthy pretests. You are not conducting a research study where you are trying to keep pre- and post-tests perfectly consistent and where you are controlling all variables. Instead, you are collecting some basic information to help you plan your unit and to be able to document what your students know and don't know beforehand. After the unit, you can do more extensive assessment to demonstrate how much they have learned, using your preassessment as baseline information.

Because these measures must be brief, you want to design them economically so that a broad range of knowledge and skill levels can be demonstrated by students. You want to make sure you are getting at higher levels of Bloom's taxonomy, as well as assessing the most basic principles. If your unit focuses on both knowledge and skills, be sure to find ways to measure both, and not just one or the other. For example, some of the best math teachers tell us that students can work lots of problems using a particular algorithm, but they have a much harder time with the more basic understanding of knowing when that procedure should and should not be used.

Third, *rely most on the information you gather systematically yourself across time.* You should weight most heavily the information you collect that is current and observable. Last year's information can be outdated or erroneous unless you can detect strong patterns through triangulation of different sources. Because your fleeting impressions can be distorted, erroneous, or forgotten if they don't conform to your first impressions, you should gather information in a systematic way. Writing samples, documentation of contributions to discussion, pretests, early homework, and journal entries are all useful sources of information.

ACCOMMODATIONS FOR DIVERSE LEARNERS IN DIAGNOSTIC ASSESSMENT

Classroom diagnostic assessments can be flexible and informal. They allow multiple methods for students to demonstrate their knowledge and skills related to the learning goals using a variety of formats and methods of expression. Given the wide range of skills and knowledge of the students in any classroom, this flexibility is crucial. You will want to accommodate your diagnostic assessments in ways that allow students to perform at their best and demonstrate all they know.

Universal design for learning (Rose & Meyer, 2002) is an important framework for understanding accommodations for diverse learners. The concept of "universal design" originated in engineering and architecture in the 1950s. Designers began building environments that from the outset eliminated obstacles or barriers for people with physical disabilities (e.g., curb cuts in sidewalks for crossing streets). As the widespread benefits (e.g., for joggers and parents with strollers) became apparent, the idea gained strength and popularity. More recently it has been applied to proactively designing instruction and assessment to reduce barriers for diverse learners.

Universal Design for Learning
A framework for understanding the types of accommodations that should be considered for diverse learners. Instruction and assessment is designed to reduce barriers by addressing multiple means of representation, multiple means of expression, and multiple means of engagement.

In education, three types of considerations must be kept in mind anytime you design your instruction and assessment (CAST, 2008). The first is **multiple means of representation,** or the methods by which material is presented to students. For example, Jocelyn, the biology teacher, used symbolic as well as print representations of science concepts in both her instruction and assessment to make complex concepts more accessible to her students. The second is **multiple means of expression,** or the methods in which students respond to your instructional and assessment tasks. For example, some students may respond better orally or with a computer than with written answers to a diagnostic question. The third consideration is **multiple means of engagement,** or the methods used to keep students' interest and

TABLE 3.9

Accommodation Considerations for Diagnostic Assessments

Issue	Type of Accommodation
Difficulty with fine motor skills	• Oral answers to questions • Use of computer
Learning English	• Use English language without complex syntax and cultural references • Check on understanding of specific vocabulary needed for the unit and offer opportunities for repeated access • Use visual cues, questions allowing short answers • Provide nontraditional opportunities to demonstrate understanding such as diagrams, concept maps, drawings • Allow use of translation dictionaries
Learning goal already mastered	• Make sure pre-unit assessment covers the most complex and abstract elements of unit content to avoid a ceiling effect
Difficulty focusing attention	• Organize the assessment content (e.g., graphic organizers, diagrams, checklists) • Allow completion one step at a time • Limit time for questions, tasks • Increase novelty of assessment tasks
Literacy skills below those of typical peers (e.g., learning disability)	• Use language without complex syntax • Check understanding of specific vocabulary needed for the unit and offer opportunities for repeated access • Use visual cues, questions allowing short answers • Use oral more than written questions • Provide nontraditional opportunities to demonstrate understanding, such as diagrams, concept maps, drawings
Lack of familiarity with school culture	• Provide opportunities for multiple types of formats beyond teacher questioning • Determine extent of knowledge of the "hidden rules" of school culture (e.g., how to ask questions, student and teacher roles)

participation strong. This last issue is more relevant to ongoing instruction and will be addressed in Chapter 4.

We have listed in Table 3.9 some considerations for accommodations in diagnostic assessments that can help address these considerations for students. We have organized them by six common issues of concern you are likely to encounter among your students.

Students with Fine Motor Difficulties

Students with physical limitations may not have the capacity to write their answers to diagnostic questions, and so you may need to accommodate their needs to get a good estimate of their knowledge and skills. They may need accommodations such as using a tape recorder to state their answers or a computer to type responses.

Students Learning English

Students who are learning English as a second language have a double burden in the classroom. They must grapple with language comprehension and expression as well as with specific content you are teaching. For this reason, you must hone your own non-verbal communication skills because ESL students rely heavily on your movements and facial expressions.

Early on, you will want to understand how your students' different language and cultural backgrounds affect their learning so that you can provide a learning environment in which they feel comfortable. Many educators recommend gathering information from parents and the ESL teacher so that you have a clearer picture of the skills of your students. Types of information specifically relevant to language that may be helpful are listed in Table 3.10.

Understanding your students' language-use skills should be a top priority. Two levels of language proficiency are important to appreciate (Rothenberg & Fisher, 2007). **Basic interpersonal communication skills (BICS)** are the informal language used to communicate in everyday social situations where many contextual cues exist (such as gestures, facial expressions, and objects) to enhance comprehension. For example, your students use BICS in the cafeteria, on the playground, and in their after-school activities such as sports or drama.

In contrast, **cognitive academic language proficiency (CALP)** requires more formal expertise in the abstract scholarly language used in academic contexts (e.g., textbooks). Fewer context cues are available, and so language alone has to carry the burden of meaning. Because it is more difficult to master, CALP can take years longer to develop than BICS. For this reason, you may be surprised that some students in your classes whose first language is not English can fluently answer oral questions and have conversations with friends, but have difficulty with more academic activities. Gathering diagnostic information on students' listening, speaking, reading, and writing skills must, therefore, take into account your students' skills in both types of language contexts.

One of the most important strategies you can use for ESL students is to simplify the language (not the content) of oral or written questions. You preserve the knowledge

BICS
Informal language used to communicate in everyday social situations where there are many contextual cues to enhance comprehension.

CALP
Formal language that requires expertise in abstract scholarly vocabulary used in academic settings in which language itself, rather than cultural cues, must bear the primary meaning.

TABLE 3.10

Background Information Helpful in Teaching Students Whose First Language Is Not English

What language is spoken at home?

To what extent do parents speak English?

How long has student been exposed to English at school? In other contexts?

Level of English language skills:
Basic interpersonal communication skills (BICS) and cognitive academic language proficiency (CALP):
- Listening (e.g., requires repetition, slower speech to understand?)
- Speaking (e.g., displays halting speech, complete sentences?)
- Reading (e.g., fluency, vocabulary levels?)
- Writing (e.g., level of complexity, grammar issues?)

BOX 3.1   EXAMPLE OF A MATH QUESTION BEFORE AND AFTER MODIFICATIONS FOR ENGLISH LANGUAGE LEARNERS

Before	After
Patty just received a letter in the mail telling about a new promotion with stuffed animals. When Patty has collected and shown proof of owning 125 stuffed animals, she will receive the new Million Dollar Bear free. Patty has 79 animals right now. Write an equation to show how many more animals Patty will need to collect to get her free Million Dollar Bear. A. $\square - 125 = 79$ B. $79 + \square = 125$ C. $79 - \square = 125$ D. $125 + 79 = \square$	A class has 79 stars. They need 125 stars. How many more stars do they need? Choose the correct equation. A. $\square - 125 = 79$ B. $79 + \square = 125$ C. $79 - \square = 125$ D. $125 + 79 = \square$

From Kopriva, R. 2008. *Improving testing for English Language Learners.* New York: Routledge. Reprinted with permission.

and skills needed to address the learning goal, but you simplify the sentence structure and vocabulary, you eliminate idiomatic expressions, and you avoid hypothetical statements. See Box 3.1 for an example.

Because each discipline has specific vocabulary, you want to be sure this vocabulary is preassessed and then focused on and learned early in any unit by your English language learners, and by your other students as well. Using as many concrete visual cues and prompts as possible for accurate preassessment as well as during later instruction is helpful (Haynes, 2007). Charts and drawings of scientific processes such as those developed for Jocelyn's biology class can help students grasp and convey concepts that they may not be able to describe verbally. In math, we often see students using number lines taped to their desks. Many teachers also have students make a representational drawing of a problem before they start to solve it. In social studies, maps and globes are helpful, as well as pictures and artifacts. In language arts classes, charts with step-by-step procedures for common writing tasks can be designed by students and posted for future use. Such posters can serve as an indicator of their understanding of the process.

Another consideration is to limit use of extended writing in demonstrating understanding. When ESL students write in English, they have to use a good bit of their attention on mechanics and grammar, limiting their ability to attend to higher-level skills related to the content. Thus, an extended writing task for a diagnostic assessment might impede these students' demonstration of their learning and its application. Offering opportunities to brainstorm in groups or individually, or to make outlines first, can help make a writing task less daunting. These accommodations help you access students' understanding of the content apart from their understanding of the English language. Such strategies will give you a more accurate sense of the student, which will help you provide better feedback and instruction.

Students Who Have Already Mastered the Learning Goals

If you have advanced students in your class, you need to keep them challenged. To get a true sense of their knowledge and skills, your diagnostic assessments must involve higher-order thinking skills that go beyond the basic content of the learning goals. If you don't allow for a wide range, they may get a perfect score without your learning the full extent of their knowledge. Researchers call this a **ceiling effect.** A ceiling effect occurs when a student attains the maximum score, or "ceiling," for that assessment. For example, if a student had a perfect score on the five cultural regions preassessment, you would know that they knew all of that content, but you wouldn't know what else they might know and where your instruction for them should begin.

Ceiling Effect

When a student attains the maximum score, or "ceiling," for an assessment, thus preventing appraisal of the full extent of the student's knowledge.

Students Who Have Difficulty Focusing Attention

Many students have difficulty paying attention and sitting still for long periods of time. To get a good estimate of their knowledge and skills during diagnostic assessment, you may need to take steps to maximize attention. Providing graphic organizers, diagrams, and checklists can help students focus. Providing directions one step at a time or having students repeat directions can also help focus attention. Breaking down the time you use for oral questions and assessment tasks into shorter segments can also be helpful. We once worked with a teacher who often divided tasks into brief timed intervals. The strategy helped all her students keep focused, and they made a game out of "beating the clock." Increasing the novelty of your assessment tasks is also useful. In some cases, if you are using written questions, each item on an assessment can be printed on a separate page so the student is not distracted by a lot of text.

Students with Literacy Skills Below Those of Typical Peers

Students with learning disabilities, as well as other students who have difficulty with reading, will need some special attention during diagnostic assessment. Multiple representations of assessment content, such as both oral and written versions with visuals, can be helpful. As for ESL students, avoiding text with complex sentence structure and vocabulary where possible is also useful. The reading level of materials you use in class for diagnostic assessment tasks can be varied. Be sure that you do not embarrass students with obviously "easy" books at lower grade levels. The media specialists at your school can help you access reading matter with grade-level content but different reading levels. This is important when you use authentic texts in diagnostic assessments of students' reading strategies. Books about sports figures and other topics of interest to older students have been written with less complex prose. Also, some educational websites have information about a given topic (e.g., the greenhouse effect) at more than one reading level.

Students Who Lack Familiarity with U.S. School Culture

Many students who come from backgrounds other than the European American middle-class culture that is dominant in most schools may have difficulties showing you what they know. Familiarity with the norms and habits of schools is not limited to students from other countries. Educators have also noted that students from low socioeconomic backgrounds often have different assumptions about appropriate behavior and learning methods, and they may not know the "hidden rules" of school culture (Payne, 2003, 2008). Different cultural assumptions can be particularly problematic at the beginning of the year, when students may be faced with a host of different traditions and norms than they are used to. A few questions to help you think about how different cultures define appropriate and inappropriate

TABLE 3.11

Questions About Typical Classroom Behavior Illustrating Possible Cultural Differences

1. What is the typical purpose and format of questions and answers?
2. What are the typical student and teacher roles?
3. Is cooperation valued over competition among students?
4. What are typical gender roles?

classroom behavior related to assessment are listed in Table 3.11, based on work by Dunlap and Weisman (2006) and Kusimo et al. (2000).

Some divergent traditions exist around teacher questioning, a common diagnostic assessment practice in the United States, but not in all cultures (Kusimo et al., 2000). For example, in some cultures, adults will never use the pedagogical technique of asking children direct questions about something the adult obviously knows. This common learning strategy in our culture seems silly to them—why would you waste your time asking a question you already know the answer to? Other cultures, such as some American Indian groups, are never expected to demonstrate skills publicly until they are completely mastered. This assumption could interfere with a teacher's desire to engage students in public conversation to detect the extent of their prior knowledge.

In some cultures, people are in the habit of pausing a few seconds when answering an oral question. This pause is meant to show the person is offering respect to the questioner by considering the question carefully. In our culture, the teacher faced with the pause may move quickly on to another student, assuming that the first doesn't know the answer. Finally, among some groups, if questions are phrased implying a choice (e.g., "Would you like to show us a cartwheel?"), students will assume they can refuse. They are more accustomed to direct commands.

Students also may not know how to explicitly ask questions as a method for accessing information, which can be another important focus for diagnostic assessment. Students who have acquired this skill tend to do better academically than students who have not (Payne, 2008). This skill may be related to students' lack of familiarity with the less casual and more formal language typically used in school, which can put them at a disadvantage.

Beyond questioning patterns and formality of language, other cultural customs may involve different roles for learners (Kusimo et al., 2000). In some cultures, students are taught to be respectful and quiet, so you may have difficulty getting them to participate in discussions or to venture an opinion of their own during informal diagnostic assessments. Some cultures, such as those in Mexico and Central America, are more oriented toward the group's goals, whereas the dominant culture in the United States is more oriented toward individual success. The more group-oriented cultures foster interdependence and working together, and so students from these cultures may be quite comfortable with cooperative group projects and activities. Using these students' strength—the ability to work together—can foster their learning and help develop a positive classroom atmosphere. Such students may not, however, be as comfortable with activities that emphasize individual competition or individual assessment. For example, some students will purposely answer a question wrong if a peer answered it wrong so the peer will not be embarrassed.

Final Thoughts on Accommodations for Diagnostic Assessment

We would like you to focus on two overall points from this section. First, you need to get to know your students and their strengths and needs related to learning in school if you are going to gather accurate information with your diagnostic assessments. Naturally, asking parents and students directly can help you gather some of this information. If you use a variety of instructional and assessment strategies in your class, you will also learn a great deal from observing students, such as their problem-solving strategies, their ability to cooperate with others, and their personal preferences. All of these can be useful as you design your instruction and assessment.

The second point we would like you to take from this section is that the accommodations you start out making for one group of students usually end up benefiting *many* students. For example, note that strategies such as using visual cues as well as oral and written information are helpful not only for English-language learners, but also for students whose literacy skills are not yet at the instructional level of the class. Such cues are probably also helpful for students who have difficulty paying attention or difficulty staying organized. In addition, your typical students will also find such materials beneficial. The more ways all students have for representing information as they learn, the more likely they are to learn it well.

✦ CASE STUDY APPLICATION

In this section we revisit one of the cases introduced in Chapter 2 to illustrate key points with a concrete example. We turn to Ebony's unit on characteristics of solids and liquids. We focus on one learning goal: *Students will demonstrate appropriate steps to test an unknown solid or liquid.* For a preassessment for this learning goal, Ebony had each student explore a solid and a liquid in zipper plastic bags inside a "feely box," where they can touch objects but not see them. Students then made a list of descriptive words corresponding to each test they think of to perform on the object. For example, some of the options could be, Does it have a shape? How big is it? Is it heavy or light? How does it feel? How does it move? She recorded their percentage of correct answers out of a maximum of six descriptive words for the solid and five for the liquid.

Ebony's preassessment results are shown in Table 3.12. Note that students are identified by number rather than by name to ensure confidentiality. Also note that Ebony ordered total scores from lowest to highest so she could look for patterns. Describe what patterns you see in the data. Are liquids or solids easier for this group of children to identify before the unit begins? What kinds of variations do you see among the students? What else would you like to know about these students?

You might notice that the majority of the class (15 on solids, 12 on liquids) got one right or less on the preassessment. You might also notice that no student demonstrates mastery of this learning goal as measured by this diagnostic assessment. We see one student who attained 100 percent on solids, but she had 0 percent on liquids, and so she definitely needs further instruction. These findings suggest that the class has lots of room for improvement on this learning goal, which is as it should be for diagnostic assessment results. If a majority of the class had scores above 80 percent, Ebony would have needed to change the learning goal to challenge the students more.

TABLE 3.12

Preassessment Results for One Learning Goal for Unit on Characteristics of Liquids and Solids

Pre-unit assessment results for learning goal *Students will take appropriate steps to test an unknown liquid or solid*

	Percent correct on Solids (6 possible)	Percent correct on Liquids (5 possible)	Total percent correct (11 possible)
Student 8	0%	0%	0%
Student 10	0%	0%	0%
Student 11	0%	0%	0%
Student 15	0%	0%	0%
Student 16	0%	20%	9%
Student 12	17%	0%	9%
Student 5	17%	0%	9%
Student 2	17%	20%	18%
Student 3	17%	20%	18%
Student 9	17%	20%	18%
Student 6	17%	20%	18%
Student 17	0%	60%	27%
Student 4	17%	40%	27%
Student 13	17%	40%	27%
Student 14	17%	40%	27%
Student 7	33%	60%	45%
Student 1	100%	0%	54%

You might also notice that four students did not describe either object with any words. As we have pointed out, when students cannot complete any element of the preassessment, you should further assess the knowledge and skills that you assume they should have mastered earlier in order to be ready for this unit. In a small group, Ebony worked with these four students to learn more about their level of understanding. She used another "feely box" task in which every student put a hand in the box in turn, and they talked about what they felt so she could see how different children observed differently. She also had each one write one descriptive word after the discussion. She found that two of the students lagged behind typical peers in vocabulary because they were not native speakers of English, and the two others had great difficulty with writing. This information helped Ebony become sensitive to these students' needs as she designed her lessons. It also alerted her that they would require additional accommodations and instruction in these areas.

KEY CHAPTER POINTS

In this chapter we have described the importance and usefulness of diagnostic assessment. We began by showing you the link between teacher expectations and their informal teaching assessment behaviors often used in diagnostic assessment. When questioning students, answering questions, or praising and criticizing student work, teachers are often unaware of the behaviors they engage in that can encourage or deflate students. When behaviors consistent with low expectations persist across the year, they can result in poor student achievement.

We next discussed the importance of choosing your sources of information about your students wisely and using triangulation as you gather that information. Then we discussed the types of information available before school starts, such as grades, standardized test scores, portfolios of student work, and eligibility for special programs. Finally, we focused on informal and more systematic methods you will use to gauge the knowledge and skills your students bring to a new unit.

We next discussed accommodations often needed for diverse learners as you design diagnostic assessments using the perspective of universal design for learning. We included several common issues (among many) that confront teachers and students in the classroom, such as students with fine motor difficulties, students learning English as a second language, students who have already mastered the learning goals (e.g., gifted students), students who have difficulty focusing attention, students with literacy skills below typical peers (e.g., learning disability), and students unfamiliar with typical school culture.

We then highlighted two important points about diagnostic assessment. First, to be an effective teacher, you need to get to know your students and their strengths, needs, and preferences. Second, just as curb cuts in sidewalks make life easier for many able-bodied people, accommodations that you design into your assessment often benefit many typical students beyond those for whom they are first designed. Finally, we returned to one of our case studies to apply the concepts from our understanding of diagnostic assessment.

CHAPTER REVIEW QUESTIONS

1. Table 3.1 lists several teacher behaviors related to low expectations for students that can occur during informal assessment. What steps can you take to ensure that you avoid these behaviors? What behaviors could you replace them with? What teacher behaviors might communicate high expectations?
2. Why is triangulation important when you are gathering information about your students?
3. What existing sources of information (e.g., school records, testing records) about your future students do you think would be important to examine to prepare for teaching? In your view, what are the pros and cons of using these types of information?
4. Choose learning goals for a unit you might be asked to teach. Design a brief pre-assessment task (or tasks) that could help you determine what your students already know about the unit content. Be sure to include skills at higher levels of Bloom's cognitive taxonomy to avoid a ceiling effect.
5. Choose other learning goals for a different unit. Design a preassessment method for measuring knowledge and understanding of the content. Then design a preassessment method for measuring skills and procedures required for that content.

6. You have given a preassessment to your class, and the results are as follows:

Student	Task 1	Task 2	Task 3
1	0%	0%	0%
2	0%	0%	0%
3	10%	10%	50%
4	20%	0%	80%
5	20%	20%	100%
6	40%	20%	100%
7	60%	40%	100%
8	60%	20%	100%
9	80%	40%	100%
10	100%	100%	100%

Describe in words what the table tells you in terms of what your next steps should be. How might these results lead you to differentiate your instruction?

7. Describe accommodations related to assessment that you have seen teachers implement for each of the groups in Table 3.9. Were these accommodations effective? Why or why not? Have you seen other types of accommodations for other types of issues students bring to the classroom?

8. Using Table 3.3, critique Ebony's diagnostic assessment process. What did she do well? How specifically might she have improved her diagnostic assessment?

9. Analyze the extent to which Ebony followed each of the four steps in designing brief pre-unit diagnostic assessments described in Figure 3.4.

Helpful Websites

http://www.cast.org

This website for the Center for Applied Special Technology (CAST) provides many resources for helping you modify your instruction and assessment using universal design for learning (UDL) principles. You can find lesson builders, UDL guidelines, and excerpts from *Teaching every student in the digital age,* as well as reports and case studies detailing effective classroom practices.

http://www.cfa.harvard.edu/smgphp/mosart/about_mosart.html

MOSART (Misconceptions-Oriented Standards-based Assessment Resources for Teachers) was funded by the National Science Foundation to provide assessment support for teachers. The website provides items linked to the K–12 science curriculum as well as a tutorial on how to use and interpret them. These items can be particularly useful for pre-unit assessment because they focus on common misconceptions.

References

CAST. 2008. *Universal design for learning guidelines version 1.0.* Wakefield, MA: Author. Retrieved April 14 from http://www.cast.org/publications/UDLguidelines/UDL_Guidelines_v1.0-Organizer.pdf.

Chapman, C., and R. King. 2005. *Differentiated assessment strategies*. Thousand Oaks, CA: Corwin Press.

Dunlap, C. A., and E. M. Weisman. 2006. *Helping English language learners succeed*. Huntington Beach, CA: Shell Educational Publishing.

Eggen, P., and D. Kauchak. 2004. *Educational psychology: Windows on classrooms*. 6th ed. Upper Saddle River, NJ: Pearson.

Haynes, J. 2007. *Getting started with English language learners*. Alexandria, VA: ASCD.

Kusimo, P., M. Ritter, K. Busick, C. Ferguson, E. Trumbull, and G. Solano-Flores. 2000. *Making assessment work for everyone: How to build on student strengths*. Southwest Educational Development Laboratory. Retrieved June 19, 2007, from http://www.sedl.org/pubs/catalog/items/t105/assessment-full.pdf.

Moon, T. 2005. The role of assessment in differentiation. *Theory into Practice* 44(3): 226–233.

Palardy, J. M. 1969. What teachers believe—What children achieve. *The Elementary School Journal* 69: 370–374.

Payne, R. 2003. *A framework for understanding poverty*. 3rd ed. Highlands, TX: aha! Process, Inc.

Payne, R. 2008. Nine powerful practices. *Educational Leadership* 65(7): 48–52.

Rakow, S. 2007. All means all: Classrooms that work for advanced learners. *National Middle School Association Middle Ground* 11(1): 10–12.

Rose, D. H., and A. Meyer. 2002. *Teaching every student in the digital age: Universal design for learning*. Alexandria, VA: Association for Supervision and Curriculum Development.

Rothenberg, C., and D. Fisher. 2007. *Teaching English language learners: A differentiated approach*. Upper Saddle River, NJ: Pearson.

Schunk, D., P. Pintrich, and J. Meece. 2008. *Motivation in education*. 3rd ed. Upper Saddle River, NJ: Pearson.

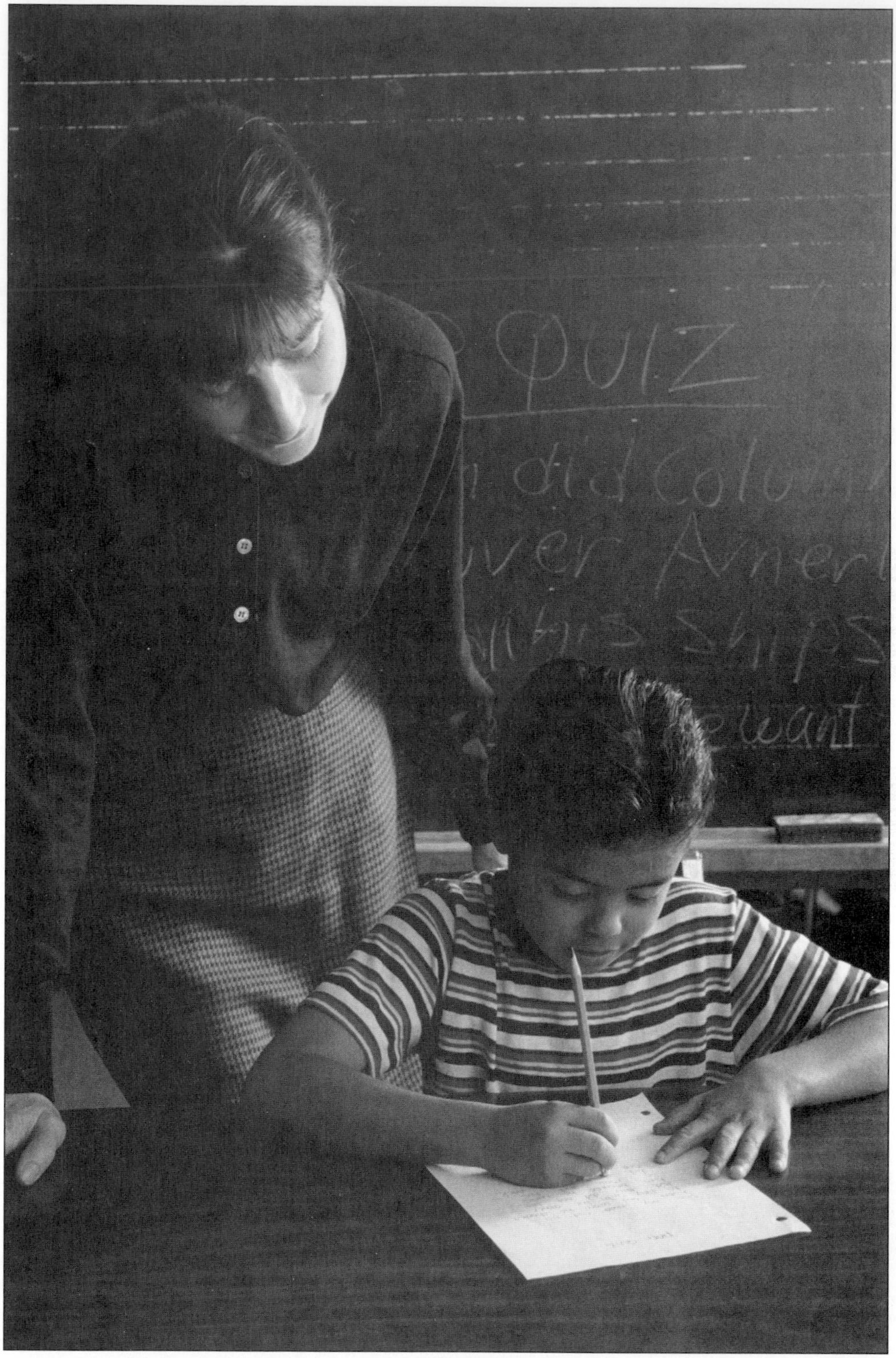
QUIZ

CHAPTER 4

FORMATIVE ASSESSMENT: ONGOING ASSESSMENT TO PROMOTE STUDENT SUCCESS

. . . students and teachers [must begin] to look to assessment as a source of insight and help instead of an occasion for meting out rewards and punishments.

–Lorrie Shepard (2000)

❖ **Chapter Learning Goals**

At the conclusion of this chapter, the reader should be able to:

- Explain how the six key elements of formative assessment can be translated into teacher actions.

- Design quality questions and a variety of formative assessment tasks.

- Provide effective feedback to students to help them close the gap between where they are and where they need to be.

- Accommodate diverse learners during formative assessment.

✦ INTRODUCTION

As a teacher preparing students to participate in our democratic society, you may find this chapter more directly helpful than any other in this text. Formative assessment, as we discussed in Chapter 1, is the monitoring of student progress during instruction that includes feedback and opportunities to improve. These frequent and more informal assessments help you get a picture of the changing knowledge, skills, and strategies of your students, and they show you how they are thinking and learning. This understanding then allows you to offer tailored feedback to students, permitting them to close the gap between where they are and where they need to be. Lorrie Shepard, whose quotation opens this chapter, cites research suggesting that the formative assessment strategies that we describe in this chapter can improve student achievement as effectively as or more effectively than many other traditional academic interventions, such as one-on-one tutoring (Shepard, 2005). In particular, a groundbreaking review by Black and Wiliam (1998) demonstrated that formative assessment can dramatically increase student achievement, especially among lower achievers.

✦ FORMATIVE ASSESSMENT: THE ESSENTIAL LINK BETWEEN TEACHING AND LEARNING

Formative assessment will be one of your most important classroom tools for preparing your students to become citizens who can ably take part in our democratic institutions. Formative assessment addresses all three of the themes we described in Chapter 1 that are crucial for fostering democratic participation.

First, formative assessment can help you provide equal access to educational opportunities for your students (Guskey, 2007). After your diagnostic assessments have assisted you in differentiating appropriate instruction for students at all levels in your classroom, formative assessment helps you check on student progress and provide mid-course correction so that students see exactly how to close the gap between where they are and where they need to reach to master each learning goal. This process is particularly helpful for closing the achievement gap because it enables *all* students to do what high-achieving students typically do on their own. Susan Brookhart (2001) found that high achievers naturally search for what they can learn from the assessments in which they participate. Lower-achieving students often need more help from the teacher in making these connections to enhance their learning and increase achievement. Formative assessment is a tool that provides such assistance (Stiggins, 2008).

Second, formative assessment helps you promote self-governing skills for democratic participation. Many traditional assessments tell you only which students your instruction was effective for, and the rest are no better off. Formative assessment lets you take students wherever they start, and then aids them *all* in making progress and getting smarter. Through carefully crafted feedback and opportunities for improvement, these practices will enhance the development of your students' self-governing skills. Self-governance comes into play when students use this information to direct their attention to the concepts and skills they next need to attain to close the gap between where they are and where they need to be. These efforts eventually lead to independence of thought as students internalize standards and depend less upon the judgment of others.

Third, formative assessment is a key to helping your students develop critical-thinking skills. Formative assessment, when used correctly, requires higher skills, such as application, analysis, and synthesis from Bloom's taxonomy (Guskey, 2007; Shepard, 2008). As your students begin to look at their work in light of the standards you show them and the comments you make about their work, they must actively struggle with applying that information to improve their work. This process involves metacognition, a crucial set of skills described in Chapter 1 and included as a type of knowledge in the revised Bloom's taxonomy (Anderson & Krathwohl, 2001). Formative assessment by its nature requires the metacognitive skills of developing awareness of and monitoring steps in problem solving or creation, offering estimates of whether answers make sense, deciding what else one needs to know, and developing judgment skills to evaluate work.

To understand how formative assessment can fulfill all these functions, we will examine its characteristics and how it works. Especially important is distinguishing formative assessment from the typical ways that assessment operates in classrooms (McMillan, 2007). The following sections of the chapter address each of the six key elements of formative assessment, which we describe as specific actions that teachers take. We will also contrast these actions with many of the assessment practices we all grew up with. Table 4.1 illustrates these elements as teacher actions.

Element 1: Make Students Aware of the Learning Goals and Evaluation Standards

A common complaint we hear from our students about both past and current teachers is "I can't figure out what the teacher wants." Students need to know what the teacher values and what quality work looks like. Too often, teachers have expectations in their heads that remain unarticulated and thus unavailable to students. If students can't have access to this expertise, they will remain dependent on the teacher for evaluation instead of being able to internalize standards themselves and use them to create better work on their own. If we want students to become lifelong learners, they need to

TABLE 4.1

Key Elements of Formative Assessment as Teacher Actions

Element	Teacher Action
1	Make students aware of learning goals and evaluation standards.
2	Provide formative tasks involving understanding and application more often than rote memorization.
3	Give feedback to students providing information on how to close the gap between where they are and the evaluation standards for which they are aiming.
4	Avoid grading formative tasks.
5	Offer students an opportunity to close the gap between where they are and the evaluation standards.
6	Use formative assessment to enhance your instruction.

develop, with the help of their teachers, internal standards of quality that allow them to self-assess. We want to help students gradually discard the idea that only teachers can or should judge the quality of their work. The first step in doing this is to ensure that students know what they are aiming for.

A number of school districts are taking this idea very seriously. They require their teachers to write the learning goal for each lesson on the board at the front of the class before the lesson starts. This practice alone, however, doesn't give students access to the elements that define a quality performance or the criteria that must be met for the learning goal to be achieved. Teachers must do more to communicate these often complex aspects of performance.

One way to communicate the elements required in a performance or assignment is to provide several positive examples of the final products or outcomes, and then work through them with the class using your scoring guide. A similar task involves having the class work together to improve an anonymous and less-than-perfect sample of an assignment. When designing the scoring guide for specific assignments related to the learning goal, some teachers also have students take part in defining with them what each level of performance looks like in concrete, clear language that students provide. Processes such as these take time, but they pay off for both students and teachers. One key benefit is that when students have a clear understanding of the criteria used for evaluation, they see the evaluation process as fair.

Ethics Alert: When you use samples of student work, students must not recognize the authors of these examples, or you are violating confidentiality. Make sure all identifying information has been removed.

This semester, one of our students provided an example of the unfairness that can result when scoring criteria are left ambiguous. In high school he had participated in chorus for four years. The chorus teacher had one grading criterion called "participation" related to her goal of enhancing students' love of music. But she never explained to the students what she expected from them. Every term this student received a low participation grade and assumed the teacher didn't like him and was just partial to a few favorite students. Based on this assumption, he felt it would be fruitless to ask what counted as good participation. This teacher missed an opportunity to be perceived as fair and impartial by laying out specific criteria that would count for participation related to her learning goal of creating lifelong music lovers. More students are willing to rise to a challenge if they know what it takes to be successful.

When students learn to focus their efforts on the learning goals, another benefit is increased autonomy. Students no longer need to rely solely on the teacher's judgment of their work, and they can start to develop confidence in their own understanding of the definition of success they are aiming for. They can learn to see critiques of their work as information about how to improve toward their own goal. Although the teacher is still ultimately responsible for guiding students and providing feedback, the power of the teacher as authority becomes shared with students.

Spending time on evaluation standards sometimes seems like a waste of time if the teacher already believes the assignment and the standards for scoring it are concrete and clear. But don't be too quick to make this decision on your own. In Table 4.2 you see a scoring guide that one high school teacher recently passed out to her class for a culminating assignment on a unit related to analysis of newspaper articles. The assignment required them, in a five-minute speech, to choose the two most important articles they had read during the unit, to describe how they defined "most important," and to describe one similarity and one difference between the two articles. She was ready to move on when hands started going up. After all of their previous discussions, she was surprised that the students wanted to know how to define "important." She turned the question back to them, and the class had a useful 10-minute discussion on the variety of definitions of important, and several ways importance could be determined. She reported that students were intrigued with the range of possibilities and came up with quite varied presentations as a result of this discussion.

Element 2: Provide Formative Tasks That Involve Understanding and Application

When you are contemplating which kinds of tasks and skills to use for formative assessment, you should avoid tasks with yes/no answers or black and white correct and incorrect responses. These types of responses are usually fairly easy for students to

TABLE 4.2

Rubric for Grading Brief Oral Presentation

Scoring for Grading Brief Presentation	0	.5	1
Definition of "most important article" is explicit.			
Explanation for why two articles you chose meet the criterion of "most important."			
One similarity between the two articles is explained.			
One difference between the two articles is explained.			
Oral presentation skills (looks at full audience; faces front, no fidgeting; voice is strong, confident; clear enunciation of words; business casual dress).			

produce on demand, and they are not usually challenging or difficult to master. One of our students had a teacher who gave back a multiple-choice exam so students could see right and wrong answers, and called this formative assessment. But true formative assessment requires spending time in dialogue between teachers and students on the gray areas (like what does "important" really mean when you are choosing an important article?), not the black and white ones. With formative assessment, teachers need to work with knowledge and skills that take practice and that are less accessible and more elusive to students, not simply cut-and-dried facts.

Formative assessment tasks can range from informal questions and discussions during class time to more complex assignments, such as term papers. Knowing when to use a particular strategy to solve a problem and when not to, learning what types of writing are persuasive and why, and understanding the difference between good and bad composition in a painting are just a few examples. In fact, almost any assignment can be used for formative assessment if it includes the teacher actions in Table 4.1. Some examples of typical formative assessment tasks used by teachers appear in Table 4.3. In the following subsections of the chapter we explore several kinds of tasks for formative assessment in more detail.

TABLE 4.3

Examples of Formative Assessment Tasks

Oral questions asking for student reasoning behind a position on a political issue.	Assign homework asking students to write three examples of persuasive techniques discussed in class that they see in television ads that evening.
Informal observations of quality of student gymnastic routines.	In theater class, have students observe and critique a video of their most recent public performance.
Ungraded quiz covering that day's biology lecture on organelles.	As students solve math problems, ask them to explain how they got their answer and why it is a reasonable answer.
Authors' chair where students share their writing and receive comments from students and teacher.	Band students record themselves individually playing a piece and have themselves and a peer look for two musical strengths and target one area for improvement.
Quick writes, or brief written answers to questions at the end of class such as, "What was the most important idea you learned today?" or "Describe which aspects of today's lesson were particularly difficult and list questions you still have."	In an art class, have students write a brief reflection about a work in progress or use a scoring guide to analyze aspects of the piece they want to improve.
In ESL class or class with English language learners, audio record a conversation designed to reach a decision or solve a problem. Have students in the group evaluate the performance and discuss communication pitfalls.	Hold individual conferences with students to check progress on a major paper or project. (See the Tracie Clinton example in Chapter 1.)

BOX 4.1 SAMPLE QUESTIONS TO ENCOURAGE HIGHER-LEVEL THINKING

Quality Questions

Comprehension (Understand):

Give an example of _____.

What is the big idea in _____?

Use your own words to explain _____.

Application (Apply):

Predict what would happen if _____.

How would you use _____ in this situation?

How would you use _____ to change this situation?

How could you apply _____ to your own (or another) experience?

Analysis (Analyze):

What are the similarities (differences) between _____ and _____?

What is evidence for (or against) _____?

Compare (contrast) _____ with _____.

What are the critical elements of _____?

Evaluation (Evaluate):

What is most important about _____? Why?

Justify your choice that _____.

Do you agree (disagree) with _____? Why?

How would you critique _____?

Synthesis (Create):

How would you design _____?

Compose/formulate/construct a _____.

What would be a good solution to _____?

Imagine you could _____.

Teacher Observations and Questions

Perhaps the most frequent teacher activities involving formative assessment are informal observations and questions as instruction proceeds. Questioning is the most flexible formative assessment technique because it can be used for individual or large- and small-group instruction, and questions can constantly be modified depending on the answers you are getting and which student you are addressing. The key is that you put some planning and forethought into these questions, and they must target the student learning you are looking for. We know several teachers who keep a sample of well-designed question stems at higher levels of Bloom's taxonomy on a laminated card that they tape to their desk, such as the one in Box 4.1.

A few simple rules, listed in Table 4.4, can help you design good questions that will elicit the information that you need to gauge student learning. Oral questions can be difficult for many students to process, so they must be concise and direct. You may want to put some of these questions in writing, especially for students who are learning English or other students who require extra visual cues. You also want your questions to be specific rather than vague so that students know exactly what you are looking for.

If you are designing questions that encourage your students to think critically and make connections, you must allow them the time they need to process the information in the question and to formulate an answer. The average wait time after a question in most classes is usually about one second. Many teachers are uncomfortable with silence in the classroom—even three seconds seems to stretch forever when it's

TABLE 4.4

Rules for Asking Questions That Enhance Formative Assessment

Questioning Rules	Example
1. **Think about the key elements of your learning goals for this class session.** • What specific concepts and skills should students be able to master? • What are their relationships to previous concepts and skills? • What evidence would let you know they have mastered them and connected them to previous learning?	**Current learning goals:** • Student will be able to compare and contrast characteristics of a utopia and dystopia. • Student will be able to use persuasive language in writing and speaking. **Previous learning goals:** • Student will be able to make connections between text read independently and prior knowledge, other texts, and the world. • Student will be able to respond to texts orally and in writing.
2. **Design brief, succinct questions, including more than half at higher levels of Bloom's taxonomy, that will provide evidence of students' understanding of the goals.** • Keep them short and direct. • Keep them specific rather than vague. • Make sure students must manipulate their knowledge to answer.	**Sample questions for discussion based on learning goals:** • What do you think is the most important characteristic of a utopia? A dystopia? Why do you think so? • (After reading an excerpt from *Fahrenheit 451*) How does this passage reflect the characteristics of a dystopia?
3. **Give students time to think about the question.** • Provide at least 3 seconds wait time. OR • Think, pair, share OR • Small-group discussion	**To address wait time:** • "In groups of three, decide which country in the world today seems more utopic; more dystopic. Develop specific reasons for your choice."
4. **Provide appropriate feedback.** • **Positive probing or redirection:** • **Acknowledging appropriateness:** • **Specific praise about student comment:**	**Possible appropriate responses:** • "Why is that characteristic of a utopia more important to you than others we have discussed?" *not* "That doesn't make sense, nobody could defend that choice." • "You are definitely on the right track; who else can add another argument for the importance of X?" *not* "OK, who's next?" • "Your argument for that characteristic is well reasoned and tight!" *not* a vague "Nice job!"

quiet. But "wait time" (usually three seconds is enough) has been shown to improve student answers. Another way to allow some thinking time is to have your students jot a brief answer on paper and then discuss it with a partner before sharing with a larger group. This procedure is often termed "Think, pair, share."

Answers to questions and student discussion are an important source of information about what students are learning. They also keep students active in the learning process and help them focus on what is important. Most teachers tend to ask basic-level questions such as definitions, requests for recall of specific information, or recitation of facts, hence the need for question prompts like those in Box 4.1. Top educators recommend that at least half of your questions require students to use basic information in new ways through reasoning at higher levels of Bloom's taxonomy.

To be more specific, Table 4.5 offers suggestions for moving toward higher-level thinking types of questions rather than focusing on definitions at the knowledge level. We often encourage our teacher candidates to "bump up" their questions from knowledge level to more challenging levels of Bloom's taxonomy. You also must remember to ask these higher-level questions of all of your students, not just your higher achievers. Sometimes doing so may require extra practice and modeling to clarify the process. This is an example of differentiating your instruction. Students who are required to make inferences and engage in complex reasoning tend to learn more. They make more connections in their minds when they use the concepts in different ways.

TABLE 4.5

Strategies for "Bumping Up" Your Questions from the Basic Knowledge Level When Working on Defining a New Concept

AVOID Knowledge-Level Examples	STRATEGY	INSTEAD Higher-Level Alternatives
"What does listless mean?"	Ask students to provide examples of concepts from their own experience rather than definitions.	"Describe a time when you felt listless."
"What is a metaphor?"	Ask students to describe similarities and differences between a new concept and an old one.	"How are metaphors and similes similar and different? Use examples from the poem to illustrate the similarities and differences."
"Define equity."	Ask students to apply the concept to something they have seen or read recently.	"Where have you seen equity demonstrated in current events you have read about or seen on TV?"
"Describe osmosis."	Ask students how they would explain this concept to a younger student.	"How could you use a visual concrete method to explain osmosis to a first grader?"
"Explain what interdependence means."	Ask students to differentiate this concept from other close concepts and give examples to illustrate the difference.	"How is interdependence different from independence and dependence? What are examples from your life that illustrate the differences between these three concepts?"

One common method that teachers use to systematically gather answers to questions from the whole class is individual white boards or chalk boards. You can use "The In and Out Game" or the "Always, Sometimes, Never Game" described in Chapter 3 as formative assessment in the midst of a new lesson and have the students write their answer on their board, then hold them up so only you can see them. You can do a quick check of the answers to get a sense of the level of understanding across the whole class. Even our college students have enjoyed using white boards and have told us that the boards keep them involved and give them an opportunity to experiment with answers without fear of being wrong in front of their peers.

Other In-class Activities

As you instruct your students, you will want to embed formative assessments into the instructional activities. We will offer a few examples so you can see the many ways you can weave formative assessment into your instruction. Our first example comes from Stephen Gundersheim, a professor of theater and former high school theater teacher. In an instructional unit on directing, he works with students to understand the impact of blocking and movement on stage through demonstrations in which students participate. To check on their grasp of the concepts, he has them create different stage pictures using other students as characters on the stage (e.g., a balanced stage, variations in strengthening or weakening different characters' stage position, relationship of power between characters, change of focus from one character to another based on blocking or movement choices). These physical demonstrations designed by the students are a wonderful teaching and learning tool that evoke discussion and allow him to know how adept students are at putting these directing principles into practice. When he wants to do more systematic checking, he asks students to answer similar types of questions on paper. Mastering these principles is crucial before moving on to other aspects of directing, so this type of formative assessment is essential.

Journals or notebooks are one of the most common in-class assignments that teachers currently use; these are excellent for formative assessment. Although our own teachers primarily used them in English classes, we know teachers who employ journals in other subjects such as theater, art, math, and science. However, to benefit the most from journals, students must be required to go beyond description and definition tasks at Bloom's "remember" level. For example, students can easily describe the procedures and results from a science experiment without understanding their significance. They need to be able to extrapolate the results from that situation to others, compare one experiment to another, or see how the experiment illustrates an important scientific principle. Unfortunately, an analysis of science notebooks by Maria Ruiz-Primo and her colleagues (2004) found many more "reporting data" or "definitions" entries than "applying concepts" or "interpreting data" entries, except in the highest performing classrooms. Journal and notebook assignments should be used to help students see the big picture and make connections. They should not be used for copying definitions or other work that doesn't require any thought or reflection.

Another important in-class formative assessment assignment is having students compare their work on a current assignment to a previous assignment. You can let students decide, or you can choose which one or two dimensions to use to rate the assignments and describe their improvement. Such comparisons can be done in pairs or individually. This kind of comparison could be a useful journal entry or standalone assignment for any teacher who provides similar assignments with slightly different content across the semester or the year. English themes, math projects, Spanish translations, science experiments, dance routines, art projects, or music pieces could be used in this way.

Quick Write

A brief written response to a question or probe.

Quick Writes   A quick write is a brief written response to a question or probe. Quick writes have been developed in the context of science units as a technique for gauging change in student understanding over time, allowing teachers to meet the learning needs of students, and obtaining valuable information for instructional changes where necessary (Bass, 2003; Green et al., 2007). Quick writes have also been used in many other learning contexts. Many teachers use a quick write at the end of class to ask students to summarize the key points of the lesson that day or to describe what questions they still have. Quick writes are easy and flexible—they can be adapted to almost any content you work with and can address any area you might want to probe with your students. When consolidating new information, quick writes have the advantage of requiring students to develop their own representations of content rather than checking a right answer, filling in a blank, or memorizing what the teacher has told them. They also provide opportunities for teacher feedback that can be easily differentiated according to the needs of the students.

Collaborative Quizzes   Quizzes are a staple of most classrooms, and they can be used for formative assessment. One variation on quizzes that we recently read about is called the collaborative quiz (Rao et al., 2002). Students take a quiz in a small group where they must agree on correct answers and report back to the class. This process can develop student reasoning skills, promote useful discussion over disagreements about answers, and help students fill in gaps in knowledge. To be effective, you must ensure that the discussion is structured so that students who have wrong answers will not be stigmatized.

Self- and Peer Assessments   Perhaps the best way for students to learn from formative assessment is to enlist them to do it for themselves. Getting students in the habit of reflecting about their work, rather than just doing it and turning it in, helps them begin to assume a more active role in applying the criteria for success. An active role increases student willingness to take more general responsibility for learning. You are encouraging them to take a metacognitive step and make observations about their work, then judge their work against what is expected. Eventually they develop the capacity to set standards and goals for their own work. Table 4.6 provides sample questions that students can ask themselves to start an internal reflective dialogue.

Students need instruction in the skill of self-assessment because most students do not automatically know how to apply evaluation standards to their own work. Remember that evaluation skills in Bloom's taxonomy are one of the most difficult cognitive levels to master. Students must know what is central and what is peripheral. They must know the vocabulary that describes the different levels of quality so they can see the differences between success and failure. Students also need feedback on their judgments to gradually become accurate.

To assist students in this process, Heidi Andrade (2008) suggests having students use different colored pencils to underline important elements in the scoring guide and then use the same color to note evidence of each element in their paper. Practice with assignments from an earlier class (with all identification removed) can also be helpful. At first you might find that poorer students tend to inflate their ratings of their performance, and better students tend to undervalue their work. But practice across time helps students develop more accurate self-assessments.

Another way that students can be involved in formative assessment is through peer assessment. Students can profit from examining others' work. It gives them practice applying the evaluation standards and ultimately will give them more

TABLE 4.6

Sample Questions for Self-Assessment Reflection

What goals do I want to accomplish with this assignment?	Do I really understand the difference between a utopia and a dystopia?
Am I executing my dance routine with proper alignment and balance?	How could I improve this paragraph to make it more persuasive?
Am I communicating what I want to with my performance of this musical piece?	How could I apply this new concept to my own life?
What skill should I work on next?	What strategies have I used successfully before that might work with this new word problem?
How will I be able to tell when I make a mistake?	How would I summarize the paragraph I just read?
Does my answer cover all parts of the question?	What are ways I can improve the next time I do something like this?
Does this answer make sense for this problem?	Do I understand and have I followed all directions?

insight into their own work. The key is to make sure that they know the goal is to offer constructive suggestions for improvement. As in self-assessment, students must be trained to understand the learning goals and the evaluation standards. They must know what to look for in the assignments they are examining. More specifically, they must learn the evaluative standards that are important to a task. This topic will be further addressed in Chapter 9 when we discuss performance tasks and scoring guides.

Peer assessment also requires training in interpersonal sensitivity. We know one elementary teacher who spends two weeks every year modeling and coaching appropriate ways to offer feedback and suggestions to peers. Only then does she let her students engage in peer assessment using a simple scoring guide to examine stories their classmates are working on. She also structures peer-assessment activities so that students discuss strengths as well as ways to improve. She asks students to describe two "pats on the back" and one suggestion each time they peer assess. You as a teacher must develop a positive climate in your classroom where students are honestly working together to improve the quality of each other's work in constructive ways. Students must feel comfortable and supported by the teacher and each other.

The hard work required in developing constructive peer and self assessment practices in your classroom will pay off. Students become more familiar with the learning goals and evaluation standards when they are asked to use them in judging their own and others' work. They develop more autonomy and independence as well as confidence in their judgment. They practice sophisticated high-level thinking skills. In addition, students receive more input on their work from a variety of points of view and learn to consider alternative perspectives seriously. Often students use more basic language in their interactions than the teacher does, which may help promote new

TABLE 4.7

Homework Strategies for Formative Assessment

1. Explain why the homework assignment is valuable in terms of reaching the learning goal.

2. Plan homework assignments that reflect the range of student needs related to the learning goal.

3. Focus on quality and not quantity, and vary the types of assignments.

4. Awareness of students' family and cultural backgrounds should be considered as you assign homework.

5. Never use homework as punishment.

6. Provide prompt feedback on how to close the gap between where students are and what they are aiming for.

understanding. Eventually this process allows students to develop the capacity to set standards and goals for their own work.

Homework

Homework can be a controversial subject because it is not always used wisely. Table 4.7 offers suggestions for making homework most effective for formative assessment purposes. In keeping with the key elements of formative assessment, you must first make sure students understand what the homework assignment is meant to accomplish in terms of the learning goal. Before you assign any homework, you want to be sure it has a clear purpose that the students understand. Students need to believe that the homework is valuable and will lead to academic improvement. As you may recall from your own personal experience, many students dislike homework and experience negative feelings while they are doing it. They haven't internalized the conviction of some adults that all homework is good for building character and developing a sense of responsibility. If students can understand directly the value and purpose of a homework assignment, negative feelings are less likely to surface about homework.

Next, you should assign homework that addresses the specific needs of your students. This usually requires flexible differentiation. For students who need practice with a skill, you can use homework to reinforce what has been taught. For students who need to be stretched to apply a skill to a new situation, you may focus on applications. Tanis Bryan and her colleagues (2001) also point out the importance of taking into account differing homework completion rates for students with disabilities, who can take up to eight times as long to complete homework as other students.

In addition, some students may require cues and prompts for completing an assignment. For example, you might develop a checklist for an assignment where students can check off each step as they complete it. You might also set up homework checking groups who work together and graph their progress across time. Finally, understanding of students' home situations can help you tailor assignments to them. For example, availability of time for homework must be considered for a student in charge of younger siblings after school or for students who must work to help support their family.

Students have reported in research that their homework is usually boring and routine. They often are required to do the same tedious tasks (e.g., answer chapter questions, do 10 math problems from the text, write definitions for the words of the week) over and over. Homework assignments that are brief but valuable will enhance interest in school and help promote mastery goals. The quality of an assignment is much more important than the quantity. Particularly useful are assignments demonstrating that students are able to apply concepts learned in class to situations in the real world. For example, in a unit on persuasive writing, students could look for persuasive strategies used in articles in a newspaper or on a website. In a unit on understanding proportions in math, you could have students measure the dimensions of one piece of furniture in a room at home and construct a drawing to scale of the room and that object.

Use of students' family and cultural background can help you develop homework assignments that are meaningful to students. When you have assignments related to family, you should be aware of the diversity in your students' lives and point out that by family you mean those people whom your students consider as family. For social studies and history units, you can ask students to find out about their family's experience with and connection to historical events. A student we know in a history class recently surprised his teacher with a battered bronze bust of Hitler that his grandfather had found in a German factory at the end of World War II. These family experiences can be compared and contrasted with other information about the events.

Family members also often have skills and knowledge that can help students move toward mastering learning goals through activities at home. Tapping such information, especially when working with students from culturally marginalized groups, can help students connect the school and home cultures and can help them feel that their home culture is valued at school. For example, family traditions related to music and art, business and trade, or farming can be applied to units in science, math, social studies, or the arts.

One problem that can arise with this approach, if you are not careful, is that students learn a lot about parts of the topic that are interesting to them, but they don't make the needed connections to the learning goals. Their understanding remains superficial. Your job is to make sure you always connect your learning activities to mastery of the skills and knowledge your students need. Your goal is not simply to keep your students entertained.

The last thing to remember about homework is that assigning it as a punishment is a guaranteed way to discourage motivation and learning. All of us remember teachers saying things like, "All right, class, since you can't settle down, I am doubling your homework tonight and you must do all the problems instead of just the even ones." Please make a quiet pledge to yourself right now *never* to do this, no matter how much your students annoy you on a bad day. Too often in the past, teachers have assumed that punishment or the threat of punishment works best to get students to comply with their requirements. Using homework as a punishment sends the message that learning activities are negative and something to avoid—not meaningful, and certainly not enjoyable. Imagine our loss if our favorite authors—Stephen King, Emily Dickinson, Toni Morrison, or Joan Didion—had perceived writing as a form of punishment because of a teacher's misuse of assessment.

Ethics Alert: Behavior problems and assessment practices should be kept separate. The purpose of assessment is for us to understand what the student understands, not to manage behavior through punishment.

Element 3: Provide Students with Feedback to Close Any Gaps

Whatever kind of formative tasks you give your students—homework, quick writes, journal writing, self-reflection—the kind of feedback you supply is crucial (Shute, 2008). Students can close the gap and reach a goal only if they know what to do next. For example, in one situation, students who received only comments and no grades actually did worse than students who received grades with minimal comments. Interviews with the students suggested that the comments they had received were too vague to be helpful in moving their learning forward (e.g., "try harder next time," or "very good") (Smith & Gorad, 2005).

So, to get more specific, your feedback must provide concrete comments that students can use to improve. In fact, some have suggested that feedback is misnamed. If the feedback is helpful, it allows students to move *forward* in their learning. Perhaps the term "feedforward" captures the dynamic and future-oriented aim of the information that should be provided in teacher feedback (Goldsmith, 2002). When you see improvements, you must also note them so your students see when they have used feedback effectively.

John Hattie and Helen Timperley (2007) have studied feedback extensively. They have concluded that it is one of the most powerful influences on student learning when it is designed to help students close the gap between their current and their desired performance. In analyzing what makes feedback effective, we have relied on elements of their analysis. In Tables 4.8 and 4.9 we contrast descriptions and examples of useful

TABLE 4.8

Characteristics of Useful Feedback

Type	Questions It Answers	Useful Examples
Information on the assignment's knowledge/ understanding (WHAT)	• What level of knowledge/understanding related to the learning goals did the student demonstrate, and what needs work? • What actions can the student take to improve that knowledge/understanding? • In what ways does this assignment show improvement over previous assignments?	• "Your understanding of musical forms needs tweaking, especially the difference between sonatas and symphonies." • "Review the musical selections from Lesson 3 in the listening lab." • "You have now clearly mastered an understanding of the causes of World War II."
Information on the assignment's skills/ strategies/procedures (HOW)	• What skills/strategies/procedures related to the learning goals did the student use well, and which need more work? • What actions can the student take to improve that skill/strategy/procedure? • What kind of improvement has occurred in progress toward learning goals? What is the reason for the improvement? • What strategies should be continued? Changed? • Is there evidence of self-monitoring and self-correction? • Is there evidence of improvement in self-monitoring? Self-correction?	• "You need to work on seeing more than one perspective on an issue." • "I suggest you may want to look at your argument from your opponent's point of view." • "You are making progress in your drawing because you are now incorporating balance into your composition." • "You did a good job keeping a steady beat in that piece. Keep it up." • I like how you noticed that you forgot to regroup in the 100's column and went back to fix it. You didn't do that last week, so you are making progress."

TABLE 4.9

Characteristics of Feedback That Are *Not* Useful

Type	Questions It Answers	*Not* Useful Examples
Judgment of the work	• Is the work good or bad?	• "Good job!" • "What a mess!"
Judgment of the student	• How does this assignment affect teacher feelings about student personal qualities?	• "What a good student you are!" • "You are so smart!" • "You will never learn!" • "Why can't you ever pay attention?"

versus potentially harmful kinds of oral and written feedback. Notice that Table 4.8 addresses both knowledge/understanding (WHAT) and skills/strategies/procedures (HOW) previously seen in Chapter 2 for designing learning goals and in Chapter 3 for designing diagnostic assessments.

In looking at the differences between Tables 4.8 and 4.9, you can see that useful feedback informs, reminds, questions, suggests, and describes. It gives students something to think about and helps them know what to do next in relation to both the knowledge/understanding and skills/strategies/procedures components of the learning goals. Poor feedback, on the other hand, offers judgments about the work or the student and not much else. Useful feedback helps students feel they are making discoveries that help them grow. Poor feedback makes them think they have made mistakes that reflect low ability or other negative character traits. As early as second grade, children can sense the difference between feedback that is descriptive or informational and feedback that is more evaluative. When students feel judged, their motivation and effort usually suffer. Often in the past when the sorting function of schools was most prominent, teachers focused on the evaluative function of feedback more seriously than the informative function. But now as we all work to help all children learn as much as they can, informative feedback must be our goal. We will now look at each of the four kinds of feedback in Tables 4.8 and 4.9 in more detail.

Information on the Assignment's Knowledge/Understanding

Feedback on basic knowledge and understanding (see Table 2.11) provides students with information about their results in relation to the evaluation criteria. If the work is incorrect or incomplete, this type of feedback provides students information on how to fix it. For example, a teacher might ask a student to get more information for a report on the civil rights movement, or she might provide a mini-lesson related to a misconception that shows up in student work. If the work is complete and correct, appropriate feedback lets the students know specifically how they have done well.

This type of feedback is powerful for students when they are allowed to use it to improve their work. Some problems can arise, however, if this is the only type of feedback you focus on. For example, students can get caught up in correcting small details (such as specific facts) and may not focus on larger issues (such as understanding a key misconception). They can make the improvements needed for this task, but not necessarily be able to apply them to other tasks in the future. Your feedback should also address progress you have seen since the last assignment to help students make connections across assignments. Focusing explicitly on progress also provides encouragement that effort is making a difference in their learning, promoting effort optimism.

Information on the Assignment's Skills, Strategies, and Procedures

Teacher feedback on skills, strategies, and procedures offers students insight into processes they can use for mastery of the learning goals and, especially with metacognitive skills, for improving their work in general. For example, the strategy of designing a paragraph with a first sentence that provides a transition from the previous paragraph is one skill students might need for successfully integrating new material into their paper on the civil rights movement. Helping students develop "triggers" that enable them to detect errors or problems in their work is one key. For example, we know one math teacher who stops her students after every problem completed in class and asks all students to evaluate whether their answer makes sense given the context of the problem. (For example, if the question is "What percent of students in the class favor capital punishment?" and your answer is 150%, something is wrong with your calculations.) Students have told her this strategy was the most valuable thing they learned in her class because it applied to so many other situations.

These kinds of strategies help students learn to monitor themselves, which is one of the most important forms of metacognition. When students are thinking about *how* they are doing their work, rather than just doing it, they will start to self-evaluate and self-correct. These skills are essential for developing independence of thought. Feedback on metacognitive skills is often best developed in conversation with students so they are given the opportunity to apply their own self-assessment skills as you appraise their work together.

Judgment of the Work

Giving students a smiley face or "good job so far!" comment or simply telling them to start again are examples of feedback that conveys a positive or negative judgment and nothing else. Teachers often make these types of judgments as they monitor students completing work during formative stages, not just when grading assignments. Teacher approval of a student's work is often seen as a powerful motivator, but if the praise is vague, it doesn't necessarily help a student achieve more. Disapproval of children's work can totally deflate them. Without additional information, judgments and evaluations of work are *not useful* for increasing student learning. Remember that facial expressions and tone of voice, as well as your comments, convey judgment.

Judgment of the Student

Praise or blame directed at students themselves and not their work is the least useful type of feedback, and can lead to many negative consequences. Avoid using labels describing student characteristics as fixed traits such as "smart," "lazy," "careless," or "annoying." Some students will try to live up to any negative label you apply. Others may try to prove a positive comment wrong if they don't want to be perceived by peers as a good student. Also avoid insincere praise. Students who are praised by teachers after completing a relatively easy task think that the teacher believes they have low ability.

Providing feedback is one of your most important opportunities for tailoring your teaching activities based on needs of individual students. Different students will need different kinds of feedback, and this is an important opportunity to differentiate your individual instruction for them. You must make sure students don't perceive the gap between where they are and where they need to be as too large, or they will find it unattainable and not worth the effort. Similarly, if you give students too many things to improve at once, you will overload them and they will get discouraged. Usually you will want to pick out only one or two areas for improvement at a time.

Technology and Feedback

Advances in technology have provided many exciting opportunities to deliver feedback in less time-consuming and more productive ways. For example, at the time of this writing, audio recording software, such as WavePad (http://www.nch.com.au/wavepad/) or the free audio software Audacity (http://audacity.sourceforge.net/), allows you to provide oral feedback using a microphone plugged into your computer. The resulting files can be distributed as .mp3 files through email, on a digital music player such as an iPod, or even on a standard audio CD. In five minutes you can offer oral comments to students on their papers or projects that are the equivalent of 2½ double-spaced pages of notes. Recently marketed inexpensive digital video cameras, such as Pure Digital's The Flip (http://theflip.com/), record 30–60 minutes of video depending on the model you buy. With such a camera you can video oral performances, physical education skills, musical pieces, recitations, and other student activities. You can move these files to a computer for editing or permanent storage, or you can immediately analyze these yourself or with the students to provide on-the-spot suggestions for improvement on the built-in video screen. Devices such as Personal Digital Assistants (PDAs), cell phones, and digital cameras are integrating features for audio and video recordings as well. Watch for other technological advances that can help you supply quality feedback to your students.

Element 4: Avoid Grading Formative Tasks

To be most useful, formative assessment should take place *before* student work is evaluated for a grade. We have found this element of formative assessment to be one of the hardest for our teacher candidates to grasp. They expect that every piece of work they turn in will come back with a grade on it, and they expect they will grade every piece of their students' work. Many teachers also get into this grading trap and believe that students will not take work seriously unless it is graded. But if students are getting useful feedback on learning tasks they value, this problem lessens. To develop more positive student attitudes, teachers often need to nudge students toward a mastery goal orientation so they begin to value the feedback they get that helps them learn more. We often offer a point or two for completion of an assignment that receives formative feedback. Then a later assignment or test that incorporates the improved product or understanding from the feedback is evaluated for a grade. Similarly, some teachers offer opportunities for students to turn in early drafts of paper for feedback. Word gets around to others that those students tended to do well on the final product. When the teacher offers the next chance for formative feedback, more students take advantage of the opportunity.

In this process, you want to ensure that students don't see identification of any areas for improvement as the sole responsibility of the teacher. In other words, a student should not be able to say, "Well, you didn't tell me to fix that on the formative assessment, so it's not fair that you mark me down on the summative assessment." Often a teacher will focus only on one or two elements during formative assessment and will let the students know that all other aspects of quality are up to them. Because formative assessment can increase a teacher's workload, you must set explicit limits.

Element 5: Offer Students an Opportunity to Close Any Gaps

All the feedback in the world won't help students learn if they aren't able to use it to make improvements in their work. Often with summative assessments, students have told us they don't even read the careful comments teachers write to justify a grade they have given. The students just look at the grade and put the paper away. If, however, the assignment is formative with feedback offering a means to improve an ultimate grade, students will likely pore over every word you offer.

Element 6: Use Formative Assessment for Enhancing Instruction

As formative assessment is incorporated into classrooms, we have already discussed how students become more aware of what the teacher is trying to accomplish. In addition, teachers become more aware of exactly how well learning is proceeding. If their formative assessment tells them students are floundering, they have a responsibility to use their expertise to address the problem. The knowledge teachers gain from monitoring student learning usually can provide them with valuable information for improving their instruction. Their instruction can then become more responsive to the needs of the specific students with whom they are working. Based on information from this type of assessment, they can make adjustments to speed up, slow down, or try a different instructional approach.

For example, Meredith Reid, a middle school teacher, was recently working with her students on personification as one kind of figure of speech. As a brief formative assessment, she had students write a sentence which personified an object in the classroom. As she walked around the room, she noticed many students weren't making meaningful personifications. For example, one student said, "The cabinet talked to the bookcase."

The student work instigated her to re-present the concept and really focus on helping students see they needed to achieve some effect or image. All of her examples had been personifications to create a colorful image (e.g. "As I wandered through the trees, they whispered my name."), but the students didn't get that point. Meredith took another step based on the feedback she was getting. "I wrote a couplet poem about my computer waking me up every night because it makes crazy noises. I explained in this poem that the computer growled, roared, screamed my name, etc. As I showed the poem to students, I asked them to really think about what I was trying to say through my personification. I then asked them if it would mean the same thing for me to just say, 'My computer talks.' Showing students the contrast between these two examples seemed to really make the connection that there had to be a purpose behind using personification. Once we had this discussion, I had students try to write a sentence personifying an object in the classroom again. This time the results were much, much better and I felt students really did understand how to use personification."

With good formative assessment, the role of the teacher changes from just delivering instruction to fostering the learning of that instruction. Teachers start to rely more on their professional expertise to help the class make progress. When they notice students aren't learning what they need to or aren't making progress with certain skills, they cannot chalk it up to "slow learners" or a "rowdy" class that won't settle down.

They take responsibility to make an instructional change. This approach leads to what we often call a "Don't blame the kid first" philosophy of teaching. Teachers, as professionals, have an obligation to look to themselves for solutions to classroom problems before they write students off as unable to learn.

✦ Accommodations for Diverse Learners for Formative Assessment

Like diagnostic assessments, formative assessments can be flexible and informal, allowing them to take a variety of forms and permitting students to use a range of methods of expression, as universal design for learning principles recommend. Therefore, most of the recommendations for accommodations for diagnostic assessment based on the considerations described in Chapter 3 (see Table 3.9) are also relevant to formative assessments. These recommendations should, therefore, be reviewed as you design formative assessments.

In addition, the third aspect of universal design, multiple means of engagement, comes into play during formative assessment and ongoing instruction to keep student participation and interest high (CAST, 2008). Suggestions closely tied to our discussion in Chapter 1 (see Figure 1.3) on how teachers promote learning goals to motivate students provide excellent means of accommodation for this purpose. In designing formative assessment tasks (our Element 2 of formative assessment), you incorporate the needs of diverse students by providing opportunities for student choice and by providing tasks that are relevant specifically to them. Offering students the choice to discuss a topic before completing an individual formative assignment allows them to build on content knowledge already acquired. This can be particularly useful if they learned some of the content in a language other than English and they discuss it in their native language. Encouraging students who have already met the learning goals to choose the most creative questions from an array of choices for their journal assignment is another example of incorporating relevance and choice to keep engagement strong. Accommodations related to choice and relevance to promote engagement are important for enhancing all students' learning.

Students who lose their way or perceive themselves as far behind get discouraged quickly, so another aspect important to multiple means of engagement is **scaffolding.** Scaffolding is temporary support of some kind allowing students to meet a challenge and increase their understanding. As the learning goal is gradually mastered, the scaffolding can be removed, just as scaffolding is removed from buildings after their construction is complete. For example, designing formative assessments early in the unit to ensure that students have first mastered the basic unit vocabulary—and only later moving to formative assessment that addresses the application of these basic concepts—may provide scaffolding for English language learners or for students with literacy skills below those of typical peers. In any class where skills are a focus, charts with step-by-step procedures for common tasks can be designed by the class and then referred to during formative assessments, if needed. Similarly, "anticipation guides" to focus attention and learning (Woelders, 2007) are scaffolding devices for developing and monitoring critical thinking. These could, for example, ask students to compare and contrast sources and evaluate bias when watching films or reading articles. Thoughtful improvisations like these can be tailored to students' needs, as well as to their interests, bringing out their best and keeping them engaged. That's why Carol Tomlinson and Amy Germundson (2007) suggest that teaching is like creating jazz—as a teacher you need "personal awareness of the moment and an understanding that allows for a range of

Scaffolding

Temporary support that allows students to meet a challenge and increase understanding.

TABLE 4.10

Accommodation Considerations for Multiple Means of Engagement for Formative Assessments

Issue	Type of Accommodation
Difficulty with fine motor skills	• Consider choice in terms of fine motor limits. • Provide scaffolding related to skill level.
Learning English	• Focus early formative assessments on ensuring that specific vocabulary of the discipline is learned. • Use cultural diversity as a resource in considering interests, relevance, and choices. • Provide opportunities for small-group discussion, possibly in native language. • Provide scaffolding related to language requirements.
Learning goal already mastered	• Increase breadth or depth of instruction and assessment. • Consider interests, relevance, and choice beyond current learning goals.
Difficulty focusing attention	• Consider interests, relevance, and choice related to novelty, degree of movement, and inclusion of hands-on tasks. • Provide scaffolding such as charts with procedural steps.
Literacy skills below those of typical peers (e.g., learning disability)	• Provide opportunities for small-group discussions. • Focus early formative assessments on ensuring that specific vocabulary of the discipline is learned. • Consider interests, relevance, choice in terms of literacy skill levels. • Provide scaffolding related to literacy skill levels (e.g., structure of tasks, language demands).
Lack of familiarity with school culture	• Provide opportunities for small-group discussions. • Consider interests, relevance, choice related to student resources. • Provide extra formative feedback as needed.

expressions to fit the situation" (p. 27). Table 4.10 summarizes accommodation considerations for formative assessments related to a sample of needs your students may have. Also remember our point in Chapter 3 that many students, not just students with these specific needs, will benefit from your considering such accommodations.

✦ CASE STUDY APPLICATION

Lynn McCarter decided to address all three learning goals (see Table 2.11) in the formative assessment she devised for her math unit on solving problems related to proportions.

BOX 4.2   MATH JOURNAL PROMPTS FOR UNIT ON SOLVING MATH PROBLEMS RELATED TO PROPORTIONS

Journal Prompt 1

A tree casts a shadow of 15 meters when a 2-meter post nearby casts a shadow of 3 meters. Find the height of the tree.

Journal Prompt 2

You have a scale drawing of a hammerhead shark that measures 23.6 cm. If the scale for the drawing is 4 cm = 3 m, how big is the actual shark?

Journal Prompt 3

You recently saw a table for $5 at the Salvation Army store that your guardian says you can buy for your room if it will fit. The dimensions of the table are 2.5 feet by 2.8 feet. You already have a scale model of your room showing 1 foot = 1.5 inch. The space where you want to put the table is 3 inches by 4.5 inches on your scale model. Should you buy it?

Responses Required for Each Prompt

- Draw a diagram of the situation depicted in this problem.
- Tell in your own words what you know and what you must do to find the solution to this problem.
- Solve the problem, showing all your work.
- Explain how you checked to make sure you worked the problem correctly.
- Explain how you know your answer is reasonable.

Her approach involves designing three equally difficult journal prompts that require students to analyze a problem, solve it, and document how they know their answer is reasonable. Each prompt addresses problems incorporating geometric concepts and similar and congruent figures, the mathematical content to be mastered in this unit. Thus the prompts constitute one measure of the skills and knowledge students should be able to demonstrate when they have mastered the learning goals.

She plans to use the first prompt as a diagnostic assessment and springboard for class discussion at the beginning of the unit. The second prompt serves as a formative assessment involving individual work and class discussion in the middle of the unit to check on student understanding and progress toward the learning goals. The final prompt will be given as a review before Lynn's summative assessment for the unit to determine what remaining aspects of the goals may need additional work. An example of the three prompts is displayed in Box 4.2.

To keep track of student progress across time, Lynn uses the same scoring guide each time to score student responses. The scoring guide is shown in Table 4.11. After the last prompt, most students should have checks in the column farthest to the right for each checklist item because students should reach mastery on each element by that time.

In addition, Lynn can examine the pattern of checks for all students in her class when she examines the students' journals after these prompts. If she notices, for example, that certain mathematical terms aren't being used correctly by a group of students, she can design a mini-lesson for them. If some students are getting stuck on a specific procedure, she can highlight that in upcoming instruction. The scores on the checklist, when scanned for the whole class, are an important source of information for designing feedback and later instruction to ensure all students meet the learning goal.

Lynn's example also illustrates several important points we have made about formative assessment. First, her journal prompts are aligned with all three of her learning

TABLE 4.11

Scoring Guide for Scoring Math Journal Prompt

	Needs Further Instruction and Guidance (list)	Minor Assistance Needed to Reach Understanding (list)	Mastery of This Element of the Problem
Diagram Is Accurate			
Explanation Demonstrates a Thorough Understanding of the Problems			
Follows Appropriate Procedures to Solve the Problem			
Uses Appropriate Units of Measurement			
Uses Proper Mathematical Terminology			
Documents Check on Reasonableness of Answer			

goals. When students respond to these prompts correctly, they will provide one kind of evidence that they have mastered the content of the learning goals. In addition, Lynn's prompts require both types of content knowledge discussed in Chapter 3—skills/strategies/procedures and knowledge/understanding. These tasks are consistent with learning goals that require skills to do certain types of problems as well as a clear understanding of the concepts involved.

Math teachers often tell us that their students learn how to solve problems fairly easily, but they have more difficulty knowing when to use a specific strategy or knowing the reasoning behind following a particular procedure. This kind of understanding, in addition to the problem solution, is facilitated by the questions Lynn asks. Because students reveal their level of understanding in their responses to these prompts as well as in class discussion following them, Lynn can provide them with useful feedback on how to close the gap between where they are and where they need to be to successfully meet the learning goals. Finally, students have an opportunity after the formative feedback from Lynn to demonstrate their understanding and show progress in learning during a summative assessment.

KEY CHAPTER POINTS

In this chapter we have described the importance of formative assessment. We presented six key elements of formative assessment as *teacher actions*. These include making students aware of the learning goals and evaluation standards, providing formative tasks that involve higher-level skills, providing feedback to students on how to close the gap between where they are and where they need to be, avoiding grades on formative tasks, offering students an opportunity to close the gap, and using formative assessment to enhance your own instruction.

We then discussed accommodations often needed for diverse learners as you design formative assessments. We focused on the universal design for learning concept of multiple means of engagement, which encourages differentiated efforts to engage students and maintain their interest. In particular we addressed the importance of using formative tasks involving choices that are relevant and interesting to students and the value of scaffolding in fostering engagement.

Finally, the case study example involved one aspect of formative assessment for Lynn McCarter's unit on solving problems related to proportions. She designed three journal prompts requiring students to solve problems and explain their work at different points in the unit.

HELPFUL WEBSITES

http://www.caroltomlinson.com/
Carol Tomlinson, one of the foremost advocates of differentiated instruction, provides articles, books, presentations, and other resources on her website.
http://www.tki.org.nz/r/assessment/one/formative_e.php
This website offers a variety of presentations from experts about formative assessment, including a general introduction, how to offer quality feedback, teacher-student conversations that enhance learning, and practical formative strategies.

CHAPTER REVIEW QUESTIONS

1. Which element or teacher action (see Table 4.1) involved in formative assessment do you believe is most important? Why do you think so?
2. Choose learning goals for a unit you might be asked to teach. Design a formative task (or tasks) that could help you determine what your students already know about the unit content. Explicitly describe how you will address the six key elements of formative assessment in Table 4.1.
3. Explain how each task in Table 4.3 requires higher-order thinking (one of the key elements of formative assessment) rather than rote memorization by students. Which levels of Bloom's taxonomy are represented by each task in Table 4.3?
4. Use the rules for asking good questions (Table 4.4) to design several questions to discover whether students are making progress toward mastering a specific learning goal that you will teach.
5. What will you do to promote an atmosphere in your classroom so that students are empowered to engage in honest and accurate self- and peer-assessment?
6. Using the recommendations in Table 4.7, design a specific homework assignment related to a learning goal that you will address in your classroom.

7. Describe tasks you have seen teachers use that enable their students to close the gap between where they are and where they need to be. What kind of feedback do teachers offer these students before they take action to close the gap?
8. Analyze the feedback you received on a paper or project in terms of the characteristics of useful and poor feedback in Tables 4.8 and 4.9. Describe how you might improve the feedback you received.
9. For the formative assessment task you designed for question 2, describe several accommodations you might make for a student whose first language is not English and for a student who has difficulty paying attention based on UDL principles described in Chapters 3 and 4.
10. Describe accommodations you have seen teachers implement for one of the groups in Table 4.10 related to multiple means of engagement. Were these accommodations effective? Why or why not?
11. Analyze Lynn McCarter's formative assessment approach in terms of how adequately it addresses the key elements of formative assessment as teacher actions (Table 4.1). How might you improve Lynn's formative assessment?

REFERENCES

Andrade, H. 2008. Self-assessment through rubrics. *Educational Leadership* 65(4): 60–63.

Bass, K. 2003. *Monitoring understanding in elementary hands-on science through short writing exercises.* Unpublished doctoral dissertation, University of Michigan.

Black, P., and D. Wiliam, 1998. Assessment and classroom learning. *Assessment in Education: Principles, Policy, and Practice* 5(1): 7–74.

Brookhart, S. 2001. Successful students' formative and summative uses of assessment information. *Assessment in Education* 8: 153–169.

Bryan, T., K. Burstein, and J. Bryan. 2001. Students with learning disabilities: Homework problems and promising practices. *Educational Psychologist* 36: 167–180.

CAST. 2008. *Universal design for learning guidelines version 1.0.* Wakefield, MA: Author. Retrieved April 14 from http://www.cast.org/publications/UDLguidelines/UDL_Guidelines_v1.0-Organizer.pdf.

Goldsmith, M. 2002. Try feedforward instead of feedback. *Leader to Leader.* Retrieved May 20, 2008, from http://www.marshallgoldsmithlibrary.com/cim/articles_print.php?aid=110.

Green, S., J. Smith, and E. K. Brown. 2007. Using quick writes as a classroom assessment tool: Prospects and problems. *Journal of Educational Research & Policy Studies* 7(2): 38–52.

Guskey, T. 2007. Formative classroom assessment and Benjamin S. Bloom: Theory, research and practice. In J. McMillan (ed.), *Formative classroom assessment: Theory into practice,* pp. 63–78. New York: Teachers College Press.

Hattie, J., and H. Timperley. 2007. The power of feedback. *Review of Educational Research* 77: 81–112.

McMillan, J. 2007. *Formative classroom assessment: Theory into practice.* New York: Teachers College Press.

Rao, S., H. Collins, and S. DiCarlo. 2002. Collaborative testing enhances student learning. *Advances in Physiology Education* 26: 37–41.

Ruiz-Primo, M., M. Li, C. Ayala, and R. Shavelson. 2004. Evaluating students' science notebooks as an assessment tool. *International Journal of Science Education* 26: 1477–1506.

Shepard, L.A., 2000. The role of assessment in a learning culture. *Educational Researcher* 29(7): 4–14 (p. 10).

Shepard, L. A. 2005. Assessment. In L. Darling-Hammond and J. Bransford (eds.), *Preparing teachers for a changing world: What teachers should learn and be able to do.* San Francisco: Jossey-Bass.

Shepard, L. 2008. Formative assessment: Caveat Emptor. In C. A. Dwyer (ed.), *The future of assessment: Shaping teaching and learning,* pp. 279–303. New York: Lawrence Erlbaum Associates.

Shute, V. 2008. Focus on formative feedback. *Review of Educational Research* 78: 153–189.

Smith, E., and S. Gorad. 2005. 'They don't give us our marks': The role of formative feedback in student progress. *Assessment in Education* 12: 21–38.

Stiggins, R. 2008. Correcting "Errors of measurement" that sabotage student learning. In C. A. Dwyer (ed.), *The future of assessment: Shaping teaching and learning,* pp. 229–243. New York: Lawrence Erlbaum Associates.

Woelders, A. 2007. "It makes you think more when you watch things": Scaffolding for historical inquiry using film in the middle school classroom. *Social Studies* 98(4): 145–152.

CHAPTER 5

PROGRESS MONITORING: ASSESSMENT AS A MOTIVATIONAL TOOL

For goals to be effective, people need summary feedback that reveals progress in relation to their goals.

—Edwin Locke and Gary Latham

❖ **Chapter Learning Goals**

At the conclusion of this chapter, the reader should be able to:

- Explain why systematic progress monitoring is a valuable aspect of classroom assessment.

- Compare and contrast mastery monitoring and general outcome measurement as approaches to systematic progress monitoring.

- Implement a progress monitoring system, including a visual component, to address gains over time toward a learning goal.

- Summarize data for groups using frequency distributions, frequency polygons, and measures of central tendency.

- Design tables that communicate information about a whole class and disaggregated groups within the class.

✦ INTRODUCTION

In this chapter we are tightening the assessment focus to help you find ways to discover and use tangible evidence of individual and class-wide growth in learning. One of the most powerful motivators we have seen in classrooms—for teachers as well as students—is concrete evidence of student progress. Remember the six students in Chapter 1 who set a goal for the specific number of words they would read in one minute and then charted their progress on a graph for 10 weeks? As they saw the numbers rise, these students not only increased their reading fluency, they also became more interested in reading and took more books home after school.

The instructional gains of these students, as well as 35 years of research (e.g., Locke & Latham, 2002; Zimmerman, 2008), provide us with concrete evidence that when learners focus on personal goals and track their own progress, they begin to develop mastery goals. As you recall from Chapter 1, mastery goals involve learning for the sake of mastery, not just working to perform well in the eyes of others. Encouraging mastery goals can lead to more positive attitudes, higher motivation, and increased effort and engagement. Mastery goals also promote independent thinking and personal responsibility, important self-governing skills for democratic participation (Urdan & Schoenfelder, 2006). This chapter will focus on several approaches you can use to capture and showcase progress across time.

→ GOAL SETTING AS THE KEY FIRST STEP

When you decide to monitor progress with your students, you must start with a specific goal. You need to know what your objective is before you can track any progress toward it. When we have appropriate goals, they direct and energize our behavior and they increase our persistence (Locke & Latham, 1990, 2002). Students who set short-term, specific goals also achieve more and have more confidence (Zimmerman, 2002, 2008). As you and your students choose goals specifically for progress monitoring, you must take into account several considerations.

Commitment

Goals work best for progress monitoring when students are committed to them. One way you can ensure commitment is by allowing students to choose the goals themselves so they are tailored to their needs and interests (see Table 5.1). As you recall from Chapter 2, Jo Ellen Hertel, the middle-school computer teacher, found that involving students in designing personal goals increased their interest in the unit. When this is not possible, students are still likely to commit to a goal if they understand its significance. For example, if a third-grade teacher explains that memorizing multiplication tables will be useful when students want to quickly determine how much money they will be paid for cat sitting when their neighbor is out of town (or for similar relevant calculations), students are more willing to work toward that goal because they see the value concretely.

Another factor that influences commitment is how official or "public" it is. Students who sign a copy of their goals, for example, are more likely to take them seriously than students who don't have an official record. The other ingredient for commitment is ensuring that students are challenged by the goal but can reach it. Do not waste time monitoring progress toward goals that are easily achieved. You also want to make sure that students don't get discouraged by an impossible goal. For progress monitoring to be motivating, you want to see steady gains across time.

TABLE 5.1

Considerations for Effective Goals for Progress Monitoring

Consideration	Suggestions
Commitment to the goal increases performance toward the goal.	• Allow students to help set their own goals. • Help students understand why the goal is important to learning. • Encourage public commitment to the goal. • Ensure that the goal is challenging but attainable for the student.
Specific and shorter-term goals work better than vague goals or urging to "Do your best" or "Try hard."	• If addressing learning goals for progress monitoring, design goals based on procedures described in Chapter 2. • Work with student to personalize goals. • Break long-range goals into subgoals that can be accomplished in a shorter period of time.

Specific, Shorter-Term Goals

You may choose learning goals that you design for a unit for monitoring progress, if they are specific enough (see Table 5.2 and the Chapter 2 discussion about specificity of learning goals). You need enough specificity for students to understand the kinds of knowledge/understanding and skills/strategies/procedures they will master. For example, the chart in Table 5.2 is an example of tracking progress toward the learning goals in a unit on gases and their properties. Notice the clearly stated learning goals and the opportunity to list evidence for the student's rating. Also notice the concrete actions students are asked to list in order to make further progress toward each goal.

TABLE 5.2

Mastery Monitoring Chart for Chemistry Unit

Chemistry Standards: Gases and Their Properties

Name: _____

Learning Goal	Don't Get It Yet*	Action**	Need More Practice*	Action**	Ready for Test*
Define pressure and explain how it is related to the motion of particles.					
Explain why gases diffuse.					
Apply gas laws to mathematically describe the relationship between temperature, pressure, and volume of an ideal gas.					
Define standard temperature and pressure (STP).					
Convert from moles of gas to volume or vice versa at STP.					
Convert from Celsius to Kelvin.					
Explain the meaning of absolute zero.					

*List evidence for your self-rating: quiz score, homework, success on review questions, etc.

**List what steps you will take to improve your preparedness for the test.

Adapted from Costa, A., & Kallick, B. 2004. *Assessment strategies for self-directed learning*. Thousand Oaks, CA: Corwin Press. p. 39. Reprinted with permission.

Requiring students to monitor their progress so carefully helps them develop the meta-cognitive skills that increase their ability to evaluate themselves.

✦ FORMATIVE TASKS AS THE FOUNDATION FOR MONITORING GROWTH

As we explained in Chapter 1, specific kinds of formative assessment strategies promote mastery goals (see Figure 1.3). We added to that foundation in Chapter 4 by introducing you to the key elements of formative assessment (see Table 4.1). As you recall, formative assessment involves assignments where mistakes are an expected part of learning, and improvement is expected across time. Such assignments might include turning in drafts of a paper or project for feedback before a final grade is given, or self-assessing at each step in an art project. So, to notice progress over time, you must use tasks designed so students can improve as they progress through them (Table 5.3).

Your next step is to decide how to track this improvement over the course of the unit of instruction and the school year. For example, to note student progress during a unit on essay writing, you can use a checklist of steps that must be in place before the final draft is complete. You can also rate each draft using the scoring guide that

TABLE 5.3

Steps Required for Examining Progress Over Time

Step	Examples
1. Set specific goal.	• I will be able to catch a ball in my hands with my elbows bent and my arms in front of my body (P.E.). • I will be able to write journal entries that show connections between the period we are studying and current events (Social Studies). • I will be able to read 100 words per minute with fewer than three errors in third-grade stories.
2. Use formative assessment: assignments where mistakes are an expected part of learning and improvement is expected across time.	• Use videos of students catching a ball and use scoring guide for self- and peer-assessment at two points during a unit (P.E.). • Progression of journal reflections across the year incorporating teacher feedback (Social Studies). • Students read aloud from an unfamiliar grade-level passage for a minute several times across the year (Elementary language arts).
3. Choose a method to track improvement over time, representing gains visually.	• Use scoring guide for catching a ball before, during and after instruction (P.E.). • On a personal chart, track changes in teacher feedback and scores on scoring guide for reflections across the year (Social Studies). • Graph changes in number of words read correctly and miscues over time (Elementary language arts).

will be employed with the final draft. Both of these methods document progress as students develop the essay.

The earlier education model discussed in Chapter 1, in which sorting and judging were the dominant influence, had a pervasive impact on the way assessment was conceived and designed. Under that model, researchers and educators devoted much time and effort to developing tests that would sort students by determining their relative position in a larger group.

Rather than simply comparing the individual student to others, the newer assessment approach looks instead for *individual growth.* You compare the individual student to him- or herself across time in relation to the learning goal. This approach is especially relevant for classroom teachers because their primary concern is growth in students' learning. Because this approach is newer, it has less historical research and accumulated standard practice associated with it. Because we believe this newer approach is the wave of the future, we want to use this chapter to describe practices found to be effective that you can adapt in your own classroom.

We believe focusing on individual growth across time, especially with a visual representation, is a key strategy for enabling you to close the achievement gap for students (often poor and minority students) who have consistently performed lower than other demographic groups in academic achievement and graduation rates in the United States. Keeping track of individual growth ensures that you know when a student is falling behind. When you see someone lagging, you can do something about it, such as changing instructional strategies, finding time for more practice, or making accommodations.

The best teachers engage in some kind of progress monitoring as the basis for differentiating their instruction for learners at different levels (Moon, 2005). If you have no way to check on who is failing to accomplish key tasks necessary to master the learning goals, you won't have the information you need to help struggling students catch up to their peers. You are trying to teach blindfolded. Progress monitoring focuses your attention squarely on your efforts and your students' efforts to master the learning goals. You are conveying to students that you won't give up on them and you will do everything you can to help them master the learning goals. This understanding helps you foster high expectations for your students. You signal to them that you expect them all to keep working and to keep learning more. And they see this work pay off as their graph or checklist illustrates tangible improvement.

Systematic progress monitoring motivates students (Bandura, 1997; Zimmerman, 2008). Children we have worked with look forward to noting their accomplishments on checklists or graphs. Some of you probably had a teacher who had you check off each multiplication table as you learned it, and you may have felt encouraged to see the growing number of checks over time. The same dynamic works when you make a "To Do" list and you cross off items as you finish them. Many students can feel overwhelmed by all they have to accomplish, so some method of monitoring lets them see that they are progressing and learning new things. Even asking students to set a goal and keep track of homework completion can enhance achievement (Trammel et al., 1994), probably because it increases the awareness necessary for developing self-control (Zimmerman, 2002). Even more important, evidence is accumulating that frequent progress monitoring and multiple opportunities for improvement are a common characteristic of high-achievement schools, even in the face of significant obstacles such as student bodies with high levels of poverty and diversity (Reeves, 2004). The advantages of systematic progress monitoring are summarized in Table 5.4.

TABLE 5.4

Advantages of Systematic Progress Monitoring

Advantages for Teachers	Advantages for Students
Provides clear signal when student falls behind or gets ahead of others	Promotes mastery goals and a sense of responsibility for own learning, especially when students keep track of their own progress
Provides foundation for differentiating instruction	Provides opportunity for setting personal goals
Provides clear framework for promoting high expectations	Makes high expectations concrete
Allows tangible picture of growth useful for communicating with students, parents, and administrators	Allows students to see tangible evidence of their own growth and develop effort optimism
Focuses teacher effort and attention on students mastering learning goals	Focuses student effort and attention on mastering learning goals

✦ TWO APPROACHES TO PROGRESS MONITORING

Stan Deno has been designing and refining methods of monitoring individual students' progress since the 1970s. He describes two approaches to tracking individual student progress (Deno, 1997). We discuss each one in turn.

Mastery Monitoring

Mastery Monitoring

A method of monitoring progress by tracking student completion of different tasks, that when completed, indicate achievement of the learning goal.

The first approach is termed **mastery monitoring.** It requires three steps: (1) choosing a learning goal or standard, (2) designing several tasks that if completed satisfactorily indicate mastery of the standard, and (3) documenting when each student completes each task. Table 5.2, which we have discussed in terms of goals for a chemistry unit, depicts a mastery monitoring approach. Similarly, in his elementary P.E. program at Orchard school, Jim Ross expects students to master the learning goal of *executing game strategies and skills* (see Table 5.5) by age 12. He has broken down this learning goal into several observable tasks, such as *moves safely within boundaries* and *receives an object from a teammate in a game*. As you can see on the checklist, he can keep track of each student's accomplishment of each task that contributes to the learning goal. The shaded column represents mastery of the learning goal. The previous skills, when mastered, should lead to this proficiency level. Note that more advanced skills are also presented in the table to challenge those who exceed mastery of the learning goal.

For mastery monitoring to make sense, the tasks you choose to monitor should each contribute new understanding and skills leading toward mastery of the learning goal. For example, you can see how *overtakes an escaping player* and *able to escape a defender* both play a role in *executing game strategies and skills.*

TABLE 5.5

Mastery Monitoring Chart for Elementary P.E. Class as of Winter Break

Orchard School   Physical Education

Learning goal: Executing game strategies and skills

Homeroom: Mr. Hussein

Name	Moves Safely Within Boundaries	Overtakes an Escaping Player	Able to Escape a Defender	Utilizes Feinting and Dodging	Escapes Multiple Defenders in a Game	Uses Team-Oriented Defensive Strategies	Manipulates Object Within Team-Oriented Game	Receives an Object from a Teammate in a Game
Student 1	Mastered 9-15	Mastered 9-15	Mastered 9-15	Mastered 10-15	Mastered 11-30			
Student 2	Mastered 9-30	Mastered 10-30	Mastered 11-30					
Student 3	Mastered 10-15	Mastered 11-30	Mastered 12-15					
Student 4	Mastered 10-15	Mastered 11-15	Mastered 12-15					
Student 5	Mastered 10-30	Mastered 11-30						
Student 6	Mastered 10-30	Mastered 11-30						
Student 7	Mastered 10-30	Mastered 11-15	Mastered 12-15					
Student 8	Mastered 11-30	Mastered 12-15						
Student 9	Mastered 12-15							
Student 10	Mastered 12-15							

If you want your students to use a graph to illustrate mastery monitoring for a specific learning goal, it could look like the graph in Figure 5.1. The number of tasks successfully accomplished is listed cumulatively from 1 to 7 on the left side of the graph, and the expected completion dates are noted across the bottom. You can see that a student who is on target for completing the tasks that lead to mastery of a learning goal is depicted in Figure 5.1. The line shows a steady increase in the number of tasks completed over time. Figure 5.2 shows a student who is getting behind and may need assistance. For this student, the graph depicts accomplishment of tasks 1–3, but the student does not master task 4, so the line flattens out between dates 3 and 4. Figure 5.3 depicts a student who has forged ahead quickly to master the learning goal

7
6
5
4
3
2
1
0
Tasks
Date 1
Date 2
Date 3
Date 4
Date 5
Date 6
Date 7
Time

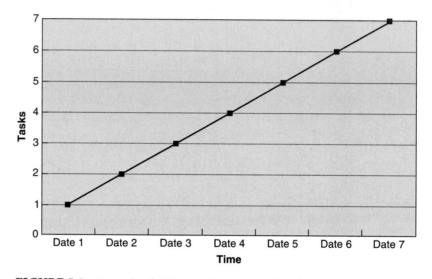

FIGURE 5.1 ***Example of a Mastery Monitoring Chart for a Student Who Accomplishes Each Task by the Expected Date***

7
6
5
4
3
2
1
0
Tasks
Date 1
Date 2
Date 3
Date 4
Date 5
Date 6
Time

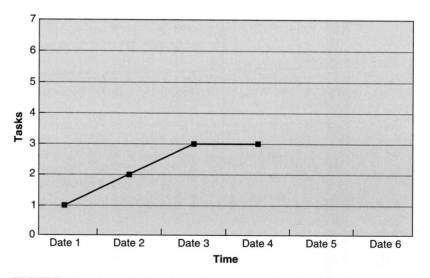

FIGURE 5.2 ***Example of a Mastery Monitoring Chart for a Student Who Has Not Successfully Completed Task 4 by the Expected Date and May Require Additional Assistance***

7
6
5
4
3
2
1
0
Tasks
Date 1
Date 2
Date 3
Date 4
Date 5
Date 6
Time

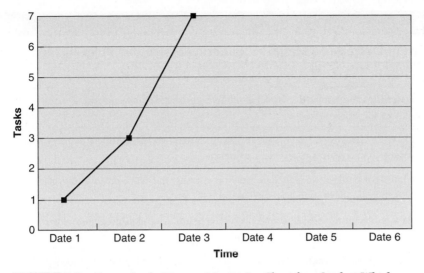

FIGURE 5.3 ***Example of a Mastery Monitoring Chart for a Student Who has Completed All Seven Tasks Before Due Date and Requires Enrichment***

and could benefit from enrichment activities. The graph shows the student successfully completed tasks 2 and 3 by the second date and all of the tasks by the third date.

> **Ethics Alert:** To protect the confidentiality of a student's performances, graphs should not be posted on classroom walls or bulletin boards. Instead, each student should have a folder or portfolio for keeping his or her mastery graphs.

The amount of time and organizational skills required for such progress monitoring can be daunting. To reduce teacher workload, we suggest that students from second or third grade and above can often be in charge of monitoring their own progress, with the teacher prompting graph updates at appropriate intervals. Checking these graphs periodically can give you and your students a snapshot of how they are progressing on accomplishing a major learning goal that spans many tasks and requires considerable time. Computer spreadsheet programs can also help organize data with students in rows and specific skills in columns. Such a setup allows for reviewing progress quickly and efficiently.

You should also be selective about which learning goals you choose for progress monitoring, and you may want to start with a small group of students first. Monitoring progress in this way can provide important insights for your decisions about what, when, and how to teach. Visual displays such as graphs can also clearly communicate to other interested parties such as parents and administrators. To summarize mastery monitoring procedures, Table 5.6 provides the steps in developing a mastery monitoring system for progress monitoring.

General Outcome Measurement
A method of monitoring progress that uses several brief yet similar tasks (e.g., reading aloud in grade-level stories for one minute) that can indicate achievement of the learning goal.

General Outcome Measurement

The second method for individual progress monitoring that Deno describes is termed **general outcome measurement.** Instead of monitoring the achievement of several sequential tasks necessary to demonstrate mastery of a learning goal (as in

TABLE 5.6

Steps in Designing a Mastery Monitoring System for Progress Monitoring

1. Select an important learning goal for which you want to track progress.

2. Determine the knowledge/understanding and/or skills/strategies/procedures required to master the learning goals.

3. Design a checklist for each student listing these knowledge/understandings and skills/strategies/procedures in a logical sequence.

4. Choose or design a sequence of assessment tasks that represent mastery of each of the knowledge/understanding and skills/strategies/procedures.

5. As a student attains each knowledge/understanding or skill/procedure, have the student check it off with the date on a personal checklist.

6. (Optional but motivating) Student designs line graph (see Figure 5.1) showing cumulative progress toward learning goal.

TABLE 5.7

Steps in Designing a General Outcome Measurement System for Progress Monitoring

1. Choose an important achievement or "general outcome" that students should work toward across a semester or school year that is consistent with your learning goals.

2. Choose or develop a brief, repeatable measure that validly represents the general outcome in the content area, and collect or design a variety of equivalent versions.

3. Develop or choose a standard method of administration and scoring for your measure so that any increase in scores can be attributed only to student growth.

4. Administer different versions of the measure at suitable intervals (e.g., once per month, once per grading period).

5. Graph the results across time to track individual progress toward the general outcome.

mastery monitoring), a teacher chooses an overarching, repeatable measure that, by itself, represents an important achievement or "general outcome" in the content area. Table 5.7 illustrates the steps you take in designing a general outcome measurement system of progress monitoring.

One way to illustrate the difference between general outcome measurement and mastery monitoring is to show how you could use them both with the same learning goal. Deno offers the example of the goal of writing an appropriate paragraph. For mastery monitoring, you could include on a checklist for each student several tasks, such as writing complete sentences with subjects and verbs, using correct spelling and punctuation, writing topic sentences, and developing supporting details. As students master each task, they get a check on their checklist and move on to the next task. For general outcome measurement, you would instead get samples of student paragraphs across time. At first the paragraphs would require much

TABLE 5.8

General Scoring Scale for Evaluating Multiple Tasks Within a Learning Goal

Score	Description of Place on Scale
4	In addition to Score 3 performance, in-depth inferences and applications that go beyond what was taught.
3	No major errors or omissions regarding any of the information and/or processes (simple or complex) that were explicitly taught.
2	No major errors or omissions regarding the simpler details and processes, but major errors or omissions regarding the more complex ideas and processes.
1	With help, a partial understanding of some of the simpler details and processes and some of the more complex ideas and processes.
0	Even with help, no understanding or skill demonstrated.

Source: Marzano, R. 2006. *Classroom assessment and grading that work*. Alexandria, VA: Association for Supervision and Curriculum Development. Copyright 2004 by Marzano & Associates. Reprinted with permission.

improvement, because students won't have mastered most of the tasks (writing complete sentences with subjects and verbs, etc.) involved. But gradually their paragraphs would become more sophisticated as the students mastered more of the key elements with practice.

The formative assessment assignment chosen by Lynn McCarter described in the case study at the end of Chapter 4 offers an example of general outcome measurement. As you may recall, she designed three equally difficult journal entry prompts that addressed mastery of all three learning goals for her math unit. She uses a different one at three different points during the unit to assess student progress.

Marzano (2006) suggests an approach similar to general outcome measurement. He offers a 5-point scoring scale that can be used when evaluating a range of tasks that could represent a learning goal (Table 5.8). Most student work can be rated from 0, which is characterized as "no understanding or skill demonstrated," to 4, "in-depth inferences and applications that go beyond what was taught," in reference to a specific standard or learning goal. Scores based on this scale will gradually improve as mastery increases on the tasks across time, documenting learning gains.

For general outcome measurement progress monitoring, graphing of results is useful and important, according to both Deno and Marzano. Deno suggests that these graphs often look like height and weight charts that pediatricians use. You are measuring a desired broad outcome that represents academic "health" as it increases across time. Student performance on your graph starts out low but then improves as instruction proceeds. Figure 5.4 illustrates a graph that tracks writing progress across a school year for Brittany, a second-grader. For each instance represented by a point on this graph, the teacher gave students a writing probe (e.g., "Yesterday a monkey climbed in our classroom window and . . .") and had them write for three minutes. She then counted words spelled correctly (WSC) for each probe and plotted it on this graph.

You can see scores for Brittany's very first writing sample from August and her last writing sample from the following April in Figure 5.5. Notice that the line in

Words Spelled Correctly
50
45
40
35
30
25
20
15
10
5
0
August
September
November
December
February
March
April

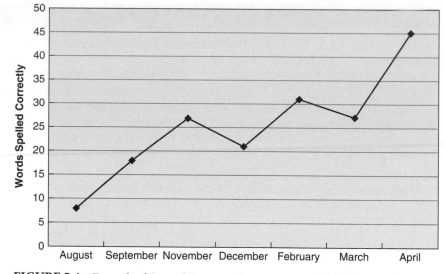

FIGURE 5.4 ***Example of General Outcome Measurement Graph for Paragraph Writing***

Brittany

The mukey gond our class. Then he went to the o

TWW 10
WSC 8

Brittany

They jump in the lake and did not take there cloths off. And they saem under watter for a long time. Then I said I am going in and I jump in and I went to the botton and I saw the milkey way and when I saw the boy

TWW - 51
WSC - 45

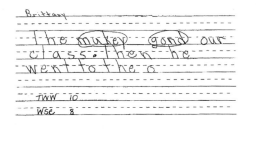

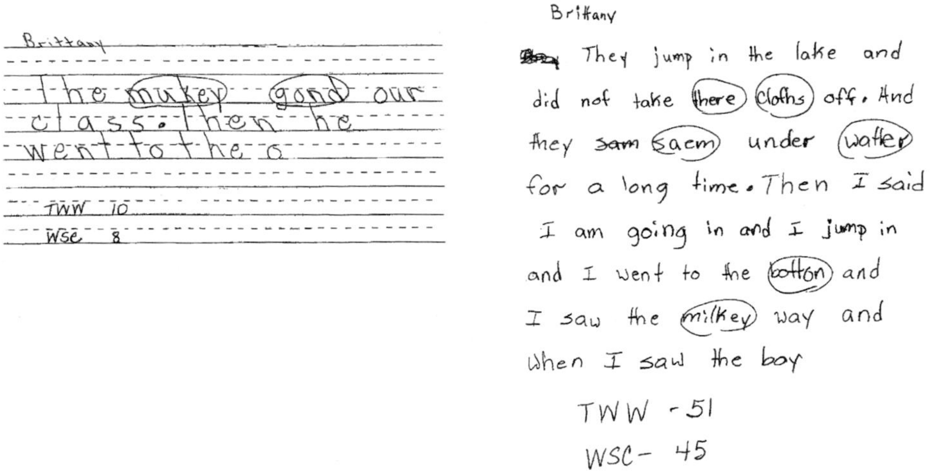

FIGURE 5.5 ***Writing Samples from August and the Following April for Brittany***

Figure 5.4 shows rising scores and slight declines, which are to be expected. The key is that overall Brittany shows considerable progress between August and the following April. And this progress can be clearly seen only because the teacher took the time to work with Brittany to make this chart. As you look at these writing samples, think about other ways you might gauge progress. Brittany's teacher also counted total words written (TWW) to note progress, although she did not include that measure on the graph.

You might instead decide to score such writing samples with a scoring guide that assigns points for each of the key elements (writing complete sentences with subjects and verbs, using correct spelling and punctuation, writing topic sentences, developing supporting details). Over time, as Brittany made progress, the points she would earn on the scoring guide would increase. The key for general outcome measurement is that you use the *same type of task* and the *same method of scoring* each time so you can legitimately compare scores across time and get a clear picture of progress.

Curriculum-Based Measurement: General Outcome Measurement for Basic Skills

Deno and his colleagues (Deno, 1985, 1997, 2003; Shinn, 1989, 1998) have devoted decades to developing measures of important general student outcomes that can be used for progress monitoring and to improve student learning. They refer to this form of general outcome measurement as **Curriculum-Based Measurement (CBM).** CBM is a system of brief assessments (each requiring between 1 and 5 minutes) in the basic skill areas of reading, math, spelling, and written expression. CBM oral reading fluency, or the number of words a student can read aloud in grade-level material correctly in one minute, has been the most widely researched (e.g., Stecker, Fuchs, & Fuchs, 2005). Reading a passage fluently encompasses several reading skills, such as decoding, recognition of sight words, comprehension, and knowledge of syntax, among others, so the number of words read correctly per minute is strongly related to general reading achievement (Baker et al., 2008).

Curriculum-Based Measurement (CBM)
One form of general outcome measurement in which frequent brief assessments are used in basic skill areas to monitor student progress and provide information for teacher decision making.

CBM has been used in both general and special education to monitor student progress and to provide information for teacher decision making. Studies have demonstrated that CBM measures are strongly related to teacher judgments of student achievement and to performance on standardized achievement tests (Baker et al., 2008). CBM measures are also sensitive to growth in achievement over time (Deno, 1997). They are also useful for diagnosing problems and designing successful interventions (Stecker et al., 2005). Directions for CBM administration and scoring can be found at http://www.aimsweb.com/measures/.

Teachers have successfully used CBM measures to track their students' acquisition of basic skills primarily in the earlier elementary grades. Teachers with whom we have worked have also found that CBM measures are useful for diagnostic assessment. For example, one teacher recently mentioned that she used results of CBM written expression probes (such as those by Brittany in Figure 5.5) to design mini-lessons about sentence structure, homophones, and grammar. A fourth-grade teacher who uses monthly CBM reading probes offers comments about their value in Box 5.1.

We recommend that beginning teachers who want to use CBM reading start first with their lower performing students to get comfortable and organized with the administration, scoring, and graphing requirements. CBM writing, math, and spelling measures can be administered to your students as a group, and so they are not as time-consuming to implement.

CBM and Responsiveness to Intervention Recently, educators have also employed CBM measures in new efforts to intervene earlier with children at risk for school failure who in the past would have been directly referred for special education. The Individuals with Disabilities Education Improvement Act of 2004 allows educators to use **responsiveness to intervention** (RTI) for assisting students. Responsiveness to intervention involves collecting data to determine whether underachieving students profit from specific instruction targeting their needs. This law, then, encourages schools to focus on effective instructional strategies and is the first special education law to provide funds for early intervention in typical classrooms.

Responsiveness to Intervention (RTI)
An approach in general education that involves collecting data to determine the degree to which underachieving students profit from specific instruction targeting their needs.

For example, elementary students can be screened at the beginning of the school year with brief CBM reading measures or other data by a group of trained volunteers or school staff. Those who fall in the lowest quarter of their class can receive focused instructional interventions in addition to regular reading instruction. Teachers then administer weekly CBM measures for several weeks to determine whether these students respond positively to the interventions. Students who do not improve would then receive a comprehensive individual evaluation for special education eligibility. Students

BOX 5.1   TEACHER COMMENTS ON ADVANTAGES OF MONTHLY CBM PROGRESS MONITORING

Instructional influence. It reminds me to check on everybody. I think with a room full of kids it's sometimes easy to get slack about it, but you really can't. I can catch those middle of the road kids, you know, the average kids who don't get a lot of attention. I can supplement and find out who needs enrichment and who needs reteaching in certain areas. It's good for me to know where my children's strengths and weaknesses are. And I know for right now, vocabulary is a real weakness for my class.

Effects on parents. If I can show them that "other fourth graders are able to read the same passage and get at least 100 words correct and your child is reading 15," they can see the deficit. That's really important because that's how people nowadays understand facts. Some parents don't take my word for it. You've got to have data.

Impact of noticing progress. Sometimes it's easy to get discouraged and not think anything you are doing is working, so it is a good measure for me. Day-to-day stuff isn't as sensitive to growth. Even the lowest students make steady little gains with CBM. For instance, I have had one special education student for two years. When she came to me she started in the 30s and now she's in the 80s. It's a morale booster for both of us.

who are responsive to the intervention would continue to be monitored in the general education classroom.

Because determination of responsiveness to intervention occurs in general education rather than special education, all teachers should be familiar with this assessment process. The potential benefits of RTI approaches include increased accountability for all learners, reduced special education referrals, and decreased overidentification of minority students for special education (National Joint Committee on Learning Disabilities, 2005; Marston et al., 2003). Thus combining CBM with responsiveness to intervention provides information to better serve students.

✦ ISSUES TO CONSIDER: PROGRESS MONITORING

So far, we have discussed the benefits of progress monitoring and described two approaches to it, mastery monitoring and general outcome measurement. Table 5.9 provides a comparison of these two approaches, as well as advantages and concerns for each approach.

Mastery monitoring is easy to implement across the curriculum, but, as Deno points out, "unfortunately, the standards of performance that are specified within mastery monitoring systems are almost always arbitrary." That is, specific evidence may not yet have accumulated showing that the skills or tasks chosen for the checklist across the unit actually do reflect growth toward the learning goal. If you use mastery monitoring, you must ensure as much as possible that the knowledge/understanding and skills/procedures you choose for your checklist will result in mastery of the learning goals they address. You must also make sure that tasks on the list are not checked off merely when completed without regard to excellence. High-quality standards of work must be required, communicated, and maintained so that students know they have truly earned each check mark denoting progress.

General outcome measurement has been used most for tracking basic skills. The idea of choosing a task that represents a desired general outcome that can be repeated more than once (with slight variations) can be adapted to other content areas such as music or art. One of our teacher candidates decided to experiment

TABLE 5.9

A Comparison of Mastery Monitoring and General Outcome Measurement

	Focus for Progress Monitoring	Graphic Display	Content	Advantages	Concerns
Mastery Monitoring	Completion of a sequence of tasks that culminates in mastery of learning goal	Checklist or graph showing increases as tasks finished appropriately	Adaptable to most content areas	Easy to design and track progress through tasks	• Difficult to be certain that links have been established between a specific sequence of tasks and mastery of important learning goals • Fails to provide information on maintenance of knowledge and skills after unit completed • Must maintain clear and high standards on each benchmark or quality of student work can slip
General Outcome Measurement	Completion of repeated administrations of tasks that show increase across time for a key general education outcome	Graph of scores showing increases as gains on the measure are made across time	Applicable to basic skills such as reading, written expression, math, and spelling	Research indicates: • Related to established measures (e.g., teacher ratings and test scores) • Sensitive to growth in achievement • Increased achievement and improved teacher decision-making	• Difficult to find appropriate repeatable measures that represent general outcomes beyond basic skills • When implemented in addition to other ongoing assessment may reduce instructional time • Effectiveness reduced if progress monitoring emphasized at the expense of explicit intervention based on it

with CBM and art (see Box 5.2). Similar procedures can be developed in other content areas. The key is to ensure that the task represents the desired outcome, that it can be completed quickly and efficiently, and that you can develop a number of versions that are equivalent.

Finding those appropriate repeatable measures that represent important general outcomes can be difficult, and this is one major concern with general outcome measurement. Mastery monitoring, on the other hand, can be flexibly applied to more

BOX 5.2   STUDENT REFLECTION ON CURRICULUM-BASED MEASUREMENT APPLICATIONS TO ART

I am thinking of ways to use the basic idea of CBM in art. One idea that comes to mind is that I could use it to track progress of students' drawing abilities over time for mastery of specific skills. I would set up a still life with two or three items and ask students to draw it and then assess specific skills, such as shadows, values, etc. If I wanted to track shading abilities, I could assess shading skills at various times throughout the year. I could vary the still life each time, but keep the same number of items so the drawing would be about the same level of difficulty each time. I would use the same rubric that focuses on shading each time and see how scores increase. It would be even nicer if I had some of the same students year after year, and then it would really give an accurate measurement of their progress. The only drawback I see is time constraints. I don't think three minutes would be appropriate; however, ten to fifteen minutes might work. I'm eager to try it out!

fields of study. Another concern with general outcome measurement has been the time required, as it must be implemented in addition to ongoing assessment requirements related to specific learning goals for units of instruction.

Systematically monitoring progress—whether using mastery monitoring or general outcome measurement—has many advantages for both students and teachers, described at the beginning of this chapter. We believe these advantages make systematic progress monitoring an important component of classroom assessment. Teachers we know agree. For instance, Tracie Clinton, third-grade teacher at Cotton Belt Elementary School, uses both types of progress monitoring in her classroom and describes in Box 5.3 what she sees as the advantages.

We urge you to begin progress monitoring by systematically choosing one learning goal or general outcome in your classroom, perhaps as part of an action research project. Focus on a specific content goal and define your strategies for choosing assessments, scoring them, and quantifying the outcomes to track across time. Your experiences and your students' reactions can help you decide how best to implement progress monitoring to improve your students' academic achievement. Recall from Chapter 1 that "Does this help my students learn?" is the overriding question for making these or any other classroom decisions.

✦ SUMMARIZING DATA FOR GROUPS

In discussing progress monitoring so far, we have focused on the individual student and described specific methods for tracking one student's progress across time using the support of visual aids such as graphs. However, you also will have occasions when you need to analyze and communicate information about your entire class. We describe a few tools to help you present this information in ways that make it easy to interpret for you and for others. Strong visual representations—whether graphs, checklists, or tables—communicate gains in a compelling way for teachers and students.

Frequency Distributions

Let's say you just gave your first test in a class, and you are sitting at your desk with a pile of graded papers with the following percent-correct scores for each student: 85, 20, 100, 90, 80, 10, 85, 60, 80, 95, 50, 75, 85, 70, 90, 75, 90, 85.

BOX 5.3 THIRD-GRADE USES AND COMMENTS ON SYSTEMATIC PROGRESS MONITORING

On General Outcome Measurement with CBM:

"Using CBM written expression once a month does take time, but it is worth it in the long run. My students enjoy seeing their progress throughout the year as they are able to monitor their growth. The CBM results provide the students as well as myself with a sneak peek in the areas they need to improve in and the areas the students are doing well in. This information is also valuable to parents during parent conferences. I try to use as many student work samples as possible when talking with parents. The CBM is a great tool for this. Also, the graphs are useful for students because they are visual. One of the standards in third grade is being able to read charts and graphs. Reading CBM graphs is good practice for the students."

On Mastery Monitoring:

"We use several other tools to measure progress over time. I use a graph in Accelerated Reader to show progress over a nine-week period. The students place a sticker in their folder every time they pass a test. I also use a similar process when looking at multiplication tables. Students move a tag according to where they are on their tables. Also, as we move through the writing process on a long assignment, the students move their tag according to where they are in writing. These procedures help with motivation as we see steady growth."

How do you make sense of these scores? Did most students do well or poorly? One of the first things you might do is reorder the tests from lowest to highest: 10, 20, 50, 60, 70, 75, 75, 80, 80, 85, 85, 85, 85, 90, 90, 90, 95, 100. Now you can quickly see the lowest and highest scores attained on your test. The distance between these is called the **range.** The range between scores in this example is 100 − 10 = 90 points. The range is useful to begin to get a sense of how the class did. A wide range, as in this case, suggests that at least one student (with a score of 10) has not mastered the goals, and that at least one student (with a score of 100) *has* mastered them. A narrow range, if the top score is high, suggests that most students did well. For example, if the range for a test is 10 and the top score is 95, then grades for that test range from 85 to 95—quite strong scores! A narrow range, if the top score is low, suggests that most students did poorly. Consider, for example, a test with a range of 10 and a top score of 70. In this instance the range of grades is 60–70, which means we still have some teaching to do.

Range
The distance between the lowest and highest scores attained on an assessment.

Because the range takes only the top and bottom score into account, you probably want to explore in a little more depth the information you get from the group of scores. A frequency distribution should be your next step. A **frequency distribution** lists the number of students who attained each score ordered from highest to lowest scores. Table 5.10, section A illustrates the frequency distribution for the set of scores with which we have been working. You can also group the scores into larger intervals for a **grouped frequency distribution,** which is displayed in Table 5.10, section B. You may recognize a grouped frequency distribution as similar to the ones that teachers sometimes post for students to show the range of grades. We, of course, discourage this practice of identifying students because it encourages students to compare themselves with others instead of focusing on their own score and progress.

Frequency Distribution
A display of the number of students who attained each score in order from lowest to highest.

Some teachers prefer a graph to a frequency distribution because it communicates the information about the pattern of frequencies visually. In that case, you would design a **frequency polygon,** which is a line graph in which the frequencies for each score are plotted as points, and a line connects those points. The scores or score

Frequency Polygon
A line graph that plots the frequencies of each score.

TABLE 5.10

Frequency Distributions for a Set of 18 Test Scores

(A)

Frequency Distribution	
Score	**Frequency**
100	1
95	1
90	3
85	4
80	2
75	2
70	1
60	1
50	1
20	1
10	1

(B)

Grouped Frequency Distribution	
Interval	**Frequency**
90–100	5
80–89	6
70–79	3
60–69	1
50–59	1
40–49	0
30–39	0
20–29	1
10–19	1
0–9	0

intervals are listed along the bottom of the graph, and the frequencies (used for plotting number of students at each score) are listed up the left side. See Figure 5.6 for a frequency polygon using the set of scores in Table 5.10.

You can see from examining the frequency polygon in Figure 5.6 that just looking at the range of scores (90 points) does not tell you enough about the pattern of scores for your students. You have two students who attained very low scores, but you have eleven students who attained a score of at least 80 percent, which you believe reflects a fairly high level of mastery, given how you constructed your assessment. If this had been a preassessment before a unit, you would probably want to redesign your unit to address more challenging goals based on this pattern of scores. If this assessment were at the midpoint of a unit, you would want to analyze what content the low-scoring students found difficult and work with them to master it.

Measures of Central Tendency

Mode
The score attained by more students than any other.

Median
A measure of central tendency that is the midpoint of a set of scores.

Another way to summarize the scores is to determine what the typical or average score is for the class using a single number. The **mode** is the score achieved by more students than any other. You can see from either Table 5.10 or Figure 5.6 that the mode for the class is 85. In this case, the mode represents only four students' scores.

A measure of central tendency that focuses on the exact midpoint of a set of scores is the **median.** The median falls exactly at the point where half of the scores are above it and half are below it. Thus, the *position* of the score in the range is more important than the *value* of the score when selecting the median. If you have an uneven number of scores, the median is whichever score falls exactly in the middle when scores are ordered from lowest to highest. If you have an even number of scores,

Frequency
0
1
2
3
4
5
6
7
8
9
10
0 5 10 15 20 25 30 35 40 45 50 55 60 65 70 75 80 85 90 95 100
Score

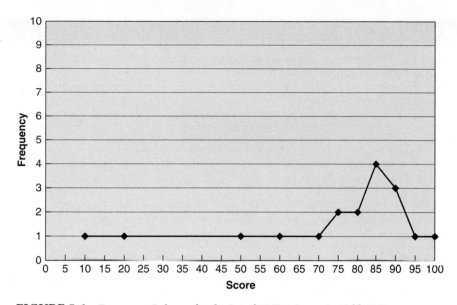

FIGURE 5.6 *Frequency Polygon for the Set of 18 Test Scores in Table 5.10*

the median is the value halfway between the middle two scores. In our example, we have 18 scores, so the median would fall between the ninth and tenth scores. Since both the ninth and tenth scores are 85, and there are no values between them, the median would be 85. (If the middle two scores had been 75 and 85, however, the median would be 80, or the value halfway between them.)

The measure of central tendency that takes into account *all* scores is the **mean.** This is the measure with which you may be the most familiar. The mean for the class is calculated by adding up every student's score, then dividing by the number of scores. In our example, 10 + 20 + 50 + 60 + 70 + 75 + 75 + 80 + 80 + 85 + 85 + 85 + 85 + 90 + 90 + 90 + 95 + 100 = 1325. When you divide this total by 18, the number of scores, the mean is 73.6. Because the mean is calculated using every score, it is used most commonly as the measure of central tendency.

Mean
A measure of central tendency that is the average of all scores in a distribution.

Shopping bag, in a tourist nigga! Bion bop, i do the money dance

Notice that the mean score of 73.6 for our example is much lower than the median score of 85. Scores that are extremely different from the others (in this case, the low scores of 10 and 20) disproportionately influence the mean. In contrast, the median is *not* influenced by extremely high or low scores (often called **outliers**) because its calculation relies only on the scores at the middle of the distribution. Sometimes teachers use the median instead of the mean for summarizing scores if an extreme score distorts the mean. When reporting measures of central tendency for certain figures, such as average national income, experts often use the median rather than the mean because the outliers who make billions of dollars a year would considerably alter the figures and give an erroneous impression. We discuss other aspects of score distributions (e.g., standard deviation) in Chapter 11.

Outliers
Extremely high or low scores that differ from typical scores.

➔ Building a Useful Table—An Analysis and Communication Tool

As we have seen, when working with data from a whole class, you need to organize the information to make sense of it. We have illustrated how you can use checklists and graphs to monitor individual progress. Now we turn to the **table** as an analysis and communication

TABLE 5.11

Steps for Designing a Table That Communicates Information About Student Performance

1. List data for each student in the column next to that student's name (or student number, when protecting confidentiality) with the scores in order from lowest to highest.

2. Give your table a title that communicates the content of the table.

3. At the top of each column, indicate what that list of scores represents. Include any information needed to interpret a score (e.g., number correct, percent correct, number of items).

4. As the last entry for each column, provide a measure of central tendency (mean or median).

5. Look for differences in performance across different subgroups (various races/ethnicities, free/reduced fee lunch vs. full pay lunch, high vs. low attendance rates, gender, levels of English proficiency, disability status), and calculate measures of central tendency for groups that may show important differences.

tool for class-wide data. The steps in designing a good table are listed in Table 5.11. We want to walk you through these steps one by one so you see the rationale for each aspect of table design. We have found in the past that many of our students do not realize how important each element of a table is for communicating information effectively.

A table allows you to visually represent relationships between different pieces of information. For the table to be useful, however, it needs to communicate what those relationships are. For example, some of our teacher candidates, when looking at the performance of their students, have designed a table that looks like this:

Eleanor	30	84
JaMarcus	10	66
Toby	10	50
Sam	20	60
LaKendra	40	95
Leah	50	90
William	40	84
Carol	50	90
LaTrellini	60	86
Buzz	40	45

We can see the relationship between each of the students and their scores, but we don't know what the scores represent, and we can't easily discern any pattern in these scores. The first step is to put the scores in some order. One common strategy is to put the scores in order from lowest to highest. We can do this for the first column of scores:

JaMarcus	10	66
Toby	10	50
Sam	20	60
Eleanor	30	84
LaKendra	40	95
William	40	84
Buzz	40	45
Leah	50	90
Carol	50	90
LaTrellini	60	86

This step provides order to the scores so you can quickly scan the range of scores and see whether they cluster together or tend to cover a wide spectrum. You can see that the scores in the first column have a 50-point range with a top score of only 60.

The table also needs a title to communicate what information is presented. Carefully labeling what each column of scores represents also provides important background for understanding what the scores can tell you:

Pre-unit Assessment and Midterm Scores for American Revolution Unit

	Percent Correct on Pre-unit Assessment	Percent Correct on Midterm Exam
JaMarcus	10	66
Toby	10	50
Sam	20	60
Eleanor	30	84
LaKendra	40	95
William	40	84
Buzz	40	45
Leah	50	90
Carol	50	90
LaTrellini	60	86

As you can see, this new information provides context for interpreting the scores. We now know that the scores are from a specific type of unit in a social studies class. We also know that the scores show the percent correct rather than the number of items correct. We understand that the scores are all quite low on the preassessment because it was completed before any of the material was taught. We can also tell that the teacher would expect progress between the first assessment and the second one. Another piece of information that would be useful, however, would be to know the total number of items in each assessment. When you have only percentages listed, you need to explain what the percentages represent. Was the midterm a major test or more like a quiz? What about the preassessment? Adding those details communicates more useful information:

Pre-unit Assessment and Midterm Scores for American Revolution Unit

	Percent Correct on Pre-unit Assessment (10 items)	Percent Correct on Midterm Exam (50 items)
JaMarcus	10	66
Toby	10	50
Sam	20	60
Eleanor	30	84
LaKendra	40	95
William	40	84
Buzz	40	45
Leah	50	90
Carol	50	90
LaTrellini	60	86

We now know that the second assessment had many more items than the first, so it was likely a fairly major assessment. We can look at students' scores individually to see whether any made gains, but the table could add means, the measure of central tendency that averages every score, so we can look at the class as a whole:

Pre-unit Assessment and Midterm Scores for American Revolution Unit

	Percent Correct on Pre-unit Assessment (10 items)	Percent Correct on Midterm Exam (50 items)
JaMarcus	10	66
Toby	10	50
Sam	20	60
Eleanor	30	84
LaKendra	40	95
William	40	84
Buzz	40	45
Leah	50	90
Carol	50	90
LaTrellini	60	86
Class mean	**35**	**75**

From this addition to the table, the scores suggest that the class as a whole has made impressive progress between the preassessment and the midterm.

Under the sorting model of education, teachers might look at the gains in this table and feel quite confident that the unit was progressing well. The difference in means between the preassessment and the midterm seems to show that the class as a whole has benefited from the teacher's instruction. The students seem to be making good progress toward the learning goal.

However, the more recent model that emphasizes helping all children to learn asks us to dig a little deeper. Did some children start with less background knowledge that might prevent them from learning all they could from this unit? Did some children make less progress than others? Can we discern any patterns in these results that will help us differentiate our instruction for the rest of the unit so we can teach the students more effectively? Because we want to explore any potential patterns in score differences, we will start by examining more closely the preassessment scores from lowest to highest to see whether any relationship between scores and students emerges.

First, you may notice that the top three scorers were girls, and the lowest three scorers were boys. You decide you need to explore this possible relationship between gender and scores more thoroughly. One way to do so would be to order the scores from lowest to highest for each gender separately. Then, to get a sense of where each group falls in relation to the other, you can calculate means for each gender. Add this information to your table:

Pre-unit Assessment and Midterm Scores for American Revolution Unit

Boys	Percent Correct on Pre-unit Assessment (10 items)	Percent Correct on Midterm Exam (50 items)
JaMarcus	10	66
Toby	10	50
Sam	20	60
William	40	84
Buzz	40	45
Boys' mean	**24**	**61**
Girls		
Eleanor	30	84
LaKendra	40	95
Leah	50	90
Carol	50	90
LaTrellini	60	86
Girls' mean	**46**	**89**
Class mean	35	75

Now you see a very strong relationship between gender and scores. On both the preassessment and the midterm, boys performed less well than girls. When you just looked at the mean for the whole class, this relationship was hidden because boys' and girls' scores were averaged together.

From this example, you can also see why examining your preassessment scores before you teach a unit can help you plan your unit and differentiate your instruction. The preassessment showed that some of the boys may have needed some different types of activities to provide background and engage their interest—perhaps a mini-lesson on important vocabulary and an ongoing journal assignment to describe the daily life of revolutionary soldiers. Similarly, several girls who showed they had already mastered some of the content could use varied activities as well, such as delving into some of the facets of revolutionary war culture (e.g., music, popular books, gender roles) that influenced the events of the war. Even after a midterm, of course, the information from the scores in the table on these gender differences can be used to differentiate your instruction to help the boys catch up and to enrich the girls' learning. All of these suggestions would, of course, be tied to your learning goals for the unit.

✦ DISAGGREGATION UNCOVERS HIDDEN TRENDS

Disaggregation of Scores
Separating the scores of a large group of students into smaller groups to determine whether differences among these groups exist.

What we have just done has a fancy name: **disaggregation of scores.** Disaggregation involves separating the scores of a large group of students into smaller meaningful groups (such as gender, disability status, or socioeconomic status) to understand better some problem or issue. Disaggregation can be done at the class level, as we have shown, to identify students who need something more (e.g., scaffolding or different ways of representing content) than your usual instructional approach. It is also done at the school, district, state, and national levels. Disaggregating academic scores helps us to better understand the needs of our students. As we saw in the example with gender, when you look only at average scores for a whole class, important information that can help to guide instruction can remain undetected.

The recent trend toward disaggregating scores has uncovered the achievement gap that we described in Chapter 1. Many schools that appeared to have high average achievement scores actually had large discrepancies among different groups. On a number of measures, students in racial, ethnic, and language minorities, as well as those at lower socioeconomic levels, tended to perform worse than other demographic groups. For example, Table 5.12 shows the results from one annual test at one elementary school in language arts disaggregated by race.

To see differences among groups more clearly, note that percentages of the total number in each disaggregated group are used for each category. For example, this school may have 600 European American students, 200 African American students, and 100 Latino

TABLE 5.12

Disaggregated Student Achievement Data for Language Arts Scores on One Test

	Third Grade		Fourth Grade	
	Advanced and Proficient	Need Improvement and Failing	Advanced and Proficient	Need Improvement and Failing
European American	65%	35%	55%	45%
African American	40%	60%	20%	80%
Latino	30%	70%	20%	80%

students. This table shows what percentage of each group, regardless of the size of that group, has met the standard. This procedure allows clearer comparisons among groups.

Reporting percentages by groups ensures that the smaller groups don't get neglected. If all 900 students had been averaged together, the high scores of the 600 European American students would have had the most influence on the total percentages of advanced and proficient students. We would not have seen the discrepancies between their scores and the scores of the other two groups.

At this point we offer a caution. Although these disaggregated test scores show *average* differences for European American students and African American students, your instructional decisions must be made for *individual* students, not for groups. Some of your African American students may be at the Need Improvement and Failing levels, but others will likely be at the Advanced and Proficient levels. The same thing can be said for your Latino students and your European American students. Disaggregation can help sensitize us to the needs of our students, but it should not be used indiscriminately.

A persistent pattern of lower achievement among minorities was one impetus behind the **No Child Left Behind Act (NCLB)** passed by the U.S. Congress and implemented nationwide since 2002. The goal was to increase academic achievement of lower performing groups and to have all students in the United States achieve proficiency in math and reading by 2014. Under NCLB, each state accepting federal assistance is required to assess students in math and reading in grades 3 through 8 each year and once in high school. (Science assessment requirements were also added in 2007–2008.) Public reporting of these results must be disaggregated by race, ethnicity, gender, disability status, migrant status, English proficiency, and status as economically disadvantaged. If any of the groups fail to make annual yearly progress (AYP), which is determined by each state, sanctions follow. We discuss NCLB at greater length in Chapter 11.

No Child Left Behind Act (NCLB)
U.S. federal law aimed to improve public schools by increasing accountability standards.

The stated purpose of disaggregation of achievement data required by NCLB has been to increase accountability of schools and teachers. Teachers and principals now pay close attention to the achievement of all groups. They have begun examining more carefully the patterns of achievement of their students using many assessment measures in classrooms. Clues from disaggregation of classroom assessment can help teachers to close the achievement gap by identifying students who lag behind. Some schools, such as J.E.B. Stuart Elementary in Richmond, VA, have weekly grade-level meetings where teachers look at disaggregated data on attendance, teacher observations, and various assessments for low achieving groups as a diagnostic tool to provide students who are behind the help they need to do better.

Sometimes data disaggregation can show that some of our assumptions may not be true about low-achieving groups. For example, the staff at one high school decided to examine their assumption that low achievement on state standardized tests was caused by high student absence rates. They disaggregated these test scores by attendance rates (high attendance vs. low attendance). They did find that a large percentage of students who were absent often did poorly. But they also found that an equally large percentage of students who had high attendance *also* did poorly on the test. This finding led to useful discussions about ways to improve the content and quality of their instruction. They began to look for other causes over which they had more influence than absences as reasons for their school's poor performance (Lachat & Smith, 2005).

→ Case Study Application

In this section, we visit Ebony Sanders's case study to reflect on the lessons it provides on monitoring progress over time and summarizing data for groups. As you recall, one learning goal in Ebony's unit on characteristics of solids and liquids is *Students will demonstrate appropriate steps to test an unknown solid or liquid.* As the preassessment for this learning goal, Ebony had each student explore a solid and a liquid in zipper plastic bags inside a "feely box," where they could touch objects but not see them. Students then made a list of descriptive words corresponding to each test they could think of to perform on the object (e.g., does it have a shape?). After instruction and exploration with a number of materials, she had students come up with rules for why one item is a liquid and one is a solid so they could later do their own specific tests on unknown objects whenever they wanted. For example, rules for one group included "If it has a definite shape in a cup but not in a zipper bag, it must be a liquid." "If it doesn't change shape, it's a solid." Then, partway through the unit, as a measure of progress she repeats the "feely box" assessment with a new liquid and a new solid. This second trial served as a mid-unit check on progress.

Now we can compare these results with the preassessment results, which are both displayed in Table 5.13. In this table, Ebony added the findings for liquids and solids together for each assessment, so the total possible number correct is 11. First note that two students withdrew from school before the mid-unit assessment was conducted.

TABLE 5.13

Preassessment and Mid-unit Assessment Results for One Learning Goal for Unit on Characteristics of Liquids and Solids

	Pre-unit and Mid-unit Assessment Results for Learning Goal *Students Will Demonstrate Appropriate Steps to Test an Unknown Solid or Liquid*		
	Percent Correct on Preassessment (11 possible)	**Percent Correct on Mid-unit Assessment (11 possible)**	**Points Gained Between Preassessment and Mid-unit Assessment**
Student 8	0%	64%	64
Student 10	0%	54%	54
Student 11	0%	27%	27
Student 15	0%	withdrew	withdrew
Student 16	9%	45%	36
Student 12	9%	64%	55
Student 5	9%	45%	36
Student 2	18%	withdrew	withdrew
Student 3	18%	36%	18
Student 9	18%	54%	36
Student 6	18%	82%	64
Student 17	27%	45%	18
Student 4	27%	45%	18
Student 13	27%	36%	9
Student 14	27%	82%	55
Student 7	45%	73%	28
Student 1	54%	27%	−27
Class mean	**18%**	**51.9%**	**32.7**

The school where Ebony worked has a high rate of student mobility, so the composition of classes changes often because students transfer in and out.

Now let's look at progress across time. Ebony's preassessment measure and her mid-unit measure were identical, except that she used a different liquid and a different solid each time. Because the measures were so similar, she believed that comparing scores on the two measures would let her know what students had learned so far on this learning goal. If you look at the class means for preassessment and mid-term assessment, you see an average gain of over 30 percentage points. This definitely shows progress for the whole class.

But as we saw in a previous example, sometimes averages for the whole class mask important differences among groups. Ebony decided to disaggregate these scores by comparing students who qualified for free or reduced-fee lunch (one measure of lower income and socioeconomic status) with students who paid full price for lunch. She did not include the two students who withdrew from the school in this analysis. (One came from each group.) You can see her findings in Table 5.14.

Notice that both groups were within three points of each other on the preassessment, a relatively insignificant difference. But you see a much larger disparity on the mid-unit assessment—more than a 20-point difference. These findings suggested to Ebony that she needed to look more closely at differences in what students had learned so far so she could decide how to close this achievement gap. She realized she needed to attend to these students more closely as she finished the unit, especially students 1 and 11. Were there certain rules about the characteristics of liquids or solids they had not yet grasped? Was some of the vocabulary of the unit difficult because of lack of previous experience? For example, one test she introduced students to for examining solids was magnetism. Did all students have necessary background knowledge about magnets?

One bright spot was that Student 8 and Student 10, who had writing difficulties, were able to perform in the average range at mid-unit. She had accommodated these two students, after consulting with her school's occupational therapist, by letting them use pencil grips that were easier to grasp and paper with raised lines. (She could have let these students report answers orally, but she wanted to be sure to work on students' weaknesses and not just rely on their strengths.) She had also worked with Student 11, the remaining student who was learning English (the other had withdrawn), by providing more visual examples, pairing her in activities with native speakers, and providing mini-lessons on unit vocabulary.

Now we can revisit some of our themes in relation to Ebony's experience, first stressing the value of critical thinking at higher levels of Bloom's taxonomy. Ebony has first graders examine unfamiliar liquids and solids and apply rules to classify them, demonstrating that even young children can be expected to go beyond memorizing facts. She also uses her assessments to promote active rather than passive learning among the students by providing for feedback and subsequent improvement before summative assessment. This also encourages the students to develop effort optimism and take charge of their learning.

In addition, by repeating the same task with different liquids and solids, Ebony uses a type of general outcome measurement. We hope you have learned from Ebony's case study that carefully analyzing and disaggregating your assessment data can yield important information that will enhance your teaching and help you move toward closing achievement gaps. As we mentioned in Chapter 1, many people just shut down when they see numbers or data. But as you have seen with Ebony's assessment data, the numbers summarizing student responses yielded important information that provided a window on her students' needs. She knew that even though her lower scoring students had made gains, they needed additional assistance to master the learning goal. The only way to maximize achievement is to hold high expectations for all students and not settle for measures of achievement that mask children left behind.

TABLE 5.14

Preassessment and Mid-unit Assessment Results Disaggregated by Lunch Status

Pre-unit and Midterm Assessment Results for Learning Goal *Students Will Demonstrate Appropriate Steps to Test an Unknown Solid or Liquid*		
Free/Reduced Lunch Students:	**Percent Correct on Pre-unit Assessment (11 items)**	**Percent Correct on Mid-unit Assessment (11 items)**
Student 10	0%	54%
Student 11	0%	27%
Student 5	9%	45%
Student 12	9%	64%
Student 3	18%	36%
Student 4	27%	45%
Student 13	27%	36%
Student 1	54%	27%
Free/Reduced-Fee Lunch Students' Mean	**18%**	**41.7%**
Regular Fee Lunch Students:		
Student 8	0%	64%
Student 16	9%	45%
Student 9	18%	54%
Student 6	18%	82%
Student 17	27%	45%
Student 14	27%	82%
Student 7	45%	73%
Regular-Fee Lunch Students' Mean	**20.6%**	**63.6%**
Class mean	18%	55%

As an additional note from this case study, you may get the idea that one assessment is all that you need to do. This would be a misconception. How many times have you heard the old adage, "Don't put all your eggs in one basket"? It definitely applies to assessment. You need more than one assessment "basket" because students have different strengths and weaknesses. For example, you may be terrible at multiple-choice questions, but you shine on essay questions. How would you feel if one of your professors gave only one assessment—a multiple-choice final exam? As a teacher, you want to give your students opportunities to work to their strengths, but you also must give them opportunities to improve their weaknesses. Helping students work on content and strategies they have difficulty with is crucial for closing achievement gaps. Also, different kinds of assessments work best for detecting different types of learning. In Chapter 6 you will learn more about why multiple assessments are needed when we discuss validity and reliability of assessments. Then, in Chapters 7, 8, and 9 you will learn more about different methods of assessment, their strengths and weaknesses, and when to use them.

KEY CHAPTER POINTS

This chapter began by explaining the requirements for examining progress over time: specific goals, formative assessment tasks where mistakes are an expected part of learning, and a method of tracking progress with visual representation of individual improvement over time. We then discussed the advantages of systematic progress monitoring for both students and teachers. Key among these were providing the knowledge needed for differentiated instruction and promoting learning goals and high expectations.

We then described two approaches to monitoring student progress. The first, mastery monitoring, tracks students across the different tasks contributing to mastery of the learning goal. The second, general outcome measurement, samples more than once a performance that represents the achievement of a learning goal. Both of these approaches work best when they include a visual representation (e.g., a graph) of progress documenting gains across time. We then described curriculum-based measurement as an example of general outcome measurement. We also compared mastery monitoring and general outcome measurement in terms of their strengths, content, advantages, and concerns.

Next we discussed the procedures needed when you summarize data for a group or class of students. We described how you can use frequency distributions and frequency polygons to get a general picture of a group of scores. We then described three measures of central tendency—mode, median, and mean—as other ways to characterize a group of scores. We also provided rules and a step-by-step example for building a table that accurately communicates information about student performance. Finally, we discussed and illustrated the importance of disaggregation of assessment data for understanding students and their instructional needs.

In the case study section, we compared student scores from Ebony's mid-unit assessment to her pre-unit assessment. In addition, we highlighted the importance of addressing higher-level thinking skills and the value of disaggregating assessment data to uncover learning differences. These last two points in particular relate to our recurring themes of teaching self-governing skills for democratic participation and providing equal access to education for all students.

HELPFUL WEBSITES

http://www.studentprogress.org/

The National Center on Student Progress Monitoring website answers questions and provides
    information, resources, a free newsletter, discussion board, and training opportunities for
    those interested in curriculum-based measurement.

http://ed.sc.gov/topics/assessment/scores/pact/2007/statescoresdemo.cfm

Most state departments of education post disaggregated scores from their statewide achievement
    tests on a website. You can examine these scores to find the types and severity of the
    achievement gaps in your state. This website features scores from the Palmetto
    Achievement Challenge Test in South Carolina.

CHAPTER REVIEW QUESTIONS

1. Why do you think formative assessment is a basic requirement for monitoring student growth across time? What characteristics of formative assessment would make it useful for this purpose?

2. Describe a situation (academic or not) when you set a goal and monitored your progress toward that goal. Would you categorize the process as closer to mastery monitoring or to general outcome measurement? Why?

3. Choose a learning goal in your content area for which you would like to set up a progress monitoring system. Using your understanding of the advantages and concerns for both mastery monitoring and general outcome measurement, describe the progress monitoring system you would design, including a visual representation, and justify your approach.

4. Think of a specific, short-term goal you would like to achieve in your personal life and describe what benchmarks you would use to monitor progress toward it. What visual representation of progress would you use and why?

5. Describe the similarities and differences between a frequency distribution and a frequency polygon.

6. Describe a situation when you would want to use a frequency distribution or a frequency polygon to examine scores of students in one of your classes.

7. Choose a learning goal in your content area and assume that the following set of scores represent student performance in your class related to that learning goal. Develop a frequency distribution, a grouped frequency distribution, and a frequency polygon for the preassessment scores. You may use a spreadsheet software program.

Student	Gender	Lunch Status	Percent Correct on Preassessment (10 items)	Percent Correct on Mid-unit Assessment (20 items)
1	M	Free	10%	35%
2	M	Full pay	30%	85%
3	F	Free	0%	25%
4	M	Free	10%	45%
5	F	Full pay	10%	55%
6	M	Full pay	20%	75%
7	M	Full pay	40%	90%
8	M	Free	20%	70%
9	F	Free	10%	35%
10	F	Full pay	10%	45%
11	M	Full pay	100%	100%
12	F	Full pay	20%	45%

8. Now calculate the mean, median, and mode for all 12 students for the preassessment. What differences do you see between mean and median? Why?

9. Now revise your frequency distribution by disaggregating the preassessment data by gender. Then make a new frequency distribution disaggregated by lunch status. Interpret what you have found in these analyses for the whole group, the gender groups, and the lunch groups. Do you see any indications that some students may not have the background knowledge required for the unit? What implications do the preassessment data have for your instructional planning? What would you do next, given the content of your learning goal?

10. One student attained a score of 100% on the pre-unit assessment. What actions should you take to differentiate instruction for this student given the content of your learning goal?

11. Now design a frequency distribution for the mid-unit assessment data for the whole class; for the gender groups; and for the lunch groups. Calculate means and medians for all groups. What implications do the mid-unit assessment data have for your instructional planning for the rest of the unit?

12. Describe at least three ways systematic progress monitoring can help you address achievement gaps in your classroom.

References

Baker, S. K., K. Smolkowski, R. Katz, H. Fien, J. Seeley, E. Kame'enui, and C. T. Beck. 2008. Reading fluency as a predictor of reading proficiency in low-performing high-poverty schools. *School Psychology Review* 37: 18–37.

Bandura, A. 1997. *Self-efficacy: The exercise of control.* New York: Freeman.

Deno, S. L. 1985. Curriculum-based measurement: The emerging alternative. *Exceptional Children* 52: 219–232.

Deno, S. L. 1997. "Whether" thou goest . . . Perspectives on progress monitoring. In E. Kame'einuii, J. Lloyd, and D. Chard (eds.), *Issues in educating students with disabilities.* Saddle River, NJ: Erlbaum.

Deno, S. L. 2003. Developments in Curriculum-Based Measurement. *Journal of Special Education* 37: 184–192.

Lachat, M. A., and S. Smith. 2005. Practices that support data use in urban high schools. *Journal of Education for Students Placed at Risk* 10: 333–349.

Locke, E., and G. Latham. 1990. *A theory of goal setting and task performance.* Englewood Cliffs, NJ: Prentice Hall.

Locke, E., and G. Latham. 2002. Building a practically useful theory of goal setting and task motivation: A 35-year odyssey. *American Psychologist* 57: 705–717.

Marston, D., P. Muyskens, M. Lau, and A. Canter. 2003. Problem-solving model for decision making with high incidence disabilities: The Minneapolis experience. *Learning Disabilities: Research and Practice* 18: 187–200.

Marzano, R. J. 2006. *Classroom assessment and grading that work.* Alexandria, VA: Association for Supervision and Curriculum Development.

Moon, T. 2005. The role of assessment in differentiation. *Theory into Practice* 44(3): 226–233.

National Research Center on Learning Disabilities. 2005. *Understanding responsiveness to intervention in learning disabilities determination.* Retrieved October 10, 2007, from http://nrcld.org/publications/papers/mellard.shtml.

Reeves, D. B. 2004. The 90/90/90 schools: A case study. In D. B., Reeves, *Accountability in action: A blueprint for learning organizations.* 2nd ed. Englewood, CO: Advanced Learning Press.

Shinn, M. R. 1989. *Curriculum-based measurement.* New York: Guilford.

Shinn, M. R. 1998. *Advanced applications of curriculum-based measurement.* New York: Guilford Press.

Stecker, P., L. Fuchs, and D. Fuchs. 2005. Using curriculum-based measurement to improve student achievement: Review of research. *Psychology in the Schools* 42: 795–819.

Trammel, D., P. Schloss, and S. Alper. 1994. Using self-recording, evaluation, and graphing to increase completion of homework assignments. *Journal of Learning Disabilities* 27(2): 75–81.

Urdan, T., and E. Schoenfelder. 2006. Classroom effects on student motivation: Goal structures, social relationships, and competence beliefs. *Journal of School Psychology* 44: 331–349.

Zimmerman, B. 2002. Becoming a self-regulated learner: An overview. *Theory into Practice* 41(2): 64–70.

Zimmerman, B. 2008. Investigating self-regulation and motivation: Historical background, methodological developments, and future prospects. *American Educational Research Journal* 45: 166–183.

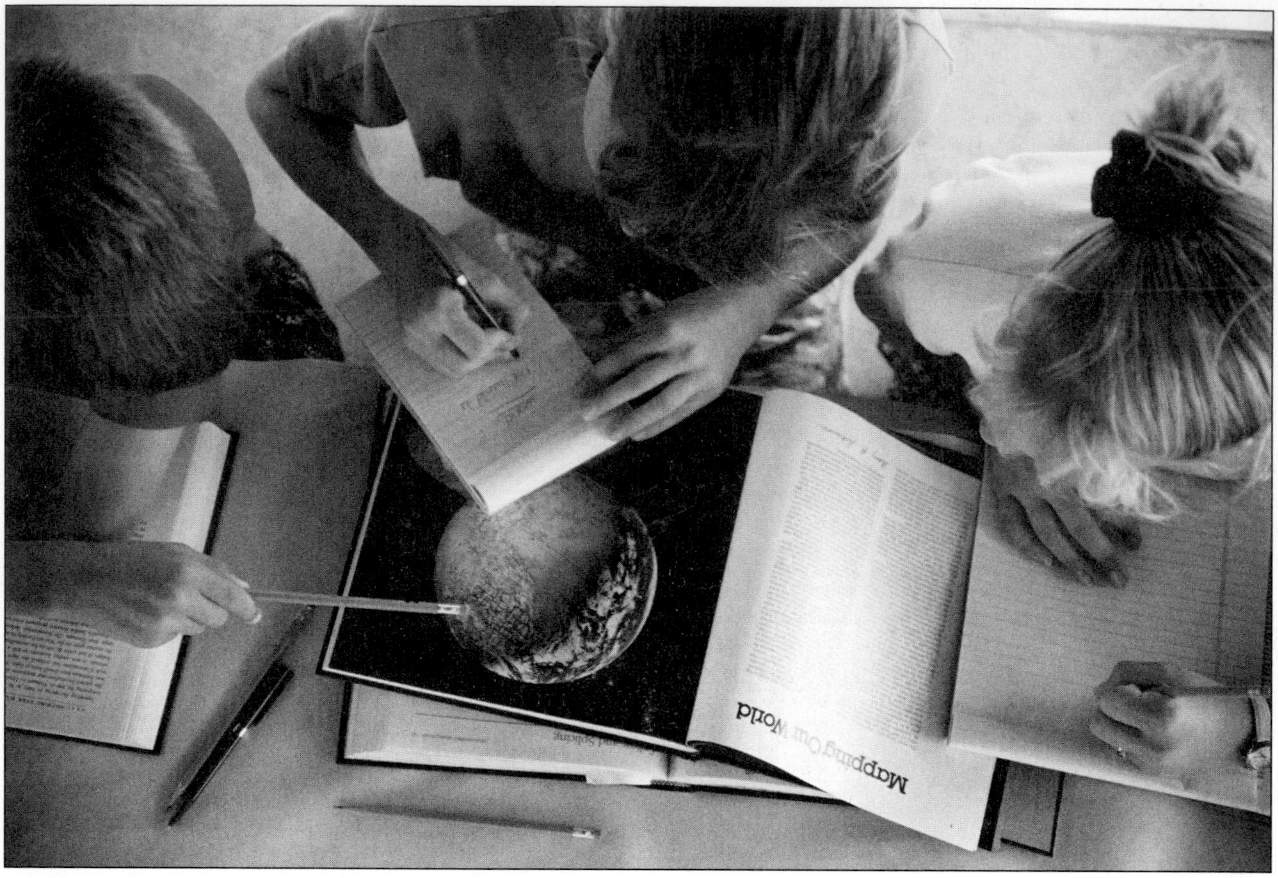
Mapping Our World

CHAPTER 6

Essential Characteristics of Assessment

Garbage in, garbage out.

–George Fuechsel

❖ **Chapter Learning Goals**

At the conclusion of this chapter, the reader should be able to do the following:

- Understand the importance of error and appraise the degree of reliability in interpreting assessment results.

- Describe how to minimize the impact of error in assessment.

- Appraise the degree of validity when interpreting assessment results.

- Distinguish how the purpose of an assessment influences its validity.

- Use four sources of evidence for validity (logic and common sense, variety of assessment formats, content-related evidence, and criterion-related evidence) to improve the validity of assessments.

- Avoid the bias pitfalls in classroom assessment.

- Create assessments representing the diversity of the classroom.

⤳ Introduction

We begin with a quotation that was widely used by technicians in the early days of computers to caution that if the data entered into a computer program are problematic or nonsensical, the computer output will also be meaningless. Just because you use a computer doesn't mean it can magically transform bad raw material into a wonderful finished product. Now the phrase is used in many situations where the quality of the "input" will affect the value of the "output."

Classroom assessment is a prime example. If you design a poor assessment (the input), you could still use its results to assign grades (the output) that seem official and objective. But you will really end up with "garbage" that does not tell you what you need to know about what students are learning. One of our students describes just such a situation: "In my freshman year of high school, my geometry teacher taught mostly triangles and the Pythagorean Theorem. However, for our final grade, he handed out directions to make a 3-dimensional dodecahedron. The key to passing the project was not to know anything about triangles, but to use sturdy paper so that when he dropped your dodecahedron on the floor, it wouldn't fall apart. If your dodecahedron fell apart . . . so did your grade." This teacher was able to put a score in the grade book for each student, but what did it really mean?

> **Ethics Alert:** This is an example of score pollution. The teacher is using a task and criteria that have little relationship to the course subject matter.

In this chapter we discuss concepts that have a strong impact on the quality of the input—the assessment opportunities you provide your students. These concepts include reliability, validity, bias, and representing diversity in your assessments. If you take great care with these concerns as you design your assessments, you will ensure that the output—the scores resulting from the responses of your students— will be of high quality and will therefore provide you with meaningful information about student learning.

→ RELIABILITY: ARE WE GETTING CONSISTENT INFORMATION?

Reliability
The degree to which scores on an assessment are consistent and stable.

Error
The element of imprecision involved in any measurement.

The first aspect of assessment that we want to consider is **reliability.** Reliability is the degree to which scores on an assessment are consistent and stable. A reliable assessment will produce roughly similar scores for a student even if the assessment is taken on different occasions, if it has slightly different items, or if it happens to be graded by a different person. The results are reproducible and not a fluke. If you *do* find significant differences in scores across these situations, they are caused by some form of error. **Error** is the element of imprecision involved in any measurement. Error can change a score in either direction from where it would actually fall. It can boost a score higher *or* decrease it. The more error, the lower the reliability of the score.

Knowing that *every single score* has an error component leads us to the logical conclusion that *no important decision about any student should be made on the basis of a single score.* This conclusion is not unique to us; professionals in assessment have long understood the role of error and the need to make decisions based on multiple assessments. For example, most college admissions decisions are based on several factors, such as high school grade-point average, letters of reference, SAT or ACT scores, and an essay.

Sources of Error

In thinking about error and testing circumstances, one of our students shared with us her experience about taking the SAT for the first time. The heat wasn't working in the scheduled classroom, and so the group was moved to the gym. The proctor used the time clock on the scoreboard to keep track of the minutes remaining for the test. Unfortunately, this clock loudly ticked off each second. To top everything off, the proctor had a big bunch of keys that jingled loudly with each step as he constantly patrolled the room. As you might imagine, this student's score was lower than she had expected, and it increased by 150 points the second time she took the SAT. Her experience illustrates error due to the occasion of testing. Factors from the assessment occasion that can introduce error into scores include environmental sources shown in Table 6.1. In the case of our student (and probably others who took the test at the same time) these sources had a negative impact on scores.

Assessment occasion is only one source of error influencing scores. Other sources of error are listed in Table 6.1. These include items as well as scoring issues. We discuss each one in turn.

TABLE 6.1

Potential Sources of Error

Source	Examples
Assessment occasion	• High or low room temperature • Disruptions (e.g., noise) • Fluctuating motivation or mood of respondent • Carelessness of respondent
Assessment items	• Number of items (too few *or* too many) • Different versions of a test
Scoring issues	• Unclear criteria for scoring • Differences between scorers or raters

Assessment Occasion

The SAT example with the ticking clock is a perfect illustration of how environmental distractions related to the specific occasion of an assessment can introduce error into the scores that students receive. You can see how noises from the clock and the keys as well as the disruption of moving from room to room could have distracted our student, producing a poorer score for her. Some variations in assessment occasion, however, do not occur during the assessment, but can still have an impact (negative *or* positive), such as class parties. We know one high school teacher who never schedules important summative assessments during prom week because of the increased potential for error.

Error in scores due to the occasion of the assessment is also influenced by the **respondent,** or the student completing the assessment. As you know from your experience, students vary from day to day and even from moment to moment in their interest in the concepts and skills being introduced, their mood, their level of energy, whether they are sick or healthy, their degree of carelessness, their level of motivation, and how their relationships with family and other significant people are going, to name a few issues. These individual variations also contribute to errors in assessment outcomes. If teachers use more frequent assessments, errors due to individual variation average out across time with many assessments.

Respondent
The student completing the assessment.

Assessment Items

Another aspect of an assessment that contributes to reliability is the pool of items. Reliability is increased to the degree that the items display **internal consistency.** Internal consistency refers to the degree that all the items in an assessment are related to one another and therefore can be assumed to measure the same thing. Internal consistency is high if all items are strongly related to each other. Internal consistency is low if they are not strongly related to each other.

Internal Consistency
The degree to which all of the items in an assessment are related to each other.

Also important to reliability is the number of items. Let us exaggerate for a moment to show the importance of the number of items. What if your professor were to create a summative, final examination for this assessment course with only one question? The one item may address *any* concept covered in *Assessment Is Essential.* Are you comfortable with a one-item test assessing everything you learned this semester? What if the test had five items? Are you comfortable yet? What if the test had from 35 to 40 items? Intuitively, you realize that a one-item or five-item test might fail to capture all the ideas that you've learned this semester. In contrast, you see that a 40-item test that is based on the learning goals associated with the text chapters could be a fairer assessment of your knowledge gained in the course. Thus, in considering consistency in test scores, use enough items to adequately cover the concepts learned.

Errors related to this type of evidence for reliability will not be problematic in classrooms if teachers assess often. Teachers usually gather information so frequently that any random error resulting from one assessment is likely to be quickly corrected with the next, which often occurs the very next day.

Scoring Issues

A third factor that contributes to reliability involves the way assessments are scored, particularly when scoring requires careful judgment. Have you ever been in a class where you compared tests with someone next to you and found that they got more points for an answer than you did, even though the answers seemed almost identical to you? Sometimes teachers may not carefully delineate the criteria they are using to score answers, and so errors in judgment can result. If the criteria for grading are not as explicit as possible (to both teacher *and* students), all sorts of extraneous factors that have nothing to do with quality of the student performance will influence the score. Significant error will be introduced to the actual scores students deserve. For example, if a teacher grades some papers at night when she is tired, she might not notice that several students left out an important point. This would be particularly likely to occur if she had not specified that the idea was worth a specific number of points when she allocated points in her scoring guide before she began grading any papers. Statement of explicit criteria in the scoring guide, such as accuracy and number of supporting facts, presence of particular kinds of arguments, or adherence to conventions of written language, make these types of problems less likely. Even when teachers are tired or distracted, if they have spelled out exactly what they are looking for, they will more likely be consistent in their scoring. You will learn more about establishing scoring criteria in Chapters 8 and 9.

Interrater Reliability
A measure of the degree of agreement between two rates.

Interrater Reliability   **Interrater reliability** is the measure of the consistency between two raters. When interrater reliability is high, the two raters strongly agree on the score that should be assigned to the same piece of work. When interrater reliability is low, the two raters disagree on what score should be assigned. We once had a student who suffered firsthand from interrater reliability problems. Her high school social studies teacher had everyone in the class rate each student's oral presentation on the connection between a current event and a historical event. Each student's final score for the project was to be the sum of 20 different peers' scores. This student had recently broken up with a boyfriend. The boyfriend convinced eight of his friends in the class to assign his former girlfriend's presentation an "F." With the inconsistency between these scores and other students' ratings, the student ended up with a "D" on the project. The teacher did not take into account the degree of error involved, so the student's grade did not reflect her level of mastery.

> **Ethics Alert:** Scoring major summative assessments, such as projects or presentations, is the responsibility of the teacher.

In contrast, most teachers know how important consistency across raters can be for making accurate judgments about student work. We have worked in several schools

TABLE 6.2

Reliability Questions for Classroom Assessment

Have I ensured that the assessment occasion is free of distractions?

Have I designed an assessment that gathers sufficient information for the decisions to be made?

Have I developed scoring criteria that are clear and unambiguous for both myself and my students?
Have I compared my scoring standards with other teachers who teach the same content?

in which a common scoring guide is used for writing. In these schools, teachers make an effort to check out their degree of interrater reliability. They practice scoring papers that range in quality from several students, and then they discuss any differences in their resulting scores in hopes of improving their consistency. These teachers want to make sure that they agree on the standards of quality and what the scores for different levels of work represent. They want to reduce errors in their scoring and increase their reliability so that they provide the most precise possible representations of their students' writing quality.

Sufficiency of Information

Recently, educators in the area of classroom assessment have suggested that for the classroom teacher, reliability may be defined as **"sufficiency of information"** (Brookhart, 2003; Smith, 2003). These authors suggest that sufficiency of information means that the teacher needs enough (that is, sufficient) information from any assessment to make a good decision based on the results. With a formative assessment, the teacher must have enough information to make good decisions about the next step in instruction. With a summative assessment, the teacher must have enough information to be able to determine the level of mastery of the learning goals for each student. Usually, your confidence in the results of your assessment and the reliability of your assessment increases as the number of items and occasions increases.

Sufficiency of Information
Ensuring the collection of adequate data to make good decisions.

An analogy that we heard once from one of our professors is helpful in understanding the idea of increasing the sample to increase sufficiency of information (and, therefore, reliability). Assume that a friend asks you how the food is at a local restaurant. If you have eaten several meals there, you will be more confident of your recommendation than if you have eaten there only once. This is because you have more sufficient information. Similarly, you will feel more confident about making decisions about student understanding of new concepts and skills if you use a sufficient sample of items related to the learning goals on different assessment occasions. See Table 6.2 for a list of reliability questions for classroom assessment.

✦ IMPROVING RELIABILITY IN CLASSROOM ASSESSMENTS

To finish our discussion of reliability, we have a few suggestions about ways to improve reliability in classroom assessments. These suggestions are listed in Table 6.3. Note that a common theme is the importance of providing many opportunities for students to demonstrate what they have learned.

TABLE 6.3

Suggestions for Improving Reliability in Classroom Assessments

	Suggestions	Examples
Assessment Occasion	• Ensure that the assessment occasion is free of distractions.	• Avoid scheduling important assessments at the same time as other important events. • Provide multiple assessment opportunities.
Assessment Items	• Ensure sufficiency of information.	• Use enough items to get a clear picture of student performance.
Scoring Issues	• Clarify scoring criteria. • Ensure interrater reliability.	• Use the most objective possible items and scoring methods. • Discuss scoring criteria with students before an assessment. • Practice scoring assessments with students. • Practice scoring assessments with other teachers. • Allow students to assist in designing scoring criteria.

The conclusion that you should provide many opportunities for assessments is a logical extension of your understanding that every score contains error. The more assessment opportunities you offer your students, the more likely you are to have a reliable picture of their performance. Across time, different sources of error cancel each other out. For example, in a chemistry class on a unit about energy transformation, you could give students (1) a set of problems calculating the energy required for several transformations, and (2) a multiple-choice quiz on the three types of transformations of matter. Some students may make careless errors on the calculation problems that lower their score. But on the multiple-choice items they make a few lucky guesses, and the error contribution instead raises their score. One assessment occasion has produced negative error and the other has produced positive error. When you average these two, you are likely closer to an accurate score than the score on either single assessment opportunity. The more scores you have, the more stable is the resulting average. The fewer scores you have, the more likely the error component is large. Box 6.1 describes

BOX 6.1   EXCERPT ON RELIABILITY CONCERNS FROM TEACHER INTERVIEW

". . . This fourth-grade teacher and her team do a number of things to ensure reliability. When they have open-ended questions on a test, all three teachers in the grade read all students' answers and scores from each teacher are compared so they gather information on interrater reliability. This teacher also uses several test questions to assess each skill so that the possibility of being lucky or unlucky is removed."

one teacher's approach to reliability in her classroom assessments that reflects these points. And, to conclude our discussion of reliability, we reiterate the point made earlier in the chapter: *No important decision about any student should be made on the basis of a single score.*

→ VALIDITY: WILL SCORES SUPPORT US IN MAKING GOOD DECISIONS?

Now we move on to validity, another concept in addition to reliability that affects the kind of "input" you provide when designing assessment opportunities for your students. **Validity** addresses whether the scores from your assessment will support you in making valid decisions about students. Like reliability, validity can be pictured on a continuum from low to high. The example of the geometry teacher who had students construct a dodecahedron for their final grade falls at the low end of the validity continuum. Scores on that assessment were not accurate, representative, or relevant to whether students had mastered the learning goals of the class, the purpose usually addressed by a final grade.

Usually teachers think about the validity of their classroom assessments intuitively. For example, if scores on a Spanish midterm test are low, and even the students most fluent in spoken Spanish earned low scores, the teacher begins to suspect that the test scores are providing questionable conclusions about the class. She may check to see if the answer key is correct or she may review the items for clarity. She might ask a student who usually earns high scores why he missed an item that the majority of students missed. The low scores of fluent students would have triggered this informal study of the validity of the test. They would cause the teacher to gather evidence on the accuracy, representativeness, and relevance of this test for its intended purpose.

Importance of Purpose in Considering Validity

Because you must always consider the intended purpose when thinking about validity, what counts as a solid indicator of validity may change from situation to situation. The ability to make an indestructible dodecahedron *could* be an assessment with high validity if the intended purpose of the assignment were to measure students' skill at constructing indestructible dodecahedrons in a physics class. Considering the purpose in judgments of validity is crucial because assessments that you design can be invalid for one purpose (geometry) and valid for another (physics).

If a test is inappropriate for its purpose, the conclusions drawn about student performance are not valid. For example, Popham (2007) suggests that many standardized tests used to determine annual yearly progress by states for No Child Left Behind may not be appropriate for their intended purpose. Often the scores on these tests cannot be specifically attributed to the effects of classroom instruction, but they *are* strongly influenced by children's social class. He suggests that we need better tests specifically designed to be sensitive to instruction if we want to use them as valid measures of students' yearly progress. Because purposes of assessments vary, you think about somewhat different issues depending on the purpose you have in mind. Table 6.4 summarizes the relationship between purpose and validity for assessment types that we have discussed.

Purpose and Validity: Formative Assessment

When you are thinking about formative assessments, your primary validity concern is the degree that the assessment *supports the learning* your students must do to master the learning goals. You develop activities in which student understanding or skills are

TABLE 6.4

Validity Concerns Depend on the Purpose of the Assessment

Formative	Summative
Degree to which the practice supports the learning required to master classroom learning goals	Degree to which the interpretation of the results provides accurate evidence about achievement of the classroom learning goals

assessed so the misconceptions or misunderstandings can be corrected. You also focus on a very narrow range of knowledge and/or skills so you can probe in depth your students' understanding. For example, in math you may focus on the process of problem solving steps and students' explanations for their choices for only one particular type of problem, such as solving geometry proofs. Formative assessment should provide a window on the students' thought processes as a guide to which next instructional steps will support their learning the most.

Purpose and Validity: Summative Classroom Assessment

When you design your classroom summative assessments, you should look at the degree to which your interpretation of student scores will give you accurate evidence about their levels of achievement of the learning goals the assessment addresses. You want to make sure the assessment representatively samples the content from the learning goals taught. It should also use formats and activities similar to those used in class. For example, as a chemistry teacher, you might teach a unit incorporating the structure of the atom, the periodic table of the elements, and the formation of chemical bonds. Your summative assessment should sample items from each of these three areas and incorporate only problems that used the calculations and formulas covered in class. If you did not cover isotopes and methods to determine the number of extra neutrons in an isotope, these should not be included on the summative test. As we noted in Chapter 2, the learning goals, instruction, and assessment must be aligned. If you had never given students the opportunity to explain why they used a certain step in solving a problem during the unit, you would not want to ask them to do so for the first time on a summative test of that unit. To draw valid conclusions about what your students have learned, you must develop items that represent the content *and* the modes of instruction in your classroom (Brookhart, 2003).

Evidence for Validity

Over the years, educational researchers have developed a number of methods to provide evidence for the validity of assessments. These procedures involve using logic as well as informal and formal collection of data, but putting the information together always involves a degree of judgment. Because the evidence required for different purposes varies, the type and extensiveness of information collected also varies significantly, especially between classroom and large-scale settings. When you make judgments about validity, you will usually be gathering information from several sources.

At the most basic level, all the information about validity that we collect examines **construct-related evidence** (Gronlund, 2006). A **construct** is the basic idea, theory, or concept that you have in mind whenever you attempt to measure something. Science achievement and reading comprehension are examples of constructs.

Construct-Related Evidence
All information collected to examine the validity of an assessment.

Construct
The basic idea, theory, or concept when measurement is attempted.

Perhaps you have designed a questionnaire as a project for a class or organization to learn about people's attitudes. You came up with items that you hope zero in on the construct you care about—people's opinion of a specific issue or a particular political figure. You always start with a construct, or idea, anytime you develop some form of measurement. Usually there are a number of possible ways to measure the same construct, and so no single measure can really capture the whole construct. See Figure 6.1 for examples of the different kinds of measures you might use to describe two constructs. Note that any one of these single measures alone cannot do a good job of summing up the whole construct. That is another reason why we recommend that *no important decision about a student should be made based on a single score.*

High-quality construct-related evidence for validity provides support for your hunch that the data you choose to collect actually *do* represent the basic concept with which you started. Because so many choices exist in measuring one construct, this type of evidence must be collected to show that *your* measure makes sense. If you have strong construct-related evidence for validity, you can assume that the data you collect will allow you to make useful and accurate **inferences** about student learning. Inferences

Inference
An assumption or conclusion based on observations and experiences.

Construct
Geometry Proficiency
Potential Measures
Accurate completion of several proofs
Accurate calculations of surface area of pyramids, cylinders, cones, and spheres
Accurate calculations of volume of pyramids, cylinders, cones, and spheres
Demonstrates understanding of triangle classifications
Accurate use of Pythagorean Theorem
Construct
Attitudes About Universal Healthcare
Potential Measures
Survey of healthcare experiences
Questionnaire on current coverage
Attitudes about personal vs. communal responsibility
Attitudes toward Medicare and Medicaid
Level of factual knowledge about healthcare alternatives

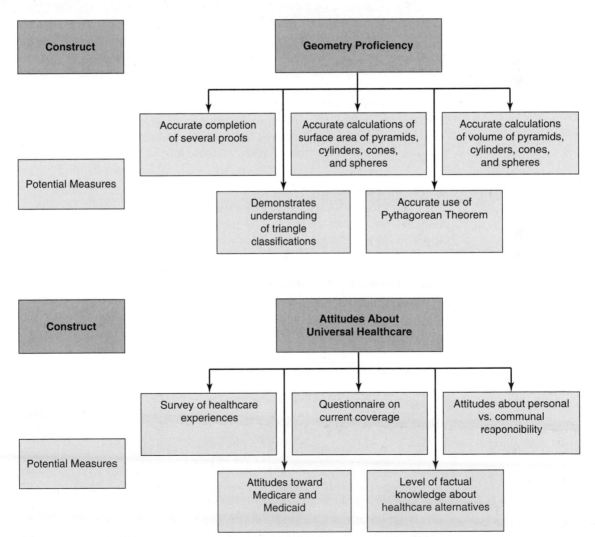

FIGURE 6.1 ***Relationship Between Constructs and Attempts to Measure Them***

are assumptions or conclusions based on observations and experience. Conclusions about student learning that result in grades are one common type of inference that teachers make. Because of different prior experience, not everyone makes the same inferences about the same observations or facts. For example, when you see someone walk down the street talking to himself, you will probably conclude he is on his cell phone. When someone who has never encountered cell phones sees him, that person may instead assume he has a possible mental disorder such as schizophrenia.

The difficulty with inferences is aggravated with assessment because every assessment provides only a small sample of student behavior. When drawing conclusions about what that sample tells us, we sometimes assume more than we should. This would be true of the geometry teacher who used the sturdiness of students' dodecahedrons for the final grade. The small sample of student behavior he chose was not the most useful for drawing inferences about general geometry skill. Gathering construct-related evidence helps us avoid such mistakes. The evidence allows us to solidly link our inferences about a measure back to the construct we started with. See Figure 6.2 depicting a visual representation of this process.

For example, constructing a sturdy dodecahedron was the measure in our earlier example. The teacher drew the inference that scores on this measure represented geometry proficiency. If he had gathered construct-related evidence for the validity of his assessment, however, he would have quickly seen that his conclusions were not valid. As a couple of possible examples, his grades on the dodecahedron project were unlikely to match up with students' scores on his earlier summative tests, and they were unlikely to correlate with their quantitative scores on the SAT. Every assessment always gives us some information, but gathering construct evidence about its validity helps us make sure it is really the information that we want and need. A number of sources, shown in Table 6.5, can be used to gather construct-related evidence for validity. Next, we discuss each one.

Logic and Common Sense

For classroom assessment, logic and common sense can provide important construct evidence for validity. In the case of the geometry teacher, if he had thought more about it, he would have realized that constructing dodecahedrons has only tenuous

Construct-related evidence
Inferences
Valid inference
No construct-related evidence
Construct:
Geometry Proficiency
Sample of student behavior assessed
Invalid inference

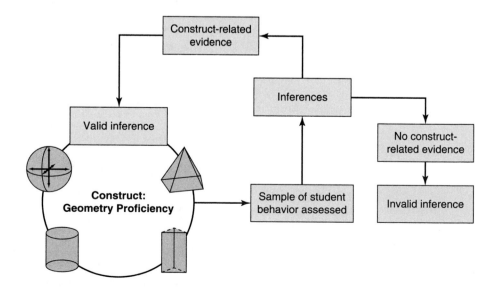

FIGURE 6.2 ***Process of Moving from Measure to Valid Inference About a Construct***

T A B L E   6 . 5
Sources of Construct-Related Evidence for Validity
Evidence based on logic and common sense
Evidence based on variety of assessment formats
Content-related evidence
Criterion-related evidence

connections to geometry proficiency. The manual dexterity required and the quality of materials (e.g., whether the paper was sturdy) are two factors involved that clearly have absolutely no relationship to geometry. These factors did, however, weigh heavily in whether students achieved success on the task.

Another common factor that can detract from construct evidence for validity is reading proficiency. Many assessments aimed at constructs such as history, or even mathematical skill, may require strong reading-comprehension skills that are irrelevant to the construct but can strongly influence scores. When assessments require skills or knowledge clearly irrelevant to the construct being measured, those assessments fall at the lower end of the validity continuum.

Additional elements of an assessment that may detract from construct validity include unclear directions, confusing items, unusual formats, and typographical errors. Each of these factors clouds score interpretation; did the student do poorly because he didn't understand the directions or because he did not learn the material? For example, one student we know misread two questions on a recent test because they both included the word "not" and he didn't notice the use of the negative (e.g., "Which of the following is NOT an amphibian?"). If the test had included only positively worded questions, his score likely would have been higher. In later chapters we provide guidelines to help you in the writing of clear directions and items. In addition, we have stated that any format that a teacher plans to use in the assessment of learning goals should also be part of instruction, thus avoiding the problem of unusual item formats.

Variety in Formats

Another common problem in the classroom that can reduce our confidence that an assessment fully addresses the relevant construct is a reliance on a single assessment format. You can see this in the dodecahedron assessment example as well. The final grade in that geometry class had only one task, and this task was unrelated to the activities students had engaged in all semester, such as solving problems related to the Pythagorean Theorem. One kind of construct-related evidence for validity, then, is checking on whether a summative assessment contains multiple assessment formats capturing the breadth and depth of the content addressed. Formative assessments, of course, may often have a single format if they address only a small portion of the knowledge and skills in a unit.

Another factor in considering formats is that some students vary in their preference for and competence with different formats. For example, you know people who always do better with multiple-choice tests, whereas others prefer sharing their understanding through writing an essay. Researchers have also demonstrated that students perform differently with different assessment formats such as teacher observations, short-answer problems, or writing in science notebooks (Shavelson et al., 1993). As a classroom teacher, you should vary the formats you use to increase the validity of your assessments and to provide opportunities for every student to shine. Of course, students must have practice in class with these various formats prior to any summative assessment.

Another important reason to vary formats is to give all students opportunities to work on improving their less developed or weaker skills. If students are encouraged to do only what they are good at, they will never get better at other assessment formats. Although we have noted that writing may impede some students from expressing their understanding of science or history, we also acknowledge the critical role of writing in conveying information. So writing should be one of an array of assessment forms during a unit. Using a range of assessment formats is crucial not only to validity, but also to conveying high expectations to your students. It can be another opportunity to help close achievement gaps.

Content-Related Evidence

Content-Related Evidence
The adequacy of the sampling of specific content, which contributes to validity.

Content-Representativeness
Ensures the assessment adequately represents the constructs addressed in the learning goals.

As we have emphasized, every assessment you design necessarily addresses only a sample of the total content that students are learning in your class. **Content-related evidence** for validity refers to the representativeness of the understanding and skills sampled. Often people term this type of evidence **content representativeness** because the key issue is ensuring that the assessment adequately represents the constructs addressed in the learning goals.

For classroom assessments, content-related evidence is easy to ensure if you align your learning goals, your instruction, and your assessment. Your assessments should address both the content of the learning goals and the cognitive processes you expect students to master. They should not address content or processes irrelevant to those goals. For example, you would not use a multiple-choice test to determine whether students can organize contradictory information into an argument on the pros and cons of imposing a national carbon tax. This would require an essay. Similarly, if your summative assessment includes writing a persuasive essay, you must also provide classroom activities that allow students to hone their persuasive writing skills, including formative assessment with feedback on how to improve. For a summative classroom assessment, we have suggested in Chapter 2 that you design a table of specifications (sometimes called a "blueprint") to visually represent how your assessment covers the content of the learning goal (see Table 2.15). When the table is completed, it should provide the evidence you need about the degree to which your assessment has content representativeness. If all learning goals are represented with items in proportion to the amount of instruction that they received, you will be able to make a positive judgment about content representativeness.

In our classes, when we discuss validity, our students always have many examples to offer from their experiences in which teachers either did not gather evidence for content representativeness of a summative classroom test or assumed their test had content representativeness when the students believed otherwise. For example, one student told us, "When I was in biology in high school, my teacher would show video after video of diseases and things which had nothing to do with our textbook. We were expected to write twenty facts on each video, and we were told our test would come from our facts. However, when test time came around, my teacher would ask questions from the textbook and not the movies." Assessments must be aligned with instruction and the learning goals if you want your students to perceive them as reasonable.

Lack of content representativeness, in fact, is the most common problem we have found among student complaints about grading and summative assessments. As a teacher, you should see this as good news, because it is a problem you can easily remedy with your own assessments. If you use a table of specifications to help align your assessment with your instruction and the learning goals, your assessments will possess content representativeness and students will believe they are fair.

TABLE 6.6	

Content-Related Evidence and Applications

Definition	Classroom Applications
Evidence that the assessment representatively samples items associated with the learning goals	• Formative: Design formative tasks that require practice and feedback and address higher-order thinking skills from the learning goals. • Summative: Design table of specifications to gauge alignment among learning goals, instruction, and assessment.

For formative classroom assessments, you must make sure that each task you spend time on contributes to student advancement toward the learning goals. You also want to allocate the most time to formative tasks essential to the most important learning goals. You probably would not design even one formative task to address the learning goal *Recall forms of poetry and definitions* (see Table 2.15). This information is at the basic knowledge ("remember") level. Students should be able to understand and recall definitions without much assistance. You should save formative assessment tasks for goals related to more complex understanding and for skills that take time, effort, and feedback to master. Table 6.6 summarizes the discussion of content-related evidence for validity.

Criterion-Related Evidence

Criterion-related evidence refers to information that examines a relationship between one assessment and some other established measure that is gathered to provide evidence of validity. For example, you would have evidence for the validity of a survey measuring values associated with a political party if people who attained high scores on that survey also indicated they always voted for that party's candidates. Researchers examining the relationship between SAT scores and college freshman grades are conducting studies to assemble evidence of the criterion-related validity of using SAT scores for predicting college performance.

As you recall, triangulation is the process of developing an accurate conclusion based on comparison of several sources. In Chapter 3 we discussed drawing conclusions about individual students using triangulation. You can also use triangulation when drawing conclusions about the validity of your tests. If you look for patterns across different assessments of similar content, you may find that your students did much worse (or much better) on one of them. For example, if the geometry teacher who gave the dodecahedron assignment had compared those scores to scores on previous geometry assessments, he would have seen that the dodecahedron scores were much lower for a number of students. Evidence for validity based on the criterion of a strong relationship to other previous assessments would have been slim.

Sometimes when students do more poorly than usual on an assessment, teachers may assume they did not study or they were not motivated. These can be dangerous assumptions because they prevent teachers from critically examining their own practices. We suggest that when your students do particularly poorly on an assessment, you use the process of triangulation with previous assessments to look for criterion-related evidence of validity. That way, instead of blaming students, you will consider whether something could instead be wrong with the validity of the test you constructed.

Comparison with previous work can also help you ensure that the assessments you design are at the right level of difficulty to challenge your students but not discourage them. Sometimes new teachers design assessments that are too hard or too easy for their students, and so the assessments are not useful. Assessments that are too easy do not give you any

Criterion-Related Evidence
Information that examines a relationship between one assessment and an established measure for the purposes of discerning validity.

TABLE 6.7

Criterion-Related Evidence and Applications

Definition	Classroom Application
Evidence of a relationship to other already established, relevant criteria	Use triangulation to determine whether results of an assessment produce patterns similar to or different from previous assessments.

information about what concepts your students find challenging, so you do not gain ideas about what they need to work on to improve. Easy assessments also convey low expectations for your students. Assessments that are too difficult are discouraging to students and do not give you information about the steps needed to get them from where they are to where they need to be. You only know they are not there yet. Comparing student performance on current assessments to their performance on previous assessments will help you identify assessment activities providing an appropriate level of challenge.

A final way to think about criterion-related evidence in classroom assessment is to use your preassessment as a criterion measure. If your summative classroom assessment for a unit is sensitive to instruction and squarely addresses the unit content, you should see evidence that all students improved greatly, in terms of the percentage correct, between the preassessment you conducted before you began the unit and the summative assessment you design at the unit's end. If, on the other hand, the percentage correct does not vary much from the preassessment to the summative assessment, you have criterion-related evidence that you are *not* measuring gains based on the instruction for the unit. Table 6.7 summarizes the discussion of criterion-related evidence for validity.

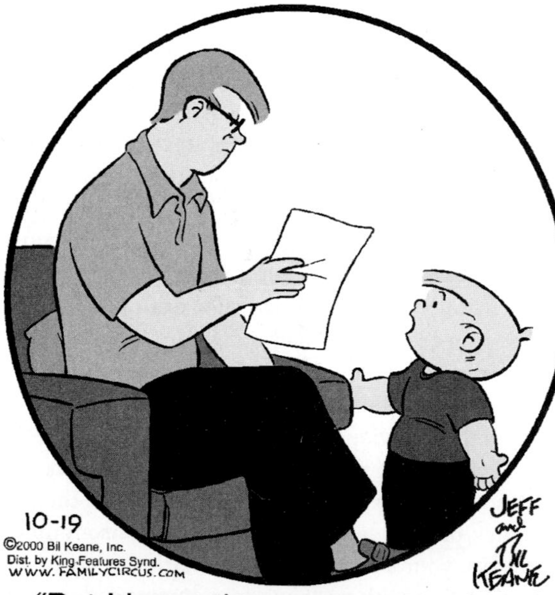
10-19
©2000 Bil Keane, Inc.
Dist. by King Features Synd.
WWW.FAMILYCIRCUS.COM
JEFF and BIL KEANE

"But I knew the answers to a lot of questions that weren't even on the test!"

FIGURE 6.3 Which type of validity evidence does this cartoon best illustrate? Why?

✦ IMPROVING VALIDITY IN CLASSROOM ASSESSMENTS

We close our section on validity by providing suggestions about methods for improving validity in classroom assessments, which are listed in Table 6.8. They stem from the four sources of validity evidence we have discussed, so they should look familiar. Because the biggest problem related to validity that we hear about from our students is problems with content-related evidence, we start with and emphasize the suggestion that you review every assessment task to ensure that it addresses the learning goals and the associated important instructional content. We believe if all teachers conducted such a review each time they designed an assessment, complaints from students about unfair assessments would plummet dramatically.

TABLE 6.8

Suggestions for Improving Validity in Classroom Assessments

Suggestions	Examples
Develop content-related evidence: Review each assessment task to ensure that it represents learning goal content and instructional activities in appropriate proportion.	• Use a streamlined table of specifications (see Chapter 2) in designing summative assessments to ensure appropriate sampling of items. • Collaborate with colleagues who teach the same content when designing assessments. • Ask whether your students must use the higher-order thinking skills required by the learning goals to complete this assessment.
Use logic and common sense.	• Ask yourself whether items tap the most important content and not just trivial content. • With formative assessments, make sure the assessment provides a window to student thought processes related to important material addressed by the learning goals. • Ask yourself whether the task requires high levels of understanding or skills unrelated to the focus of your assessment (e.g., strong reading comprehension). • Ask students for feedback on clarity, accuracy, and relevance of the assessments you use.
Use a variety of assessment formats.	• Use multiple assessment formats for both formative and summative assessments. • Check to see whether students perform similarly when you assess the same understanding or skill in different ways.
Develop criterion-related evidence: Triangulate results of the most recent assessment task with previous tasks to examine patterns of performance.	• Check on how students did compared to their performance on similar assessments in this or other units. • Check whether this assessment as a whole is much easier or much harder than previous assessments. • Compare student scores on the preassessment with scores on the summative assessment to see if your summative assessment is sensitive to instruction.

→ RELATIONSHIP BETWEEN RELIABILITY AND VALIDITY

We have now explained reliability and validity as two attributes that affect the quality of the "input" you invest in designing your assessments. As you recall, reliability involves minimizing random errors that can mistakenly increase or decrease the true score a student should receive. To reduce the impact of random errors that can lower reliability, you do your best to ensure the assessment occasion is free of distractions, you ensure the number and types of assessment tasks give you sufficient information, and you provide clear scoring criteria to support consistency in your grading.

Validity, on the other hand, relates to the degree of confidence you have that the inferences you are making based on assessment results are accurate. The primary way to ensure validity in classroom assessment is alignment among learning goals, instruction, and assessment. One factor that could affect the degree of confidence about your inferences could be scores that are not reproducible because they are plagued by random errors. If scores are highly unreliable, then validity is also limited. High reliability is necessary for high validity.

For example, one of our students recounted an incident involving a summative assessment from her high school calculus class. The test she had to take consisted of two very complex problems. The teacher gave credit for each problem only if the student had the right answer. Our student received no credit for one of the two problems because she made a simple mistake in addition, even though she had followed all the necessary steps and used the correct formulas. Her score on this test, because of her random calculation error and the limited number of problems, had low reliability and resulted in a failing grade. This score also caused the teacher to make an invalid inference about the student's calculus skills. This incident illustrates the necessity of high reliability for high validity.

Simply having high reliability on an assessment, however, cannot guarantee that the inferences you make about that assessment will be valid ones. You can readily see this if we alter the calculus example. Consider what would happen if the summative test the teacher designed had 20 items instead of 2 and used several types of tasks to increase the sufficiency of information. Suppose she also gave students as much time as they needed, ensured the environment was free of distractions, and had clear scoring criteria. These actions would definitely improve the reliability of the assessment. However, if the content were algebra instead of calculus, no matter how high the reliability, the scores on the assessment would not help the teacher make valid decisions about her students' achievement of calculus learning goals. The teacher would not have carefully aligned the assessment with the learning goals and the instruction, and so the inferences she could make would not be related to the construct about which she needed information. These examples illustrate why assessment theorists assert that reliability is a necessary but not sufficient condition for validity.

→ AVOIDING BIAS IN ASSESSMENTS

Bias
An inclination or preference that interferes with impartiality.

A **bias** is an inclination or a preference that interferes with impartiality. For example, you might have a bias against chocolate chip cookies compared to oatmeal cookies, so if you were judging cookies in a local contest, you would find it hard to be impartial if you had to rate both kinds. Bias can creep into the assessments teachers design and score, but it is rarely intentional or conscious. Most teachers we know bend over backwards to be fair and give students the benefit of the doubt. Sometimes, however, an item or an activity can put one group at a disadvantage so that the scores they receive are systematically lower than their actual scores would be. This systematic bias will lower the validity of your assessment.

As our culture diversifies, the danger of unintentional bias increases. As of the 2000 census, almost 20 percent of the people over age 5 in the United States spoke a language other than English at home, and by 2005, the Hispanic/Latino population increased to 14.4 percent of the total population to become our largest minority. Furthermore, family structure is changing, with 20 million children living with single parents (including more than 3 million with single fathers) and 5.6 million with grandparents. Such changes suggest that for us to provide equal access to education for all students, we must become familiar with and respond to the increasing diversity of life and language experiences in our classrooms. Attention to this issue is particularly important because statistics continue to demonstrate that teacher education students are overwhelmingly European American and female. We discuss some of the possible bias pitfalls so that you can avoid them in your own classroom. Table 6.9 summarizes the pitfalls.

Unfair Penalization

Unfair penalization refers to the inadvertent bias of putting students who are not familiar with the content, examples, or language of an assessment at a disadvantage compared to those who are familiar with them. For example, an assessment that you

Unfair Penalization

Comparing students who are unfamiliar with content, examples, or language of an assessment to students who are.

TABLE 6.9

Bias Pitfalls in Classroom Assessment

Pitfall	Definition	Example
Unfair penalization	Using content, examples, or language based on life experiences in an assessment that puts groups who are unfamiliar with them at a disadvantage	Using exclusively American holidays such as Thanksgiving or the 4th of July as the basis for an essay on family experiences
Lack of opportunity to learn	Using assessments that do not take into account absences or other systematic differences among groups in exposure to the curriculum	Testing students who leave the classroom for special classes on the content they missed without providing compensatory experiences
Teacher bias	Systematic but usually unintentional teacher preferences (e.g., microaggressions, preferential interaction patterns, scoring biases) that can influence assessments	Formative assessment: Asking questions requiring higher-order thinking skills of only the students who raise their hands Summative assessment: Inadvertently marking down papers with messy handwriting

design for an English class could involve a topic that males in your class may have more experience and knowledge about than females, such as their perspective on how the rules about football could influence other social interactions. This topic choice may then influence the quality of the essays differentially for the two genders if the females had less experience on which to draw. Similarly, in a social studies class you may choose to ask students to write a letter to a person living during the U.S. Civil War as an assessment. But you generate the list of eligible correspondents off the top of your head and happen to limit it to famous officers or civic leaders who come to mind quickly, all of whom happen to be European American and most of whom happen to be male. Because your female students and your minority students may have a harder time identifying with and picturing these figures and their interests, they could be at a disadvantage in completing the assignment. You must make sure your activities and assessments take into account important differences in your students' life experiences. These include variations ranging from exposure to different types of climate (e.g., snow), to family experiences (e.g., vacations, exposure to cultural events), to typical interaction patterns (e.g., methods of problem solving).

We were reminded of unfair penalization recently when we gave a picture vocabulary test to a bright young African American kindergartener who lived in subsidized housing in the middle of a city. The procedure involved showing him pictures and asking him to identify them. He flew through dozens of pictures until he encountered a saddle for a horse. He was suddenly completely stumped, perhaps because he had never had the opportunity to see horseback riders. For this city, riding stables could be found only out in the countryside and tended to draw an upper middle class and wealthy clientele.

In thinking about unfair penalization related to language, the suggestions we made in Chapter 3 for accommodating English language learners are worth revisiting because such accommodations are intended to reduce unfair penalization. For example, you should consciously use visual as well as verbal representations of content, and you should avoid complex syntax and exclusively U.S. cultural references. In formative assessments, you should also make sure all the vocabulary building blocks necessary for the unit content are in place for your English language learners.

Opportunity to Learn

Another factor that can introduce bias into assessments is a systematic difference among students in their opportunity to learn the content of the curriculum. For example, if your preassessment shows some students are far behind the rest in their ability to use and interpret maps for the unit on the five regions of the United States, they would not be able to benefit from any new instruction requiring map interpretation until you had taken the time to teach this prerequisite skill. Another factor related to opportunity to learn is attendance. Students who are absent often are at a disadvantage because they do not receive the same amount of instruction as other students. Often the students who are absent the most are also students who lag behind their peers. Similarly, students who have no supervision in the evenings or no parental encouragement to complete homework are at a disadvantage in their opportunities to learn. Awareness of the bias that fewer opportunities to learn can breed will sensitize you to the needs of your students. Efforts to equalize the opportunity to learn for all your students are one more way to work to close achievement gaps. For example, we know several teachers who allow students who have a disorganized home environment to come to their classrooms as soon as the bus drops them in the morning to work on homework and ask questions rather than waiting outside until the bell rings.

Teacher Bias

Teachers are human, and all humans are susceptible to bias. You know from your own experience that sometimes teachers have favorite students, and sometimes certain students feel they could never do anything right in the eyes of a particular teacher. But if you asked those teachers, they would probably believe that they are doing their best to be fair. Bias is rarely intentional.

Because teachers don't intend to show bias, many authors suggest that the first step in reducing our biases is to bring our own social identities to our awareness so we can see the limits of our experience (e.g., Bell et al., 1997; Sue et al., 2007). Willingness to scrutinize our own assumptions, values, and habits generates self-awareness that can provide insights enhancing our empathy. This in turn may help us accommodate diversity in the classroom successfully. Analyzing your own group membership, history, and experiences allows for increased sensitivity to the kinds of assumptions you make about your students. For example, teacher candidates who have been to foreign countries where they do not speak the language find they later have more empathy for the English language learners in their own classrooms than candidates who have never had such experiences. Or breaking a leg and using a wheelchair can provide surprising new insights into the barriers facing students with physical disabilities to which a candidate otherwise would have been oblivious. You can see how broadening your experience allows you to notice some unconscious biases you may have had. We will now address some aspects of teacher bias that may help sensitize you to the needs of students.

Microaggressions

Seemingly innocent questions or comments arising from lack of awareness of our own biases can damage our relationships with others from different backgrounds and be perceived as **"microaggressions"** (Sue et al., 2007). Microaggressions are "brief, everyday exchanges that send denigrating messages . . ." (p. 273). For example, when a middle-class European American asks an Asian American or Latino American, "Where are you from?" the question implies that the person is a perpetual foreigner, and it negates their American heritage. Several of our Asian American friends born in the United States have told us they encounter this question frequently, and it is often repeated, "But where are you *really* from?" when they say they are from the United States.

Another common microaggression that we find among our teacher candidates is a statement such as "I am color blind," or "When I look at my students, I don't see color." Such comments deny a person's racial or ethnic experiences and implicitly insist that assimilation to the dominant culture is required (Sue et al., 2007). If you say you don't "see" color, you are probably trying to communicate that you are fair and do your best not to discriminate on the basis of color. However, recognizing that race is perceived differently depending on one's position in society is an important step in the process of becoming culturally sensitive.

A possible outgrowth of such comments (and the beliefs behind them) is insensitivity in designing assessments. One of our African American friends told us about a teacher of one of her sons who professed not to "see" color. When she had students design a self-portrait with construction paper, she had only buff colored paper for the faces and blue for the eyes. When some people don't "see" color, they tend to ignore facets of culture and experience beyond their own limited perspective. Their behaviors can inadvertently alienate their students of color and marginalize them. When students feel like they don't belong, their achievement usually suffers. When academic performance is depressed for such children, the achievement gap continues to widen.

Microaggression
Brief, everyday remark that inadvertently sends a denigrating message to the receiver.

Because we want to *narrow* achievement gaps, we must avoid letting our own background and assumptions limit the learning experiences we provide. We must learn how the cultural background of our students can influence their identity and learning so we can take advantage of it in our teaching and in creating an inclusive, welcoming classroom.

At the same time, we must avoid unconscious negative stereotypes that sometimes can accompany a limited understanding of another culture. For example, Paul Gorski (2008) describes and debunks several myths of the "culture of poverty," such as assuming poor people have low motivation. Such stereotypes can derail high expectations and undermine our efforts to promote achievement for every child. As you might imagine, the balance is difficult to achieve. Gradually, with intentional thoughtful awareness, you will build an understanding of your students, their families, and the local community that can help you teach so your students can reach their maximum potential.

Observing Interaction Patterns

Beyond analyzing our own identities and experiences, we can use other ways to challenge our implicit biases. For example, we once worked with a student teacher in kindergarten to analyze a videotape of herself teaching a lesson. During an informal formative assessment to see whether her students could make predictions about what might happen next in a story, one African American boy gave a suggestion. She didn't acknowledge his response. A few seconds later a European American girl paraphrased the same suggestion, and the student teacher quickly offered enthusiastic praise. You could see the African American boy on the videotape squirm in frustration. As we talked about the incident, the student teacher was embarrassed. She had not intentionally ignored the boy and would not even have believed it had happened if it hadn't been captured on videotape. But such patterns of interaction may be more frequent than we realize. We have observed similar incidents with female students receiving less positive teacher attention than males and Latino students receiving less attention than their European American peers in several elementary and secondary classes. Such incidents underscore the need for teachers to check systematically on their interaction patterns with students.

When we began teaching at the college level, we had a similar experience. Another professor observed our class and used an informal seating chart to monitor the students who made contributions to the discussion. He pointed out after class that even though the majority of the class was female, the majority of the students participating were male. He suggested several strategies we regularly continue to use (and suggest to our own teacher candidates), such as allowing students to write down or discuss an answer in pairs before the teacher calls on random students, or noting check marks on a seating chart as students participate to ensure that no one is left out. Because class participation can be crucial during formative assessment, allowing all students opportunities to respond and receive feedback is necessary, especially when you keep the goal of equal access to education for all in mind. Every one of us must be willing to examine our assumptions and our behavior objectively to avoid bias. See Table 6.10 for suggestions on avoiding teacher bias.

Scoring Biases

Not only can unintended bias influence classroom interactions and formative assessment, it can also affect scoring of summative assessments. Numerous studies have been conducted over the years investigating scoring biases (see Fiske & Taylor, 1991). We

TABLE 6.10

Suggestions for Avoiding Teacher Bias

In General

Analyze the limits of your own assumptions, values, and experience and make an effort to expand them:
- Read widely about other cultures, social classes, ethnicities, and races.
- Seek out experiences with people unlike yourself by traveling and doing volunteer work.

During Classroom Interaction for Formative Assessment

Monitor teacher attention on a seating chart using checks or + and – for teacher comments.

Have a peer observe and monitor interactions using a seating chart.

Videotape and analyze interaction with students for positive and negative teacher attention and appropriate feedback.

During Scoring of Summative Assessments

When possible, remove clues to the identity of the student whose work you are grading.

When possible, have students type work they turn in to avoid penalizing hard-to-read handwriting.

Provide frequent and varied assessments.

Collaborate with peers in designing and scoring assessments to detect bias.

Use scoring guides with clear expectations to help prevent bias.

want to alert you to some of these findings so you can avoid scoring bias in your own classroom. In these studies, two groups usually rate the same essay or assignment. Additional information about the student who completed the assignment is varied between the two groups to see if it changes perceptions of the quality of the work. For example, when one group is told the student is "excellent" and the other group is told that the student is "weak," those who believe they are grading the work of an "excellent" student assign higher grades than those who think they are grading the "weak" student. Similarly, when raters are given a photo of a student, those who receive an attractive photo usually grade higher than those given an unattractive one. Research such as this impels us to recommend that whenever possible, you grade assignments without knowing the identity of the student.

Similarly, messy handwriting, length of a paper, and grammatical errors can strongly influence grades, even when the teacher doesn't intend it. A close friend who teaches fourth grade has what he calls a "handwriting fixation" with which he grapples. He recently caught himself just before lowering the grade for a student who wrote every cursive "m" with two humps instead of three. To bring home the point about how easily biases can emerge, we know one professor who has his students grade the same essay for practice every semester. Some students looked at a messy version and others had a neat version. Every single semester, the neat version emerges with a higher grade.

Another factor that can have impact on grading is the variance in political or social perspectives of teachers and students (Barbour, 2007). Teachers we know do their best to grade fairly, but they sometimes agonize about how to maintain impartiality and see this potential bias as an important ethical dilemma. A good scoring guide helps enormously, and in Chapters 8 and 9 we discuss how to design scoring guides that help you to maintain consistency and objectivity.

As you review Table 6.10, you will notice the repetition of a few recommendations that we made to enhance reliability and validity—such as providing frequent and varied assessments and collaborating with peers on designing and scoring assessments. This is because bias can influence the validity of the inferences we make about students based on their test scores. Does a high score on a writing assignment reflect that the student has mastered the writing strategies you have taught, or is the high score because of the student's neat handwriting? The safeguards we offer will help you catch yourself and your implicit biases as you reflect on variations in the outcomes of your assessments.

→ REPRESENTING THE DIVERSITY OF THE CLASSROOM

Your awareness of the diversity in your classroom and your conscientious efforts to represent these variations in your assessment is another method of avoiding potential bias. Such efforts also help you create a cohesive, welcoming classroom to students who have sometimes been overlooked or marginalized. We once observed a math lesson in a fourth-grade classroom where a teacher designed word problems teaching a new concept. In each problem, she used the names of each of her own students by saying things like "Shakira has 21 CDs and Aisha wants her to . . ." The students clearly loved this approach and laughed and cheered when they heard their names. The teacher's tactic helped her students personally "own" the activities, and they clearly felt valued and included. However, what would happen if this teacher had consistently left someone out because a name was hard to pronounce or because she unconsciously didn't like that child much? Think about how you might feel when put in the place of the marginalized student.

As a teacher, you should do your best to make each student feel like an integral and significant part of the learning community you create. Your efforts will pay off. You will help all your students develop positive self-images. You will also help them learn how to live in our pluralistic society with respect and appreciation for others who are different.

Many of your assessment activities provide opportunities to expose your students to varieties of scenarios, photographs, stories, and cultural practices reflecting the diverse students in your classroom and beyond. Based on Macmillan-McGraw Hill's (1993) efforts to reflect diversity in textbooks and other instructional materials, in Table 6.11 we offer three types of problems to avoid as you design assessments and activities.

Stereotypical Representation

Stereotypical Representation
Depicting social groups in an oversimplified manner.

Stereotypical representation involves depicting social groups in an oversimplified, clichéd manner in your formative and summative assessments. For example, if your early childhood students were learning about the instruments in the orchestra, you might want to be sure to include photographs of women playing brass instruments and African Americans playing strings as you developed activities for assessments. Our students tell us that typical stereotypes in music depict males playing brass instruments, females playing stringed instruments, with African Americans few and far

TABLE 6.11

Problems to Avoid When Designing Assessments

Consideration	Definition	Example
Stereotypical representation	Depiction of groups in an oversimplified, clichéd manner	A math word problem that involves calculations about Juan picking lettuce or grapes
Contextual invisibility	Underrepresentation of certain groups, customs, or lifestyles in curricular or assessment materials	Using only typically European American names as examples in assessments
Historical distortions	Presenting a single interpretation of an issue, perpetuating oversimplification of complex issues, or avoiding controversial topics	Describing slavery exclusively in terms of economic "need" and avoiding a moral perspective

Adapted from Macmillan-McGraw Hill. 1993. *Reflecting diversity: Multicultural guidelines for educational publishing professional.*

between. Stereotypical depictions can implicitly narrow students' understanding of possibilities and limit their aspirations.

A few years ago, one of our friends was paid by an editor in New York to systematically review assessment items in texts to look for stereotypical representations of groups and correct them. She told us one of the most common changes she made involved modifying images of passive females who sat and watched males do things. Similarly, males are often portrayed as lacking empathy, never crying, and showing little interest in fashion, cooking, or children. Expanding the variety of male and female interests and roles in assessment examples can go a long way toward broader acceptance of a range of behaviors, regardless of gender. Acceptance of broader gender roles should also help decrease the widespread verbal and physical harassment reported by males who exhibit behaviors and interests beyond the typically narrow male stereotype. Designing assessments that convey inclusiveness contributes to developing more inclusive classrooms.

A number of other stereotypes should be avoided as you design assessments. Depictions of the elderly as inactive, such as using images of grandparents in rocking chairs on the porch, can convey stereotypes. Portrayals of people with mental and physical disabilities have often been limited or, when they are included, have been depicted in a helpless role. You should include these groups in a variety of roles, not solely as recipients of assistance from others. Racial stereotypes have often crept into instructional materials, with depictions of people of color in low-paying jobs such as farm workers or janitors rather than as bank presidents or globe-trotting executives.

The language you use in assessments can also convey stereotypes. For example, research has shown that when an author uses a term such as "mankind," most people picture only men (Switzer, 1990). When the term is changed to "humankind," people tend to think of both genders. Using terms that include both genders whenever possible conveys a more inclusive message. For example, changing the singular to the

TABLE 6.12

Avoiding Sexist Language

Avoid	Change To
"mankind"	"humankind"
"man" (as plural)	"human" "people"
"man-made"	"manufactured," "handmade"
"They will man the table for the bake sale."	"They will staff the table for the bake sale."
"Everyone should know his vote counts."	"People should know their votes count."
"salesman," "policeman," "chairman," "fireman"	"salesperson," "police officer," "chair," "firefighter"
Making female identity passive: "American colonists brought their wives and children to America." "Women were given the vote after the First World War." "John Jones took his wife to California to look for a new house."	"Colonist families came to America." "Women won the vote after the First World War." "John and Sarah Jones went to California to look for a new house."

Adapted from Macmillan-McGraw Hill. 1993. *Reflecting diversity: Multicultural guidelines for educational publishing professionals.* Used with permission.

plural whenever possible allows both genders to be represented. See Table 6.12 for examples of methods for avoiding sexist language and the hidden assumption of female passivity.

Contextual Invisibility

Contextual Invisibility
The concept that certain groups, customs, or lifestyles are not represented in assessment materials.

Contextual invisibility means that certain groups, customs, or lifestyles are not represented or are underrepresented in your assessment materials (Macmillan-McGraw Hill, 1993). Underrepresentation implies that these groups, customs, or lifestyles are less important, and it marginalizes them. For instance, examples of males in parenting roles are often much less visible in instructional materials than examples of males actively involved in work outside the home, hinting that nurturing roles are less valued for men in our society. Similarly, when using names in assessments, many teachers are inclined to stick with common European American names such as Tom or Mary. In the movie *Stand and Deliver,* Jaime Escalante combats contextual invisibility by pointing out to his students that the Mayans recognized and used the important concept of zero well before the Greeks, Romans, or Europeans. Emphasizing the contributions of multiple groups beyond European Americans to the development of our culture helps students appreciate a pluralistic society.

Historical Distortions

Historical Distortion
Presenting a single interpretation of an issue, perpetuating over-simplification of complex issues, or avoiding controversial topics.

Historical distortion involves presenting a single interpretation of an issue, perpetuating oversimplification of complex issues, or avoiding controversial topics (Macmillan-McGraw Hill, 1993). Historical distortions can occur with past or present issues. The term "historical" used in the definition probably refers to the need to avoid the typically

Eurocentric and male perspective that has dominated much historical and contemporary analysis of political and historical events. For example, in an analysis of textbooks for English language learners, Ndura (2004) reports that controversial topics, such as prejudice or racial and ethnic conflict, were avoided in all texts reviewed. She reports,

> We hear about the Navajo code talkers [' contribution to World War II] . . . but nothing about why their recognition was delayed over three decades. We hear the pleading voice of Chief Joseph, but nothing about why he and his people had to go to war. The Universal Declaration of Human Rights is presented, but there is no discussion of those rights that are often infringed upon in the lives of many immigrants and people of color. . . . The Civil Rights Movement is featured as a piece of history with no extension to today's struggles. The Lewis and Clark story is told from a White man's perspective. The voices of York, the male slave, Sacagawea, the female Indian helper, and of the Indians they met on the expedition are all silenced.

As we mentioned in Chapter 1, varied, meaningful and challenging assessment tasks encourage students to develop mastery goals and increased motivation. Engaging tasks that grapple with controversial issues can be ideally suited to preventing historical distortion. For example, to encourage perception of multiple perspectives on current or historical events, you might assign different students to look at different groups' perceptions when designing a web quest about a controversial issue. You can also explore conflicts through mini-debates, class discussions, or persuasive essays required to address opposing views. Such activities have the added benefit of requiring complex thinking at the highest levels of Bloom's taxonomy.

If instead you gloss over controversial subjects, you deny your students opportunities to develop the critical thinking skills essential for active democratic participation. Exploring controversy and understanding it from several points of view may also allow students to develop confidence to contribute to solutions. A recent study found that classroom opportunities such as learning about things in society that need to be changed, focusing on issues students care about, and encouraging students to discuss and make up their own minds about political and social issues help students develop stronger commitments to participation in civic affairs (Kahne & Sporte, 2007).

✦ KEEPING THE THREE DEMOCRATIC VALUES IN MIND

In this chapter we have discussed some wide-ranging recommendations to develop reliable, valid, and unbiased formative and summative assessments. All our recommendations are based on the assumption that development of top-notch assessments will allow you to obtain accurate and fair information on your students' progress toward the learning goals. We now turn to the connection between this emphasis on good assessment design and scoring to our three themes related to preparing students for democratic participation.

Equal Access to Educational Opportunity

If you have frequent, high-quality assessment information from your students, you will make better decisions about how best to teach them. You will know who is falling behind as soon as it happens, and you will know what they need to catch up. Reliable scoring of assessments also explicitly holds all students to the same criteria so that you are able to maintain clearly spelled out, high expectations for everyone. Valid assessments closely aligned with your learning goals also promote equal access because you can be certain you are addressing the appropriate content based on the standards your students need to be successful. Finally, unbiased assessments that provide inclusive perspectives promote student motivation and engagement and help avoid marginalization of groups who have typically been underrepresented. These are often the groups who lag behind peers, so enhancing their motivation and sense of belonging can lead to accelerated progress in working to close achievement gaps.

Skills for Democratic Participation

Frequent assessment leads to high reliability. Relying, when practical, on student input into your frequent assessments and their scoring guides can help you design a range of assessment activities that are varied, often creative, and perceived as fair. In our own classes we often have students take a crack at designing items for summative assessments. Such efforts promote students' internalization of responsibility for their own learning when they start thinking like teachers and developing an internal critic. Development of a sense of responsibility is one of the important self-governing skills needed for democratic participation.

Furthermore, in efforts to avoid traditional biases, you can design assessment tasks relating to student concerns and current social issues that include exposure to varied perspectives. Opportunities for student exposure to and discussion of different sides of issues promote development of independent thought and a more activist orientation, skills which have been shown to increase civic participation.

Development of Critical Thinking Skills

To be valid, assessments for all students must involve an array of thinking skills that require much more than the minimal memorization of facts at the knowledge level of Bloom's taxonomy. We believe that children at all levels can be challenged with critical thinking skills at the higher levels of Bloom's. For example, we know one teacher who always makes sure to ask her kindergarteners some tough questions involving evaluation and application about the fables and fairy tales they read together (e.g., "What would you do if the wolf from *The Three Little Pigs* came to YOUR house?"). She believes it is never too early to encourage her students to use higher-order thinking skills. We have also stressed that you can avoid historical distortions leading to marginalization of students in your class and encourage mastery goals with assessments incorporating current and historical events with multiple points of view. Such activities sharpen critical thinking skills, and they also increase engagement among different groups of students who come from a variety of backgrounds and cultures.

→ CASE STUDY APPLICATION

We now return to Maria Mensik's secondary English unit on utopias and dystopias. We discuss it in terms of lessons about reliability, validity, avoiding bias, and representing diversity.

Maria designed a table of specifications (Table 6.13) that included her learning goals and descriptions of the assessments she designed related to each one. Such a procedure is an excellent way to provide content evidence for the validity of the assessments designed for a unit. As you recall, this is the most important validity issue for classroom teachers. Such a table is very useful for ensuring alignment between the assessments and the learning goals. It also illustrates whether each learning goal has effective assessment coverage. As you examine this table, you see Maria is devoting

TABLE 6.13

Table of Specifications for Assessments in Utopia and Dystopia Unit

Learning Goal and Percentage of the Unit It Covers	Assessment Items Addressing Each Learning Goal	
	Knowledge-Level Items	Above Knowledge Level
1. Student will be able to compare and contrast characteristics of a utopia and dystopia. 60%		1. Formative assessment on characteristics of utopias and dystopias 2. 10 multiple-choice items 3. 4 essay items 4. Performance assessment on creating a society
2. Student will be able to compare and contrast multiple works concerning utopia/dystopia, paying particular attention to the role of the government and the role of the individual. 30%		1. Formative assessment on characteristics of utopias and dystopias 2. Multiple-choice items 1–3 3. Essay items 1–3
3. Student will be able to use persuasive language in writing and/or speaking. 10%		1. Essay item 4 2. Performance assessment on creating a society

60 percent of the unit to the first learning goal; consequently, the majority of her assessment also addresses this learning goal. In addition, you see she has also taken important steps to make sure each of her assessments requires higher than knowledge-level cognitive skills to complete. For example, she requires students to use comprehension, analysis, and evaluation skills from Bloom's by comparing and contrasting the characteristics of utopias and dystopias, choosing the most important characteristics, and describing how different pieces of literature exemplify them in her formative assessment.

Notice that each learning goal has more than one assessment addressing it, and the assessments require different kinds of skills and activities. Sufficiency of information, the key issue for reliability of classroom assessments, requires multiple assessments. With this variety, Maria will have evidence to determine whether different assessments addressing the same learning goal result in similar levels of performance among students. If she finds consistent patterns, she will be able to conclude that random error does not contribute in a major way to the obtained scores of her students.

The other reliability issue important to consider in classroom assessments relates to scoring. Maria has a range of assessment tasks. She includes multiple-choice items, which have a clear-cut correct answer, as well as essay items and a performance task, which can be more susceptible to random error associated with making judgments. She must pay careful attention to her scoring criteria and procedures to ensure she grades them consistently and reliably. Ideally, consulting with another teacher to examine interrater reliability could also be helpful if time permits. We know of several schools where interrater reliability is addressed in team meetings (see Box 6.1). Chapters 8 and 9 provide discussion of procedures for construction of scoring guides that enhance reliability.

Maria's use of diverse forms of assessment will support the validity of her decisions about students' achievement of learning goals. Whether students are good at multiple-choice tests is *not* the focus of an assessment. Rather, the focus is on whether students show an understanding of the *concepts* tested in the multiple-choice format. Some students best express their knowledge by being assessed with essay questions. Others best express their grasp of new concepts when assessed by multiple-choice items. Strong teachers use a mix of formats to assess student achievement because such variety is more likely to provide valid inferences about student mastery of the learning goals.

In terms of avoiding bias, Maria addresses the opportunity to learn by ensuring that students who don't have computers at home will not be penalized by assignments requiring technology such as PowerPoint slides. She plans to allocate class time in the computer lab to complete the PowerPoint or other figures needed for any assignments requiring computer technology. She will also ensure that students will not be tested on content and skills that have not been thoroughly addressed in class—an issue of validity. She will take care to reduce any systematic scoring bias on her part through designing scoring guides with relevant criteria, and she will spend time working with students to clarify her scoring guides for them and for herself.

In terms of representing the diversity of the classroom, Maria began by including writings by both male and female authors as resources (see Table 6.14). However, she noticed most of these seemed to represent a Eurocentric perspective. After doing a little research with an eye toward representing a wider range of groups, Maria decided to add readings on Chinese notions of utopia/dystopia (e.g., Chairman Mao's *Little Red Book*) and the seventeenth-century social experiments begun by Jesuits in what are now Paraguay, Argentina, and Brazil, as well as Roland Joffe's film *The Mission*. She also decided to make explicit in class discussions and assessments some of the underlying tensions at work in any society between freedom and equality and between political majorities and minorities. She intends to address issues of politics and power directly. In addition, she decided to offer students opportunities to do research on sometimes marginalized perspectives and found information on feminist utopias, Jewish utopias, and musical utopias to get them started in thinking about potential topics. These additions fit well within the framework of Maria's learning goals, and the added complexity will stretch students' critical thinking skills. The additions also provide more conflicting perspectives and controversial issues that can deepen and enrich student understanding of the facets of utopias and dystopias and the implications for their lives and for their own civic participation.

TABLE 6.14

Resources for Unit on Utopia and Dystopia

Literature	Films
Declaration of Independence	*Gattaca*
Utopia, by Thomas More	*The Truman Show*
1984, by George Orwell	*I, Robot*
Fahrenheit 451, by Ray Bradbury	*Pleasantville*
The Giver, by Lois Lowry	
"The ones who walk away from Omelas" by Ursula LeGuin	

Key Chapter Points

We began this chapter by introducing four concepts that strongly influence assessment quality. The first of these was reliability, or the degree to which scores on an assessment are consistent and stable. We discussed three sources of error: assessment occasion, assessment items, and scoring issues. We then suggested a number of ways to improve reliability in classroom assessments, the most important of which is to provide multiple assessment opportunities to ensure sufficiency of information.

Next, we turned to a discussion of the validity of assessments, or the extent to which an assessment provides an accurate, representative, and relevant measure of student performance for its intended purpose. We discussed construct-related evidence as the foundation for supporting validity. Because translating a construct into an assessment can take so many forms, checks on whether your assessment accurately represents the construct are crucial. We then described four sources for gathering construct-related evidence: evidence based on logic and common sense, evidence based on variety of formats, content-related evidence, and criterion-related evidence. Next, using these four sources of evidence, we described a number of ways to improve the validity of classroom assessments. Finally, in discussing the relationship between reliability and validity, we made the case that reliability is a necessary but not sufficient condition for validity.

The next issue described in this chapter to consider when designing assessments was avoiding bias. We discussed the bias pitfalls of unfair penalization, lack of opportunity to learn, and teacher bias. In discussing teacher bias, several issues were considered including microaggressions, the importance of monitoring interaction patterns with students, and scoring biases.

Finally, we discussed the importance of representing the diversity of the classroom in assessments. Problems to avoid include stereotypical representation (depiction of groups in an oversimplified, clichéd manner), contextual invisibility (underrepresentation of certain groups, customs, or lifestyles in curricular or assessment materials), and historical distortions (presenting a single interpretation of an issue, perpetuating oversimplification of complex issues, or avoiding controversial topics).

In the case study section, we reviewed the table of specifications for Maria Mensik's unit on utopias and dystopias to examine evidence for reliability and validity of her assessments. We also discussed her efforts to represent diversity in her assessments.

Helpful Websites

http://www.ncel.org/sdrs/areas/issues/methods/assment/as500.htm
This section of the North Central Educational Laboratory website provides resources and video
    clips related to enhancing the quality of assessments to support student learning.
http://www.understandingprejudice.org/
The Understanding Prejudice website provides resources, interactive activities, and
    demonstrations that provide a variety of perspectives on prejudice, stereotypes, and
    appreciation of diversity. It was established with funding from the National Science
    Foundation and McGraw-Hill Higher Education.

Chapter Review Questions

1. Employing concepts from the section of the chapter on reliability, explain in your own words why no important decision about any student should be made on the basis of a single score.

2. Why is it important to explain that every score has an error component when sharing a summative test score with parents or students?

3. Decide whether these student concerns are caused by problems with reliability (R) or validity (V), and explain your reasoning:

V R	The teacher tested us on the whole chapter, but she forgot to go over one section, so the scores on the test of many students were much lower than they should have been.
V R	I had handed in a completed rough draft and she gave me a few comments on how to improve what she herself called "a well-written paper." After editing my paper and incorporating all of her comments, I turned in my final draft. She returned the paper a week later with a failing grade.
V R	In my algebra class, all of the questions on tests were multiple choice and essay even though during class we mostly worked problems.
V R	In one of my high school classes, we would have short readings for homework. To quiz us on the readings, the teacher would ask specific questions such as "The word missing from this sentence is _____." He didn't test our overall understanding.
V R	In ninth grade I had a teacher who gave only one test for the entire semester. I am not a good test taker, I get nervous and draw a blank. Everything I knew left me and I received a low grade in the class even though I was there every day, did all my homework and assignments, and participated regularly.

4. Think about a recent major classroom assessment you have completed in your college classes. Did you feel it was a valid assessment? Explain why or why not, demonstrating your understanding of at least two sources of validity evidence.

5. For another recent major classroom assessment you have completed, describe the specific information your teacher ideally should have collected as evidence for the validity of the assessment. Explain how you know whether such evidence was collected or not. Would such evidence make the teacher more or less confident of the decisions he or she made about the meaning of the scores?

6. Why is content-related evidence the most important source of evidence for validity in classroom assessment?

7. If you were chosen to debate whether validity or reliability is more important for assessment, which side would you choose? Explain the reasoning for your choice.

8. Think about your own experiences with people who are different from you. Describe areas where you believe your experience is limited and could lead to unintentional bias on your part as a classroom teacher.

9. Identify examples of microaggressions that you have observed or that have been directed at you.

10. Describe classroom examples you have observed of unfair penalization, lack of opportunity to learn, and teacher bias. With each example, describe what group was targeted and what you would have done to rectify the situation.

11. Examine a textbook in your content area for stereotypical representation, contextual invisibility, and historical distortions. Under each heading, provide a list of specific examples.

12. In your estimation, does Maria provide sufficient content-related evidence for the validity of her assessments in the unit on utopias and dystopias? Justify your answer. What additional evidence would be useful?

REFERENCES

Barbour, J. 2007. Grading on the guilty-liberal standard. *Chronicle of Higher Education* 53(42): (ERIC Document Reproduction Service NO. EJ770974). Retrieved June 10, 2008 from ERIC database.

Bell, L., S. Washington, G. Weinstein, and B. Love. 1997. Knowing ourselves as instructors. In M. Adams, L. Bell, & P. Griffin (eds.), *Teaching for diversity and social justice: A sourcebook*, pp. 299–310. New York: Routledge.

Brookhart, S. 2003. Developing measurement theory for classroom assessment purposes and uses. *Educational Measurement: Issues and Practices* 22 (4): 5–12.

Fiske, S., and S. Taylor. 1991. *Social cognition*. 2nd ed. Reading, MA: Addison Wesley.

Gorski, P. 2008. The myth of the "culture of poverty." *Educational Leadership* 65 (7): 32–36.

Gronlund, N. 2006. *Assessment of student achievement*. 8th ed. New York: Allyn and Bacon.

Kahne, J., and S. Sporte. 2007. *Educating for democracy: Lessons from Chicago*. Chicago: Consortium on Chicago School Research. Retrieved October 2, 2007 from http://ccsr.uchicago.edu/content/publications.php?pub_id=117.

Macmillan-McGraw Hill. 1993. *Reflecting diversity: Multicultural guidelines for educational publishing professionals*. New York: Author.

Ndura, E. 2004. ESL and cultural bias: An analysis of elementary through high school textbooks in the Western United States of America. *Language, Culture, and Curriculum* 17 (2): 143–153.

Popham, W. J. April, 2007. Instructional insensitivity of tests: Accountability's dire drawback. Paper presented at the annual meeting of the American Educational Research Association, Chicago, IL.

Shavelson, R., G. Baxter, and X. Gao. 1993. Sampling variability of performance assessments. *Journal of Educational Measurement* 30: 215–232.

Smith, J. 2003. Reconsidering reliability in classroom assessment and grading. *Educational Measurement: Issues and Practices* 22 (4): 26–33.

Sue, D., C. Capodilupo, G. Torino, J. Bucceri, A. Holder, K. Nadal, and M. Esquilin. 2007. Racial microaggressions in everyday life. *American Psychologist* 62: 271–286.

Switzer, J. 1990. The impact of generic word choices. *Sex Roles* 22: 69.

CHAPTER 7

TEACHER-MADE ASSESSMENTS: MULTIPLE-CHOICE AND OTHER SELECTED-RESPONSE ITEMS

Perhaps the most common argument proponents of alternative assessment bring against the use of [selected-response items] is this: [they] measure only recall and other lower-order thinking skills whereas alternative methods of assessment require students to exhibit the higher-order skills such as critical thinking, analysis, synthesis, reasoning, and problem solving. If this were true, it would be a very damning argument indeed, but neither assertion is altogether accurate.

–William Sanders and Sandra Horn (1995)

❖ **Chapter Learning Goals**

At the conclusion of this chapter, the reader should be able to do the following:

- Describe the formats, benefits, and weaknesses of three types of selected-response items: multiple-choice, true-false, and matching.

- Use guidelines to write items in each format across the range of cognitive skills from "remember" to "create."

- Explain the use of interpretive exercises to assess higher-level cognitive strategies using selected-response formats.

- Avoid item-writing errors that are often overlooked by teachers.

- Format selected-response items and arrange them in an assessment.

- Describe methods to involve students in the development of items.

- Accommodate the selected-response format for diverse learners.

→ INTRODUCTION

In this and the next two chapters, we examine three forms of assessment: **selected-response** (e.g., multiple-choice, true-false, and matching), **constructed-response** (e.g., short answer and essays), and **performance assessments** (e.g., science experiments, music auditions, speeches). Used in combination, these forms of assessment will provide you with information for making valid decisions about your students. As we begin our look at these various forms of assessment, we start with the following guiding thoughts:

- A student should get an item or task correct because the student understands the material, not because we gave clues to the answer or because the student guesses well.
- A student should miss an item because the student does *not* understand the material, not because we wrote confusing items or tasks, tricked the student, or asked for trivial information.

These guiding thoughts apply whether we are talking about true-false items, multiple-choice questions, essay questions, or performance tasks. They remind us that the purpose of our tests is to find out what our students know and are able to do.

In this chapter we focus on selected-response items. Selected-response items offer choices from which a student decides on an answer. We look at three types of selected-response formats: multiple-choice, true-false, and matching.

ALIGNING ITEMS WITH LEARNING GOALS AND THINKING SKILLS

A first step in developing a test is to prepare a table of specifications based on the learning goals that you covered during instruction (see Table 2.15). Based on the learning goals addressed in the unit, the table of specifications will ensure that you focus your test development efforts on items related to instruction. The table of specifications also prevents you from including test items based on learning goals that had to be modified during the unit. Finally, the alignment between your instruction and the test items will support you in making valid decisions about whether students have met the learning goals associated with the instructional unit.

SELECTED-RESPONSE FORMATS

Having developed a table of specifications, you are now ready to consider the formats you can use in writing the items.

Multiple-Choice Formats

Stem
The premise of a multiple choice item, usually a question or an incomplete statement.

Options
Potential answers including one correct response.

Distracters
Incorrect options in multiple choice items.

Conventional multiple-choice items begin with a **stem** and offer three to five answer **options.** The stem takes the form of a question or an incomplete statement (Figure 7.1). Options are the potential answers, with one correct response and several plausible incorrect responses. Incorrect responses are referred to as **distracters** because they capture the attention of students who have not mastered the material. (This choice of term is conventional but unfortunate because it sounds like teachers are trying to trick students.) In Figure 7.1(a), Olive Crews, a high-school teacher, used the following question format: What are the class boundaries when the class limits are 8–12? In Figure 7.1(b), Rodney Grantham, who teaches Spanish to high school students, used the completion format: Mis amigos son __________.

Alternate-Choice Item
Selected-response item with only two options.

A second multiple-choice format is the **alternate-choice item.** This type of question has only two options instead of the three to five options of the conventional multiple choice. An example is shown in Figure 7.2. Experts suggest that conventional multiple-choice

a
b
1. What are the class boundaries when the class limits are 8–12?
8. Mis amigos son __________.
Stems
a. 7–13
b. 7.5–12.5*
c. 8.5–12.5
d. 10
Options
a. cómica
b. cómico
c. cómicas
d. cómicos*
Olive Crews
Rodney Grantham

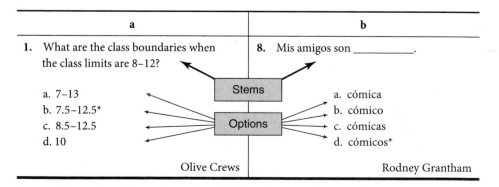

FIGURE 7.1 ***Examples of the (a) Question Format and (b) Completion Format for Multiple-Choice Items***

5. In a food chain, rabbits are ____________________.

   a. consumers*
   b. producers

FIGURE 7.2 *An Example of an Alternate-Choice Item*

1.
2.
3.
4.
5.
6.

8. Look at the different kinds of animals in the pictures above. Which three of these animals have a very large number of young every time they reproduce? ← Stem

   A) 1, 2, and 4
   B) 1, 4, and 6
   C) 3, 5, and 6*
   D) 4, 5, and 6

   } Options with choices grouped into sets

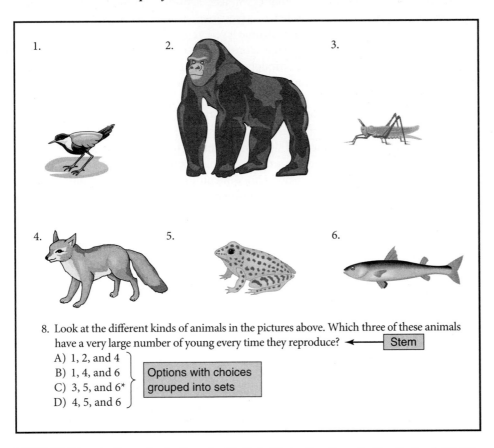

FIGURE 7.3 *An Example of a Complex Multiple-Choice Item from the Fourth-Grade NAEP Science Assessment*

Adapted from the National Center for Educational Statistics. 2005. NAEP question. Reprinted with permission.

items with three to five options often actually function as alternate-choice items because they usually have only one plausible distracter (Haladyna & Downing, 1993). In the food chain item, the choices are consumers and producers. As you recall from elementary science class, food chains are composed of producers, consumers, and decomposers. "Decomposers" is not a useful option, however, because these organisms are primarily fungi and bacteria. Little would be gained by including decomposers as an option because students would quickly eliminate this implausible distracter.

Complex Multiple Choice
Selected response item with stem followed by choices grouped into more than one set.

The third multiple-choice format is **complex multiple choice.** This type of item consists of a stem followed by choices that are grouped into sets (Figure 7.3). The complex multiple-choice format is more difficult than other formats. The student must consider each option, but also each combination within an option; so getting the answer correct may depend on logical skills more than mastery of the content. A student could know the material; however, in the juggling of the combinations within the options, the

student might select the wrong answer. This type of format, then, can violate our guiding thought that students should miss an item only if they do not understand the material, and so we do not recommend it.

The example of the complex multiple-choice format in Figure 7.3 is from the fourth-grade science assessment of the National Assessment of Educational Progress (NAEP), a national test administered to a representative sample of students in grades 4, 8, and 12 (Greenwald, Persky, Campbell, & Mazzeo, 1999). The NAEP Assessment provides descriptive information about examinees' achievement in such areas as reading, writing, mathematics, and science. Assessment results are reported by student groups (e.g., gender, ethnicity, family income level) at the state and national level. Items on the test include multiple-choice, short constructed-response, extended constructed-response, and performance tasks. Throughout this chapter we will use examples from NAEP to illustrate the application of item-writing guidelines we are discussing.

When to Use the Multiple-Choice Format

The multiple-choice format can be useful to assess learning when an instructional unit covers a broad range of content. This format can be used to assess students in the cognitive processes of remembering, understanding, applying, and analyzing. However, the processes of evaluating and creating are difficult to assess with the multiple-choice format and may require use of essays and other performance assessments, which are the topics of Chapters 8 and 9.

Some experts suggest that the multiple-choice or alternate-choice format may be particularly useful for assessing students with special needs. Myers and Pearson (1996) found that students who were unable to complete typical portfolio entries *were* able to demonstrate what they had learned by correctly completing some multiple-choice items. They note that "data from multiple choice tests provided significant information about students at the low end of the scale on some performance tasks." Thus they suggest that "data from multiple choice tests may turn out to be useful sources of information on students who provide only minimal performance data in portfolios."

Advantages and Disadvantages of the Multiple-Choice Format

Using multiple-choice questions has the advantage of potentially broader coverage of the learning goals. Multiple-choice items take less time to complete because the answer options are provided. Essay questions and performance tasks require time for students to organize their ideas and record them. Given that multiple-choice items can be answered quickly, you can ask more questions and therefore represent the content more adequately with a wide range of multiple-choice items rather than with a few essay questions.

Using a greater number of multiple-choice items in a test, as contrasted with a limited number of essay items, will also likely produce higher reliability. For example, if you develop 35 multiple-choice items from the learning goals based on a unit, you are likely to sample the range of material covered in that unit. In contrast, for a test that uses only essay questions, you will not be able to ask about as many topics as you did for the multiple-choice test. Writing out responses takes more time for students; so fewer essay questions can be asked. With 35 multiple-choice items, a student's performance is less likely to depend on luck. If you touch on only 6–8 topics in a test using essay questions, you might select the topics that students struggled with and you might omit topics that they did grasp. The greater number of multiple-choice items allows you to sample from a broader range of topics, making it less likely that students' scores will be influenced because you sampled topics that they did not grasp or omitted concepts that they did learn.

Another advantage of multiple-choice and selected-response items is scoring efficiency. The teacher creates an answer key and does not have to make a judgment about the quality of each student's response.

Dissatisfaction with multiple-choice items in the past has focused on their assumed reliance on factual content only. As noted in the quote at the beginning of the chapter, assessment experts contend that measuring students' ability to analyze, synthesize information, make comparisons, draw inferences, and evaluate ideas are all possible with multiple-choice items (e.g., Sanders & Horn, 1995; Worthen & Spandel, 1991). Assessing such complex skills, however, generally requires the use of the interpretive exercise, an item format that we will discuss at the end of this section.

We need to say that we are not advocating exclusive use of multiple-choice assessment items. The advantages of other types of items are addressed in future chapters. Each type of assessment item has advantages and disadvantages. Accordingly, multiple forms of assessment are needed for a balanced picture of student achievement.

A potential disadvantage of the multiple-choice format is the lack of student motivation when assessed in this manner. We have seen the excitement of students as they participated in a debate about social issues, which showcased their understanding of the debate format and the social issues being debated. Such engagement is not often seen when students complete a multiple-choice test or an essay test. Assessments that energize students are more likely to promote student motivation and encourage students to achieve learning goals.

True-False Formats

True-false items provide a statement, also referred to as a proposition, and the student must determine whether the statement is correct or incorrect. An example of a true-false item is the following:

True-False Items
Items that provide a statement that the student must determine to be correct or incorrect.

T* **F** One acceptable syllable pattern for a limerick is 9-9-5-5-9.

Sometimes the answer options are Yes/No or Correct/Incorrect.

A variation of the true-false format is to have students correct the false part of a statement. For example, the question on the syllables pattern for limericks might read as follows:

T **F*** One acceptable syllable pattern for a limerick is <u>8-8-9-9-8</u>.

Then the students would be instructed, "For false statements, correct the underlined part of the item to make the statement true." In this case a student might change the pattern to 8-8-6-6-8 or some other variation that falls within the general syllable pattern for limericks. The requirement to correct the underlined part of the statement reduces the effect of guessing, but it requires more detailed scoring and, thus, increases the amount of grading time.

Another form of the true-false item is the **multiple true-false** (Figure 7.4). This format combines the multiple-choice and true-false formats. In the multiple true-false

Multiple True-False Items
Several choices follow a scenario or question and the student indicates whether each choice is correct or incorrect.

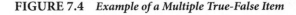

A farmer has a small pond that has recently had a lot of algae growth. Which of the following statements are actions the farmer might take and the possible results? Indicate whether each statement is true (T) or false (F).

T F* 5. Adding fertilizer will kill the algae.
T* F 6. Adding small fish to the pond will reduce the amount of algae.
T F* 7. Introducing small fish to the pond will attract herbivores.

FIGURE 7.4 ***Example of a Multiple True-False Item***

item, several choices follow a question or scenario, and the student indicates whether each choice is true or false.

When to Use the True-False Format

Intuitively, it appears that the true-false item would be useful for assessing young students. However, critics of true-false items raise the concern that the presentation of a false statement may have a detrimental impact on students' learning because appearing in print on a test can lend plausibility to erroneous information. Because this **negative-suggestion** effect would most likely apply to young children, true-false items should be used only with older students.

Negative-Suggestion Effect
Concern that appearance in print lends plausibility to erroneous information.

Advantages and Disadvantages of the True-False Format

Like multiple-choice items, true-false items have the advantage that more items can be included in the test. Because students have only two options to consider, they can answer even more true-false items in a test than multiple-choice items. True-false items allow you to assess many facts, concepts, and other material covered in an instructional unit.

Problems with guessing pose limitations to simple true-false items. A student who is guessing an answer has a 50/50 chance of getting the item correct. In contrast, if you use a multiple-choice item with four options, a student has only a 1 in 4 chance of guessing correctly. Thus, scores on true-false tests can be influenced by guessing.

Another potential disadvantage of the true-false format is that it is generally associated with lower cognitive levels than the multiple-choice format (Downing et al., 1995). However, consider the example about the limerick syllable pattern, which requires students to determine whether the pattern fits the form for limericks, a thinking skill at least at the understanding level of Bloom's taxonomy.

Matching Formats

Matching Format
Two parallel columns of items (termed premises and answers) are listed and the student indicates which items from each column belong together in pairs.

A final form of selected response is **matching.** As shown in Figure 7.5, in a matching exercise two columns are formed. In the left-hand column, you list a set of premises (e.g., statements, questions, phrases). In the right-hand column, you list the answers (sometimes referred to as responses). Generally, the premises, or lengthier phrases,

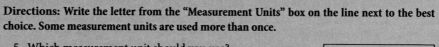

Directions: Write the letter from the "Measurement Units" box on the line next to the best choice. Some measurement units are used more than once.

5. Which measurement unit should you use?

_______ 1. length of the playground
_______ 2. the height of a house
_______ 3. the distance between cities
_______ 4. the length of a baby
_______ 5. the tip of a pencil
_______ 6. the width of your hand

Measurement Units
a. centimeter
b. kilometer
c. meter
d. millimeter

PREMISES **ANSWERS**

FIGURE 7.5 ***Example of a Matching Item***

should be placed on the left. The answers, or briefer phrases, appear on the right. In Figure 7.5, the answer column contains the measurement units and the premise column lists the objects (e.g., house, playground) to be measured.

When to Use the Matching Format

The matching format is useful when the learning goal requires students to connect two types of facts. An example is linking countries and their major exports. This example, however, addresses only knowledge-level cognitive skills. To address comprehension, analysis, or application, you would need to modify the task. For example, if you want students to categorize information, a skill at the analysis level, the premises might be examples and the answers might be categories. Figure 7.6 illustrates this approach with responses that are categories of organisms and premises that are examples to be categorized. For the items to address higher-order thinking, however, the examples (e.g., mushroom) should be new to the students, and they should not have been used during instruction.

Advantages and Disadvantages of the Matching Format

As was the case for multiple-choice and true-false, the matching format allows a teacher to assess a broad span of student learning. Students can quickly read a premise, scan the responses for the correct answer, record their responses, and move to the next problem. Although this format is criticized for mainly assessing at the knowledge level, the cognitive skill students use with matching items may require analysis or application levels if students assign novel examples to broader categories, as shown in Figures 7.5 and 7.6. This format can thus provide evidence that students have mastered skills, such as classification, in a quick but reliable way. The challenge with this format is the difficulty in writing matching items that require more complex thinking.

Interpretive Exercises and Assessing Higher-Level Cognitive Levels

The **interpretive exercise** is a selected-response item preceded by material a student must interpret to answer the question. A set of directions should indicate which items require the student to use the material. Next comes the interpretive material. Types of interpretive materials include graphs, reading passages, diagrams, maps, and chemical equations. The interpretive material should be new to the students, but it should require the same understanding and skills that were the focus of the learning goals. The student must analyze the interpretive material (e.g., graph, picture) to answer questions that follow. That is, students should not be able to answer the question

Interpretive Exercise

A selected-response item preceded by material the student must analyze or interpret to answer the question.

Directions: Write the letter from the "Types of Organisms" box on the line next to the best choice. Some organism types are used more than once.

_____ 1. apple tree

_____ 2. fox

_____ 3. mold

_____ 4. mushroom

_____ 5. rabbit

Types of Organisms

a. consumer
b. decomposer
c. producer

FIGURE 7.6   *Example of a Matching Item That Requires Categorization*

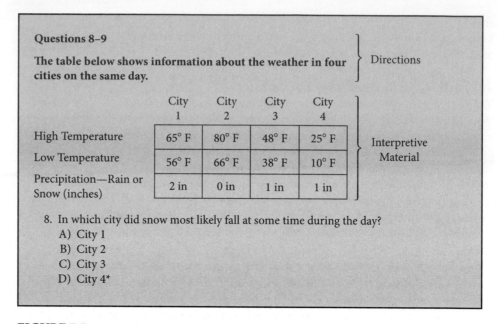

Questions 8–9

The table below shows information about the weather in four cities on the same day. ⎫ Directions

	City 1	City 2	City 3	City 4
High Temperature	65° F	80° F	48° F	25° F
Low Temperature	56° F	66° F	38° F	10° F
Precipitation—Rain or Snow (inches)	2 in	0 in	1 in	1 in

⎫ Interpretive Material

8. In which city did snow most likely fall at some time during the day?
   A) City 1
   B) City 2
   C) City 3
   D) City 4*

FIGURE 7.7   *Example of an Interpretive Exercise for Science*

SOURCE: National Center for Educational Statistics. 2005. NAEP question. Reprinted with permission.

without reference to the graph or picture. The multiple-choice item in Figure 7.7 is an interpretive exercise used in the NAEP science assessment for fourth grade.

When to Use the Interpretive Exercise Format

The interpretive exercise is useful for measuring higher-level thinking. This format lends itself particularly well to assessing procedural knowledge, such as how to read graphs and diagrams. The exercise in Figure 7.7, for example, requires students to comprehend the graph elements (rows, columns, cells, headers), read the information in the table, analyze the information, and draw conclusions.

Advantages and Disadvantages of the Interpretive Exercise Format

In addition to measuring higher-order thinking skills, interpretive exercises allow a teacher to assess concepts in more depth than the typical multiple-choice item. When you design an interpretive exercise, you should include at least two or three questions addressing the introductory material. Doing so takes full advantage of the chart, table, or passage you are using. Several questions make more efficient use of your time in carefully selecting a passage or a table and the students' time in interpreting the introductory material during the test. For example, Figure 7.7 could also be used to ask the following:

- What was the high temperature for City 1?
- Which city had the highest temperature?

Our students see interpretive exercises as more interesting because, to assess higher cognitive levels, the interpretive exercises require application of knowledge to new situations students have not encountered in class. For example, in English, new material could be a poem in a style studied in class, but by a different author. In social studies, the interpretive material could be a document or letter from a certain time period, as in Laura Clark's example from an eighth-grade unit on the Civil War (Figure 7.8).

Also, with increased use of computers for instruction and assessment, interpretive materials now can include movement of graphics and the inclusion of sound. The

Read the following entry of a soldier's diary. From the information he provides, determine which "side" this soldier is fighting for. Then answer the questions based on his view of the Civil War.

We get further and further from home everyday. After we lost the first big battle, my old job at the factory does not seem so bad. Morale is low. We are tired. However, more supplies and troops are coming which helps to build our strength. Gen. Grant says we move out tomorrow towards the Mississippi River. I hope we succeed in our mission.

1. Which state do you think this soldier is from?
   A. Maryland*
   B. New Mexico
   C. Virginia

2. How might this soldier defend his reason for going to war?
   A. Federalism*
   B. Fifth Amendment
   C. Fugitive Slave Act

3. To which political party would this soldier most likely belong?
   A. Constitutional Union
   B. Democratic
   C. Republican*

FIGURE 7.8 *Example of an Interpretive Exercise That Uses a Fictional Entry from a Soldier's Diary*

Use the following animated figure to answer item 2.

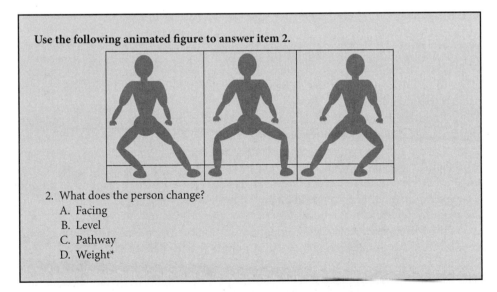

2. What does the person change?
   A. Facing
   B. Level
   C. Pathway
   D. Weight*

FIGURE 7.9 *Example of an Interpretive Exercise That Uses Movement*

SOURCE: South Carolina Arts Assessment Program (SCAAP). 2002. Reprinted with permission.

South Carolina Arts Assessment Program (SCAAP) administers a computer-based test on the Internet (Yap, 2005). Administration of a test by computer allows animation or video clips to be used as interpretive material. For example, in a sample test for dance, an animated stick figure (Figure 7.9) shifts its weight to the left, moves to an upright position, shifts to its right knee, and returns to the upright position. Then the student must determine which element of dance is demonstrated.

3. Look at the rhythm patterns below. Which of the 4 rhythm patterns matches the one you hear?

A.
B.
C.
D.

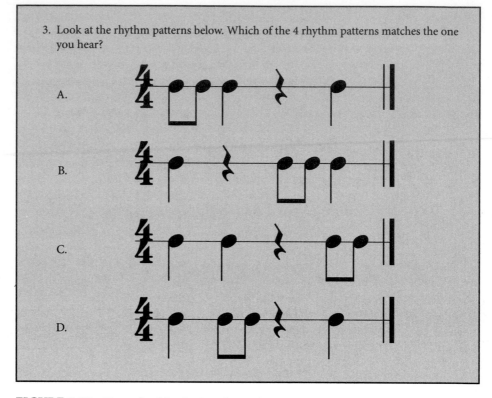

FIGURE 7.10 ***Example of the Options for an Interpretive Exercise in Music***

SOURCE: South Carolina Arts Assessment Program (SCAAP). 2002. Reprinted with permission.

Sound is also incorporated into the interpretive exercises in music for the SCAAP (Yap et al., 2005). To answer the item shown in Figure 7.10, fourth-grade students listen to a music clip; then the students select the option that matches the rhythm pattern that they heard.

Another advantage of the interpretive exercise is that after you have designed an exercise addressing important information related to one of your learning goals, you can use many variations of the same basic item as you modify your tests for new groups of students. You can change the interpretive material (e.g., a different poem, music clip, map, or literary passage), and/or you can change some of the questions about the interpretive material (e.g., offer different rhythm patterns to choose, require different distances to be calculated).

This format, however, takes more administration time than other selected-response item formats. For example, the NAEP fourth-grade science item in Figure 7.11 requires students to read the problem, draw conclusions about Julio's pulse rate, then analyze each bar graph to determine if it represents the pattern of Julio's pulse rate. Because this takes more time than other selected-response formats, the number of such items must be limited.

→ Guidelines for Item Development

To help you to develop clear items, we first present some general guidelines for item development that apply to the various selected-response formats. Subsequently, we offer rules specific to each of the item formats.

1. Julio wanted to know how his pulse rate changed when he ran very fast. Julio measured his pulse rate before he started running, while he was running, and two minutes after he stopped running. Which graph best shows how Julio's pulse rate changed?
A)
Pulse rate (beats per minute)
Before running
During running
After running
B)
Pulse rate (beats per minute)
Before running
During running
After running
C)
Pulse rate (beats per minute)
Before running
During running
After running
D)*
Pulse rate (beats per minute)
Before running
During running
After running

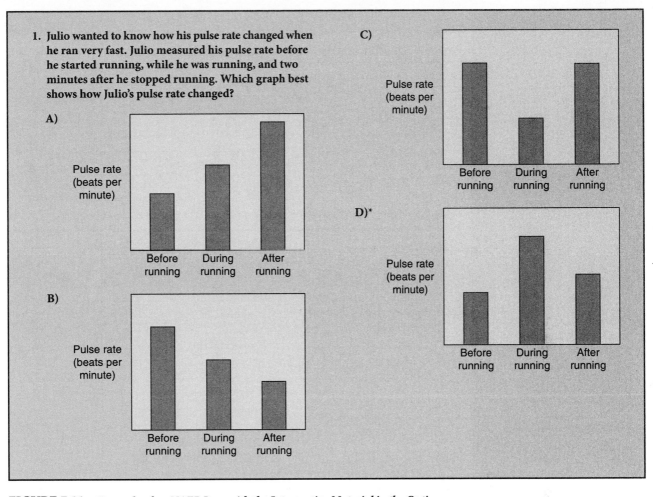

FIGURE 7.11 ***Example of an NAEP Item with the Interpretive Material in the Options***

SOURCE: National Center for Educational Statistics. 2005. NAEP question. Reprinted with permission.

General Guidelines for All Selected-Response Formats

General guidelines to apply in the development of selected-response items include assessing important content across cognitive levels, keeping reading skills at an appropriate level, following the conventions of written language, portraying the diversity of your classroom, avoiding the introduction of bias, and omitting humor in a testing situation. Table 7.1 lists the general guidelines.

Assess Important Content Across the Range of Cognitive Levels

The items in your assessment should be based on the subject-area content standards and represent a range of cognitive skills (e.g., remember, understand, apply, analyze, etc.). Developing your table of specifications will help you to meet this requirement.

Not all content, however, is equal. Each item should be based on important content to learn, and you should avoid trivial content. For example, we know of an instructor of a literacy course who included in her final examination a test item about the technical term for the ə symbol. The symbol, referred to as a schwa, is found in the pronunciation key of dictionaries. Such a practice is similar to instructors who

TABLE 7.1

General Guidelines for Writing Selected-Response Items

Each item should assess important content across the range of cognitive levels.

An assessment should not require advanced reading skills unless it is a test of literacy skills.

Selected-response items should follow the conventions of written language (e.g., spelling, grammar, and punctuation).

Items in a test should portray the diversity of the classroom.

Avoid introducing bias in an assessment.

The use of humor in a test is not advised.

write test items asking about details from a caption accompanying a diagram or information addressed in a footnote. Items should address the key facts, concepts, and procedures addressed in an instructional unit.

You should also incorporate novel material that has not been discussed explicitly in class. In Figure 7.5, for example, the objects that are to be measured (e.g., length of a playground, height of a house) should be different than the objects used during instruction. Also, keep the content of each item independent from content of other items on the test. For example, refer to the eighth-grade items from the NAEP civics item shown in Figure 7.12. After a student answers item 4, the student might think that the answer to 4 should be the basis for answering item 5, thus influencing the student's answer to item 5. If the student got the first one wrong, the student would also get the second one wrong.

Keep the Reading Level Simple

A critical issue in developing a test is its reading level. As we discussed in Chapter 6, complex reading or writing demands in a science assessment might lower scores of students because of unfamiliar language or demands of writing rather than because of the students' lack of understanding. Because irrelevant skills influenced the score, the validity of the assessment is questionable. Thus, an assessment should not require advanced reading skills unless it is a test of literacy skills.

You can use the spelling and grammar tool in Microsoft Office Word 2007 to get an estimate of the reading level for a test item. As shown in Figure 7.13, highlight the text for which you want to get a reading level, click the Review tab, and click the Spelling & Grammar option. A pop-up window states that Word has completed checking the selection and asks whether you want it to check the rest of the document. When you select No, the pop-up with the readability statistics appears.

For example, the entry from the soldier's diary in Figure 7.8 has a Flesch-Kincaid Grade Level index of 4.0, which means a fourth-grade student should understand the passage. Therefore, the eighth-grade students in Laura Clark's history class should be able to read the entry. The Flesch Reading Ease has a 100-point scale. As the score increases, the document is easier to read. With a score of 82.2, the soldier's diary is fairly easy to read. The scores for both readability indices are based on the average number of syllables per word and the number of words per sentence. Thus, you can

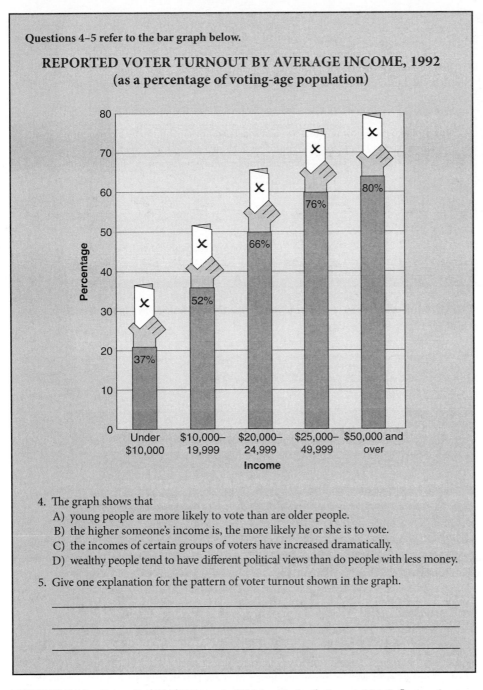

Questions 4–5 refer to the bar graph below.

REPORTED VOTER TURNOUT BY AVERAGE INCOME, 1992
(as a percentage of voting-age population)

80
70
60
50
40
30
20
10
0
Percentage
37%
52%
66%
76%
80%
Under $10,000
$10,000–19,999
$20,000–24,999
$25,000–49,999
$50,000 and over
Income

4. The graph shows that
   A) young people are more likely to vote than are older people.
   B) the higher someone's income is, the more likely he or she is to vote.
   C) the incomes of certain groups of voters have increased dramatically.
   D) wealthy people tend to have different political views than do people with less money.

5. Give one explanation for the pattern of voter turnout shown in the graph.

___

___

___

FIGURE 7.12 ***Example of NAEP Items in Which a Student's Answer May Influence Answers to Other Items***

SOURCE: National Center for Educational Statistics. 2005. NAEP questions. Reprinted with permission.

control the reading level required by your assessments by keeping vocabulary simple and by attending to the length of the sentences.

Another factor possibly contributing to reading demands is the use of negatives in an item. In developing items, when possible, word the stem positively and avoid negatives such as *not* or *except*. Sometimes, however, you want to know if students

Read the following entry of a soldier's diary. From the information he provides, determine which "side" this soldier is fighting for. Then answer the questions based on his view of the Civil War.
1. Which state do you think this soldier is from? (8.4.1)
A. Maryland*
B. New Mexico
C. Virginia
Readability Statistics

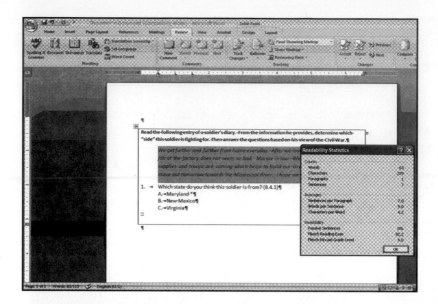

FIGURE 7.13 ***Illustration of the Calculation of the Grade Level of Test Materials***

Reprinted with permission of Microsoft.

11. Which of the following is a problem that could NOT be solved by one nation alone?
    A) National debt
    B) Highway traffic
    C) Ocean pollution*
    D) Government corruption

FIGURE 7.14 ***An Item That Uses NOT in the Stem***

SOURCE: National Center for Educational Statistics. 2005. NAEP question. Reprinted with permission.

recognize a non-example. If a negative word is used, write it in boldface and/or capitalized: **NOT** or **EXCEPT.** The word "NOT" appears in all capitals in the eighth-grade civics item from NAEP in Figure 7.14.

Use Conventions of Written Language in Writing Items

Selected-response items should follow the conventions of written language (e.g., spelling, grammar, and punctuation). For multiple-choice, alternate-choice, or interpretive exercise formats, when the item is an incomplete statement, as in Figure 7.1(b), the options should begin with a lowercase letter—unless the first word is a proper noun—and the stem should end with the appropriate punctuation mark (e.g., period). When the item is a question, if the options are complete sentences (such as in Figure 7.15), capitalize and punctuate as appropriate for each sentence. One more convention: when the item is a question and the options are phrases, capitalize the first word of the phrase (see Figure 7.14). Given the need to follow conventions of language, prior to finalizing a test, you should edit and proof all items.

After a workshop on writing multiple-choice items, a teacher approached us and stated that she did not worry about capitalization because she used ALL CAPS for her tests. She appeared to be seeking our approval for her use of ALL CAPS. However, we

Question 5 refers to the quote below.

Sojourner Truth said these words in 1852.

I hears talk about the constitution and rights of man. I come up and I takes hold of this constitution. It looks mighty big. And I feels for my rights, but they not there.

5. What did Sojourner Truth want to communicate with her words?
   A) Poor people did not know what was written in the Constitution.
   B) African Americans were not allowed to read the Constitution.
   C) The Constitution did not talk about the rights of African Americans.*
   D) The Constitution needed to talk about the rights of Native Americans.

FIGURE 7.15 *Fourth-Grade NAEP History Item with Options Written in Complete Sentences*
SOURCE: National Center for Educational Statistics. 2005. NAEP question. Reprinted with permission.

14. A farmer thinks that the vegetables on her farm are not getting enough water. Her son suggests that they use water from the nearby ocean to water the vegetables. Is this a good idea?
    A) Yes, because there is plenty of ocean water.
    B) Yes, because ocean water has many natural fertilizers.
    C) No, because ocean water is too salty for plants grown on land.*
    D) No, because ocean water is much more polluted than rainwater.

FIGURE 7.16 *NAEP Science Item That Challenges Stereotypes*
SOURCE: National Center for Educational Statistics. 2005. NAEP question. Reprinted with permission.

stated that her tests serve as models of the conventions of language and her unique use of capitalization did not provide appropriate models. In addition, the use of ALL CAPS is likely to make reading more difficult (Thompson & Thurlow, 2002), thus increasing reader fatigue.

Depict Diversity in Items

As discussed in Chapter 6, items in a test should portray the diversity of the classroom. Interpretive exercises use scenarios, tables, and pictures to provide context for a problem. Therefore, the images or data should depict the diversity of the classroom and the culture at large. To avoid bias, you should attend to whether the items introduce stereotypical representation, support contextual invisibility, or portray historical distortions (see Chapter 6). For example, do items foster stereotypes in areas such as interests, dress, activities, and professions? Or are stereotypes challenged—for example, by portraying senior citizens as energetic participants in activities? Are African American females presented in a variety of professions, such as medicine or law? In images and narrative, are classrooms diverse in composition, including, for example, students of African, Asian, European, and Hispanic origins? Stop for a moment and read the fourth-grade NAEP science item in Figure 7.16.

Were you expecting the farmer to be a woman? For most of us, the phrase "her farm" was a surprise. As soon as we read "A farmer thinks . . ." we had formed a mental image of a male farmer. When we came to the phrase "her farm," we had to shift our

BOX 7.1

A Reflection on Reviewing Test Items for Stereotypes

One of the word problems in the test described a girl who wanted to buy a new pair of jeans and babysat to earn the money she needed. This scenario may promote the idea that babysitting is typical for girls, or that girls are usually preoccupied by clothes. Therefore, a male was chosen as the character of this word problem. Additionally, the objective of buying a new pair of jeans was replaced with the one of buying a new pair of ice skates, because ice-skating is not typical for just one gender and does not have any stereotypical connotations.

Original Item:

Directions: Read the following sentences and use the information provided to answer questions 22, 23, and 24. Indicate your response by circling the letter next to the best answer.

Mary wants a new pair of jeans and she started babysitting to earn the amount of money she needs. On Monday, Mary babysat for 2 hours, and she earned 8 dollars. On Tuesday, she babysat for 5 hours, and she earned 20 dollars. The jeans Mary would like to buy cost 40 dollars.

22. How many more hours does she need to babysit to be able to buy the new jeans?
    A. 3*
    B. 10
    C. 12
    D. 40

Revised Item:

Sam wants new ice skates and he started babysitting to earn the amount of money he needs. On Monday, Sam babysat for 2 hours, and he earned 8 dollars. On Tuesday, he babysat for 5 hours, and he earned 20 dollars. The skates Sam would like to buy cost 40 dollars.

22. How many more hours does he need to babysit to be able to buy the new skates?
    A. 3*
    B. 10
    C. 12
    D. 40

image, evidence of our unintentional stereotyping. Being aware of potential sources of bias will help you to represent the diversity of your students' cultures.

Awareness of the issue of bias in selected-response items led Diana Luminiţa Mîndrilă, a special education teacher, to edit one of her interpretive exercises to avoid stereotyping. As shown in Box 7.1, originally the interpretive exercise described a young girl who was babysitting to earn money to buy some new clothes. Diana's insight was that the description "may promote the idea that babysitting is typical for girls, or that girls are usually preoccupied with clothes." She subsequently edited the item to remove the potential for stereotyping.

In another instance, one of our students developed an interpretive exercise that required students to translate a French passage based on the story of Cinderella. Before using such interpretive materials, we should step back and ask whether the passage is appropriate or whether it promotes stereotypes of passive females waiting for their prince to rescue them.

At this point you might wonder whether it is ever appropriate to portray people in a typical role, such as a female nurse or male lawyer. The answer is that you want to achieve balance. For example, teachers are often females; however, some teachers are male. So, in our presentation of teachers, we describe teachers as females and as males. Where we start to stereotype is when we *always* portray a farmer as male, a teacher as female, or a babysitter as female.

In terms of contextual invisibility, review both your instructional unit and its assessment to see whether you include the broad range of peoples contributing to the narrative of history. Does, for example, an instructional unit on art in culture portray

Answer questions 5–7 based on the following excerpt from Beverly Buchanan's artist statement.

My work is about, I think, responses. My response to what I'm calling GROUNDINGS. A process of creating objects that relate to but are not reproductions of structures, houses mainly lived in now or abandoned that served as home or an emotional grounding. What's important for me is the total look of the piece. Each section must relate to the whole structure. There are new groundings, but old ones help me ask questions and see possible stories as answers. Groundings are everywhere. I'm trying to make houses and other objects that show what some of them might look like now and in the past. (Buchanan, 2007)

7. Which of the following artist quotes would Beverly Buchanan most agree with based on her artist statement?
   A. "Painting is easy when you don't know how, but very difficult when you do." Edgar Degas
   B. "Great things are not done by impulse, but a series of small things brought together." Vincent Van Gogh*
   C. "I feel there is something unexplored about woman that only a woman can explore." Georgia O'Keeffe

FIGURE 7.17 *Visual Arts Item About the Works of Beverly Buchanan, an African American Artist*

the contributions of women artists? If so, does the assessment for the unit gauge student learning about the role of women artists? A visual arts unit by Leslie Drews, an art teacher, provides an illustration of making visible the contributions of women in the arts. In Leslie's unit, she draws from the works of Beverly Buchanan, an African American artist. The interpretive exercise in Figure 7.17 requires students to analyze a quote from Buchanan's artist statement and then compare its meaning to quotes from other artists—both male and female. In this manner, Leslie contributes to lifting the veil of contextual invisibility and acknowledging the works of women and African American artists.

Review the NAEP history item in Figure 7.18. Which people are the focus of this question? Asking fourth-grade students about the Sinaguan people reminds students that American history is multicultural with many diverse people contributing to the story of the United States of America.

Historical distortions occur when instructional units and assessment materials present only one interpretation of an issue or avoid sensitive topics. For example, a social studies standard might indicate that students should be able to do the following:

> Summarize the Holocaust and its impact on European society and Jewish culture, including Nazi policies to eliminate the Jews and other minorities, the "Final Solution," and the war crimes trials at Nuremberg. (SCDE, 2005, p. 58)

Although focus would naturally be on Nazi actions and atrocities, historical completeness would require acknowledging the refusal of some countries to help Jewish refugees fleeing the Third Reich (United States Holocaust Memorial Museum, 2007c). Similarly, when allied forces liberated prisoners in concentration camps, they did not free all those who were persecuted by the Nazis. Rather, allied forces transferred some of the gay men who were liberated from concentration camps to German prisons to serve the remainder of their sentences (United States Holocaust Memorial Museum, 2007a).

Questions 1–2 refer to the picture below.

1. The remains of this Sinaguan cliff house tell us something about the way ancient people lived in what is now the southwestern part of the United States. Which of the activities below would be the best way to learn how the Sinaguan people lived in ancient times?
   A) Talk to people living near the cliff houses
   B) Study letters and diaries left in the cliff houses
   C) Camp out in the cliff houses for a couple of days
   D) Study tools, bones, and pottery left in the cliff houses*

FIGURE 7.18   *NAEP Item That Presents the Multicultural Aspect of United States History*

Adapted from National Center for Educational Statistics. 2005. NAEP question. Reprinted with permission.

An assessment that includes only Item A in Figure 7.19 would contribute to historical distortion about the role of various countries in the liberation of prisoners in the Nazi camps. Inclusion of Items B and C in the test would create a more balanced view of the United States and allied forces in their treatment of those who were persecuted by the Nazis. Notice that we did not indicate that Item B or C should replace Item A. Such a change would also be historical distortion. The challenge for the teacher is to develop instructional units and assessments that present the multiple aspects of history and culture.

The twelfth-grade NAEP civics item in Figure 7.20 avoids historical distortion by including both facts: President Eisenhower did act to protect the rights of African American students to attend an all-white school, even though he had originally opposed

A	B	C

6. Which country contributed most to liberating Jews and others from Nazi concentration camps?
  a. Italy
  b. Japan
  c. United States of America*
	11. Which country did **NOT** provide help to Jewish refugees on the *St. Louis*?
	  a. Belgium
	  b. Denmark
	  c. United States of America*
		15. Allied forces transferred members from which group to German prisons after their liberation from the concentration camps?
		  a. Gay men*
		  b. Jews
		  c. Soviets

FIGURE 7.19   *Multiple-Choice Items That Relate to Historical Distortions*

Questions 17–19 are based on the passage below.

On May 17, 1954, in *Brown v. Board of Education,* the Supreme Court ruled that laws mandating racially segregated public school systems were unconstitutional. The Supreme Court later argued that federal courts should take steps to bring about the integration of segregated school systems "with all deliberate speed."

In 1957, Governor Orval Faubus of Arkansas called on the National Guard to turn away nine African American students as they attempted to enter Central High School in Little Rock. President Eisenhower, who did not support the *Brown* decision, called out federal troops to protect the rights of the African American students to attend the school.

18. President Eisenhower called out federal troops because he
  A) had a long career in the military.
  B) believed that the governor needed his assistance.
  C) was required by the Constitution to enforce the rule of law.*
  D) wanted to show that the federal government would protect the rights of protesters.

FIGURE 7.20   *NAEP Item That Presents Balanced View of a Historical Event*

SOURCE: National Center for Educational Statistics. 2005. NAEP question. Reprinted with permission.

the Supreme Court's decision in the case. Thus, the item presents a balanced view of a historical event.

Avoid Bias

In addition to representing diversity, you should avoid introducing bias in an assessment. For example, the fourth-grade science item from NAEP in Figure 7.21 may introduce bias because of the options offered. Students may not have had equal opportunity to be familiar with the instruments. The options use language likely to be known by students in upper middle class homes or wealthy schools. Whether students from low-income homes or underfunded schools have access to such equipment is questionable because such science equipment is expensive and, in the case of the "periscope" option, obscure.

Evidence of bias in this item, however, is equivocal. The NAEP website also provides statistics on the percentage of students who correctly answered an item. Percentage correct is provided for various student groups. The science item in Figure 7.21 was correctly answered by 90 percent of students not eligible for free and reduced-fee lunch versus 81 percent of students who received free or reduced-fee lunch (National Center for Educational Statistics [NCES], 2005). Percentage correct was 90 percent for

1. If you wanted to be able to look at the stars, the planets, and the Moon more closely, what should you use?
   A) Magnifying glass
   B) Microscope
   C) Periscope
   D) Telescope*

FIGURE 7.21 *An Item That Might Exhibit Bias for Students from Low-Income Homes and Schools*

Adapted from National Center for Educational Statistics. 2005. NAEP question. Reprinted with permission.

white students, 79 percent for African American students, and 82 percent for Hispanic students. Reviewing items to determine if the concepts are addressed in instruction and the language is accessible to all students helps to avoid bias.

Avoid Humor in a Test Setting

In developing items in general, one more issue should be considered. An assessment is a serious endeavor to determine which concepts and skills students have learned and which materials they have not yet mastered. Given this fact, the use of humor in a test is not advised, although some writers indicate it may be permissible (Haladyna, Downing, & Rodriquez, 2002). We know of an instance where a ninth-grade teacher candidate infused humor into one of his geometry tests. A student who did not do well on the test, however, shared the test and its misguided humor with her parents. The parents complained to the supervising teacher and the teacher candidate was reprimanded. Humor during instruction can lessen the stress of learning new materials; however, humor has the potential to interfere with students' focus during an assessment.

Guidelines for Specific Item Formats

Multiple-Choice Format

Table 7.2 shows guidelines specific to writing multiple-choice items. In this section, we elaborate on the guidelines and provide examples of their application.

Write Clear Stems   One key to developing effective multiple-choice items is to ensure that the stem clearly conveys what the test taker should do with the item. The stem

TABLE 7.2

Guidelines for Writing Multiple-Choice Items

Write a clear stem for the multiple-choice item.

Develop distracters that provide insight into student learning.

Develop reasonable options.

Arrange multiple-choice options in a logical order.

Avoid providing clues to an answer.

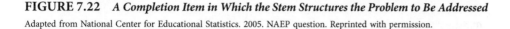

3. Peace treaties are usually signed by
   A) cities.
   B) countries.*
   C) states.
   D) townships.

FIGURE 7.22   *A Completion Item in Which the Stem Structures the Problem to Be Addressed*

Adapted from National Center for Educational Statistics. 2005. NAEP question. Reprinted with permission.

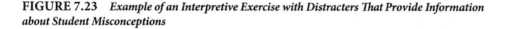

Use the following poem to answer question 8.

In a patch of snow
A lone purple crocus blooms.
Winter _____.

8. Which is the *best* ending for the poem?
   A. is done
   B. melts away*
   C. winds blow

FIGURE 7.23   *Example of an Interpretive Exercise with Distracters That Provide Information about Student Misconceptions*

must structure the problem to be addressed. This is often best accomplished by having the stem ask a direct question, especially for beginning item writers. Stems should also be fairly short and the vocabulary simple. In the fourth-grade NAEP civics item in Figure 7.22, the problem to be addressed is who the signatory parties in a peace treaty are, so it communicates clearly what students should do with the item. When the item uses the completion format, the omitted information should occur at the end, or near the end, of the stem as shown in Figure 7.22.

Develop Distracters That Provide Insight into Student Learning   In designing options for selected-response items, develop distracters that can help you understand students' thinking. Student choice of a distracter can provide diagnostic information about *why* a student missed an item if distracters include misconceptions, faulty algorithms, or incomplete calculations (Clarke et al., 2006). If the distracters contain common misconceptions or errors typically made by students with partial knowledge, a test with multiple-choice items can serve as a formative assessment that informs later instructional decisions. For example, in Figure 7.23, option B is the correct answer because the phrase "melts away" completes the vignette described in the haiku and provides the appropriate number of syllables (i.e., 5 syllables on the first line, 7 syllables on the second line, and 5 syllables on the third line). If a student chose option A, the teacher knows that the student likely realizes the poem must have meaning (i.e., Winter is done); however, the student may not understand the 5-7-5 syllable pattern required for a haiku. Option C indicates that the student may not understand the syllable pattern and may think that haiku must rhyme.

In addition, the options provided should be conceptually similar. In the fourth-grade NAEP item in Figure 7.24, the options are conceptually similar: in options A,

2. Which shows 3/4 of the picture shaded?

A) B) C) D)

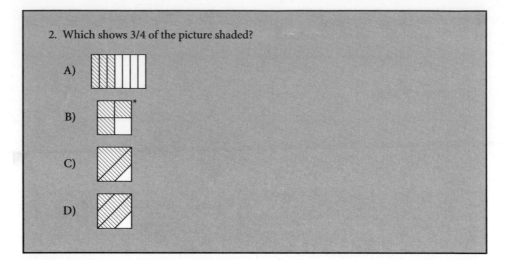

FIGURE 7.24 ***Example of an NAEP Multiple-Choice Item with Distracters That Provide Information About Student Misconceptions***

SOURCE: National Center for Educational Statistics. 2005. NAEP question. Reprinted with permission.

Most children begin to walk unassisted at
a. 6–8 months.
b. 9–12 months. ← Overlapping options
c. 12–16 months. ←

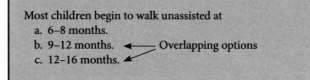

FIGURE 7.25 ***Item with Overlapping Options***

B, and D, three parts of the figure are shaded. In option A, however, the shaded parts are 3 of 7, not 3 of 4. In option D, 3 of 4 parts are shaded; however, the shaded parts are not of equal size. These options, then, provide information about the partial knowledge that students have and implications for additional instruction on fractions.

Develop Reasonable Options In writing the options, develop as many plausible ones as you can, but make sure none are preposterous. Sometimes, in an effort to generate the typical four or five options, teachers come up with absurd options that no one would ever choose. These provide no useful information about student thinking and increase the reading load. Research indicates that three options (i.e., two plausible distracters and one right answer) are adequate for multiple-choice items (Haladyna, 2004). Another important consideration is that the choices are independent; that is, the choices should not overlap (Figure 7.25).

If you use *None of the above* and *All of the above*, do so carefully. A problem with this format is that for a four-option item, if two options are correct, the test-wise student knows to select *All of the above*. This is so even if the student does not know whether the third option is correct. Another concern with *None of the above* and *All of the above* is that teachers tend to include these options only when they are the correct answer. If you use these options as the correct answers, you should also use them as distracters in some items. We suggest that you use *All of the above* and *None of the above* sparingly.

Arrange Multiple-Choice Options in a Logical Order Once developed, the options should be arranged in a logical order (e.g., alphabetically, numerically, chronologically,

	Charcoal	Carbon Dioxide
Formula	C	CO_2
State at Room Temperature	Solid	Gas
Soluble in Water	No	Yes
Combustible in Air	Yes	No

14. Based on the information in the table above, which is a reasonable hypothesis regarding elements and their compounds?
    A) An element retains its physical and chemical properties when it is combined into a compound.
    B) When an element reacts to form a compound, its chemical properties are changed but its physical properties are not.
    C) When an element reacts to form a compound, its physical properties are changed but its chemical properties are not.
    D) Both the chemical and physical properties of a compound are different from the properties of the elements of which it is composed.*

FIGURE 7.26   *Example of a Science Multiple-Choice Item with Options Arranged Shortest to Longest*

SOURCE: National Center for Educational Statistics. 2005. NAEP question. Reprinted with permission.

shortest to longest). The options are ordered from shortest to longest in the interpretive exercise from twelfth-grade NAEP science shown in Figure 7.26.

Arranging items in numerical order is another helpful strategy. In the eighth-grade mathematics item in Figure 7.27, the options for the interpretive exercise have been arranged in numerical order. If students know an answer, we want them to be able to select it and move on. Little is gained if students spend time searching through a set of options for an answer. A student who knows that the answer is 1.4 will select the response and quickly move to the next problem.

For ease of reading, options should be listed in one column or in a single row. As you see in Figure 7.28, teachers at times will incorrectly format the answer options into two columns. A student could easily understand that he lives in North America and, if a teacher has students record their answers on a separate answer sheet, the student might record a "b." A teacher might inaccurately interpret the student's response to mean the student does not even know the continent on which he lives. In actuality, the formatting of the options likely confused the student. Thus, options should be listed in one column or arranged in a single row.

You might wonder if ordering options in a logical manner makes a difference. A history teacher shared with us that his students noticed when he started organizing options logically. At the beginning of a test, students asked the teacher whether there was a pattern to the answers. When the teacher told his class he arranged the choices in alphabetical order and by length of answer, the students looked at him a bit astonished. They appeared a little surprised at the amount of thought and effort that had gone into making the test. Perhaps the greatest advantage of arranging options in logical order is that it conveys to students that you are not trying to trick them with a confusing order for the answers.

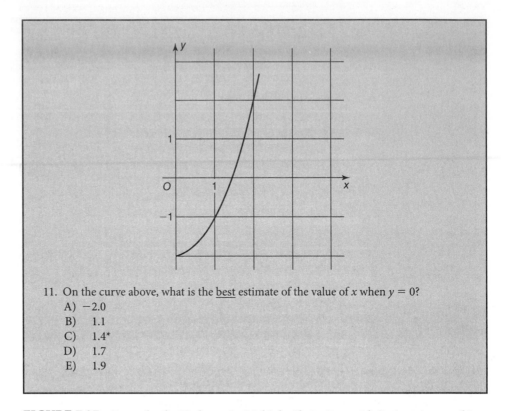

11. On the curve above, what is the <u>best</u> estimate of the value of x when $y = 0$?
    A) −2.0
    B)   1.1
    C)   1.4*
    D)   1.7
    E)   1.9

FIGURE 7.27   *Example of a Mathematics Multiple-Choice Item with Options Arranged in Numerical Order*

SOURCE: National Center for Educational Statistics. 2005. NAEP question. Reprinted with permission.

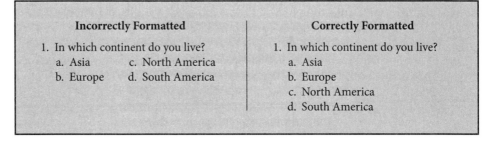

Incorrectly Formatted	Correctly Formatted
1. In which continent do you live?	1. In which continent do you live?
a. Asia c. North America	a. Asia
b. Europe d. South America	b. Europe
	c. North America
	d. South America

FIGURE 7.28   *Example of Incorrect and Correct Arrangement of Options for a Multiple-Choice Item*

Avoid Providing Clues to the Answer   In writing multiple-choice items, avoid providing clues to the answer. For example, use of the article *an* can lead a student to ignore any options that begin with consonants. As shown in Figure 7.29, use of "a(n)" can eliminate this type of grammatical clue. Similarly, to rule out an option, teachers sometimes add the qualifier *always* or *never*. Students soon learn that such absolutes are rarely true and quickly eliminate such choices.

Another habit in item writing is the tendency to make the correct response the longest response, as was the case in Figure 7.26. Students who are test-wise will pick up on this tendency and use it when they must guess an answer. To avoid this problem, some authors recommend keeping options about the same length. Another possibility

8. A living thing that uses the energy from the sun to make its own food is a(n) _____.
   A) bird
   B) frog
   C) insect
   D) tree*

FIGURE 7.29   *Example of an Item That Avoids Grammar Clues*

1. Type casting usually involves _____.
   A. playing a part similar to oneself*
   B. having a young actor play an old person
   C. the director casting himself/herself in the play
   D. playing a character totally different from one's own personality

FIGURE 7.30   *SCAAP Theater Item with Options Arranged from Short to Long*
SOURCE: South Carolina Arts Assessment Program (SCAAP). 2002. Reprinted with permission.

12. A green tree frog lives in a forest. How does the frog's green color help it to survive?
    A) By keeping the frog cool
    B) By helping the frog find other frogs
    C) By allowing the frog to make its own food
    D) By making the frog hard to see when sitting on leaves*

FIGURE 7.31   *Example of an NAEP Science Item That Avoids Giving Clues to the Answer*
SOURCE: National Center for Educational Statistics. 2005. NAEP question. Reprinted with permission.

is to follow our previous recommendation to arrange options that are phrases or complete sentences from shortest to longest, as you see in Figure 7.30. If you do so, you will quickly notice if the correct answer is typically last, and you can revise some options.

Another clue to an answer can occur when a teacher includes a distracter that is silly or outrageous. Quick elimination of that choice enables students to zero in on the plausible answers. Our previous discussion on the inappropriate use of humor during an assessment also recommends against using ridiculous distracters.

Finally, teachers sometimes repeat a word from the stem in the correct option. The fourth-grade science item from NAEP, shown in Figure 7.31, shows an instance where the writers avoided this mistake. If the writers had written option D as "By making the frog hard to see when sitting on green leaves," the student would have been directed to the answer because "green" would appear in both the stem and the answer. To avoid giving clues to items, attend to issues of grammar, qualifiers (e.g., all, none), lengthy choice options, implausible distracters, and repetition of words in the stem and the correct response.

True-False Format

Guidelines specific to writing true-false items are shown in Table 7.3. In this section, we discuss these guidelines and provide examples of their application.

TABLE 7.3
Guidelines for Writing True-False Items
Use interpretive material to develop true-false items that span the cognitive levels.
In writing a true-false item, you should not mix partially true with partially false statements.
Balance the number of items that are true and the items that are false.
Avoid providing clues that involve the use of qualifiers.

Develop True-False Items That Span the Range of Cognitive Levels   Use of interpretive material can raise the cognitive level of an item from remember to apply or analyze. Figure 7.32 shows an example. In item 8, for example, the student will need to balance the equations before answering true or false. Such thinking requires students to *apply* the procedures for balancing chemical equations.

Avoid True-False Items That Are Partially True and Partially False   In writing a true-false item, you should not mix partly true with partly false statements. In Figure 7.33, the first part of the statement is true (Foxes are carnivores); however, the second part of the statement (that serve as decomposers in a food chain) is false, because foxes are consumers. Your students are left with a dilemma. If they mark the item as true, and you count their response wrong, then the students' grades might not reflect their knowledge of carnivores. True-false statements should be all true or all false.

Balance the Number of True and False Items   As you develop items, you should make sure you balance the number of items that are true and the number of items that are false. However, people who do not know an answer tend to use the true response, so it can be beneficial to use slightly more false than true statements.

Use the following chemical equation to answer items 6–9. Circle T if the statement is true and F if the statement is false.

$$NaOH + H_2SO_4 \rightarrow Na_2SO_4 + H_2O$$

6. T* F   Water is one product of this chemical reaction.
7. T F*   Sodium sulfate is a reagent in this chemical equation.
8. T F*   The balanced equation will have 8 oxygen atoms.
9. T* F   The same elements will be present in the balanced equation.

FIGURE 7.32   *Example of the Use of Interpretive Material to Assess Higher-Order Cognitive Skills with True-False Items*

T F*   Foxes are carnivores that serve as decomposers in a food chain.

FIGURE 7.33   *TF Item That Is Partially True and Partially False*

TABLE 7.4

Guidelines for Writing Matching Items

The premises and responses should be arranged in a logical order (e.g., alphabetically, numerically, chronologically).

Matching items should be arranged on the same page.

Use no more matching items than 10 to 15 for older students and 5 to 6 items for younger students.

To avoid giving clues to an answer, make the options homogeneous.

Limit guessing by using answers more than once or having more answers than premises so that students cannot get items correct through the process of elimination.

Avoid Providing Clues to the Answer   As with multiple-choice items, the use of qualifiers (e.g., none, all) cue students that the statement is likely false because few rules, guidelines, or concepts are appropriately described in such absolute terms. Thus, the statement *All bodies that orbit the sun are called "planets."* gives a clue to students that any exception to this general statement makes it false.

Matching Items

Guidelines for writing matching items are shown in Table 7.4. In this section, we discuss these guidelines and examine examples of their application.

Arrange Matching Options in a Logical Order   The premises and responses should be arranged in a logical order (e.g., alphabetically, numerically, chronologically). Consider a matching exercise in which a student is to match significant historical events with the major figures involved with each. Ordering the list of historical figures alphabetically by name will assist the student in locating the appropriate person associated with an event and then moving to the next event. You may be inclined to say, "I want my students to search out the material; so it makes sense to jumble the names instead of alphabetizing them." But recall our introductory guiding thought suggesting that students should miss an item only if they do not know the answer. If students miss an item because they had difficulty finding the answer in a long, jumbled list of names, we do not know what they actually understand.

Also, matching items should be arranged on a single page so students do not have to flip back and forth between pages when answering the items. When considering the number of matching items, you should limit yourself to no more than 10 to 15 per exercise if you teach older students. For elementary students, you should use a maximum of 5 or 6 items. Also, in the directions prior to the matching items, state whether each answer option is to be used once or if options are used more than once.

Avoid Providing Clues to the Answer   To avoid providing clues for matching items, you should make the responses homogeneous. In Figure 7.6 the answers are all general categories of organisms associated with a food chain. The premises are all specific instances of organisms in a food chain. Thus, the response options of consumers, decomposers, and producers are all plausible answers for the premises.

Another method to avoid clues is to use the answers more than once or have more answers than premises. Having a limited number of answers means each will be used several times. Thus, students cannot use the process of elimination and save an item they are unsure of to see which response is left and must be the correct answer. For example, in Figure 7.5, the answer "meter" might be used for both "length of the playground" and "the height of a house." Having more answers than premises will also prevent the process of elimination from providing the right answer. Getting matching items right by the process of elimination violates the guiding thought at the beginning of the chapter that students should get items correct only if they know the material, not because they find clues to guide them to the right answer.

As was true for multiple-choice and true-false items, the use of interpretive material can raise the cognitive level of an item from lower cognitive levels (e.g., knowledge) to higher ones. As Figure 7.34 shows, a student must remember the value of each coin and then combine the values of the coins to come to the total.

Put the letter of the correct numerical amount in the blank to the left of each row of coins.
1.______
2.______
3.______
4.______
5.______
a. .50
b. .75
c. $1.00

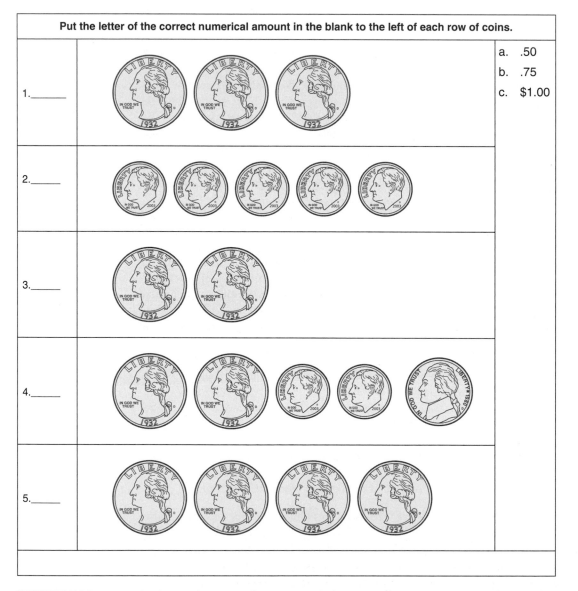

FIGURE 7.34 ***Example of a Matching Item That Engages Students in Cognitive Skills at the Understanding Level or Higher***

→ PITFALLS TO AVOID: TOP CHALLENGES IN DESIGNING SELECTED-RESPONSE ITEMS

We next highlight critical guidelines often overlooked by teachers. The first type of challenge relates to focusing on trivia in our test items. The fix is to address important content tied to the learning goals. For this guideline, contrast the item in the Poor Design column with the item in the Better Design column in Figure 7.35.

In the novel, *A Wrinkle in Time,* Calvin O'Keefe *does* have red hair. However, focusing on such minor details trivializes students' experience in reading a book about the theme of conformity. In this book, Madeleine L'Engle (1962) describes a society in which the citizens have the same type of house and yard and act the same as their peers. Everything happens in rhythm. As some children bounce their balls, the skipping ropes of others hit the sidewalks—in *perfect* rhythm. In this town, mothers simultaneously appear at the doors of their identical houses to call their children in from play. L'Engle uses this scene to convey a powerful message about conformity that you would want students to understand as a key part of using the book to address your learning goals.

Take a moment to contrast the two items accompanying the second common error of writing items—requiring students only to remember facts. To fix this problem we must use items at higher levels of cognition. The item in the Better Design column reminds us that with the use of interpretive material (e.g., music, stories, diagrams), we can write items that assess more complex cognitive skills. Also remember that interpretive material can be combined with matching and true-false items to require application of higher-level cognitive skills. Again, we must emphasize that it is appropriate to require students to analyze materials in an assessment only if instruction and learning activities engaged students in similar forms of analysis.

The third difficult challenge is writing good distracters. Sometimes you will find it easy to design a good question and the answer for it, but thinking of plausible distracters is difficult. Sometimes the ones you design will be easy to eliminate because they are not plausible (e.g., using recent popular songs as choices for the national anthem). Other times they may be too complicated or confusing, or they overlap with the correct answer. We suggest you concentrate on designing two clear distracters that can give you insight into student thinking rather than generating three or four just to have a larger number for students to choose from.

To avoid the poor-design issues associated with the last common error in Figure 7.35, you should follow the conventions of written language. Notice that the options in the poor example are complete statements, yet they do not have correct capitalization or punctuation. This focus on the conventions of language is not just an idiosyncratic quirk of ours. Recall that use of ALL CAPS makes reading more difficult and might contribute to reader fatigue. Students also see the conventions of language modeled when we use appropriate grammar and correctly capitalize and punctuate items.

→ CONSTRUCTING THE ASSESSMENT

Having followed all the guidelines for writing items, you are now ready to organize them into a test. As Table 7.5 shows, the first step you should take is to prepare test directions. Be sure to indicate how students are to respond to items. Are they to transfer their answers to an answer sheet? Writing answers on an answer sheet should be reserved for older students because young students may make mistakes in transferring their answers. You should also provide new directions for each type of item format

Common Errors	Poor Design	Fixes	Better Design
Focusing on trivia	5. In *A Wrinkle in Time*, what was the color of Calvin's hair? a. Black b. Blond c. Brown d. Red*	**Address important content**	5. Which theme is developed in *A Wrinkle in Time* when the children visit Camazotz? a. Ambition b. Conformity* c. Truth
Requiring students only to remember facts	8. A limerick is a a. 3-line poem about nature. b. 5-line poem about something funny.* c. 9-line poem that describes a person.	**Incorporate higher levels of cognitive skills**	**Use the following poem to answer items 8–11.** There once were some very naughty cats Who gave chase to some terrified rats. The rats grew tired, And a bull dog they hired. Now the chase is on for the cats! 8. The above poem is a a. cinquain. b. haiku. c. limerick.*
Using implausible or confusing distracters	What is the national anthem of the United States? a. No Air b. Dream Big c. Stop and Stare d. The Star-Spangled Banner*	**Use plausible distracters**	What is the national anthem of the United States? a. America, The Beautiful b. God Bless America c. The Star-Spangled Banner* d. This Land Is Your Land
Ignoring the conventions of written language in formatting items	4. Annette completes an experiment in which she applies different amounts of fertilizer to her tomato plants. She applies one scoop of fertilizer to one plant, two scoops to the second plant, and three scoops to the third. During the growing season she records the weight of tomatoes she harvests from each plant. Which of the following is true? A. the fertilizer is a control variable B. the experiment lacks an independent variable C. the weight of the tomatoes is the dependent variable*	**Apply the conventions of written language**	4. Annette completes an experiment in which she applies different amounts of fertilizer to her tomato plants. She applies one scoop of fertilizer to one plant, two scoops to the second plant, and three scoops to the third. During the growing season she records the weight of tomatoes she harvests from each plant. Which of the following is true? A. The fertilizer is a control variable. B. The experiment lacks an independent variable. C. The weight of the tomatoes is the dependent variable.*

**Sample question from Naturalization Self-Test at www.uscis.gov

FIGURE 7.35 *Common Errors in Designing Selected-Response Items*

TABLE 7.5

Guidelines for Constructing the Assessment

Prepare test directions that tell students how to answer the items and the number of points each item is worth.

Provide new directions for each type of item format (e.g., multiple-choice, matching, essay).

Order items from the easiest format to the most difficult.

Load the beginning of each section of the test with easier items to lower the anxiety level of students.

Place items in the test so that you do not have patterns in correct answers (AABBCCAA).

Vary the location of the right answer so that the correct answer is fairly evenly distributed across the options.

(e.g., multiple-choice, matching, essay). For example, at the beginning of a group of matching items, you should tell students whether each answer is used only once. In the directions for each section, you also should specify the number of points that each item is worth. For example, will multiple-choice items be worth 5 points each and an essay question 15 points? Imagine a student's surprise to find out that in hurriedly writing a response to an essay question, she missed 10 of 15 points, lowering her grade on the test. If the student had known the importance of the essay question, and the number of points associated with it, perhaps she would have appropriately allocated her time.

In formatting your assessment, order items from the easiest format to the most difficult. A possible order would be true-false, matching, multiple choice, short answer, then essays. Also, group similarly formatted questions together. Put your true-false items together, the multiple-choice items together, etc. If items switch from matching to true-false and back to matching, followed by multiple choice and culminating with more true-false, the student is likely to be committing cognitive resources to switching between formats instead of using those resources for addressing the concepts and principles addressed by the assessment.

Because students are fairly sensitive to knowing whether they answered an item correctly, you should load the beginning of each section of the test with easier items to lower the anxiety level of students. Sometimes people who develop tests spiral the items by difficulty. They format the test so it begins with an easier item, moves to a harder item, provides another harder item, then returns to an easier item, moving again through the progression of easier to harder. Why do they do this? We have administered standardized tests of reading achievement to individual students in which the items strictly moved from easy to hard and did not spiral by level of difficulty. In taking the test, a student reads a passage, then states the answer to a question. The examiner terminates the test when the student misses five items in a row. Requiring students to continue answering items when they knew they were not able to answer them was hard for both the students and us. Had the test developers spiraled the items, the occasional easy item would present students with some success and perhaps bolster their performance as they progressed through the test.

Selected-response items should be placed in the test so the items do not have patterns in correct answers (e.g., A A B B C C or T T F T T F). You also should vary the location of the right answer according to the number of choices. You should have roughly the same number of correct answers that are associated with the options A, B, C, and D. Test-wise students quickly pick up on patterns and recognize, for example, when a teacher rarely uses option A. Or, test-wise students quickly grasp when a teacher uses a repeating answer pattern to make grading easier. When a student gets an item correct, it should be because the student knows the answer, not because we gave clues.

→ THE VALUE OF STUDENT-GENERATED ITEMS AND CRITICAL THINKING

If you teach students in upper-elementary grades or higher, consider involving students in the development of some items. This idea is not as farfetched as it may seem initially. Such a practice is consistent with math exercises in which students are given a number sentence and then asked to give an example of a story that fits the problem. Such tasks allow students to practice the skill of establishing a problem consistent with a mathematics operation.

In one of our classes, a kindergarten teacher shared her experience in writing multiple-choice items with her students. Students helped in formulating the wording of some of the questions for a life science unit on the characteristics of organisms. In one instance, the teacher could not decide if she should use the word "regurgitate" or the words "cough up" to tell how the mother penguin feeds the baby. As we discussed earlier, difficult-to-read test items should not be used because they can interfere with students' expression of their knowledge in science, social studies, or mathematics. The teacher addressed the issue of readability by involving her kindergarten students in the selection of key terms for inclusion in the multiple-choice items. In the case of the penguin example, the children voted, and the word "regurgitate" was the one they wanted included. The teacher indicated that the involvement of her kindergarteners in developing the questions gave them ownership. In addition, to reduce reading demands for her kindergarteners, the teacher administered the assessment orally.

Involving students in designing items offers the potential to deepen their understanding of the learning goals that are the focus of the assessment. For example, as students in social studies learn to write interpretive exercises that use graphs to show trends, the students also begin to understand the manner in which they should approach a line graph in an interpretive exercise on a test they are taking. The possibility also exists that students will begin to look at items in published tests in a more analytic manner. Thus, a skill you have taught and assessed in your classroom may generalize to other testing situations. Engaging students analytically also assists them in acquiring the ability to think critically—an important skill for citizens in a democracy.

Student development of items will also help you understand their depth of knowledge and their misconceptions. For example, we have worked with our teaching assistants to develop tests for our undergraduate courses in assessment. Our teaching assistants, who are advanced doctoral students, follow the item-writing guidelines in preparing items for a test; however, their initial items focus on less-important concepts and skills than those we consider to be key ideas. This item-writing experience gives us insights into our teaching assistants' grasp of the concepts. Also, if a student has marked the wrong option as the answer, or cannot develop an item related to the learning goals, you have information about concepts the student has not mastered.

Writing selected-response items is a complex task; so if you plan to involve students in writing items, you should model the skill of item writing. At first your students' items are likely to require only remembering of factual knowledge. However, if you model for students the construction of an interpretive exercise, they can begin to develop items that require analysis or application. A group activity might involve students analyzing some well-written examples and differentiating them from problematic items. Then students should practice writing items in small groups and, ultimately, begin writing items on their own.

The items students develop can be used for formative purposes and used as practice for a summative assessment. However, you should not use student items on a summative test because at least some already know the correct answer; therefore, they would not have to use higher thinking skills to answer. Also, errors students made in writing items may make the item unclear to their peers. Another reason for not using student-developed items in a summative test is that students will have unequal access to the answers to the items. As they write their items, students will likely share them with their friends, so some students will have seen several of the items and other students will have seen few of the items.

→ ACCOMMODATIONS FOR DIVERSE LEARNERS: SELECTED-RESPONSE ITEMS

Individual teachers, as well as state testing programs, have developed a multitude of methods in which diverse student needs can be accommodated to help ensure that the performance of students on an examination depends only on their understanding of the content the examination measures. In this section we consider methods for accommodating (i.e., differentiating) assessments that use selected-response items to gauge student attainment of learning goals. We examine each of the student considerations first described in Chapter 3 and then discuss appropriate accommodations for them related to the selected-response formats presented in this chapter.

Students with Fine Motor Difficulties

Circling the letter of an answer or filling in a bubble might provide challenges for those with disabilities related to fine motor skills. As shown in Table 7.6, possible accommodations for students with fine motor difficulties might include allowing the student to state the answer response with someone else recording the response. Another option is for the student to complete the test on the computer if assistive devices are available.

Students with Sensory Challenges

Students with visual impairments might benefit from enhancing the legibility of the printed test material. For example, use of large-font type or Braille might be required. Students with auditory challenges might benefit from having the test directions signed.

Students Learning English

For students who are learning English, the challenge presented is the reading load associated with the selected-response items in a test. You should consider limiting the reading demands by using plain language. Writing a test in plain language requires a teacher to reduce wordiness and use common words. The teacher should avoid ambiguous language, irregularly spelled words, proper names, and irregular naming conventions. The teacher also should arrange headings and graphics to clarify the importance of information and the order for reviewing the information.

TABLE 7.6

Accommodation Considerations for Selected-Response Items

Issue	Type of Accommodation
Difficulty with fine motor skills	• Allow oral answers to questions. • Allow use of computer.
Sensory challenges (e.g., visual, auditory)	• Provide signing of oral directions for students with auditory impairments. • Enhance legibility. • Limit use of graphics to only those that contain information being assessed. • Use large print or Braille for visual impairments.
Learning English	• Provide task directions in student's first language and in English. • Limit reading demands by using plain language. • Allow use of bilingual dictionaries. • Use visual cues. • Use alternate choice items.
Learning goal already mastered	• Use interpretive exercises to engage student at the analysis and application levels of cognition.
Difficulty focusing attention	• Repeat directions. • Use alternate-choice items rather than multiple choice. • Enhance legibility. • Present one item per page. • Highlight critical information in the test directions. • Teach student to highlight critical material in the test. • Reduce distractibility by limiting graphics to only those that contain information being assessed. • Include frequent breaks. • Administer test individually or in a small group. • Extend testing time.
Literacy skills below those of typical peers (e.g., learning disability)	• Limit reading demands by using plain language. • Use visual cues. • Enhance legibility. • Use readers or audiotapes to administer the directions and items, except in the case of a reading test. • Highlight critical information in the test directions. • Teach student to highlight critical material in the test. • Extend time for completing task.
Lack of familiarity with school culture	• Use plain language. • Use visual cues.

Visual cues in the form of photographs and graphics might provide information that clarifies the meaning of the text for students who are learning English. These students might also benefit from the use of bilingual dictionaries if the assessment is focused on areas other than reading. Several teachers we know with experience with English language learners also suggest that students learning English sometimes respond more positively to written language when it is presented one sentence at a time rather than in a continuous paragraph. The teacher should also consider use of alternate-choice items to reduce the reading load.

Students Who Have Already Mastered the Learning Goals

One reason for including interpretive exercises in a test is to challenge students who have mastered the basics in a subject area. A bad solution is to give these students *more* items. Students who are quick learners enjoy a challenge; however, they do not perceive doing more of the same as a challenge.

Students Who Have Difficulty Focusing Attention

Students who have difficulty focusing their attention are likely to benefit from accommodations that limit the amount of information that a student must filter in answering a question. For example, a teacher can enhance a student's focus by highlighting critical information in test directions and teaching the student to highlight important material in the test items.

A student's ability to focus can be improved by enhancing legibility of the test items. As discussed in Chapter 3, legibility can be improved, for example, by using left-justified text and standard uppercase and lowercase type, rather than *italics* or ALL CAPS, and by using only a few words per line (Thompson & Thurlow, 2002). Use of blank space anchors the text on the paper. Thus, presenting only one item per page or administering one item at a time might enhance a student's ability to focus. Students who face challenges in focusing also are likely to benefit from having frequent breaks, individual administration of the test, and extension of the testing time.

Students with Literacy Skills Below Those of Typical Peers

As with students who are learning English, the reading load of a selected-response test presents challenges to students whose literacy skills are below those of their peers. These students also will benefit from the use of plain language, visual cues, and enhanced legibility. Oral administration of the test directions and items might assist a student in showing understanding in subject areas such as history or science. Oral administration of a reading test, however, changes a reading comprehension test to a receptive language test; therefore, thoughtful consideration is required for you to decide what you are testing. If you are assessing concepts about social studies, an oral administration of the test will not influence your interpretation of scores in terms of social studies concepts.

Also consider teaching students with challenges in the area of literacy to highlight critical information in test directions and items. Such an accommodation will likely require an extension of testing time.

Students Who Lack Familiarity with School Culture

For students with a lack of familiarity with school culture, performance on a test with selected-response items will benefit from the use of plain language. In addition, student understanding will benefit from visual cues that clarify the meaning of the text or the intent of the test item.

→ CASE STUDY APPLICATION

In discussing Maria Mensik's English unit on utopias and dystopias, she notes that her learning goals go beyond the knowledge level and so her assessments require application, analysis, synthesis, and even a little evaluation (refer to Table 2.16). With goals that require analytic thought (e.g., compare and contrast), Maria includes selected-response items that go beyond knowledge and engage students in analysis. Maria uses interpretive exercises to provide material for her students to analyze within the context of utopias and dystopias. For example, as shown in Figure 7.36, students read brief statements made by imaginary people and indicate whether the statement is consistent with living in a utopian or dystopian society. Notice that the items use a matching format in which students select "U" for utopias and "D" for dystopias. Also notice that by using statements (i.e., interpretive material) for her students to analyze, Maria engages students in categorizing the statements according to utopian and dystopian characteristics, such as the role of the individual and the role of government.

Maria's assessment reminds us of one other key issue relating to instruction and assessment. Assessment must follow instruction. This means that this type of analytic exercise had to be part of instruction prior to being used to assess students' understanding of utopias and dystopias. Use of the statements as interpretive material allows Maria to determine whether students understand the characteristics of utopian and dystopian societies and can apply them when reviewing various narrative forms. Prior to the assessment, students must have practice in classifying literary works into descriptions of these two forms of society. They gain practice in discussing the films that were part of instruction. Perhaps they pretend to be a citizen in a utopian society and write about their daily life in their journals. On another day they might write from the point of view of a citizen in a dystopian society. Using the types of items shown in Figure 7.36 would be inappropriate if a teacher uses lecture and reading and omits opportunities for analyzing whether given scenarios or literary selections were primarily utopian or dystopian.

Read the following statements made by imaginary people. Based on what we have learned about the characteristics of utopian and dystopian societies and literature, decide if the imaginary person lives in a utopia or dystopia.

If the imaginary person lives in a utopia, circle U.

If the imaginary person lives in a dystopia, circle D.

U* D   Hiking in the great outdoors is what I like to do with my free time. Not only do I enjoy its beauty, but I also feel like I can really learn a lot from nature.

U D*   As the mayor of our town, I'm pleased to report that crime has dropped considerably, largely due to the fact that our police can now monitor every portion of our city with real-time video surveillance.

FIGURE 7.36   *A Set of Items That Uses an Alternative Matching Format*

Key Chapter Points

In this chapter we described three forms of selected-response items: multiple-choice, true-false, and matching. We presented three types of multiple-choice items: conventional multiple-choice, alternate-choice, and complex multiple-choice. We next discussed that multiple-choice items should be used when your instructional unit covers a broad array of facts, concepts, and strategies. We noted that critics of multiple-choice items argue this item format assesses students' ability to remember facts. We emphasized, however, that multiple-choice items can assess cognitive skills of analysis and application.

In the section on true-false items, we described the typical true-false item and the multiple true-false item. True-false items allow a teacher to assess a broad range of facts, concepts, and other material covered in a unit; however, guessing can be a problem with this item form.

In the section on matching items, we first discussed the item format: premises (e.g., statements or question phrases) in the left-hand column and answers (i.e., responses) in the right-hand column. Matching allows you to assess a broad range of facts and concepts associated with your learning goals (as is true of multiple-choice and true-false items). Although criticized for assessing only recall of facts, matching items can assess analysis and application.

In the next section we described interpretive exercises. In an interpretive exercise, a selected-response item is preceded by material that a student must interpret to answer the question. Examples of interpretive material include reading passages, diagrams, graphs, timelines, and reproductions of paintings. This type of selected-response item allows a teacher to assess students' ability to apply, analyze, and evaluate factual, conceptual, and procedural knowledge. Interpretive material can be used in combination with matching, true-false, and multiple-choice formats.

We then provided general guidelines for writing items. We stated that items *should* (a) assess important content across the range of cognitive levels, (b) follow the conventions of written language, and (c) portray the diversity of your classroom. Items *should not* require advanced reading skills (unless you are assessing reading), introduce bias, or attempt humor. Subsequently we discussed item-writing guidelines for each of the specific formats. We next reexamined critical guidelines that teachers often overlook in designing items such as focusing on important content across the range of cognitive levels.

We next presented guidelines for constructing the assessment, including directions, point values, and beginning the test and each section with easier items. In the section on student-generated items, we discussed the benefit of teaching students to develop selected-response items. In the section on diverse learners, we reviewed issues to consider in developing tests with selected-response items. In the last section of the chapter, we examined Maria's case study for lessons about selected-response items. In the next two chapters we discuss forms of assessment that complement selected-response items.

Helpful Websites

http://nces.ed.gov/nationsreportcard/
A website with items from the National Assessment of Educational Progress (NAEP). Includes items in the subject areas of civics, economics, geography, mathematics, reading, science, United States history, and writing. All NAEP questions in this chapter come from this website.
http://www.scaap.ed.sc.edu/
A website with sample selected-response items for the South Carolina Arts Assessment Programs. Arts areas assessed include dance, music, theater, and the visual arts. SCAAP art questions in this chapter come from this website.

CHAPTER REVIEW QUESTIONS

1. What are the similarities between conventional multiple-choice, alternate multiple-choice, and interpretive exercises? What are the differences between these item formats?
2. Revisit the NAEP item in Figure 7.7. Write the options for the question "What was the high temperature for City 1?" Why did you select those options?
3. Review the NAEP item about graphs in Figure 7.11. How might we edit the item to make it more simple to read?
4. In the NAEP item about the Sinaguan culture in Figure 7.18, could you argue that the photograph is not needed to answer the question? Explain.
5. In the graphing item from NAEP shown in Figure 7.27, why is Option A a plausible distracter?
6. Put the following countries and continents in the selected-response format that you would use to assess whether students could link these continents and countries.
   Continents: Asia, Europe, Africa, South America
   Countries: Brazil, Spain, Uganda, Korea, England, Sudan

Use the following item from the fourth-grade NAEP History Assessment to answer questions 7 and 8.

---

3. Indentured servants were different from slaves because indentured servants
   A) came from the West Indies
   B) were freed at the end of their term
   C) were paid less money
   D) did much easier work

Source: National Center for Educational Statistics (2005). NAEP question.

7. Which item-writing guidelines were followed in developing this item?
8. Which item-writing guidelines were NOT followed in developing this item?
9. A student in your class has difficulty focusing on tasks. What type of accommodations may be helpful when assessing this student?
10. Design an interpretive exercise with at least two questions based on content addressing a learning goal in your area. Be creative about choosing the interpretive material on which the questions are based.
11. Explain why it is important to use new examples that students haven't seen before when designing selected-response items. How does this practice differ from including items whose content is not addressed in the learning goals or instruction?

REFERENCES

Buchanan, B. 2007. *Artist's statement.* Retrieved October 26, 2007 from http://www.beverlybuchanan.com/statement.html.

Clarke, N., S. Stow, C. Ruebling, and F. Kaynoa. 2006. Developing standards-based curricula and assessments: Lessons for the field. *The Clearing House* 79(6): 258–261.

Downing, S. M., R. A. Baranowski, L. J. Grosso, and J. R. Norcini. 1995. Item type and cognitive ability measured: The validity evidence for multiple true-false items in medical specialty certification. *Applied Measurement in Education* 8: 189–199.

Greenwald, E., H. Persky, J. Campbell, and J. Mazzeo. 1999. *The NAEP 1998 writing report card for the nation and the states* (NCES 1999–462). Washington, DC: U.S. Government Printing Office.

Haladyna, T. 2004. *Developing and validating multiple-choice test items*. 3rd ed. Hillsdale, Lawrence Erlbaum Associates.

Haladyna, T. M., and S. M. Downing. 1993. How many options is enough for a multiple-choice item? *Educational and Psychological Measurement* 53: 999–1010.

Haladyna, T., S. Downing, and M. Rodriguez. 2002. A review of multiple-choice item-writing guidelines for classroom assessment. *Applied Measurement in Education* 15(3): 309–334.

L'Engle, M. (1962). *A Wrinkle in Time*. New York, NY: Ferrar, Strauss, and Giroux.

Microsoft Office Word 2007. 2007. *Test your document's readability*. Redmond, WA: Author.

Myers, M., and P. D. Pearson. 1996. Performance assessment and the literacy unit of the New Standards Project. *Assessing Writing* 3(1): 5–29.

National Center for Educational Statistics. 2005. *NAEP questions*. Retrieved June 19, 2008 from http://nces.ed.gov/nationsreportcard/itmrls/.

Sanders, W., and P. Horn. 1995. Educational assessment reassessed. *Education Policy Analysis Archives* 3(6). Retrieved October 11, 2007 from http://epaa.asu.edu/epaa/v3n6.html.

South Carolina Arts Assessment Program (SCAAP). 2002. *Sample test*. Retrieved October 26, 2007 from http://www.scaap.ed.sc.edu/sampletest/.

South Carolina Department of Education. 2005. *South Carolina social studies academic standards*. Retrieved June 2, 2008 from http://ed.sc.gov/agency/offices/cso/standards/ss/.

Thompson, S., and M. Thurlow. 2002. *Universally designed assessments: Better tests for everyone!* NCEO Policy Directions No. 14. Minneapolis, MN: National Center on Educational Outcomes.

United States Holocaust Memorial Museum. 2007a. *Press Kit: Nazi persecution of homosexuals, 1933–1945*. Retrieved October 26, 2007 from http://www.ushmm.org/museum/press/kits/details.php?content=nazi_persecution_of_homosexuals&page=02-background.

United States Holocaust Memorial Museum. 2007b. Voyage of the Saint Louis. *Holocaust Encyclopedia*. Retrieved September 9, 2007 from http://www.ushmm.org/wlc/article.php?lang=en&ModuleId=10005267.

United States Holocaust Memorial Museum. 2007c. Wartime fate of the passengers of the St. Louis. *Holocaust Encyclopedia*. Retrieved September 9, 2007 from http://www.ushmm.org/wlc/article.php?lang=en&ModuleId=10005431.

Worthen, B., and V. Spandel. 1991. Putting the standardized test debate in perspective. *Educational Leadership* 48(5): 65–69.

Yap, C. 2005. *Technical documentation for the South Carolina Arts Assessment Project (SCAAP): Entry-level dance & theatre assessment field test 2005*. Columbia: University of South Carolina, Office of Program Evaluation.

Yap, C., M. Moore, and P. Peng. 2005. *Technical documentation for the South Carolina Arts Assessment Project (SCAAP) Year 3: 4th-grade music and visual arts assessments*. Columbia: University of South Carolina, Office of Program Evaluation.

CHAPTER 8

TEACHER-MADE ASSESSMENTS: SHORT ANSWER AND ESSAY

Many issues that confront individuals and society have no generally agreed-on answers. Yet understanding issues like these constitutes much of what is genuinely vital in education

–Robert M. Thorndike

❖ **Chapter Learning Goals**

At the conclusion of this chapter, the reader should be able to do the following:

- Describe the format and structure of two types of constructed-response items: short answer and essay.

- State the advantages and disadvantages of each type of constructed-response format and explain when they should be used.

- Apply general guidelines when writing constructed-response items across the range of cognitive skills, from remember to create.

- Format constructed-response items and arrange them in an assessment.

- Describe methods to involve students in the development of items.

- Describe ways to accommodate the constructed-response format for diverse learners.

✦ INTRODUCTION

The quote from Thorndike reminds us that many questions can be answered from more than one point of view. For many, a hallmark of a democratic society is the freedom to express diverse opinions. The ability to present an argument and to justify decisions are key skills. Thus, in assessing students' understanding of complex topics, at times you will want to use an assessment format that requires this range of thinking skills and allows students to express their understanding in their own words. **Constructed-response items,** such as short-answer items and essays, offer such a framework. This approach can be contrasted with selected-response items (see Chapter 7), which provide possible answers from which a student chooses.

We have observed firsthand the power of essays to engage students in critical thinking. In a unit on historical fiction, students in one of our sixth-grade classes read *Friedrich* (Richter, 1987), a novel about two friends, one a Jewish boy and the other a Christian boy, growing up during the rise of Nazism. The book portrays the different fates of the boys as they grew into their teens as the Nazi movement grew in power. Students also read *Sadako and the Thousand Paper Cranes* (Coerr, 1977), which related the story of a Japanese girl who developed leukemia from the fallout from the nuclear bomb dropped on Hiroshima. Students then wrote an essay in which they argued whether contemporary society visits such injustices on groups of people. Students' essays were graded not on the position they took but on their use of evidence to develop their argument. In grappling with an issue with no simple, generally agreed upon answer, the students worked on the critical skills necessary for participation in a democratic society.

✦ ALIGNING ITEMS WITH LEARNING GOALS AND THINKING SKILLS

In considering the use of constructed-response items for formative assessment or in a test, you first should review the learning goals and cognitive strategies that are the focus of your instruction. Constructed-response items will be useful in assessing student achievement of the learning goals associated with application, analysis, evaluation, and creation. For example, if one learning goal for students is to "Establish and use criteria for making judgments about works of art" (Ohio State Department of Education, 2003), then the assessment will require students to develop criteria and apply them in critiquing paintings or sculptures. The constructed-response format lends itself well to assessment of students' ability to engage in the cognitive process of evaluation.

✦ CONSTRUCTED-RESPONSE FORMATS

Three forms of constructed-response assessments are the short answer, the essay, and the performance task. In this chapter we focus on short-answer and essay forms. We discuss performance tasks in Chapter 9.

Short-Answer Formats

Short-Answer Items

Items that require students to supply short responses such as a single word, a phrase, or a few sentences.

Short-answer items take the form of a question or an incomplete statement. Student responses may be a single word, a phrase, or a few sentences. In Figure 8.1, the first item is written as a question. The second item is written as an incomplete statement and requires only a single-word response. The science item from NAEP shown in Figure 8.2 is an example of a short-answer item that requires students to write a few sentences.

When to Use the Short-Answer Format

The short-answer format can be used to assess student understanding of knowledge and concepts that can be expressed in brief form. Although student responses are short, this does not mean short-answer items assess only recall of information. Instead, short-answer items can assess the full range of student knowledge. Revisit the NAEP science item in Figure 8.2. To answer the question, students must analyze the diagram, think about methods for measuring volume, and supply their own answer.

Question Format:

What is the English translation of the following sentence?
Yo voy al parque.

Incomplete Statement Format:

Student Choices for Ice Cream
Number of Students
0
2
4
6
8
10
12
14
Vanilla
Chocolate
Strawberry
Ice Cream Flavors

The flavor of ice cream that the most students ordered was ________________.

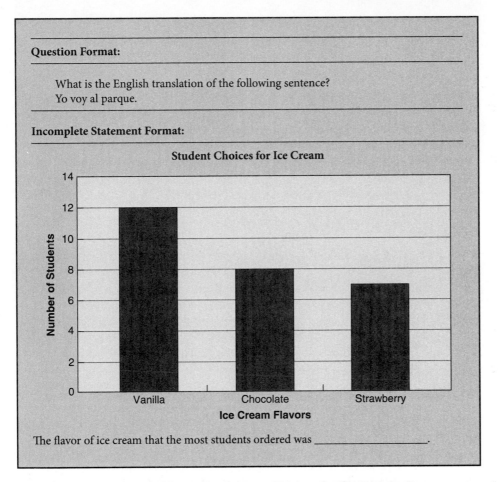

FIGURE 8.1 ***Question and Incomplete Statement Formats for Short-Answer Items***

Advantages and Disadvantages of the Short-Answer Format

A distinct advantage of short-answer items is that guessing contributes little to score error. Also, a test can include more short-answer items than is possible with longer essays or other performance tasks. Thus, a test can better sample a wide range of concepts and strategies associated with the learning goals of an instructional unit.

A disadvantage is that when you score a short-answer item, you must judge each response as correct or incorrect. Many of the student responses will include exactly the information you are looking for. Some responses, however, will have some variation that you must decide is correct or not. An example is the listing of possible answers shown in Figure 8.3 to the question posed in Figure 8.2. The need to make a judgment will add to the amount of time it takes to score responses. When grading 70 tests or more, you may very well find it difficult to remain consistent in judging variations. Later in this chapter we discuss some methods for avoiding such inconsistencies.

Essay Formats

Essay items consist of a stem (i.e., a **prompt**) that presents students with a question or task. This format requires students to organize information in formulating a response to the task or question. Some essay items limit the content of the answer and the form

Essay Items
Prompts that present students with a question or task that require a paragraph or more in response.

Prompt
The directions for an essay.

5. You are going to the park on a hot day and need to take some water with you. You have three different bottles, as shown in the picture below. You want to choose the bottle that will hold the most water. Explain how you can find out which bottle holds the most water.

FIGURE 8.2   *An Example of a Short-Answer Item from the Fourth-Grade NAEP Science Assessment*

SOURCE: National Center for Educational Statistics. 2005. NAEP question. Reprinted with permission.

Complete

Student demonstrates an understanding of how to measure and compare the volumes of three different bottles by outlining a method for finding which bottle holds the most water.

  a. The bottles are filled with water and the water is measured in a graduated cylinder, measuring cup, or other measuring device to see which bottle holds the most water.
  b. Using a displacement method, each bottle is filled with water. Then placing each bottle into a measured volume of water, the amount of displaced water is measured. The bottle displacing the most water has the greatest volume.
  c. Filling one bottle with water and pouring it into the other bottles, the one that holds the most water can be determined.
  d. Weighing the bottles with and without water, the bottle that holds the greatest weight in water can be determined.
  e. Student fills each bottle at the same constant rate to determine which takes longest to fill.

FIGURE 8.3   *Possible Complete Answers for the Short-Answer Item from the Fourth-Grade NAEP Science Assessment (Figure 8.2)*

SOURCE: National Center for Educational Statistics. 2005. NAEP question. Reprinted with permission.

Question 13 is based on the situation described below.

Teresia is a small country that has been invaded by its neighbor Corollia. The king of Teresia is a long-standing United States ally who has been living in exile since the Corollian invasion. Teresia is an important exporter of uranium; it sends most of its supply to members of the European Union. The king appeals to the United States and the United Nations for military help in driving Corollia from his country.

13. Identify two pieces of information NOT given above that you would need before you could decide whether or not the United States military should help Teresia. Explain why each piece of information would be important.

1)

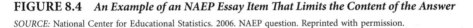

_____

_____

_____

_____

2)

_____

_____

_____

_____

FIGURE 8.4 *An Example of an NAEP Essay Item That Limits the Content of the Answer*

SOURCE: National Center for Educational Statistics. 2006. NAEP question. Reprinted with permission.

of the response. In the eighth-grade NAEP civics item in Figure 8.4, the question is structured to limit the students' response to two types of information needed and a justification of the importance of that information.

In other instances, essays allow students to organize information to express their own ideas. For example, the essay prompt in Figure 8.5 establishes a purpose for the writer—that is, to persuade a friend that the writer's position on registering to vote is the right one. However, the intent of this task is to assess students' ability to build a persuasive argument, not to see if they can provide correct factual information. This essay allows flexibility for students in the choice of arguments and type of support provided for them.

When to Use the Essay Format

Writers in the field of assessment consistently state that essay items should not be used to assess students' ability to remember factual or conceptual knowledge (Hogan & Murphy, 2007). Rather, essay items should focus on assessing learning goals associated with developing ideas, organizing a logical argument, creating a plan of action, explaining a solution to a problem, or demonstrating original thinking.

Advantages and Disadvantages of the Essay Format

Essay items allow a teacher to assess students' ability to recall, organize, and synthesize concepts that were the focus of an instructional unit. Use of essays allows a teacher to complete an in-depth assessment of student learning for a limited scope of content. Look back at the essay question in Figure 8.4 related to United States involvement in

1. Your school is sponsoring a voter registration drive for 18-year-old high school students. You and three of your friends are talking about the project. Your friends say the following,

Friend 1: "I'm working on the young voters' registration drive. Are you going to come to it and register? You're all 18, so you can do it. We're trying to help increase the number of young people who vote and it shouldn't be too hard—I read that the percentage of 18- to 20-year-olds who vote increased in recent years. We want that percentage to keep going up."

Friend 2: "I'll be there. People should vote as soon as they turn 18. It's one of the responsibilities of living in a democracy."

Friend 3: "I don't know if people should even bother to register. One vote in an election isn't going to change anything."

Do you agree with friend 2 or 3? Write a response to your friends in which you explain whether you will or will not register to vote. Be sure to explain why and support your position with examples from your reading or experience. Try to convince the friend with whom you disagree that your position is the right one.

FIGURE 8.5 *An Example of a Persuasive Essay Item from the Twelfth-Grade NAEP Writing Assessment*

SOURCE: National Center for Educational Statistics. 2005. NAEP question. Reprinted with permission.

the conflict between Teresia and Corollia. In responding to the item in an essay format, the student must

1. Provide the additional information required for making decisions about involvement in conflicts.
2. Justify the importance of the required information.
3. Compose a brief answer.

A disadvantage of essays is that they assess less broadly than other formats, even though they probe in more depth. In a multiple-choice format, the student reviews the options with plausible types of information and justifications and selects an acceptable response. Most students can answer a multiple-choice item in about one minute. The essay in Figure 8.5, in contrast, will require between 15 and 30 minutes to compose. To balance the need for in-depth coverage of concepts with the need for broad sampling of ideas that are the focus of the learning goals, one option we recommend is to use both multiple-choice and essay items in a test.

✤ GUIDELINES FOR ITEM DEVELOPMENT

We now turn to guidelines for developing items in constructed-response formats. We begin with some general guidelines and then turn to specific guidelines related to the short-answer and essay formats.

General Guidelines for All Constructed-Response Formats

Table 8.1 contains general guidelines for all constructed-response items. They are consistent with our overall approach to classroom assessment, and you will see some familiar but important themes.

TABLE 8.1

General Guidelines for Writing Constructed-Response Items

Develop items requiring the same knowledge, concepts, and cognitive skills as practiced during instruction.

Incorporate novelty so that the task requires students to generalize the skills and concepts presented during instruction.

Keep the language simple.

Consider the developmental level of students in terms of the complexity of the task and the length of the response.

Assess the Same Knowledge, Concepts, and Cognitive Skills Emphasized in Class

Items should be written to be consistent with the learning goals and instruction associated with a unit. In the case of essays, during instruction you will need to model the use of factual and conceptual knowledge to develop new ideas, build arguments, or defend views. You may review with your students some examples of essays written in previous years (removing all identifying information). Students also need to practice writing essays with formative feedback from you before they begin to use this format in a summative assessment. This may seem like a lot of work; however, after your students learn to use the essay format, your instruction about writing essays will not have to be as in-depth in preparing students for subsequent tests.

Incorporate Novelty

If you use the same constructed-response items in your assessment that you used in class activities, the cognitive strategy you tap is remembering. By including novel material as an integral part of a constructed-response task, you will be able to write short-answer items and essay prompts that require students to analyze, evaluate, and create. By novel material, we are not suggesting you should assess students on new concepts and strategies that were not part of a learning unit. Instead, we mean new examples related to the concepts being learned. For example, during instruction you might engage students in the interpretation of political cartoons. An essay item, then, would have students interpret a political cartoon from the same historical period, but a cartoon the students had not discussed in class. Students would analyze the new cartoon and link it to events occurring in the historical period that is the focus of the instructional unit.

Keep the Language Simple

To promote clarity in writing items, you should keep the language as simple as possible for students at all levels. This means you should use vocabulary your students understand. This also requires you to attend to the complexity of phrases and sentence structure. For example, in Figure 8.6, the short-answer item for second-grade students should be edited to remove the term "approximate" unless the word is part of vocabulary taught in science and mathematics. Also, the phrase "in this picture" can be cut because the directions tell the students to use the diagram.

Consider the Developmental Level of Students

The developmental level of students (e.g., breadth of vocabulary, degree of cognitive complexity) must be considered in writing constructed-response items. The level of

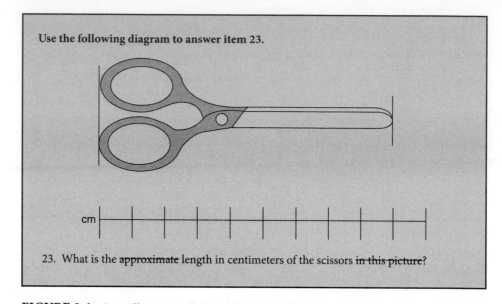

Use the following diagram to answer item 23.

cm

23. What is the ~~approximate~~ length in centimeters of the scissors ~~in this picture~~?

FIGURE 8.6   *Item Illustrating the Need for Simple Language*

student development should be reflected in the complexity of the item and the length of the expected response. For example, topics for younger students might refer to specific situations (e.g., school rules), whereas older students can write about more abstract concepts (e.g., civil liberties).

Guidelines for Specific Item Formats

Now we turn to rules for developing specific item formats, and we start with short-answer items.

Developing Short-Answer Items

Our rules for short-answer items appear in Table 8.2.

Determine Whether Short-Answer Format Is Best   First, you must decide whether an item functions better as a short-answer item or a multiple-choice item. Look at item 3 in Figure 8.7. When the item is offered as a multiple-choice item, students have various equations to analyze to determine which equation models the rate plan. By contrast,

TABLE 8.2

Guidelines for Writing Short-Answer Items

Determine whether an item should be short answer or multiple choice.

Use interpretive material to develop items that engage students at the higher cognitive levels.

Keep the stem brief.

Word the item so that only one answer is correct.

Omit only key words and phrases when using the completion form of short answer.

Avoid clues to answers.

Multiple-Choice

Use the following information to answer item 3.

A cellular phone company charges monthly rates according to the following plan:

- Monthly fee of $23.95
- The first 100 minutes of calling time are free
- $0.08 charge per minute of calling time over 100 minutes

3. If c is the total monthly cost, and m is the number of minutes of calling time, which equation models this rate plan when m is greater than 100 minutes?

    A. $c = 0.08m - 76.05$
    B. $c = 0.08(m - 100) - 23.95$
    C. $c = 23.95 + 0.08(m - 100)$*
    D. $c = 23.95 + 0.08m$

Short-Answer

3. A cellular phone company charges monthly rates according to the following plan:

    - Monthly fee of $23.95
    - The first 100 minutes of calling time are free
    - $0.08 charge per minute of calling time over 100 minutes

    If c is the total monthly cost, and m is the number of minutes of calling time, write the equation that models this rate plan when m is greater than 100 minutes.

FIGURE 8.7   *Example of the Cognitive Demands for a Short-Answer Versus Multiple-Choice Item*

SOURCE: South Carolina Department of Education. 2007. PACT math release items: Grade 8. From http://ed.sc.gov/agency/offices/assessment/pact/PACTMathReleaseItems.html. Reprinted with permission.

the short-answer version of the item requires students to create an equation to model the rate plan. Both versions of the item are challenging; however, the short-answer item requires more of the students. If your learning goal is for students to be able to analyze information to determine the appropriate model, and your instruction involves students analyzing verbal information and determining the correct equation, a multiple-choice item might be appropriate. However, if your learning goals and instruction focus on students writing (creating) a linear model, then the short-answer version is more appropriate for assessing student knowledge.

Engage Students at Higher Cognitive Levels   Let's dispel the myth that short-answer items necessarily focus on the simple recall of facts. The modeling of an equation in Figure 8.7 and the calculating of density in Figure 8.8 both require students to use cognitive levels higher than remembering. If combined with interpretive materials, such as charts, quotes, or short musical pieces, an item may require the student to analyze the material prior to answering the item.

Conversely, we do not want you to think that writing an item in short-answer form will always increase the cognitive level of the item. Look at the science item in Figure 8.8. Cover the answer options and read the item in a short-answer form. Notice that your answer to the question is going to be sample 1, 2, 3, or 4. The multiple-choice form simply gives you a method for recording your response. So, sometimes the cognitive level will not be influenced by the use of short-answer items versus multiple-choice items.

Use Brief Stems   In writing short-answer items, keep the stem brief. Notice the format of our examples that use interpretive material. A set of directions introduces the interpretive material, indicating that the student should use the following material to answer the

Use the following information to answer item 13.

The following table shows properties of four different sample materials. One of these materials is cork, a type of wood that floats in water.

Physical Properties

Sample Number	Mass	Volume
1	89 g	10 mL
2	26 g	10 mL
3	24 g	100 mL
4	160 g	100 mL

13. Given that the density of water is 1 g/mL, which of the samples is *most* likely cork?
   A. 1
   B. 2
   C. 3*
   D. 4

Cover the answer options to see the item requires the same cognitive skills whether written as a short-answer item or multiple-choice item.

FIGURE 8.8   *Example of an Item with Similar Cognitive Demands for a Short-Answer or Multiple-Choice Item*

SOURCE: California Department of Education. 2008. *California standards test released test questions: Grade 8 science.* From http://www.cde.ca.gov/ta/tg/sr/css05rtq.asp. Reprinted with permission.

Use the following information to answer item 16.

A teacher had students in her class count for 15 seconds how many times they blink both eyes. They created the ordered stem-and-leaf plot given below using the data.

```
6 | 0 3
5 | 1 2 5 7
4 | 1 3 3 6
3 | 1 3 4 5 5 6 7 7 7 8 9
2 | 0 5 6 9
3 | 9 means 39 blinks
```

16. What is the mode for blinking? ← Original version

16. Write the number that is the mode for blinking. ← Edited version

FIGURE 8.9   *Example of the Edits Required for a Short-Answer Item*

Adapted from the South Carolina Department of Education. 2007. PACT math release items: Grade 6. From http://ed.sc.gov/agency/offices/assessment/pact/PACTMathReleaseItems.html. Reprinted with permission.

item. Next is the interpretive material, which includes scenarios, diagrams, and tables, followed by the item number and a stem that presents the problem. In Figure 8.9 in which students are to interpret a stem-and-leaf plot, the stem is "Write the number that is the mode for blinking." Setting the stem apart from and after the interpretive material serves to highlight the actual problem; thus, a student does not have to search for the question.

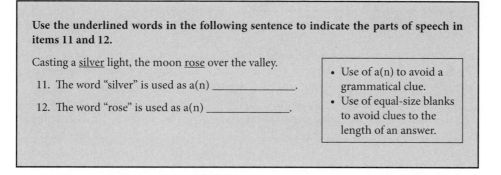

Use the underlined words in the following sentence to indicate the parts of speech in items 11 and 12.

Casting a <u>silver</u> light, the moon <u>rose</u> over the valley.

11. The word "silver" is used as a(n) _____.

12. The word "rose" is used as a(n) _____.

- Use of a(n) to avoid a grammatical clue.
- Use of equal-size blanks to avoid clues to the length of an answer.

FIGURE 8.10 *An Example of Avoiding a Grammatical Clue*

Ensure Only One Answer Is Correct   In some ways, the greatest challenge is to write short answer items that avoid ambiguous answers. The item should be worded so that only one answer is correct. To help you meet this challenge, we suggest looking at the short-answer as if it were a selected-response item. Then ask yourself, "What is the right answer?" Next ask yourself, "What are the possible wrong answers a student might use?" Is your item written so that only the right answer can complete the response? For example, for Figure 8.9, we first wrote, "What is the mode for blinking?" However, with a little thought, we realized some students would write, "The most frequently occurring number." Well, those students would be correct. But we want to know whether the student can read the stem-and-leaf plot to determine the most frequently occurring response for number of blinks. We then edit the item to read, "Write the number that is the mode for blinking."

Omit Only Key Words and Phrases   For the completion form, the word or phrase that has been omitted should consist of key concepts rather than trivial details. In addition, the omitted material should be near the end of the incomplete statement. A quick look back at the bar graph item in Figure 8.1 shows the blank at the end of the incomplete statement.

Avoid Clues to the Answer   Grammatical clues can inappropriately point students to a correct answer. In Figure 8.10, the issue of appropriate use of "a" or "an" before a word with an initial consonant or vowel is handled by using the "a(n)" designation. In addition, avoid letting blanks in a completion item offer hints as to the length of the response or the number of words that are needed to complete the statement. Instead, place only one blank of a standard size at the end of the completion-form item to avoid clues.

Developing Content-Based Essay Items

Essays may be used to assess students' content knowledge (**content-based essays**) or their writing skills (writing prompts). In this section we provide guidelines for developing content-based essay items (see Table 8.3).

Content-Based Essay

A prompt that presents students with a question or task requiring one or more paragraphs about a subject area.

TABLE 8.3

Guidelines for Developing Content-Based Essay Items

Write directions that clearly define the task.

Write the prompt to focus students on the key ideas they should address in their response.

Use formatting features, such as bullets and ALL CAPS, to clarify the task.

Write Directions That Define the Task Clearly As was true for short-answer items, your first challenge is to write the essay item so the task is clearly defined for the student. One way to do so is to identify the cognitive process you want to assess by beginning the essay question with a verb that cues that cognitive process for answering. Using Table 2.9 from Chapter 2, choose verbs at the comprehension levels and higher. Examples include *summarize, compare, provide original examples of, predict what would happen if.*

In the NAEP mathematics item in Figure 8.11, students analyze a graph to indicate the activity that would be occurring during each time interval. Notice the use of

Marisa's Bicycle Trip
Speed (miles per hour)
10
8
6
4
2
0
20
40
60
80
Time (minutes)

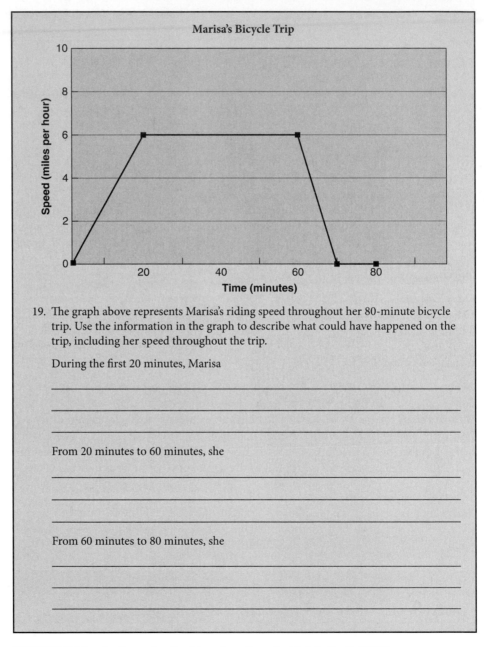

19. The graph above represents Marisa's riding speed throughout her 80-minute bicycle trip. Use the information in the graph to describe what could have happened on the trip, including her speed throughout the trip.

During the first 20 minutes, Marisa

____

____

____

From 20 minutes to 60 minutes, she

____

____

____

From 60 minutes to 80 minutes, she

____

____

____

FIGURE 8.11 ***An Example of an Essay Item from the Eighth-Grade NAEP Mathematics Assessment***

SOURCE: National Center for Educational Statistics. 2005. NAEP question. Reprinted with permission.

the term "describe" in the directions for the mathematics item. If you relied only on the verb "describe" to determine the cognitive processes a student is using to solve the problem, you would miss the need for the student to analyze the graph and make the biking activities consistent with the graph. Sometimes the meaning of the verb depends in part on the context of the task, and the task demands can make the actual cognitive process higher. "Describe" means analyze in this case.

Using terms such as *when, where,* or *list* will result in essays based on students remembering factual information, which can be more effectively done with selected-response items. Essays, however, can be developed that require students to both recall factual information and apply the information to a novel context. For example, to respond to the essay item in Figure 8.12, students must recall the meaning of the terms associated with the elements of art. They then apply the terms in an analysis of artist Laura McFadden's pen and ink drawing.

Focus Students on the Key Ideas to Address in Their Response   In writing the essay prompt, you should focus on the specific points students should concentrate on. Notice how the item writer focuses students in Figure 8.13 by specifying the elements of the answer. These will then provide the basis for creating a scoring guide. When you specify the elements of a good answer, you ensure that the requirements of the task are clear to you and to your students.

Use Formatting Features to Clarify the Task   Attention to the formatting of essay items can also clarify the task. For example, clarity can be enhanced through the use of bullets to draw students' attention to the aspects of the essay that they must address. The prompt in Figure 8.13 uses bullets to highlight the countries about which the student might write. In addition, the prompt uses the letters "a," "b," and "c" to list (and highlight) the three aspects of the task the student must address.

Using ALL CAPS or italics can bring emphasis when exceptions are being made, as in Figure 8.4. The use of ALL CAPS in the direction to "Identify two pieces of information NOT given above that you would need before you could decide whether or not the United States military should help Teresia" cues students to take careful note of the exception.

Structuring responses also may contribute to item clarity. The NAEP mathematics bicycling item (Figure 8.11) provides an illustration. Notice the problem is structured to draw students' attention to three time periods in the bicycle trip. The developers of the item could have stopped after writing, "The graph above represents Marisa's riding speed throughout her 80-minute bicycle trip. Use the information in the graph to describe what could have happened on the trip, including her speed throughout the trip." Such a response format requires the students to create their own framework for their response. The item developer, however, then used paragraph starters, such as "During the first 20 minutes, Marisa . . ." to structure the task and direct the students to the relevant time spans. This presents a slightly different task in that students have the structure of the response provided.

Providing such paragraph starters may make some teachers wince because they prefer that students write their own short paragraph to convey the information. However, the bicycling item is from a mathematics assessment, so the developer of the item did not want students' writing abilities to influence their mathematics scores.

Developing Writing Prompts
Now we turn to the development of prompts that focus on assessing students' writing skills. Writing prompts are used in NAEP to assess three forms of writing: narrative,

A CONVERSATION REMEMBERED

The pen and ink drawing below, *A Conversation Remembered*, is by artist Laura McFadden. In an essay, describe Laura's work using the elements and principles of design.

Also, discuss your response to the painting and how the artist uses the elements and principles of design to create the response.

Elements and Principles of Design

Color	Line	Shape	Value
Contrast	Movement	Space	
Emphasis	Pattern	Texture	

FIGURE 8.12 *Essay Task That Requires Students to Remember Art Terms in Analyzing Laura McFadden's* **A Conversation Remembered**

Reprinted with permission.

34. Each of the following world regions was a "hot spot" in the 1900s.

    - Israel
    - The Korean Peninsula
    - Vietnam
    - The Persian Gulf

    Select one world region from the list and answer the following three questions about conflict in that area.

    a. Identify the area you selected and summarize the conflict that occurred. In your summary, identify the major participants in the conflict.
    b. Explain the historical reasons for the conflict.
    c. Explain why the conflict has had a major effect on the rest of the world.

FIGURE 8.13 *A Released History Item from the 2004 PACT Social Studies Field Test*

SOURCE: South Carolina Department of Education. 2004b. Reprinted with permission.

informative, and persuasive (NCES, 2008). **Narrative writing** includes stories or personal essays. Students use **informative writing** to describe ideas, convey messages, and provide instructions. Informative writing includes reports, reviews, and letters. Students use **persuasive writing** to influence the reader to take action or create change. Examples of each type of prompt appear in Table 8.4, and Table 8.5 lists guidelines for constructing them.

Develop Interesting Prompts   To create writing prompts that will encourage students to enjoy writing and to excel at it, your first consideration is to create topics of interest to students. You will also want the writing prompts to be of interest to you because you will dedicate a substantial amount of time to reading your students' thoughts on a topic. Also, bias can creep into your scoring of essays if you become bored with a topic; so develop essay prompts that are likely to stimulate thought.

Incorporate Key Elements   In developing writing prompts, you should consider the following elements:

Subject	Who or what the response is about
Occasion	The situation that requires the response to be written
Audience	Who the readers will be
Purpose	The intent of the writing, i.e., inform, narrate, persuade
Writer's role	The role the student assumes in the writing (e.g., a friend, student, concerned citizen)
Form	The type of writing, e.g., poem, letter, realistic fiction (Albertson, 1998; Nitko & Brookhart, 2007)

We apply these elements to the prompt in Figure 8.14. The subjects of the prompt are the student writer and a person whom the student has read about or seen in a movie. The occasion is a day the student would spend with this person. The audience is not specified; however, the prompt was part of a high school exit examination and students would be aware that raters would read their essays. The purpose is for students to write a narrative in which they explain how they would spend the day with this

Narrative Writing
A composition that relates a story or a personal experience.

Informative Writing
A composition that describes ideas, conveys messages, or provides instructions.

Persuasive Writing
A composition that attempts to influence the reader to take action or create change.

TABLE 8.4

Examples of Prompts Used to Assess Writing Skills

Forms of Writing	Examples of Prompts	Grade Levels
Narrative	One morning a child looks out the window and discovers that a huge castle has appeared overnight. The child rushes outside to the castle and hears strange sounds coming from it. Someone is living in the castle! The castle door creaks open. The child goes in. Write a story about who the child meets and what happens inside the castle.	Fourth Grade
Informative	Your school has a program in which a twelfth grader acts as a mentor for a tenth grader at the beginning of each school year. The mentor's job is to help the tenth grader have a successful experience at your school. The tenth grader you are working with is worried about being able to write well enough for high school classes. Write a letter to your tenth grader explaining what kind of writing is expected in high school classes and what the student can do to be a successful writer in high school. As you plan your response, think about your own writing experiences. How would you describe "good" writing? What advice about writing has been helpful to you? What writing techniques do you use?	Twelfth Grade
Persuasive	Many people think that students are not learning enough in school. They want to shorten most school vacations and make students spend more of the year in school. Other people think that lengthening the school year and shortening vacations is a bad idea because students use their vacations to learn important things outside of school. What is your opinion? Write a letter to your school board either in favor of or against lengthening the school year. Give specific reasons to support your opinion that will convince the school board to agree with you.	Eighth Grade

National Center for Educational Statistics. 2005. *NAEP questions*. http://nces.ed.gov/nationsreportcard/itmrls/.

person and why it would be so special. The form of the writing is a narrative. Notice how this prompt uses bullets to focus students on key qualities to include in their writing. Not every element is directly evident in the prompt because these elements serve to help you in developing prompts. They are not meant to dictate the structure of your prompts.

TABLE 8.5

Guidelines for Developing Writing Prompts

Develop prompts that are interesting to your students and you.

Incorporate the elements of subject, occasion, audience, purpose, writer's role, and form.

Focus on cultural and social experiences in which students have participated.

Avoid prompts that require students to (a) write about their personal values or their religious beliefs or (b) criticize others.

WRITING

Write your response on the lined pages in your test booklet. Use only the lines provided in your test booklet. Do not write beyond the lines or in the margins.

Writing Prompt

If you could spend a day with a person you have read about or seen in a movie, who would that person be? How would you spend your day with that person?

Write an essay in which you explain how you would spend your day with this person and why it would be so special. Include detailed descriptions and explanations to support your ideas.

As you write, be sure to

- consider the audience.
- develop your response around a clear central idea.
- use specific details and examples to support your central idea.
- organize your ideas into a clear introduction, body, and conclusion.
- use smooth transitions so that there is a logical progression of ideas.
- use a variety of sentence structures.
- check for correct sentence structure.
- check for errors in capitalization, punctuation, spelling, and grammar.

FIGURE 8.14 *Example of a Narrative Writing Prompt*

SOURCE: South Carolina Department of Education. 2006. *South Carolina High School Assessment Program.* From http://ed.sc.gov/agency/offices/assessment/programs/hsap/releaseitems.html. Reprinted with permission.

Focus on Students' Cultural or Social Experiences   If the purpose of an assessment is to gauge the quality of student writing, the prompt should not require the students to use content area or other specialized knowledge. To avoid bias, writing prompts should not require students to write about cultural or social experiences in which they have not participated (Arter & Chappuis, 2007; Johnson et al., 2009). Instead, you should develop prompts that are reasonably within all students' realm of experiences.

Avoid Prompts Addressing Personal Values, Religious Beliefs, or Criticism   Writing prompts should avoid asking students to write about personal values or religious beliefs because some students and their parents may find such questions intrusive (Johnson et al., 2009; Nitko & Brookhart, 2007). Prompts that require students to criticize their parents or community members may create controversy that will take time away from instruction and student learning.

Constructing the Assessment

As we discussed, a limitation of constructed-response items is the amount of time that it takes for students to respond to each item. Constructed-response items require students to recall relevant information, organize the information, and write a response. These demands call for more time for students to respond, and they limit the number of test items and scope of concepts and skills that can be assessed.

If a teacher uses only one essay to assess students, the grades students earn may reflect (1) their knowledge *or* (2) the particular topic the teacher chose (Dunbar et al., 1991). Consider the narrative writing prompt in which a student writes about spending the day with a person read about in a book or seen in a movie (Figure 8.14). This topic may have been of little interest to some students, and their lackluster writing would reflect their disinterest in the topic. If students had an additional prompt in which they write about a day of discoveries they had personally experienced, their score might differ.

The best fix for this problem is twofold. First, any test that focuses on factual and conceptual knowledge in a content area should be a mix of short-answer items, multiple-choice items, and essays. The use of these three different item formats allows broader sampling of the concepts and skills developed in a learning unit. Second, in the case of essays used to assess writing skills, students should write several essays during a grading period for the teacher to assess students' overall achievement in writing comprehensively.

Scoring the Assessment

A common criticism of assessing with short-answer items and essays is that the scoring will be subjective. That is, some people think the score assigned to a constructed-response item is primarily influenced by a teacher's personal preferences. However, use of scoring tools like those described in the following sections will help you to score fairly.

Scoring Short Answers

Scoring short-answer items is fairly straightforward. To prepare for scoring short-answer items, review the instructional materials (e.g., lesson plans, texts, learning centers) that guided student learning. From these materials, develop a scoring key with all the possible answers. For an example of one such list, revisit the list of complete answers for the question related to determining the volume of liquid in a set of bottles (Figure 8.3). Developing the key will help to ensure that a teacher considers all possible answers and will apply the answers consistently across students.

Scoring Essays

Essay tests pose greater challenges in scoring than do selected-response items and short-answer items. A critical tool developed to address these challenges is the **scoring guide.** A scoring guide presents the elements of a performance to be scored. These elements are referred to as **performance criteria.** The checklist, the analytic rubric, and the holistic rubric are three forms of scoring guides.

Scoring Guide
An instrument that specifies the criteria for rating responses.

Performance Criteria
The key elements of a performance specified in a scoring guide.

Checklist

Score	Description

Content:

_____ Presents a comprehensive, in-depth understanding of the subject content.

_____ Defines, describes, and identifies the terms, concepts, principles, events, interactions, changes, or patterns completely and accurately.

_____ Uses subject-appropriate terminology to discuss the primary concepts or principles related to the topic.

Note. May include a minor error, but it does not detract or interfere with the overall response.

Supporting Details:

_____ Develops the central idea by fully integrating prior knowledge or by extensively referencing primary sources (as appropriate).

_____ Provides a variety of facts (to explore the major and minor issues).

_____ Incorporates specific, relevant examples to illustrate a point, and ties examples, facts, and arguments to the main concepts or principles.

Analysis, Explanation, Justification:

_____ Thoroughly analyzes the significance of a term, concept, principle, event, interaction, change, or pattern by drawing conclusions, making inferences, and/or making predictions.

_____ Conclusions, inferences, and/or predictions are consistent with the supporting details.

Note. Student receives 1 point for each complete and accurate descriptor or criterion in the checklist.

FIGURE 8.15 *Checklist for Scoring a Social Studies Item*

Creighton, S. 2006. *Examining alternative scoring rubrics on a statewide test: The impact of different scoring methods on science and social studies performance assessments.* Unpublished doctoral dissertation, University of South Carolina, Columbia. Reprinted with permission.

A **checklist** is a list of key task elements that are organized in a logical sequence. A checklist allows a teacher to document the presence (or absence) of important dimensions of a performance task. The teacher indicates the presence of observed dimensions by placing a check in the appropriate blank. Figure 8.15 is a checklist for scoring the history item about world conflict. Note that for each criterion the student receives 1 point.

Analytic rubrics identify criteria to use in reviewing the qualities of a student's performance. Notice that the analytic rubric in Figure 8.16 has six performance criteria (e.g., *has five lines, tells a funny story*). In the analytic rubric, **proficiency levels** accompany each performance criterion. Proficiency levels provide a description of each level of that performance criterion along a continuum. For example, in the rubric for scoring limericks in Figure 8.16, the highest proficiency level of the performance criterion *tells a funny story* is "The story that the limerick tells is complete *and* funny." In this rubric, one performance criterion has two proficiency levels and the others have three.

When using this analytic rubric, a teacher would assign a score for each performance criterion. Thus, a student would get six scores. These scores may be reported separately or added for a total score.

Checklist
Key elements of a task organized in a logical sequence allowing confirmation of each element.

Analytic Ruberic
A scoring guide that contains one or more performance criteria for evaluating a task with proficiency levels for each criterion.

Proficiency Levels
The description of each level of quality of a performance criterion.

Student Name:		Date:	
Performance Criteria	**Proficiency Levels**		
Has five lines	**0** Limerick does not have 5 lines.	**1** Limerick has 5 lines.	
Tells a funny story	**1** The story that the limerick tells is incomplete and is not funny.	**2** The story that the limerick tells is incomplete *or* is not funny.	**3** The story that the limerick tells is complete *and* funny.
Has correct rhyming pattern	**1** Limerick does not rhyme.	**2** Limerick has some rhymes, but the rhyming pattern is not correct.	**3** Limerick has correct rhyming pattern (AABBA).
Has correct capitalization	**1** Capitals are not used or are used incorrectly.	**2** Capitals are sometimes correctly used.	**3** Capitals are correctly used in the poem and title.
Has correct punctuation	**1** Limerick is not punctuated or is punctuated incorrectly.	**2** Limerick has some correct punctuation.	**3** Limerick is correctly punctuated.
Contains descriptive words	**1** Specific nouns, adjectives, and adverbs to "paint a picture" for the reader are not used.	**2** The selection of specific nouns, adjectives, and adverbs to "paint a picture" for the reader is attempted.	**3** Specific nouns, adjectives, and adverbs to "paint a picture" for the reader are effectively selected.

FIGURE 8.16   *Analytic Rubric for Scoring a Limerick*

Reprinted with permission from *Put to the Test: Tools and Techniques for Classroom Assessment* by Susan Agruso, Robert Johnson, Therese M. Kuhs, and Diane Monrad. Copyright © 2001 by Susan Agruso, Robert Johnson, Therese M. Kuhs, and Diane Monrad. Published by Heinemann, Portsmouth, NH. All rights reserved.

Holistic Rubric

A scoring guide that provides a single score representing overall quality across several criteria.

In contrast to an analytic rubric, a **holistic rubric** provides a single score that represents overall quality across *several* performance criteria. The scoring guide shown in Figure 8.17 is an example of a holistic rubric. Take a moment to read the highest quality level (i.e., 4 points) of the holistic rubric. Similar to the checklist, this scoring guide describes student responses in terms of the performance criteria *content, supporting details,* and *analysis*. Unlike the analytic rubric, the performance criteria are not separated into their own categories with points assigned for each one. Instead, all performance criteria are joined together to describe general proficiency levels on the essay. Thus, in scoring holistically a teacher arrives at a single overall judgment of quality.

Figures 8.18 and 8.19 show two rubrics for scoring writing prompts. Figure 8.18 is an analytic rubric with four performance criteria (i.e., *content/development, organization, voice,* and *conventions*). Figure 8.19 presents a holistic rubric for scoring student writing. Notice that for the holistic rubric a student would receive only one score between 1 and 6.

Holistic Rubric

Score	Description
4 points	**Superior Achievement** The response presents a comprehensive, in-depth understanding of the subject content. Using subject-appropriate terminology, the response completely and accurately defines, describes, or identifies the primary terms, concepts or principles, events, changes, or patterns. The response develops the central idea by extensively referencing and integrating prior knowledge, citing relevant details from primary sources, incorporating appropriate examples to illustrate a point, and/or providing a variety of facts that support the premise. The response includes a thorough analysis of the significant events by drawing conclusions, making inferences, and/or making predictions that are consistent with the supporting details. The response may include a minor error in the subject content, but it does not detract or interfere with the overall response.
3 points	**Commendable Achievement** The response adequately presents an accurate understanding of the subject content. Using subject-appropriate terminology, the response generally defines, describes, or identifies the primary terms, concepts, principles, events, changes, or patterns; however, more specific details are needed. The response adequately develops the central idea by referencing primary sources, appropriate examples, and a variety of facts that support the premise. The response includes an analysis of significant events by drawing conclusions, making inferences, and/or making predictions that are generally consistent with the supporting details. The response may include minor errors in subject content, but these errors do not detract or interfere with the overall response.
2 points	**Limited Achievement** The response presents a limited understanding of the subject content. The response provides a vague description of a term, concept, principle, event, change, or pattern. It includes attempts to use some subject-appropriate terminology to discuss the concepts; however, details are sparse. The response minimally develops the central idea by referencing basic facts or examples. Examples may be vague or not clearly connected to the central idea, or the response includes insufficient or inaccurate examples. The response provides partially incorrect information. The response draws conclusions, makes inferences, or makes predictions that are incomplete, partially inaccurate, or inconsistent with supporting details. One or more errors in content interfere with the student's presentation.
1 point	**Minimal Achievement** The response reflects little understanding of the subject content; the presentation is brief and includes unrelated general statements. Using little, if any, subject-appropriate terminology, the response minimally defines, describes, or identifies the primary terms, concepts, principles, events, changes, or patterns. The response attempts to provide a central idea by referencing prior knowledge, but these references are sparse, incomplete, inaccurate, and/or unclear. The response may include a fact or an example that is irrelevant or only loosely related to the discussion. The response may attempt to explain or analyze the significance of an issue, but it is irrelevant; or, the response does not include an analysis. The response may or may not include conclusions, inferences, and/or predictions; or they may be irrelevant or inaccurate. Serious errors in the content interfere with the student's presentation.
0 points	**No Achievement** The response is blank, inaccurate, too vague, missing, unreadable, or illegible.

FIGURE 8.17 *Holistic Rubric for Scoring a Social Studies Item*

Creighton, S. 2006. *Examining alternative scoring rubrics on a statewide test: The impact of different scoring methods on science and social studies performance assessments.* Unpublished doctoral dissertation, University of South Carolina, Columbia. Reprinted with permission.

	Performance Criteria				
	Score	**Content/Development**	**Organization**	**Voice**	**Conventions**
Proficiency Levels	4	• Presents a clear central idea about the topic. • Fully develops the central idea with specific, relevant details. • Sustains focus on central idea throughout the writing.	• Has a clear introduction, body, and conclusion. • Provides a smooth progression of ideas throughout the writing.		• Minor errors in standard written English may be present.
	3	• Presents a central idea about the topic. • Develops the central idea but details are general, or the elaboration may be uneven. • Focus may shift slightly, but is generally sustained.	• Has an introduction, body, and conclusion. • Provides a logical progression of ideas throughout the writing.	• Uses precise and/or vivid vocabulary appropriate for the topic. • Phrasing is effective, not predictable or obvious. • Varies sentence structure to promote rhythmic reading. • Strongly aware of audience and task; tone is consistent and appropriate.	• Errors in standard written English may be present; however, these errors do not interfere with the writer's meaning.
	2	• Central idea may be unclear. • Details may be sparse; more information is needed to clarify the central idea. • Focus may shift or be lost, causing confusion for the reader.	• Attempts an introduction, body, and conclusion; however, one of these components could be weak or ineffective. • Provides a simplistic or repetitious progression of ideas throughout the writing.	• Uses both general and precise vocabulary. • Phrasing may not be effective, and may be predictable or obvious. • Some sentence variety results in reading that is somewhat rhythmic; may be mechanical. • Aware of audience and task; tone is appropriate.	• A pattern of errors in more than one category (e.g., capitalization, spelling, punctuation, sentence formation) of standard written English is present; these errors interfere somewhat with the writer's meaning.
	1	• There is no clear central idea. • Details are absent or confusing. • There is no sense of focus.	• Attempts an introduction, body, and conclusion; however, more than one of these components could be absent or confusing. • Presents information in a random or illogical order throughout the writing.	• Uses simple vocabulary. • Phrasing repetitive or confusing. • There is little sentence variety; reading is monotonous. • There is little awareness of audience and task; tone may be inappropriate.	• Frequent and serious errors in more than one category (e.g., capitalization, spelling, punctuation, sentence formation) of standard written English are present; these errors severely interfere with the writer's meaning.
	B	Blank			
	OT	Off Topic			
	IS	Insufficient amount of original writing to evaluate			
	UR	Unreadable or illegible			

FIGURE 8.18 ***Example of an Analytic Rubric for Writing***

South Carolina Department of Education. 2004a. *Extended response scoring rubric.* http://ed.sc.gov/agency/offices/assessment/pact/rubrics.html. Reprinted with permission. For the purposes of scoring Conventions, "interference" is defined as that which would impede meaning for a reader other than an educator or professional reader.

6 Points	The writing is focused, purposeful, and reflects insight into the writing situation. The paper conveys a sense of completeness and wholeness with adherence to the main idea, and its organizational pattern provides for a logical progression of ideas. The support is substantial, specific, relevant, concrete, and/or illustrative. The paper demonstrates a commitment to and an involvement with the subject, clarity in presentation of ideas, and may use creative writing strategies appropriate to the purpose of the paper. The writing demonstrates a mature command of language (word choice) with freshness of expression. Sentence structure is varied, and sentences are complete except when fragments are used purposefully. Few, if any, convention errors occur in mechanics, usage, and punctuation.
5 Points	The writing focuses on the topic, and its organizational pattern provides for a progression of ideas, although some lapses may occur. The paper conveys a sense of completeness or wholeness. The support is ample. The writing demonstrates a mature command of language, including precision in word choice. There is variation in sentence structure, and, with rare exceptions, sentences are complete except when fragments are used purposefully. The paper generally follows the conventions of mechanics, usage, and spelling.
4 Points	The writing is generally focused on the topic but may include extraneous or loosely related material. An organizational pattern is apparent, although some lapses may occur. The paper exhibits some sense of completeness or wholeness. The support, including word choice, is adequate, although development may be uneven. There is little variation in sentence structure, and most sentences are complete. The paper generally follows the conventions of mechanics, usage, and spelling.
3 Points	The writing is generally focused on the topic but may include extraneous or loosely related material. An organizational pattern has been attempted, but the paper may lack a sense of completeness or wholeness. Some support is

included, but development is erratic. Word choice is adequate but may be limited, predictable, or occasionally vague. There is little, if any, variation in sentence structure. Knowledge of the conventions of mechanics and usage is usually demonstrated, and commonly used words are usually spelled correctly.

2 Points The writing is related to the topic but includes extraneous or loosely related material. Little evidence of an organizational pattern may be demonstrated, and the paper may lack a sense of completeness or wholeness. Development of support is inadequate or illogical. Word choice is limited, inappropriate, or vague. There is little, if any, variation in sentence structure, and gross errors in sentence structure may occur. Errors in basic conventions of mechanics and usage may occur, and commonly used words may be misspelled.

1 Point The writing may only minimally address the topic. The paper is a fragmentary or incoherent listing of related ideas or sentences or both. Little, if any, development of support or an organizational pattern or both is apparent. Limited or inappropriate word choice may obscure meaning. Gross errors in sentence structure and usage may impede communication. Frequent and blatant errors may occur in the basic conventions of mechanics and usage, and commonly used words may be misspelled.

Unscorable

The paper is unscorable because

- the response is not related to what the prompt requested the student to do.
- the response is simply a rewording of the prompt.
- the response is a copy of a published work.
- the student refused to write.
- the response is illegible.
- the response is incomprehensible (words are arranged in such a way that no meaning is conveyed).
- the response contains an insufficient amount of writing to determine if the student was attempting to address the prompt.
- the writing folder is blank.

FIGURE 8.19 *Example of a Holistic Rubric for Writing*

SOURCE: Florida Department of Education. 2005. *Florida Writing Assessment Program (FLORIDA WRITES!).* http://www.fldoe.org/asp/fw/fwaprubr.asp. Reprinted with permission.

TABLE 8.6

Guidelines for Developing Scoring Guides

Decide whether a checklist, analytic rubric, or holistic rubric is appropriate for reviewing student responses (see Table 8.7).

For all scoring guides: Determine a small number of non-overlapping performance criteria that students should demonstrate in their responses.

For analytic and holistic rubrics: Develop a continuum of proficiency levels from least to most skilled for each performance criterion.
- Use parallel language to describe achievement across the levels of proficiency.
- Avoid use of negative language.
- Design descriptive rather than evaluative proficiency levels that can be clearly distinguished from one another.

Developing a Scoring Guide

All scoring guides have several basic steps in their construction. Table 8.6 provides guidelines for developing checklists, analytic rubrics, and holistic rubrics.

Decide Whether a Checklist, an Analytic Rubric, or a Holistic Rubric Is Appropriate

A first major decision is to determine which type of scoring guide is appropriate. Aspects to consider in determining the appropriate type of scoring guide are shown in Table 8.7. For example, in terms of communicating expectations, a checklist might be used to convey several elements required in an essay. A holistic rubric can serve to communicate the levels of overall quality of an essay, whereas an analytic rubric could serve to provide information about levels of quality on each performance criterion. Other aspects to consider include the degree to which each scoring guide supports student self-assessment, provides feedback to students, and supports communication across faculty.

Determine the Performance Criteria

Whether using a checklist, analytic rubric, or holistic rubric, a critical step in developing a scoring guide is to determine the performance criteria that provide the framework for scoring. The performance criteria must be consistent with the learning goals associated with instruction. An example can be found in the essay item related to major conflicts (Figure 8.13) and the potential scoring guides (Figures 8.15 and 8.17). Notice that the performance criteria in the scoring guides imply the learning goals addressed (a) an understanding of the events that occurred (i.e., *content*), (b) the ability to provide details to support statements (i.e., *supporting details*), and (c) the capability to analyze information to draw conclusions (i.e., *analysis*). Also notice that these performance criteria parallel the directions in the item (Figure 8.13).

To make scoring guides manageable, they must have a limited number of performance criteria (e.g., 4–6) and they should be limited to one page at the very most. Anything more complex is difficult for students to use effectively in monitoring their work. In the content-based essay item in social studies, only three performance criteria—*content, supporting details,* and *analysis*—were used. For scoring writing prompts, we looked at the performance criteria of *content/development, organization, voice,* and *conventions*. In deciding the performance criteria for your scoring guides, you should look at the task directions to see the qualities that you told your students they should address. In addition,

TABLE 8.7

Aspects of Checklists, Holistic Rubrics, and Analytic Rubrics to Consider in Selecting a Scoring Guide

	Checklist	Holistic Rubric	Analytic Rubric
Description	Simple list of requirements to check off if present.	A single score represents overall quality across several criteria.	Separate scores are provided for each criterion.
Communicate Expectations to Students	Useful when more than two or three unambiguous elements (e.g., page length, format) are required in the product.	Useful when communicating a general impression of the levels of overall quality for the product.	Useful when each criterion has important distinctions among the levels of a quality performance that students must learn.
Student Self-Assessment	Allows self-check on presence of unambiguous criteria.	Allows self-check on overall performance.	Allows self-check on quality of each criterion.
Feedback to Students	Offers feedback on presence or absence of unambiguous criteria.	Offers feedback providing a general impression of the product.	Offers feedback with detail and precision on all criteria.
Communication Among Faculty Across Sections/ Courses	Provides information on basic elements required.	Provides general grading guidelines.	Provides most information about requirements to facilitate consistency in grading.
Optimal Use	Best used with assignments with several clear-cut components; drafts or preliminary work.	Best used with brief assignments carrying less grading weight.	Best used with products involving complex learning outcomes; opportunities for formative assessment and improvement.
Advantages	Easiest to design.	Scoring is simple and quick.	Provides most information to teacher and student.

you will find it helpful to think about the qualities you will see in a top-notch essay. The qualities you are looking for in your students' essays will be the performance criteria.

Unfortunately, sometimes performance criteria focus on less relevant aspects of a performance, such as *length, neatness,* and *punctuality.* Ideally, a scoring guide focuses on the dimensions of an essay that are the focus of the learning outcomes. When we include performance criteria that assess frivolous aspects of a student essay, such as neatness, error is introduced to the scores.

Developing a Checklist

Having established the performance criteria of interest, let's consider the elements to develop in checklists.

List the Key Performance Criteria To develop a checklist, you list the performance criteria with a space beside each (see Figure 8.15). Each criterion should be a key quality of the essay. For example, in the checklist for the social studies item, one criterion includes "Presents a comprehensive, in-depth understanding of the subject content." These criteria should be organized in a logical sequence. Notice that for the *supporting details* domain in the checklist, the criteria are in the following order:

_____   Develops the central idea by fully integrating prior knowledge or by extensively referencing primary sources (as appropriate).

_____   Provides a variety of facts (to explore the major and minor issues).

_____   Incorporates specific, relevant examples to illustrate a point and ties examples, facts, and arguments to the main concepts or principles.

In front of each criterion, you put a blank to check off to show whether the student has mastered the skill.

Developing an Analytic or Holistic Rubric

Whereas a checklist requires you to list only the performance criteria, analytic and holistic rubrics require you to describe the performance criteria along a continuum of proficiency levels from least to most skilled.

Develop a Continuum of Proficiency Levels for the Performance Criteria   To establish the proficiency levels, descriptors should use consistent wording across all levels of achievement for that criterion. For example, notice in Figure 8.18 the parallelism of the language of the highest and lowest levels of proficiency for the performance criterion of *content/development*. Each proficiency level describes qualities related to a clear central idea, the use of details, and sustaining of focus.

The descriptors at each proficiency level should avoid evaluative labels and instead use language that elaborates on each performance criterion. For example, the following descriptors for the *title* criterion address the degree that the title summarizes the main idea:

Criterion	Proficiency Levels		
	0	1	2
Title	Needs a title that summarizes the main idea.	Title needs to more accurately summarize the main idea.	Title summarizes the main idea.

Evaluative descriptors such as "poor," "OK," or "excellent" do not communicate to students the need to align the title with the central idea. Thus, in developing a scoring guide you should write descriptors characterizing what a response looks like at each level of proficiency rather than merely using evaluative terms.

Another issue in the development of descriptors is to avoid negative language. Negative language may harm student motivation. If descriptors are written to illustrate a learning continuum, the scale will not present the lowest levels as "failure" and higher levels as "success." One way to handle this issue is to describe what the student should do rather than what is lacking in the response. The following descriptor is from the lowest proficiency level of a holistic rubric. The performance criteria focus on story structure (i.e., beginning, middle, and end), sentence formation (i.e., complete sentences), and conventions (i.e., capitalization).

> I should put events in the right order to have a clear beginning, middle, and end for my story. I should use complete sentences in my story. I should use capitals to start sentences and for people's names. (Gredler & Johnson, 2004)

The emphasis in the descriptors is on what the student should do in future story writing.

You should also determine the appropriate number of proficiency levels for each performance criterion. Each proficiency level must be clearly distinguishable from the others if your rubric is to be useful (Lane & Stone, 2006). Sometimes our teacher candidates believe they should have the same number of proficiency levels for all performance criteria. However, you should develop the number of proficiency levels you can describe distinctly enough that your assignment of scores will be consistent. The analytic rubric in Figure 8.18 makes our point. Those who developed the rubric could describe only three proficiency levels for *voice* and wisely did not write a level 4 descriptor that could not be distinguishable from the level 3 descriptor.

The scoring rubric should be drafted as the essay item is being developed. You will then be able to ensure alignment between them. For content-based essay items, developing the scoring guide will be facilitated by first reviewing the materials on which the test is based. The scoring of content-based essays can be facilitated by developing a model answer or an outline of key points. In addition, before scoring, read a sample of the responses to determine whether your expectations are realistic. Based on the review, make any necessary edits to the scoring guide.

Factors Contributing Error to Essay Scores

As previously noted, rubrics were developed to address the error that a scorer's judgment can introduce into student scores. Many factors other than content knowledge or writing ability can influence students' essay scores, and studies over the past century have identified some of the challenges we face as teachers when scoring essay items. Table 8.8 provides a list of the challenges, as well as possible solutions that have been suggested to address them.

TABLE 8.8

Factors Contributing Error to Essay Scores and Recommended Solutions

Scoring Challenges	Possible Solutions
Teacher unreliability	Carefully frame question, develop a scoring guide, provide a model answer or outline of key points, identify examples of various levels of proficiency, and recalibrate often.
Halo effect	Remove identifying marks and grade anonymously.
Test-to-test carryover effects	Recalibrate by reviewing the scoring guide and rereading a sample of previously scored papers. After completing the scoring of one essay item, shuffle student papers before scoring the next item.
Item-to-item carryover effects	Score the same question for all students before moving to next item.
Other issues: language mechanics, handwriting effects, essay length	Note on the scoring guide that these criteria are not the focus of scoring for content-based essay items.

Teacher Unreliability   Probably the most common criticism of essays is the unreliability of teacher scores. Nearly a century ago two studies showed the unreliability of the scoring of students' work in English and mathematics (Starch & Elliot, 1912; Starch & Elliot, 1913). As we have become more aware over the years of the various factors that contribute error to scores, we have developed methods for reducing that error. For instance, to reduce error due to teacher judgment, in addition to carefully designing a scoring guide, you should frame the question to focus student attention on the key issues. When the question is overly broad, students' answers will diverge and require more teacher judgment about the correctness of the response. The use of bullets in Figure 8.13 provides an example of framing the question to focus students' attention. To improve your scoring, you can select examples of student work for each proficiency level. These serve as anchors as you grade.

Halo Effect   The halo effect occurs when teachers' judgments about one aspect of a student influence their judgments about other qualities of that student. In such an instance, a teacher may score an essay more leniently for a student who is generally a strong student. On the other hand, the teacher might score a different student severely because of perceptions that the student is weaker (Nitko & Brookhart, 2007). The best way to guard against the halo effect is to mask students' names when scoring.

Test-to-Test Carryover   Test-to-test carryover occurs when a teacher inadvertently compares a student's response to the responses of other students whose papers precede the student's essay. This may occur after the teacher scores a series of exemplary responses, then the teacher reads an essay that meets the pre-stated expectations, but appears somewhat lackluster compared to the others (e.g., Daly & Dickson-Markman, 1982; Hopkins, 1998). The tendency is for this response to be evaluated too severely. To remedy such a problem, the teacher can recalibrate by reviewing the scoring guide and rereading some of the essays scored earlier.

Item-to-Item Carryover   Similar to test-to-test carryover, item-to-item carryover occurs in the rating of multiple essay questions within a test (Bracht, 1967, as cited in Hopkins, 1998). A student might write an exceptional answer to the first question, which establishes the mindset to assume above-average answers by the student on subsequent questions. A solution to this problem is to score all students' responses to one essay item before scoring the next item.

Additional Factors Contributing Error to Scores   Language mechanics, essay length, and handwriting sometimes contribute error to scores (e.g., Chase, 1986; Grobe, 1981; Markham, 1976; Stewart & Grobe, 1979). In the assessment of writing, language mechanics (i.e., conventions) may be relevant and, if this is the case, a performance criterion related to mechanics should be included in the scoring guide (see Figure 8.18). But handwriting quality and essay length should *not* influence writing scores. In the case of content-based essays, none of these three factors (mechanics, length, handwriting) should influence scores, and the scoring guide should explicitly state this point.

The teachers and teacher candidates with whom we work struggle with the issue of not including in scoring guides such criteria as spelling, language mechanics, and neatness. They want these criteria to carry some weight so students will attend to them. One method that serves as a halfway point is to include the criteria, but apply a low weight to them. For example, if the criterion of neatness counts 3 points out of a possible 100 points, you establish the expectation of neatness without greatly changing the student's final score. Even if a student misses all three points for neatness, the student's grade will remain an "A" or "A−" if the essay is of high quality.

⇥ Pitfalls to Avoid: Top Common Challenges in Constructed-Response Items and Scoring Guides

We next highlight the biggest challenges for teachers as they design constructed-response items and scoring guides. These challenges are listed in Figure 8.20.

Essay Pitfalls

Requiring Higher-Order Thinking Aligned with Learning Goals

When we addressed the pitfalls in writing multiple-choice items, our first example was failing to address important content tied to the learning goals. Avoiding this problem with essay questions is even more important because an essay covers fewer topics in more depth than a group of multiple-choice items requiring similar testing time. If you write an essay prompt that doesn't relate to critical content or skills, your assessment does not do justice to your instruction or to student learning.

In addition, requiring students to employ higher-order thinking skills is also crucial. Essay questions are more time-consuming to score, as well as more susceptible

Common Errors	Poor Design	Fixes	Better Design
Requiring students to list facts in response to an essay item.	List and explain the factors leading to World War I.	**Include items that require use of higher-order thinking skills aligned with learning goals.**	1. In your opinion, of the factors leading to World War I discussed in class, which factor do you believe was most important? Support your answer with at least three examples of evidence from the chapter and lectures.
Writing prompts that are broad or vague.	Compare President Nixon to President Reagan.	**Clearly define the task.**	2. Compare President Nixon to President Reagan in terms of the similarities and differences in their foreign policy initiatives.
Lacking consistency in criteria addressed in the task directions and the scoring guide.	No statement about the importance of writing conventions in task directions but included in scoring.	**Align scoring guide and task directions.**	Number of points for writing conventions specified in both task directions and rubric.
Evaluative terms used in scoring guide.	"Bad title."	**Use descriptors that foster learning rather than evaluative terms.**	"Title needs to more accurately summarize the main idea."
Frivolous or untaught performance criteria included.	Neatness, length (frivolous). Creativity (if not taught).	**Align performance criteria with instruction and learning goals.**	Persuasiveness. Organization around central idea. Creativity (if taught).

FIGURE 8.20   *Top Challenges in Designing Constructed-Response Items and Scoring Guides*

to error in scoring than selected-response or short-answer items. This means you want to use essays only when you are tapping understanding and skills you can't assess with more direct, less error-prone methods.

Making sure you are appraising higher-order thinking skills can be tricky. Recently, one of our teacher candidates developed a history essay prompt that required students to list and explain the factors leading to World War I. Although such an essay prompt might appear to require students to use critical thinking skills from higher levels of Bloom's taxonomy, the factors leading to the war had been thoroughly discussed in class. For such an essay, students could simply list facts memorized from class instruction. To avoid using essays for listing memorized facts, decide whether the essay question requires students to recall a list of facts based on instruction or whether students are required to analyze new material or evaluate a situation from a different perspective.

Clearly Defining the Task

At times, our teacher candidates design essay questions that don't clearly communicate what they want their students to address in their answers. In fact, there has been a time or two when we, too, received essays we did not anticipate given the question we asked. We recheck the question and then, in hindsight, can see how someone might interpret it differently. Often you will have a clear purpose for the question in your mind that doesn't allow you to see the ambiguity your question may present to someone who hasn't organized the material the way you have or who doesn't know as much as you do about it. To avoid this pitfall, you must clearly define the task for your students. If you think three examples is enough to bolster an argument about the most important cause of World War I, specify that you want three; don't make students guess how much support for their argument is enough. If you want students to compare the foreign policy of two presidents rather than their approaches to monetary policy or social programs, make sure you specify the dimension for comparison.

Scoring Guide Pitfalls

Aligning the Scoring Guide and Task Directions

Having inconsistent task directions and criteria for the scoring guide is a common mistake. For example, you may develop an essay prompt that requires students to analyze facsimiles of historical documents (such as diary entries and letters to family members) to examine the views of citizens about historical events. If your directions do not instruct students about following the conventions of written language, yet you have this criterion in your scoring rubric, the misalignment may result in students feeling the assessment was unfair. One way to handle this issue is to make the scoring guide a part of the task directions. At the end of the task directions, you make a statement such as the following: "Use the attached analytic rubric to guide you in completing the task. I will use the rubric to grade your essay."

Using Descriptors Rather Than Evaluative Terms

Look back at the scoring guides in this chapter. The proficiency levels are described using language that elaborates on each criterion and they avoid evaluative language. For example, "Title needs to more accurately summarize the main idea" communicates what is expected (and how to improve) much better than "poor title." As you write performance criteria and proficiency levels, focus on descriptors that help students learn, rather than on evaluative terms that only convey judgment.

Avoiding Frivolous or Untaught Performance Criteria

Performance criteria are critical components of the scoring guide. They frame students' evaluation of the work as well as yours, and they tie the performance explicitly to the learning goals. When you include unrelated or untaught performance criteria on a scoring guide, you distract students from the primary goals. In addition, your assessment appears unfair because it isn't aligned with what you taught.

One factor that often turns up in essay rubrics is "creativity." If you have explicitly spent time in your instructional activities addressing creativity through asking thought-provoking questions, providing freedom to take risks, focusing on applying language in unusual ways, and teaching strategies to escape typical ways of seeing or doing, then such a criterion is warranted. If you have not designed instructional activities that address creativity, making creativity an important criterion for scoring is not defensible.

✦ THE VALUE OF STUDENT-GENERATED ITEMS AND CRITICAL THINKING

Recall that one of the first guidelines for developing writing prompts was to create topics of interest to both students and yourself. By involving students in developing ideas for essays, you are more likely to generate topics of interest. Students can help in identifying key concepts in content areas. If students help you do this, they begin to learn to tease out what is important for themselves.

Students also can contribute to developing rubrics. After an essay prompt is developed, you can work with students to identify key criteria for assessing their responses. A benefit of student involvement in developing checklists and rubrics is the discussion of the criteria. Evaluative criteria are often very abstract concepts. For example, the first time we encountered the criterion of *voice* we had little clue to its meaning. Only with the help of a rubric did we understand that elements of *voice* include the following:

- Precise and/or vivid vocabulary appropriate for the topic
- Effective rather than predictable or obvious phrasing
- Varied sentence structure to promote rhythmic reading
- Awareness of audience and task; consistent and appropriate tone

During the development of a checklist or rubric, discussing important features of an essay and linking each feature with your scoring criteria will help students understand the connection between the rubric and the qualities they are aiming for in their essays. This involvement serves as useful instructional time because the development process helps students understand and internalize the elements of quality essays.

✦ ACCOMMODATIONS FOR DIVERSE LEARNERS: CONSTRUCTED-RESPONSE ITEMS

In Chapter 7 we described various forms of test accommodations that may assist diverse learners in your class to complete an examination with multiple-choice, true-false, and matching items. In this chapter we focus on accommodations that may assist your students in completing short-answer items and essays. We do not repeat suggestions that we offered in Chapter 7, so you may want to revisit Table 7.6 to gain additional ideas of the accommodations diverse learners may benefit from.

A critical issue in accommodations for diverse learners is the demand of writing when short-answer items and essays are used to assess student learning. Writing can

TABLE 8.9

Accommodation Considerations for Constructed-Response Items

Issue	Type of Accommodation
Difficulty with fine motor skills	• Use speech-recognition software for word processing.
Sensory challenges (e.g., visual, auditory)	• Enhance legibility of prompt for visual impairments. • Read prompt aloud or present it in Braille. • Allow use of Braille or dictation for response.
Learning English	• Allow use of spell check and grammar check in word-processing program. • Allow use of bilingual dictionary. • Explicitly discuss rubric and criteria.
Learning goal already mastered	• Write prompts to engage student at the evaluation and creation levels of cognition.
Difficulty focusing attention	• Explicitly discuss rubric and criteria. • Review sample essays.
Literacy skills below those of typical peers (e.g., learning disability)	• Allow use of spell check and grammar check in word-processing program. • Explicitly discuss rubric and criteria. • Review sample essays.
Lack of familiarity with school culture	• Explicitly discuss rubric and criteria. • Review sample essays.

present physical demands for these learners in terms of manually recording thoughts on paper. Writing also presents cognitive demands in terms of organizing the ideas a student wants to use in a response. In examining the accommodations for diverse learners, we consider the need for the assessment to avoid interfering with a student demonstrating achievement of learning goals. See Table 8.9 for accommodation suggestions for several groups of diverse learners.

→ CASE STUDY APPLICATION

Two examples of Maria Mensik's essay questions from her unit on utopias and dystopias are shown in Table 8.10, and the rubric for scoring the essays is presented in Figure 8.21. The essay prompts and rubric display many of the features discussed in the guidelines. Note how carefully these questions are aligned with the learning goals (see Table 2.16) and the explicitness of the writing tasks. In the first essay, Maria directs students to support their answer with three characteristics of utopia or dystopia and relate these to examples from works they have read. She even provides an example to show students how to link their viewpoint with examples of utopias or dystopias in those works. In the second essay, the number of examples required and the societal aspects to address are specified. Furthermore, Maria emphasizes the explicit focus of the task by stating, "A good essay will briefly describe the aspect, then use persuasive language to tell other people why they will want to live there."

TABLE 8.10

Essay Questions on Utopia/Dystopia Unit

1. Given what we know about utopia—that it is an ideal place, state, or condition—we know that the existence of a utopia is impossible. Conversely, a dystopia often reflects a society taken to the worst possible extreme. Given the two extremes, do you think the United States is more utopic or dystopic? Support your answer with three characteristics of utopia or dystopia and relate these reasons to examples from works we have read. (Example: You might say that the United States is more like a dystopia when police want to use video surveillances to monitor public places. In *1984*, we see constant surveillance when the government uses telescreens to monitor the citizens of Oceania.)

2. Each group in this class has created a version of a utopian society. Write an (individual) 2–3 page essay that will persuade other classmates that they would want to move to your group's community. Your essay should describe at least three societal aspects. One must be the government, and two others can be chosen from work, family, religion, education, attitude toward technology, or others on which your group has focused. A good essay will briefly describe the aspect, then use persuasive language to tell other people why they will want to live there.

Performance Criteria	Proficiency Levels		
Description	**6** Describes fewer than 3 aspects and/or the descriptions are very limited.	**9** Describes 3 aspects; however, descriptions are vague and need more detail.	**12** Clearly describes 3 aspects with vivid, detailed language.
Persuasion	**6** Support for position is limited or missing.	**9** Position supported but some reasons or examples are not relevant or well-chosen.	**12** Position supported with relevant reasons and well-chosen examples.
Organization	**2** Is disorganized and lacks transitions.	**4** Is organized, but may lack some transitions.	**6** Is focused and well organized, with effective use of transitions.
Mechanics	**2** Frequent errors in grammar, spelling, or punctuation. These errors inhibit understanding.	**4** Errors in grammar, spelling, or punctuation do not inhibit understanding.	**6** Few errors in grammar, spelling, or punctuation. These errors do not inhibit understanding.

FIGURE 8.21 *Rubric for Scoring Students' Essays*
Reprinted with permission.

Maria limits the scoring guide to four criteria: *description, persuasion, organization,* and *mechanics.* The criteria *description* and *persuasion* most directly relate to the unit learning goals. When students write persuasively about the United States as a utopia or dystopia, the *description* dimension of the task requires them to support their argument by providing examples of either utopic or dystopic qualities. Similarly, in the second essay students must describe the utopian qualities of the society that they create. The descriptions the students provide will help Maria to gauge whether students have developed an understanding of the *utopia* concept. The language and arguments the students use in their essays will allow Maria to assess their grasp of writing persuasively.

The criteria of *organization* and *mechanics* are less directly related to the unit. However, these two criteria are part of the content standards for writing in most states. Many English language arts teachers will address *organization* and *mechanics* (i.e., *conventions*) in their instruction all year long. Thus, including them in the scoring guide makes sense.

The *organization* and *mechanics* criteria are generic in that they will apply across writing assessments throughout the course of the year. However, given their indirect relation to the learning goals of the unit, the lower weighting of *organization* and *mechanics* (12 total possible points) as compared to *description* and *persuasion* (24 possible points) helps to ensure most of the grade for these essays will be based on the learning goals that are specifically the focus of the unit.

Also notice that the proficiency levels for each performance criterion use specific language to establish a continuum of performance. Descriptors for *persuasion,* for example, state the following:

- Support for position is limited or missing.
- Position supported, but some reasons or examples are not relevant or well chosen.
- Position supported with relevant reasons and well-chosen examples.

The descriptors avoid evaluative terms, such as "poor," "good," and "excellent." In addition, the four criteria address key qualities and do not focus on criteria that are frivolous (e.g., neatness) or untaught (e.g., creativity).

KEY CHAPTER POINTS

In this chapter we looked at various forms of constructed-response items, such as short answer and essay formats. Short-answer items take the form of a question or an incomplete statement, and student responses may be a single word, a phrase, or a few sentences. A teacher can use the short-answer format to assess student understanding of knowledge and concepts that are limited in scope. Essay items pose a question for students to answer or present a task to which students respond. Essay items should be used to assess learning goals associated with cognitive processes related to analysis, evaluation, and synthesis.

General guidelines for item development include assessing knowledge and cognitive skills associated with class instruction, using new interpretive material, keeping the language in the items simple, and attending to the developmental level of students.

In preparing content-based essay items, we stated that teachers should write directions that define the task clearly, focus students on the key ideas to address in their response, and use formatting features to clarify the task. In developing prompts for which writing skills are the focus, we suggested developing interesting prompts, incorporating key elements, focusing on students' cultural or social experiences, and avoiding prompts addressing personal values, religious beliefs, or criticism.

We next turned to scoring constructed-response items. Short-answer items can be scored by reviewing your instructional materials and using this information to prepare a list of answers. Essays and writing prompts require you to develop a scoring guide to identify important elements that should be evident in student responses. We then described the checklist, analytic rubric, and holistic rubric as three scoring frameworks. Checklists and analytic rubrics allow a teacher to report a score for each criterion. In the case of a holistic rubric, the criteria are integrated to describe students' responses for each proficiency level, and a teacher can report only one overall score.

We next discussed factors contributing error to students' essay scores. We then turned to identifying common pitfalls in developing essay items and scoring guides. After identifying students as a valuable resource in developing essays and scoring guides, we pointed out that short-answer and essay item formats present physical and cognitive demands that may interfere with student expression of knowledge. Such demands can be lessened if you plan for accommodations in your instruction and assessment. The case study section addressed application of the guidelines for essays and analytic rubrics.

HELPFUL WEBSITES

http://nces.ed.gov/nationsreportcard/
A website with constructed-response items and scoring guides from the National Assessment of
    Educational Progress (NAEP). Includes items in the subject areas of civics, economics,
    geography, mathematics, reading, science, United States history, and writing. All NAEP
    questions and rubrics in this chapter come from this website.
http://rubistar.4teachers.org/index.php
A website that provides templates for constructing rubrics. You also can look at rubrics made by
    teachers.

CHAPTER REVIEW QUESTIONS

1. For a test item to engage the students at the understanding cognitive level or higher, the interpretive material must be new. Suppose that during instruction you used the bar graph item in Figure 8.1. As you prepare a test on interpretation of graphs, how could you change the interpretive material in the bar graph item so your students must use the understanding cognitive level or higher?

2. Use the elements of a prompt from the "Developing Writing Prompts" section to review the persuasive writing prompt in Table 8.4. The persuasive prompt addresses which elements? Support your answer. Which elements are absent? Support your answer.

3. Read the descriptor for the rating level of 1 for the *voice* criterion in Figure 8.18. Rewrite the descriptor to use positive language.

4. A student in your class has difficulty with spelling, and her errors in spelling interfere with the meaning of her writing. What form of accommodation would be appropriate?

5. What criteria would you include in a scoring guide for the essay about Laura McFadden's pen and ink drawing? Refer to Figure 8.12. Would you use a checklist, analytic rubric, or holistic rubric? Why?

6. Design an essay prompt and an analytic rubric for a writing assignment that you might assign in your class. Which guidelines did you find hardest to follow?

7. Revisit the accommodations for selected-response tests in Table 7.6 of Chapter 7. Select two of the accommodations for students who have difficulty focusing attention that would apply to a test that used essays. State why the accommodations would be useful for this group of diverse learners.
8. Download one of the writing prompts from the NAEP website: http://nces.ed.gov/ nationsreportcard/ITMRLS/searchresults.asp. Write two of the strengths of the prompt according to the guidelines that we have presented.

REFERENCES

Albertson, B. 1998. *Creating effective writing prompts.* Newark: Delaware Reading and Writing Project, Delaware Center for Teacher Education, University of Delaware.

Arter, J., and J. Chappuis. 2007. *Creating and recognizing quality rubrics.* Upper Saddle River, NJ: Pearson Education.

California Department of Education. 2008. *California standards test released test questions: Grade 8 science.* Retrieved February 18, 2008, from http://www.cde.ca.gov/ta/tg/sr/css05rtq.asp.

Chase, C. 1986. Essay test scoring: Interaction of relevant variables. *Journal of Educational Measurement* 23: 33–41.

Coerr, E. 1977. *Sadako and the thousand paper cranes.* New York: Puffin Books.

Creighton, S. 2006. *Examining alternative scoring rubrics on a statewide test: The impact of different scoring methods on science and social studies performance assessments.* Unpublished doctoral dissertation, University of South Carolina, Columbia.

Daly, J., and F. Dickson-Markman. 1982. Contrast effects in evaluating essays. *Journal of Educational Measurement* 19(4): 309–316.

Dunbar, S., D. Koretz, and H. Hoover. 1991. Quality control in the development and use of performance assessments. *Applied Measurement in Education* 4(4): 289–303.

Florida Department of Education. 2005. *Florida Writing Assessment Program (FLORIDA WRITES!).* Retrieved December 26 from http://www.fldoe.org/asp/fw/fwaprubr.asp.

Gredler, M., and R. Johnson. 2004. *Assessment in the literacy classroom.* Needham Heights, MA: Allyn & Bacon.

Grobe, C. 1981. Syntactic maturity, mechanics, and vocabulary as predictors of quality ratings. *Research in the Teaching of English* 13: 207–215.

Hogan, T., and G. Murphy. 2007. Recommendations for preparing and scoring constructed-response items: What the experts say. *Applied Measurement in Education* 20(4): 427–441.

Hopkins, K. 1998. *Educational and psychological measurement and evaluation.* 8th ed. Englewood Cliffs, NJ: Allyn and Bacon.

Hopkins, K. D., J. C. Stanley, and B. R. Hopkins. 1990. *Educational and psychological measurement and evaluation.* Englewood Cliffs, NJ: Prentice Hall.

Johnson, R., J. Penny, and B. Gordon. 2009. *Assessing performance: Developing, scoring, and validating performance tasks.* New York: Guilford Publications.

Kuhs, T., Johnson, R., Agruso, S., and Monsod, D. 2001. *Put to the Test: Tools and Techniques for Classroom Assessment.* Portsmouth, NH: Heinemann.

Lane, S., and C. Stone. 2006. Performance assessment. In R. Brennan (ed.), *Educational measurement,* 4th ed., pp. 387–431. Westport, CT: American Council on Education and Praeger Publishers.

Markham, L. 1976. Influences of handwriting quality on teacher evaluation of written work. *American Educational Research Journal* 13: 277–284.

National Center for Educational Statistics. 2005. *NAEP questions.* Retrieved June 19, 2008, from http://nces.ed.gov/nationsreportcard/itmrls/.

National Center for Educational Statistics. 2008. *What does the NAEP Writing Assessment measure?* Retrieved June 19, 2008, from http://nces.ed.gov/nationsreportcard/writing/whatmeasure.asp.

Nitko, A., and S. Brookhart. 2007. *Educational assessment of students.* 5th ed. Upper Saddle River, NJ: Pearson.

Ohio State Department of Education. 2003. *Academic content standards: K–12 fine arts.* Retrieved June 11, 2007, from http://www.ode.state.oh.us/GD/Templates/Pages/ODE/ODEDetail.aspx?page=3&TopicRelationID=336&ContentID=1388&Content=12661.

Richter, H. 1987. *Friedrich.* New York: Puffin Books.

South Carolina Department of Education. 2004a. *Extended response scoring rubric.* Retrieved May 24, 2008, from http://ed.sc.gov/agency/offices/assessment/pact/rubrics.html.

South Carolina Department of Education. 2004b. *Released PACT history item.* Columbia, SC: Author.

South Carolina Department of Education. 2006. *South Carolina High School Assessment Program: Release form.* Retrieved July 1, 2008, from http://ed.sc.gov/agency/offices/assessment/programs/hsap/releaseitems.html.

South Carolina Department of Education. 2007. *PACT math release items.* Retrieved February 18, 2008, from http://ed.sc.gov/agency/offices/assessment/pact/PACTMathReleaseItems.html.

Starch, D., and E. Elliot. 1912. Reliability of grading high school work in English. *School Review* 20: 442–457.

Starch, D., and E. Elliot. 1913. Reliability of grading high school work in mathematics. *School Review* 21: 254–259.

Stewart, M., and C. Grobe. 1979. Syntactic maturity, mechanics of writing, and teachers' quality ratings. *Research in the Teaching of English* 13: 207–215.

Thorndike, R. 2005. *Measurement and evaluation in psychology and education.* 7th ed. Upper Saddle River, NJ: Pearson Education.

CHAPTER 9

TEACHER-MADE ASSESSMENTS: PERFORMANCE ASSESSMENTS

We cannot be said to "understand" something unless we can employ it wisely, fluently, flexibly, and aptly in particular and diverse contexts.

–Grant Wiggins

❖ **Chapter Learning Goals**

At the conclusion of this chapter, the reader should be able to do the following:

- Describe the two forms of response in performance assessments.

- Align the learning goals and the form of assessment.

- Describe when to use performance assessments.

- Explain the advantages and disadvantages of performance assessments.

- Apply general guidelines to develop performance assessments that require students to use the cognitive strategies of apply, analyze, evaluate, and create.

- Design methods for scoring performance assessments.

- Involve students in the development of performance assessments.

- Describe ways to accommodate the performance assessment format for diverse learners.

✦ INTRODUCTION

Now that we have described teacher-made selected-response and constructed-response formats for designing assessments in Chapters 7 and 8, we move on to the most complex teacher-designed assessment type. **Performance assessments** require students to construct a response to a task or prompt to demonstrate their achievement of a learning goal. In the previous chapter, we noted that the essay is a special case of a performance assessment. In responding to an essay prompt, students retrieve the required facts and concepts, organize this information, and construct a written response. However, not all performance assessments require a written response. In music, for example, students sing or play an instrument. In masonry, students might lay a brick corner.

To illustrate the power of performance assessments, let us take you into one of our classes. Actually, we are taking you into the media center at Germanton Elementary. In the biography section of the media center, you see a group of fifth-grade students standing by the bookshelves. At each shelf a student counts the books from left to right. After counting five books, the student pulls the fifth book, reads the title to determine who the biography is about, and sometimes reads the blurb inside the book cover. Each student then tells another student, who is serving as a recorder, the ethnicity of the person who is the focus of the biography. The student then returns the book to the shelf, counts five books, and pulls the next biography. After completing this process for each of the shelves in the biography section, the students return to the classroom to compile their data. In the classroom, the students graph their results, showing that a majority of the biographies focused on European Americans. Students then write a brief report about their findings and present the report to the media specialist.

What was the purpose of this exercise? The students had just completed a learning unit on the use of pie charts and bar graphs to show patterns in data. Why bother with students actually counting the biographies? Why not simply give students some fabricated data to graph? Enhancing the meaningfulness of a problem is a key quality in performance assessment (Johnson et al., 2009). By involving students in the data collection, we make real the use of visual representations of data to detect patterns and answer significant questions. This particular exercise also involves students in examining equity in representing the diversity of our culture—linking their critical thinking skills with issues relevant to participation in a democracy.

Process

The procedure a student uses to complete a performance task.

In performance assessment, the form of response required of students may be a **process** (e.g., delivering a speech) or a product (e.g., a house plan). Process should be the focus of a performance assessment when (a) the act of performing is the target learning outcome, (b) the performance is a series of procedures that can be observed, or (c) a diagnosis of performance might improve learning outcomes (Gronlund, 2004). For example, in elementary schools, when a student engages in the process of retelling a story, the teacher can examine the student's ability to capture the main idea of the text, identify key details of the narrative, and use this information to summarize the story.

Product

The tangible outcome or end result of a performance task.

A **product,** on the other hand, should be the focus of learning outcomes when (a) a product is the primary outcome of a performance, (b) the product has observable characteristics that can be used in evaluating the student's response, and (c) variations exist in the procedures for producing the response (Gronlund, 2004). For example, in the visual arts the student engages in a process to create a sculpture; however, the focus should be the qualities expressed in the final product.

A systematic method for scoring student responses must accompany any performance assessment. In Chapter 8, we described three types of scoring guides: checklists, holistic rubrics, and analytic rubrics. We will revisit analytic rubrics later in this chapter as the preferable means of scoring performance assessments.

✦ ALIGNING ITEMS WITH LEARNING GOALS AND THINKING SKILLS

As with any item type, a critical component of developing a quality performance assessment is the alignment of the task with the understanding and skills that were the focus of instruction. Figure 9.1 presents an example of how content of learning goals can affect the selection of performance tasks versus selected-response, short-answer, or essay formats. As shown, to assess whether a student uses appropriate instruments and tools safely and accurately, a teacher will need to use a performance assessment and observe the student in the process of conducting a scientific investigation. However, the teacher can use selected-response items to assess students' learning to classify observations as quantitative or qualitative or to categorize statements as observations, predictions, or inferences.

Standard 4-1:
The student will demonstrate an understanding of scientific inquiry, including the processes, skills, and mathematical thinking necessary to conduct a simple scientific investigation.

Indicators (i.e., Learning Goals)	Possible Assessment Formats
4-1.1 Classify observations as either quantitative or qualitative.	Selected Response
4-1.2 Use appropriate instruments and tools (including a compass, an anemometer, mirrors, and a prism) safely and accurately when conducting simple investigations.	Performance Assessment
4-1.3 Summarize the characteristics of a simple scientific investigation that represent a fair test (including a question that identifies the problem, a prediction that indicates a possible outcome, a process that tests one manipulated variable at a time, and results that are communicated and explained).	Essay
4-1.4 Distinguish among observations, predictions, and inferences.	Selected Response
4-1.5 Recognize the correct placement of variables on a line graph.	Selected Response
4-1.6 Construct and interpret diagrams, tables, and graphs made from recorded measurements and observations.	Performance Assessment
4-1.7 Use appropriate safety procedures when conducting investigations. (SCDE, 2005, p. 31)	Performance Assessment

FIGURE 9.1 *Aligning Content Standards and Learning Goals with Assessment Forms*

Adapted from South Carolina Department of Education. 2005. *South Carolina science academic standards*. Columbia, S.C.: Author. From http://ed.sc.gov/agency/offices/cso/standards/science/. Reprinted with permission.

✦ When to Use Performance Assessments

In deciding whether to use a performance assessment, the first issue to consider is whether the learning goals to be assessed require students to use higher-level cognitive strategies such as evaluation or creation. If, for example, you want to assess whether students can incorporate the elements and principles of the visual arts into a drawing, a task that engages students in producing an actual drawing is necessary. A test that uses multiple-choice items can tap into a student's ability to analyze a drawing and identify elements displayed in the piece. However, a test that relies solely on multiple-choice items cannot inform you about a student's ability to create. Writers in the field of assessment agree that performance assessment should be used to assess students' use of higher-level cognitive strategies (Hogan & Murphy, 2007).

Another issue to think about is your goals for the development of student understanding. Consider the example of the students investigating the diversity in the biography section in the school media center. Their understanding, in part, could have been assessed using multiple-choice items, or the teacher could have provided the frequency counts for the types of vegetables or fruits displayed in textbooks. Instead, students were engaged in the more meaningful task of investigating the representation of the diversity of our society, summarizing the data in graphs, and writing a written report with recommendations. Performance assessments are best utilized when the consequences broaden your students' understanding and contribute to their development.

→ Advantages and Disadvantages of Performance Assessments

A major advantage of performance assessment is the potential to engage students in more cognitively complex, relevant tasks in which they must organize information in formulating a response. Performance tasks allow a teacher to assess students' understanding and skills in depth. Such tasks require students to recall, organize, and synthesize concepts that were the focus of a learning unit. Also, performance tasks can be embedded in contexts that contribute to the meaningfulness of a task. Consider, for example, students demonstrating their achievements in public speaking when they host the morning newscast on their school's closed-circuit television broadcast. The context of a broadcast makes the task more authentic to the students.

In terms of disadvantages, we should talk about the time required for students to complete a performance task. Having students actually collect the data on biographies, generate the appropriate graphs, write the report, and present their findings to the media specialist consumed several class periods. We would have taken perhaps one class period if we simply handed our students a set of data and asked them to put the information into the appropriate graph form and write an interpretation. Given the demand on time, we suggest using performance assessments primarily in the culminating activities of a unit when you need to assess students' abilities to analyze, evaluate, and create. As the opening quotation suggests, a performance assessment should give your students an opportunity to demonstrate their deeper understanding of the learning goals by employing it "wisely, fluently, flexibly, and aptly" in a carefully chosen context.

A second disadvantage in the use of performance assessment lies with the difficulty of achieving high reliability in scoring. As a teacher grades numerous student responses, the teacher's scoring may become more severe (or sometimes more lenient). For some students, the grade might reflect the teacher becoming fatigued rather than the quality of the performance. All is not lost, however, because we have learned to develop scoring guides that will improve the consistency of our grading of performance tasks. We will examine scoring guides more closely in a later section.

→ Guidelines for Task Development

In this section, we provide guidelines that contribute to a well-designed performance task (see Table 9.1).

Specify the Understanding and Skills to Be Addressed

As you begin writing the task prompt, you should specify the understanding and skills to be addressed in the student response. Here we mean both the knowledge the student will demonstrate and the cognitive processes the student will use. In Figure 9.2, Gloria Ham, a high school Spanish teacher, identifies the content that is the focus of the task *Libro de Niños Sobre el Medio Ambiente*. Gloria's task engages students in application of conventions of Spanish language to create a book. She identifies the focus to be sentence structure, verb tenses, and vocabulary. By explicitly specifying the content, as

TABLE 9.1

Guidelines for Developing Performance Assessment Prompts

Specify the content knowledge and cognitive strategies the student must demonstrate in responding to the prompt.

Create a task that is meaningful to the students.

Determine the format (i.e., oral, demonstration, or product) of the final form of the student's response.

Consider the supplies and resources to complete the task.

Address the degree of structure appropriate for this task.

Keep the reading demands at a level that ensures clarity of the task directions.

Address logistics in the task directions.

LIBRO DE NIÑOS SOBRE EL MEDIO AMBIENTE

[Children's Book About the Environment]

Gloria Ham

Assignment:

- Option 1: You will write a book for small children (5–7-year-olds). You will write it in story form to educate and/or persuade small children to protect the environment, do community service, and/or be aware of our role in society.
- Option 2: You will write a children's story that is a retelling of a well-known fairy tale. It shouldn't be a direct translation of the fairy tale, but your own original story.

Structure, grammar, and vocabulary:

- You should use simple and compound sentences and they should follow the structures that we have studied in Units One and Two.
- Your verbs should include the subjunctive and the indicative moods in all tenses and forms necessary to tell the story.
- Make sure to include vocabulary, conjunctions of time, phrases and expressions from Unit Two.

Your book . . .

- Should be an original story.
- Should be bilingual.
- Should include minimum 6 – maximum 10 pages (in Spanish and same number in English), plus front and back covers.
- Should have an illustration on each page. The illustrations must be appropriate for small children (bright, colorful, and big). You may use original pictures or drawings, appropriate clip art, pictures from a fairy tale, etc.
- Should have at least one sentence per page, but not more than five sentences per page.
- Should include a title page with a graphic and fancy lettering, the title, author's name, illustrator's name, and the year.
- Due on November 13.

Submit a rough draft for corrections (20 points)

- Typed, double spaced.
- Due on November 1.

We will go to one of the elementary schools in the district to read our books.

FIGURE 9.2 *A Performance Task for Students in a High School Spanish Class*

Reprinted with permission.

Gloria did, you can determine whether the task addresses the knowledge, skills, and strategies that were the focus of instruction. In addition, a review of the content requirements allows you to make sure the cognitive strategies required for the task engage students in analyzing, evaluating, and creating.

In some instances, teachers write performance tasks to assess student learning across content areas. As discussed in Chapter 8, assessing student development of writing skills can be integrated with assessing their content knowledge. In Figure 9.3, the prompt for an art class directs students to create a painting in one of the artistic styles they have studied. In addition, students develop a placard describing the elements of the painting. In this task, the teacher assesses in an integrated way her students' learning in both the visual arts and writing.

Build Meaningfulness into the Task

Meaningfulness is considered a critical element to incorporate into performance assessments. In the task shown in Figure 9.4, a high school mathematics teacher, Denise Derrick, establishes a scenario in which students must use their skills in developing

We have been studying several artistic styles, such as cubism, impressionism, and pointillism. We are going to turn our classroom into an art gallery for when your families come to our school's open house. Galleries usually have a variety of art styles in their exhibits and hanging beside each piece is a placard that tells about the artwork. Your contribution to our gallery is to create a painting of some person or event in your life using one of the styles of art that we studied. Also, write a description of what it is that your family member should see in your painting that will help him or her understand which style you used. Your description should address the elements and principles of the visual arts. In writing your description, be sure to follow the conventions of written language that we have studied.

FIGURE 9.3 *Performance Task That Integrates Art and Writing Skills*

QUADRATIC RELATIONS AND CONIC SECTIONS

Denise Derrick

Objective: The student will analyze a situation involving a nonlinear real-life problem and devise a method to solve the problem.

Directions:
    You are the director of the Disaster Preparedness Agency for Richland County. It is your job to assess the situation when a disaster occurs and make decisions regarding evacuations for any affected areas in the county. On December 10, a toxic spill involving chlorine gas occurs at one of the local industries. The gas is lethal when inhaled. You immediately consult with local climatologists regarding wind patterns and are informed that due to prevailing wind patterns, the gas can be expected to spread in dangerous levels for 20 miles in all directions. Beyond the 20 miles, everyone will be safe. There is a hospital located 11 miles east and 17 miles north of the point of origin of the leak. If you don't evacuate the hospital, will the patients be safe? If you do evacuate and it is not necessary, there will be a tremendous financial loss and unnecessary suffering for patients.

Do you evacuate the hospital?
    After having studied the four conic shapes: parabolas, circles, ellipses, and hyperbolas, choose one of the shapes to help you make your decision. Write an algebraic model equation/inequality to represent the affected or unaffected area; show the calculations necessary to make your decision; and defend your decision by writing an explanation of your procedures.

FIGURE 9.4 *A Mathematics Performance Task That Incorporates "Meaningfulness"*
Reprinted with permission.

¿ C Ó M O   L L E G O ?

Carmen Nazario

Standard 1.1   Students engage in conversations, provide and obtain information, express feelings and emotions, and exchange opinions.

We have been studying how to identify places, give addresses, request directions, and give instructions.

Our room will be transformed into "Downtown E. L. W."

Situation: Imagine that you are lost in "Downtown E. L. W." You will be given two starting and two ending points. Your partner and you will take turns requesting directions and giving instructions in Spanish on how to get to your final destination.

You will be graded according to the following rubric:

Performance Criteria	Proficiency Levels			Weight	Score
	0	**1**	**2**		
Request directions.	Student does not know how to ask for directions.	Student asks for directions but with some difficulty.	Student asks for directions with no difficulty.	2	
Follow directions.	Student can't follow directions given by partner.	Student can follow directions with some difficulty.	Student can follow directions without hesitation.	3	
Use of affirmative *tu* commands.	Commands are barely or not used.	Commands are used but not consistently.	Commands are correctly used throughout.	5	
Use of prepositional phrases to express location.	Prepositions are not used correctly.	Prepositions used but with some mistakes.	Prepositions used correctly.	5	
Identifying places.	Student can't identify places in and around the destination.	Student identifies places but with some difficulty.	Student can identify the places without mistakes.	5	
Accuracy in the giving of instructions.	Instructions were not clear or accurate.	Instructions were clear but with some mistakes.	Instructions were very clear and accurate.	5	

Earned points_____
Total possible points: 50

FIGURE 9.5   *A Spanish Performance Assessment That Incorporates the Element of "Meaningfulness"*
Reprinted with permission.

algebraic models to make a decision about evacuating areas of a county that may be affected by a toxic spill. In "Quadratic Relations and Conic Sections," students see real-life implications for the algebraic skills they are developing.

Carmen Nazario, a middle-school Spanish teacher, incorporated meaningfulness into the task she developed in which students ask for directions and provide directions in Spanish (Figure 9.5). Students in her class recognize giving directions as a necessary skill and, thus, the task is likely to be more meaningful to students than textbook exercises at the end of a unit.

Ethics Alert: In the "¿Cómo Llego?" task in Figure 9.5, the grade of the student depends in part on the quality of the instructions he receives in Spanish from his partner. Because the student's grade should be based only on his understanding of directions stated in the correct Spanish form, the teacher will need to correct any directions in which the Spanish is incorrect. Then the grade of the student who is receiving directions will represent his understanding of directions stated in Spanish.

Audiences and Meaningfulness

Contributing to meaningfulness of the "¿Cómo Llego?" task in Figure 9.5, is the use of students' peers as the audience for their performances. In our teaching, we have experienced the excitement of students who had articles published by their local newspapers about their visits to museums. As students wrote the articles, they knew the community was their audience. Contrast the meaningfulness of writing for a community-wide audience with completing short-answer items or writing brief essays that only a teacher will see.

If students are engaged in a content-area task, potential audiences extend beyond the teacher or other students to other writers, mathematicians, artists, and scientists. These audiences impose realistic demands for the task. For example, in "Libro de Niños Sobre el Medio Ambiente" (Figure 9.2), the teacher indicates the high school students will read their books to elementary students. This audience has implications in terms of vocabulary: the students in the Spanish class will need to use vocabulary appropriate for elementary students. In the art example (Figure 9.3), students will need to use language their parents or guardians will understand when they read the placard.

Context and Meaningfulness

Context is another element that potentially contributes to the meaningfulness of a task by providing a setting and a purpose that realistically focus and constrain the task. The example at the beginning of the chapter focused on the media center as the setting and had the purpose of using students' skills in creating graphs to summarize their findings about the diversity reflected in the biography collection.

Context can be provided by the subject area being studied, the themes associated with learning units, or students' personal experiences (Kuhs et al., 2001). In the task shown in Figure 9.6, Angela Black, a fourth-grade teacher, uses the subject area being studied—organizing data in graphical display—as the context. She also links the task to students' personal experiences when she bases the data on a survey about the sports that fifth-grade students liked to watch on television. Linking the task to students' personal experiences is one of the most effective ways to enhance meaningfulness (Ovando, 2005).

Determine the Response Format

In the prompt directions you should specify the form the response should take. Some learning goals may best be assessed by attending to the processes in which a student engages in responding to a performance task (Table 9.2). For other learning goals, a product is the best response form to gauge achievement. A review of the types of activities in Table 9.2 reminds us that student assessments can include an array of forms.

DATA ANALYSIS AND PROBABILITY

Angela Black

Student Name:_____   Date:_____

Standard: Mathematics Grade 4: Data Analysis and Probability

Standard 4-6.3: Organize data in graphical displays (tables, line graphs, bar graphs with scale increments greater than one).

We have been learning about collecting data, interpreting (reading) the data, organizing the data for a reader, and the different types of graphs that are used for data.

You will create a graph using Microsoft Excel from the data that were collected in class from the survey on the sports that fifth-grade students liked to watch on television. The graph should represent the data clearly and meet the grading categories in the rubric.

   Directions:

1. Bring collected data to Computer Class during Related Arts time.
2. Enter data into Microsoft Excel spreadsheet.
3. Create graph using Chart Wizard.
4. Label and adjust graph to make graph clear and accurate to the reader.
5. Attach your graph to this sheet before turning it in.

FIGURE 9.6   *A Data Analysis Performance Task That Links to Students' Personal Experiences*

Reprinted with permission.

The "¿Cómo Llego?" task in Figure 9.5 engages students in providing directions using Spanish—an example of a process performance task. Other process tasks include making patterns with math manipulatives, passing a basketball, and playing a musical passage. The outcomes in the previous performance tasks in which students write a bilingual children's book (Figure 9.2) and create a graph (Figure 9.6) are examples of products.

Today, the distinction between process and product can become blurred because students' responses or demonstrations can be recorded and scored later. Previously, students' performances of a play or a dance could be observed and evaluated only at the time students engaged in the process. We do not advocate delayed scoring because the amount of time required to grade a recorded performance is likely to be added to the time spent watching the original presentation.

TABLE 9.2

Examples of Process and Product Performance Tasks

Processes		Products
Oral	**Demonstration**	
• Delivering a newscast	• Performing a play	• Play script
• Interviewing a senior citizen	• Searching for websites related to a topic	• Floor plan
• Retelling a story	• Applying first-aid skills	• Spreadsheet
• Modeling a decision-making process	• Operating a fire extinguisher	• Musical score
• Reciting a memorized poem or speech	• Performing a dance choreographed by a student	• Scale model
		• Timelines
		• Written reports

Consider the Materials and Resources Required

Performance assessments frequently go beyond the pencil and paper modes of response. In the examples we have seen thus far, students needed access to computer programs to create graphs, clip art to use as illustrations for a children's book, and art supplies. Not all students have the resources at home to complete such tasks; in planning a performance assessment, you need to consider the availability of these resources to ensure that all students have equal access.

Address the Degree of Structure for a Task

You should also consider the amount of structure needed by your students for the task. One method to provide structure is to use numbers or bullets to outline critical procedural steps in a task. As shown in Figure 9.7, Frank Harrison, a high school English teacher, numbers the steps students should follow in writing a poem. Notice the use of bullets in "Libro de Niños Sobre el Medio Ambiente" in Figure 9.2 and the use of numbers in "Data Analysis and Probability" in Figure 9.6. These formats guide students as they complete a task.

In the sonnet task, Frank also developed a grid for added structure to guide students as they write. The grid indicates the number of lines, the stresses, and the rhyming pattern. Finally, when scoring guides are provided with the task, as done in "¿Cómo Llego?," the guide provides structure by highlighting for students the critical features to incorporate into their responses.

Another way to help students structure and visualize the performance task is to show examples of responses completed by students in previous years. Reviewing and discussing the qualities of exemplary responses will help to make the directions and rubric more concrete for your students. We stress the use of multiple models because if you show only one example, students may be led to think the model is *the right answer*. If you use such models, you should show several versions of exemplary responses.

Monitor the Reading Demands

As you develop a performance assessment, you will also want to pay attention to language used in the prompt. Instructions often require a heavy cognitive processing load based on the reading required. Text is used to describe the problem, place it within a context, and specify the form of the students' responses. In constructing a prompt, you need to attend to choice of words and sentence structure of the prompt. After drafting your prompt, reread it to see whether you can use less-demanding vocabulary and whether you can add graphics or other visual organizational tools to reduce reliance on language alone (e.g., the grid used in the sonnet lesson in Figure 9.7). Also check the structure of sentences to see if you can simplify them.

In Chapter 7 we described how to check the reading level of your test materials using the Spelling and Grammar feature in Microsoft Word. The analysis in Word indicated that the grade-level readability is 8.5 for the NAEP science item in Figure 9.8. Given the item is for the twelfth-grade NAEP, the reading level should be appropriate for the students.

Address Logistics in the Task Directions

A final element to consider is the logistics of the task, or a listing of your expectations in terms of the due date, the number of pages for any written responses, the acceptable font, the length of time for oral responses or demonstrations, and the point value for the task.

SONNET SEQUENCE: ENGLISH III COLLEGE PREP

Frank Harrison

Instructions: Write a Petrarchan sonnet about any topic, character, theme, setting, period, etc., you've encountered thus far in your study of American literature. Use your text, required novels, summer reading, videos shown in class, and/or class discussions/notes for sources.

1. Write exactly fourteen lines, putting one syllable in each box of the grid below.
2. In the first eight lines, describe a problem, introduce an issue, or pose a question.

3. In the last six lines, resolve the problem, make general comments or conclusions, or answer the question.
4. The grid will help you as you draft your sonnet. Follow the pattern for stressed and unstressed syllables shown along the top of the grid.
5. Follow the pattern for end rhymes shown along the right side of the grid.
6. Final drafts should be typed and double-spaced.

"−" indicates an unstressed syllable; "ʹ"indicates a stressed syllable

	−	ʹ	−	ʹ	−	ʹ	−	ʹ	−	ʹ	
1											A
2											b
3											B
4											a
5											a
6											b
7											b
8											a
9											c
10											d
11											e
12											c
13											d
14											e

FIGURE 9.7 *An English Performance Task That Uses a Grid to Guide Student Development of a Sonnet*
Reprinted with permission.

When students are working on long-term projects, teachers should review students' progress at several points during the process. (We have addressed some of the benefits of such formative assessment in Chapter 4.) Periodic reviews also teach students to pace themselves and not wait until the last minute to complete a task. No one wants to grade projects done the night before.

Another benefit to incorporating checkpoints and working with students during the process is to reduce the likelihood of shoddy last-minute work or even plagiarism. For

Questions 4–5 refer to the following investigation.

A student took a sample of water from a pond and examined it under a microscope. She identified several species of protozoans, including two species of *Paramecium* that are known to eat the same food. The student decided to examine the water sample every day for a week. She added food for the *Paramecia* each day and counted the number of each species. Her findings are summarized in the table below.

Number of *Paramecia* in Pond Water Sample

Day	Species *S*	Species *T*
1	50	50
2	60	80
3	100	90
4	150	60
5	160	50
6	160	30
7	160	20

4. Using the axes below, construct a graph showing the number of each species of *Paramecium* the student found each day. Be sure to label the axes.

FIGURE 9.8   *An NAEP Science Task for Twelfth-Grade Students*

SOURCE: National Center for Educational Statistics. 2005. NAEP questions. From http://nces.ed.gov/nationsreportcard/ itmrls/. Reprinted with permission.

example, after reading and discussing a historical novel, students in one class prepared to write their own historical novelettes. To frame the collection of information about a time period, the teacher prepared a chart with the headers of historical events, clothing, food, etc. (Kuhs et al., 2001). Students used the chart to take notes about people during the historical period that was the focus of their novel. After reviewing their notes with the teacher, students then began writing a five-chapter novelette. The student reviewed each 3- to 4-page chapter with the teacher and revised as needed. At the end of the process, students had an original novelette of approximately 15 pages. Think of the different position of the students if the teacher had simply instructed them to write a historical novelette, assigned a due date for the final project, and not monitored student work as they progressed.

→ SCORING THE ASSESSMENT

In this section we examine the elements of the scoring guides accompanying performance tasks. To supplement this information, you should review the section on scoring guides in Chapter 8.

The teachers in our examples for this chapter favored analytic rubrics to score the performance tasks. Analytic rubrics list separate performance criteria for reviewing students' responses. For example, in the rubric for the task "Sonnet Sequence: English III College Prep," the teacher includes criteria related to number of lines, rhyming pattern, syllable patterns, etc. (see Figure 9.9). Thus, students receive a score for each performance criterion. Because performance tasks are usually complex with several performance criteria to be addressed, we recommend analytic rubrics for providing the clearest scoring and feedback for students.

Student Name:			Date	
Performance Criteria	**Proficiency Levels**			
	0	**1**	**2**	**3**
Has 14 lines	Sonnet does not have 14 lines.	Sonnet does have 14 lines.		
Has correct rhyming pattern		Sonnet does not rhyme.	Sonnet has some rhymes, but the rhyming pattern is not correct.	Sonnet has correct rhyming pattern.
Ten syllables per line with alternating stressed/unstressed syllables		No regular pattern of syllables.	Some lines are ten syllables and some alternate stresses.	All lines are ten syllables and alternate stresses.
Is about a topic covered in class		The sonnet does not deal with a topic covered in class.	The sonnet attempts to deal with a topic covered in class, but it is underdeveloped or unclear.	The sonnet's topic is directly related to a topic covered in class and is well-developed.
Last 6 lines comment on the first 8 lines		No identifiable comment (shift).	An obvious attempt is made to make a comment, but it is underdeveloped or unclear.	A clear and clever shift is evident where the second portion of the sonnet comments on the first.
Correct grammar and conventions		Sonnet contains errors in grammar, punctuation, or spelling that distract the reader.	Sonnet contains a few errors in grammar, punctuation, or spelling, but they don't distract the reader.	Sonnet has correct grammar, punctuation, and spelling.
Contains descriptive words		Specific nouns, adjectives, and adverbs that paint a picture for the reader are not used.	The selection of specific nouns, adjectives, and adverbs that paint a picture for the reader is attempted.	Specific nouns, adjectives, and adverbs that paint a picture for the reader are effectively selected.
Correct format		Not typed.	Typed, but not double-spaced.	Typed and double-spaced

FIGURE 9.9 *The Scoring Guide Used with the Task "Sonnet Sequence: English III College Prep"*

Reprinted with permission.

Accompanying each performance criterion is a scale with numerical ratings and a descriptor for each proficiency level. Notice in the rubric for writing a sonnet (Figure 9.9), the performance criterion for rhyming pattern has a scale that ranges from 1 to 3. (The teacher did not include a rating of 0 for this criterion.) The descriptor that accompanies the proficiency level of 3 is *Sonnet has correct rhyming pattern;* whereas for the proficiency level of 2, the descriptor is *Sonnet has some rhymes, but the rhyming pattern is not correct.*

Weighting Performance Criteria

You may find that some performance criteria in your scoring guide are more important than others and choose to weight the critical ones more heavily (Arter & Chappuis, 2007). For example, in the rubric for the "¿Cómo Llego?" task in Figure 9.5, the teacher assigned a weight of 2 to the student's request for information, but assigned a weight of 5 to the student's accuracy in giving instructions. A student who gets the highest proficiency level for requesting directions receives a score of 4 (i.e., a rating of $2 \times$ a weight of 2). So, a student with the top proficiency level for each performance criterion would receive 50 points $(4+6+10+10+10+10)$.

Attaching a Grade Scale

Teachers in our classes have found attaching a grade scale with the rubric useful when a performance assessment serves as a summative assessment. Look at the rubric that Angela Black developed for her performance task "Data Analysis and Probability" (Figure 9.10). She added a grading scale so that students would know the points required for each grade. Adding such a scale avoids confusion in expectations for grades.

How do you determine the range of scores for an A or B? Look again at the rubric (Figure 9.10) for "Data Analysis and Probability." Of course, a student who earns the top rating for all the criteria would earn an A; so the maximum score required for an A is 18 (i.e., $4+3+4+4+3$). What about the lowest score for an A? Look at each criterion and think about what rating is essential for an A. Perhaps you think that losing a point for labeling each axis and the design is a bare minimum for an A. If so, your low score is 15 $(4+3+3+3+2)$ and the score range for an A is 15–18 points. A high B would be 14 points. Then you must decide what score ratings would be acceptable for the lowest score in the B range. For example, is a rating of 3 acceptable for the data criterion? If students can earn 2 for the title, labeling the X axis, labeling the Y axis, and design, then combined with the 3 for data, you have a minimum score of 11 $(3+2+2+2+2)$. You systematically review each criterion and decide the rating that is acceptable for each grade. Then add the ratings to get your score range for an overall grade.

Sometimes you must convert letter grades to numerical scores. Letter grades from rubrics can be converted to numerical grades that parallel those given on report cards. One method we have used in our classrooms is to post the following scale:

Letter Grade	Numerical Grade
A+	100
A	96
A−	94
B+	92
B	88
B−	84

Performance Criteria	Proficiency Levels				Score
	1	2	3	4	
Data	Data in the table need to be organized, accurate, and easy to read.	Data in the table are somewhat organized, accurate, and easy to read.	Data in the table are organized, accurate, and easy to read.	Data in the table are well organized, accurate, and easy to read.	
Title	A title that clearly relates to the data should be printed at the top of the graph.	Title is somewhat related to the data; it is present at the top of the graph.	Title clearly relates to the data graphed and is printed at the top of the graph.		
Labeling of X axis	The X axis needs an accurate and clear label that describes the units.	The X axis has a label, but the label is not clear or accurate.	The X axis has a clear label that describes the units, but the label lacks accuracy.	The X axis has an accurate and clear label that describes the units.	
Labeling of Y axis	The Y axis needs an accurate and clear label that describes the units.	The Y axis has a label, but the label is not clear or accurate.	The Y axis has a clear label that describes the units, but the label lacks accuracy.	The Y axis has an accurate and clear label that describes the units.	
Design	The graph is plain. It needs an attractive design. Colors that go well together should be used to make the graph more readable.	The graph is somewhat plain. It needs an attractive design. Or Colors should be used that make the graph more readable.	The graph has an attractive design. Colors that go well together are used to make the graph more readable.		

TOTAL SCORE: _____

Grading:
15–18 Points = A
11–14 Points = B
7–10 Points = C
3–6 Points = D
Less than 3 points = F

FIGURE 9.10   *Analytic Rubric and Grading Scale for the Task "Data Analysis and Probability"*

Reprinted with permission.

Students then use the conversion chart and calculate their grades from performance tasks and their other grades during a nine-week grading period.

✦ PITFALLS TO AVOID: TOP CHALLENGES IN PERFORMANCE ASSESSMENTS

In Figure 9.11, we highlight the biggest challenges for teachers as they design performance tasks and the rubrics for them.

Keep the Task Related to Learning Goals

Sometimes teachers get so excited about a performance task that the original learning goals are lost. For example, a performance task in a history class involved students in the development of posters modeled after propaganda posters from World War I and World War II (Angle, 2007). However, the students' propaganda posters, while in the style of the war years, were designed to create support for clean-up day at the school and did not deal with the historical content associated with these wars. Instead of assessing student knowledge and understanding of World War I or World War II, the

Common Errors	Poor Design	Fixes	Better Design
Developing a task that generates excitement but is detached from the learning goals.	We have been studying the use of propaganda posters in WWI and WWII. Develop a propaganda poster that will get students involved in the upcoming clean-up day at school.	**Keep the task related to learning goals.**	We have been studying the use of propaganda posters in WWI and WWII. Develop a poster that America could have used for anti-German propaganda.
Assigning a task without providing students with practice in the knowledge and skills required in the task.	A school prepares students for the annual science fair by sending home a booklet on how to do a science fair project.	**Incorporate all the elements of the task into instruction and class activities.**	Preparation for the science fair is integrated with science instruction and activities. Prior to the science fair, in class activities, teachers and students conduct experiments, record the outcomes, and write summaries of their findings.
Including too many criteria in a rubric.	To guide students in writing a novelette, a teacher developed a checklist with 15 criteria that reflected the skills learned during the year.	**Limit the number of criteria in the scoring guide.**	The teacher focused the checklist on the criteria of character and plot development, voice, and conventions.

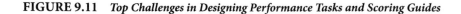

FIGURE 9.11   *Top Challenges in Designing Performance Tasks and Scoring Guides*

performance task emphasized the propaganda aspects of the lesson. This type of error also occurs when teachers find an interesting activity on the Internet but forget to check the alignment with their learning goals. Care must be taken to align the activities in the performance task with the learning goals.

Provide Practice Before Assigning the Task

A second error that teachers make is to misalign their instruction and the performance task. Let's use the "Sonnet Sequence: English III College Prep" in Figure 9.7 as an example. If the teacher's learning activities are confined to students reading sonnets and analyzing their structure, then the students are not necessarily prepared to create a sonnet. To align instruction and the performance task, students need to engage in writing sonnets as part of the learning experience.

Limit the Number of Performance Criteria in the Rubric

Earlier in our teaching careers, we thought that a scoring guide should list every single performance criterion relevant for a task. Recall the novelettes students wrote after studying historical fiction. The scoring guide for the task was a checklist in which the performance criteria were based on the learning goals for writing for the year. Students used the list to guide their writing of each chapter. A major problem with the checklist was its length of 10+ performance criteria. The checklist attempted to cover *everything* our students learned about writing. Later we realized the value of identifying *critical* performance criteria. For students in primary grades, 1 to 3 performance criteria are the maximum to which students can attend, given their level of cognitive development. Elementary and middle school students can attend to 3 to 5 criteria, and high school students can attend to 5 to 7.

A final note: You will benefit from revisiting Chapter 8 where we presented common challenges in the development of essays and scoring guides (see Figure 8.20). We noted the importance of assessing higher-order thinking skills, clearly communicating the task to students, aligning the criteria in the scoring guide and task directions, avoiding criteria that are frivolous (e.g., neatness) or untaught (e.g., creativity), and steering clear of evaluative terms, such as "poor" and "excellent" in the descriptors of the scoring guide. These guidelines will also assist you in developing prompts and scoring guides for performance assessments.

✦ The Value of Student-Generated Items and Critical Thinking

Performance assessments allow you to gauge student understanding of complex concepts and skills. The meaningfulness of the task to students is a central quality of this form of assessment. To establish meaningfulness, a teacher specifies an audience for the task and provides a context. Establishing an audience and context, however, increases the cognitive load of the task. Students have to read directions and then determine the demands of the task. To keep the task directions and response requirements from becoming too overwhelming, we recommend you draft the task and then review it with students to put it into their language. This process supports you in making valid decisions about student learning because your students are more likely to clearly understand the task. Students benefit from being engaged in a process that allows them to see the meaning of the directions and the form their response should take. If students are similarly engaged in developing the scoring guide, they are more likely to see the connections between the task expectations and the way their response will be scored.

Developing or reviewing the task and scoring guide with students helps them to internalize the criteria and develop a metacognitive awareness of the critical elements they should attend to in a task (Shepard, 2006). In developing these skills, students can more easily take responsibility for their own learning and develop the self-governing skills needed for participation in civic culture.

Also consider involving your students in brainstorming the form (i.e., oral, demonstration, or product) of the performance assessment. Use Table 9.2 to show students the possible forms an assessment might take. Then discuss potential assessment activities and the reasons some would be appropriate and others not. For example, if you are studying visual artists' use of the elements of art to create a response in the viewer, a timeline about an artist's life would be inappropriate. Instead, you might discuss the appropriateness of an assessment in which your students write journal reflections on artists and the responses the artists' work provokes. Such participation in decision making gives students a sense of control over their learning, which promotes mastery goals and increases how much they value the tasks (Urdan & Schoenfelder, 2006).

✦ ACCOMMODATIONS FOR DIVERSE LEARNERS: PERFORMANCE TASKS

When diverse learners use writing in their response to a performance task, the challenges they face will be the same as those discussed in Chapter 8 for short-answer and essay items. Also relevant are the accommodations related to reading demands and the testing environment discussed in Chapter 7 about tests with selected-response items. So, you will want to revisit Table 7.6 and Table 8.9 to gain additional ideas for accommodations that diverse learners may benefit from when completing constructed-response assessments.

Because not all forms of performance assessment require writing, we expand our consideration of accommodations here. Products such as photographs, graphs, and framing for a house do not require written responses. Neither do process-oriented assessments, such as story retelling (an oral assessment) or application of first-aid skills (a demonstration).

Before considering the needs of specific groups of diverse learners, we want to discuss a few issues relevant to all learners. For example, *all* students grade 2 and above are likely to benefit from having a set of written directions and a copy of the rubric. Often our directions are communicated orally and students have to recall the various tasks they must complete. Their memory, like ours, is faulty, so students will benefit from having directions presented in both written and oral forms. Similarly, providing a rubric with the task and discussing it will benefit all students.

As you write the performance assessment, use plain language (i.e., simple vocabulary and sentence structure). We are not suggesting you "dummy down" your tasks. For instance, it is appropriate to use the new vocabulary terms that are part of the learning unit. Our point here is that as you write a performance task, keep simplicity and clarity in mind. If you have the choice between writing two simple sentences or combining them into one complex sentence, choose the simpler structure of two sentences.

As you plan an assessment, decide whether, for all students, the *form* of the assessment (i.e., oral, demonstration, or product) is the only appropriate manner to gauge student achievement of learning goals. For example, if you have a student with

TABLE 9.3	

Accommodation Considerations for Performance Tasks

Issue	Type of Accommodation
Difficulty with fine motor skills	• Use assistive devices to control tools (e.g., paint brushes). • Use head/eye controlled input pointers for computer.
Sensory challenges (e.g., visual, auditory)	• Provide speech/communication devices for students with speech production impairments. • Provide a translator for students who are deaf and/or have speech production impairments. • Use software that allows students with visual impairments to zoom in on the contents of a computer document. • Use screen reader programs to present computer graphics and text as speech.
Learning English	• Provide voice-recorded and written directions.
Learning goal already mastered	• Engage student in multimedia representations of knowledge.
Difficulty focusing attention	• Provide structure within the task (e.g., list of steps to complete). • Keep oral assessments and demonstrations to a short period of time.
Literacy skills below those of typical peers (e.g., learning disability)	• Keep oral assessments and demonstrations to a short time frame. • Provide voice-recorded and written directions.
Lack of familiarity with school culture	• Allow much of the task to be completed in class. • Ensure necessary resources are accessible to all.

a speech impairment, is retelling a story the only method to assess her understanding? If so, you may need to consider speech production devices for students with severe impairments. Also ask yourself whether you might on some occasions allow the student to write a brief paragraph about the story she read.

You should also consider whether the *activity* you developed is the only possible mode for students to use in demonstrating their knowledge. A well-intentioned teacher may decide that during the year all students will present a newscast on the school's closed-circuit broadcast. However, the stress of being broadcast on closed-circuit television will have a negative effect on some students' performance. Students who are English language learners and students with speech impairments may perform poorly in such a situation; however, they may be quite effective in a small-group setting. We want to provide an opportunity for students to demonstrate their achievement of learning goals, and this may be achieved using different forms of performance assessment or different types of activities for different students.

Students with Fine Motor Difficulties

In accommodating a performance assessment for students with impaired fine motor skills, determine whether assistive devices will allow students to use the tools needed to complete a task. For example, some students may benefit from hand grips that can be used with pencils or paint brushes. Some performance tasks may require students to use a computer to work on a spreadsheet or use graphics to develop a presentation. However, lack of fine motor control may make work at the computer difficult. An assistive device referred to as a head pointer allows students to complete such activities.

Students with Sensory Challenges

Responding orally or demonstrating a skill may pose challenges to students with sensory challenges. For oral assessments, students with speech impairments may require speech/communication devices or the assistance of translators to respond to the task. In completing a task that requires the use of a computer, students with visual impairments may need software to zoom in on relevant text or to read graphics on a computer screen.

Students Learning English

Students who are learning English may benefit from having directions in print and voice recorded. Because directions require time for mental processing, having the directions in both forms gives students the resources to process the information at their own pace.

Students Who Have Already Mastered the Learning Goals

Performance tasks can engage students who have mastered many of the learning goals associated with an instructional unit. Consider having gifted students portray their understanding using a multimedia format. For example, a student may write a poem in the style of poems the class is studying, design a PowerPoint presentation to contrast this type to others, or choose a favorite poet who writes this type of poem to showcase on a personal website. Meaningful extensions or alternative assessments can expand learning.

Students Who Have Difficulty Focusing Attention

Building structure into the performance task may be an appropriate accommodation for students who have difficulty focusing their attention. The need for structure is related to the complexity of the task. For example, providing a visual that organizes a task, such as the grid in Figure 9.7 that organizes the key building blocks of a sonnet, can help students be more systematic in their approach. Designing checkpoints for completing a complex performance task will also benefit students who lose focus and need structure to complete the task by a deadline.

You should also establish reasonable expectations for the time frame for an oral response or a demonstration. Students who have challenges maintaining focus may perform appropriately if they are required to give a 5-minute speech, but they may have more difficulty delivering a 15-minute speech. Usually the length of a speech is not the focus of typical learning goals. Instead, learning goals for a speech address whether a student includes relevant details to support main ideas, illustrates main ideas through anecdotes and examples, or cites appropriate information sources (Virginia Department of Education, 2003). If your learning goals address the latter, deemphasizing the length of time in the rubric is reasonable.

Students with Literacy Skills Below Those of Typical Peers (e.g., Learning Disability)

Oral language skills present challenges for some students. To assist these students, keep oral assessments and demonstrations to a short time frame.

Students Who Lack Familiarity with School Culture

Students who lack familiarity with school culture may lack the resources required to complete a task at home. For this reason much of the work should be completed at school. In addition, thorough explanation of requirements through examples and discussion can be particularly helpful for students who may not be familiar with your typical expectations.

→ CASE STUDY APPLICATION

For this chapter we return to the high school English unit on utopias and dystopias. Maria Mensik develops a performance task (see Figure 9.12) for her unit addressing the guidelines we have presented in this chapter. She identifies the content by listing the learning goals at the beginning of the task. Thus, the focus of the assessment is whether students can compare and contrast characteristics of utopias and dystopias and use persuasive language in their writing and speaking. The response form for the task includes a PowerPoint slideshow (i.e., a product) and a presentation (i.e., a process). To establish meaningfulness, Maria uses the theme of the unit to provide the context of the task, and she specifies the audience for the students' responses will be their peers and their teacher. Using the Microsoft Word review tool, we find the Flesch-Kincaid reading level is 11.3, a demanding level. She may want to review and edit the prompt, shortening sentences and simplifying vocabulary where possible. Finally, she specifies such logistics as the use of PowerPoint, presentation length of 10 to 12 minutes, and the requirement that each member participate in the presentation.

Recall that a scoring guide is a critical component of any performance assessment. For her performance assessment, Maria develops a three-part rubric with performance criteria for Presentation Content, Presentation Quality, and Individual

---

Student Will Be Able To (SWBAT) compare and contrast characteristics of a utopia and dystopia.

SWBAT use persuasive language in writing and/or speaking.

Assignment:

Based on the characteristics we have learned about utopias and dystopias, work together in groups (3–4 people) to apply your knowledge and create your own society.

An anonymous billionaire has donated a large, remote island and practically unlimited funds to your group so that you may create a new society. Your new country exists in the present time, on earth, and all natural laws apply—anything else is up for debate. Name your country and give it a meaningful motto or creed. Then, create some form of government and fully describe at least two other institutions or aspects of society like work, family, religion, education, entertainment, or technology (including the government, your group should present as many institutions as there are group members). These institutions should represent your motto. Finally, your group must present your country to the class (each group member should present an institution or aspect) and the class will vote to determine which new society is "best." An important part of this assignment is persuading others why they might want to become a citizen of your new country.

Group presentations will take the form of a PowerPoint presentation. Presentations should be 10–12 minutes long, and each member must present information. The group will receive a grade and each individual will receive a grade. Keep in mind public speaking concerns we have discussed like clarity, volume, and eye contact.

FIGURE 9.12 *Maria's Performance Task for Utopias and Dystopias*

Reprinted with permission.

Component (see Figures 9.13–9.15). When Maria includes the rubric with the task directions, it can provide students some structure for completing the task. Maria's rubric reminds us of the possibility of weighting the evaluative criteria. Notice for the performance criterion of *persuasive language,* at the highest proficiency level a student

Presentation Content *Performance Criteria*	*Proficiency Levels*			
Country Name	0 No	1 Yes		
Country Motto	0 No motto, or motto does not describe any beliefs.	1 Motto makes an attempt to describe society, but it is unclear.	2 Motto describes the basic beliefs of the society.	
Description of Utopic Societal Institutions	1–3 Descriptions are lacking or missing, or the government is not addressed. Fewer than one instance per institution. Little or no attempt to consider utopic characteristics.	4–6 Descriptions are less developed. Fewer than two instances per institution. Explanations and examples frequently do not exhibit utopic characteristics.	7–9 Descriptions are less developed and not all of the institutions have three instances. The institutions are less clearly utopic. Explanations and examples sometimes only imply that they are meant to be utopic.	10–12 Thoroughly describes each institution (one of which must be the government) and gives three instances of how each institution would function in a typical citizen's life. Through explanation and/or example, the institutions exhibit students' thorough knowledge of utopic characteristics.
Persuasive Language	1–5 Little or no attempt to use persuasive language. States opinion, but no reasons or support.	6–10 Attempts persuasive language, but only one or two reasons given without support.	11–15 Persuasive language needs polishing. Gives several reasons, but some reasons or examples need more support or are not relevant or well chosen.	16–20 Effectively uses persuasive language. Gives several relevant, well-chosen, and well-supported reasons as to why the position is superior.
Organization	1–3 Information is disorganized and lacks transitions.	4–6 Information is organized, but it may lack some transitions. Reasons and examples are not effectively organized.	7–9 Logical progression from one point to another. Reasons and examples are listed and integrated. Obvious and meaningful transitions.	

FIGURE 9.13 *Rubric Section for Scoring the Content in the Presentation*

Reprinted with permission.

Presentation Quality *Performance Criteria*	*Proficiency Levels*		
Visuals	1–3 Slides are very hard to read/see. Effects are distracting.	4–6 Slides are not as easy to read/see as they could be. A few distractions.	7–9 Slides are easy to see and read. Effects enhance rather than distract.
Mechanics	1–3 Frequent errors in grammar, spelling, or punctuation. These errors inhibit understanding.	4–6 Errors in grammar, spelling, or punctuation do not inhibit understanding.	7–9 Few errors in grammar, spelling, or punctuation. These errors do not inhibit understanding.

FIGURE 9.14 *Rubric Section for Scoring the Quality of the Presentation*
Reprinted with permission.

Individual Component *Performance Criteria*	*Proficiency Levels*		
Preparedness	1 Speaker gets lost in the presentation.	2 Speaker needs to practice a few more times.	3 Speaker knows and is comfortable with the material.
Clarity	1 Speaker mumbles, is unintelligible, or speaks too quickly.	2 Speaker attempts to enunciate, but occasionally slips. Speed needs work.	3 Speaker enunciates well. Speed is appropriate.
Volume	1 Only people right next to the speaker can hear.	2 People in the middle can hear the speaker.	3 People in the back can hear the speaker.
Body Language	1 Speaker does not attempt to make eye contact, reads the slides, and fidgets.	2 Speaker tries to make some eye contact, mostly uses the slide for reference, and tries to use appropriate movements.	3 Speaker makes eye contact, does not read the slides, does not fidget, and uses appropriate movements like pointing.

FIGURE 9.15 *Rubric Section for Scoring the Individual Contribution to a Presentation*
Reprinted with permission.

might earn from 16 to 20 points and for the lowest level from 1 to 5 points. A student's score for *country motto*, in contrast, can be a maximum of 2 points and a minimum of 0 points. The differences in possible points make sense because persuasive writing is a key component of the learning unit, and the motto is less central.

Notice also that Maria includes a section in the rubric for an individual component (see Figure 9.15). Group projects teach our students to work together to accomplish a goal, a key skill in a democracy. However, if the students are to be graded, the teacher must include some aspects of the task that students complete individually. This is important because we want a student's grade to reflect his or her learning. The grade should not reflect which group the student was in. Members of a group bring different levels of participation to a task. Some students contribute and others do little. As a teacher you can monitor participation levels. In addition, some groups will function better than others. Focusing on whether each individual has met the learning goals is the key to judgment. Therefore, incorporating tasks individuals can complete independently of the group is important. As we saw in previous chapters, Maria also assesses individual mastery through several other summative assessments targeting the learning goals.

> **Ethics Alert:** When students are assessed for their work in a group, you must include an individual component of the assessment that allows you to gauge each student's achievement of the learning goals. A student's grade should not be largely determined by the group to which the student was assigned.

KEY CHAPTER POINTS

In this chapter we learned that performance assessments require students to respond to a prompt by constructing a product (e.g., balanced spreadsheet) or engaging in a process (e.g., debating). In considering when to use a performance task, we indicated that performance tasks, like essays, lend themselves to assessing students' abilities to analyze, evaluate, and create.

In our discussion about the advantages and disadvantages of performance assessment, we noted that performance assessments engage students in cognitively complex tasks in which they identify relevant information, organize the information, and develop a response. A disadvantage of performance assessment is the amount of time required to move through the process.

We next presented issues to consider as you develop a task, which included content of the learning unit, meaningfulness, response form, materials needed, the degree of structure, language level, and logistics. We discussed the value of using analytic rubrics for scoring performance assessments, and we recommended use of weighting to allow a teacher to allocate more points for the most important criteria.

In our discussion on pitfalls to avoid in developing tasks and scoring guides, we noted the importance of aligning the task to the learning goals for the instructional unit and students practicing the skills required before completion of the task. We also cautioned against using too many criteria in the scoring guide. We suggested involving students in reviewing directions and rubrics and in brainstorming ideas for performance tasks.

Finally, we described accommodations to consider with performance assessments related to alternative forms of demonstrating understanding and alternative task structures. The case study illustrated implementation of the guidelines for designing performance assessments and the rubrics for scoring them.

HELPFUL WEBSITES

http://www.intranet.cps.k12.il.us/assessments/Ideas_and_Rubrics/Assessment_Tasks/Ideas_Tasks/
   ideas_tasks.html
An extensive list of activities to consider in designing your performance tasks. Lists tasks in the
   visual and performing arts, health and physical development, language arts, mathematics,
   biological and physical sciences, and social science. Published by Chicago Public Schools.
http://palm.sri.com/palm/
A website with mathematics performance assessments and scoring guides aligned with the
   mathematics standards of the National Council of Teachers of Mathematics (NCTM).
http://pals.sri.com/
Website with science performance assessments for grades K–12. Each performance assessment
   has student directions and response forms, administration procedures, scoring rubrics,
   and examples of student work.

CHAPTER REVIEW QUESTIONS

1. Name an example of a real-life performance assessment for each of the three
   forms: oral, demonstration, and products.
2. Which type of assessment—selected response, essay, or performance assessment—
   can be used to gauge student achievement of the following learning goals?

   Measurement and Geometry
   1.0 Students choose appropriate units of measure and use ratios to convert
       within and between measurement systems to solve problems:
   1.1 Compare weights, capacities, geometric measures, times, and temperatures
       within and between measurement systems (e.g., miles per hour and feet per
       second, cubic inches to cubic centimeters).
   1.2 Construct and read drawings and models made to scale (California, 1997,
       p. 32).

3. Reread the example of the performance task involving students collecting
   information about the diversity of biographies in the school media center.
   Which of the guidelines in developing a performance are evident in the task?
   Which guidelines are not evident?
4. A colleague asks you, What is the greatest advantage of using performance
   assessments? What would you tell him? Be sure to provide support in your
   answer.
5. Following is a section of the rubric from Figure 9.13. Label each part of the rubric.

			_____ label	
Persuasive Language _____ **label**	1–5	6–10	11–15	16–20
	Little or no attempt to use persuasive language. States opinion, but no support.	Attempts to use persuasive language, but only on a limited basis. Only one or two reasons given.	Persuasive language needs polishing. Gives several reasons, but they are unclear or tentative.	Effectively uses persuasive language, like opinion and argument. Gives several reasons as to why the position is superior.

6. What criteria would you use in a rubric for the visual arts performance task in Figure 9.3? Which criteria would you weight more than others?

7. Review the grading scale in Figure 9.10. What would be a reasonable grading scale for the rubric for scoring sonnets (Figure 9.9)?

8. A teacher and students read limericks and then identify common characteristics of the poems. Subsequently, the teacher assigns a performance task in which the students must write an original limerick. What type of common error does this exemplify?

9. After finding a copy of a performance assessment and accompanying rubric from the Internet or from a teacher, analyze whether and how it avoided the most common errors for designing performance assessments and rubrics described in Chapters 8 and 9.

10. Design a performance assessment that addresses one or more key learning goals in your content area. Make sure you carefully address each of the guidelines for development of performance tasks.

11. Design an analytic rubric for the performance assessment you designed in item 10. Include the relevant number of performance criteria for the age group you work with. Carefully label each proficiency level for each performance criterion using guidelines in Chapters 8 and 9.

REFERENCES

Angle, M. 2007. *An investigation of construct validity in teaching American history portfolios.* Unpublished doctoral dissertation, University of South Carolina, Columbia.

Arter, J., and J. Chappuis. 2007. *Creating and recognizing quality rubrics.* Upper Saddle River, NJ: Pearson Education.

Arter, J., and J. McTighe. 2001. *Scoring rubrics in the classroom: Using performance criteria for assessing and improving student performance.* Thousand Oaks, CA: Corwin Press.

California State Board of Education. 1997. *Mathematics content standards for California Public Schools kindergarten through grade twelve.* Retrieved April 18, 2008, from http://www.cde.ca.gov/re/pn/fd/.

Gredler, M., and R. Johnson. 2004. *Assessment in the literacy classroom.* Needham Heights, MA: Allyn & Bacon.

Gronlund, N. 2004. *Writing instructional objectives for teaching and assessment.* 7th ed. Upper Saddle River, NJ: Pearson Education.

Hogan, T., and G. Murphy. 2007. Recommendations for preparing and scoring constructed-response items: What the experts say. *Applied Measurement in Education* 20(4): 427–441.

Johnson, R., J. Penny, and B. Gordon. 2009. *Assessing performance: Developing, scoring, and validating performance tasks.* New York: Guilford Publications.

Kuhs, T., R. Johnson, S. Agruso, and D. Monrad. 2001. *Put to the test: Tools and techniques for classroom assessment.* Portsmouth, NH: Heinemann.

Ovando, C. 2005. Language diversity and education. In J. Banks and C. Banks (eds.), *Multicultural education: Issues and perspectives,* 5th ed., pp. 289–313. New York: Wiley.

Shepard, L. 2006. Classroom assessment. In R. Brennan (ed.), *Educational measurement,* 4th ed., pp. 623–646. Westport, CT: American Council on Education and Praeger Publishers.

South Carolina Department of Education. 2005. *South Carolina science academic standards.* Columbia, SC: Author. Retrieved May 2, 2008, from http://ed.sc.gov/agency/offices/cso/standards/science/.

Urdan, T., and E. Schoenfelder. 2006. Classroom effects on student motivation: Goal structures, social relationships, and competence beliefs. *Journal of School Psychology* 44:331–349.

Virginia Department of Education. 2003. *English standards of learning curriculum framework.* Retrieved September 7, 2006, from http://www.pen.k12.va.us/VDOE/Instruction/English/englishCF.html.

Wiggins, G. 1993. *Assessing student performance.* San Francisco: Jossey-Bass.

CHAPTER 10

GRADING AND COMMUNICATING ABOUT STUDENT ACHIEVEMENT

Teachers are asked to nurture learning and growth; yet they are also asked to be judges at report card time. In most endeavors in life, the advocate is not also the judge.

–Dale Whittington

❖ **Chapter Learning Goals**

At the conclusion of this chapter, the reader should be able to do the following:

- Explain why difficulties arise in the grading process.

- Develop a thoughtful process for determining grades that avoid these difficulties.

- Differentiate between norm-referenced and criterion-referenced grading practices.

- Compare different types of summarizing systems (e.g., letter grades, standards-based, percentages, "not yet" grading).

- Distinguish among different purposes for portfolios.

- Describe key portfolio implementation issues.

- Explain the advantages and limitations of portfolios.

→ INTRODUCTION

In Chapter 1 we touched on grading as one area where we have found teachers often have difficulty agreeing about what practices are ethical. We recently asked more than 100 teachers to write about a situation related to classroom assessment where they found it difficult to know what was the right or wrong thing to do. About 40 percent of them described a dilemma related to grading. This category had the largest number of responses by far—issues related to large-scale standardized testing was a distant second with only about 20 percent of the responses. You, too, can no doubt draw on personal experiences where a grade caused some conflict. In this chapter, we address the thorny issue of grading and do our best to give you practical guidelines to help you grade confidently and fairly. We define a **grade** as a score, letter, or narrative that summarizes the teacher's judgment of student achievement of the relevant learning goals.

→ WHY DOES GRADING CAUSE SO MANY PROBLEMS?

First, we discuss several reasons why grading frequently seems to produce predicaments and quandaries for teachers. Table 10.1 presents some issues that we will consider.

TABLE 10.1

A Few Reasons Why Grading Can Cause Problems for Teachers

Grading brings into conflict teachers' role as student advocate vs. their role as evaluator and judge of student achievement.

Grades are a powerful symbol and have the capacity to impact students profoundly in positive and negative ways.

Teachers rarely agree on how to determine grades.

Grades represent different things to different people.

TABLE 10.2

Practices That Overstress the Advocate and Nurturer Role

1. Giving numerous extra credit opportunities.

2. Emphasizing work completion rather than quality of the work.

3. Raising grades because of high effort.

4. Providing easy rather than challenging assessments to "build self-esteem."

Advocate Versus Evaluator

As the opening quotation for this chapter points out, teachers often wrestle with their grading practices because of the tension between their role as nurturers and advocates for students versus their role as graders and judges. Many teachers who take their advocate role seriously are reluctant to give bad grades because they fear the grade may demoralize a student. For example, one teacher we know had a bright but troubled student who never got assignments in on time. The points he lost for late work caused him to fail the quarter, and the teacher blamed himself the next marking period when the student completely gave up. Similarly, other teachers we know want to nurture and encourage borderline students by incorporating points for good effort even if a student has not met the standard required for the higher grade. But at some later point a teacher may find parents on her doorstep, demanding an explanation for the discrepancy between their child's grades and the test scores when that student fails to pass the large-scale high-stakes exam in the spring. Based on the grades, the parents had assumed their child had been doing just fine. But those grades did not communicate their child's performance relative to the larger world. Table 10.2 describes practices that, when taken to extremes, will overemphasize the advocate role and thus convey an unwarranted impression of mastery. Think for a moment about how such practices can foster what former President George W. Bush termed "the soft bigotry of low expectations," especially when they are employed with low-performing poor and minority students.

On the other hand, when teachers stress their power as an evaluator more, they can intimidate or disillusion students, which can interfere with learning. Practices used by teachers who take their role as "sorter" of students too seriously may actually impede mastery of the learning goals because such actions can demoralize students and reduce their motivation. When teachers engage in practices intended solely to separate the most mentally agile students from their peers, they are not focusing on

TABLE 10.3

Practices That Overstress the Judging and Sorting Role of Teachers

1. Test questions covering obscure points or skills/understanding not addressed in learning goals.

2. Test question intentionally designed to mislead the test taker to provide the wrong answer ("trick" questions).

3. Making tests too long to complete in the available time allotted.

4. Comments suggesting that doing well is very rare. ("I hardly ever give an 'A.'")

their duty to encourage every student to learn. Table 10.3 describes several such practices that often appear unnecessarily punitive to students. Such practices can undermine the integrity of the student teacher relationship. Teachers instead must take their role seriously as an adult authority figure who uses power fairly.

Finding the right balance between the advocate role and the judge role can be difficult. If teachers accentuate advocacy too much when assigning grades, they may overestimate level of mastery by always giving students "the benefit of the doubt." If they emphasize judging too much, they may end up sorting students based on the understanding and skills they bring to class rather than focusing on teaching everyone the new content to master. The middle ground requires development of assessment practices and grading policies that explicitly take into account *both* of these important roles.

Symbolic Value of Grades

In our competitive culture, grades loom large. We all have stories about the impact a grade has had on us. We still can picture a pop quiz with an angry-looking purple "F" on it handed back to us in fifth grade. Similarly, a colleague of ours recently had to do some serious counseling with her ninth-grade son who received what looked like a pretty arbitrary "D−" on his first essay in English. The son decided he was a terrible student and a poor writer and knew he should never have taken any Advanced Placement courses. Our friend later discovered the teacher had given *everyone* a bad grade, regardless of the actual quality of their work, to "motivate" them. Bad grades and the judgment they imply can leave an emotional residue that colors self-perception and motivation. For students who habitually receive bad grades, this effect is multiplied exponentially. (Recall our misbehaving student from Chapter 1 who told us, "It's better to be bad than dumb.")

> **Ethics Alert:** No teacher should *ever* assign artificially low grades to "motivate" students. Instead, grades should communicate what students know.

Such stories, the numerous blog entries we have encountered about perceived unfair grading, and perhaps some experiences in your own academic career illustrate the intense impact grades can have on our psyches. As one student pointed out, "OK, that grade, that's me. I am the grade. I did that" (Thomas & Oldfather, 1997). Thus another reason grading practices so often cause problems is the sway they hold over us and our sense of self-worth. This relevance to our ego magnifies the effects of the judgments that accompany the translation of assessments into grades. As teachers, we must remember the power grades possess so we grade thoughtfully and judiciously.

Lack of Agreement on the Judgment Process

Grades are based on judgment, and judgments by their nature have a subjective element. The range in judgment is reflected in the enormous variation in what different teachers consider important as they formulate grades. Some teachers use only one or two important assessments, whereas others may use dozens. Some teachers give great weight to homework, and others stress tests or projects more. There probably are as many disparities related to which academic work should count toward grades (and how much it should count) as there are teachers.

In addition, teachers also vary on which *nonacademic* elements they include in a grade. Some teachers have a personal philosophy that takes student effort into account; others do not. Some teachers penalize students for lack of participation or for absences. Others consider how they perceive students' abilities and whether they are making the most of them. To exacerbate matters, most teachers are not methodical about weighing these nonacademic factors. They may give a little boost to one student whose parents are going through a divorce, or they may inadvertently be a little easier (or harder) on a "suck-up." And they are usually not explicit and systematic about how they consider nonacademic issues such as ability, effort, and attitude. Rarely, for example, does a teacher note a score on "attitude" or "effort" each day for every student.

You can see that the judgments teachers make in assigning grades may be influenced by a number of considerations that do not directly relate to mastery of the learning goals. These judgments are unique for each teacher, and many struggle with these decisions (Zoeckler, 2007). Furthermore, most school district grading policies do not explicitly address the weight that should be assigned to different types of assignments or the role of nonacademic considerations. With the tremendous range of academic and nonacademic factors influencing the grading process in different ways for different teachers, you can see why students and their parents can sometimes see grades as capricious or unfair.

Ambiguous Meaning of Grades

One basic reason so many variations in grading practices arise is that a grade may represent fundamentally different things to different people. For example, Janet Pilcher (1994) found in several case studies that parents assumed grades reflected only whether their child had mastered course content, and they questioned the interpretability of grades that included considerations of effort. Teachers, on the other hand, believed they should adjust grades for ability, effort, and attitude, and they did so. (The students, as you might guess, thought teachers should include effort when it improved their grade, but not when it penalized them.)

Similarly, Robert Marzano, who frequently presents workshops on grading, begins by asking the assembled teachers if they, themselves, have ever received a grade that did not accurately represent their achievement. Most of the time, every hand goes up (Marzano, 2000). And in our own classrooms, teacher candidates hotly debate the pros and cons of whether a grade should ever include considerations other than the degree of mastery of the learning goals.

James Allen (2009) suggests a way to reach consensus about the meaning of grades. He recommends that when grading, we as teachers consider the following: "If I was given a student's transcript with a single letter grade listed next to the subject I teach, what would be the most logical interpretation I could make about what the grade represents about the student's knowledge of that academic subject?" He believes this question should focus us on the essential meaning each grade should communicate.

You can see that Allen's question assumes the primary purpose of grading is to communicate about levels of student *achievement*. Most members of the assessment community in education strongly agree (Brookhart, 2004; Guskey & Bailey, 2001; Marzano, 2000, 2006; O'Connor, 2002). Surveys of practicing teachers, however, suggest that many nonetheless weight heavily some factors unrelated to level of achievement (e.g., Brookhart, 1994; Cross & Frary, 1999; McMillan et al., 2002). These findings illustrate some of the dimensions of this ongoing struggle.

✦ THE GRADING DECISION PROCESS

With the complexities and pitfalls in mind that can make grading decisions difficult, we turn to discussing guidelines that should enable you to make fair and accurate decisions when grading your students. These principles will help guide you safely through the minefield grading decisions often present. They summarize and synthesize current recommendations for best practice (Brookhart, 2004; Guskey & Bailey, 2001; Gronlund, 2006; Marzano, 2000, 2006; O'Connor, 2002; Shepard, 2006; Winger, 2005). The guidelines are presented in Table 10.4.

TABLE 10.4

Guidelines for Fair and Accurate Grading Decisions

1. Learn and follow your school district's grading policy.

2. Design a written policy in which you base grades on summative assessments that address your learning goals derived from the standards.

3. Ensure quality of assessment by having sufficient information (reliability) and by using different types of assessments that address the learning goals (validity).

4. Communicate with and involve students in developing standards of performance for graded assessments.

5. Allow recent and consistent performance to carry more weight than strict averages.

6. Avoid unduly weighting factors unrelated to a student's mastery of the learning goals, such as the following:
   - Effort
   - Participation
   - Attitude or behavior
   - Aptitude or ability
   - Improvement
   - Extra credit
   - Late work
   - Zeroes
   - Group grades

7. Avoid using grades as rewards and punishments.

8. Review borderline cases carefully.

Follow School District Grading Policy

School districts develop grading policies to guide teachers; and in formulating your own grading practices, you should carefully follow the policy to which your district adheres. A review of grading policies posted online by districts in several states reveals that these documents vary widely in what they include and their degree of specificity. Most discuss purposes for grades, suggestions of the types of assessments that should be used in grading, and the grading system (e.g., 93–100 = A). Some go further and specify the minimum number of grades necessary per marking period, the weights that should be applied to different types of assignments, and even what to do in borderline cases. Because of the tremendous variation across school districts, you must familiarize yourself early on with your own district's requirements and use them as the foundation for constructing your own policy.

Base Grading on Summative Assessments

Students have a right to know your grading policy. A clearly spelled-out grading policy also protects you. If your policy is arbitrary and unstated, it can be perceived as capricious or unfair and may even lead to legal action against you. Make sure you formulate your grading policy in writing and provide it to your students and their parents.

In designing your policy, we recommend that you build on the bedrock assumption that the grade you assign represents your evaluation of each student against the learning goals based on the standards and benchmarks available for your subject and grade level (Brookhart, 2004; Marzano, 2006; O'Connor, 2002). In the teaching profession, our models of instruction and assessment are "anchored" to learning goals based on standards (Brookhart, 2004). With the learning goals as the focus of your evaluation, your assessments—and therefore your overall evaluations of your students—must be aligned with these goals, as we discussed in Chapter 2. Studies examining different grading criteria across a number of school districts indicate that academic achievement is the primary and most frequent factor used in formulating grades (Marzano, 2000). Gronlund (2006) gets to the point when he states, "Letter grades without an achievement referent tend to have little meaning."

In addition, grades should be based on summative rather than formative assessments. Because formative assessments are designed to provide feedback to help students learn, grades on formative assessments penalize students who do not master everything quickly. In addition, feedback on formative assessment is one of your best opportunities to play the advocate role for your students. You do all you can to help them make progress and learn more as they practice skills and master complex ideas. You encourage them to take the next step and note their progress. Remember also that formative assessments enhance mastery goals, which increase motivation and help students take responsibility for their own achievement. Students will be more likely to do their best on your summative assessments if they have been able to make progress on the formative ones.

Then, after formative assessments have helped students do all they can to narrow the gap between where they started and where they need to be to master a learning goal, you can administer summative assessments to ascertain mastery. At this time, your role changes from advocate to evaluator and judge of student achievement.

Let's look at an example of the progression from formative assessment *for* learning to summative assessment *of* learning. Consider a unit including a learning goal covering the causes and course of the Civil War and its effects on the American people. One learning focus could be examination of the different cultures at the time (e.g., enslaved people, Southern plantation owners, Northern city dwellers). Formative assessments could include student journal entries, documentation of progress on personal research for a culminating project, and use of Venn diagrams to compare and contrast beliefs and practices, material adaptations to the environment, and social organizations. These could allow students to work on reasoning and research skills as well as to organize and master the content of the unit.

Summative assessments for grading purposes could then include students independently constructing a Venn diagram (addressing a different focus from any earlier Venn diagrams), and projects or presentations on specific persons of the time, focusing on their relationship to their culture and the impact of the war. Tests and quizzes could also be administered at several points during the unit, and they might use excerpts from original sources, asking students to explain their significance or compare perspectives of people. The summative assessments would cover similar content to the formative assessments, but they would also provide novel opportunities for students to summarize their understanding of the period and its cultures and to apply their knowledge to new examples to demonstrate mastery. Grades for the unit based on these summative assessments would then reflect the degree to which each student had met the learning goals. This is because the instruction, as well as both formative and summative assessments, would have been carefully aligned with those goals.

Ensure Quality of Assessment

As discussed in Chapter 6, sufficiency of information is the key to ensuring reliability in your classroom assessment. You need enough information to assure yourself that you have a reasonable sample of each student's performance. Having enough different kinds of assignments addressing the learning goals through different assessment methods is important for ensuring the validity of the inferences you make about each student. You don't want to use only tests, because some students do not do their best work on tests, and you want other methods of determining their ability to apply what they have learned. You also don't want to use only projects, because these tend to focus in depth in only one area of the learning goals. You need a range of different types of assignments across the different areas of strength and weakness of your students and across the different understanding and skills addressed in the unit.

For example, Greenville County Schools in South Carolina specify that middle school English Language Arts teachers should base 50 percent of a student's grade on 12 minor grades per marking period. Minor grades might be based on classwork, quizzes, journals, or informal presentations. The other 50 percent should be based on 3 or 4 major tests, formal writing assignments, or research-based projects. This district specifies weightings and types of assignments in all subjects and at all grade levels to increase consistency in grading across teachers. See Table 10.5 for the specifications for English Language Arts across grade levels. Notice how the weight of major assessments increases as students move up in grade level.

Paradoxically, most teachers grade too many things, rather than too few. One principal we know is on a crusade to get teachers to substantially reduce the 40–50 items he finds in their grade books each marking period. He wants them to focus on fewer, more meaningful assessments. For example, if you give a grade on every homework and in-class assignment, you have lots of grades to summarize at the end of the marking period. But most of these activities should probably be considered practice, or formative assessment, rather than summative assessment. As such, they are not usually effective for checking on true mastery of the learning goals. Marzano (2006) recommends no fewer than four assessments per topic in each grading period, adding another when you are uncertain about a student's level of performance in relation to the learning goals. Carefully choosing several different types of summative assessment

TABLE 10.5

Greenville County Schools Grade Weighting for English Language Arts at Elementary, Middle, and High School Levels

	Minor Assessments	Major Assessments	Other
Elementary Reading	**(7) 60%** Comprehension Strategies and Skills, Retelling Protocols, Responses to Literature, Observations, Checklists, Name Test, Portfolio, HM Theme Skills Test, etc.	**(2) 40%** Selection Assessments and Novel/Chapter Book Tests 20%; Integrated Themes Skills Test 20%	
Elementary Language Arts (Writing, Research, Communication and Language Skills)	**(7) 60%** Response Journals, Learning Logs, Writer's Craft, Writing Conventions, Writing Process, Writing Rubrics, Research Process, Reference Materials, Use of Technology, Presentation Rubrics, Writing Prompts, Constructed Responses, Anecdotal Records, Observation Checklists, etc.	**30% (1) Writing Portfolio** **(1) Major Test**	**Spelling: (8–9) 10%**
Middle School English Language Arts	**(12) 50%** Including but not limited to quizzes (vocabulary, reading, skill based), small writing assignments, journals, write to learn assignments, informal oral presentations, other class work.	**(3–4) 50%** Including but not limited to tests, formal writing, portfolios, research-based products, culminating products	
High School English Language Arts	**(12) 40%** Including but not limited to quizzes (vocabulary, reading, skill based), small writing assignments, journals, write to learn assignments, informal oral presentations, other class work.	**(3–4) 60%** Tests, formal writing, research-based products, culminating products	

Reprinted with permission of the Greenville County SC School District.

can save you grading time, and your summative assessments will allow students to thoughtfully demonstrate what they have learned.

Involve Students

As we have discussed previously—in relation to formative assessment, designing rubrics, and progress monitoring—involving students in the assessment process fosters their development of mastery goals and a sense of ownership of their learning. It also helps to ensure that your grading is perceived as fair. At a minimum, before any summative assignment or project is due, you must inform students of the specific characteristics you are looking for in it. We will never forget our frustration as students when we received a paper back with 10 points marked off for not including a diagram we had not known was expected and had therefore not included. Those of us in the class never saw the rubric until we found it stapled to our paper with our (unsatisfactory) grade.

We also recommend you share with your students a clear picture of the types of questions you will ask on exams as well as a sense of the areas of content on which the exam will focus and the relative weight of the different areas. We have found that providing students with a list of topics or learning goals and the number of questions or percentage of points on each one helps reduce anxiety and gives students an understanding of the relative importance of different topics.

Remember also the benefits of not just informing students about how assessments will be graded, but also allowing students to help discuss and contribute to some aspects of assessments. Discussing and defining criteria on a rubric using good and poor models can help students clarify and internalize the standards of quality. Designing sample questions can help students take a teacher's perspective on what's important and how to think critically.

Weigh Recent and Consistent Performance Most Heavily

When you are combining into a grade the set of assessments for each student for a marking period, you must keep in the forefront of your mind your primary goal of providing an accurate representation of each student's level of mastery. This assumption implies that a simple average of the grades collected from the first week to the last during the marking period may not be your best interpretation of a student's performance. One of the most robust educational research findings is that learning of new skills increases incrementally across time; therefore, more weight should be given to assessments later in the learning sequence (Guskey & Bailey, 2001; Marzano, 2006; O'Connor, 2002). This suggestion is consistent with our recommendation to rely primarily on summative assessments in formulating grades. They are completed *after* students have had opportunities to practice and consolidate skills.

Looking at the consistency of student performance is also a key consideration in providing the most accurate reflection of mastery. As you learned in Chapter 6 from our discussion of reliability, any measurement of student learning has some error. If one score deviates from a student's typical performance, there may be a chance that some kind of error is detracting from that score's consistency.

One extreme score (or outlier) can distort the mean, as we demonstrated in Chapter 5. For this reason, some teachers use median scores rather than average scores when calculating grades. Use of the median reduces the effect of a low test score on the final grade. However, the use of the median can also reduce the effect of a test that a student aced (i.e., made a 100) on a final grade, if that score is significantly different from other scores. You can see the difference between mean and median grading in Table 10.6. Considering consistency and recency can help you assign grades that

TABLE 10.6

Calculating Grades Based on Median Scores Versus Mean Scores

	Consistent Student	Inconsistent Student A	Inconsistent Student B
Test Grade	82	82	82
Presentation	85	85	100
Quiz Grades	83	83	83
Venn Diagrams	80	40	80
Mean	82.5	72.5	86.25
Median	82.5	82.5	82.5

capture more accurately the level of student achievement (Marzano, 2006; O'Connor, 2002). However, you must not build disincentives into your grading policy. Students may take advantage of a median-based grading policy and "take a break" on the last assessment or two without affecting their grade if they have done well on a majority of the earlier ones (see Inconsistent Student A).

Avoid Unduly Weighting Factors Unrelated to Mastery of the Learning Goals

One of the basic tenets of this text is that assessments (and grading) should primarily reflect mastery of the learning goals. Yet many teachers believe that other factors, particularly effort, should also be explicitly considered when calculating grades. Instead, we suggest these factors should contribute to grades indirectly rather than directly (Brookhart, 2004). For example, a student who spends hours revising a paper based on your formative feedback (thus investing high effort) will probably earn a better grade on the final product than a student who invests low effort by making only a few superficial changes at the last minute before turning in the paper. The teacher of these two students need not explicitly assign points for effort in the final grade. The two final papers already differ in quality based solely on the grading criteria for the assignment.

We will discuss several factors in turn and the rationales against allowing them to influence your calculation of grades directly. We are not absolute purists, because we do believe some of these factors can play a *minor* role. However, to avoid score pollution, we suggest nonachievement factors should count for 10 percent or less of a grade. This approach provides some flexibility, because you can draw student attention to nonacademic factors without significantly detracting from the strong link you need to establish between grades and mastery of the learning goals. Two or three points on a 100-point assignment do not much alter a grade. Another approach is to report nonachievement factors independently from grades for academics by giving a separate grade or report on "work habits" (Winger, 2005). Either approach does not detract from the key point we are driving home: grades should primarily represent level of achievement of the learning goals.

Effort

The most common nonachievement factor teachers like to include in grades is effort (Marzano, 2000). We have heard teachers say that students who work hard should receive a higher grade than students at the same level of mastery who do not try hard. Similarly, many teachers also believe that they should lower the grade for "lack of effort" if a student turns in no homework but gets "A"s on summative assessments.

Teachers like to take effort into account because they feel they can then use grades as a motivational tool to increase effort (Gronlund, 2006). However, measuring effort is not easy. Some teachers try to look at specific behaviors, such as turning in homework. But a student may not turn in homework because he is the sole caretaker of his siblings every night after school, or because she has already mastered the material and doesn't need additional practice. Besides, if homework is considered formative assessment, scores on it should make a minimal contribution to the total grade.

Others look at demeanor of students during class. But most students at one time or another have pretended to be diligent when their minds were a million miles away. Having a systematic means of choosing behaviors that represent effort and assigning points for their presence or absence would be time consuming, not to mention controversial. But simply adding a few points to one student's grade and subtracting a few from another's depending on your momentary perception of effort is arbitrary and unfair.

We believe other, more effective methods for increasing effort exist than assigning a bad grade. For example, as we have discussed throughout this text, use of formative assessment, student involvement in decision making, and challenging, relevant assessment tasks have been shown to increase mastery goals on the part of students and enhance motivation and persistence (Ames, 1992; Schunk et al., 2008). Ultimately, effort will be reflected directly in the level of mastery attained on the learning goals. Students who invest effort to take advantage of feedback on formative assessments and revise their work or sharpen their thinking will perform better on the summative assessments you provide.

Participation

Some teachers like to allocate some percentage of the grade to participation because they believe students learn more when they actively take part in classroom activities, and participation enlivens instruction. However, defining participation (like defining effort) can be a difficult task. If you simply count the number of times students speak up in class without regard to the quality of their comments, you could be encouraging a lot of talk without a lot of thought. Also, introverts and students from cultures that discourage assertive speaking from children are penalized unfairly if they participate less than other students.

Jeffrey Smith and his colleagues (2001) suggest instead that you consider "contribution" as a small percentage of the grade rather than participation. You can clearly specify to your students what counts as a contribution, including a range of possibilities, such as bringing in articles or artifacts that offer new information on what the class is studying, asking an important question, and making comments in class or in written work that relate the subject matter to previous topics of study. These authors suggest you note contributions weekly in your grade book, but we know of at least one teacher who passes out "Constructive Contribution" slips at appropriate moments and has students keep track of them until the end of each marking period. If you use this type of approach, it should count for 10 percent or less of the grade.

Attitude or Behavior

Teachers sometimes include attitude or behavior as a factor in grading, sometimes weighted quite heavily (Marzano, 2000). They naturally prefer students who conform to their rules and have a positive attitude and may tend to favor them when it's time to calculate grades. Such considerations dilute the key role of grades as an indicator of *achievement*. Similar to the problems with considering effort, figuring out systematic and fair ways to quantify teachers' range of impressions of "appropriate" attitudes and behavior is daunting. Usually, attitudes and behaviors are more effectively addressed in the teacher's day-to-day classroom management plans.

In addition, researchers have found some systematic patterns suggesting that behavior is taken into account in grading more often in "troubled" schools, where discipline is a problem and teachers may be concerned more with compliance than with fostering achievement (Howley et al., 2001). Because these schools tend to serve students from poorer and minority backgrounds, the emphasis on behavior issues may overshadow and interfere with encouraging the advances in learning that must be gained to close achievement gaps. In other words, when the focus on discipline and control is manifested in grades, high expectations for achievement may drift to lesser status.

Cheating is one of the most difficult issues related to behavior and grading because it concerns both behavior and achievement. You should have a clear policy on cheating (usually determined at the school or district level) that addresses plagiarism, cheating on tests, and other academic dishonesty issues, as well as their consequences. Carefully explaining this policy to students with explicit examples educates them about appropriate academic behavior and demonstrates that you take cheating seriously. Because cheating involves achievement concerns as well as behavioral ones, academic consequences should be applied (O'Connor, 2002). Such consequences would probably include, for example, a reduction in grade on the assignment. Notice we stated a reduction in grade, not assigning a zero. Again, the issue is moderation. Just as effort or participation should have a minor effect on grades, so should behavior have a minor effect. Lowering the student's grade, and/or having the student complete another task to show *actual* achievement, communicates that cheating doesn't have a role in education *and* maintains the overall integrity of the student's grade.

Aptitude or Ability

Some teachers, in their role as advocate, believe they must give a student of "low ability" high grades even if the student doesn't meet the learning goals as long as the student is "working to potential." On the other hand, teachers may believe that a student with high ability should not receive an "A," even if the student masters the learning goals, if the student is *not* "working to potential." If you had this perspective and these two students were in your classroom, you might give the first student an "A" and the second a "B" for similar performances on summative assessments. We exaggerate a bit here to show how this would distort the usefulness of the grades in communicating levels of mastery.

In addition, experts in cognition over a number of years have found aptitude or ability very elusive and difficult to measure apart from achievement (see Chapter 11). We as teachers, then, should hesitate to jump to conclusions about the learning potential of students in our classrooms. As we noted in Chapter 3, conveying high expectations for all students is important. In addition, if we are modeling mastery goals for our students, we must help them internalize the conviction that they can learn new things and master new challenges.

Improvement

Sometimes teachers see a student improve across a marking period and want to give that student's grade a boost because an average grade doesn't reflect the gains. If you follow our suggestion to weight recent and consistent performance more heavily than strict averages, this problem is considerably diminished. In addition, if you rely on formative assessments to help students move toward mastery of the learning goals, improvement across time should be expected from *everyone,* and scores on the summative assessments should accurately reflect gains the students have made.

Extra Credit

Sometimes teachers offer extra credit assignments. We (and probably most other teachers) also find a few students pleading for extra credit opportunities if they are worried about a grade, especially as the end of the term approaches. If you do offer extra credit, it must be offered to all students. It should also be crafted as an opportunity for showing mastery of some aspect of the learning goals rather than busywork (e.g., bringing in photos from magazines). Finally, it should contribute a very small amount to a final grade. If students do not do the extra credit assignment, they should not be penalized.

Late Work

Most teachers have policies for penalizing students who turn in work after the due date. In addition to encouraging responsibility among students, specific due dates and late penalties allow us to sequence instruction based on knowing exactly which content students have mastered. They also ensure our grading workload is manageable. Often, however, penalties are so severe (e.g., 10% for each day late) that they reduce student motivation—why turn in something four or five days late if you will get an "F" on it anyway? We agree with Marzano (2000), who suggests that teachers deduct no more than 1 percent or 2 percent per day with a maximum of 10 percent. We also recommend that permission for extensions be secured before the due date. Using this approach ensures that a grade still primarily represents the quality of the work. Rectifying frequent tardiness is, however, important to address as part of developing a sense of responsibility and the other personal qualities that contribute to academic success. But punitive grading has not been shown to be effective for accomplishing this (Guskey & Bailey, 2001; O'Connor, 2002). Instead, supporting students by learning why their work is late and establishing assistance or supervision of make-up work can be more helpful in addressing the problem.

Zeroes

Teachers sometimes assign zeroes for missing assignments or for misbehavior. But if grades are to communicate the level of achievement, zeroes may significantly distort them. Such distortion is particularly significant if grades are averaged. A zero is an outlier that noticeably lowers the mean. In Table 10.7 we changed one of Inconsistent Student A's grades (from Table 10.6) to zero. Note the mean fell from 75 to 62.5, while the median remained the same. Zeroes have an enormous impact because there is a much bigger numerical distance between them and the next higher grade—usually at least 50 points—than there is between any other two grades. For example, the distance between any "B" and an "A" on a grading scale (where 90–100 = A and 80–89 = B) is only 10 points. For this reason, some schools have grading policies that require teachers to give no score lower than one point less than the lowest "D."

Group Grades

If a grade is meant to represent the individual's level of mastery of the learning goals, you can already see the argument against all students in a group receiving exactly the same score on a group project intended as a summative assessment. Chances are the

TABLE 10.7

Showing the Impact of Zeroes on Mean Versus Median Scores

	Consistent Student	Inconsistent Student A
Test Grade	82	82
Presentation	85	85
Quiz Grades	83	83
Venn Diagrams	80	0
Mean	82.5	62.5
Median	82.5	82.5

score will represent the performance level of some, but probably not all, students in the group. If you want to use a team project in your classes, it should be designed to have a large individual accountability component and a smaller group component. For example, in a group presentation, individuals can be scored on their delivery and content contribution, and then a smaller group score related to some aspects of the overall presentation might be given. The key in designing group projects is keeping in mind the understanding and skills you want individuals to demonstrate.

Avoid Using Grades as Rewards and Punishments

From the points we have made about grading so far, you can see that we dilute the meaning of grades when we use them for purposes other than communicating the level of mastery. Because grades are one source of power teachers have over students, we may sometimes be tempted to use grades as incentives for motivation and compliance or as punishments when students don't conform to our expectations. Do your best to avoid this temptation.

To understand why, let us consider grades as punishments. The research is clear. No studies have found that low grades are effective as punishments (Guskey & Bailey, 2001; O'Connor, 2002). Because grades are connected to self-concept and carry emotional meaning, a low grade usually causes students to question their abilities (recall our colleague's son with the D− on his first English essay), to withdraw, or to disparage the importance of the grade and the importance of learning. Rather than punitively assigning a zero for uncompleted homework, a more effective approach could be to consider an assignment as "incomplete" and to require additional (sometimes supervised) work (Guskey & Bailey, 2001). Conversely, to consider using positive grades as a reward apart from an indication of mastery of learning goals can encourage students to focus on getting the grade rather than getting the learning. For example, we know an English teacher who guaranteed students at least a "B" on a paper if they followed all formatting directions, which, by the way, were not addressed in the learning goals for the class. Many of her students focused more carefully on the formatting than on the content. Such an approach emphasizes performance goals over mastery goals, so the importance of acquiring understanding and skills may take a back seat to figuring out how to get the best grade.

Review Borderline Cases Carefully

No matter what process you use in determining grades, you will always have borderline cases. And because any measurements related to achievement contain error, you know you must rely on judgment as you examine scores in the grade book. We believe you must review borderline cases carefully, bearing in mind the grade you assign should be your best judgment of the student's level of mastery. If you have implemented Guideline 5 (Table 10.4) to make sure recent and consistent performance carries the most weight in the grade, this problem may already be mitigated somewhat. For additional guidance, you may need to consider which evidence is most important in relation to the goals in the course. For example, a paper that demonstrates application of course concepts to a practical setting may reflect mastery more comprehensively than quiz or test grades. Through this process, focus on mastery rather than on effort or other nonachievement considerations. If you are still wavering after review, it is reasonable to give the student the benefit of the doubt and the higher grade (Gronlund, 2006). Whatever decision you make should be applied to students consistently. Table 10.8 details the components of an effective grading policy based on our guidelines that should be communicated to and discussed with students.

TABLE 10.8

Elements of an Effective Grading Policy to Communicate to Students

Describes formative assessments and their purpose and distinguishes them from summative assessments

Provides descriptions of summative assessments, including
- Detailed scoring guide with criteria and weights
- Due dates

Explains grading scale, including
- Cutoff points for final grade levels
- Amount each assessment contributes to final grade
- Borderline policy

Addresses cheating

Addresses consequences for late work

Addresses extra credit, if any

A Special Case: Students with Disabilities

Many teachers we have worked with have worried extensively about grading students with disabilities. One middle school science teacher we know has said that trying to grade students fairly who receive special education services is one of the hardest parts of her job. Figuring a grade is difficult when you are teaching eighth-grade standards to a student who reads at the second-grade level, and you don't simply want to put a string of "F"s in the grade book.

Dennis Munk and William Bursuck (2003) have worked extensively to address this dilemma. They suggest that the key is collaborating with the team that designs the student's **Individualized Education Plan (IEP).** The IEP is the program designed each year for students with disabilities by the parents and teachers who work with each student. It defines the student's current level of performance and contains goals and how they will be measured, as well as the specific services provided to the student, including any modifications of the typical program or accommodations to enhance access.

Recognizing that grades can serve different purposes and mean different things to different people, these authors recommend the IEP team explicitly decide what each grade should signify for a special education student. During the IEP process, they suggest parents and teachers should openly discuss what each grade should represent. For example, they could agree for a mainstream science class that the student should be graded on three rather than five key assignments, and improvement across the semester will count for a certain percentage of the grade. This agreement is written into the IEP as a grading modification. Then the teacher applies that system in calculating a grade for the student. Monk and Bursuck suggest that providing a "menu" of grading adaptations or modifications for special education students can encourage more access to grade-level curriculum as well as support these students' efforts toward success. Grading modifications are helpful for dispelling any ambiguity about what a student's grade represents. They allow teachers to use different but explicit criteria with students who would have great difficulty meeting standard learning goals. In our experience, many teachers aren't aware grading adaptations can be written into the IEP.

Individualized Education Plan (IEP)

The program designed each year for a student with disabilities. The program is designed by the teachers who work with the student and the student's parents.

Ethics Alert: Parents must participate in this decision-making process about grades. If parents are not made aware of modifications to grading, they may be surprised if their child does not do well on a state test. Remember, the role of the grade is to communicate to others (e.g., parents) about a student's achievements.

Grading as a Skill

Learning to grade consistently and fairly is a complex set of skills that requires careful thought and practice (Brookhart, 2004). This issue doesn't come into play when you are grading multiple-choice tests with only one correct answer. But when you are scoring writing assignments or performance assessments, your first step in fair grading is to be sure to formulate a clear scoring guide to delineate key elements of quality for you as well as your students, as we discussed in Chapters 8 and 9. You must then take special care to apply the criteria from the scoring guide consistently. The first few times you grade a set of papers or projects, we recommend reviewing the suggestions for avoiding the pitfalls listed in Table 8.8 in Chapter 8.

Types of Grading Approaches

We now turn to the more technical considerations in converting performance on assessments into grades. Two issues are important at this point: the basis for comparison and the type of summarizing system you intend to use. For most teachers, these are determined by school or district grading policies.

Basis for Comparison

From the beginning, you must decide whether you assign grades based on comparing student work to a specific criterion or standard of mastery (**criterion-referenced grading**) or to the work of the other students you are teaching at the same time (**norm-referenced grading**).

Criterion-Referenced Grading
A grading process in which student work is compared to a specific criterion or standard of mastery.

Norm-Referenced Grading
The assignment of grades according to a pre-specified distribution (e.g., exactly 10% will receive an "A").

Criterion-Referenced Grading

A criterion-referenced grade is determined by comparing a student's performance to an absolute standard. Most of us have experienced criterion-referenced grading when we completed the driver's licensing examination; we wanted to get at least 85 percent correct (the absolute standard) to pass the test. In the classroom, we might review the tasks we will be using to assess student learning and decide that a percentage grade of at least 90 percent (the standard) is required for an "A."

We recommend criterion-referenced grading. If you have aligned your instruction and your assessment with the learning goals, combined scores should provide a strong indicator of each student's level of mastery of the learning goals. In addition, with criterion-referenced grading, any number of students can attain high grades if they have demonstrated mastery. Criterion-referenced grading stresses mastery and lessens competition among students. For criterion-referenced grading to be most effective, you must be sure to keep your expectations high and your learning goals challenging.

Also, notice that one student's grade of "A" does not depend on the number of other students who earned an "A." In fact, if you were teaching a class of gifted students, they might all earn "A." This is not the case with norm-referenced grading.

Norm-Referenced Grading

Norm-referenced grading, sometimes referred to as "grading on the curve," requires you to arbitrarily decide how many students can achieve each letter grade. For example, you may decide the grades in your classroom should approximate a normal distribution:

10% of the students will get an "A" and 10% will receive an "F."
20% will get a "B" and 20% will earn a "D."
40% will receive a "C" (Frisbie & Waltman, 1992).

Unfortunately, if 15 percent of your students have high levels of mastery, 5 percent of them must receive a "B" if you are using the 10 percent cutoff. This approach is clearly arbitrary, and the meaning of an "A" will vary with every new group of students. A student's grade depends on how many people do better. You can see why norm-referenced grading often weakens the morale and effort of poorer performing students. It also functions as a method of "sorting" students from best to worst and thus fosters competition among students. We recently heard from a student who was taking a class where the teacher used norm-referenced grading. He told us that as students finished each exam, they would make as much noise as possible when leaving the classroom—dropping books, scraping their chairs, slamming the door—to distract the remaining students and interfere with their concentration in hopes of lowering their grades.

In our own classes, we often ask students which form of grading they prefer. Surprisingly, we always have a few who favor norm-referenced grading. They inevitably reveal they have had several classes where everyone would have failed tests if criterion-referenced grading were used, so norm-referenced grading was their only shot at doing well. But if you align your assessment with your instruction and use formative assessment with feedback to help students improve before the summative assessments, students should not be failing your tests in droves.

Types of Summarizing Systems

After you have chosen and weighted your summative assessments in terms of the contribution they represent to mastery of the learning goals, you must choose a way to combine them for a grade. Several methods exist, and often the method is chosen at the school or district level.

Letter Grades

Letter grades are the most familiar method of summarizing student achievement. For many years, teachers have used letter grades, from "A" to "F," for individual assignments and then have combined them for final grades, usually weighting more important assignments more heavily than less important ones.

Even though letter grades are so common, the actual meaning of letter grades may vary and even confuse. Sometimes the label for each of the five grade categories can suggest a norm-referenced interpretation (e.g., "C" = Average), whereas at other times it can suggest a criterion-referenced interpretation (e.g., "C" = Satisfactory) (Guskey & Bailey, 2001). If you grade using a criterion-referenced approach, the labels conveying the meaning of your grades should be consistent with this approach.

Standards-Based

To tie grading categories more closely to standards on which learning goals are based, some school districts have abandoned letter-grade categories for categories that indicate degree of mastery on the standards. They explicitly design assessments

Benchmark Tests
Assessments tied explicitly to academic standards and administered at regular intervals to determine the extent of student mastery.

termed **benchmarks** that indicate levels of proficiency in meeting the standards, and grades are based on these benchmarks. Grading status is then assigned based on categories such as *below basic, basic, proficient,* and *advanced* or *beginning, progressing, proficient,* and *exceptional.* Some educators find this approach particularly useful for connecting student performance to the standards and view it as the best approach for capturing student performance (Marzano, 2006; O'Connor, 2002). For example, when you design scoring guides, the categories can be tied explicitly to the proficiency levels of the standards (see Table 5.8). For this approach to be effective, the standards designated must be broad enough to communicate an overall sense of student achievement, but narrow enough to provide useful information for future learning (Guskey & Bailey, 2001).

Percentage

A common method for summarizing grades is to calculate the percentage of total points earned on each assessment. After weighting assignments proportionally, letter grades can then be assigned based on specified ranges, or in some schools, the percentages themselves are reported. Many teachers prefer using percentages because they believe they can make finer discriminations between students with a 100-point range than with the 5-point letter grade range (i.e., A–F). Because of the error involved in all measurement, however, the difference between a 72 and a 75 may not actually be meaningful. In addition, a score of 100 percent, especially if it is on an easy test, may not necessarily equate to complete mastery of the material. You can't necessarily assume that the percentage correct increases directly with the degree of mastery of the learning goals (McMillan, 2007). In addition, students may perform quite differently on the different learning goals addressed during a marking period, and a single total doesn't allow a picture of strengths and needs in these different areas.

Total Points

A point system is another method teachers often use in calculating grades. The outcome is similar to the percentage method. Instead of weighting assignments after the percentage correct is calculated to get a total, you assign a weighted proportion of the total points to each assignment at the beginning of the term. For example, instead of weighting the percentage correct on a test twice as much as the percentage correct on a quiz, you simply have a quiz worth 20 points and a test worth 40 points. You add up all the points, calculate the percentage of total points earned, and assign grades on this basis. The drawbacks of this method are similar to those for the percentage system.

Other Methods for Summarizing Grades

Grades as a summary representation of achievement have a long tradition, but they also have significant problems, as we have seen. In a standards-focused educational environment, grades based on percentage or total points may not link achievement clearly enough with standards. In addition, single grades may have included characteristics of students other than achievement, such as effort and ability. Other methods for summarizing grades have been proposed, and we describe two of these. Although they are not widely used at this time and may have logistical concerns, they illustrate efforts to remedy some of the unease teachers, parents, and students have expressed about traditional grading systems. They provide ideas about possible directions schools may take in the future.

"Not Yet" Grading   **"Not yet" grading** assumes not all students learn at the same pace, but all students will learn. On benchmark assessments tied to grade-level standards, students receive an "A," a "B," or "NY" for each learning goal. "Not Yet" implies all students will reach the goal when they put in more work, conveying high expectations and promoting the connection between student effort and achievement. These systems also offer students systematic opportunities to improve their "NY" grades, so this approach is one way to capture the positive results of differentiated instruction and formative assessment. Students who did not do well on an assessment the first time may need different instructional strategies or more time. Instead of assuming the fault is in the student, this approach provides more opportunities to master the content, thus encouraging rather than demoralizing anyone who tends to lag behind peers. You may protest that this method is not "fair" to those who do well on the first try. But we must remember that in providing equal access to educational opportunity, we have an obligation to help *all* students learn rather than merely sorting them into "strong" or "slow" learners.

"Not Yet" Grading
A grading system in which students receive either an "A", "B", or "NY" (not yet) for each learning goal.

Narrative Reports   Rather than using report cards with a single letter grade for each subject, some elementary schools have teachers write **narrative reports** describing student achievement and progress each marking period. The difficulty of combining a range of disparate factors into one letter or number is thus eliminated. Teachers can describe student work habits, reasoning skills, communication skills, and other facets of learning and performance that may not be captured by a single grade in a content area. This type of summary of student achievement can work effectively when teachers employ a structured approach that addresses specific learning goals in their reports (Guskey & Bailey, 2001). Otherwise, narrative reports can be too vague in their descriptions to pinpoint achievement strengths and needs. Narrative reports are rarely used in middle and high schools because they are quite time consuming for teachers who may have more than 100 students each term. In addition, earning credits toward graduation requires more explicit tracking of accumulated understanding and skills.

Narrative Reports
Written descriptions of student achievement and progress.

We next turn to a discussion of portfolios. Portfolio assessment is a popular and growing means of documenting and communicating about learning in a more comprehensive way than a single grade or score might offer.

✦ PORTFOLIOS AND COMMUNICATING ABOUT ACHIEVEMENT

A **portfolio** is a purposefully organized collection of student work. We believe that the key words in the definition are "purposefully organized." We have seen many teachers collect a variety of student work in individual folders without a clear rationale in mind. However, a portfolio is most valuable when work samples are chosen by teachers and students with a clear objective (Belgrad et al., 2008).

Portfolio
A purposefully organized collection of student work.

Portfolio Purposes

Because portfolios require time and energy, they should be used only if they enhance communication about learning. Therese Kuhs and her colleagues (2001) suggest that teachers ask themselves, "What is it I want to know about student learning that I cannot find out in another way?" and "What can a portfolio tell about student learning that cannot be told by a single performance task?" We thus first turn to the purposes portfolios can serve so you get a clear picture of the functions they can perform.

Growth Portfolios

Growth Portfolio

An organized collection of students' work gathered to document development and growth over time.

If you intend to promote mastery goals among the students in your classroom, a growth portfolio could be a helpful strategy. The **growth portfolio** is designed to document student growth over time. It therefore contains items such as progress monitoring charts and graphs tracking progress toward specified goals, samples of similar assignments (e.g., lab reports, critiques, perspective drawings, descriptive paragraphs) across time, and performance assessments, plus other projects, including early drafts and final product, with the feedback from earlier drafts incorporated.

In our own teaching, we have used portfolios to document student growth in writing. At the beginning of each school year, our third-grade students wrote a fictional story. These stories generally consisted of four or five sentences on 1-inch lined paper. By the end of the year, stories had greatly improved. They often filled two or more pages of regular notebook paper. Students now established a setting, developed a character, presented a problem, and brought the problem to a resolution. They also had learned to follow the conventions for capitalization, punctuation, quotations for dialogue, and paragraphing. At the year-end conference, parents viewed their child's learning progression through the stories, which dramatically illustrated their child's growth. Thus, in our experience, a portfolio of student writing can be a powerful method for documenting and communicating about learning.

Another essential element of growth portfolios is focused student reflection. For example, students may be asked to describe their strengths and weaknesses at the beginning of the year and then note how they have changed, using evidence from the items collected over several months in the portfolio. Students may choose a personal goal and then later describe how portfolio entries illustrate their progress toward reaching that goal. Sometimes students write a "biography" of a piece of work that describes the development over time of the assignment. These types of assignments help students focus on their own progress and improvement rather than comparing themselves to others, a key element of promoting mastery goals. Stronger mastery goals then tend to increase student motivation, enhance persistence, and increase student willingness to attempt challenging tasks (see Chapter 1).

Reflective assignments also encourage students to take responsibility for their own learning by providing them with opportunities to think about their work as meaningful evidence of their learning rather than as arbitrary assignments to get out of the way. Growth portfolios also allow students to personalize the learning goals and to internalize the standards for evaluation, which help them develop the self-governing skills needed for continued learning and, ultimately, for democratic participation.

Showcase Portfolios

Showcase Portfolio

An organized collection of students' work designed to illustrate their finest accomplishments in meeting learning goals.

The **showcase portfolio** is designed to display a collection of work illustrating students' finest accomplishments in meeting the learning goals. It therefore contains only the best examples of student work. For example, a math showcase portfolio might show a student's most effective attempts related to specific problem-solving abilities and communication skills (Kuhs, 1997). A writing showcase portfolio might show a student's best writing for different purposes, such as one journal entry on current events, one poem or piece of fiction, one persuasive essay, and one nonfiction report.

If you decide to use showcase portfolios, you must be sure students have more than one opportunity to complete each type of assignment. One goal for the showcase portfolio is to encourage students to learn to apply the evaluation standards to their work, a strategy we have suggested can help students develop self-governing skills. For this reason, students usually choose the portfolio entries from categories designated by the teacher. They must, therefore, have several pieces to compare in order to choose the one they believe represents their best work. A reflective piece explaining why each item was chosen for the showcase portfolio can reinforce students' use and internalization of the standards.

Documentation Portfolios

Some states and school districts, because of dissatisfaction with large-scale standardized tests, have made an effort to use portfolios for large-scale assessment for reports to government agencies and the public. The **documentation portfolio** is intended to provide an evaluation of student achievement status for accountability purposes. Entries for these portfolios must be strictly standardized so they are comparable across students and classrooms. Entries may include performance assessments and written assignments, as well as teacher-completed checklists (especially in the early grades). Entries are determined at administrative levels rather than by teachers and/or students. In contrast to growth and showcase portfolios, student self-assessment is not usually an essential component. Documentation portfolios are also sometimes employed by classroom teachers for evaluating levels of student achievement. Table 10.9 presents an overview of the three types of portfolios.

Documentation Portfolio

An organized collection of students' work that provides information for evaluating achievement status for accountability purposes.

TABLE 10.9

Types of Portfolios

Type of Portfolio	Purpose	Types of Entries	Importance of Standardized Entries and Procedures	Importance of Student Self-assessment	Who Chooses Entries?
Growth	Show progress over time	• Progress monitoring charts and graphs tracking progress toward specified goals • Samples of similar assignments (e.g., lab reports, critiques) across time • Performance assessments or other projects, including early drafts and final product with feedback incorporated • Student reflections on progress	Low	High	Teacher and student
Showcase	Demonstrate best accomplishments	A student's best work, such as the following: • Most effective attempts related to specific problem-solving abilities and communication skills in math • Best writing for different purposes in language arts • Best pinch pot, best hand-built pot, and best thrown pot in art class on pottery • Student reflection on rationale for entries	Low	High	Student
Documentation	Provide a record of student achievement status	Comparable entries across students and classrooms, such as • Performance assessments • Written assignments • Teacher-completed checklists (especially in the early grades)	High	Low	Administrators

Implementation Issues

Several issues must be addressed if you decide to implement some variation of growth or showcase portfolios in your classroom. These issues are not as salient for documentation portfolios required by external authorities.

What's the Point?

The first issue you face is deciding exactly what you want to get out of implementing portfolios. You must make sure you design the system to provide information on student learning that you are not getting in other ways. For this reason, the decision cannot be taken lightly. Using portfolios often requires considerable effort and significant modification of your teaching practices. For example, when you choose to use growth portfolios, your primary purpose is to help students focus on their own progress in ways they may never have done before. You must teach students the skills and strategies they need to monitor their progress and reflect on their growth. You must design class work and assignments with this focus in mind, so you must ensure that you structure formative assessment and student self-assessment into your teaching. We recommend that you initiate portfolios with only one subject area because of the intense work required.

In addition, a strong focus is necessary. You must concentrate portfolio work on specific learning goals that you address in your curriculum (Belgrad et al., 2008). For example, learning goals in mathematics that lend themselves to documentation by portfolio could include "collects and uses data to support conclusions" or "makes generalizations and creates classification systems" (Kuhs et al., 2001). "Uses persuasive language in writing" or "demonstrates the ability to write in a variety of formats" could be learning goals in language arts that are appropriate. These topics are broad enough that progress across a whole semester or year can be addressed.

Student Involvement

Another issue in getting started is to foster meaningful student participation. Students, too, need to understand what they will get out of developing portfolios. Helping students feel responsible for their work is a key issue facing teachers today, and portfolios can help. Preparing an opening statement for the portfolio at the beginning of the year, such as describing themselves and what they hope to gain in school this year ("Who are you and why are you here?"), focuses students on ownership of their work and provides a benchmark for examining progress later (Benson & Barnett, 2005). Some of the suggestions we have made for promoting mastery goals are also relevant here. Allowing students choice and control in the types of items to be included is one step. Another factor we have discussed in terms of fostering mastery goals is relevance. Students need to understand why the work they are doing is important and has value for them and their future. Involving them in analyzing their own work related to learning goals whose significance they understand helps make their efforts meaningful and relevant.

Systematically requiring student reflection is probably the most important aspect of generating student engagement in the portfolio process. Involving students in explaining and reviewing the process of creating their entries as well as evaluating their products is useful. These reflections should allow them to analyze their work in comparison to the learning goals, to see their strengths and weaknesses, and to develop new strategies to improve future efforts.

One important job of the teacher is to help students see how such efforts foster significant insights that expand their learning, and three guidelines are recommended (Fernsten & Fernsten, 2005). First, you must create a supportive environment in which you encourage candid reflection, even if student revelations don't correspond to your ideas of appropriate strategies (e.g., doing a large project at the last minute). Only honest dialogue about work habits or study strategies can lead to new learning insights.

Second, you must take special care in designing effective prompts for student reflection. These should be based on the learning goals for the portfolio entries. For example, if students are to use imagery in their writing, you might ask them how and why they chose the imagery they used rather than asking a vague question about the writing process. Similarly, if an entry requires revision after formative feedback, you might ask students to specify the changes made and how they helped the student move toward mastery of the learning goals.

Third, for effective student reflection, you and your students must develop a common language. Your modeling of the language to use when analyzing work is crucial in the early stages (Gredler & Johnson, 2004). You must also designate periods for specific instruction related to student learning of evaluation and reflection skills. Such instruction could include class discussions involving careful analysis of work samples based on scoring guides and comparison of one piece to another. Discussion and examples of appropriate goals that can be monitored across time can also be helpful. Opportunities for students to examine samples of portfolios and generate their own questions about them may help make the process more concrete for them.

Logistics

After you have clearly established a purpose and have your students involved, you must choose work samples on which to focus, incorporate the portfolio process into your instructional activities, and decide how to organize and store the portfolios.

Choosing Work Samples   Bailey and Guskey (2001) suggest that the most effective approach in selecting pieces for inclusion involves a "combination of teacher direction and student selection." For example, for growth portfolios, teachers may mandate certain progress monitoring charts be included (e.g., documenting writing fluency growth), but students may also choose an additional goal and a personal method to monitor progress toward it. For showcase portfolios, a language arts teacher may specify that three types of writing progress will be monitored, but students may be able to choose which three out of the four types of writing studied they want to represent, and they also decide which pieces constitute their best work. Sometimes teachers specify a few entries that must be included (e.g., monthly performance of scales on audiotape for instrumental music students, written reflection on progress in a specified area in art). These are added to other entries students choose, including favorite pieces, work related to their special interests, or items into which they put the most effort or learned the most. In addition, items chosen collaboratively by students and teachers can be included (Gredler & Johnson, 2004).

Portfolio Classroom Activities   Portfolios require instructional time. As discussed, you must first help your students become comfortable with the common language and the skills required for appropriate reflection about portfolio entries. You must also address the understanding and skills required for developing each entry and its connection to the learning goals. Then you should build into your classroom routine periodic opportunities to employ these skills to develop the content of the portfolios and the reflections about the entries.

Organizing and Storing Portfolios   Portfolios can be harbored in file folders, large envelopes, large cereal boxes, or pizza boxes (unused). Another possibility is for students to keep their work in a computer file, an MP3 file, or on a CD or DVD.

TABLE 10.10

Growth Portfolio Reflection Form

Portfolio Reflection

Assignment: _____ **(attached if using paper copies)**

Date: _____

1. What is the main thing I learned from this assignment/performance?

2. What was strongest about my work on this assignment?

3. In what specific ways have I improved from the last assignment (or last draft of this assignment)?

4. What problems did I encounter and how did I solve them?

5. Which aspect of my performance do I need to work on most?

6. What specifically will I do to improve this aspect?

Developing password-protected sites such as MySpace for portfolio purposes (perhaps "MyAchievementSpace") are among other interesting possibilities (Callison, 2007). The sequence of materials in the portfolio should be clearly specified from the beginning. For example, a growth portfolio is usually organized chronologically, whereas a show-case portfolio is organized by using a consistent order for the different types of entries. You may want to keep specific forms in each student's file that they complete as they include a piece of work in their portfolio. For example, in a growth portfolio, variations on the form in Table 10.10 could be employed in art, music, or physical education, as well as for writing, math, science, or social studies. Students can refer back to older reflections when considering new entries or examining their progress.

Evaluation

The evaluation approach to portfolios depends on the type of portfolio. For growth and showcase portfolios, the emphasis is on student self-evaluation and reflection rather than on using portfolios for traditional grades. The key to encouraging accurate student self-evaluation is establishing clear criteria and providing practice with these skills. If you include a learning goal related to self-assessment or reflection, the most recent portfolio entries in which students demonstrate these skills may be used as a summative assessment for grading purposes. You must make clear what you are looking for in these reflections, preferably with discussion of examples using a well-designed scoring guide. Then the early reflections for the portfolio should serve as formative assessments on which the same rubric is used, and feedback and suggestions for improvement are offered. Many other key items in growth and showcase portfolios (e.g., persuasive essays, performance assessments) probably serve as summative assessments in their own right and therefore will have been graded separately by the teacher.

If you do want to assign grades using portfolio assignments, developing a written assessment plan such as the one depicted in Table 10.11 for a social studies unit can be helpful (Rushton & Juola-Rushton, 2007). Such a plan provides an opportunity for

TABLE 10.11

Portfolio Assessment Plan

Learning Goal	Student Assignment Choice	Score	Teacher Assignment Choice	Score
Students will be able to appraise the impact of significant political features of the Roman Empire on civilization today.	Essay: Julius Caesar: Ruthless dictator or ambitious reformer?		Venn diagrams with paragraph summaries comparing Roman citizenship, law, and governmental structures to those of the U.S.A.	
Students will be able to evaluate the Roman Empire's legacy in the arts.	PowerPoint on an architectural feature (e.g., column, arch) then and now.		Design a Roman villa for your family project.	

both teachers and students to choose entries that exemplify the student's level of performance for each learning goal.

Documentation portfolios, in contrast to growth and showcase portfolios, are formally designed to demonstrate student level of mastery of the learning goals, and entries are not usually a matter of student or teacher choice because of the need for standardization across many students. Currently, judges assessing large-scale use of documentation portfolios have difficulty scoring portfolios consistently, but efforts are continuing to improve reliability by improving training and scoring guides (Azzam, 2008). The variations in conditions under which the entries in the portfolios are developed may also cloud the meaning of scores. Circumstances often vary between students and between classrooms. For example, the amount of support students have received from others may fluctuate from classroom to classroom, and revision opportunities may also differ (Gredler & Johnson, 2004). Such discrepancies may detract from the validity of the judgments made about students' level of mastery.

Communication Beyond Student and Teacher

Many educators view portfolios as an effective vehicle for communicating with parents and others about student achievement. This process can also encourage students to take responsibility for their learning, one of the major goals of preparing students for democratic participation. Portfolio conferences involving parents or guardians with their student and the teacher can be an excellent vehicle for communication between school and home. In particular, **student-led conferences,** in which students take the primary responsibility for explaining their own strengths, needs, and progress to their parents or others, exemplify efforts to aim toward improved communication (e.g., Bailey & Guskey, 2001; Benson & Barnett, 2005; Stiggins & Chappius, 2005). When students are responsible for explaining their own learning and progress to their parents or other interested people, they begin to see more clearly the connection between their own actions and their outcomes. A formal and public presentation of evidence of their learning requires them to see themselves in a new light. They become accountable for learning rather than seeing the evaluative process as beyond their control or their interest.

Student-Led Conferences
A conference where students take primary responsibility for explaining their own strengths, needs, and progress to their parents or others.

Our own experience in parenting leads us to endorse student-led conferences. We, like most parents, often had only a very sketchy picture of what went on in the classroom and would have loved to know more about our child's school activities and learning process. A weekly folder, occasional paper, or annual open house just aren't enough to convey the complex learning going on in any classroom. So one big advantage of student-led conferences is parents being able to understand the range and depth of their child's experiences by hearing their child discuss their learning in the context of tangible ongoing classroom assignments.

Student-led conferences may also change the relationship between student and teacher or student and parent in a positive way (Stiggins, 2008). The student and the teacher form an alliance as they work together to face the challenge of showcasing the student's work to others. And parents' new understanding of their child may open up new opportunities for communication that continue over time.

Student-led conferences have advantages for improving communication between home and school and enhancing student ownership of learning. But they also require intense planning and careful structuring of the conference process (Bailey & Guskey, 2001). Students must possess a clear understanding of the learning goals. Portfolio items must illustrate the student's progress toward these learning goals, and students should be able to explain why. Role-playing (both a good conference and a bad conference) and discussion are often needed so students develop the self-presentation skills they need to lead the conference. Conference plans or checklists for student-led conferences, such as the one shown in Figure 10.1, are also helpful to keep everyone focused on the procedure.

Portfolio Conference Plan

Language Arts Grade 3

☐ Introduce parent/guardian to teacher.

☐ Get portfolio and explain your learning goals in reading and writing, including your personal goal and why you chose it.

☐ Find your graph for writing progress. Explain how the graph shows your writing has improved since the beginning of the year.

☐ Find your best example of writing to describe something. Explain how your paragraphs use a topic sentence with supporting details.

☐ Find your copy of your favorite poem. Explain how the author chose words to convey ideas (e.g., imagery, figures of speech).

☐ Find your reading log. Describe examples of the four major types of literary texts (fiction, literary nonfiction, poetry, and drama) that you have read.

☐ Explain the ways you have made progress in reading so far this year.

☐ With your parent and teacher, write down two things you still want to work on in reading and writing:

_____

_____

Your signature: _____

Parent/guardian signature: _____

Teacher's signature: _____

FIGURE 10.1   *Student-Led Conference Plan for Grade Three Language Arts*

Portfolio Advantages and Limitations

To summarize our discussion of portfolios, see Table 10.12 for some advantages and limitations. By far the most important advantage of portfolios is opportunities for student ownership of learning based on development of self-assessment skills and the focus on individual progress across time. Implementing portfolios as a centerpiece of your instruction can profoundly affect students' approach to learning by providing a structure for promoting mastery goals and self-governing skills. If, however, the portfolio process lacks a clear focus, omits student self-evaluation, and is not integrated with your instruction, these benefits will not materialize.

Portfolios can also be used flexibly by teachers to differentiate instruction to meet individual student needs. Portfolio assessment has been used successfully with a wide range of students, including those with cognitive disabilities (Klein-Ezell & Ezell, 2004). Student control over learning and these opportunities for individualization are particularly useful for students who lag behind peers. Their experience of academic success increases confidence, perhaps rekindling their motivation to learn and ultimately contributing to closing achievement gaps (Stiggins & Chappius, 2005).

Designing an effective portfolio system does, however, require a considerable investment of time for both teachers and students. In addition, although individual assignments may serve a summative grading purpose, we don't recommend the portfolio itself receive a summative grade. Typical inconsistency in scoring makes the interpretation of the degree of student learning problematic when based on only one combined grade for a portfolio. Although using a rubric will help improve consistency of scoring, portfolios may be best suited for communication purposes.

TABLE 10.12

Advantages and Limitations of Portfolios

Advantages	Limitations
Provide opportunities for student ownership of learning through self-evaluation and focus on own progress.	Superficial understanding of portfolios can lead to random collections of documents without a clear purpose or effective student reflection.
Provide comprehensive evidence of progress over time, mastery of learning goals, and opportunities for formative assessment.	Difficult to use for summative grading purposes because of lack of consistency in grading and variation in conditions under which entries are developed.
Provide opportunities for differentiated instruction based on curriculum, student interests, and levels of understanding.	Require considerable investment of time for planning, training students, providing feedback, organizing conferences.
Provide opportunities for in-depth communication with parents and others about student learning and progress.	Management tasks may require time that detracts from attention to mastering learning goals.

In fact, the final strength of portfolios is their ability to communicate to parents and other interested adults about the complexities of student learning. In the earlier sections on grading in this chapter, we pointed out the difficulty of trying to summarize a student's academic achievement with a single letter or number. Portfolios provide multidimensional, tangible evidence of students' learning outcomes, their approach to learning, and their self-evaluation of their progress, strengths, and needs. This comprehensive picture can communicate more compellingly than a single grade the reality and context of each student's achievement.

KEY CHAPTER POINTS

We began the chapter by discussing the difficulty teachers often have in grading students fairly. First, grading brings into conflict the teacher's role as advocate of the student versus the role as evaluator of student achievement. Second, grades are a powerful symbol and have the capacity to impact students profoundly in positive and negative ways. Third, teachers rarely agree on how to determine grades. And fourth, grades represent different things to different people.

Next we described the grading decision process, including recommended guidelines for fair and accurate grading decisions. These include learning and following your school district's grading policy, designing a written policy in which you base grades on summative assessments that address learning goals based on standards, ensuring quality by having sufficient information (reliability) and by using different types of assessments (validity), communicating with and involving students in developing standards of performance, weighting recent and consistent performance most heavily, avoiding unduly weighting factors unrelated to a student's mastery of the learning goals (e.g., effort, participation), avoiding using grades as rewards and punishments, and reviewing borderline cases carefully.

We next described the elements of an effective grading policy that should be communicated to students. We also discussed methods for grading students with disabilities through designing an explicit agreement with the IEP team.

Subsequently, we discussed types of grading approaches such as the basis for student comparisons (criterion-referenced or norm-referenced) and the types of summarizing systems. Letter grades and percentages were discussed, as well as more recently developed approaches such as "not yet" grading and narrative reports.

The next section of the chapter was devoted to portfolio assessment, a popular and growing means of documenting and communicating about learning in a more comprehensive way than a single grade or score can offer. We first discussed three purposes or approaches to portfolios (growth portfolios, showcase portfolios, and documentation portfolios). Implementation issues were then described, including deciding what purpose the portfolio should serve, choosing the learning goals to address, and involving students. Then we described logistical issues. Evaluation of portfolios and using portfolios to communicate with parents were explained next. Finally, the advantages and limitations of portfolios were discussed.

HELPFUL WEBSITES

http://www.guilderlandschools.org/district/General_Info/Grading.htm
The Guilderland, New York Central School District grading policies provide explicit
    guidelines for elementary, middle, and high school teachers, including purposes of

grades, type of criteria, borderline cases, weighting of grades, and number of grades required per marking period.

http://essdack.org/?q=digitalportfolios

This site for the Educational Services and Staff Development Association of Central Kansas presents information about designing digital portfolios and provides a related blog.

CHAPTER REVIEW QUESTIONS

1. Describe personal examples of the tension that can occur between the teacher roles of advocate versus evaluator. How did you see this tension exhibited in terms of grading?
2. Survey two other teachers or teacher candidates and compare the elements they consider in grading and the weight they assign these elements. On what elements do they agree and disagree with you?
3. Generate examples that illustrate why factors unrelated to mastery of the learning goals (e.g., effort, participation) should *not* be heavily weighted in the grading process.
4. Do you believe that some factors unrelated to mastery of the learning goals *should* be weighted heavily in grading? Justify your position, taking into account the arguments in the chapter against such practices.
5. Describe several strategies you could use in your classroom other than grades to increase student motivation.
6. Using Table 10.8, design a grading policy that you could distribute to students in your classroom.
7. How would you go about determining the grading policy you would use for a student with an IEP who reads two grade levels below the rest of your class?
8. Why do most educators recommend criterion-referenced grading over norm-referenced grading practices?
9. Which type of summarizing system (letter grades, percentages, "not yet" grading, etc.) would you prefer to use in your classroom? Explain why.
10. Compare and contrast the different purposes for portfolios. Which approach do you prefer and why?
11. Addressing the implementation issues described in the chapter, describe a portfolio system you might consider adopting in your classroom.
12. Addressing the advantages and limitations of portfolios, explain why you are likely (or not likely) to implement portfolios in your classroom.

REFERENCES

Allen, J. G. 2009. Grades as valid measures of academic achievement of classroom learning. In K. Cauley and G. Pannozzo (eds.), *Annual Editions Educational Psychology*, 23rd ed., pp. 203–208.

Ames, C. 1992. Classrooms: Goals, structures, and student motivation. *Journal of Educational Psychology* 84(3): 261–271.

Azzam, A. 2008. Left behind—By design. *Educational Leadership* 65(4): 91–92.

Bailey, J., and T. Guskey. 2001. *Implementing student-led conferences*. Thousand Oaks, CA: Corwin Press.

Belgrad, S., K. Burke, and R. Fogarty. 2008. *The portfolio connection: Student work linked to standards*. 3rd ed. Thousand Oaks, CA: Corwin Press.

320   Chapter 10   Grading and Communicating About Student Achievement

Benson, B. P., and S. P. Barnett. 2005. *Student-led conferencing using showcase portfolios.* Thousand Oaks, CA: Corwin Press.

Brookhart, S. 1994. Teachers' grading: Practice and theory. *Applied Measurement in Education* 7: 279–301.

Brookhart, S. 2004. *Grading.* Upper Saddle River, NJ: Pearson Merrill Prentice Hall.

Callison, D. 2007. Portfolio revisited with digital considerations. *School Library Media Activities Monthly* 23(6): 43–46.

Cross, C. 1997. Hard questions, "standard answers." *Basic Education* 42(3): 1–3.

Cross, L. H., and R. B. Frary. 1999. Hodgepodge grading: Endorsed by students and teachers alike. *Applied Measurement in Education* 12(1): 53–72.

Fernsten, L., and J. Fernsten. 2005. Portfolio assessment and reflection: Enhancing learning through effective practice. *Reflective Practice* 6: 303–309.

Frisbie, D., and K. Waltman. 1992. Developing a personal grading plan. *Educational Measurement: Issues and Practices* 11(3): 35–42.

Gredler, M., and R. Johnson. 2004. *Assessment in the literacy classroom.* Boston: Pearson.

Gronlund, N. 2006. *Assessment of student achievement.* 8th ed. Boston: Pearson.

Guskey, T., and J. Bailey. 2001. *Developing grading and reporting systems for student learning.* Thousand Oaks, CA: Corwin Press.

Howley, A., P. Kusimo, and L. Parrott. 2001. Grading and the ethos of effort. *Learning Environments Research* 3: 229–246.

Klein-Ezell, C., and D. Ezell. 2004. Use of portfolio assessment with students with cognitive disabilities. *Assessment for Effective Intervention* 30(4): 15–24.

Kuhs, T. 1997. *Measure for measure: Using portfolios in K–8 mathematics.* Portsmouth, NH: Heinemann.

Kuhs, T., R. Johnson, S. Agruso, and D. Monrad. 2001. *Put to the test.* Portsmouth, NH: Heinemann.

Marzano, R. 2000. *Transforming classroom grading.* Alexandria, VA: Association for Supervision and Curriculum Development.

Marzano, R. 2006. *Classroom assessments that work.* Alexandria, VA: Association for Supervision and Curriculum Development.

McMillan, J. 2007. *Classroom assessment.* Boston: Pearson Allyn & Bacon.

McMillan, J., S. Myran, and D. Workman. 2002. Elementary teachers' classroom assessment and grading practices. *Journal of Educational Research* 95(4): 203–213.

Munk, D., and W. Bursuck. 2003. Grading students with disabilities. *Educational Leadership* 61(2): 38–43.

O'Connor, K. 2002. *How to grade for learning: Linking grades to standards.* Glenview, IL: Pearson SkyLight.

Pilcher, J. 1994. The value-driven meaning of grades. *Educational Assessment* 2(1): 69–88.

Rushton, S., and A. M. Juola-Rushton. 2007. Performance assessment in the early grades. In P. Jones, J. Carr, and R. Ataya, eds. *A pig don't get fatter the more you weigh it.* New York: Teacher's College Press, pp. 29–38.

Schunk, D., P. Pintrich, and J. Meece. 2008. *Motivation in education: Theory, research, and applications.* 3rd ed. Upper Saddle River, NJ: Pearson.

Shepard, L. A. 2006. Classroom assessment. In R. L. Brennan (ed.), *Educational measurement,* 4th ed., pp. 623–646. Westport, CT: American Council on Education/ Praeger Publishers.

Smith, G., L. Smith, and R. DeLisi. 2001. *Natural classroom assessment.* Thousand Oaks, CA: Corwin Press.

Stiggins, R. 2008. *An introduction to student-involved assessment for learning.* 5th ed. Boston: Pearson.

Stiggins, R., and J. Chappuis. 2005. Using student-involved classroom assessment to close achievement gaps. *Theory into Practice* 44(1): 11–18.

Thomas, S., and P. Oldfather. 1997. Intrinsic motivations, literacy, and assessment practices: "That's my grade. That's me." *Educational Psychologist* 32(2): 107–123.

Urdan, T., and E. Schoenfelder. 2006. Classroom effects on student motivation: Goal structures, social relationships, and competence beliefs. *Journal of School Psychology* 44: 331–349.

Whittington, D. 1999. Making room for values and fairness: Teaching reliability and validity in the classroom context. *Educational Measurement: Issues and Practice* 18(1): 14–27.

Winger, T. 2005. Grading to communicate. *Educational Leadership* 63(3): 61–65.

Zoeckler, L. G. 2007. Moral aspects of grading: A study of high school English teachers' perceptions. *American Secondary Education* 35(2): 83–102.

CHAPTER 11

LARGE-SCALE STANDARDIZED TESTS AND THE CLASSROOM

As long as learning is connected with earning, as long as certain jobs can only be reached through exams, so long must we take this examination system seriously.

–E. M. Forster, British novelist and essayist

What gets inspected is respected.

–Marilyn Rahming, Principal, Pineview Elementary School

❖ **Chapter Learning Goals**

At the conclusion of this chapter, the reader should be able to do the following:

- Explain differences between norm- and criterion-referenced scoring and between aptitude and achievement tests.

- Refute common misconceptions about large-scale standardized tests and describe practices that enhance their benefits and reduce their pitfalls.

- Prepare students for optimal performance on large-scale tests.

- Explain the types of accommodations available for testing of diverse learners.

- Interpret the results of norm-referenced tests using percentiles, normal curve equivalents, and stanines.

- Critique the use of grade- and age-equivalent scores.

- Interpret results of tests using criterion-referenced scoring.

- Explain the results of large-scale tests to students and parents and formulate ways to use the results of large-scale tests in the classroom.

✦ INTRODUCTION

This chapter addresses large-scale, standardized, summative tests. They are the focus of possibly the most controversial discussions in education today, with passionate defenders and detractors. One key reason large-scale tests loom so large in the national discourse on education is that they are the primary means by which states assess student performance to meet the requirements of the No Child Left Behind Act (NCLB) of 2001. They are also used for high-stakes decisions related to college and graduate school entry and for access to some special programs.

As you may recall from Chapter 5, the goal of NCLB is to increase academic achievement of lower-performing groups and to have all students in the United States achieve proficiency in math and reading by 2014. Each state accepting federal assistance is required to assess students in math and reading in grades 3 through 8

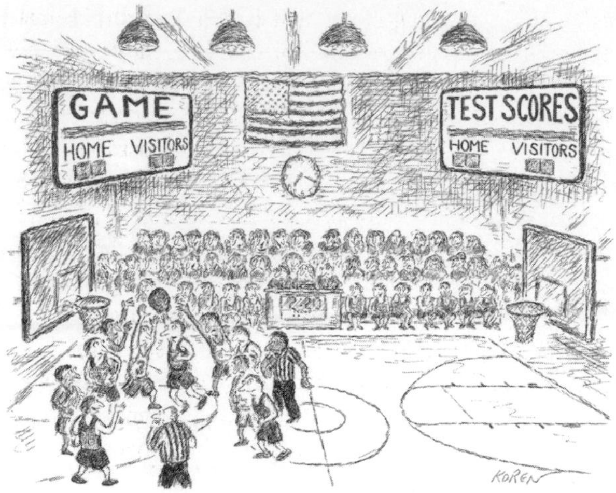
GAME
HOME VISITORS
TEST SCORES
HOME VISITORS
KOREN

FIGURE 11.1

each year and once in high school. Science must also be assessed at least once in elementary, middle, and high school. The results must be disaggregated by major ethnicity groups, disability status, English proficiency, and status as economically disadvantaged. These results are reported publicly. If any of the groups in a school fail to make annual yearly progress (AYP) two years in a row, the school is designated as needing improvement, and students may transfer to another public school in the district. If the school continues to fail to make annual yearly progress, other corrective actions must be taken, eventually leading to "restructuring" the school with curriculum and staff changes.

Because such important consequences result from these tests, they have become high-stakes assessments. With so much riding on the results, these tests definitely get "inspected." If "respect" equates to crowding other issues out of the spotlight, these tests do that, too. The cartoon in Figure 11.1 underlines the burgeoning prominence of such test scores.

To begin navigating this high-profile controversy, you must become familiar with large-scale summative assessments. Thus, we devote this chapter to the issues surrounding them. We first describe some basic definitions and misconceptions related to large-scale standardized tests, then we appraise their benefits and pitfalls. Next, we explain preparation for and administration of these tests, including accommodations that can be made for diverse learners. We also discuss how to interpret these tests and describe how classroom teachers can use the results.

Definitions Related to Large-Scale Standardized Testing

Before we discuss the controversy around large-scale summative testing, we will provide some important background and basic terms. We differentiate among different ways of scoring these tests, and we describe several kinds of large-scale tests.

Criterion-Referenced Scoring and Norm-Referenced Scoring

Criterion-Referenced Scoring
A scoring process that compares an individual student's score to predefined standards.

Large-scale standardized tests can be scored in two different ways. **Criterion-referenced scoring** compares the individual student's score to predefined standards. The scores provide information about the degree to which test content is mastered (similar to criterion-referenced grading in Chapter 10). For example, most states set a criterion level of performance for their accountability tests at each grade that represents proficiency. If students reach this predetermined score, they are categorized as "proficient" or "meeting standards." Criterion-referenced scoring is also termed standards-based scoring in education because students' outcomes determine whether they meet the standards the state has chosen for levels of understanding and skills for that subject and grade.

When we address criterion-referenced scoring in our classes, we ask students for examples from their own experiences. An example often given is the test to get a driver's license. You must obtain a score at or above a certain cutoff level to pass it. Our students think of this example because that cutoff score still looms large in their memories, especially if they had to take the test more than once. Most teachers grade classroom summative tests using criterion-referenced scoring. If a teacher sets the cutoff score at 94 percent correct for an A, everyone above that score receives an A, even if it is half of the class.

Norm-referenced scoring, on the other hand, compares individual scores to the scores of a group of students who has taken the test. Instead of indicating level of content mastered, scores indicate standing relative to that group. Your score reflects a comparison to people taking the test rather than to the amount of content learned. The score you are assigned depends on where your performance (number of items correct) fits in the range of scores obtained by a group, called the **norm group.**

Norm-Referenced Scoring
Compares a student's score to a group of other students who have taken the test.

Norm Group
A carefully constructed sample of test takers used for evaluating the scores of others.

When we ask our students for examples from their experience that illustrate norm-referenced scoring, they mention their high school class rank or their band or football team's annual ranking. These examples also illustrate why careful attention must be directed to just who composes the norm group. If you had 10 National Merit Semi-Finalists in your graduating class, your class rank is likely to be higher than if you had 40.

Similarly, your scores may look very different if you are compared to a norm group of students from a nationwide sample rather than to **local norms,** which are based on school district or state performance. Figure 11.2 illustrates this point. It represents the distribution of test scores along a continuum of low scores (on the left), average scores (in the middle), and high scores (on the right). If your school district is above the national average, your scores will be lower when compared to local norms.

Local Norm
A norm group made up of test takers from a restricted area (e.g., school district).

National test takers
Local test takers
Your score
1 5 10 20 30 40 50 60 70 80 90 95 99
Percentile ranks for national test takers
Percentile ranks for local test takers
1 5 10 20 30 40 50 60 70 80 90 95 99

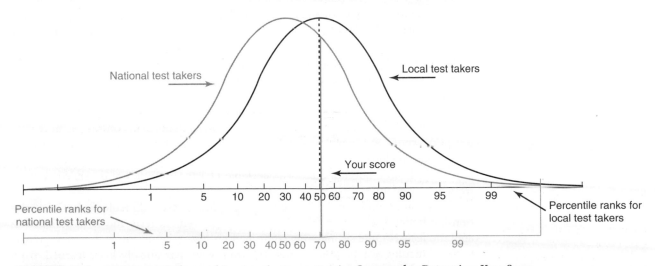

FIGURE 11.2 *With Norm-Referenced Scoring, the Group You Are Compared to Determines Your Score*

For example, in Figure 11.2, your test score at the 70th percentile nationally (see the lighter gray scale) will be at the 50th percentile locally (see the dark scale). If, instead, your school district is below the national average, your scores will be higher when compared to local norms than when compared to national norms.

A test using norm-referenced scoring is not useful unless the norm group is composed of a representative sample of individuals from the entire population of the type of people expected to take that test. If a test is used only in one school district, local norms will suffice. If a test is used widely across the whole country, the sample of students for the norm group should also represent the student population in the United States in terms of demographics, geography, race, gender, age, and socioeconomic and cultural factors.

If the norm group does not include a representative sample, using that sample's distribution of scores to interpret scores in your school will provide misleading information and lead to decisions that lack validity. For example, one of our students found a published norm-referenced test whose norm group consisted of students from only two states, yet the test developer suggested the norms based on this group could be applied to students across the United States. Similarly, questions have been raised about the legitimacy of comparing English language learners to norm groups made up of native English speakers (Solorzano, 2008).

Because people know that norm- and criterion-referenced scoring require different processes for interpreting scores, they assume that you cannot use both methods on the same test. Many tests offer only one or the other kind of scoring option. However, any test can be scored both ways if (1) appropriate criteria for acceptable performance have been specified (for criterion-referenced scoring), and (2) if representative norms have been developed (for norm-referenced scoring). Sometimes people are interested in indicators of content mastery *and* comparisons to a national or state norm group for the same set of scores.

Achievement Tests and Aptitude Tests

Achievement Test

A test that measures how much students have learned in academic content areas.

Aptitude Test

A test that estimates a student's potential or capacity for learning.

The large-scale summative tests used by each state for No Child Left Behind are achievement tests. **Achievement tests** are designed to measure how much students have learned in various academic content areas such as science or math. **Aptitude tests,** in contrast, attempt to estimate students' potential or capacity for learning apart from what they have already achieved and with less reference to specific academic content. Intelligence tests or ability tests are other common names for aptitude tests.

The two types of tests often have a different look. Aptitude tests cover a broader range of life experiences than achievement tests do. They often focus on learning that has occurred informally and incidentally. For example, aptitude tests may include solving puzzles, determining which geometric figure in a series would occur next, or questions about solving problems related to interpersonal relations. In contrast, achievement tests focus more on formal learning in school subjects such as math, English, or history. They would include questions related to solving math equations or comprehension of an excerpt from a novel or a report. See Table 11.1 for examples of possible questions from achievement versus aptitude tests.

As you might imagine, devising a pure aptitude test is difficult. In fact, the relationship between scores on tests designed as achievement tests and tests designed as aptitude tests is quite strong. This confirmed positive relationship is due in large part to the difficulty of separating "potential" from what has already been learned, from background factors and experience, and from motivation.

TABLE 11.1

Questions Similar to Those on Aptitude Versus Achievement Tests

Aptitude	Achievement
What's the right thing to do if you see a car accident?	Explain the difference between the rotation and the revolution of the earth.
What is the next number in the following series? 5 10 20 40	If there are five ducks in the water and three fly away, how many ducks are left?

Although schools sometimes use aptitude tests for placement of students in special education or gifted programs, many are moving toward gathering a much wider variety of information about students, including their response to academic interventions (see Chapter 5). This change makes sense to us because we have found in our school experiences that aptitude tests did not have much use for determining the best ways to help children learn. We view aptitude tests as having a limited classroom role because they provide general information that cannot be translated into practical ways to help teachers work effectively with their students. English language versions of aptitude tests are especially problematic for students of limited English proficiency (Solorzano, 2008). In contrast, information from an achievement test related to specific academic strengths and needs in a subject area is much more useful for planning instruction. In our experience, especially when scores on aptitude tests are low, they can unintentionally and harmfully lower teacher expectations without providing compensatory gains in information about how to help students learn.

✦ MISCONCEPTIONS RELATED TO LARGE-SCALE TESTING

In our years of teaching, we have found that teacher candidates have certain misconceptions about large-scale standardized tests, especially published norm-referenced tests. Table 11.2 lists the five most common misconceptions.

TABLE 11.2

Misconceptions About Standardized Tests

1. The obtained score always accurately represents the test taker's true score.

2. Only commercially published multiple-choice tests can be standardized.

3. Norm-referenced tests always compare people who took the test at the same time.

4. Standardized tests with multiple-choice items address only basic facts at the knowledge level of Bloom's taxonomy.

5. Teachers should be able to use large-scale test results to address individual student needs in the classroom.

Misconception 1. Obtained Score Represents the True Score

Many of our students believe the scores on standardized tests must be interpreted literally. That is, they believe each score pinpoints precisely a student's true level of competence in the subject area tested. Yet you know from our discussion of reliability in Chapter 6 that any obtained score has some degree of error that makes it only an estimate of proficiency. In fact, test developers use information they have collected on the reliability of their tests to provide an estimate of how much error can be assumed to occur on a given test. Called the **standard error of measurement (SEM),** this estimate indicates the average magnitude of error for the test.

Standard Error of Measurement (SEM)
An estimated amount of error for a test.

Confidence Interval
The range of scores determined by the SEM that a student would attain if the test were taken many times.

When we were trained to administer individual standardized tests, our professors recommended we never give parents or children the obtained score, but always provide them instead with a range of scores, called a **confidence interval,** determined by the standard error of measurement. To determine the range covered by the confidence interval, you add the SEM to the obtained score to get the high end of the range, and you subtract it from the obtained score to get the low end of the range. For example, if the standard error of measurement for a test was 3 points, and the student's obtained score was a 70, we would report the score was likely to be in the range of 67 to 73. This practice helps people understand error is involved every time a student takes a test. Some score reports for achievement tests also follow this practice by showing a figure with band or range of scores indicated rather than only a single score. In Figure 11.3 we have one student's individual profile for the TerraNova Achievement Test. You can see on the first two pages that the scores are presented on the right as midpoints within a confidence interval.

Ethics Alert: The report is simulated and the student's name is fictional. Providing an actual student's report would violate confidentiality. As teachers, we should share student test scores only with the student, his or her parents, and other school faculty with a need to know.

Misconception 2. Only Commercially Published Multiple-Choice Tests Can Be Standardized

As we discussed in Chapter 1, an assessment is standardized if it is administered, scored, and interpreted exactly the same for everyone who takes it. This practice is essential for large-scale summative assessments because they compare large numbers of students across districts, states, or countries. For such comparisons to be valid, equivalence in administration and scoring is necessary.

Many large-scale standardized tests do employ multiple-choice questions, but many also include essays or performance assessments. For example, the SAT is a nationally standardized test that includes an essay. These essays are standardized in their administration with the same instructions and time limit for all test takers. Their scoring also requires standardization, which is achieved through extensive training of the teachers who score the essays.

We must remember that the practice of standardization with noncommercial methods of assessment can also be useful in an individual classroom. For example, if you are using some form of general outcome measurement to monitor progress, such as curriculum-based measures of reading or writing (see Chapter 5), you will also use standardized administration and scoring so you can logically compare one score with another score from a later time. Standardization allows you to compare "apples and

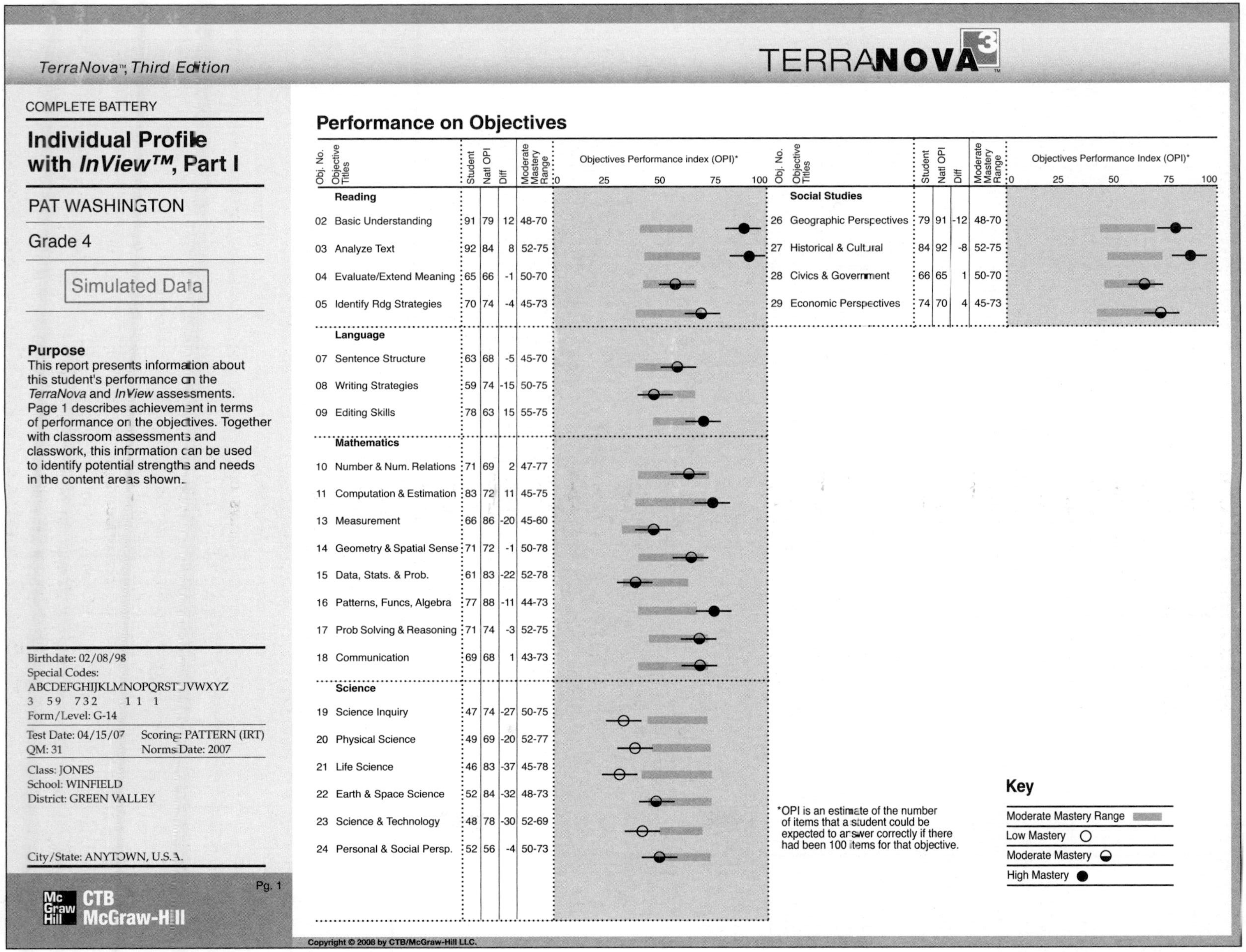

TerraNova™, *Third Edition*

TERRANOVA 3™

COMPLETE BATTERY

Individual Profile with *InView*™, Part I

PAT WASHINGTON

Grade 4

Simulated Data

Purpose
This report presents information about this student's performance on the *TerraNova* and *InView* assessments. Page 1 describes achievement in terms of performance on the objectives. Together with classroom assessments and classwork, this information can be used to identify potential strengths and needs in the content areas shown.

Birthdate: 02/08/98
Special Codes:
ABCDEFGHIJKLMNOPQRSTUVWXYZ
3 59 732 1 1 1
Form/Level: G-14

Test Date: 04/15/07 Scoring: PATTERN (IRT)
QM: 31 Norms Date: 2007

Class: JONES
School: WINFIELD
District: GREEN VALLEY

City/State: ANYTOWN, U.S.A.

Pg. 1

CTB McGraw-Hill

Performance on Objectives

Obj. No.	Objective Titles	Student	Natl OPI	Diff	Moderate Mastery Range
	Reading				
02	Basic Understanding	91	79	12	48-70
03	Analyze Text	92	84	8	52-75
04	Evaluate/Extend Meaning	65	66	-1	50-70
05	Identify Rdg Strategies	70	74	-4	45-73
	Language				
07	Sentence Structure	63	68	-5	45-70
08	Writing Strategies	59	74	-15	50-75
09	Editing Skills	78	63	15	55-75
	Mathematics				
10	Number & Num. Relations	71	69	2	47-77
11	Computation & Estimation	83	72	11	45-75
13	Measurement	66	86	-20	45-60
14	Geometry & Spatial Sense	71	72	-1	50-78
15	Data, Stats. & Prob.	61	83	-22	52-78
16	Patterns, Funcs, Algebra	77	88	-11	44-73
17	Prob Solving & Reasoning	71	74	-3	52-75
18	Communication	69	68	1	43-73
	Science				
19	Science Inquiry	47	74	-27	50-75
20	Physical Science	49	69	-20	52-77
21	Life Science	46	83	-37	45-78
22	Earth & Space Science	52	84	-32	48-73
23	Science & Technology	48	78	-30	52-69
24	Personal & Social Persp.	52	56	-4	50-73

Obj. No.	Objective Titles	Student	Natl OPI	Diff	Moderate Mastery Range
	Social Studies				
26	Geographic Perspectives	79	91	-12	48-70
27	Historical & Cultural	84	92	-8	52-75
28	Civics & Government	66	65	1	50-70
29	Economic Perspectives	74	70	4	45-73

Objectives Performance Index (OPI)*
0
25
50
75
100

*OPI is an estimate of the number of items that a student could be expected to answer correctly if there had been 100 items for that objective.

Key
Moderate Mastery Range
Low Mastery ○
Moderate Mastery ◒
High Mastery ●

FIGURE 11.3 *TerraNova Test Scores for Fictitious Students*

(Continued)

TerraNova™, *Third Edition*

TERRANOVA 3™

COMPLETE BATTERY

Individual Profile with *InView*™, Part I

Simulated Data

Norm-Referenced Scores	Scale Score	DIFF[1]	Anticipated Normal Curve Equiv.	Obtained Normal Curve Equiv.	Anticipated National Percentile	National Percentile	National Percentile Range
Reading	664		35	47	23	45	32-56
—							
—							
Language	678	Above	34	57	22	64	53-72
—							
—							
Mathematics	674		41	48	29	47	37-60
—							
—							
Total Score**	679	Above	35	55	24	59	50-66
Science	668		36	45	26	41	36-50
Social Studies	662		38	43	28	37	27-48
—							
—							

National Percentile Scale
1
10
25
50
75
90
99
1
2
3
4
5
6
7
8
9
National Stanine Scale

**Total Score consists of Reading, Language, and Mathematics.
[1]Above or Below appears when there is a significant difference.

Skills and abilities the student demonstrates:

Reading...
Students use context clues and structural analysis to determine word meaning. They recognize homonyms and antonyms in grade-level text. They identify important details, sequence, cause and effect, and lessons embedded in the text. They interpret characters' feelings and apply information to new situations. In written responses, they can express an opinion and support it. Integrate the use of analogies to generalize an idea; identify paraphrases of concepts or ideas in text; indicate specific thought processes that lead to an answer; demonstrate understanding of an implied theme; assess intent of passage information; and provide justification for answers.
The student demonstrated some understanding of the knowledge, skills, and abilities in this content area.

Language Arts...
Students identify irrelevant sentences in paragraphs and select the best place to insert new information. They recognize faulty sentence construction. They can combine simple sentences with conjunctions and use simple subordination of phrases/clauses. They identify reference sources. They recognize correct conventions for dates, closings, and place names in informal correspondence. Understand logical development in paragraph structure; identify essential information from notes; recognize the effect of prepositional phrases on subject-verb agreement; find and correct errors when editing simple narratives; correct run-on and incomplete sentences; eliminate all errors when editing their own work.
The student demonstrated some of the knowledge, skills, and abilities in this content area.

Mathematics...
Students identify even and odd numbers; subtract whole numbers with regrouping; multiply and divide by one-digit numbers; identify simple fractions; measure with ruler to nearest inch; tell time to nearest fifteen minutes; recognize symmetry; subdivide shapes; complete bar graphs; extend numerical and geometric patterns; apply simple logical reasoning. Locate decimals on a number line; apply basic number theory; compute with decimals and fractions; measure to the nearest quarter-inch; read scale drawings; find areas; identify results of geometric transformations; construct and label bar graphs; find simple probabilities; find averages; use patterns in data to solve problems; use multiple strategies and concepts to solve unfamiliar problems; express mathematical ideas and explain the problem-solving process.
The student demonstrated some of the knowledge, skills, and abilities in this content area.

In Science...
Students are familiar with the life cycles of plants and animals. They can identify an example of a cold-blooded animal. They infer what once existed from fossil evidence. They recognize the term habitat. They understand the water cycle. They know science and society issues such as recycling and sources of pollution. They can sequence technological advances. They extrapolate data, devise a simple classification scheme, and determine the purpose of a simple experiment. Differentiate between instinctive and learned behavior; develop a working understanding of the structure of the Earth; create a better understanding of terms such as decomposers, fossil fuel, eclipse, and buoyancy; interpret more detailed graphs and tables; understand experimentation.
The student demonstrated little of the knowledge, skills, and abilities in this content area.

In Social Studies...
Students demonstrate skills in organizing information. They use time lines, product and global maps, and cardinal directions. They understand simple cause and effect relationships and historical documents. They sequence events, associate holidays with events, and classify natural resources. They compare life in different times and understand some economic concepts related to products, jobs, and the environment. They give some detail in written responses. Synthesize information from sources such as maps and charts; create a better understanding of the democratic process, the basic principles our government was founded on, as well as roles and responsibilities of government and citizens; recognize patterns and similarities in different historical times; understand global and environmental issues; locate continents and major countries; summarize information from multiple sources in early American history; describe how geography affected the development of the colonial economy; thoroughly understand both sides of an issue.
The student demonstrated most of the knowledge, skills, and abilities in this content area.

For more information, visit CTB's website, CTB.com/TerraNova3

Purpose
Page 2 of this report presents obtained norm-referenced information (*TerraNova*) and anticipated norm-referenced information (InView), as well as descriptions of the skills and abilities the student demonstrated, and the skills and abilities the student can work toward to show academic growth.

Birthdate: 02/08/98
Special Codes:
ABCDEFGHIJKLMNOPQRSTUVWXYZ
3 5 9 7 3 2 1 1 1
Form/Level: G-14

Test Date: 04/15/07 Scoring: PATTERN (IRT)
QM: 31 Norms Date: 2007

Class: JONES
School: WINFIELD
District: GREEN VALLEY

City/State: ANYTOWN, U.S.A.

Mc Graw Hill CTB McGraw-Hill

Pg. 2

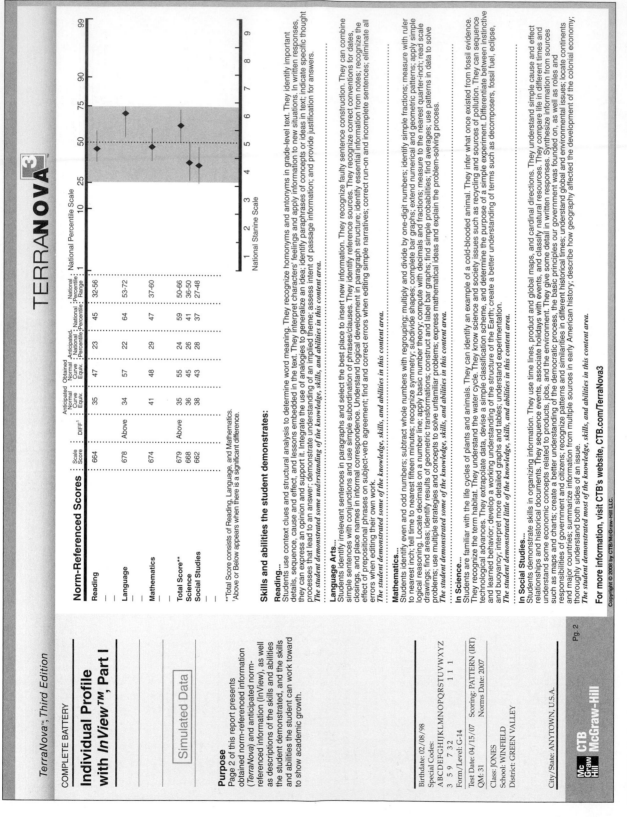

FIGURE 11.3 *TerraNova Test Scores for Fictitious Students*

(Continued)

TerraNova™, *Third Edition*

TERRANOVA 3™

Individual Profile with *InView*™, Part II

PAT WASHINGTON

Grade 4

Simulated Data

Purpose
Part II of this report provides details regarding this student's performance on *InView*.

Birthdate: 02/08/98
Special Codes:
ABCDEFGHIJKLMNOPQRSTUVWXYZ
3 59 732 1 1 1
Form/Level: G-14

Test Date: 04/15/07 Scoring: PATTERN (IRT)
QM: 31 Norms Date: 2007

Class: JONES
School: WINFIELD
District: GREEN VALLEY

City/State: ANYTOWN, U.S.A.

Pg. 3

CTB McGraw-Hill

Norm-Referenced Scores

	GE	NCE	SS	NS	NP by Age	NP by Grade
Sequences	78	66	567	6	54	61
Analogies	69	78	687	7	51	48
Quantitative Reasoning	88	89	568	5	64	75
Total Non-Verbal Score	70	78	687	7	80	74
Verbal Reasoning-Words	65	66	677	6	65	63
Verbal Reasoning-Context	77	56	766	8	88	78
Total Verbal Score	89	79	789	5	70	65
Total Score	78	80	599	6	85	77

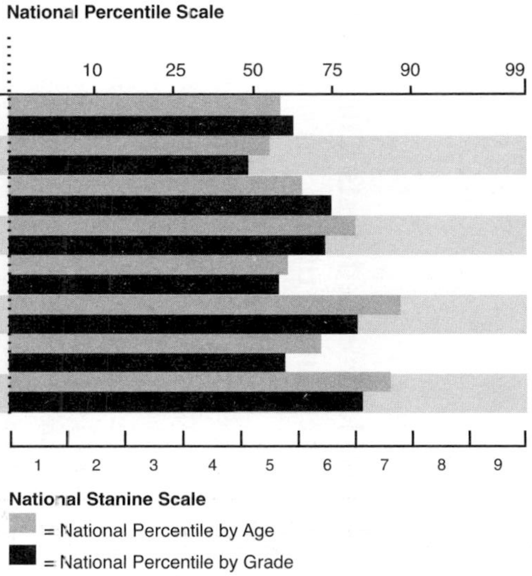

National Percentile Scale
10
25
50
75
90
99
1
2
3
4
5
6
7
8
9
National Stanine Scale
= National Percentile by Age
= National Percentile by Grade

CSI (Range) = 111 (92–127)
Cognitive Skills Index requires student birthdate and Total Score.

Observations

InView consists of five tests that measure cognitive ability. The five tests are Sequences, Analogies, Quantitative Reasoning, Verbal Reasoning-Words, and Verbal Reasoning-Context. Explanations of what these tests measure can be found on the next page. All five tests are combined to create a Total Score. Sequences, Analogies, and Quantitative Reasoning are combined to yield a Total Non-Verbal Score; Verbal Reasoning-Words and Verbal Reasoning-Context are combined to create a Total Verbal Score.

Displayed on the left are the norm-referenced scores for every content area tested. The National Percentile by Age and the National Percentile by Grade are listed in the last two columns. A National Percentile by Age is based on the student's cognitive ability with respect to students of the same age, regardless of their grade in school. A National Percentile by Grade compares a student with other students in the same grade, regardless of their ages. Displayed on the right is a graph of both National Percentile scores. For example, in Sequences, the National Percentile by Age is 54 and the National Percentile by Grade is 61. This can be interpreted to mean that with respect to age, this student scored higher than 54 percent of the students nationally who are at the same age. With respect to grade, this student scored higher than 61 percent of the students nationally who are in the same grade.

The **Cognitive Skills Index** (CSI), which is shown beneath the table, is an age-dependent standardized score based on an individual's performance on *InView*. This score indicates a student's overall cognitive ability relative to other students for the same age without regard to grade. The CSI has a mean of 100 and a standard deviation of 16. This means that two-thirds of the students in the national norm group had CSI scores between 84 and 116. The CSI range indicates that if the student had taken the test numerous times, two-thirds of the scores would have fallen within the range shown.

FIGURE 11.3 *TerraNova Test Scores for Fictitious Students*

apples" rather than "apples and oranges." The equivalence of administration and scoring methods supplies you with the confidence that you can attribute gains to student growth as you see scores improve across time. Without standardization, gains could be attributed to irrelevant things such as changes in your directions, variations in time for the assessment, or idiosyncratic scoring.

Misconception 3. Norm-Referenced Tests Compare People Who Took the Test at the Same Time

Our previous discussion of norm groups should have alerted you that norm groups for most published norm-referenced tests take the test *before* current students take the same test. Test publishers must expend great effort and expense in developing representative norms, so they don't usually do it every year. If you examine reports of your own norm-referenced tests, you can usually find a date for the norms used. One interesting fact about norm-referenced aptitude tests is that as years go by, people seem to do better on them. When tests are re-normed, average scores are higher for the new norm group than for the previous norm group (Flynn, 1999). Students who take the test and are compared to the new norm group must then get a higher score to be in the average range than students who took it the year before with the old norms.

Misconception 4. Standardized Tests with Multiple-Choice Formats Address Basic Facts Only

In Chapter 7 we shared several methods for developing multiple-choice items that address higher-level cognitive skills, such as comprehension, analysis, application, and evaluation. One especially helpful approach to increasing the level of cognitive skills required is the use of interpretive exercises, where students analyze introductory information (e.g., passages to read or graphs) to answer questions. Many published standardized tests incorporate interpretive exercises and other items going well beyond basic facts.

The widely held but mistaken belief about the inability of the multiple-choice format to tap critical thinking skills is the most dangerous misconception on our list. People who believe multiple-choice items address only knowledge-level skills may needlessly disparage the tests based on false assumptions that they are undemanding and lack challenge. If teachers believe this misconception, they may spend unnecessary time on drills of basic facts rather than stimulating children with more complex and interesting assignments that expand their horizons and help them develop the skills they need for participating in civic life.

Misconception 5. Using Large-Scale Tests to Address Individual Student Needs

One misconception about large-scale tests is that they should provide useful diagnostic information on individual students for teachers to use in classrooms. As you may recall from Chapter 1, the purpose of large-scale tests is to provide a "panoramic view" covering content spanning a year or more. When you assess so broadly, only a few items on each concept or skill can be included. These few items cannot generate the detailed information teachers need for planning lessons or figuring out which concepts a student may be missing. Large-scale tests instead provide a general picture useful for showing how a group of students compares to standards, how a school or district compares to others, and how performance from one year compares to the next. Thus, their primary purpose is to generate information for accountability, planning, and resource allocation, not for instructional uses for individual teachers and students. Diagnostic and formative assessments are much better suited to these purposes.

→ BENEFITS AND PITFALLS OF LARGE-SCALE ASSESSMENTS

We will discuss the complexities of large-scale assessments primarily in the context of No Child Left Behind. Since the law was implemented, researchers have begun to gather information about its intended and unintended impact on education in the United States. We can glean some important lessons from these trends that apply to other high-stakes tests as well.

As we begin to sort out the issues associated with the increased use of large-scale achievement tests, we must remember the basic purpose of the NCLB law. It started with very good intentions—closing the widely acknowledged achievement gaps that have developed in the United States. The law had bipartisan support in Congress because everyone supports this important goal. We address three issues related to large-scale assessments: comparisons, curriculum concerns, and addressing improvement. Table 11.3 summarizes these issues.

Comparisons

One of the most important benefits of large-scale tests is their standardization, which is implemented to allow systematic, meaningful comparisons across different groups on the same content. Evidence has begun to accumulate that the large-scale tests initiated to comply with the NCLB legislation have helped school districts focus on struggling children by using disaggregated data to compare groups and pinpoint weaknesses. Districts that previously looked only at average scores often

TABLE 11.3

Benefits and Pitfalls Related to Use of Large-Scale Tests for NCLB Accountability

Issue	Benefit	Pitfall
Comparisons	Allows comparisons across demographic groups within a state, providing opportunities to find and fix achievement gaps.	Nonequivalent standards across states inhibit state-to-state comparisons and may encourage weakening of standards.
Curriculum	Focuses educators on alignment between standards, curriculum, and instruction and assessment.	May narrow the curriculum excessively: "teaching to the test" instead of to the standards.
Addressing Improvement	Focus on enhancing learning: Test scores seen as providing one piece of information useful for improving educational processes.	Focus on increasing scores: Test scores seen as the all-important outcome, minimizing focus on educational processes needed to improve learning.

discovered that minority or poor children in their districts were not faring as well as their middle-class European American peers. In a recent analysis, *Time* magazine suggested that spotlighting "the plight of the nation's underserved kids" is NCLB's "biggest achievement" (Wallis & Steptoe, 2007). One principal we know who is an expert on working with low-achieving African American children attributes the burgeoning number of requests he gets to consult with other schools about how to enhance achievement of African American males to NCLB and the awareness it has generated. Working to close achievement gaps is an important assessment focus we have stressed throughout this text as necessary for preparing students for participation in a democratic society.

Unfortunately, different states require different levels of proficiency on their large-scale tests. Because levels of quality are determined by each state, wide variations in what students know and can do to be "proficient" for NCLB occur (Nichols & Berliner, 2007; Wallis & Steptoe, 2007). For example, to achieve proficiency in Wyoming, you must perform significantly better than you have to in Oklahoma. The lower Oklahoma standards make it appear that more students are proficient. One way this happens is through variations in the reading difficulty of items. For example, two states may both require fourth graders to be able to distinguish between fact and opinion, but one state may use simple sentences for this task while another uses complex passages. Even with standardized administration and scoring, you can only compare scores *within* a state and not *across* states when this is the case.

Paradoxically, states with higher requirements for proficiency find themselves at a disadvantage with NCLB accountability. Fewer of their students, compared to other states, meet annual goals, and so they are more likely to miss annual yearly progress targets and to receive sanctions. The fact that standards of proficiency declined in 30 states between 2000 and 2006 is a worrisome trend suggesting possible "watering down" of expectations under the pressure of NCLB sanctions (Wallis & Steptoe, 2007). To address this issue, some national policy groups are making the case for international benchmarks (McNeil, 2008).

We can draw lessons from these events about the importance of comparisons for large-scale tests. For any standardized large-scale test taken by your students, whether norm- or criterion-referenced, you should know the basic facts about the test. If the test uses criterion-referenced scoring, you should know the understanding and skills required for attaining proficiency so you know what your students must aim for. If the test uses norm-referenced scoring, you should know whether the norm group is appropriate for your students. For tests with either (or both) kinds of scoring interpretations, you and your fellow teachers and administrators should be able to use the scores to disaggregate the data for use in pinpointing groups who may need extra attention. Familiarity with standards and understanding what comparisons are meaningful will help you keep these tests in perspective.

Curriculum Concerns

The second issue related to the high-stakes test controversy we must address is curriculum concerns. How do these tests affect the curriculum? Several studies have suggested that NCLB assessments have influenced educators to develop policies and programs that better align curriculum and instruction with state standards and assessments (Center on Education Policy, 2006). Other research suggests that a well-designed exit exam, another type of high-stakes test, can produce positive impact on curriculum alignment, improve the quality of instruction, and generate positive attitudes and useful dialogue among teachers (Yeh, 2005). Most assessment experts believe alignment between learning goals, instruction, and assessment ensures that instruction addresses the understanding and skills students need to learn. It also helps guarantee that students are fairly assessed on that specific content, and it helps keep standards high for all students, as discussed in Chapter 2. NCLB outcomes related to enhancing alignment, then, suggest a positive influence of high-stakes tests on instruction consistent with recommendations for best practice.

On the other hand, evidence suggests that curriculum is narrowing excessively as a result of the NCLB focus on math, reading, and science (Au, 2007). Educators fear subjects not tested, such as art, history, or the skills needed for democratic participation, will not be taught. We have anecdotal indicators of this, such as recent complaints we heard from a middle school principal that student handwriting is becoming impossible to decipher because elementary schools no longer teach cursive writing because "it's not in the standards." Broader evidence comes from a study that queried educators from all 50 states. In that study, 71 percent of the respondents reported they had increased time for reading and math and decreased time for science and social studies in response to NCLB (Center on Education Policy, 2006). Even more alarming, this curriculum narrowing occurred more in high-poverty districts (97%) than in others (55–59%). Critics of high-stakes tests have suggested teachers perceive pressure to "teach to the test" and therefore spend time having students drill on facts as they eliminate more demanding activities they see as unlikely to contribute to increasing scores. These lackluster strategies in turn reduce student interest and motivation, leading to further depression of educational achievement.

Such actions, however, are not effective and they do not increase either test scores *or* student achievement. To buttress this point, research is emerging suggesting that teachers who teach to high standards (and *not* to the test) have students who excel on large-scale tests. A study in the Chicago public schools analyzed teachers' assignments to students in math and writing in Grades 3, 6, and 8 (Newman et al., 2001). They found teachers who gave more challenging work had students who made larger than average gains on annual standardized tests. Similarly, Reeves (2004) studied schools with 90 percent low-income and ethnic minority students, yet with 90 percent also achieving mastery on annual state or district tests. He found schools with these characteristics emphasized higher-order thinking, in particular by requiring performance assessments with written responses demonstrating students' thinking processes. Finally, studies show teachers who take time to systematically develop formative assessment strategies have students who do better on general ability tests or end-of-year tests (e.g., Wiliam et al., 2004). Formative assessment and more challenging work involving critical thinking allow students to develop and apply multiple, flexible strategies so they can capitalize on their strengths and compensate for their weaknesses when confronted with the broad content of a large-scale test (Sternberg, 2008).

These findings suggest a lesson to take away from the controversy about the impact of large-scale high-stakes tests on curriculum. "Teaching to the test" by focusing on knowledge-level thinking and rote memory learning is a no-win strategy. Students are shortchanged, class is boring for teacher and learners, and test scores will not rise. Instead, providing students with thought-provoking work and tasks with real-world applications aligned to standards and learning goals will be more effective. The other element, of course, is plenty of formative assessment along the way so students receive feedback on how to close the gap between where they are and where they need to be and are provided opportunities to improve. See Box 11.1 for the experience of one of our own colleagues who took this path.

BOX 11.1

Preparing Students for Annual Large-Scale Tests?

In her fourth year of teaching, Barbara Blackburn was assigned two language arts classes filled with students who had scored below average on the annual large-scale test the year before. The principal provided her with lots of "test prep" materials and told her this was a "make or break" year for the students. She found her students responded much better to activities aligned with standards but with real-life implications, such as using the state driver's manual and *USA Today*

for teaching reading, and stressing writing for authentic purposes (e.g., writing editorials). So she ended up using only about a third of the material in the test prep notebooks. At the end of the year, when test scores were received, the principal called Barbara into his office. She was apprehensive, worrying her students had failed because she had not spent enough time specifically on preparation for the tests. Instead, the principal was overjoyed. Almost all the students in those language arts classes had achieved proficiency. He was eager to know how Barbara had worked this miracle.

Addressing Improvement

The third issue we must address related to the high-stakes test controversy is improvement. The point of implementing NCLB was to improve the nation's schools and close achievement gaps. Has the use of large-scale tests enhanced achievement, narrowed achievement gaps, and helped improve schools that fail to make annual yearly progress? Evidence is currently mixed.

Extensive studies of all 50 states by the Center on Education policy (2007, 2008) report scores on reading and math have climbed since NCLB was enacted in 2002. They also report evidence that achievement gaps between groups are narrowing. The authors temper the reports, however, by stating they cannot necessarily attribute these gains to NCLB because many schools have implemented other significant policies to increase student achievement since NCLB began. The impact of NCLB is entangled with the impact of these other programs.

Critics believe the problems with NCLB overshadow any gains, even if gains can be directly attributed to this law. They believe NCLB accountability tests have become an end in themselves, rather than a check on the real goal, which is enhanced understanding and skills for all children. As a farmer relative of ours is fond of saying, "The hogs won't gain weight just because you weigh them more often."

An inordinate focus on the "weighing" (in this case, the NCLB accountability test) can lead to problems. As you already know from our discussions of reliability and validity in Chapter 6, you should never make important decisions on the basis of one test because error is always involved. In addition, the fact that these test scores are used to decide on significant sanctions leads to great pressure to enhance scores without necessarily enhancing student achievement (which we termed score pollution in Chapter 1). This trend has been called "Campbell's Law" (Nichols & Berliner, 2007). Donald Campbell, a social psychologist, philosopher of science, and social researcher, pointed out that when a single social indicator is increasingly used to make important decisions, it will also come under increasing pressure to be corrupted and will become less and less useful as an indicator of progress. Examples of augmenting scores at state and local levels using unethical means (e.g., teachers reviewing specific test content before the test) are documented by Nichols and Berliner. Their examples provide confirmation of such pressure and evidence the scores themselves may not always be an accurate and valid indicator of student achievement gains.

In our view, if the results of any large-scale assessments are to be at all useful for addressing educational improvement, the focus must be on increasing *learning*, and not simply on increasing test scores. Test scores must be seen merely as one indicator of broader learning, and not as an end in themselves. After all, when students have left school and become adults participating in a democratic society, they are judged on their accomplishments and their character, not on their test scores. We lose sight of these larger issues when we focus on improving test scores rather than on developing all facets of learning. From this larger perspective, test scores can provide general information used to modify educational programs and procedures put in place by schools. Results can generate ideas for improving teaching and learning at the school, district, and state level. Examples could include using scores to decide to increase staff development in areas where a school shows weakness, or using scores to see whether programs in place are having the intended impact on learning. When scores are used to provide clues about how to fine-tune educational processes, they are used formatively rather than summatively.

In contrast, efforts will be superficial and test results will become less valid and less useful if educators merely aim to increase scores. Examples include teachers reviewing specific test content before the test, schools removing less able students from testing, or districts focusing interventions only on students close to the proficiency cutoff while ignoring lower achievers. Such practices may influence test scores, but they will not enhance overall achievement for all students.

Ethics Alert: All these practices contribute to score pollution and may warrant an ethics review of a teacher.

Unfortunately, much of the funding to augment student achievement originally promised for NCLB implementation was not included in the final version of the law. This lack of funds exacerbates the problem. As one of our colleagues (a superintendent of schools) says, the stress on testing and the lack of funding for equipping teachers to help children learn is like "trying to kill a lion with a toothpick." Lack of resources may produce shallow (but less expensive) efforts to increase *scores,* but it hampers comprehensive efforts to design significant reforms to enhance *learning.* More emphasis needs to be placed on finding resources and strategies to help schools and teachers bolster learning rather than on punishing schools that do not make annual yearly progress.

The problem of resources is intensified by the wide disparity in school funding in the United States. Whereas Asian and European countries fund all schools equally, in the United States, wealthy school districts commonly spend $3 for every $1 that poor school districts spend. Furthermore, the richest 10 percent of school districts outspend the poorest 10 percent by nearly a 10 to 1 ratio (Darling-Hammond, 2007). Poverty level and minority status strongly predict the percentage of students not meeting proficiency levels for NCLB. These characteristics of students also strongly predict low levels of resources in their schools. Thus, attempts to sever the strong relationship between poverty and low achievement must consider the disparities in resources between rich and poor school districts.

→ PREPARATION FOR AND ADMINISTRATION OF LARGE-SCALE TESTS

We now turn to the subject of preparing your students for large-scale tests, and then we offer a brief discussion of issues related to administration of these tests. Although we are addressing these topics in this chapter on large-scale tests, we ask you to place the information in the broader context of all classroom testing.

TABLE 11.4

Suggestions for Test Preparation

1. Know the standards and teach them.

2. Promote mastery goals throughout the year to enhance student motivation.

3. Foster appropriate attitudes toward tests.

4. Teach students general strategies for taking tests.

Preparation for Tests

We build our suggestions around the basic question we urged you to use in Chapter 1 to judge all your assessment practices: Will this help my students learn? We believe any efforts you make to prepare your students for large-scale (or any other) tests should be judged by the value of the learning your students acquire. Remember, our goal isn't to improve test scores, it is to improve learning. Using this question to guide your decisions also helps you avoid score pollution, one of the important ethical principles we have discussed. We offer several suggestions in the following sections listed in Table 11.4.

Know the Standards and Teach Them

The most important strategy for helping your students do well on large-scale tests is to know the instructional content standards for which you are responsible and to teach that content to your students. Table 11.5 suggests several ways to address instructional content standards. Collaborating with other teachers on designing instruction and assessment tied to the standards is an effective means for developing familiarity with the standards and related teaching activities.

You should also help your students become familiar with the standards. As we discussed in Chapter 4, one of the first actions you should take in designing good instruction and assessment is to make students aware of the learning goals you are working on together. Doing so encourages students to become more autonomous learners and lets them set their sights on clear targets. Discussing how learning the content addressing the standards enables your students to excel, not only in your

TABLE 11.5

Suggestions for Knowing and Teaching the Standards

1. Collaborate with other teachers to design instruction and assessments aligned with the standards.

2. Make students aware of the learning goals and evaluation standards you are working on together.

3. Use instructional activities and assessments promoting higher-order thinking and application to new situations.

4. Provide equal access by differentiating instruction using more than one method of gaining and demonstrating learning.

classroom but also on large-scale tests and in their daily life, and can provide meaning as well as a larger context to your classroom activities. It can also help students see the large-scale tests as nonthreatening and more connected to their ongoing work (Taylor & Nolan, 2008).

Another part of knowing and teaching the standards is stressing instruction and assessment activities in your classroom that address higher-order thinking skills, especially if you want students to use the learning they acquire in your classroom in other contexts. They must be able to apply concepts they are learning to novel situations if they are to use them effectively in large-scale assessments, or, of course, in daily life or for future work or learning.

A final issue related to knowing the standards and teaching them is providing equal access to the content for all of your students. Using differentiated instruction, including supplying students with alternative methods of gaining information and demonstrating their learning, are key strategies.

Promote Mastery Goals Throughout the Year

Motivation is a crucial, but intangible, ingredient in students doing their best in any evaluative situation, including large-scale testing. Some schools or teachers may go all out right before large-scale testing time with pep assemblies or exhortations emphasizing to students how important it is for them to do well. Such practices can backfire, however, by raising stress levels and producing too much anxiety. We recommend you don't blow these tests out of proportion. A better strategy is to focus on enhancing mastery goals throughout the school year. Refer often to Figure 1.1 in Chapter 1 as you design your instruction and assessment. This figure provides guidelines for designing meaningful and challenging tasks, for encouraging student participation in decision making, and for helping students focus on personal goals and track their own progress as you employ formative assessment. Each of these elements enhances students' motivation and increases their effort to do well at whatever challenges (including tests) come their way.

Foster Appropriate Attitudes Toward Large-Scale Tests

If you want your students to take a serious but positive approach to large-scale tests, you must first examine your own attitudes. If you see these assessments as a waste of time, or if they raise your anxiety level, you will unintentionally communicate your feelings to your students. You should neither apologize for nor complain about these tests. The goal for both you and your students is to see these tests as useful. Students should know the results will be *most* useful if they do their best. To accomplish this, explain the test and its purpose. The "panoramic view" of learning provided by these tests offers information to help decision makers improve learning. Across time, the tests can also provide valuable information about individual students and their progress in the curriculum. In addition, without the standardized test scores, we have no way of answering this fundamental question: How are your students doing as compared to others? With this information, we can examine our areas of strengths and our areas to improve. If both you and the students see value in the test results, attitudes can be positive, and excessive anxiety is reduced.

Another factor in generating positive and confident attitudes toward large-scale tests is to make sure students understand that the tests are integrated with what you do every day. They are explicitly connected to your regular learning goals, instruction, and assessment; they are not a foreign and difficult trial by fire. A matter-of-fact remark to this effect every so often can help students put these assessments in perspective.

TABLE 11.6

Skills Useful for Taking Tests

1. Use time wisely.	• Answer all easier items your first time through the test while skipping the harder ones. • Give yourself enough time to address all questions (e.g., allocate more time for questions with more points).
2. Determine exactly what each question asks.	• Focus on key words in the question. • With multiple-choice questions, don't choose an answer just because it's a true statement. It must also answer the question. • With essay questions, don't answer a different question or provide superfluous information. • Consult the scoring guide, if available.
3. Avoid careless mistakes.	• Read directions carefully. • Mark answers carefully, especially if they are on a separate sheet. • For questions involving calculations, estimate the answer to be sure yours makes sense. • Make sure you have answered all parts of each question.
4. Use logic.	• With multiple-choice questions, read all choices and eliminate incorrect answers (distracters) before choosing the correct answer. • Make sure you take into account any words that reverse the meaning of a question such as "LEAST," "NOT," or "EXCEPT." • With complex multiple-choice items, eliminate any single answer first, as well as multiple answer choices that include the single answer.
5. Use shrewd guessing.	• Be sure to answer all questions, especially if you can eliminate at least one alternative.

Some educators also recommend occasionally showing students released items from previous tests related to a learning goal you are working on. Such a practice familiarizes students with the format and style of the test as well as reassuring them about the familiar content.

Teach Students General Strategies for Taking Tests

Equal access to education for all students includes equal access to skills that are useful when taking tests of all kinds. Some students pick up these skills on their own. Others have parents who can provide expensive test-preparation coaching. We have found that even a number of our teacher candidates are not yet aware of all of these strategies, so as a college student, you may find a useful tip or two among our suggestions. Table 11.6 lists key strategies.

Administration of Large-Scale Tests

Teachers usually administer large-scale tests to their own students. The rules are easy to follow—the chief concern is following the directions *exactly*. If a test is norm-referenced, you cannot use the norm group for valid comparisons unless your group takes the test under the same circumstances as the norm group. Also, the only way results from different classrooms, schools, and states can be compared fairly is if the conditions under which all students take the test are the same.

Testing directions go into detail about the arrangement of desks and the classroom (e.g., educational posters or academic information on the classroom walls must be covered), how to pass out the tests, whether students can have scratch paper, and how to time the test precisely. Written instructions you read aloud to the students are also provided. If you and your students remember these procedures are designed to make the test fair and to allow useful interpretations, they will make sense and not feel intimidating to students.

→ Large-Scale Test Accommodations for Diverse Learners

Now that we have discussed the importance of standardization with the administration of large-scale tests, we must also point out that a few exceptions to these strict standardization practices, called **testing accommodations,** are permitted for certain children with disabilities and for students with limited English proficiency. Accommodations are formally chosen by a team of educators that includes classroom teachers and others who regularly work with designated children. Each state has a list of acceptable accommodations your team of educators may use for making accommodations decisions based on students' demonstrated needs. These accommodations should be in place for all assessments, not just for large-scale assessments. The accommodations should be consistent with those incorporated into typical classroom practices throughout the year (Thompson et al., 2002).

Testing Accommodations
Exceptions to the strict standardization practices that allow students to demonstrate their learning without altering the basic meaning of the score.

The purpose of such accommodations is to allow students to demonstrate their understanding and skills without being unfairly restricted by a disability or limited English proficiency. For example, one of the most common accommodations is extending the amount of time available for an assessment. Extra time can remove an obstacle to doing well for those who work slowly because of either a disability or limited proficiency with English.

No accommodation is supposed to change the constructs the test measures. Change to the content brings into question the validity of the student's results and eliminates the value of the comparisons that can be made with them. For example, simplification of test questions or eliminating some alternatives could alter the meaning of a student's test score. This practice would be considered a **testing modification,** or a change made to the testing process that *does* change the construct being measured.

Testing Modification
A change in the testing procedures that alters the meaning of the score.

Sometimes, a modification depends on the content of the test. If a reading comprehension test is read aloud to a student, the test no longer measures the construct of *reading* comprehension. Instead, it measures *listening* comprehension. Similarly, using spell-check devices for a test measuring writing skills, or using a calculator for a test measuring math computation skills, are testing modifications because they alter the interpretations that can be made about students' level of proficiency based on the test results.

The most common testing accommodations are grouped into four categories: flexibility in scheduling, flexibility in the setting in which the test is administered, changes in the method of presentation of the test, and changes in the method of student response to the test. The effectiveness of accommodations should be regularly evaluated by the team working with any student who receives them. Table 11.7 lists examples of accommodations.

TABLE 11.7

Examples of Common Testing Accommodations for Use with Students with Disabilities or Students with Limited English Proficiency

Type of Accommodation	Examples
Flexibility in timing/scheduling of the test	• Extended time • Multiple sessions • Break after specified time period (e.g., 30 minutes)
Flexibility of the setting for the test	• Separate room • Small-group administration • Adaptive furniture or special lighting
Changes in the presentation of the test	• Large print • Braille • One question per page • Sign language interpreter • Examiner can repeat or explain directions in native language • Revised directions (e.g., verbs highlighted) • Use of assistive technology (e.g., audiotape, visual magnification device, computer) • Use of dictionary
Changes in the method of response	• Marking answers in test booklet instead of on answer sheet • Use of word processor • Provide oral rather than written answers • Provide answers in native language

✦ RELIABILITY AND VALIDITY IN LARGE-SCALE TESTS

We discussed the importance of reliability and validity in designing high-quality classroom assessments in Chapter 6. Researchers who work with large-scale summative assessments have devised measures to examine these concerns. Such evidence is extremely important for large-scale assessments. Many of these tests are used for making decisions with important consequences (e.g., retention in grade, placements in special education or gifted programs), so they are referred to as high-stakes tests.

Technical manuals describing evidence for reliability and validity are available for most published standardized norm-referenced tests, and they are an important indicator of the quality of the test. Table 11.8 lists several questions that should be addressed for any large-scale test used for important decisions.

Reliability

To examine reliability related to assessment occasion, test developers have a group of students take the same test twice, usually several weeks apart. They then conduct calculations to see how much variation occurs between the two scores for each student.

T A B L E   1 1 . 8

Questions That Should Be Addressed in the Technical Manual for a Large-Scale Test

Reliability

- Is test-retest reliability high for this assessment?

- Is internal consistency high for this assessment?

Validity

- What empirical evidence is available for the legitimacy of comparing results of this test across persons, classrooms, and schools?

- Has a table of specifications been provided to gauge alignment between local learning goals and this assessment?

- Is the process used in consulting experts and reviewing major textbooks in the development of test content described?

- Is empirical evidence of relationships to other established, relevant criteria based on logic and theories provided?

The resulting measure of stability is termed **test-retest reliability.** Another form of reliability provides a measure of internal consistency by comparing student scores on items within the test. An example of this is to split the test in half, correlating students' scores on even items with their scores on the odd items.

Test-Retest Reliability
The degree of stability between two administrations of the same test to the same students.

Validity

Designers and evaluators of large-scale tests also assemble evidence supporting the accuracy of test score interpretations. They must make sure that the norm group is appropriate and that the test content representatively samples the subject areas addressed. This process should be carefully described in the technical manual, and a table of specifications is often provided. Large-scale tests of achievement in a particular subject usually cover a broader range of material than is covered in any one school district's assessments. The degree of overlap between the large-scale test's coverage and local coverage can vary. The degree of overlap should be considered when drawing inferences about children's achievement. The test publisher must demonstrate in the technical manual that evidence relating this test to other established measures shows it is an accurate, representative, and relevant measure of student performance for the intended purpose.

✦ INTERPRETING NORM-REFERENCED TESTS

We hope the foregoing discussion has provided you with a context for understanding the use of large-scale tests today. The results of these tests, as well as the pros and cons, are frequently discussed in public discourse as well as in schools. To be an informed participant in the dialogue (part of *your* responsibility as a citizen living in a democracy), you need to know how to interpret them. You also need to understand these test scores for your own use, as well as for explaining them to students and their parents.

Foundational Issues in Interpretation of Test Scores

Quantifying a person's level of academic achievement is much more difficult than measuring something concrete about that person, such as height or weight. These physical measurements start with a zero that means absolutely none of the trait, and the intervals between each level of measurement are equal. These characteristics allow you to say that a person who is six feet tall is twice as tall as a person who is three feet tall. With academic achievement, though, you cannot say with certainty that a person who gets 50 percent of the test items correct knows half as much as someone who got 100 percent. We cannot be sure tests measure equal intervals, and there can be no absolute zero representing no achievement at all. Complicating the picture further, people do not agree on exactly what levels or even what kinds of mastery constitute academic achievement.

Educators have persisted in their efforts to quantify achievement, though, because they know we need some shared basis for understanding—a common frame of reference. Quantifying achievement in some way allows for comparisons across types of instruction, locales, and student characteristics. We are no longer a nation of small family farmers where impressionistic judgments of teachers or parents suffice. If the content and the measurement methods are left vague, enormous variations in what counts as high achievement will occur, and some students will be shortchanged. Educators have developed several means for deriving meaning from test scores. We begin with norm-referenced interpretations.

Importance of the Norm Group

As you recall, the focus for comparison when using a norm-referenced interpretation of scores is the performance of other students who form the norm group, not the amount of content mastered. Most commercial, nationally known norm-referenced achievement tests such as the Terra Nova, Metropolitan Achievement Test, Iowa Test of Basic Skills, or Stanford Achievement Test, use a national sample of thousands of students chosen to represent the whole population of the United States.

Characteristics of the norm group can be summarized so you can get a clearer picture of it. As we discussed in Chapter 5, information on distributions of scores for groups of students, including norm groups, can be described using measures of central tendency (e.g., the mean). Other useful methods of summarizing data that take into account how much variation occurs within the group are the range and the **standard deviation.** As you recall from Chapter 5, the range is simply the difference between the lowest and highest scores earned on a test. The standard deviation for a group of scores is the average distance between the individual scores and the mean of the group. If the scores are widely dispersed across the whole range of scores, the standard deviation will be larger, as in Distribution A of Figure 11.4. If, instead, the scores cluster fairly close to the mean, as in Distribution B, the standard deviation will be smaller. As you can see from Figure 11.4, the means for these two groups of scores are the same, so you can also see that knowing the standard deviation adds new information to your understanding of the overall pattern of the group.

Educators use the mean and standard deviation of the norm group to derive meaningful scores for individuals. To do so, they rely on the concept of the **normal curve** or **normal distribution.** A normal distribution is the theoretically bell-shaped curve thought to characterize many attributes in nature and many human traits. When you have a large sample, whatever you are measuring, whether achievement or height, the measurements or scores tend to follow a predictable pattern. For example, if you are measuring height, most people fall in the middle of the distribution of scores—most

Standard Deviation
The average distance between the individual scores and the mean of the group score.

Normal Curve or Normal Distribution
The theoretically bell-shaped curve that characterizes most traits and attributes.

B
A
10 15 20 25 30 35 40 45 50 55 60 65 70 75 80 85 90

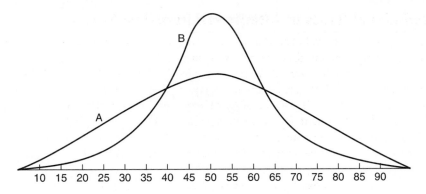

FIGURE 11.4 ***Two Sets of Scores with the Same Mean but Different Standard Deviations***

Many
Some
None
Number of People
2%
14%
34%
34%
14%
2%
None of the characteristic
2 SDs below mean
1 SD below mean
Mean
1 SD above mean
2 SDs above mean
Highest level of the characteristic
Characteristic Being Measured

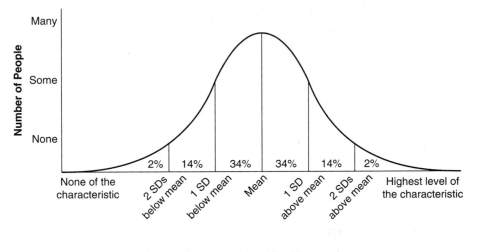

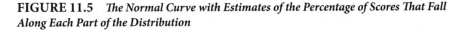

FIGURE 11.5 ***The Normal Curve with Estimates of the Percentage of Scores That Fall Along Each Part of the Distribution***

of us are about average in height. As you move away from the mean in either direction, fewer and fewer people appear, until only a very few can be found either at the extreme short end of the height continuum or at the extreme tall end. Figure 11.5 presents the normal distribution.

When you transform a large group of raw scores to the bell shape of the normal distribution, the pattern becomes regular and predictable. As you see in Figure 11.5, 68 percent of a group of scores is predicted to fall within one standard deviation on either side of the mean. Even though each normalized distribution has its own mean and standard deviation, the pattern of percentages of scores across the normal distribution always stays constant. If you know the mean and standard deviation of the norm group, you can estimate with accuracy the percentage of scores that will lie along each part of the range of possible scores. Whether the mean of the norm group is 15 or 50, 50 percent of the scores will always lie at or below that mean for the group. Similarly, whether the standard deviation is 15 or 50, 16 percent of the scores will always fall at or below one standard deviation below the mean.

Distribution of Test Scores
Number of Students
0
1
2
3
4
5
6
7
8
9
1
2
3
4
5
6
7
8
9
10
11
Test Scores

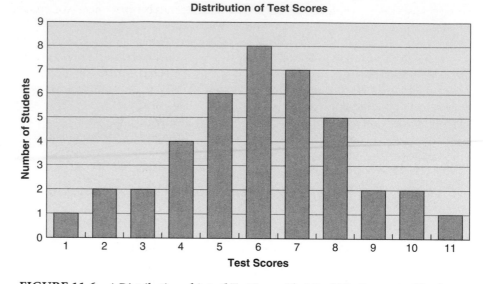

FIGURE 11.6 *A Distribution of Actual Test Scores That Could Be Represented by the Normal Curve*

It can be hard to remember that the foundation of this smooth curve consists of the actual test scores for a group of test takers. For example, in Figure 11.6 you see a pattern of actual scores that could underlie a normalized distribution like that in Figure 11.5. You can see that one person earned a score of 1 on this test, and six people earned a score of 5. Remember, when you look at a normal distribution (Figures 11.2, 11.4, 11.5), it actually represents a group of real test takers' scores.

Comparing the Individual to the Norm Group

The mean and standard deviation of the norm group's scores give us information about the norm group that helps us interpret an individual's score. This information determines where your students fall compared to the distribution found in the norm group. You can see how this approach could be used to serve the "sorting" function of schools previously described in Chapter 1. Norm-referenced interpretations rank students as "higher" or "lower" than peers in their performance on a test.

Percentile Rank

Percentile or Percentile Rank
A score that indicates the percentage of students in the norm group at or below the same score.

In our experience, the most common type of score used in schools is percentile rank. A **percentile** or **percentile rank** indicates the percentage of students in the norm group at or below the same score as your student. By looking at Figure 11.5, you can see that a student who scores at the mean is at the 50th percentile. If you add up the percentages of the number of students who scored below the mean (2% plus 14% plus 34%), you arrive at 50 percent. If instead your student's score is one standard deviation below the mean, you can see that the student's score is at the 16th percentile because 2 percent plus 14 percent of the norm group was at the same score or below.

Percentile ranks range between 1 and 99.9. They reflect the pattern shown in the normal curve. Typically, average scores are considered to range between the 25th and 75th percentiles. Because more students are clustered around the middle of the distribution, the distance between percentile ranks is smaller near the mean than at the extremes. Because percentile ranks don't have equal intervals between them, you should not add them or do other calculations with them.

Sometimes our teacher candidates confuse percentile ranks with percentage correct. Remember that percentile rank tells you your students' relative standing compared to *students* in the norm group. So, if your SAT percentile rank is 87 for the critical reading section, you did better on the test than 87 percent of the students in the norm group. Percentile rank therefore provides a *norm*-referenced interpretation of scores. Percentage correct instead provides an indicator of the amount of *content* mastered and therefore can be used only in *criterion*-referenced interpretations.

Instead of providing a single percentile rank score, many commercial test designers now provide a range of percentile scores incorporating the standard error of measurement for each section of a test. These are called **percentile bands, confidence intervals,** or **percentile ranges.** The higher the reliability of a test, the narrower the band appears. Percentile bands are useful for determining individual students' strengths and weaknesses. If the bands overlap across different parts of the test, differences appearing in the specific percentile score on each part are likely due to measurement error. If the bands do not overlap, a real difference in performance is more likely.

For example, if you return to the Terra Nova results in Figure 11.3, Pat Washington's percentile bands are pictured on the right on page 2. You can see that his social studies percentile band does not overlap with his language percentile band, suggesting a real difference for him between these areas. On the other hand, his reading, language, and mathematics percentile bands *do* overlap, suggesting they are not significantly different. Also notice the average range (25th–75th percentile) is shaded on the national percentile scale. You can see that all of Pat's scores fall within the average range, even though his language score is his strongest and his social studies score is his weakest.

Whenever we explain percentile ranks and percentile bands to our students, we are reminded of a poignant story told to us by one of our teacher candidates. During the class on interpreting standardized test scores, another student, who happened to be a P.E. major, wondered aloud why the class needed to learn to interpret these scores. This candidate spoke about her brother and told the story that appears in Box 11.2.

Percentile Bands

A range of percentile scores that incorporate the standard error of measurement.

BOX 11.2

Story

My brother was having a really hard time in the eighth grade. He was beaten up, food was thrown at him in the cafeteria, and he was taunted in the hallways. He began to find ways to avoid going to school because it was such a horrible experience. Some days he would pretend to leave for the bus stop, but then hide in the woods until everyone else had left the house. He had missed 41 days of school, off and on, before my parents found out. Near the end of the year, the principal called a meeting with all of my brother's teachers and my parents. The meeting's purpose was to confirm he would have to repeat the eighth grade due to the absences. During the meeting, the band director was looking through my brother's permanent record. He noticed all my brother's large-scale test scores were at or above the 95th percentile in every subject, which he pointed out to those in the meeting. Everyone was surprised, because my brother was doing so poorly in his classes. The whole mood of the meeting changed. The group decided what my brother needed was a fresh start in a new environment. They pulled strings so he would not be retained, provided he did not miss any more days, but could enter ninth grade at a high school with an International Baccalaureate Program rather than suffer through another year at the same junior high school. After graduating from the IB program with honors, he earned an undergraduate engineering degree and took a job designing silicon chips. He has lots of friends and is happy, but if it hadn't been for that music teacher, his life could have been very different!

2%
14%
34%
34%
14%
2%
Standard deviations
−3 −2 −1 0 1 2 3
Normal curve equivalents
1 10 20 30 40 50 60 70 80 90 99
Percentile ranks
0.1 2 16 50 84 98 99.9
Stanines
1 2 3 4 5 6 7 8 9

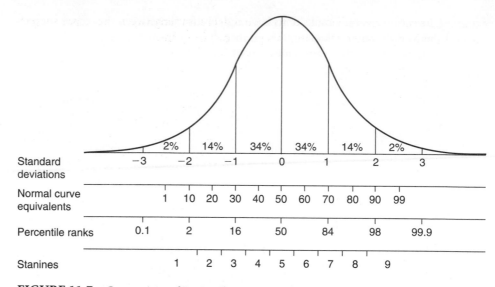

FIGURE 11.7 *Comparison of Percentiles, NCEs, and Stanines*

Normal Curve Equivalent

Normal Curve Equivalent
A scale ranging between 1 and 99.9 that has equal intervals between all of the scores on the continuum.

Because percentile ranks do not represent equal intervals along the low-to-high dimension of scores, educators developed a type of score termed **normal curve equivalent (NCE).** This scale also ranges between 1 and 99.9, but it has equal intervals between all the scores along the continuum, spreading out those scores that cluster around the middle. Equal intervals allow adding and averaging, which cannot be done with percentile ranks. Normal curve equivalents are also required for reporting results of some federal education programs for evaluation purposes. You can compare normal curve equivalents to percentile ranks in Figure 11.7. Note especially the differences near the middle of the distribution. If you return to Pat Washington's scores in Figure 11.3, you will see NCE scores as well as percentile rank scores in the columns on page 2. "Anticipated" NCEs and percentile ranks are based on predictions from the aptitude test results described on page 3 of the figure.

Stanines

Stanine
A standardized score that indicates where a student's score falls in relation to the norm group when the distribution of the scores is divided into nine equal parts.

Whereas normal curve equivalents divide the distribution of the norm group's scores into 99 equal parts, **stanines** divide the norm group's scores into only 9 equal parts, with 1 representing scores in the lowest part and 9 representing scores in the highest part. Scores around the middle of the distribution are represented by a stanine of 5 (see Figure 11.7). With only 9 scores possible, a stanine score therefore represents an approximate score within a range rather than pinpointing a single score. Because stanine scores fall in a range, they often fluctuate less across time than percentile ranks or normal curve equivalents, which fall at a single point. For this reason, many teachers find them useful for examining student performance across years to see if a student's relative standing changes compared to peers. Teachers can also use stanines to compare student performance across different kinds of test content. For example, a student who attains a stanine of five in math and a stanine of two in English appears stronger in math. Generally, a difference of two stanines suggests a significant difference in performance, whether across years on the same test or between two different types of tests taken the same year. For example, in Figure 11.3 you can see the stanine range for Pat Washington's scores at the bottom of the figure on the right of page 2. His stanine score for social studies is four, and his stanine score for language is six, again suggesting a significant difference between his performance in these two areas.

Other Standard Scores

Test score reports may also include a **scale score,** which is based on where a student's performance falls using the arbitrary numbers the test's designers have assigned for its mean and standard deviation. For example, the mean of many IQ tests is 100 and the standard deviation is 15. If your score is one standard deviation above the mean, your scale score would be 115, calculated by adding one standard deviation to the mean score. On the other hand, the mean of each section of the SAT is 500 with a standard deviation of 100, whereas the mean of the ACT is 21 and the standard deviation is 5. If your score was exactly one standard deviation above the mean on these tests, your scale score would be different for each test (600 on the SAT and 26 on the ACT) because each test company uses these different scales. Yet for every one of these norm-referenced tests, the mean always falls at the 50th percentile, an NCE of 50, or a stanine of 5. For teachers, parents, and students, we find it more useful and less confusing to use percentile ranks, NCEs, or stanines, because they do not vary across different tests.

Scale Score

A score that classifies a student's performance based on arbitrary numbers that the test designers have assigned for its mean and standard deviation.

Grade Equivalent (or Age Equivalent) Scores and Their Problems

Grade equivalent scores provide you with a number that represents the grade level at which the median student gets the same number of questions correct as your student. Grade equivalents are expressed in grade levels divided by tenths of the year. Therefore, a student with a grade equivalent score of 10.2 attained a score roughly similar to a typical student in the second month of tenth grade. Age equivalent scores work the same way, except your student is compared to students of different ages rather than in different grades. Thus, an age equivalent score of 10.2 indicates your student attained a number correct similar to a typical student who is 10.2 years old.

Grade Equivalent Score

A number representing the grade level at which the median student gets the same number of questions correct as your student.

Some people believe that grade and age equivalent scores are easy to understand, and so they like to use them. However, grade and age equivalent scores foster incorrect interpretations of scores, so we strongly recommend against their use. For example, a grade equivalent score of 3.6 reached by your student who is at the 2.6 grade level right now does *not* mean she is performing like a third grader. Nor does it mean she can do third-grade work. It also does not even necessarily mean she is performing above grade level. Performance for second graders will fall across a range of scores much lower and much higher than the exact point in the year that they take a test. (Remember that average scores fall in the wide range between the 25th and 75th percentiles.) Assuming that 2.6 is where students should be ignores the statistical fact that about half of the students in second grade will always be above this median point and about half will always be below.

We have heard many parents brag about their children based on their faulty understanding of grade equivalent scores. Recently, one father mentioned that his son, who is in fourth grade, was "reading at the 12th-grade level." He did not realize that no 12th graders even took the same test his son took—it was designed for fourth graders, not 12th graders. The grade equivalent scores for 12th graders for that 4th-grade test were most likely estimated by testing some 3rd- and 5th-grade students. Values for 6th grade and above would be **extrapolated,** or estimated outside the known range, based on the medians for these three grades. Commonly, grade equivalent scores are extrapolated when real data do not exist. Students should be compared only to others in the same grade who took the same test. Grade equivalent scores vary unpredictably across ages for the same test and across different tests. They

Extrapolated

Estimated outside the known range.

are not systematically derived from the characteristics of the norm group like stanines, percentile ranks, or normal curve equivalents. Therefore, grade equivalent scores are seldom useful for interpreting individual students' scores on tests or subtests, for comparing scores on different types of tests, or for exploring growth across time (Sattler, 1992). Many test publishers are eliminating the reporting of age or grade equivalent scores for these reasons.

✦ INTERPRETING CRITERION-REFERENCED TESTS

Most of the large-scale tests used to determine Annual Yearly Progress for No Child Left Behind (NCLB) use criterion-referenced interpretations. Criterion-referenced interpretations focus on content mastery as the source of comparison rather than performance of peers. The tests for NCLB are designed to focus explicitly on the content of each state's established academic standards. To derive meaning from resulting scores, the types of concepts and skills the tests address must be detailed and clear.

To develop interpretations from these tests, criteria for performance levels are chosen at the state level. These performance levels are usually termed, for example, "below basic," "basic," "proficient," and "advanced." Cutoff scores are set for each performance level by a panel of teachers and other educators. These educators review each item on the test to determine the score required to be at each performance level. For NCLB requirements, states report the percentage of students who attain a score of "proficient" or above. As we mentioned, the degree of mastery for each level varies significantly from state to state, so comparisons across states by level of proficiency do not yield consistent information.

✦ INTERPRETING LARGE-SCALE TESTS FOR STUDENTS AND PARENTS

To help you to summarize the most important points related to interpreting large-scale test scores, we now turn to the steps to take in explaining them to students and parents. (You have probably heard one way to learn something really well is to explain it to someone else, and that is likely to happen as you begin summarizing test scores for others.) One middle school teacher we know has listed the common questions he gets about large-scale tests, and these are presented in Table 11.9. As you can see, parents

TABLE 11.9

One Teacher's List of Parents' Common Questions About Large-Scale Tests

1. What is the required score to pass this test?

2. What does this score actually mean?

3. How was this score calculated?

4. What was the average score other students received?

5. Has my child made progress since last year?

TABLE 11.10

Key Large-Scale Test Interpretation Rules for Students and Parents

1. Explain the purpose of the test and exactly what it measures.

2. Explain the basis for comparison of the student's scores.

3. Explain the influence of error on scores.

4. Choose one type of score (e.g., percentiles, stanines, proficiency level), explain how it works, and then use that type of score to describe all parts of the test.

5. Place the scores in the larger context.

6. Work with the parent and student as partners in designing recommendations for what the next steps should be given the information you have all gleaned from these scores.

want to put these scores in context (e.g., What is required to pass? What was the average of other students? Has my child made progress?). They also need some basic information about the test (What does this score mean?) and how scores are derived (How was this score calculated?).

To answer these questions satisfactorily, we have devised a few rules for you to follow. These are useful steps for you to take when interpreting scores for your own use of test scores, and they can be especially helpful as you think about sharing test results with your students and their parents. We have followed these rules ourselves in many parent conferences. Table 11.10 shows a summary of the rules.

Explain Purpose and Content

The first step is for you to clearly understand and be able to communicate the purpose of the test and the content it measures. Many schools administer more than one large-scale test. Some of these may be criterion-referenced tests such as those used for NCLB, exit exams, or end-of grade tests that focus on content mastery. Others may be nationally norm-referenced aptitude or achievement tests. Others may be designed to capture progress with a certain skill across time using benchmarks for progress. You need to know and be able to explain the differences among these types of tests and how they are used by your school.

Explain the Basis for Comparison

You should be clear on the type of interpretation used for each test your students take. If the test uses a norm-referenced interpretation, you should be familiar with the characteristics of the students in the norm group and when results from the norm group were established. If the test uses a criterion-referenced interpretation, you should understand the cutoff points and characteristics of the understanding and skills assumed at each level.

Explain the Influence of Error on Scores

Anyone who receives test scores from teachers needs to know there is error in all measurement. Thus, a single score should be thought of as an *estimate* of performance. If the

Over-Interpretation
Incorrect assumptions and conclusions that are not warranted by the available data.

test score report illustrates percentile bands, these can be used to explain the range of error around each score. Specific score numbers should not be overinterpreted. **Over-interpretation** occurs when conclusions are drawn that are not warranted by the data. For example, if a student scores at the 45th percentile in math and at the 55th percentile in language arts on a nationally normed large-scale test, you should not conclude the student is "below average" in math. In addition, if you take the standard error of measurement into account, you would see that a student has a good chance of scoring higher than the 45th percentile if the mathematics test were taken again. (Of course, the percentile band will also show the student may score lower if that student were to take the test again.) Using percentile bands or stanines to explain scores helps reduce overinterpretation.

Choose One Type of Score to Explain All Parts of the Test

As you can see from the score report in Figure 11.3, test designers provide many types of scores to choose from when explaining test results. To avoid confusion and to simplify the process, choose just one type of score to discuss and use it for every part of the test. This strategy allows reasonable comparisons across the parts of the test.

Many teachers prefer to use percentile ranks when explaining norm-referenced test scores to students and parents. Percentile ranks are easy to explain if you suggest they visualize 100 students lined up across the back of the room you are in according to their score, with the lowest student (Student 1) at the left end and the highest student (Student 100) at the right end. If your student's score is at the 75th percentile, you can point to your estimate of where the 75th student would be along that wall to help explain the meaning of the score. Then be sure to place these specific ranks in the broader context of the percentile bands computed for them to show how they are estimations of true performance.

Stanines are an alternative score to use with students and parents for norm-referenced interpretations, especially when examining scores across time. If a student has made a year's growth in a year's time, that student should fall in the same stanine as the previous year. If the student has made more impressive gains, the stanine scores will be higher than the year before. If the student has lost ground compared to peers, the stanine score will be lower than the previous year. Avoid using grade-equivalent scores or normal curve equivalent scores in interpreting scores to students and parents. In our experience, they cause confusion.

For criterion-referenced or standards-based test interpretations, you will use proficiency levels to explain each student's test results. Explain the scale used to the parents—for example, stating that students' scores go from the lowest proficiency level, which is Below Basic, to Basic, to Proficient, to Advanced as the highest proficiency level. Be sure you have a clear understanding of the specific knowledge and skills expected at each level. This understanding will help you explain clearly the strengths or needs the student has regarding particular content from your state standards.

Put the Scores in the Larger Context

As you should recall from Chapter 6, no decisions about students should be made on the basis of a single score because of potential problems with error in any test. Large-scale test scores are no exception. You must take the time to put these scores in the context of what else you know about this student's typical performance. Samples of student work, comparisons to past large-scale test performance, and comparison among different parts of a large-scale test help you fill out the complete picture of a student's level of understanding and skills. Many educators suggest that students and their parents should be enlisted in the process of providing this context. Encouraging your students to fully participate can foster in them a sense of responsibility for their own learning, an important step in developing mastery goals for enhanced motivation.

Work as Partners to Determine Next Steps

As patterns emerge, the information can be used to enable everyone involved to get a clear picture of the student and to determine next steps. At all times, you must take the stance that you, your students, and their families are partners in helping the students achieve at the highest possible levels. For example, if trends across several years suggest a student's vocabulary is not keeping pace with the student's other language arts learning, you might together set up a reading program with specific goals involving choices of books and activities to enhance vocabulary. If, instead, a student's math concepts scores tend to fall below the student's math computation scores, you can work with that student to devise more opportunities to articulate the concepts behind the computations (e.g., explaining on homework assignments why the student's answer is a reasonable estimate of the correct answer). Encouraging analysis of patterns helps students and their parents grasp the results of large-scale tests. It also affords opportunities for everyone to use them most effectively.

→ USING LARGE-SCALE TEST RESULTS IN THE CLASSROOM

Patterns of scores and trends across time can also be used as you design lessons and plan instruction. Going beyond the examples we described previously, you can use such information for differentiating instruction with academic tasks in the classroom. If you teach a high school math class, for example, you might find that some of your students have stronger scores in language arts than in math. This information could lead you to institute math journals in which students describe the design and solution of authentic problems and/or explain the math concepts you are working on together.

Similarly, noting different levels of reading comprehension skills among your students can alert you to differentiate methods for your students to obtain content (e.g., through websites or books that provide differing reading levels on specific subjects). Thus, large-scale tests can provide information about the range of skills among your students. This range may also alert you to monitor particular students who fall either far above or far below others as a first step toward determining whether provision of special education or gifted programs is needed.

Test scores from a single year can be useful for examining common trends across a whole group of students. You may find similar patterns among a large group of students, not just patterns within an individual student's scores. For example, if you teach fifth grade, and you notice that fifth graders at your school tended to have low scores in science compared to other subjects last year, you will want to take a hard look at your own science instruction to make sure your coverage is sufficient. You will want to make sure students have the necessary prior knowledge to engage in the activities you plan. You should also ensure they understand and can apply the key science

TABLE 11.11

Uses of Large-Scale Tests for Classroom Teachers

Determine general strengths and needs of individuals for
- Partnering with student and family to enhance achievement
- Differentiating instructional tasks

Examine trends of scores for a group of students to
- Identify common patterns (e.g., general weakness in science or reading comprehension) that need to be taken into account when designing instruction
- Learn the range of skills in the class to anticipate materials and types of strategies that may be required
- Alert you to monitor students significantly different from peers as a first step in determining whether additional special programs are needed

process skills, such as careful observation. Encouraging your school to sponsor faculty workshops related to effective methods for teaching science and instituting family science nights could also be helpful.

Large-scale test results, because they provide only a broad sweep across the content without a lot of detail, cannot be used for precise diagnostic purposes. From large-scale test results, for example, you can see whether students tend to do better in math computation than in math concepts, but the results don't give you enough information to know specifically which math concepts to teach or how to teach them. Instead, you must design your classroom diagnostic and formative assessments for that purpose. Large-scale test results can point you in the right direction and provide clues to orient your classroom approach. They are most useful for providing general information about trends within and across years and across subject content for groups and individual students. Table 11.11 summarizes the ways you can use large-scale test scores to add to your understanding of your students' academic abilities and skills.

KEY CHAPTER POINTS

We began this chapter by introducing you to important concepts related to large-scale standardized testing, including differences between norm-referenced and criterion-referenced scoring and between aptitude and achievement tests. We then described several commonly held misconceptions related to large-scale testing.

Next, we described the benefits and pitfalls of large-scale tests, using the tests designed by the states for examining compliance with the No Child Left Behind (NCLB) legislation. Benefits included using comparisons across demographic groups to find and fix achievement gaps; promoting the alignment of standards, curriculum, instruction, and assessment; and focusing on improving education. Pitfalls included nonequivalent performance standards across states that may weaken expectations for student achievement, excessive narrowing of the curriculum, and a focus on improving scores without improving learning.

We then provided suggestions for preparation of students for large-scale testing, which included knowing and teaching the standards, promoting mastery goals throughout the year, fostering appropriate attitudes toward testing, and teaching students general strategies for taking tests. We went on to describe accommodations that may be used for students with disabilities and for English language learners to allow students to demonstrate their understanding and skills of the construct tested without being unfairly restricted by a disability or by limited English proficiency.

We next discussed reliability and validity in the context of large-scale tests, then turned to interpreting norm-referenced tests, showing how the mean and standard deviation of the norm group are used to compare your students' scores to those of the norm group using percentile ranks, percentile bands, normal curve equivalents, and stanines. We next explained why grade and age equivalent scores are problematic.

We moved on to interpreting criterion-referenced tests and then discussed the steps in interpreting large-scale tests for students and parents. Finally, we talked about the ways that classroom teachers can use large-scale testing results in their work.

HELPFUL WEBSITES

http://www.cep-dc.org/

The Center on Education Policy is a national, independent advocate for public education and for more effective public schools. The website provides recent research on current topics such as No Child Left Behind and standards-based education reform. The organization is funded by charitable foundations and does not represent special interest groups. Its goal is to provide information to help citizens understand various perspectives on current educational issues.

www.centerforpubliceducation.org

The Center for Public Education website is an initiative of the National School Board Association. It offers up-to-date, balanced information on research involving current issues in public education, such as high-stakes testing. It also provides access to summaries of recent education reports, polls, and surveys related to improving student achievement and the role of public schools in society.

CHAPTER REVIEW QUESTIONS

1. Describe examples of the influence of large-scale high-stakes tests based on your experience.
2. Explain the difference between norm-referenced and criterion-referenced interpretations of test scores. Give an example of each not found in this chapter.
3. Explain the difference between aptitude and achievement tests, with examples from your own experience. Do you believe tests purely measuring aptitude can be developed? Why or why not?
4. Give an example of one of the five misconceptions about large-scale tests that you or someone you know has encountered. Explain how you would refute this misconception now.
5. Describe specific actions you as a teacher will take in your classroom to ensure you avoid the three pitfalls of large-scale standardized tests described in the chapter.
6. Based on the discussion of appropriate preparation practices for large-scale tests, describe test preparation practices you believe would NOT be appropriate. How might these practices contribute to score pollution?
7. If you have several students in one of your classes who are learning English, what accommodations might you request for them when taking tests throughout the year?
8. Describe the strengths and limitations in using percentile ranks, normal curve equivalents, stanines, and scale scores. Which would you prefer to use when

interpreting large-scale test results? Complete the table below to answer this question.

Type of Score	Strengths	Limitations
Percentile rank		
Percentile band		
Normal curve equivalent		
Stanine		
Scale score		
Grade- or age-equivalent		

9. Provide two reasons for not using grade- or age-equivalent scores when interpreting large-scale test results.
10. Address the points in Table 11.10 for the test results in Figure 11.3.
11. If a student's score falls one standard deviation above the mean, what will be her percentile rank?
12. Describe at least two specific ways you might use the results of large-scale tests for individual students. Describe two specific ways you might use the results for a whole class.

References

Au, W. 2007. High-stakes testing and curricular control: A qualitative metasynthesis. *Educational Researcher* 36: 258–267.

Center on Education Policy. 2006, March. *From the capital to the classroom. Year 4 of the No Child Left Behind Act.* Washington, DC. Retrieved October 23, 2007, from http://www.cep-dc.org/index.cfm?fuseaction=Page.viewPage&pageId=497&parentID=481.

Center on Education Policy. 2007, June. *Answering the question that matters most: Has student achievement increased since No Child Left Behind?* Washington, DC. Retrieved November 2, 2007, from http://www.cep-dc.org/document/docWindow.cfm?fuseaction=document.viewDocument&documentid=200&documentFormatId=3620.

Center on Education Policy. 2008, June. *Has student achievement increased since 2002? State test score trends through 2006–07.* Retrieved June 25, 2008, from http://www.cep-dc.org/document/docWindow.cfm?fuseaction=document.viewDocument&documentid=241&documentFormatId=3769.

Darling-Hammond, L. 2007. The flat earth and education: How America's commitment to equity will determine our future. *Educational Researcher* 36: 318–334.

Flynn, J. R. 1999. Searching for justice: The discovery of IQ gains over time. *American Psychologist* 54: 5–20.

McNeil, M. 2008. Benchmarks momentum on increase. *Education Week* 27(27): 1, 12–13.

Newman, F., A. Bryk, and J. Nagoaka. 2001. *Authentic intellectual work and standardized tests: Conflict or coexistence?* Chicago: Consortium on Chicago School Research. Retrieved November 5, 2007, from http://ccsr.uchicago.edu/content/publications.php?pub_id=38.

Nichols, S., and D. Berliner. 2007. *Collateral damage: How high-stakes testing corrupts America's schools.* Cambridge, MA: Harvard Education Press.

Reeves, D. B. 2004. The 90/90/90 schools: A case study. In D. B. Reeves, *Accountability in action: A blueprint for learning organizations,* 2nd ed. Englewood, CO: Advanced Learning Press.

Sattler, J. 1992. *Assessment of Children.* 3rd ed. San Diego: Jerome M. Sattler, Publisher, Inc.

Solorzano, R. W. 2008. High stakes testing: Issues, implications, and remedies for English language learners. *Review of Educational Research* 78: 260–329.

Sternberg, R. 2008. Assessing what matters. *Educational Leadership* 65(4): 20–26.

Taylor, C., and S. Nolan. 2008. *Classroom assessment: Supporting teaching and learning in real classrooms.* Saddle River, NJ: Pearson Education.

Thompson, S., C. Johnstone, and M. Thurlow. 2002. *Universal design applied to large scale assessments* (Synthesis Report 44). Minneapolis, MN: University of Minnesota, National Center on Educational Outcomes. Retrieved November 13, 2007, from http://education. umn.edu/NCEO/OnlinePubs/Synthesis44.html.

Wallis, C., and S. Steptoe. 2007. How to fix No Child Left Behind. *Time* 169(23): 34–41.

Wiliam, D., C. Lee, C. Harrison, and P. Black. 2004. Teachers developing assessment for learning: Impact on student achievement. *Assessment in Education* 11: 49–65.

Yeh, S. 2005. Limiting the unintended consequences of high-stakes testing. *Education Policy Analysis Archives* 13: 43. Retrieved October 23, 2007, from http://epaa.asu.edu/epaa/ v13n43/.

CHAPTER 12

TYING IT ALL TOGETHER

We can, whenever and wherever we choose, successfully teach all children whose schooling is of interest to us. We already know more than we need to do that. Whether or not we do it must finally depend on how we feel about the fact that we haven't so far.

–Ron Edmonds

❖ **Chapter Learning Goals**

At the conclusion of this chapter, the reader should be able to do the following:

- Explain the importance of six essential guidelines for effective classroom assessment for ensuring all children learn to their potential.

- Describe how these guidelines will foster equal access to knowledge, development of self-governing skills, and critical thinking proficiencies important for democratic participation.

- Develop efficient strategies to make the most of student and teacher assessment activities.

- Compare and contrast the Knowledge Is Power Program (KIPP) in Charlotte, NC, and the Center for Inquiry classroom assessment strategies promoting skills for democratic participation.

- Set a personal goal for integrating assessment strategies to promote skills for democratic participation.

→ INTRODUCTION

We wholeheartedly agree with the quotation beginning this chapter—we already know what to do to successfully teach all children. In fact, we now know even more about what makes for effective schools than we did when Edmonds wrote those words in 1979. In particular, studies of schools and classrooms have shown that effective classroom assessment practices can be one of the most important ingredients for enhancing student achievement (Reeves, 2004; Wiliam et al., 2004). Throughout this book we have acquainted you with classroom assessment practices to motivate students and help them learn to their full potential. In this chapter we take the opportunity to review some key guidelines, discuss issues related to efficiency in assessment practices, show you illustrative examples from real classrooms, and help you set goals for your own classroom assessment practices to equip your students to become lifelong learners and active participants in a democratic society.

→ SIX ESSENTIAL GUIDELINES

We now turn to six fundamental guidelines evolved from conversations between other teachers and ourselves about the assessment essentials needed by teacher candidates as they begin their careers. Although our expertise comes from many

TABLE 12.1

Six Essential Assessment Guidelines

1. Begin with the end in mind: Have clear, high expectations for developing understanding and skills that can be flexibly used across contexts.

2. Find out what students know: Use diagnostic assessment supporting differentiated instruction.

3. Check as you go: Use flexible formative assessment to help students close the gap between where they are and where they need to be.

4. Teach students to check as you go: Teach self- and peer-assessment to promote internalization of goals and performance criteria.

5. Use rubrics creatively to reinforce attainment of student learning goals: Set clear and concrete criteria for excellence.

6. Assess yourself: Regularly reflect on ways to enhance student learning.

fields, from music and theater to English and biology, and from elementary through college levels, critical themes converge that guide effective teachers.

These guidelines are based on the foundational assumption that teachers must be reflective in their practice and aware of the instructional climate they are creating in their classroom. Reflective teachers weigh what they do against the question we introduced in Chapter 1: "Will this help my students learn?" Their primary purpose for assessment is formative rather than summative in nature. They use assessment to be advocates who help their students learn more, not simply evaluators who gauge where students are and assign grades accordingly. Using this approach, assessment becomes a fluid, continuing activity intertwined with instruction rather than mere documentation of student levels of attainment on end-of-unit tests.

Teachers sometimes struggle to provide rationales for their grading practices and their assessment strategies. When they explain how and why they assess, they tend to give more weight to their individual experiences, beliefs, and external pressures than to principles of effective assessment (McMillan, 2003). We hope these guidelines, which are based on principles of effective assessment, can serve as an important source for the justification of the assessment practices you put in place in your classroom. We believe they should coincide with, rather than contradict, your beliefs about assessment and your experiences with it. Table 12.1 lists the guidelines.

Guideline 1. Begin with the End in Mind

We borrow our first guideline from Chapter 2 and from Stephen Covey, who wrote the popular self-help book titled *The Seven Habits of Highly Effective People.* Covey's second habit is to "Begin with the end in mind." We believe his principle is fundamental for designing and implementing effective assessment practices.

Simply put, beginning with the end in mind suggests you start with a clear understanding, based on your learning goals and the curriculum, of what you ultimately want your students to know and be able to do after your instruction. This principle is consistent with the backward design model of Wiggins and McTighe (1998) in which you first focus on the end goals. You need a well-developed mental image of what you want to accomplish before you set out to accomplish it.

A problem we sometimes see with teacher candidates is that they can be captivated by interesting topics or activities (e.g., "I want to do a zoo unit." or "I want to design several lessons around the upcoming election.") without having learning goals to anchor and guide their planning. With clear goals, you can easily capitalize on the teaching potential of creative strategies, materials, and topics (the zoo or the election). A laser-like focus on the end you have in mind is crucial for separating wheat from chaff as you design engaging instruction and figure out how to maximize learning. Remember that merely offering appealing activities such as games does not guarantee high motivation or strong learning (Sanford et al., 2007). You should build all your instructional and assessment activities on the foundation of your learning goals and your curriculum. This habit will make it easy to justify clearly to yourself and others why you are doing what you are doing in your classroom.

Fostering High Expectations

One important benefit of clear learning goals is that they help you maintain high expectations and standards. Sometimes teachers modify assignments to make them easier if students complain, or they see students lose interest and, as a result, they relent on a standard. Sometimes standards of quality can also suffer if a teacher focuses too much on "raising self-esteem" and "helping kids feel good about themselves" without realizing that a feeling of self-esteem does not necessarily lead to quality accomplishments. Instead, research shows the reverse is true: accomplishments based on hard work and mastery of high standards lead to stronger self-esteem (Leary, 1999; Marsh & Craven, 1997).

Fostering Applications to New Contexts

Another key facet of beginning with the end in mind involves making certain the ends you choose involve understanding beyond rote memorization. Such effort is important so students can apply their knowledge beyond the explicit context of the lesson to other situations. At several points in the text we have helped you see ways to design assessments addressing higher-order thinking and application of concepts to novel situations. Encouraging students to explain why they are solving a problem in a particular way, requiring them to find disconfirming as well as confirming evidence for a position, and having them generalize an idea to a new situation are important ways to challenge students to extend their thinking. In designing informal discussion questions, in developing rubrics, and in creating assessments from multiple-choice to performance tasks, we have stressed that you must ensure students can understand the principles behind your activities and not just the activities themselves. Learning goals help you keep the big picture in mind as you guide students through this process.

We once worked with an intern who confirmed this recommendation but also showed it is sometimes easier said than done. She had provided a worksheet with carefully varied shapes on it for her students to practice calculating perimeters of different dimensions and sizes. When two students finished early, she asked them to calculate the perimeter of the worksheet itself. They insisted they could not do it and seemed at a complete loss. Because they had applied the procedure only to figures on worksheets, they did not see how it could also be applied to shapes in the real world. This story illustrates well how teachers must intentionally vary their instructional and assessment activities to help students see the range of ways an idea or procedure can be used. The learning goals you choose must keep these ends in mind.

Fostering Overarching Personal Goals

Clear goals may come from your personal aims and teaching identity, as well as from the national or state standards you use to guide instruction. For example, several music teachers we know want more than anything to instill a love of music in their students, and they keep this goal in mind as they design each lesson. Other teachers stress pride in doing a good job as a goal and encourage students to believe that several drafts of an essay should be the norm and not the exception. Others emphasize the importance of seeing the classroom as a supportive community for learning, encouraging students to rely on each other and celebrating their diversity. We also hope many aim to equip their students as well-informed, active participants in a democracy. The point is to articulate for yourself the overarching personal goals you care about so you can build in activities to support them every day.

Guideline 2. Find Out What Students Know

Diagnostic assessment allows you to learn what your students already know, and its results should guide your instructional activities. High student mobility, coupled with the wide range of experience and understanding found among students in every classroom, makes diagnostic activities imperative. Accurately understanding what your students know and are able to do is critical to designing instruction that challenges but does not overwhelm them.

As discussed at length in Chapter 3, before teaching a skill or concept, a teacher must examine prerequisite knowledge needed for working with new material. This includes knowledge and skills not directly related to content that are also crucial for student success. For example, we worked with a student teacher in social studies who discovered that the students in his history classes did not know how to take notes, but realized this only after he had delivered a 15-minute lecture a couple of weeks into the term. Because he was reflective about his practice, he took the time to examine the notes they did have to devise a template to help structure later note-taking efforts. If he had known from the beginning that note-taking was a weak skill, he could have addressed it sooner.

Diagnostic assessment is also one of the most important strategies you can use to guarantee that all your students have an equal opportunity to learn what you want to teach them, an important function of schooling in a democracy. If students' prior knowledge, including cultural as well as school experiences, is not taken into account, they may lack the ability to take full advantage of the classroom activities. At the beginning of one school year we worked with a kindergartener who had never seen a book before and didn't know which side was up, how to hold it, or how to turn pages. Familiarity with different types of materials—books, maps, computers—can vary greatly among your students.

Also remember that diagnostic activities are the important first step in documenting the growth students make across time. Sometimes progress is difficult to detect from day to day, so seeing progress over longer periods can be important to the motivation of both students and teachers. Documenting the earliest student performance allows you to make these gains visible and concrete.

Guideline 3. Check as You Go

Monitoring students' progress during instruction, including giving them feedback to close the gap between where they are and where they need to be, is our next indispensable assessment guideline. In the past, many of us assumed assessment occurs only at the end of a unit. Many teachers and students continue to think of assessment in this way. In your classroom, you must change the meaning of assessment from something dreaded to something that is a natural part of the learning process. Using formative strategies allows assessment to become an opportunity for providing insights about learning and ways to improve. It's no longer a source of anxiety resulting in an irrevocable stamp of approval or disapproval. In Chapter 4 of the text, we explained why we believe that "checking as you go" using formative assessment is essential. Evidence continues to accumulate that, when used correctly, it is one of the most effective interventions available to enhance student achievement.

Guideline 4. Teach Students to Check as You Go

Fostering the ability of students to assess themselves is one of the ultimate goals of instruction. As students begin to self-assess, they must take a more active role and figure out concrete ways that ensure they personally can meet the goals. Helping students learn to self-assess also teaches them to look beyond their own point of view and see themselves in relation to a standard. As students eventually clarify and internalize the standard, they will not be as dependent on authorities to make corrections or judgments concerning their work. They will no longer see the standards as arbitrary and external but as something they have worked through, perhaps contributed to, and now own. They will eventually be able to use standards and feedback they have encountered to articulate goals to set for themselves. Also, remember that students who participate in self-evaluation become more interested in applying the criteria and improving, and they become less interested in getting specific grades for assignments, an important advance for promoting mastery goals.

Teachers can use simple strategies regularly to create a climate that promotes self-assessment. For example, asking informal questions during class that encourage students to analyze their work together and alone can be effective. A music teacher we know peppers her instruction with questions such as "Did everyone match as we clapped the rhythm, or was there a disagreement?" or "Was everyone silent on the rests?" or "How can we improve our performance?" This helps students to begin to actively apply standards of quality to engage in self-reflection and gain insight into their performance. Student conferences such as those described in Chapter 1 used by third-grade teacher Tracie Clinton also can help advance student self-assessment. They also allow for teacher monitoring of student progress toward effective self-assessment.

As students start to see the value of active self-assessment for their growth, they will also see value in seeking the perceptions and opinions of others as one more way to improve their own work and their learning. Incorporating peer assessment into your classroom during the formative assessment process provides opportunities for your students to reinforce among each other the value of making discoveries (not mistakes) on the learning journey. Peer assessment affords more opportunities for interpreting and internalizing standards, for understanding diverse perspectives, and for learning appropriate ways to offer and accept feedback. These are all skills that students will need as they move beyond the classroom.

One teacher we know always uses peer assessment with student writing. She credits this practice for the excellent showing her students made in a recent state poetry contest. Her students write their first draft, receive a critique from another student, develop another draft, receive another critique, and so on, until each student is satisfied with a final draft. As each new perspective is taken into account, the students make more changes to transform their work, and then they want more feedback. She has heard students bragging (not complaining) about the number of drafts they have been through. Compare this classroom climate to typical situations where many students try to get by with as little effort as possible.

Guideline 5. Use Rubrics to Reinforce Attainment of the Learning Goals

We believe rubrics, or scoring guides providing descriptions of different levels of performance in relation to a standard, are vital to effective classroom assessment. If you want students to move beyond simple tasks and memorization of facts, you need learning activities that require students to manipulate ideas through thinking, writing, and other complex understanding and skills. Rubrics are a valuable technique to help students systematically work through and understand the characteristics of excellent work for these more complex tasks. They aid students in envisioning the goal and analyzing the parts that will add up to the whole. With an eye to the important understandings and skills in your learning goals, you can construct rubrics to help both you and your students remember what is important.

As discussed in Chapter 8, useful rubrics must communicate the central features of a quality performance. You must figure out how to put into words the elusive factors that determine writing is "vivid" or "concise" or that a project is "well-organized" or "creative." One of the best ways to do this is to have a discussion with your students to help you define the levels of quality. Structuring assessment activities with rubrics is a useful way to get students in the habit of thinking about and evaluating their own and each others' work, so that formative and self-assessment automatically become incorporated into the process.

Guideline 6. Assess Yourself

All teachers have some obvious as well as more subtle influences on their students. As you think of your own teachers, you can remember ways you would like to emulate some and avoid the mistakes of others. The point is, we as teachers are significant models for our students each day they are in our classrooms. Ideally, we need to show them how to be effective learners. One of the best ways to do this as a teacher is to practice what you preach. As a teacher, you can demonstrate your commitment to assessment *for* learning by regularly obtaining and analyzing feedback on your own practice in view of your students and, at times, with their assistance.

We explained in Chapters 3 and 4 that actively seeking information from your monitoring of student learning allows you to become more responsive to individual student needs. In addition, explaining to students how you are changing your practice based on information you have collected shows them you find formative assessment indispensable, just as they should. You want to know when your instructional strategies are successful, and you want to change any strategies that are not. You can use action research (Chapter 1) to collect information to check on your own effectiveness and to search actively for solutions to problems arising in your classroom.

The inquiry stance incorporating action research also helps you avoid "blaming the kid first." As professionals, we know we should use self-assessment and analysis to solve classroom problems before we give up on students. Yet, we sometimes tend to attribute problems that arise to unchangeable student traits and then feel that remedying them is beyond our control. For example, analysis of diaries kept by 40 student teachers showed they tended to explain the sources of their difficulties most frequently in terms of pupils' cognitive or affective characteristics rather than in terms of their own methods, the lessons, or the instructional content (Penso, 2002). Using an inquiry stance and action research can allow a more proactive and less passive response to problems. A formative-assessment approach to learning setbacks or classroom difficulties may take more than one "draft." To get things right, several rounds of trial and error may be required for ourselves, as well as for our students. If students aren't learning or making progress with certain skills, we must take personal responsibility for coming up with new ways to deal with problems, just as we encourage our students to take responsibility for their own learning. The challenge and joy of teaching is finding ways to reach all students. We suggest teachers model formative assessment by regularly assessing themselves and, when problems arise, checking their instructional toolbox for new solutions for reaching their goals.

We believe these six principles can be the foundation for excellent assessment that promotes student growth. By now you understand well that assessment is not just an afterthought at the end of the term. It is an ongoing process intertwined with your classroom activities.

→ ASSESSMENT EFFECTIVENESS AND EFFICIENCY

One formative task in our assessment classes is to have teacher candidates write reflections about how they are relating what they are learning to their own experiences. One comment they often make relates to time. They wonder how a new teacher can carve out the time to incorporate these fundamental assessment guidelines. They perhaps don't realize that, according to estimates, many teachers already spend a third or more of their time on assessment (Stiggins & Conklin, 1992).

In our own experience and in our discussions with teachers who incorporate the six guidelines, we find that several commonsense efficiency strategies can help manage as well as reduce the assessment load. Table 12.2 lists suggestions for keeping assessment efficient and effective.

TABLE 12.2

Efficiency Strategies for Effective Assessment

Strategy	Examples
Choose assessment opportunities selectively.	• Rely on assessments aligned with instruction and learning goals that tell you what you need to know to move forward. • Use instructional activities that can also serve a formative assessment purpose.
Selectively analyze student work.	• Award points for homework on a random basis. • Rotate which students' work is analyzed each day.
Carefully target the feedback you provide.	• Choose only one element for feedback and vary it across time. • Choose only each student's most problematic element for feedback.
Build in time for self- and peer review and feedback.	• Have students take responsibility for comparing their work to a standard and make changes consistent with it.
Structure record keeping to encourage student self-monitoring.	• Provide progress monitoring tools and class time for updates.
Develop an "assessment bank."	• Designate a computer file or notebook for selectively collecting materials from a variety of sources.
Enlist students in assessment design.	• Clarify rubric criteria with students. • Encourage student input into characterizations of each level of a rubric. • Provide opportunities for students to design sample questions.

Choose Assessment Opportunities Selectively

You must prioritize any assessment you consider in terms of whether it provides information to assist your teaching and whether it helps your students learn (the big Chapter 1 question). You want to make sure all assessments, whether formative or summative, are aligned with instruction and learning goals and tell you what you need to know to move forward. You don't want to waste any assessment energy on irrelevant material or tasks that don't help you understand what students need next. One way many teachers accomplish this goal is to use instructional activities that can also serve a formative assessment purpose.

Assessment in conjunction with activities where students are engaged in the learning process is very efficient. For example, Jesse Schlicher and Naomi Elkin, two seventh-grade math teachers, set up grocery store "stations" in their classrooms when they are teaching a learning goal related to applying rates to unit cost. At each station, students find two or three grocery items (e.g., different types of muffin mixes, jars of cheese vs. meat spaghetti sauces, cans of fruit). Each student answers three or four questions about the products (e.g., What is the unit price? Which is the best deal? Which would you buy and why?). A sample of one of the activities to complete is illustrated in Figure 12.1. The teachers can circulate among stations to see which elements of problem solving are causing difficulty, and they can quickly check the written results for patterns of errors. The class also discusses answers together at the end of the activity.

These teachers use the information from these activities to plan future lessons. For example, problems several students struggle on are used for a warm-up the next day. In addition they put challenge problems at each station to see how students do when they boost the level a bit. A variety of similar assessment items can be developed easily based on comparison of generic store brands to name brands. Such work has the side benefit of helping students become discerning consumers.

Selectively Analyze Student Work

As we discussed in Chapter 10, we recommend that you not grade every single piece of work students complete for you. You need sufficient and varied opportunities so you have reliable information on each student, but you must also be selective. Some of the teachers and teacher candidates we know insist students will not do any work for which they don't get a grade (clear evidence that they are *not* motivated by mastery goals). We

---

Station 2

Slices or Chunks?

Price of Kroger Pineapple Chunks: $1.89

Price of Dole Pineapple Slices: $3.29

1. What is the price per ounce for the Kroger Pineapple Chunks? **(show the rate!)**
2. What is the price per ounce of the Dole Pineapple Slices? **(show the rate!)**
3. Which is the better buy?
4. Why might someone choose to purchase the more expensive product?

FIGURE 12.1 *Classroom Activity and Formative Assessment for Seventh-Grade Math Unit Learning Goal, "Apply ratios, rates, and proportions to discounts, taxes, tips, interest, unit costs, and similar shapes."*

wean our own students from expecting every piece of work to be graded by assigning homework almost every day, but we award points for it on a random basis. We always collect the work and read through it to look for patterns of errors in thinking or use of skills, but that usually goes quickly compared to scoring every paper. On average, we give points for roughly half of the assignments. To ensure quality work, we often use homework questions as part of the foundation for more involved exam questions. When we do assign points for homework, if students do not get full credit, they can redo the assignment. These practices usually stimulate students to produce quality work consistently even when points aren't awarded. We also encourage them to think about the benefits of their changing work habits in terms of development of mastery goals.

Grading and feedback on student writing can be a particularly problematic and time-consuming area for teachers. For example, if eighth graders write just 15 minutes per day, a class of 25 students produces an average of 375 sentences (Heward et al., 1991). If you multiply this by several classes, providing feedback can be overwhelming for a teacher. However, with selective checking it can be managed. Heward and his colleagues suggest a strategy: The teacher reads and evaluates 20–25% of the papers written each day. All students' papers are returned the next day, and the teacher uses the work she evaluated to develop instruction, similar examples, and feedback for groups of students who need to work on those particular writing skills. (We caution teachers not to use too many bad examples directly from student work to avoid discouraging them.) Because this strategy is useful for differentiating instruction, sometimes the whole class and sometimes smaller groups will be involved, depending on need. Students can receive points for producing writing each day (or on random days). The whole class can receive additional bonus points if a high percentage of the papers evaluated on a given day meet the criteria the teacher emphasized in a classwide daily lesson. A small sample of representative students' work can provide information about understanding and skills to work on with a larger group, and this procedure can be generalized to most subject matter. The teacher can also use this process with other methods of examining student understanding, such as small discussion groups or informal teacher conferences.

Carefully Target the Feedback You Provide

You now realize the importance of teacher feedback in helping students learn how to close the gap between where they are and where they need to be. As you also know from our Chapter 4 discussion, effective feedback can require considerable time and effort on the part of teachers. Student work can fall short of the standards you set for quality in many ways. But if you try to address every element of effective writing or every aspect of successful defending in a soccer game, both you and the students will be overwhelmed. Instead, concentrating on one focus for feedback at a time can ensure your feedback is brief, targeted, and clear. Both you and the students will be able to focus on that element and work toward improvement. For example, a high school band director might focus only on helping the ensemble produce a more balanced sound with several pieces during a practice session. A drama teacher might choose to give feedback on students' efforts to use their voices to convey elements of the character's personality. Similarly, some teachers we know allow their students to help choose a focus for improving their writing. The students have furnished ideas such as using colorful verbs or incorporating interesting metaphors.

Another way to narrow your focus for feedback is to zero in on the most problematic aspect of the work you are examining and then offer suggestions for improving that. Using this approach, your focus may change from student to student, but you are still limiting the scope of your comments to concentrate on improving one element of the work. Even with a narrowed focus for explicit feedback, you should also try to point out at least one exemplary aspect of student work to reinforce and review previous instruction.

Build in Time for Self- and Peer Review

Students can help you streamline the assessment process. Used carefully, students' self-assessment can decrease the amount of time you must spend examining student work. For example, elementary teachers who have students needing additional spelling practice could benefit from a student self-correction strategy described by Okyere and Heron (1991). Students are first taught four proofreading marks (e.g., the symbol ^ with a letter above it means the letter should be inserted at that point in a word). Appropriate spelling words are identified by the teacher tailored to each student's needs to allow for differentiated instruction. Each student then takes a spelling test at the spelling center by listening to their own set of words on a tape recorder or computer and then writing these words. They then look at the words as they are correctly spelled and correct their own spelling using the proofreading marks. Finally, they rewrite any words they had misspelled correctly. The authors report that students who use the self-correction strategy outperform students who use more traditional spelling approaches. The procedures for this self-correction approach could also be adapted to other subject matter. The basic idea is to have students explicitly take responsibility for comparing their work to a standard and making changes consistent with that standard.

This approach can also be used with less clear-cut content. For example, in our own classes, we encourage teacher candidates in class, and then later on their own, to compare projects they are designing to the criteria on the rubric for the assignment. They are often surprised to notice they have forgotten a section or have not addressed a specific point clearly. Similarly, the math teacher we mentioned in Chapter 4 who reminds students to think about whether their answers make sense is encouraging students to take more responsibility for assessing themselves. When students can self-correct some of the more glaring problems in their work, you are able to focus on more complex and subtle aspects.

Structure Record Keeping to Encourage Student Self-Monitoring

Concrete proof of student progress is a potent motivator for teachers as well as students (Bandura, 1997; Locke & Latham, 2002). Employing graphs, charts, tables, and checklists to track progress toward learning goals across time has been shown to be effective for documenting progress. In our experience, from second grade on, students can be put in charge of keeping records of their progress on at least one learning goal. Remember, however, when using student self-monitoring, you must be very selective in choosing only the most important learning goals.

After a goal has been chosen for a group of students, you can develop the progress monitoring tool (e.g., a checklist), make copies for each student, and designate a folder for each student for keeping key assignments and the monitoring sheet. Periodically you can provide class time for students to update their checklist. Such procedures not only rescue you from tedious paperwork, they also encourage students to focus on their goals and internalize a sense of responsibility for their work. In addition, they allow students to see tangible evidence of their growth, which helps them develop a connection between their effort and their results, which we discussed as "effort optimism" in Chapter 1.

Develop an "Assessment Bank"

Designing key assessments that represent learning goals, require higher-order thinking, *and* engage students can be a challenging and time-consuming undertaking. An **assessment bank**—an organized collection of assessments that can be modified and reused with different content and different groups—can assist you in maintaining high standards for your assessment.

Assessment Bank

An organized collection of assessments that can be modified and reused with different content and different groups.

You should start now to develop your assessment bank. Think about categories (including content and assessment type) you want to include, and then set up a computer file or a notebook organized with a section for each category. Within these categories you should list learning goals and arrange the examples you collect by learning goal for easy access later.

You will find many and varied sources for assessment material (see Table 12.3). For example, we recently designed a rubric for concept maps related to motivation by finding four concept-map rubrics online and taking the best points from each, modifying the wording to suit our learning goals. In addition, checking out a range of textbooks in your content area may offer you projects, thoughtful questions, or other activities different from the ones provided by the textbooks you may use. National association websites such as the National Science Teacher's Association and the National Council of Teachers of English also provide many resources for assessment and instruction, and most states' large-scale testing websites provide examples of released items. Don't forget the website of the National Assessment of Educational Progress.

With so many possible sources of assessments and rubrics, you must be very selective in choosing what to include in your assessment bank. If you are not discriminating, you will end up amassing a huge amount of information that overwhelms you rather than supports you in designing effective assessment for your particular needs. Remember to select items that address higher-order thinking, and organize them by key learning goals. These items will serve as a jumping-off point to stimulate you in designing assessment tailored to your students' needs, which often vary from class to class and year to year. The carefully selected foundation of material in your assessment bank should provide fresh ideas as you reexamine your learning goals, instruction, and assessment with each new class.

Perhaps the most important source for your assessment bank is the assessments and rubrics you design yourself. Your assessment efficiency can be increased if you design assessments such as interpretive exercises, essay questions, or performance assessments that can be used flexibly. For example, with interpretive exercises developed to check on student graph-reading skills, you can substitute different graphs for

TABLE 12.3

Sources for Assessment Banks

Materials from teachers you know in your content area

World Wide Web

Textbooks and assessment texts in your area

National association websites

Large-scale state testing websites with released items

Assessments and rubrics you design and refine

different groups of students, modifying the basic questions to address each graph's content. As long as students have not seen the content of the graph before, such items can allow you to check on this competency. Similarly, many teachers develop performance assessments that can be tweaked to address different types of content. For example, one social studies teacher we know developed a performance assessment requiring students to design a page of a newspaper reflecting a historical period studied in the class. The assignment calls for different articles displaying both news and commentary as well as pictures, drawings, or political cartoons reflecting the period studied. He uses this assignment only once per class, but he has used it for a variety of significant periods in U.S. history. His effort to develop a clear assignment and effective rubric has paid off because he can use and refine the basic elements many times. Such item "shells" or "models" can be the foundation for a systematic and efficient approach to item writing (Haladyna, 1994; Johnson et al., 2009).

Enlist Students in Assessment Design

Enlisting students in the early phases of designing assessments and rubrics can be useful in promoting learning, and it can save you time and prevent misunderstanding. Student involvement can also help tailor the assessments and scoring guides to student needs.

Some teachers we know take time to discuss and clarify criteria on their rubrics with their students. In the process, students often supply concrete terms and phrases that pin down different levels of quality the teacher might not have generated alone. These teachers start by showing students a bare-bones rubric for a project. They next ask for student questions and comments in an effort to expand and clarify what is most important to the work. They then incorporate these comments into a revised rubric. These teachers indicate the time invested in this process is well worth it. Students' work improves because the discussions have given them a clearer understanding of the standards on which their work will be judged (Andrade, 2008). They also understand the rationale behind those requirements better as they use them to revise their work (Saddler & Andrade, 2004).

Sometimes students also have useful suggestions for designing assessments or test questions. As we mentioned in Chapter 4, having students design test questions requires them to take the perspective of the teacher and use high-level thinking skills to formulate questions showing flexible understanding of key aspects of the learning goals. We know of one teacher who took this idea too far, however. She had her students each design a final exam and answer their own questions. The problem with this approach is that students can easily concentrate only on what they know best and avoid important facets of the material that should also be addressed. A more balanced approach to involving students in designing assessment allows for meaningful contributions but not total control.

➔ ASSESSMENT IN THE CONTEXT OF A DEMOCRATIC SOCIETY: CLASSROOM EXAMPLES

We now turn to actual classrooms to demonstrate assessment practices in action that incorporate the essential assessment guidelines and promote the understanding and skills needed for participation in a democratic society. We visit two schools with very different approaches and assumptions about teaching and learning. We use them to illustrate how the elements of effective classroom assessment can encompass various teaching philosophies and teaching methods. We describe some of the typical assessment practices at each school and illustrate how they address our three themes (equal access to educational opportunity, promotion of self-governing skills, and development of critical thinking skills) related to preparation for democratic participation.

Center for Inquiry

We first visit the Center for Inquiry, a small elementary magnet school from kindergarten to fifth grade established as a partnership between a public school district and a university in Columbia, SC. The mission of the staff, parents, and students is to develop "as more thoughtful, caring and intelligent people who delight in learning and are committed to creating a more compassionate, equitable, knowledgeable and democratic world." This mission statement explicitly emphasizes developing mastery goals ("people who delight in learning") and skills for activist democratic participation ("creating a more compassionate, equitable, knowledgeable and democratic world") throughout their curriculum. The school also focuses on inquiry-based instruction, so classes center around hands-on learning experiences, high-interest studies, and integrated curriculum. At the Center for Inquiry, 26.5 percent of the students are African American, 1.5 percent are Hispanic, 72 percent are European American, and 6 percent are eligible for free or reduced-fee lunch. Table 12.4 shows a rough outline of the daily schedule for Mr. O'Keefe's current third-grade class.

Aligning Goals, Instruction, and Assessment
Because the teachers organize their curriculum using broad concepts across disciplines, they weave multiple state standards through their learning activities and instructional units, rather than teaching them in discrete pieces. Their use of "kidwatching" as diagnostic and formative assessment also helps them determine a flexible order for teaching

TABLE 12.4

Sample Schedule from a Center for Inquiry Third-Grade Class

Time	Activity	Description
8:10–8:45	Exploration	Children work in areas of personal interest (e.g., make entries in class journals, read independently, play chess) and interact with the teacher and each other informally.
8:45–9:30	Morning Meeting	Teacher and students engage in wide-ranging discussion (e.g., current events, science, music) to foster connections between school content and personal lives.
9:30–11:00	Reading Workshop (MWF) and Writing Workshop (TTh)	Reading Workshop includes read-alouds, independent reading, reading conferences, and literature study groups. Writing Workshop includes activities at all phases in the writing cycle, from choosing a topic, to learning and sharing skills and strategies of good writers, to self-editing and author's circle.
11:00–12:00	Lunch and Recess	
12:00–12:15	Chapter Book Read-Aloud	Teacher chooses selections to read that are tied to aspects of the curriculum.
12:15–1:15	Math Workshop	Children investigate the purposes, processes, and content of the mathematical system in natural contexts (e.g., calculating the most economical plan for a field trip or interpreting results of a survey they designed).
1:15–2:30	Focused Studies (Science or Social Studies Units)	Children explore integrated units of study related to broad themes such as change, cycles, or systems, which include emphasis on the central role of oral and written language.
2:30–2:50	Reflection, Friendship Circle, and Homework	The class gathers materials to take home; then they reflect on the day together.

the standards depending more on children's interests and needs than on the more specific scope and sequence formats used in many traditional schools.

These teachers also have overarching personal and schoolwide learning goals related to their shared philosophy of fostering a culture of inquiry to guide the structure of their classroom activities and their assessments. This philosophy involves intentionally designing learning experiences connected to life outside the classroom based on broad, integrative concepts that involve collaboration of teachers and students in the learning process.

Key Assessment Practices

Kidwatching
An informal assessment technique requiring teachers to watch carefully and listen closely with the goal of providing optimal learning experiences tailored to each child.

At the heart of all assessment taking place at the Center for Inquiry is **kidwatching** (see Table 12.5). Kidwatching requires teachers to "watch carefully and listen closely in order to provide optimal experiences for learning" (Mills et al., 2004). Mr. O'Keefe always has a clipboard handy with a two-column sheet listing student names in the first column and space for comments in the second. He jots down notes about student questions, their reactions to activities, his reflections about next steps for them, and other details that help him get to know every student's preferences, strengths and needs, and learning breakthroughs.

The significance of kidwatching at the Center for Inquiry clearly dovetails with our emphasis throughout this text on the importance of formative assessment. Kidwatching offers a framework for formative data collection that is personalized yet systematic. Examining these notes can bring out patterns to help the learning process move forward. For example, Mr. O'Keefe might notice that one child writes about the same topic during several consecutive writing workshops, and so suggests a new genre the next time. Kidwatching is also indispensable for diagnostic assessment. Mr. O'Keefe says he would find it very difficult to begin teaching each fall without first holding a reading conference and having a written conversation with each student in

TABLE 12.5

Key Assessment Practices at the Center for Inquiry

Kidwatching: Assessment strategy requiring teachers to watch carefully and listen closely to provide optimal learning experiences. Sample sources for kidwatching include the following:

Reading Conferences	Teacher listens to and tape-records a student reading a book. Both listen to the tape together and discuss their insights on the student's strengths, needs, and preferences as a reader.
Written Conversations	Teacher and student hold a back and forth discussion in writing about a book the student or the class is reading.
Morning Math Messages	Teacher designs a math challenge related to the class's current math investigations. Students work individually on the morning message, then one child describes the strategies he used to solve the challenge. Other students then respond with *questions, connections,* and/or *appreciations.*
Strategy Sharing	At the end of the writing workshop, several authors describe a writing strategy they believe others might be able to use, or describe a writing dilemma they are experiencing and solicit advice from classmates.

his class. Kidwatching occurs during structured assessment opportunities as well as more unstructured observations over the course of a day.

Morning math messages and strategy sharing allow students to engage in thoughtful reflection together. Individual comments provide clues to how each student approaches problems, how they learn from each other, and what next steps should be taken in the learning process. Making connections (e.g., "It looks like you are using the rounding strategy we learned last week." or "I found that I can use strong verbs in writing nonfiction, not just fiction.") is a particularly effective tool for helping students generalize from one situation to another.

Not only is kidwatching used for diagnostic and formative assessment at the Center for Inquiry, it is also used for summative assessment. Rather than using report cards with letter grades, teachers at the Center instead issue narrative progress reports (first and third nine weeks) and standards-based reports (second and fourth nine weeks). The narrative reports include a description of the child's growth as a writer, reader, mathematician, and scientist/social scientist, as well as the child's growth as a learner in general. Teachers rely heavily on their kidwatching notes to assemble a picture of each student's learning. They also include a description of goals to work toward next. In addition, the students and their parents each write an evaluation of the student's growth over that period and goals for the next one. Videotaping is also used to capture learning and share student achievement with family members.

As you think about these individualized assessment strategies, they may appear overwhelming to undertake all at once with a whole class—or several classes—of students. But remember the teachers at the Center have evolved their practices across time and did not implement all of these practices at once in all their classes. Instead, they tried different approaches at different times and gradually incorporated and modified assessments to give them the most valuable information about students.

In addition, they intertwine assessment strategies with learning activities. For example, paired written conversation is an instructional activity that helps students clarify and sharpen their thinking and become more fluent writers. It also provides rich opportunities to gather information about their prediction and analysis skills and other aspects of student reading comprehension and writing patterns.

Teachers Assessing Themselves

Teachers at the Center for Inquiry hold a regular weekly meeting to examine their classroom practices together using videotapes, examples of student work, and a range of current issues related to teaching. They have reflected on many aspects of their work, including development of the features of a supportive and effective learning community, improving the assessment and celebration of student achievement, and fostering a community of inquiry among both students and teachers (Jennings, 2001).

Connections to Fostering Democratic Participation

Classroom assessment practices at the Center for Inquiry also illustrate our three democratic themes.

Equal Access to Educational Opportunity   Because assessment and instruction at the Center for Inquiry are individualized and tied closely to students' initial levels of understanding and skills, equal access is fostered. Typically, barriers to participation (such as less-developed reading or writing skills) can interfere with the accessibility of new learning for students who lag behind peers. But at the Center for Inquiry, activities that don't require specific entry-level skills coupled with kidwatching that provides tailored information on each child allow for considerable differentiation of instruction. For example, the writing workshop allows attention to specific needs through authors' circles and individual writing conferences. During the math workshop, the students work together in groups and coach each other in problem solving, so children at all levels benefit.

Another opportunity for providing additional literacy experiences for students who need them is the weekly Literacy Club after school. Activities for this targeted small group include fellowship and a snack, word games, and intensive reading and writing activities aimed at accelerating growth, such as helping each other learn to use effective strategies when encountering a difficult passage in the text. When the class is working on a literature study of a particular book, Mr. O'Keefe has Literacy Club students read ahead with coaching on strategies so they can participate more independently and successfully with peers.

Development of Self-Governing Skills   The Center for Inquiry encourages mastery goals through specific classroom practices. As you recall, when students are guided by mastery goals, they are motivated to understand and master learning tasks. They focus on their own progress, looking inward rather than comparing themselves to peers for confirmation of their learning, and they recognize the value of effort in increasing learning. Classrooms promoting mastery goals provide varied, meaningful, and challenging tasks, offer student opportunities to participate in decision making, and encourage students to focus on personal goals and track their own progress (Ames, 1992). In Table 12.6 you see listed some of the strategies used at the Center for Inquiry supporting each classroom element that fosters mastery goals among students.

First, the Center for Inquiry explicitly builds curriculum based on the students' ideas and interests. The focus on kidwatching as assessment can facilitate thoughtful attention to student concerns and evolving interests. For example, Ms. Shamlin (2001) describes the evolution of a unit on growth and change over time in her kindergarten class, which began based on a student comment about changes she was observing in the school. Then after a visit to the zoo to observe and develop hypotheses related to growth and change of animals, another student suggested the class members design expert projects on animals. As these projects were progressing, several students noticed their animal lived in a rain forest. Student interest in rain forests next led to a study of rain forests and then a social action project to collect aluminum cans to raise money

TABLE 12.6

Center for Inquiry Assessment Strategies to Enhance Mastery Goals

Classroom Element	Center for Inquiry Strategies
Varied, meaningful, challenging tasks	• Building curriculum based on students' ideas and interests • Designing thematic units across disciplines that address real-world issues • Using kidwatching to embed assessment into instructional tasks
Students participate in decision making	• Student input into directions that learning takes • Self- and peer-assessment opportunities
Students focus on personal goals, track own progress	• Personalized individual assessment through kidwatching • Student goal setting • Progress across time documented through videos, academic products, kidwatching records

for a rain forest protection organization. Because these explorations were grounded in the natural progression of student interests, they also addressed real-world issues. These engaging instructional units also incorporated key state standards related to reading, writing, science, and social studies.

Second, at the Center for Inquiry, student participation in decision making, not only about instruction but also about assessment, is part of everyday classroom life. For example, when Ms. Shamlin's class was designing the expert projects on animals, she negotiated with them the required criteria and a list of suggestions. When Mr. O'Keefe conducts reading conferences, he first solicits the students' perceptions about themselves as readers. When students participate in strategy-sharing sessions after the writing workshop, they, themselves, decide which strategies are worth sharing. And, at report-card time, students complete a self-assessment of their progress during that marking period.

Finally, the individualized assessment embodied in the various kidwatching strategies encourages students to focus on their own progress and not to compare themselves to other students. In fact, the students would have a difficult time making such comparisons because most assessments, such as reading conferences and written conversations, are geared to the individual student's level, interests, and needs.

All these elements contribute to Center for Inquiry students developing mastery goals and high motivation for academic tasks. They know their opinions and questions are valued. They know how to take action to achieve a goal. They are practicing the self-governing skills necessary to make good decisions and to develop control over their own lives as they become active, contributing citizens.

Development of Critical Thinking Skills   As we discussed in Chapter 1, providing opportunities to learn to make good judgments and critically analyze information we receive is one of the essential functions of schools. Throughout the text we have addressed methods for you to design high-quality assessment requiring higher-order thinking by students. The assessment strategies at the Center for Inquiry provide additional concrete examples of fostering critical thinking among students. For example, in reading conferences, students discuss with their teachers their own strengths and needs as readers. Such work engages them from the start in developing their metacognitive skills by engaging in the *analyze* cognitive strategies of Bloom's taxonomy. Similarly, a morning math message not only calls for students to solve a challenging problem, it also requires them to respond to each other by questioning an answer they think may be wrong, by considering more than one way to solve a problem, or by making a creative connection to another issue that could shed light on the challenge. Such work employs all the cognitive processes from *understand* to *apply* to *analyze* to *evaluate* to *create*.

Knowledge Is Power Program (KIPP)

We next visit the Knowledge Is Power Program (KIPP), a newly established public charter middle school beginning with fifth grade, in Charlotte, NC. The mission of this school is "to prepare students to thrive in the nation's finest high schools and colleges by cultivating the habits, character skills, and knowledge necessary for success." It will also "provide an education which enables students to lead full lives and empowers them to be future leaders of Charlotte and agents of change in the world beyond." This mission statement emphasizes cultivation of the constellation of behaviors accompanying success in the larger society, including leadership skills for democratic participation. KIPP Charlotte is one of 60 KIPP schools around the country focusing on underserved students, primarily in urban settings. At KIPP Charlotte, 95 percent of

TABLE 12.7

Typical Schedule at KIPP Charlotte

Time	Activity
7:30–8:00 a.m.	Morning Meeting: All students and staff have breakfast, announcements, discussion of whole school issues, and silent reflection.
8:00–9:20	Math
9:25–10:45	English
10:50–12:15	History
12:15–1:15	Lunch with all students and staff
1:15–2:30	Study hall and "No Shortcuts" (reading intervention for lowest third of students)
2:35–4:00	Science
4:00–5:00	Silent sustained reading (SSR) and "No Excuses" (math intervention for lowest third of students)

the students are African American, 5 percent are Hispanic, and 65 percent are eligible for free or reduced-fee lunch.

We focus on the fifth-grade class. These students are termed "the Pride of 2015" because they will begin college in 2015, and each class is a family (as in a pride of lions). The outline of a sample daily schedule appears in Table 12.7. Notice the school day is much longer than the typical middle-school day. This is because all KIPP schools accept many students with poor academic records—the average KIPP student starts fifth grade at the 34th percentile in reading and the 44th percentile in math. To enable KIPP students to catch up to peers, they spend 60 percent more time in school than average public school students. In addition to the longer day, "KIPPsters" attend school every other Saturday and for three weeks during the summer.

Aligning Goals, Instruction, and Assessment

During a week in June, well before school started, the KIPP Charlotte teachers developed their curriculum using the backward design approach described in Chapter 2. They used the state standards as their broad learning goals describing what they wanted students to know and be able to do after a year's instruction. They broke each of these learning goals down into a series of **objectives,** or narrower, concrete descriptions of desired understanding and skills that could be measured with some precision. They then worked backward from the objectives to design assessments and then lessons. To keep students and teachers clearly focused, in each classroom the objective to be addressed each day is written on the board. The teachers have also designed their assessments keyed to each objective.

Objectives

Measurable and concrete descriptions of desired skills that are derived from learning goals.

Key Assessment Strategies

The foundational assessment strategies are all directly tied to the objectives and the state standards from which they are drawn. The KIPP Charlotte approach thus strongly emphasizes alignment between learning goals and assessment, and it prevents meandering to topics not directly tied to the learning goals. Using assessments formatively

TABLE 12.8	
Key Assessment Strategies at KIPP Charlotte	
Diagnostic Assessments	At the beginning of the school year, all students take a diagnostic assessment designed by the teachers directly aligned with the state standards in each discipline.
Benchmark Tests	Every six weeks in each core subject, students take a test tied to the standards worked on during that marking period. For each subject, students receive results keyed to each objective with a grade of "A" (90%), "B" (80%), or "NY" (Not Yet—below 80%).
Mastery Quizzes	For each "NY" objective, students re-study or request tutoring to improve and are then allowed to take a mastery quiz on that objective so they learn the material and improve their grade.
Exit Tickets	Most days at the end of the science and math periods (and to a lesser extent, English and History), students are asked to complete an exit ticket requiring them to work a problem or summarize what they learned that day. These are used to check understanding and plan instruction.
Checks for Understanding	During instruction, teachers frequently ask for thumbs up if students agree or thumbs down if they don't.

to carefully keep track of student performance on each objective also helps shape the next steps in instruction. You can see key assessment strategies in Table 12.8.

These assessments offer a range of information for teachers and students to enhance learning. For example, the diagnostic tests let Ms. Adams, the math teacher, know that she needed to start with third- and fourth-grade objectives because her fifth graders needed a thorough review. The diagnostic tests also determine which students needed more intense intervention, and the lowest third of the class receives extra instruction in math and reading. Similarly, tracking benchmark test results (Figure 12.2) allows students and teachers to determine strengths and weaknesses and to work to improve in specific areas by later taking mastery quizzes. At first, the teachers weren't sure whether students would appreciate such detailed feedback, but as Mr. Pomis, the science teacher, told us, "The more we share the more they get excited about it."

Teachers Assessing Themselves

These assessments provide rich material for teacher reflection leading to instructional modifications. For specific objectives on which students perform poorly, the teachers design additional lessons and assessments. The teachers also discuss schoolwide issues during common planning times. One recent discussion addressed ways to emphasize writing more across all four core subject areas.

Connections to Fostering Democratic Participation

Throughout this text, we have aimed to explain how effective classroom assessment practices connect to the larger goal of preparing students to take their place as active participants in a democratic society. Classroom assessment practices at KIPP Charlotte illustrate the themes we have stressed.

I Am a Meteorologist.

I am a science genius.
My name is Keyshawn Davis.
My overall average on Benchmark One is 86%.

Number	Description	B 1	Mastery Quiz
Objective 1	I can explain how the sun heats the earth during day and night.	80%	
Objective 2	I can explain how the sun heats the earth during the four seasons.	60%	80%
Objective 3	I can explain how the sun heats the land, water, and air.	100%	
Objective 4	I can identify major air masses in North America.	60%	90%
Objective 5	I can create a bar graph.	100%	
Objective 6	I can draw conclusions from a bar graph and data table.	100%	
Objective 7	I can explain that intelligence is not fixed; hard work increases intelligence.	100%	

I strive for 100%.

FIGURE 12.2   *Sample Student Results After Benchmark One in Science and Subsequent Mastery Quiz*

Equal Access to Educational Opportunity   One important way all KIPP schools focus on closing the achievement gap and providing equal access to educational opportunity is through extra instructional time allowing for accelerated learning. Because many KIPPsters start fifth grade well behind typical peers, a basic necessity is to provide a 60 percent longer school day than typical middle schools so that they will have more time to catch up. They must make more than a year's growth in a year's time. In addition, KIPP Charlotte provides extensive intervention programs in math and English for the lowest third of the class during times that do not interfere with the four core courses.

Another element related to KIPP Charlotte efforts to help students close the achievement gap is a culture of high expectations. For example, when Ms. Young's English students were designing sentences using the prefix "bi," one of the students offered a sentence with the word "bicycle." She stopped him saying, "Why did you use bicycle? You forfeited an opportunity to expand your vocabulary," because he did not choose a less-common word.

Toward the end of science class, Mr. Pomis said, "If your table is super focused, you'll get the homework first." This statement conveyed the belief that getting the homework was something to be anticipated with excitement, not something to dread. Similarly, when asking a question, he paused as hands flew up saying, "I'm waiting for 100%," communicating the assumption that every student should know the answer and should be participating.

The use of "Not Yet" grading by all KIPP Charlotte teachers also sends a message of high expectations. On benchmark tests, students receive an "A," a "B," or "NY" for each objective. "Not Yet" implies the student certainly will reach the objective when the student puts in more work. Providing opportunities to work on "NY" objectives also conveys the expectation that everyone will reach them.

A recent independent evaluation of a national sample of KIPP schools showed students who spent fifth through seventh grades at a KIPP school improved on the Stanford Achievement Test, a nationally norm-referenced large-scale achievement test, from average scores at the 34th percentile to average scores at the 58th percentile in reading. In math they grew from the 44th percentile to the 83rd percentile in those three years.

Development of Self-Governing Skills KIPP Charlotte teachers also encourage mastery goals through a number of classroom practices. In Table 12.9 you see some of the strategies used at KIPP Charlotte supporting each classroom element fostering mastery goals among students.

A few examples illustrate tasks building on students' ideas and interests. When learning how to construct timelines in history, Ms. Flowers first had students design a timeline based on their own lives. In English class, Ms. Young had students generate topics for their persuasive essays. Some of these topics appear in Table 12.10. Similarly,

TABLE 12.9

KIPP Charlotte Assessment Strategies That Embody Classroom Elements to Enhance Mastery Goals

Classroom Element	KIPP Charlotte Strategies
Varied, meaningful, challenging tasks	• Challenging tasks requiring higher-order thinking aligned with state standards. • Building tasks based on students' ideas and interests.
Students participate in decision making	• Students decide when they are ready to take mastery quizzes. • Self-assessment opportunities during instruction. • Classes "co-investigate" benchmark test trends and problem-solve next steps.
Students focus on personal goals, track own progress	• Alignment of curriculum and assessment allows specific articulation of each student's strengths and needs for personalized goal setting. • Progress across time documented on spreadsheets for each objective in each of the four core subjects.

TABLE 12.10

Student-Generated Persuasive Writing Topics

Should KIPPsters have more days at school?

Should KIPPsters have the opportunity to eat dinner with teachers every Friday?

Should KIPPsters create their own lunch menu?

Should KIPPsters be allowed to work in groups during study hall?

when students do independent reading, they complete written questions about their book, such as "Explain how this book connects to your life." and "To whom would you recommend this book and why?"

In relation to the second classroom element, student participation in decision making, the assessments at KIPP are set up so that students must make crucial decisions about their learning. They can individually decide how to study for and when to take mastery quizzes to improve their grades on benchmark tests. After benchmark tests, an entire class "co-investigates" the resulting data on a class spreadsheet. They discuss trends, major successes and shortcomings, and areas on which the class should focus. As a class, they look for root causes of poor performance and problem solve how to address them.

In relation to the third classroom element, personal goals and progress monitoring, students are encouraged in every core subject to focus on their individual goals and track their own progress toward meeting the state standards. The careful alignment of the benchmark assessments to the standards allows students to see their strengths and weaknesses clearly. The "Not Yet" grading system and the use of mastery quizzes allows them to work toward their personal goals and master the understanding and skills they personally need.

Development of Critical Thinking Skills   The ability to think critically is essential for citizens of a democracy. The assessment strategies at KIPP Charlotte provide some examples of fostering critical thinking among students.

Students are challenged to think critically with many types of writing assignments. In science, at the end of a unit, students write five-paragraph information essays to summarize what they have learned about, for example, meteorology. In English, they construct persuasive essays. This focus on nonfiction writing helps students learn to formulate ideas with clarity and precision. It also provides teachers with insights about student strategy use, thinking processes, and what challenges and misconceptions remain. This information is invaluable for identifying obstacles—vocabulary issues, reasoning problems, writing fluency—to student learning to be addressed later in instruction.

To encourage analysis skills, teachers design mastery quizzes to cover more than one skill (e.g., both ordering and estimating in math). In the directions, students are told to do only the items addressing the skill on which they are working. Thus they must be able to discriminate among different types of problems, which requires them to move up a level from solving problems to analyzing characteristics of problems related to different skills.

Similarly, in English class, Ms. Young often asks students to describe strategies they found useful in completing a homework assignment. Students must think not merely about appropriate answers to questions, they must also decide which steps they took to arrive at them were most effective. Stressing these metacognitive skills helps students monitor themselves so they become more efficient at learning.

✦ KEY TO ASSESSMENT IN THE CONTEXT OF DEMOCRATIC PARTICIPATION

As we look at what our two schools have in common, we see that formative assessment—checking where students are in relation to the learning goals, providing feedback, and then offering opportunities for improvement—is the key. We believe that formative assessment is the foundation on which skills for democratic participation can be built. Using formative assessment also addresses all three themes we have woven throughout this book, about using assessment practices to help students become effective citizens in a democracy (see Table 12.11).

TABLE 12.11

Formative Assessment and Promoting Democratic Values

Formative Assessment Characteristic	Democratic Theme Addressed
• Helps struggling students most by making standards of evaluation more understandable and concrete • Reduces negative feedback by focusing on opportunities for improvement	Equal access to educational opportunity
• Emphasizes monitoring of self-improvement across time • Encourages internalization of standards of quality work • Fosters mastery goals	Development of self-governing skills (such as independent thought and a sense of responsibility) for democratic participation
• Requires complex tasks requiring higher-order thinking skills • Increases student analysis of own work rather than relying only on external standards	Development of critical thinking skills that enable good decision making

Formative Assessment and Equal Access

First, formative assessment helps struggling students the most, because it allows them to articulate what stronger students tend to do on their own as they compare their work to the expected standards. A focus on feedback and opportunities to improve also reduces the negative criticism struggling students frequently receive, discouraging them about what they cannot do. For example, at both KIPP, with "Not Yet" grading, and the Center for Inquiry with narrative report cards, poorer performing students are not irrevocably labeled as failing. *All* students, wherever they start, can focus on making progress and learning more. They can feel positive about their ongoing development as learners by seeing their progress across time. Effective formative assessment helps you provide equal access to knowledge and close achievement gaps because it allows all students to make the most of the learning context.

Formative Assessment and Self-Governing Skills

Second, formative assessment, because it provides opportunities to close the gap between where students are and where they need to be, emphasizes student monitoring of their own improvement across time. With opportunities to make progress, students also begin to develop concrete ways to understand and internalize the standards of quality for their efforts. They no longer passively rely on the teacher to be the sole judge of their work. They begin to develop the mastery goals that increase motivation to make them lifelong learners. For example, both KIPP Charlotte and the Center for Inquiry encourage student decision making and a focus on individual students' learning gains. These aspects of formative assessment facilitate mastery goals and the habits of mind needed to cultivate the lifelong curiosity and desire for knowledge required for active functioning in a democratic society.

Formative Assessment and Critical Thinking

Third, formative assessment requires students to engage in critical thinking and use thinking skills at the higher levels of Bloom's taxonomy. At KIPP Charlotte and the

Center for Inquiry, students engage in frequent writing tasks and other complex assignments as formative assessment. Finally, because formative assessment involves comparing one's own work to a standard for the purpose of improvement, engaging in self- and peer-assessment fosters the growth of critical thinking. Activities such as strategy sharing, checks for understanding, and student contributions to rubric development are examples we have seen at our two schools.

We hope this review has consolidated your understanding about formative assessment and the many ways formative assessment can be embedded in your classroom practice. As a guide for applying formative assessment across learning activities, Table 12.12 provides formative strategies for informal classroom activities, Table 12.13 offers strategies for adapting quizzes and tests for formative purposes, and Table 12.14 lists some suggestions for formative assessment related to performance products.

TABLE 12.12

Formative Assessment Strategies for Informal Classroom Activities

Oral questions requiring student justification of their answers.

Oral questions at higher levels of Bloom's taxonomy (see Box 4.1 and Tables 4.4 and 4.5 in Chapter 4).

Journal writing requiring application of concepts, interpretation of data, making connections.

Quick writes to key questions about learning as homework or at the end of class (e.g., exit or entry tickets).

Instructional tasks that build in opportunities for formative assessment (e.g., grocery store "stations," reading conversations).

Use of white boards or hand signals for student answers or reactions during instruction.

TABLE 12.13

Strategies for Adapting Quizzes and Tests for Formative Purposes

Ungraded quizzes.

Collaborative quizzes where students must agree on the correct answer.

Morning math messages where students work on a problem or challenge alone, then share questions, connections, appreciations.

Label test questions by content area and allow students to analyze strengths and weaknesses of their results across the content areas tested.

After feedback on a test or quiz, provide an opportunity for students to close the gap between where they are and where they need to be using mastery quizzes or other methods.

TABLE 12.14

Strategies for Formative Assessment Related to Performance Products

Discuss rubric criteria and their application to sample products.

Authors' Chair where students share writing and receive feedback from classmates and teachers.

Observation and critique of videotaped performance or activity with individuals or groups (e.g., music, dance, art, reading, ESL classes).

Critical reflection by student on a work in progress using rubric for the product.

Individual conferences with students to check progress on major product.

✦ NOW IT'S YOUR TURN: SETTING PERSONAL GOALS FOR CLASSROOM ASSESSMENT

We have learned many important lessons about human behavior throughout our careers in education. One of the most important, as we discussed in Chapter 5, is the effectiveness of setting goals and monitoring progress for achieving important ends—including efforts to help us become better teachers. When you write down your goals, you make them tangible. Explicit goal setting allows you to develop a clear personal vision of what you want to accomplish based on a strong rationale for why you want to accomplish it. Monitoring progress toward your goal also provides feedback and reinforcement that keeps you on track and bolsters your persistence (Locke & Latham, 2002). In terms of usefulness of application to work settings, goal setting is one of the highest-rated theories of motivation (Latham et al., 1997). We would like you to take a few moments now to follow a few steps to set a goal to incorporate assessment strategies that foster preparation for democratic life among your students.

Personal Goal-Setting Steps

As you think about one or more goals, we suggest following several steps recommended for personal goals for teachers and students (Radar, 2005). These steps incorporate the important issues we emphasized related to goal setting in Chapter 5.

1. Choose a Specific Goal and Write It Down

In thinking about designing a goal, you should explore assessment strategies you have never tried, and you should focus on the next term when you will be teaching. Your personal goal should also fit well with your teaching style, your subject matter, your overarching personal goals, and the age group with which you work. The best goals are as specific as possible so you have a clear picture of what you are aiming for, and you can tell when you have accomplished it. They are measurable in some way. They should also challenge you and not be too easy to attain. For example, if you wrote a goal simply stating, "I will use formative assessment," you are not being specific enough to have a tangible ambition to set your sights on, and if you ask your class a couple of "Why?" questions one day, you would be able to reach it. If, instead, you write something like "I will design a rubric with my speech students to use for self-assessment of video clips of a speech as they are preparing it for presentation," you have something a lot more concrete (and challenging) to work from.

If you think you lack the understanding and skills to use some of the types of formative assessment, you are not alone. A gap between understanding and use of effective strategies often occurs as teachers try new formative practices (Gearhart et al., 2006). If you think you need more training, exposure, or experience, you can develop a goal providing for that. For example, your initial goal might be to (1) find two teachers at your school who use students to help design rubrics for self-assessment, and (2) secure their permission to allow you to observe the process during your planning period. The key is first choosing a specific goal to accomplish that fits you and your school environment and then getting it down on paper. This action fosters your commitment to achieve the goal (Locke & Latham, 2002).

2. Decide a Time When Your Goal Will Be Achieved

Specifying a target date to achieve your goal adds to its specificity and helps you focus your effort and commitment. Shorter-term goals are easier to shoot for and accomplish than longer-term goals. We recommend a four- to six-week time frame for accomplishing most personal goals as reasonable for teachers. Six weeks doesn't seem so far away that you find it hard to be motivated, yet it is distant enough so you can undertake the sustained and comprehensive action needed for a nontrivial goal.

3. Develop a Plan

Making a list of obstacles that may impede completion of your goal along with actions to take to eliminate those threats is the first important step in developing your plan. This step helps you foresee problems you may run into and gives you an opportunity to anticipate ways to deal with them and make them manageable. It also increases the likelihood of success, so your motivation increases. For example, you may expect you will have difficulty finding time to squeeze out of your busy schedule to spend with students to design that rubric for your speech class. Pull out your weekly planner and decide right away which of your usual activities you might shorten or forgo so this activity can be scheduled.

After you have identified and dealt with potential obstacles, you can make a list of the actions you will take to reach the goal. For example, consultation with other teachers could be useful, as well as developing documents or figures to support the process. One of the actions you list should be reviewing progress toward your goal each week. In fact, you may want to design a mastery monitoring checklist or graph (Chapter 5) to help you plot your progress toward the goal. Each time you complete an action, you can then tangibly see your movement toward the goal.

4. Self-Evaluate

Here we find again the importance of teacher reflection. The inquiry stance we have talked about since Chapter 1 can aid you as you aim to reach new personal goals associated with designing classroom assessments fostering the understanding and skills students need to become responsible citizens in a democracy. A formative-assessment approach to dealing with setbacks realistically acknowledges that reaching your goal may require some trial and error.

We hope that as you have studied this text, you have learned new skills to help you achieve your goals as a professional who meets students where they are and helps all students learn to their potential. Perhaps more important, we hope we have convinced you why that aspiration is so crucial for our future, our children's future, and the future of democratic societies around the world.

KEY CHAPTER POINTS

We began the chapter with six fundamental guidelines for effective classroom assessment: begin with the end in mind, find out what students know, check as you go, teach students to check as you go, use rubrics creatively to reinforce attainment of learning goals, and assess yourself.

Next, we discussed the issue of efficiency in classroom assessment. We described a number of strategies to help reduce the assessment load, including choosing assessment opportunities and grading selectively, choosing a single focus for feedback, encouraging student record keeping, developing an assessment bank, using a modified table of specifications for tests, and enlisting students to help design assessment items and scoring guides.

We followed with classroom examples of assessment practices to foster skills for democratic participation. We introduced the Center for Inquiry and the KIPP Charlotte program. Even though teachers at these two schools have different assumptions and philosophies underlying their work, they all use their assessment practices to provide equal access to educational opportunity and to foster self-governing skills and critical thinking skills among students.

Next, we discussed the importance of formative assessment in fostering preparation for democratic life. Finally, we laid out steps for personal goal setting so you could develop a specific goal for your own practice. The steps include choosing a specific goal and writing it down, deciding on a deadline for achieving your goal, developing a plan of action, and self-evaluating. These steps should enable you to design and carry out effective assessments useful for you and your students.

CHAPTER REVIEW QUESTIONS

1. Think about the six essential guidelines for assessment. Which do you believe is most important, and why do you think so?
2. Describe at least two reasons why beginning with the end in mind is crucial to effective instruction.
3. Why is self- and peer assessment helpful for preparing students for participating in a democratic society? Use a specific example from your own discipline to support your argument.
4. Think about three typical assessment practices in your own discipline. How can the strategies for efficiency (Table 12.2) be applied to make these typical practices more efficient?
5. Go to the World Wide Web and find at least three sources you could use for your own assessment bank. Print URLs, sample items, and the learning goals they address.
6. Find three other specific sources (e.g., texts, practicing teachers, professional organizations) for your assessment bank and provide sample items from them.
7. In your opinion, what strategies are most helpful for closing achievement gaps?
8. Describe two specific ways you might incorporate kidwatching into your classroom assessment practices.
9. Compare the philosophy and methods of KIPP Charlotte and the Center for Inquiry. How do they each promote mastery goals? Which approach are you most comfortable with and why?
10. Describe one classroom assessment practice from each of the two schools that you might be willing to incorporate into your own teaching. Why do you think this practice would work for you?

11. What evidence for the six essential guidelines for assessment do you see among practices at KIPP Charlotte and the Center for Inquiry?
12. Design a specific, challenging short-term goal related to incorporating assessment strategies fostering skills for democratic participation among your students using the four steps for personal goal setting at the end of the chapter.

HELPFUL WEBSITES

http://www.nsta.org/
The National Science Teachers Association website has a wealth of resources targeted to different grade levels that can contribute to your assessment notebook, as well as listserv connections, publications, and recommendations on lessons and materials.
http://www.ncte.org/
The National Council of Teachers of English website has teaching resource collections related to many aspects of teaching English, including classroom assessments. It also features materials related to a wide range of topics from grammar to poetry.

REFERENCES

Ames, C. 1992. Classrooms: Goals, structures, and student motivation. *Journal of Educational Psychology* 84(3): 261–271.

Andrade, H. 2008. Self-assessment through rubrics. *Educational Leadership* 65: 60–63.

Bandura, A. 1997. *Self-efficacy: The exercise of control.* New York: Freeman.

Edmonds, R. 1979. Effective schools for the urban poor. *Educational Leadership* 37: 23.

Gearhart, M., S. Nagashima, J. Pfotenhauer, S. Clark, C. Schwab, T. Vendlinski, E. Osmundson, J. Herman, and D. Bernbaum. 2006. Developing expertise with classroom assessment in K–12 science: Learning to interpret student work. *Educational Assessment* 11(3 & 4): 237–263.

Haladyna, T. 1994. *Developing and validating multiple-choice test items.* Hillsdale, NJ: Lawrence Erlbaum Associates.

Heward, W., T. Heron, R. Gardner, and R. Prayzer. 1991. Two strategies for improving students' writing skills. In G. Stoner, M. Shinn, and H. Walker (eds.), *Interventions for achievement and behavior problems*, pp. 379–398. Silver Spring, MD: National Association of School Psychologists.

Jennings, L. 2001. Inquiry for professional development and continual school renewal. In H. Mills and A. Donnelly (eds.), *From the ground up: Creating a culture of inquiry*, pp. 33–54. Portsmouth, NH: Heinemann.

Johnson, R., J. Penny, and B. Gordon. 2009. *Assessing performance: Developing, scoring, and validating performance tasks.* New York: Guilford Publications.

Latham, G., S. Daghighi, and E. Locke. 1997. Implications of goal-setting theory for faculty motivation. In J. Bess (ed.), *Teaching well and liking it*, pp. 125–142. Baltimore: Johns Hopkins.

Leary, M. R. 1999. Making sense of self-esteem. *Current Directions in Psychological Science* 8: 32–35.

Locke, E., and G. Latham. 2002. Building a practically useful theory of goal setting and task motivation: A 35-year odyssey. *American Psychologist* 57: 705–717.

Marsh, H. W., and R. Craven. 1997. Academic self-concept: Beyond the dustbowl. In G. D. Phye (ed.), *Handbook of classroom assessment: Learning, achievement, and adjustment.* San Diego, CA: Academic Press.

McMillan, J. 2003. Understanding and improving teachers' classroom assessment decision making: Implications for theory and practice. *Educational Measurement: Issues and Practice* 22(4): 34–37.

O'Keefe, T. 2005. Knowing kids through written conversation. *School Talk* 11(1): 4.

Okyere, B., and T. Heron. 1991. Use of self-correction to improve spelling in regular education classrooms. In G. Stoner, M. Shinn, and H. Walker (eds.), *Interventions for achievement and behavior problems,* pp. 399–413. Silver Spring, MD: National Association of School Psychologists.

Penso, S. 2002. Pedagogical content knowledge: How do student teachers identify and describe the causes of their pupils' learning difficulties? *Asia-Pacific Journal of Teacher Education* 30: 25–37.

Radar, L. 2005. Goal setting for students and teachers. Six steps to success. *Clearing House* 78(3): 123–126.

Reeves, D. B. 2004. The 90/90/90 schools: A case study. In D. B. Reeves (ed.), *Accountability in action: A blueprint for learning organizations.* 2nd ed. pp. 185–208. Englewood, CO: Advanced Learning Press.

Saddler, B., and H. Andrade. 2004. The writing rubric. *Educational Leadership* 62: 48–52.

Sanford, R., M. Ulicsak, K. Facer, and T. Rudd. 2007. Teaching with games. Learning, media and technology 32(1): 101–105.

Shamlin, M. 2001. Creating curriculum with and for children. In H. Mills and A. Donnelly (eds.), *From the ground up: Creating a culture of inquiry,* pp. 55–77. Portsmouth, NH: Heinemann.

Stiggins, R., and N. Conklin. 1992. *In teachers' hands: Investigating the practices of classroom assessment.* Albany: State University of New York Press.

Wiliam, D., C. Lee, C. Harrison, and P. Black. 2004. Teachers developing assessment for learning: Impact on student achievement. *Assessment in Education* 11: 49–65.

GLOSSARY

A

achievement gap   The disparity in performance between student groups (e.g., ethnicity, gender, and/or socioeconomic status) on achievement measures such as large-scale tests and graduation rates.

achievement tests   Instruments designed to measure how much students have learned in various academic content areas, such as science or math.

action research   The process of examining and improving teaching practices and student outcomes using an inquiry stance.

affective domain   Responses related to students' emotional or internal reaction to subject matter.

alignment   The adjustment of one element or object in relation to others.

alternate-choice item   Type of question that has only two options instead of the three to five options of a conventional multiple-choice item.

analytic rubric   A scoring guide that contains one or more performance criteria for evaluating a task and proficiency levels for each criterion.

aptitude tests   Instruments that estimate students' potential or capacity for learning apart from what they have already achieved and with less reference to specific academic content.

assessment   The variety of methods used to determine what students know and are able to do before, during, and after instruction.

assessment bank   An organized collection of assessments that can be modified and reused with different content and different groups.

B

backward design   A process of planning instruction and assessment. After learning goals are identified, assessments measuring student achievement of learning goals are designed, and only then is instruction developed.

basic interpersonal communication skills (BICS)   The informal language used to communicate in everyday social situations where many contextual cues exist (such as gestures, facial expressions, and objects) to enhance comprehension.

benchmark tests   Assessments tied explicitly to academic standards and administered at regular intervals to determine extent of student mastery.

bias   An inclination or a preference that interferes with impartiality.

C

ceiling effect   Occurs when a student attains the maximum score or "ceiling" for an assessment and thus prevents appraisal of the full extent of the student's knowledge.

checklist   A list of key elements of a task organized in a logical sequence allowing confirmation of each element.

cognitive academic language proficiency (CALP)   The formal language that requires expertise in abstract scholarly vocabulary used in academic settings in which language itself, rather than contextual cues, must bear the primary meaning.

cognitive domain   Processes related to thinking and reasoning.

complex multiple-choice   A type of selected-response item that consists of a stem followed by choices that are grouped into more than one set.

confidence interval   The range of scores that a student would attain if the test were taken many times.

construct   The basic idea, theory, or concept in mind whenever measurement is attempted.

construct-related evidence   All information collected to examine the validity of an assessment.

constructed-response items   Questions in which students must create the response rather than select one provided. Examples include short-answer and essay items.

content-based essays   A prompt that presents students with a question or task that assesses student knowledge in a subject area. Students respond in a paragraph or several paragraphs.

content-related evidence   Refers to the adequacy of the sampling of specific content, which contributes to validity.

content representativeness   Ensuring that the assessment adequately represents the constructs addressed in the learning goals.

contextual invisibility   The concept that certain groups, customs, or lifestyles are not represented or are under-represented in curriculum and assessment materials.

conventional multiple-choice items   Questions that begin with a stem and offer three to five answer options.

criterion-referenced grading   A grading process in which student work is compared to a specific criterion or standard of mastery.

criterion-referenced scoring   A scoring process in which the individual student's score is compared to predefined standards. Also termed standards-based scoring.

criterion-related evidence Information that examines a relationship between one assessment and an established measure for the purposes of discerning validity.

curriculum-based measurement One form of general outcome measurement in which frequent brief assessments are used in the basic skill areas of reading, math, spelling, and written expression to monitor student progress and provide information for teacher decision making.

D

diagnostic assessment Assessment at the early stages of a school year or a unit that provides the teacher with information about what students already know and are able to do.

differentiation or differentiated instruction Using students' current understanding and skills, readiness levels, and interests to tailor instruction to meet individual needs.

disaggregation of scores Separating the scores of a large group of students into smaller, more meaningful groups (such as gender, disability status, or socioeconomic status) to determine whether differences among these groups exist related to achievement.

distracters Incorrect options in multiple-choice questions.

documentation portfolio An organized body of student work that provides information for evaluating student achievement status for accountability purposes.

E

effort optimism The idea that effort brings rewards. For example, if you work hard in school, you will learn more.

environmental sources of error Extraneous factors in the assessment context that can influence scores on an assessment.

error The element of imprecision involved in any measurement.

essay item A prompt that presents students with a question or task to which the student responds in a paragraph or several paragraphs.

extrapolated Estimated outside the known range.

F

formative assessment Monitoring student progress during instruction and learning activities, which includes feedback and opportunities to improve.

frequency distribution A display of the number of students who attained each score, ordered from lowest to highest score.

frequency polygon A line graph in which the frequencies for each score are plotted as points, and a line connects those points.

G

general outcome measurement A method of monitoring progress that uses several brief, similar tasks (e.g., reading aloud in grade-level stories for one minute) that can indicate achievement of a learning goal.

grade equivalent score A number representing the grade level at which the median students get the same number of questions correct as your student.

grouped frequency distribution A frequency distribution that groups scores in intervals (e.g., all scores in the 90–100% range are plotted together as one point on the distribution).

growth portfolio An organized collection of student work gathered to document student development of skills and strategies over time.

H

halo effect Effect that occurs when a teacher's judgments about one aspect of a student influence the teacher's judgments about other qualities of that student.

historical distortion Presenting a single interpretation of an issue, perpetuating oversimplification of complex issues, or avoiding controversial topics.

holistic rubric A scoring guide that provides a single score representing overall quality across several criteria.

I

individualized education plan (IEP) The program designed each year for a student with disabilities by the parents and teachers who work with that student.

inferences Assumptions or conclusions based on observations and experience.

informative writing A composition in which the author describes ideas, conveys messages, or provides instructions.

inquiry stance An approach to dealing with challenges in the classroom that involves identifying problems, collecting relevant data, making judgments, and then modifying practices based on the process to bring about improvement in teaching and learning.

internal consistency The degree to which all items in an assessment are related to one another and therefore can be assumed to measure the same thing.

interpretive exercise A selected-response item that is preceded by material that a student must analyze to answer the question.

interrater reliability The measure of the agreement between two raters.

item-to-item carryover Effect that occurs when a teacher's scoring of an essay is influenced by a student's performance on the previous essay items in the same test.

J–K

kidwatching An informal assessment technique requiring teachers to watch carefully and listen closely in an effort to provide optimal experiences for learning.

L

learning goals Learning outcomes, objectives, aims, and targets.

local norm A norm group made up of test takers from a restricted area (e.g., school district).

M

mastery goals   Academic goals that focus on a desire to understand and accomplish the task and that assume ability can increase.

mastery monitoring   A method of monitoring progress by tracking student completion of several different tasks that, when all are completed, indicates achievement of the learning goal.

matching format   Assessment form in which two parallel columns of items (termed premises and responses) are listed and the student indicates which items from each column belong together in pairs.

mean   A measure of central tendency that is the average of all scores in a distribution. It is calculated by adding all scores together, then dividing by the number of scores.

median   A measure of central tendency that is the exact midpoint of a set of scores.

metacognition   The process of analyzing and thinking about one's own thinking, enabling such skills as monitoring progress, staying on task, and self-correcting errors.

microaggressions   Brief, everyday remarks or behaviors that inadvertently send denigrating messages to the receiver.

misalignment   Occurs when learning goals, instruction, and/or assessment are not congruent.

mode   The score achieved by more students than any other.

morning math messages   A math challenge each morning related to the class's current math investigations.

multiple means of engagement   The variety of possible methods used to keep student interest and participation strong in a universal design for learning framework.

multiple means of expression   The variety of possible methods in which students may respond to instruction or assessment tasks in a universal design for learning framework.

multiple means of representation   The variety of possible methods by which instructional or assessment material is presented to students in a universal design for learning framework.

multiple true-false items   Several choices follow a scenario or question and the student indicates whether each choice is correct or incorrect.

N

narrative reports   Written descriptions of student achievement and progress each marking period.

narrative writing   A form of composition in which the author relates a story or personal experience.

negative suggestion effect   Concern that appearance in print lends plausibility to erroneous information.

No Child Left Behind Act (NCLB)   U.S. federal law aimed to improve public schools by increasing accountability standards.

normal curve or normal distribution   The theoretically bell-shaped curve thought to characterize many attributes in nature and many human traits.

normal curve equivalent (NCE)   A scale ranging between 1 and 99.9 that has equal intervals between all the scores along the continuum.

norm group   The group chosen by a test designer for the initial administration of a test to obtain a distribution of typical scores. Subsequently, test takers' performances are compared to the scores of the norm group to determine their percentile ranks and similar scores when using a norm-referenced scoring system.

norm-referenced grading   Assigning grades according to a distribution (e.g., 10% of the students will get an "A," 20% will get a "B," 40% will receive a "C").

"Not Yet" grading   A grading system in which students receive an "A," a "B," or "NY" (not yet) for each learning goal. "NY" implies that all students will reach the goal when they put in more work, conveying high expectations and promoting the connection between student effort and achievement.

O

objectives   Measurable and concrete descriptions of desired skills that are derived from learning goals.

options   The potential answers with one correct response and several plausible incorrect responses in the multiple-choice assessment format.

outliers   Extremely high or low scores differing from typical scores.

overinterpretation   Incorrect assumptions and conclusions drawn when interpreting scores that are not warranted by the data available.

P

percentile or **percentile rank**   A score indicating the percentage of students in the norm group at or below the same score.

percentile bands   A range of percentile scores that incorporates the standard error of measurement.

performance assessments   Assessments that require students to construct a response to a task or prompt or to otherwise demonstrate their achievement of a learning goal.

performance criteria   The key elements of a performance specified in a scoring guide.

performance goals   Academic goals that focus on performing well in front of others and that assume ability is fixed. Often contrasted with mastery goals.

persuasive writing   A composition in which the author attempts to influence the reader to take action or create change.

portfolio   A purposefully organized collection of student work.

process   The procedure a student uses to complete a performance task.

product   The tangible outcome or end result of a performance task.

proficiency levels   The description of each level of quality of a performance criterion along a continuum in an analytic or holistic rubric.

prompt   The stem (i.e., directions) of an essay.

psychomotor domain   Processes related to perceptual and motor skills.

Q–R

range   The distance between the lowest and highest scores attained on an assessment.

reliability The degree to which scores on an assessment are consistent and stable.

respondent The student completing the assessment.

responsiveness to intervention (RTI) An approach in general education that involves collecting data to determine the degree to which underachieving students profit from specific instruction targeting their needs.

rubric Scoring guide with information about levels of quality.

S

scaffolding Temporary support allowing students to meet a challenge and increase their understanding. Examples include pictorial or graphic organizers, note-taking guides, breakdown of task into smaller components.

scale score A score classifying a student's performance on a test based on the arbitrary numbers that the test's designers have assigned for its mean and standard deviation.

scoring guides Instruments that specify criteria for rating examinee responses. These include checklists, analytic rubrics, and holistic rubrics.

self-assessment Process in which students evaluate their own work, usually during formative assessment.

short-answer items Items in which students supply short responses, such as a single word, a phrase, or a few sentences.

showcase portfolio An organized collection of student work designed to illustrate their finest accomplishments in meeting the learning goals.

standard error of measurement (SEM) An estimate indicating the average magnitude of error for a test.

standard deviation The average distance between the individual scores and the mean of the group score.

standardized test A test that is administered, scored, and interpreted the same way for everyone taking it.

standards-based grading Grading based on an interpretation of a student's degree of mastery of the learning goals, sometimes based on periodic benchmark tests.

stanine A standardized score indicating where a student's score falls in relation to the norm group when the distribution of scores is divided into nine equal parts. Stanine scores have a mean of five and a standard deviation of two.

stem The premise of a multiple-choice item that usually takes the form of a question or an incomplete statement.

stereotypical representation Depicting social groups in an oversimplified, clichéd manner in assessments.

strategy sharing A discussion at the end of writing workshops when students share a strategy or procedure they found useful in their writing that day.

student-led conference A conference in which students take the primary responsibility for explaining their own strengths, needs, and progress to their parents or others.

sufficiency of information Ensuring the collection of adequate data to make good decisions.

summative assessment A summing up of what the students know and are able to do after instruction is completed.

T

table A visual representation of relationships between different pieces of information.

table of specifications A chart that lists the test content and specifies the number or percentage of test items that cover each content area.

taxonomy A classification framework.

testing accommodations Exceptions to strict standardization practices allowing students to demonstrate their learning without altering the basic meaning of the score.

testing modification Changes in testing procedures (e.g., simplification of test questions or eliminating some alternatives) that could alter the meaning of a student's test score.

test-retest reliability A measure of the degree of stability between two administrations of the same test to the same students.

test-to-test carryover Effect that occurs when a teacher inadvertently compares a student's response to the responses of other students whose papers precede the student's essay.

triangulation The process of developing an accurate conclusion based on several sources.

trick questions Questions intentionally designed to mislead the test taker to provide the wrong answer.

true-false format Items that provide a statement, also referred to as a proposition, that the student must determine to be correct or incorrect.

true score The score that would represent the actual degree of understanding or skill shown on the assessment if it were perfectly accurate.

U

unfair penalization Putting students who are not familiar with the content, examples, or language of an assessment at a disadvantage compared to those who are familiar with them.

universal design for learning (UDL) A framework for understanding the types of accommodations that should be considered for diverse learners. The focus is on proactively designing instruction and assessment to reduce barriers by focusing on three areas: multiple means of representation, multiple means of expression, and multiple means of engagement.

V

validity The extent to which an assessment supports accurate, representative, and relevant inferences (e.g., conclusions, prediction) about student performance.

W–X–Y–Z

writing prompt An item that presents students with a task that is used to assess student skills and strategies in composing narrative, informative, and persuasive essays.

written conversations A learning and assessment strategy involving a back and forth discussion in writing on a single sheet of paper with a single pencil about a book or article of interest.

INDEX

Note: The italicized *f* and *t* following page numbers refer to figures and tables, respectively.

Q

R

S

U

V

W